THE ENLIGHTENMENT OF VAIROCANA

BUDDHIST TRADITION SERIES

Edited by

ALEX WAYMAN

VOLUME 18

Vairocana in Bodhisattva form

Further explanation :

This photo of a bronze from the MS remains of Ferdinand Lessing was formerly dubbed Amitāyus. The hand position in the lap depicts the 'space-mudrā' of Vairocana, here a Tenth-Stage Bodhisattva. Fire control is shown by the shoulder flames. A circular form at belly represents water, reflecting the face of a warrior, the sentry in the west. At the heart position is a conch-shell, oriented right, emitting the 'unstruck sound' (anāhata-nāda). It is held up by scarves suggesting lotus petals.

THE ENLIGHTENMENT OF
VAIROCANA

BOOK I

Study of the Vairocanābhisaṁbodhitantra

ALEX WAYMAN

BOOK II

Study of the Mahāvairocana-Sūtra

R. TAJIMA

MOTILAL BANARSIDASS PUBLISHERS
PRIVATE LIMITED • DELHI

First Indian Edition : 1992

ISBN : 81-208-0640-9

Also available at:
Motilal Banarsidass
41 U.A., Bungalow Road, Jawahar Nagar, Delhi 110 007
120 Royapettah High Road, Mylapore, Madras 600 004
16 St. Mark's Road, Bangalore 560 001
Ashok Rajpath, Patna 800 004
Chowk, Varanasi 221 001

PRINTED IN INDIA
BY JAINENDRA PRAKASH JAIN AT SHRI JAINENDRA PRESS, A-45, NARAINA INDUSTRIAL AREA, PHASE I, NEW DELHI 110 028 AND PUBLISHED BY NARENDRA PRAKASH JAIN FOR MOTILAL BANARSIDASS PUBLISHERS PVT. LTD., BUNGALOW ROAD, JAWAHAR NAGAR, DELHI 110 007

Foreword

Since the present editor of the Buddhist Traditions series is himself the author of Part I of this Vairocana scripture study, while editor of Part II of another study of this scripture, The *Enlightenment of Vairocana,* it is possible in this Foreword to advise the reader on his approach to these two studies--Wayman's on the Indo-Tibetan side—*Study of Vairocanābhisambodhi Tantra* and Tajima's on the Sino-Japanese side—*Study of the Mahāvairocana Sūtra.*

After reading the outset of Wayman's introduction in his part and likewise in Tajima's introduction, the reader would do well to go directly to the scripture, reading the translation of the scripture's Chapter One in Tajima's study, then reading the translation of the scripture's Chapter Two in Wayman's study. Then the reader can take up any of the further introductory materials in Wayman's and Tajima's respective studies; Wayman's presentations of certain subsequent chapters and Tajima's brief digest of all the chapters beginning with the second one. After such perusal, the reader may do well to re-read Chapters One and Two of the scripture, along with all the commentarial annotation herein presented. He will then be prepared for any further technicalities of the system found in Part I and Part II, constituting the two studies, which will be noticed to be independent in their nature. The reader hopefully will partake of a wondrous scripture which has intricate ramifications with a host of Mahāyāna texts.

A.W.

Table of Contents

BOOK I

STUDY OF THE VAIROCANĀBHISAMBODHI TANTRA

BOOK II

STUDY OF THE MAHĀVAIROCANA-SŪTRA (DAINICHIKYŌ)

INTRODUCTION

The scripture here to be treated is known by abbreviated title in the Indo-Tibetan tradition as the *Vairocanābhisambodhi-tantra* and in the Sino-Japanese tradition as the *Mahāvairocana-sūtra*. My study, herein deals with the Indo-Tibetan tradition. R. Tajima's study, to follow, deals with the Sino-Japanese tradition.

This is carefully crafted, profound Buddhist scripture, enjoying a remarkable success since it was composed in the Sanskrit language. The composer had a knack for creating quotable verses, cited as far apart as Java, Nepal and Tibet. The scripture is sophisticated, resistant to a quick understanding, and taking much for granted in the back ground of the reader. It has echoes of the most popular of the Mahāyāna scriptures, such as the *Avataṁsaka* and the *Saddharma-puṇḍarīka,* which help account for its successful movement to China, then to become a revered scripture in Japan, particularly in its esoteric schools.

My study sets forth that the composer may have headed a committee instrumental in turn to a more hieratic Buddhist art as the Ellora caves began to be carved out in Maharashtra and that this new era was probably influenced by the iconographical depictions of the scripture's Chapter II, hence was composed in the mid-sixth century, A.D. My Indo-Tibetan approach takes the large Chapter II as the core of the scripture, so I have translated it with elaborate citations of the commentary and with various introductions.

It is the thesis of the present study that the unknown composer was a Brahmin convert to Mahāyāna Buddhism, who helped popularize the buddhist form of the Brahmanical *homa*, or fire sacrifice, the chapter on which being well treated herein. As a Tantra the scripture shows the way of becoming a Buddha in the present body, with a foundation of compassion (*karuṇā*). As a Tantra it is quite different from what is generally understood as the class of Buddhist Tantra, indeed with enlightened contents separated by a chasm from the material found in certain modern "introductions" to Buddhist Tantra.

Here it is believed that all those favourable factors, including the healthy kind of profundity and the beauty of religious message, as well as the influence on Buddhist art, amounted to a powerful impetus continuing after the lifetime of this Brahmin composer, both in Buddhist art and in the survival of this scripture by translation along with commentary into Asian languages; and by the aforementioned citation in texts of distant countries.

I should mention that for the Tibetan version of the scripture and Buddhaguhya's commentary on the scripture's words I have employed only the Peking-Kanjur-Tanjur in the photographic edition (PTT), whose catalog lists the chapters of the scripture. This is because this edition contains both the old form of Buddhaguhya's commentary and the later revised form. The Derge edition, while accessible, contains only the revised edition of the commentary. Since the unrevised, early form is what I have correlated with the scripture, while rejecting certain solutions of the revised edition, I employed the Peking version exclusively, while also consulting the revised edition in order to evaluate it. The words of the scripture were verified by the commentary. Even so, the present work does not lose sight of the basic scripture as the primary document.

This Vairocana scripture has many references to what the Buddhists call the 'Dharmadhātu': accordingly, I present a large treatment of this matter in my introduction. It is said to be the source of mantra power, which the Buddhas have learned to use. It is claimed in this tradition that the *ācāryas'* initiations (*abhiṣeka*) in the three *maṇḍalas* (of Body, Speech, and Mind) of this scripture, draw their power from the Dharmadhātu. Hence these rituals are not 'meaningless' except for those who find them 'meaningless'; while for those who by dint of personal merits can employ the power of the Dharmadhātu, the rites are 'meaningful'. This scripture has much material on the topic of mantra, and many illustrations, starting with Chapter Two.

The scriptural rite has a "preliminary service" of six months preceding 'initiation' in the *maṇḍalas*. This goes with a theory of six elements of man—a teaching that is found in earliest Buddhism. The first five elements, in the order, earth, water, fire, wind, space (*ākāśa*), are allotted respective colors, geometrical forms, and mantras for the symbolism of the human body as a *Stūpa;* and go respectively with the first five months, in each of which, various syllables among the 'hundred syllables' are used. This rite is first depicted in what both the Tibetan and Chinese versions number Chapter Five, and my work presents the requisite information. Besides, my work presents the chapter called "Fruit of Placing the Hundred Letters" with Buddhaguhya's comments; and this chapter deals with the sixth month's fruit of the drill in the preceding five months. This fruit consists of various aims such as prosperity; and the chapter especially shows how the five elements can be used for curing illnesses.

The scripture has a theory of 'stages', called in Chapter One the 'ten minds', which appear to be ten stages of penetrating the Dharmadhātu. In the Indo-Tibetan tradition the ten stages are ten Bodhisattva Stages. In the Sino-Japanese tradition, Kūkai attempts to associate various sects with various stages, setting his own Shingon at the highest level, the tenth stage. Apart from these associations, his basic treatment of the ten stages appears to be consistent with the scripture itself. In any case, the ten minds implicate different kinds of persons in the sense of spiritual progress. My introductions also treat these matters.

The *Vairocana-tantra* has many descriptions of deities, along with their gestures (*mudrā*) and mantras. It has not been possible to present the complete descriptions of all of them in the present work. However, much data is presented. The descriptions of the deity Vairocana are consistently that of the Bodhisattva form, while the Dharmakāya form of this deity is apparently not susceptible to being depicted iconographically. The important role of Śākyamuni in this scripture is explainable as the Nirmāṇakāya of Vairocana Buddha, while the Bodhisattava form used for Vairocana in the center of the main *maṇḍala* of Chapter Two is taken by Buddhaguhya to be the Sambhogakāya of Vairocana.

There is much information on both male and female deities. For example this Tantra's depiction of Avalokiteśvara and the entourage of feminine deities indicated that the later theory and iconography of Tārā divinities starts here. Vajrapāṇi's of set feminine divinities shows their role of bringing persons onto the Buddhist path by threats and forcible dragging. Among Śākyamuni's group are female deities symbolic of his enlightenment; the set of mundane deities goes with his old epithet "teacher of gods and men".

The large Chapter Two has two parts, 'the single means' and 'the several means'. Since this distinction is of great importance for understanding the message of this scripture, I have a special introductory section devoted to the difference between these two parts.

The great emphasis of this scripture upon persons, whether called 'śrāvakas', 'pratyekabuddhas', or 'bodhisattvas'; or 'buddhas', 'complete buddhas', and so on, is due to its position that what is drawn from the Dharmadhātu depends on who does the drawing and utilization. There is a special treatment of the 'ācārya' meaning the hierophant who is performing the 'preliminary service' of six months and then goes through the three *maṇḍala* initiations. While the chapters "Reality of the Ācārya" and "Array of Letters" are brief, they are sufficiently important for my presentation with commentarial expansion. The ācārya must place 32 Letters in different parts of his body. Hence the scripture is very demanding of the qualifications of this hierophant before he is deemed competent to initiate the disciples.

The foregoing should clarify why the present author deems it a great privilege to delve into this scripture. It is an abstruse text, yet justifying every effort to unravel its intentions. As the various sections of my study grew, bit by bit, they amounted to an eye-opening exercise directed to endless vistas. To grasp this text even partially is the presence of a great mind, an immersion in a powerful current of religious creativity, a return by some mystery to an era when a master held all the essential doctrines and lore, so to say in the palm of his graceful hand.

This study, as a companion to the English version of Tajima's study of the same scripture, was encouraged by Shree N. P. Jain of the publishing firm Motilal Banarasidass, Delhi. My wife, Hideko, gave me invaluable help, e.g. by acquainting me with Kambayashi's introduction to a Japanese version of the scripture, or by furnishing information about the Sino-Japanese readings at certain spots. I regret the many delays in finishing this study, and can acknowledge that the scripture being exposed is both fascinating and difficult, resistant to a short-time application. If this remarkable scripture has been treated with a modicum of success, this is indeed a reward for so dwelling upon a wonder.

BOOK I

STUDY OF THE VAIROCANĀBHISAṀBODHITANTRA

ALEX WAYMAN

PART I

TEXTUAL STUDIES

1. BACKGROUND OF THE SCRIPTURE

Here there are two topics: (1) the title and its implications; (2) sources of the scripture.

(1) ***The title and its implications.*** The present study is devoted to a remarkable Buddhist scripture whose title in its fullest form is found in the catalogs of the Tibetan canons in this manner: *Mahāvairōcanābhisambōdhi - vikurvatādhisṭhāna - vaipulyasūtra indrarāja-nāmadharmaparyāya.* The main part of the title ends with the term *adhiṣṭhāna.* The part beginning with *vaipulya* is an alternate way of saying it a Mahāyāna Buddhist scripture; thus *dharmaparyāya*—'Buddhist terms'—namely, the King Indra of long scriptures (*vaipulyasūtra*). This part is replaced with the word *tantra* in the way Buddhaguhya explains the title. According to his comments ('B-comm.')[1] on the title's main part, dropping the word *mahā* ('great'), *vairocanābhisambodhi* means the Manifest Enlightenment (*abhisambodhi*) of Vairocana. *Vikurvitādhiṣṭhāna* means the empowerment (*adhiṣṭhāna)* 'materialized' (*vikurvita*) (in the inexhaustible Body, inexhaustible Speech, and inexhaustible Mind). Hence, the title according to this commentator amounts to the "Tantra about the manifest enlightenment of Vairocana, and about the empowerment materialized."[2]

The main part of the scripture's title suits the attributed meanings of the Buddha's title '*tathāgata*'. That is to say, the meaning that the Buddhas have 'gone' (*gata*), the same way (*tathā),* is in this scripture's terminology "the Manifest Enlightenment of Vairocana". The meaning that the Buddha preaches (or performs in the world) as (*tathā*) he learned (*āgata*) (what or how), is the scripture's "empowerment materialized".[3] This suggests that the Mahāyāna teaching of Buddha bodies is also associated with the title. According to Buddhaguhya, the Dharmakāya is the Tathāgata, and amounts to the Nirvāṇa without fixed abode (i.e., not limited to the passive Nirvāṇa or the turbulent Samsāra);[4] hence is not realized by 'form' (*rūpa*) or 'sound' (*ghoṣa*).[5] The Buddha body displaying the Manifest Enlightenment to the great Bodhisattvas such as Samantabhadra is the Sambhogakāya. The appearance in this world of the "empowerment materialized" is the Nirmāṇakāya.[6] Hence there is the teaching that the two 'formal' bodies (Sambhogakāya and Nirmāṇakāya) come from the Dharmakāya.[7] The scripture (Tib. Chap. X, 'Wheel of Syllables') declares: "I am called Lord of the World; I am first of the world, and teach the Dharma...."[8] Buddhaguhya cites this in his *Concise Commentary* and claims that *'first of the world'* signifies the two Buddha bodies, called Sambhogakāya and Nirmāṇakāya. The Bhagavat is called 'Lord of the World' in the First Eon in the evolving phase, because teaching the Dharma that is supreme, etc; while the outsiders intend Brahmā, Viṣṇu, or Śiva (see Chap. II, n. 18).[9]

The term *abhisambodhi* has been discussed by commentators. They say there is a sequence of five kinds of it, with the fifth one constituting the achievement of Complete: Buddhahood as Mahāvairocana, the Sambhogakāya.[10] Buddhaguhya, in his *Concise Commentary* identifies the 'Right Complete Enlightenment' (*samyaksaṃbodhi*) with 'omniscient wisdom' (*sarvajñajñāṇa*), and at that place gives an explanation of the scripture's Chap. One formula with three things stipulated for that 'omniscient wisdom' (the Sanskrit under 'Sanskrit citations', *infra.*). The 'root' *(mūla),* great compassion (*mahākaruṇā*), is the 'entrance cause' (*praveśakāraṇa*). The '(primary) cause' (*hetuka*), mind of enlightenment (*bodhicitta*) is the 'material cause' (*upādāna-hetu*). The 'conclusion' (*paryavasāna*), the five (text: 'six') perfections (*pāramitā),* are the 'cooperating condition' (*sahakāri-pratyaya).*[11]

As to the word *tantra,* Buddhaguhya explains: "This 'intrinsic *maṇḍala*' is the *tantra* of this *tantra.*"[12] The 'intrinsic *maṇḍala*' means the five Buddhas (see Chap. II, n. 19).

The part *vikurvitādhiṣṭhāna*, namely, the inexhaustible Body, Speech, and Mind, controls the scripture's organization by establishing the procedure for the candidates or performers, pre-eminently the 'master' (*ācārya*), who should affiliate their human body, speech, and mind with those three 'mysteries' of the lord Vairocana. Buddhaguhya's commentary shows how the scripture's chapters go with this procedure of affiliation, for which there is the word *samaya* (pledge, linkage). Thus, after the first chapter devoted to a Mahāyāna introduction, sets of chapters are devoted to the '*maṇḍala* of the lord's inexhaustible Body', '*maṇḍala* of the lord's inexhaustible Speech', '*maṇḍala* of the lord's inexhaustible Mind', and 'observances for all three *maṇḍalas*'. There follow chapters on 'the hundred syllables', constituting the preliminary service in six months meant to precede the *maṇḍala*. Finally, there are chapters on the fruition promised for the affiliation with the three 'mysteries', *tantra* generalities, and the foundation of *homa*.

The most common abbreviated reference to the scripture is *Mahāvairocana-sūtra*, the *Dainichikyō* of Japan, where it is still a sacred scripture in the esoteric schools. The Sanskrit texts cite the scripture as *Vairocanābhisambodhi* or as *Vairocanābhisambodhi-tantra*. My main abbreviated reference is V-A-T, since this study is based on Indo-Tibetan materials in which the scripture is a *tantra*. I also use the abbreviation V-A-S for the Sino-Japanese text called a *sūtra*. When referring to the text generally, I prefer the term 'scripture'.

As to the 'original' title, the present writer proposes that neither of the words '*sūtra*', '*tantra*' were included. The scripture-composer may not have liked calling it a *sūtra,* since its tantric materials of *maṇḍala, mantra,* and mudrā far exceed the brief *dhāraṇī* chapters in certain Mahāyāna *sūtras.* He may not have liked calling it a *tantra,* since these ritual-filled treatises have only fleeting references to the scripture-composer's dominant concern—the 'great compassion' (*mahākaruṇā*), and basing the tantric practices on the older Buddhist precepts. The old name seems to be: *Vairocanābhisambodhivikurvitādhiṣṭhāna*.

(2) ***Sources of the scripture.*** The ethics of early Buddhism are taken for granted. So also the Abhidharma teachings of elements (*dhātu*) and worlds (*loka*) as are presented respectively in chapters one and three of Vasubandhu's *Abhidharmakośa.* The theory of man's constituents, such as the six elements—earth, water, fire, wind, space, and understanding (*vijñāna*)—alluded to in the Pāli canonical scripture called *Anāthapiṇḍikavāda Sutta* on the occasion when Sāriputta preached to the dying Anāthapiṇḍika; and also alluded to in the *Dhātuvibhaṅga-sutta.*[13]

Among Mahāyāna scriptures the first to mention is the third scripture in the *Ratnakūṭa* collection, called the *Tathāgatācintyaguhyanirdeśa.* After my attention was called to this scripture by an article of Yoritomi's,[14] I consulted it in the Derge Kanjur edition. Its chaps. one, two, and three deal respectively with the secret of the Bodhisattva's Body, Speech, and Mind; and its chaps. seven, eight, and nine, deal respectively with the secret of the Tathāgata's Body, Speech, and Mind. Its chap. ten tells the merits of Vajrapāṇi, Master of the Secret Ones. At Ka, 195a-7 of the Derge edition is the remark: "all dharmas have 'A' as their gate." This *sūtra* toward the end has a *dhāraṇī* chapter. All these facts so well dovetail with the contents of the V-A-T as to lead to a conclusion that the *Tathāgataguhya* in its entirety is a basic source.

Portions of the *Avataṃsaka* scripture collection also apply. Near the beginning of the V-A-T there is mention of the inexhaustible Body, Speech, and Mind, which Buddhaguhya relates to the *sūtra* "Arising of the Tathāgata" in the *Avataṃsaka* collection (see in this Study the section "Beings and their Minds"). Besides, the ten stages according to the *Daśabhūmika-sūtra* are assumed, and there are explicit references to stages in the V-A-T.

The *Saddharmapuṇḍarīka-sūtra*—its five chapters 24-28—are implicated, according to my section "Composition and Influence of the Scripture".

The *Prajñāpāramitā* scriptural attitude is here for its teaching of 'Prajñāpāramitā' as the Mother of the Buddhas and Bodhisattvas; the *Aṣṭasāhasrikā* suffices for this feature in this kind of Mahāyāna literature. The *Saptaśatikā* might be involved for the theory of 'sameness wisdom' (*samatā-jñānā*).

The Tathāgatagarbha scripture translated as "Lion's Roar of Queen Śrīmālā", in its theory of three kinds of *garbha* is implicated in the V-A-T chapters on the Secret Maṇḍala, according to our section "the Dharmadhātu", part on '(D) Comparative Essay'. This Tathāgatagarbha scripture also explains the V-A-T's teaching about abandoning the body; cf. V-A-T, Chap. II, tr., n. 28.

Some Japanese scholars investigated a tantric scripture which Kōbō Daishi brought back from China to his native Japan, whose title is Sanskritized as *Deśāntapālapati-dhāraṇī-sūtra* (Nanjo 978) and which incorporates an early Mahāyāna scriputre named *Dhāraṇīśvararāja-sūtra.*[15] This is because they noticed in this tantric scripture the equivalent to the celebrated formula of V-A-T, Chap. I, namely, "Omniscience has compassion as a root, mind of enlightenment as a (primary) cause, and has the means as a conclusion." However, S. Katsumata pointed out that this tantric scripture must be later than the *Vairocanābhisambodhi,*[16] and thus has its own explanations for the members of the formula.[17]

The special placement of Avalokiteśvara, Vajrapāṇi, and Acala in the first rank of the *maṇḍala* of V-A-T, Chap. II, suggests that scriptures dealing with these three deities either precede or are contemporary with the V-A-T. It so happens that the Tibetan canon of Tantra, which places the V-A-T in the Caryā-tantra, also includes in that class a tantra of Vajrapāṇi—the *Vajrapāṇy-abhiṣeka;* and a tantra of Acala—the *Ārya-Acala-Mahākrodharāja-kalpa,* which has been edited by J. Oshika.[18] The association of such an Acala tantra with the V-A-T is highly probable, because V-A-T, Chap. III, devoted to overcoming demonic obstacles, is really a chapter of Acala, named twice in Chap. III, and according to Buddhaguhya's commentary on that chapter, having the role of overcoming the demons of the four elements. That Acala tantra has this significant passage:[19]

/ ' og tu khro bo chen po ni /
/ mi g'yo ba ni stobs po che /
/ phyag na ral gri zur gyis gzigs /
/ 'chi bdag mthar byed mṅon sum bźin /
/ me yi dkyil 'khor la bźugs pa /
/ ruṅ daṅ cig sbyar bar bya /

Beneath [the two vajradhara-s] (draw) an
Acala of great power (*mahābala*), holding
a curved sword in his hand and looking through
the corner (of his eye), appearing like a
direct vision of the Ender of Death, dwelling
in the circle of fire, and add him together
with the wind (circle).

The importance of this passage is not only to link this form of Acala with V-A-T, Chap. III, but also to clear up a mystery of the Caryā-tantra class, to wit, that while there is no tantra of Yamāntaka in the Kanjur Rgyud section of Caryā-tantra, there are several commentaries in the Tanjur Rgyud section of Caryā-tantra that are obviously on Yamāntaka as a *krodha* form of Mañjuśrī, while there is no obvious commentary on Acala by this name.[20] It may well be that it is Acala who is this Yamāntaka of the Caryā-tantra class; but since it is a feature of tantric ritual that the performer who would identify himself with a furious deity (*krodha*) ordinarily identifies himself first with a gentle bodhisattva (here) Mañjuśrī, it follows that those particular commentaries must have been composed by persons who used a form of Mañjuśrī for generating an Acala-type angry deity. Besides, this same Acala-tantra earlier had defined Acala this way:[21]

/ mi g'yo ba źes mṅon par brjod /
/ mi g'yo ba yi sa thob pa /

The definition of 'Acala' is attainment of
the *acala-bhūmi* = the Eighth Bodhisattva Stage).

This definition agrees with calling Acala "of great power" (*mahābala*) because the Eighth Stage is associated with Bodhisattva powers called *vaśitā*.[22]

And that theory of 'Acala' shows some Yogācāra Buddhism in the background, because the *Bhāṣya* on Asaṅga's *Abhidharma-samuccaya* cites the Sanskrit *gāthā*-s that are employed in Asaṅga's *Mahāyānasaṃgraha,* including:[23]

> bodhisattve vaśiprāpte 'dhimuktivaśād yataḥ /
> tathābhāvaḥ pṛthivyādau dhyāyinām copalabhyate //
> When the Bodhisattva has obtained power (=attained Eighth Stage) through the power of *adhimukti,* and also in the case of the meditators (*dhyāyin,* i.e., in the four Dhyāna-s), the entity as it (really) is, is apprehended, i.e., (the elements) earth, and so on.

Not only does this passage associate the 'Acala' stage with contemplation of the elements, but it brings in the terminology of *adhimukti*. The stage of Adhimukticaryā according to the V-A-T is so different a conception from that found in the Prajñāpāramitā exegesis called *Abhisamayālamkāra* that Buddhaguhya experienced some obvious embarrassment in discussing it—as is exposed in my section on 'Stages' in the present work. But the above verse from the *Mahāyānasaṃgraha* seems to agree with the V-A-T, first chapter, in usage of the term *adhimukti*.

Among the tantric works that are feasibly in the background of V-A-T, it is reasonable to include the *Subāhu-paripṛcchā-tantra*, because Buddhaguhya, chief commentator on the V-A-T in the Tibetan Tanjur, has composed a work on the concise meaning of the *Subāhu* as well as a work on the words in their order. Having surveyed Buddhaguhya's commentaries on this Tantra, I can testify to this Tantra having more elementary and less subtle matters than the V-A-T. While it is not obviously affiliated with a particular chapter of the V-A-T, it appears to survey demonology and its attendant divination, as well as fundamental Buddhist topics such as 'non-self' (*anātma*) in a way that is taken for granted in the V-A-T itself. Thus, in the Derge, Rgyud 'grel (commentary on Tantra), Vol. Thu, f. 57a-5, on the Tantra's words, "One should take recourse with faith to the Three Jewels", Buddhaguhya comments, "One should observe the Buddha, listen to the Dharma, and pay respect to the Saṃgha" (saṅs rgyas la blta ba daṅ chos ñan pa daṅ /

dge'dun la rim gro bya ba'i don to). I presume that what he means by "observe the Buddha" is to use images, temple banners (*taṅka*) and the like; or in Buddhist meditation, take the body of the Buddha as a support for the meditative praxis.

My present work in section 10, "Chapter V and the Preliminary Service" points out that a Kanjur tantric work called *Dhyānottara-paṭalakrama,* enjoying a detailed commentary by Buddhaguhya, is affiliated with V-A-T, Chap. V, while Tibetan Tradition states that this particular Kanjur tantra is a portion of a lost tantra called the *Vajroṣṇīṣa.* The *Dhyānottara* is presumably either contemporary with the V-A-T or a utilized predecessor.

We must assume that the scripture-composer employed some treatises on Tantra generalities, explaining *mudrā*, *mantra*, *maṇḍala*, vows, homa, and the like. In all likelihood, there was an accompanying ritual manual that incorporated essentials of *mudrā*, etc., from such preceding works. For example, the *homa* chapter of the V-A-T is mainly given over to names of different fires, and tells virtually nothing of how to conduct a *homa.* Among the appended chapters to the V-A-T, Tibetan version, that are not in the Chinese version of the scripture, are four detailed chapters on the four *homas*, which are presumably based on preceding works. Of these possible preceding treatises, one may point to the *Mañjuśrī-mūla-tantra* and the *Susiddhikara-tantra*, preserved in Asian translations. The *Mañjuśrī-mūla-tantra*, (or *-kalpa*) is often mentioned as a later work due to the last part which consists of Buddhist legendary history probably composed in the ninth century, A.D. However, the first two of the three volumes as edited by T. Gaṇapati Sāstrī and published under title of *Āryamañjuśrīmūlakalpa,* at Trivandrum; Part I, 1920; II, 1922, consists of much older material, perhaps belonging to the fourth century, A.D. I cite its Homa chapter in my Study on the V-A-T Homa chapter, in the present work. The fact that the V-A-T, Chap. II, in its *maṇḍala,* allots the whole second rank to Śākyamuni as teacher of gods and men, surrounded by the constellations, and so on, seems to have behind it the role of Śākyamuni in the *Mañjuśrīmūla-tantra.*[24]

Among the scriptures mentioned above, there are *sūtras* entirely free from formulas to be muttered called *dhāraṇī, sūtras* with a *dhāraṇī* chapter, and scriptures entirely given over to tantric materials. All three kinds must be assumed in the background of the V-A-T.

Some peculiarities of the V-A-T have unknown sources, especially some theories of the first chapter. Here the exposition of sixty minds is without parallel in Buddhist sources.

We must also assume the Buddhist art tradition; to depict not only Gautama Buddha but also Bodhisattvas, etc. with increasingly defined forms, described in such treatises as the *Mañjuśrī-mūlatantra*.

Finally, some non-Buddhist sources are indicated in my study of the Homa chapter.

2. COMPOSITION AND INFLUENCE OF THE SCRIPTURE

This section has the thesis that the *Vairocanābhisambodhi*, whether called a *sūtra* (V-A-S) or a *tantra* (V-A-T) was composed in mid-sixth century in Mahārāshtra.

Composer. The composer was probably a Brahmin convert to Buddhism, the logical conclusion from his content in the 'Homa chapter' (included in the present work). He was convinced by the Mahāyāna stress on compassion (*karuṇā*) and eager to combine this feature with *maṇḍala* ritual, according to the stress on *karuṇā* in his first chapter and to his devoting the 'single means' of the second chapter to the *Mahākaruṇāgarbhodbhava-maṇḍala* (the M-K-G-Maṇḍala). He was a follower of the deity Vajrapāṇi as can be seen by his having Vajrapāṇi as the interlocutor throughout the V-A-T and including Vajrapāṇi in the central part of the M-K-G-Maṇḍala. The content of certain chapters indicated that the composer was an expert in the making of gestures called *mudrā* and recitation of the *mantras* for deities. He had a penchant for the names, thus in the first chapter listing sixty mundane minds, in the second chapter listing the food offerings, in the 'Homa chapter' listing the names of 'fires'; generally in the V-A-T giving the names of things and of deities. He had a talent for creating quotable verses, a number of which have been cited as far apart as in the old Javanese text *Sang Hyang Kamahāyānikan* and in the Nepalese text, Kuladatta's *Kriyāsaṃgraha*; and which are frequently cited in Tibetan tantric literature, such as in Bu-ston's tantric surveys and in Tsoṅ-kha-pa's *Sṅags rim chen mo*. His writing is subtle and sophisticated. By his zeal and influence, he may well have played an outstanding role in the artistic innovations in the Mahārāshtra caves in the Buddhist portion of Ellora, and at Kanheri; and perhaps was responsible, along with his colleagues, for the fixed iconographical molds of various deities, as against the narrative style of the Ajanta and Aurangabad art depictions. By strength of personality and conviction he may have been a successful fund raiser for the artistic embellishment of the monastic establishments.

Date of composition. As to the date of the V-A-T, this has partly to do with the iconographical descriptions of the deities in the second and some later chapters; and with material in the Homa chapter. Also that the V-A-T uses the old Buddha name Saṃkusumita. The dating involves the influence of the *sūtra* in various places of India and outside of India, assuming that it must have had a powerful role at the outset. Also relevant is the difference between the Sino-Japanese version of the *sūtra* on the one hand, and the Tibetan version on the other.

There had been a long artistic quiescence at Ajanta (about four centuries). Debala Mitra explains in her *Ajanta* that the prolific new period of cave construction and artistic hewing was the second half of the fifth century and first half of the sixth. The Vākāṭakas, related matrimonially to the Imperial Guptas of North India, sponsored this wondrous outpouring of art, especially during A.D. 457-500, when Ajanta Caves 16 and 17 were sponsored. The artistic embellishment of the Buddhist Aurangabad caves apparently took place in the sixth and seventh centuries, but the rulership is variously stated in modern works; thus "Early Western Chālukyas" with capital at Badami from *circa* 520 A.D., supposedly governing north Deccan from *circa* 520-600 A.D. But if the merchants mainly paid for the artistic embellishment, it does not matter who were the rulers if they did not interfere. Debala Mitra mentions the "Early Western Chālukyas" (sixth century to the eighth century, A.D.) during whose reign the twelve Elūra caves mostly sprang up, indeed starting around the mid-sixth century.[25]

M.K. Dhavalikar has argued that the earliest images of Tārā are in the caves at Kanheri, Nasik, Ellora, Aurangabad and Ajanta of Western India, all ascribable to 6th-7th centuries A.D. That the merchants and mariners of the western coast invoked Tārā for protection during their trading with the Mediterranean world and were the first to sponsor carvings of Tārā images.[26]

The theory of fire lineage in the Sūtra's Homa chapter begins somewhat like the *Vāyu-purāṇa's* Agni-vaṃśa chapter. Winternitz says that the *Vāyu-purāṇa* attained its present content in the fifth century, A.D.[27] Thus, its present form was available to the sūtra-composer to draw upon in the mid-sixth century, according to the theory of this essay, when the Elūra caves began to be hewed. The Sūtra's second chapter must have been significantly influential for the new art in order that a set of its verses be widely cited later on (as was mentioned, in Java and in Nepal), that the text be available at the variously widely separated places of India where Asian legends claimed it was found or recovered, that it be worthy of the reverence accorded it in China and Japan. Finally, the scripture itself went through some modification in time especially as concerns its chapters, because the difference between the chapter titles in the Chinese and Tibetan versions suggests that the original composition had few or no chapter titles. Then the Chinese version would get an appendix of five chapters that are not in the Tibetan version, while the Tibetan version translates a text that had seven extra chapters not in Chinese. Also it precedes the **Deśāntapālapati-dhāraṇī-sūtra.*[28]

Taking all those facts into consideration, I have placed the composition at mid-sixth century, holding that it could not have been earlier and could not have been later.[29]

Place of composition. First, where it could not be composed. The scripture could not be composed in most of South India, especially Tamilnadu, because in both its first and second chapters it uses in a list of Hindu gods a name which in the original Sanskrit must have been Skanda (Tib. *skem byed*). The equivalent Chinese means "son of Īśvara"—not Viśvakarman (see Tajima's note). The name Kārttikeya, which in So. Indian is used instead of Skanda for the "son of Śiva", is rendered into Tibetan as Smin-drug-pa (nursed by the six star-nurses of the Pleiades) in the Buddhist dictionary *Mahāvyutpatti.* Kālidāsa, prominently associated with the city of Ujjayinī (Ujjain), when relying on the mythology of the *Skandotpatti-parvādhyāya* of the *Mahābhārata* in his great poem *Kumārasambhava*,[30] uses the name Skanda but not Kārttikeya, either here or anywhere else in his works.[31]

The V-A-T could not be composed in most of North India because it uses among its Buddha names two—Dundubhinirghoṣa (instead of Akṣobhya) and Saṃkusumita (instead of Amoghasiddhi)—that are unknown in the North Indian Buddhist works such as the

Sādhanamālā and the *Niṣpannayogāvalī,* containing numerous names of deities. The Buddha name Saṃkusumita is also used in the *Mañjuśrī-mūla-tantra,*[32] which is earlier except for its last section devoted to Buddhist chronicles. The form Kusumita is found in old texts of the Malay Archipelago as Amoghasiddhi's heaven.[33] Since Buddha Saṃkusumita is in the *Saddharmapuṇḍarīka,*[34] it is the old name.

Next, where the V-A-T could be composed. The area that would escape the non-possible area of India sketched above, and be a feasible place because of Buddhist art considerations, is a belt across India just south of the Narmadā and Mahānadī rivers, including what is now called Mahārāshtra and Orissa. Now, the position of the present work is that the V-A-T had an important role on both sides of that belt, but that the influence in Orissa was later than that of Mahārāshtra.

Mahārāshtra as the area of composition. I first allude to a north-south line of an ancient road,[35] running from Ujjayinī to Mahiṣmatī (between the Vindhya mountains and the Narmadā river), passing by Aurangabad, and terminating at pratiṣṭhāna (Paithan) which was the capital of the Śātavāhana of the Deccan. The part of this line in the Deccan is on the eastern-most side of the hilly region called Sahyadri, roughly the modern Mahārāshtra. It was along this line in the Deccan that grew up the celebrated Buddhist art centers of Ajanta, Aurangabad, and the Buddhist portion of Ellora (Elūra). Another possibility is the western-most side of this same Sahyadri where there is another series of Buddhist caves, Bhaja and Karla; and in the Bombay district other sites, pre-eminently Kanheri.

Debala Mitra treats the Mahārāshtra sites (covering Bhaja, Bedsa, Karla, Junnar, Kondane, Kondivte, Kanheri, Nasik, Pitalkhora, Ajanta, Aurangabad, Ellora, Sopara).[36] At Kanheri in the Bombay district is an elaborate treatment of Avalokiteśvara (Cave 90; in Mitra's work, photo 106), with a goddess on each side of Avalokiteśvara. According to the V-A-T, Chapter Two, verses 81-83, the two goddesses should be a green Tārā (on the right) and Bhṛkutī, three-eyed (third eye faintly visible in the photo) (on the left). The figure directly above Avalokiteśvara's head is Amitābha, according to V-A-T, II, 80. There are some differences too; e.g., in the scripture Avalokiteśvara is seated, at Kanheri standing. The same group of images is found at Elūra, Cave II (locally called 'Do thal'), with Avalokiteśvara now seated in dhyana asana in the north wall, agreeing with the scripture's direction, and besides being flanked by Tārā and Bhṛkurtī, had a Buddha overhead (presumably Amitābha).[37] This Cave also has features it shares with Cave 12 ('Tin Thal') of having various Buddhas, each of which is flanked by Avalokiteśvara and Vajrapāṇi.[38] This agrees with the V-A-T, II, first rank with Buddhas in the center, and Avalokiteśvara and Vajrapāṇi in No. and So. as the only Bodhisattvas placed in this rank by the scripture.

There is a clear affiliation between the Buddhist part of Elūra and Kanheri according to Mitra, observing that Cave 5 of Elūra has in the nave two low narrow benches, shared alone by the Darbar cave at Kanheri.[39] Mitra points out that the Kanheri caves are situated on a hill on the western sea-board, with accessibility to the thriving ports with modern names of Sopara and Kalyan, whose merchants liberally supported the Buddhist establishments.[40] A modern road closely parallels the old one from the ports of Sopara and Kalyan through the Nasik region and Pithalkhorn at the Indradri crossing, then through Ellora and Devagiri (capital of the Yadava kings), ending at Paithan, near Aurangabad.[41] This shows that an artistic director of caves in Kanheri and Elūra probably had a monasterial residence at both places, perhaps spending parts of the year at each one in accordance with the seasons.

According to our theory that the V-A-T, especially Chapter II, translated herein, was a kind of early manual for the turn to hieratic art in Elūra, Kanheri, and so on, it could act as an impetus reaching beyond and lifetime of the composer. Thus the scripture had an esteemed status whereby it made its way to other places, eventually to be translated into Chinese and to become a sacred scripture of the esoteric schools of Japan. The mid-sixth century where I place the composition is perhaps the last time a Buddhist scripture could gain such reverence, since soon thereafter there would be a turn in India to the commentarial stage.

Orissa. Debala Mitra explains that when Hsüan-tsang visited Orissa in about A.D. 639, it was divided into three principalities—Oḍra, Koṅgoda, and Kaliṅga; and that a large part of then Kaliṅga is now within Andhra Pradesh.[42] She discusses the *vihāra* called Ratnagiri that was built during the Gupta period in the kingdom of Oḍiviśa (=Oḍra) (district Cuttack) on the crest of a hill near the sea; in which were kept three sets of Mahāyāna and Hīnayāna texts. It was built by king Buddhapakṣa, who is identified by Nalinakṣa Dutt with the Gupta King Narasimhagupta Bālāditya (first half of the sixth century A.D.).[43] Mitra says that the excavations at the Ratnagiri hill agree with the late Gupta attribution.[44]

Professor Motohiro Yoritomi of Kyoto, Japan, has been engaged in excavations, permitted by the Indian authorities, in the Ratnagiri area; and has published several reports in the Japanese language of the findings by others and himself about the Buddhist art of Orissa. In an article[45] he describes two Vairocana images that have been found and that are in the style of V-A-S with the two hands in what he terms *samādhi* gesture *(mudrā)*. One found at Lalitagiri has its hair tied up high in crown style (the *jaṭāmukuṭa)*[46] and has an inscription, namaḥ samantabuddhānām A vīra HŪṂ KHAṂ, which occurs in chapter six (both Chinese and Tibetan) in a context where the *samādhi* means the diamond play victorious over the four Māra-s, the non-apprehension of the six destinies, and omniscience. Hence, in the *mantra* the term *vīra* (O hero!) refers to the Enlightenment body. The other Vairocana image was found at Ratnagiri (in the 'fourth temple'). It is in the style of the M-K-G-maṇḍala, with hair knot and jewel crown;[47] and is flanked by Avalokiteśvara of the Vajradharma form, and Vajrasattva (here substituting for Vajrapāṇi). Professor Yoritomi told the present writer in Sept. 1983 at Kyoto, when he kindly furnished this and other relevant publications, as well as photos taken of these Vairocana images of Orissa, that these Vairocana images belong to the 9th-10th centuries. This is a clear indication that Orissa could not be the location of the V-A-T composition, but that after the Buddhist art impetus had run its course in Mahārāshtra, it moved to Orissa, especially the part called Oḍiviśa or Oḍra, where it would again flourish, now with Orissa style. Of course, if these images be accepted as Vairocana ones, it shows the popularity of the relevant cult and suggests the study of the V-A-T.

Now we turn to an earlier period of Orissa with the story of Śubhakarasiṃha (637-735 A.D.).[48] According to the Chinese chronicles he was a native of 'Central India' and his parents left the troubles of that place for a part of India which the Shingon priest Kambayashi calls Udra. Rajendralala Mitra explains: "Unquestionably the word Orissa is a corruption of the Sanskrit *Oḍra-deśa,* the country of the Oḍras or Uḍras; but who the Oḍras were, remains yet to be determined."[49] According to Biswarup Das, Śubhakarasimha's parents must have come from Assam; and there was a close political tie between Assam and Orissa. Śubhakarasimha's parents were apparently vassal kings of the Assam regime, presumably using the name Bhauma; while the later Buddhist rulers of Orissa starting in the last quarter of the eighth century were independent kings using the word Kara in their names.[50]

According to the story as Kambayashi tells it, when Śubhakarasiṃha was 13 years old, his parents arranged for him to assume the throne, whereupon he had to combat with arms his jealous brothers who revolted; in disgust he renounced the throne to an elder brother, and his mother gave him permission to become a monk. Chou Yi-liang's article has this important bit of information: "He went southward to the sea where he came to a superb monastery and there obtained the *Saddharmapuṇḍarīkasamādhi*."[51] Our previous information makes it practically certain that the monastery was the Ratnagiri one. Chou Yi-liang, to explain this *samādhi*, appealed to the MOCHIZUKI Buddhist encyclopedia for an explanation that it involved reciting the Lotus Sutra for 21 days with aim of seeing the Bodhisattva Samantabhadra. Anyway, the *Saddharmapuṇḍarīkasamādhi* is explicitly mentioned in the Lotus Sūtra, Chap. 24 (Hurvitz's translation).[52] "The Bodhisattva Fine Sound" (Gadgadasvara), near the beginning. This chapter starts with Śākyamuni using a ray from his ūrṇakośa to illumine the world sphere "Adorned with rays of Vairocana" in the Eastern quarter. In that realm was a Buddha with a long name including 'rājasaṃkusumita', a name among the five Buddhas of V-A-T. Later the Buddha Śākyamuni converses with Mañjuśrī.[53] Later the Buddha mentions a Buddha of the past with a long name including 'dundubhisvara' a name among the five Buddhas of V-A-T. Then Chap. 25 of the Lotus Sūtra is on Avalokiteśvara, who is important in the 2d chapter of V-A-T. Chap. 26 is on Dhāraṇī, of which there is also much in the V-A-T. Chap. 27 again refers to the world sphere "Adorned with rays of Vairocana" and the Buddha whose long name includes 'rājasaṃkusumita'. Finally, chap. 28 is on the Bodhisattva Samantabhadra, who also has an important role in the V-A-T (later we shall show his identification with Vajrapāṇi). Now, Kambayashi mentions that the founders of the Tendai sect of Japan held that the V-A-T is the esoteric counterpart to the Lotus Sūtra, while the 'Tip of the Vajra' (nickname for *Tattvasaṃgraha*) is the esoteric counterpart to the *Avataṃsaka* (the Ch. Hua-yen; Ja. Kegon).[54] The meaning may well be that the V-A-T is the esoteric counterpart to the final chapters of the Lotus Sūtra.

The foregoing information about the implication of the *Saddharmapuṇḍarīkasamādhi* which Śubhakarasiṃha obtained at a monastery which was presumably Ratnagiri, makes it reasonable to assume that a copy of the V-A-T was available to him, perhaps copied from the text in the Ratnagiri library. In short, it is likely that Śubhakarasiṃha already had a copy of the V-A-T when he was a young man.

Chou Yi-liang reports that Śubhakarasiṃha boarded a merchant ship by which he visited several countries.[55] He would naturally start out from the Orissa port, and the first country was probably Ceylon.[56] It may well be that his incessant travels over a period of years were in part to get authentic explanations of the V-A-S, which would later in China become the basis of his oral commentary on the V-A-S taken down by I-Hsing. His biography, in Kambayashi's version, shows that in time he proceeded to Nalandā University and studied Tantra from Dharmagupta, from whom he learned the esoteric practice of the mantras and mudrā-s; but the account does not claim that he received any explanation of the V-A-S at Nalandā. Many years later,[57] deciding to go to China, he carried his books on the back of a camel, and wandered into Gandhara. Here near the Stūpa of Kaniṣka (the Bodhisattva) Mañjuśrī presented him with the ritual method of the Sūtra (i.e., the V-A-S). (This refers to the ritual appendix in five chapters). Tajima points out that both Śubhakarasiṃha and Vajrabodhi translated this into Chinese.[58] The story given by Chou Yi-liang continues that he proceeded to the Jade Gate, where the Chinese Emperor had arranged for an emissary, a certain General, to meet him and conduct him to Ch'ang-An.[59] He arrived there in 716 A.D. when he was already about 80 years old. He stayed in China for 20 years translating various works, especially the V-A-S and its Appendix, and died at the age of 98, having been a monk for 80 years.

Valabhī. Notice the legend which Tajima reports of a country called P'o-lou-lo (Japanese, Borora) where the Sūtra (the V-A-S) was obtained. It is difficult to avoid the conclusion that this country was the site of Valabhī (or Vallabhī) (in Gujarat country), a great center of learning which rivalled Nalandā at the time of Hsüan-tsang's visit and which he called Fa-la-pi and also Pe-lo-lo. B.N. Chaudhury, *Buddhist Centres*, mentions that the name Valabhī is rather late; and that a 5th century inscription discovered in the ruins there calls it the kingdom of Balabhadra.[60] It is easy to take this name as the original for the Asian transcription that the Japanese pronounce Borora. For the position of Valabhī, see C. Collin Davies, *An Historical Atlas*, India in 640 A.D. which includes Valabhī in

Harṣa's Empire.[61] As to the old travel from the south to Valabhī, it presumbly is closely paralleled by the modern road, perhaps had Mahiṣmarī as the junction point. Moti Chandra reports that Valabhī fell during 750-70 A.D. by Arab attacks from the sea.[62] However, Debala Mitra shows that even after the fall of the Maitraka line of rulers, who has sponsored the flourishing Buddhist establishments, various Buddhist activities continued, and around the ninth century the cult of the Buddhist goddess Tārā was strong there, with her name used for a town Tārāpura.[63] The legend associating the V-A-T with Valabhī at least shows that the scripture had made its way north to this center of learning, where it was accessible for copying by anyone so interested.

Tibet. Here the role of the V-A-T became important through a quarrel about the character of tantric works as a corpus. Probably this was an issue as well in India, because there was presumably a collection of such works at Nalandā and at Vikramaśīla and so some sort of classification scheme. Following the indications in commentaries translated from Sanskrit and oral advice of the pandits who came to Tibet and assisted the translators while bringing in their lineages, the Tibetan canon of Tantra was arranged in the four classes called Kriyā, Caryā, Yoga, and Anuttarayoga. This aid from India practically stopped with the downfall of Buddhist institutions in No. India around 1200 A.D. When the Tibetans were left with a huge amount of translated Tantras and commentaries on them, and the numerous lineages going with a large pantheon of deities, while themselves being divided into sometimes hostile sects, various quarrels arose about these Tantras. A chief dispute had to do with the relation of Mahāyāna to the Tantra, and can be stated this way: For the tantric aim of becoming a Buddha by the quick route, i.e., in the present life, in contrast to the prospect of three incalculable eons for doing it, are some of these Tantras better for the purpose? And what is the relation to the Mahāyāna? Without going into the many complications, it is a fact that the Tibetan sects generally had a practice based on the 'higher Tantras', i.e., the Yoga and Anuttarayoga, and as time went on, practically just with Tantras of the Anuttarayoga-tantra class. This involved a theory that only the 'higher Tantras' have this quickening method of Buddhahood. In actuality there were too many books and details of *Maṇḍala*-ritual, accompanied with a plenitude of lineage and commentaries. There arose a theory in some quarters that the 'higher Tantras' were associated with the Great Vehicle *(mahāyāna)* as though the two lower ones were not. Bu-ston (1290-1364 A.D.), editor of the Kanjur and Tanjur (the Tibetan canon of scriptures and exegetical treatises), although writing his main Tantra commentaries on the two 'higher Tantras' tried to combat that theory, with an Indian ally in the author Ratnākaraśānti.[64] Bu-ston wrote three Tantra survey books, in which he made many citations from the two 'lower Tantras', especially the V-A-T which is included in the Caryā Tantra group as the chief one of its Tantras. Thereby he could show that the Mahāyāna-type Buddhism is the basis for all the Tantras that can be counted as 'Buddhist'. His Vol.Pha (collected works) includes a 32-folio work on the *Mahākaruṇā-garbha-maṇḍalavidhi* described in the V-A-T; and his Vol. Tsa includes a 32-folio work on the *maṇḍala* arrangement of Caryā-tantra works beginning with the V-A-T. Tsoṅ-kha-pa (1357-1419) continued Bu-ston's stress on the importance of all four Tantra classes, including in his tantric compendium *Sṅags rim chen mo* many citations from the V-A-T. This re-evaluation of the Tantra classes involved a theory that each one of the four Tantra classes shows the way to become a Complete Buddha (and so in shorter time than the non-tantric methods, possibly in this very life).[65]

The V-A-T is of course an excellent work to prove these points, because it starts out with Mahāyāna Buddhism and claims the 'Nirvāṇa of no fixed abode' (*apratiṣṭhitanirvāṇa*) as a practical goal for the *ācārya* (the 'master' or 'hierophant'). The V-A-T, Chap. I indicates this potentiality of man in its well known formula which I referred to above ('the title and its implications', and 'sources of the scripture'), but must be repeated here for clarification: "The omniscient wisdom has compassion as a root, mind of enlightenment as a (primary) cause, and has the means as a conclusion."[66] Indeed, this relates to the scripture's title, as was explained above.

The part of the title *Vairocanābhisaṃbodhi* (Manifest Enlightenment of Vairocana) has the 'mind of enlightenment' (*bodhicitta*) as a (*primary*) cause. The next part of the title *vikurvitādhiṣṭhanā* (the Empowerment materialized) has 'great compassion' *(mahākaruṇa)* as root. Those are the two modes of the *sarvajña-jñāna* (Omniscient Wisdom). So when it then says: "has the means as a conclusion" both Buddhaguhya's commentary and the Chinese commentary by Śubhakarasiṃha and I-hsing are right, but one-sided. Buddhaguhya claimed it means the perfections *(pāramitā)* of giving (*dāna*) and so on, since these bring fulfilment to the 'mind of enlightenment.'[67] The Chinese commentary said that this is the source of the three mysteries.[68] So Buddhaguhya gave an interpretation agreeing with *Vairocanābhisaṃbodhi* while the Chinese commentary agrees with *Vikurvitādhiṣṭhāna*. To get the scripture's own explanation of the phrase "has the means as a conclusion" one must read past Chapter I because most of the remaining chapters either deal with the *maṇḍalas* of Body, Speech and Mind, or the preparation for them. Hence, in particular, "the means as a conclusion" stands for the five Buddhas who are the 'intrinsic *maṇḍala*' of this scripture. All this shows how the V-A-T, when properly understood and followed, can serve the purpose of speeding up enlightenment as well as do the so called 'higher Tantras'.

China and Japan. For information on the role of the V-A-S in the Far East, one may consult R. Tajima's *Study of the Mahāvairocana-sūtra*. There are also various works dealing with the V-A-S within the theoretical framework of the Japanese Shingon; and here Hakeda's *Kūkai* may be mentioned.[69] Speaking generally, the V-A-S is combined with the theory of another Tantra called *Tattvasaṃgraha* (in Japanese the *Kongō-chō-kyō*, Sūtra on the Tip of the Diamond), since the two scriptures are the respective sources of the two large Mandara—the Garbha (from the *Mahāvairocana-sūtra)* and the Vajradhātu (from the *Tattvasaṃgraha*), displayed in elaborate temple hangings in Japan. The V-A-S is still a sacred scripture to the esoteric schools of Japan. There has been much research on this scripture in Japanese-language works.

Sanskrit citations. The original Sanskrit for the entire scripture is not extant. However, there are a number of citations in texts that have preserved the original Sanskrit of some important passages. I have myself traced eighteen verses of the V-A-T, all from its Chapter II, in a Nepalese work the *Kriyā-saṃgraha* by Kuladatta; and have elsewhere published these with technical apparatus, including the Tibetan version for each.[70] I shall give these here with just the Sanskrit and verse numbers as found in Chapter II translated in this book:

tvaṃ deve śaktībhūtāsi sarvabuddhena tāyinā/
caryānayaviśeṣeṣu bhūmipāramitāsu ca// (II, 15)
yathā mārabalabhagnaṃ śakyasimhena tāyinā/
tathā mārabalabhagnaṃ jitvā maṇḍalaṃ lekhayāmy aham//(II,16)
adya yuṣmābhir atulā labhā labdhvā mahātmabhiḥ/
yena yūyaṃ jinaiḥ sarvai saputrair iha śāsanaiḥ // (II, 49)
sarve parigṛhītās tu jāyāmānā mahātmabhiḥ /
tena yūyaṃ mahāyāne sujātā hi bhaviṣyatha //(II, 50)
esa mārgavaraḥ śrīmān mahāyānamahodayaḥ /
yena yūyaṃ gamiṣyante bhaviṣyatha tathāgatāh // (II, 57)
svayambhuvo mahābhāgāḥ sarvalokasya cetiyāḥ /
astināstivyatikrānta-m-ākāśam iva nirmalaṃ// (II, 58)
gambhīram sarvatarkebhir apratarkyamanālayaṃ /
sarvaprapañcarahitaṃ prapañcebhiḥ prapañcitaṃ // (II, 59)
karmakriyādirahitam satyadvaya (samā) śritaṃ

idaṃ yānavaraṃ śreṣṭhaṃ labhiṣyatha naye sthitāḥ // (II, 60)
sarvajñānāṃ kadā loke saṃbhavo jayate na vā /
udumbarasyaiva kusumaḥ kadācit karhicid bhavet // (II, 144)
tato 'pi durlabhotpādo mantracaryānayasya hi /
yena sattvārtham atulaṃ kartuśakto hy anivṛtaḥ// (II, 145)
anekakalpakoṭibhir yat kṛtaṃ pāpakaṃ puraṭi /
tatsarvaṃ hi kṣayaṃ yāti dṛṣṭvā maṇḍalam īdṛśaṃ // (II, 146)
kim utānantayaśasāṃ mantracaryānaye sthitāḥ /
yad apy anuttarapāde japan vai mantrān tāyināṃ // (II, 147)
ucchannā durgatis teṣām sarvaduḥkhasya sambhavāḥ /
yeṣām (vai) caryāvare 'smin matir anyaṃ na niścalā// (II, 148)
ajñānapaṭalaṃ vatsa apanītaṃ mayā tava /
śalākikair vaidyarajyair yathā lokasya taimiraṃ // (II, 229)
pratibimbasamā dharmāḥ svacchāḥ śuddhā hy anāvilāh /
agrāhyā-n-anabhilāpyā hetukarmasamudbhavāḥ // (II, 230)
adyaprabhṛti (lokasya) dharmacakraṃ pravarttaya /
āpūrya (hi) samantāc ca dharmaśaṅkham anuttaraṃ// (II, 234)
na te kāryā vimatir vā nirvisaṅkena cetasā /
prakāśya sadā loke mantracaryānayavidhiṃ // (II, 235)
evaṃ kṛtajño buddhānām upa (ka) rīti gīyate /
te ca vajradharāḥ sarve rakṣanti tava sarvaśaḥ // (II, 236)

Various ones among those verses are found in the old Javanese work *Sang Hyang Kamahayanan Mantranaya;* and there were attempts by scholars to correct the Sanskrit.[71] The verses II, 57, 58, 59, 60 are equivalent to verses 6, 7, 8, 9 of the Javanese text (SHKM); verses II, 229, 230 are equivalent to its verses 16 and 17; verses II, 234, 235, 236 are equivalent to its verses 20, 21, 22. Besides, the SHKM has equivalents to other verses of V-A-T, Chap. II, that were not in the Kriyā-saṃgraha set. Again using the Chap. II verse numbers of the present work, SHKM, 1=II, 4; SHKM, 2=II, 5; SHKM, 3=II, 6; SHKM, 4=II, 7; SHKM, 5ab=II, 8ab; SKHM, 18=II 230cd-231ab. One may conclude that the V-A-T, especially its Chap. II, has contributed to the tantrism as far away as Java and Nepal.

Probably the most important passage of V-A-T, Chap. I is found in Sanskrit cited in Kamalaśīla's *Bhāvanākrama* (I): tad etat sarvajnānaṃ karuṇāmūlaṃ bodhicittahetukam upāyaparyavasānam ("The omniscient wisdom has Compassion for a root, has the Mind of Enlightenment for a cause, and has the Means for a conclusion").

The tantric Candrakīrti's *Pradipoddyotana* cites V-A-T, Chap. VII (of the Tibetan canon version), entitled "Establishing the *samādhi* of the gods" for this passage:

devatārupam api guhyakādhipate dividhaṃ pariśuddham aśuddhaṃ ca iti / tat pariśuddham adhigatarūpam sarvanimittāpagatam

apari(śuddha)ṃ sarvanimittaṃ rūpavarṇasaṃsthānaś ca taıra
divividhena devatārūpeṇa dvividhakāryaniṣpattir bhavati /
sanimittena sanimittā siddhir upajāyate /
animittenānimittā siddhir iṣṭā jinavaraiḥ //
sadā animitte sthitvā sanimittaṃ prasādhyate /
tasmāt sarvaprakāreṇa vinimittaṃ sevyate /

O master of the secret folk, there are two kinds of divine form—pure and impure. The pure kind is realized form, free from all signs. The impure kind has all signs, with color-and-shape forms. Now, two purposes go with those two kinds of divine form.

The holy Jinas have maintained that the kind
with signs generates *siddhi* with signs; and that
the kind without signs, the *siddhi* without signs.
When one is always stationed in the signless kind, he
can also bring to success the one with signs. Therefore,
by all means one should take recourse to the non-signed.

The work in which this is cited, the *Pradīpoddyotana*, is a commentary on the *Guhyasamājatantra* in the Anuttarayogatantra class of tantra.[72] The citation of this V-A-T passage from a chapter in a set of tantra generality chapters (see the list of Buddhaguhya's commentarial chapters) suggests that the V-A-T scriptural influence extends powerfully in the later tantra commentaries, even when on tantras of quite different subject matter than the content of the V-A-T. Other works cite the V-A-T, but as Sanskrit is not available for the bulk of the Tibetan Tanjur commentaries, I shall not go further with the topic. Enough has been shown as to indicate that the V-A-T enjoyed remarkable success as a Buddhist scripture, whether one wishes to call it a Sūtra or a Tantra.

3. MAKE-UP OF THE SCRIPTURE

Here there are three topics: (1) editions, (2) chapters, (3) appendices.

(1) ***Editions.*** The *Vairocanābhisaṃbodhi* is a scripture translated into Chinese, then into Korean and Japanese. It was translated into Tibetan and then into Mongolian. It has been translated from Tibetan into Japanese. The original Sanskrit is lost; and only excerpts from citations in Sanskrit texts have shown up. Here I shall list only a few important editions and dates.

c. 550 A.D. Composition of the original scripture, *Vairocanābhisaṃbodhi,* or *Vairocanābhisaṃbodhi-vikurvitādhiṣṭhana*, in the Sanskrit language, in the area of present-day Mahārāshtra.

674 A.D. Death of the Chinese Wu-hsing who had procured at Nālandā University in India a copy of the scripture's Sanskrit text after which it, along with other texts he had collected, was brought to China.

724-25 A.D. Translation of Wu-hsing's copy into Chinese by the India Śubhakarasiṃha (637-735 A.D.) with the help of the Chinese I-hsing.

c.760-70 A.D. Translation into Tibetan of Buddhaguhya's commentary on V-A-T with personal direction of Buddhaguhya.

c.775-800 A.D. Translation of the scripture V-A-T and Buddhaguhya's 'Concise Commentary' into Tibetan by Sīlendrabodhi and Dpal-brtsegs.

For further information, consult R. Tajima, *A Study of the Mahāvairocana-sūtra.*

(2) ***Chapters of the scripture.*** The 29 chapters of the Tibetan version are equivalent to the 31 chapters of the Sino-Japanese version. The correlating table given below shows various differences between the Chinese and the Tibetan in the titles of the chapters. Most of the differences are inconsequential. A number of the Tibetan titles are shorter, even when agreeing on the main words. The following appear to be the most salient differences between the two versions ('Ch' for Chinese; 'T' for Tibetan).

1. The three T chapters 7, 8, 9 are equivalent to the three chapters 28, 29, 30 which is a striking difference in placement.

2. Ch makes two chapters, 6, 7, where T has one chapter 6; and does this again, Ch 27, 31, for T 29.

3. Three chapters have material differences in the titles:

(a) Ch I emphasizes the *bodhicitta* (Mind of Enlightenment); T 1 goes with the list of minds found in the first chapter.

(b) Ch 22 has a good descriptive title "Recitation that preserves the accomplishment by the hundred Syllables", while T 24 is ambiguous as "self goal".

(c) Ch 27 " The manner of celebrating mundane and supramundane homa" is correct, while T 29 "Bodhisattva mantra practice" is inappropriate, since the chapter for the most part deals with different kinds of fire.

Besides those special divergences of chapter titles between T and Ch, there is a rather startling reference in Vajravarman's commentary on the *Sarvadurgatipariśodhana-tantra* called *Sundarālaṃkāra* (PTT. Vol. 76, p. 134-4-1,2,3,4), where he quotes the V-A-T by name, and explicitly the 33rd chapter (sum cu rtsa gsum pa): "Here, the bodhisattvas are to turn away from taking life,.... " citing sentences from V-A-T, T chap. 20, Ch chap. 18! The foregoing evidence suggests that originally the V-A-S or V-A-T had short or no chapter titles; that the Chinese titles reflect some editing in China. Also, the Chinese and Tibetan version reflect two different manuscript lineages. It is curious that some chapters are long, others quite short, thus five brief chapters on the 'hundred syllables' (Ch 19-23;T 21-25) but Vajravarman's text of the V-A-S must have had even further breakdowns of the presently longer chapters.

(3)***Appendices of the scripture.*** There are the Tibetan scripture appendix and the Sino-Japanese ritual appendix. First, for the scriptural appendix to the Tibetan version. Here there are seven chapters which this tradition calls 'continuation tantra' *(uttaratantra)* and which is lacking in Sino-Japanese. Buddhaguhya's commentary on the V-A-T does not comment on the 'continuation tantra' but does mention it in a manner that alludes to the last chapter on 'Arising of the Tathāgata'. In the Peking canon (PTT), Vol. 5, the seven chapters have these page references: Chap. XXX, 271-5-2; XXXI, 273-4-2; XXXII, 274-4-3; XXXIII, 275-2-2; XXXIV, 276-1-1; XXXV,276-4 -4; XXXVI, 277-1-3.

Correlation of Chinese and Tibetan Chapters of the Scripture.[73]

Chinese chapter titles in English			*Tibetan chapter titles in* English
Access to the Shingon gate for residence in the Bodhicitta	1	1	Different minds
Access to the maṇḍala with comprehensive conditions and mantras	2	2	Access to the maṇḍala
Suppression of obstacles	3	3	Suppression of demons
Storehouse of current mantras	4	4	Treasury of general mantras
Worldly siddhi	5	5	Working for mundane siddhi

Manifestation of siddhi	6	6	Reality of fulfilling siddhi
Accomplishment of siddhi	7	7	Establishing deity samādhi
Maṇḍala praxis by setting in motion the wheel of syllables	8	8	Samādhi without signs
The mystic mudrās	9	9	Reality of mundane and supramundane recitation
The wheel of syllables	10	10	The wheel of syllables
The esoteric maṇḍala	11	11	The mudrā
Method of access to the esoteric maṇḍala	12	12	Setting in motion the Dharma syllables
Access to the status of esoteric maṇḍala	13	13	The secret maṇḍala
The eight esoteric mudrās	14	14	Entering the secret maṇḍala
Observances prescribed for those practicing the vidyā	15	15	Eight secret mudrā
True wisdom of the ācārya	16	16	Guidance in the secret maṇḍala
Placement of the syllables	17	17	Observances of the vidyā
Points of instruction as a means	18	18	Reality of the ācārya
Explaining the production of the hundred syllables	19	19	Array of letters
Effect which corresponds to the hundred syllables	20	20	Method of instructing the Bodhisattvas
Fulfillment of the state of of the hundred syllables	21	21	Teaching the origin of the hundred syllables
Recitation that preserves the accomplishment by the hundred syllables	22	22	Fruitional praxis
The mantra method of the hundred syllables	23	23	Fruit of placing the hundred syllables
Explaining the nature of bodhi	24	24	Self goal
The triple samaya	25	25	Mantra rite of the hundred syllables
Explanation of the term Tathāgata	26	26	Teaching the nature of enlightenment
The manner of celebrating mundane and supramundane homa	27	27	Practice of the three samaya
Explaining the samādhi of the main deity	28	28	The Tathāgata
Explaining the samādhi without signs	29	29	Bodhisattva mantra practice
Mundane and supramundane recitation	30		
The transmission	31		

The chapters XXX to XXXIII are on *homa*, respectively for appeasing, prosperity, controlling and drastic purpose. They are a 'continuation' of Tibetan chap. XXIX, which I have studied in this work as the "Homa chapter".

Chapter XXXIV, 'Contemplating the vowel development and initiation', clearly takes its content from other works. It has a famous verse in Tibetan translation: "Whatever natures have arisen through causes, their cause the Tathāgata has declared and whatever is their cessation--speaking thus is the great ascetic *(mahāśramaṇa).*" This is immediately followed by a verse with Yogācāra flavor: "Since dependence on another *(Paratantra)* is not, while the perfect *(pariniṣpanna)* becomes otherwise, there are two (i.e. dependency and imaginary) which are not, but the two characterize the eight *vijñana.*"

Chapter XXXV, 'Rite of Recitation', rather brief, is a kind of introduction to Tantra, starting with the Bodhisattva vow and going to a few celebrated mantras that are in many other Tantras.

The final Chap. XXXVI, Empowering the great maṇḍala (called) 'Arising of the Tathāgata', can be taken as a 'continuation tantra' both for Chap. XXVIII ('The Tathāgata') from which it repeats the verse definitions of 'Bodhisattva', 'Tathāgata', 'Buddha', and 'Saṃbuddha'; and for the Chaps. XIII-XVI on the 'Secret Maṇḍala' on behalf of which it attempts to expand the depiction of the external form of this *maṇḍala.* Its size (227-1-3 to 284-3-1) is slightly longer than the largest chapter of the basic V-A-T, namely Chap. II (translated in this study); and can be interpreted as attempting to do for the 'Secret Maṇḍala', what Chap. II does for the *Mahākaruṇāgarbhodbhava-maṇḍala.*

Of the seven 'continuation tantra' chapters, I presume the first six liberally borrow from other texts, while the seventh (Chap. XXXVI) appears to be an original attempt of exposition. In order to be accepted as a 'continuation tantra' it should be admitted that this set of seven chapters was composed sometime after the original scripture (as herein held, in mid-sixth century A.D. and in Mahārāshtra), and composed in the same place at whatever time; but not necessarily by one person. The set of seven may well have been composed by colleagues, one a *homa* specialist who composed the four *homa* chapters; another, composing the two generality chapters XXXIV and XXXV; and still another, writing the large chapter XXXVI. Since this set of seven chapters was not translated into Chinese, it follows that its composition is after the basic text was procured by the Chinese Wu-hsing at Nālandā University (he died in 674 A.D.) and prior to the translation into Tibetan of Buddhaguhya's commentaries, *c.* 760-70, hence it was composed *c.* last quarter of seventh century, or first quarter of eighth century, and probably composed in an area different from the original movement of the scripture, hence presumably either in Bengal or in Nepal, where the scripture plus these extra chapters would be readily available to the Buddhist pandits who brought texts to Tibet.

Next, for the scriptural appendix to the Sino-Japanese version. This tradition groups the chapters of the V-A-S into six parts' (Ch. *kuan*) without titles, and classifies the ritual appendix as 'part seven'. In Chinese the oral teaching of Śubhakarasiṃha, taken down by I-Hsing (Tajima has the French transcription Yi-hing), for the basic scripture is continued for the five chapters of ritual appendix (Taishō No. 1797, as entered in Tajima's bibliography). This ritual appendix was apparently brought to China independently by Vajrabodhi and Śubhakarasiṃha where each translated it (see Tajima, "Plan of the Dainichikyō"). Now, a modern Japanese scholar has shown that the Tibetan canon has an approximately equivalent work, not in the scripture section (Kanjur), but in the commentarial section (Tanjur), namely, the *Mahāvairocanābhisambodhisambaddhapūjāvidhi,* by Dpal-bzaṅ rab-dga', translated by Padmākaravarma and Rin-chen bzaṅ-po.[74] The fact that this ritual appendix exists in both Chinese and Tibetan in approximately equal form, was translated into Chinese independently of the basic scripture, while in Tibet it is preserved as a commentary—suggests that rather soon after the original composition of the scripture (as herein, mid-sixth century) a ritual handbook was added to help in coordinating scriptural chapters in a ritual sense. In the beginning, this treatise was recognized as not part of the original scripture, yet closely bound up with it by using the scripture's mantras and terminology. There existed slightly different versions of this same ritual handbook. The initial form of this ritual handbook may be as early as beginning of seventh century; the recension in the Tibetan Tanjur is obviously much later. Now I shall take only a few points from each of the five chapters of the Tibetan version to give an idea of the contents.

Chap. I. "Situation for being instructed in the praxis of mantra" *(sṇags kyi spyod pa'i bslab pa'i gnas)*. This title does not mean actual instruction in mantra, but rather the practices that get the disciple into the situation where he merits receiving this mantra instruction from the guru. In fact, it goes with the V-A-T, Chap. One, the Mahāyāna instruction in generating compassion, getting rid of bad minds among the 60 minds delineated in Chap. One. So here one must learn to honor the guru, restrain the six sense organs to achieve *samādhi,* enhance one's merits and dispel one's faults. One avoids gatherings of persons, and resorts to places appropriate for meditation. One delights in the Dharma, and craves the fruits promised by the rite.

Chap. II. "Teaching the protection" (*bsruṅ ba bstan pa*). This goes with V-A-T, Chap. Two, Part II, 'The Several Means', which has a number of protective mantras (which are given in my translation, herein). Here, in the Peking edition (PTT), p. 216-5-6 ff. the author gives the *mudrā* with palms upon the other, with thumbs coming up to a point (the *mudrā* of vairocana in the Garbha-maṇḍala), saying it arises from the Dharmadhātu, is the 'great seal' (mahāmudrā) which purifies the Dharmadhātu, and has as *mantra* the first of the set in the Chap. Two, Part II, Namaḥ samantabuddhānām/ dharmadhātusvabhāva ātmako 'ham/ (cf. my translation, with note 147; Buddhaguhya mentions only that it is the 'entrance' and involves voidness).

Chap. III. "Teaching the rite of offerings" (*mchod pa'i cho ga bstan pa*). This goes with V-A-T, Chap. Three, 'Suppression of Demons'. As in the V-A-T, one must adopt the lord Acala as a protective deity. As we learned from Buddhaguhya's commentary, the demons have the colors of the elements. Here, the elements are imagined in the order wind (black), fire (red), water (white), and earth (yellow). The officiant imagines a series of offerings, and invites the Jina and his spiritual sons to partake of them. One employs mantras and mudrā-s. To the Japanese version of the ritual appendix, the Shingon priest R. Kambayashi adds a note on three kinds of offerings: (1) exterior, namely, flowers, food, place decorations, (2) offering of praxis, namely by one's discipline, confession of sins, and so on, (3) interior, i.e., offering of mind, by comprehending the doctrine and by dwelling on the letter "A".

Chap. IV. "Teaching the rite of recitation" (*bzlas brjod k yi cho ga bstan pa*). This goes with Tibetan chap. of V-A-T, no. 9,

'Mundane and Supramundane Recitation'. Buddhaguhya's commentary is Chap. 28. This is on the "four members of muttering". One is transformed into such a deity as Mañjughoṣa, and imagines such a deity in front; one imagines one's own mind (the bodhicitta) as a moon-maṇḍala in the heart of that deity in front; and imagines syllables upon that moon-maṇḍala. The syllable there on which one dwells might be the syllable "A", colored yellow. And having 'dwelling in the flame', i.e., the tip of flame in the deity's heart, which the text (PTT, p. 220-4-3) says has a pure light that destroys the deity of ignorance. These members of muttering lead to occult success (*siddhi*), here said to be of three kinds: appeasing, prosperity, dreadful, related to geometrical forms of *homa*.

Chap. V. "Career upward toward reality" (*de kho na ñid la lhag par mos pa*). This goes with the two V-A-T Chaps. 7-8, 'Samādhi of the gods' and 'Samādhi without signs', which in Buddhaguhya's commentary are Chapters 26-27. One aspires to have the immense knowledge of the Buddhas and Bodhisattvas; and hopes that all sentient beings may have their aspirations fulfilled. One vows to never fall away from the Mahāyāna. Imbued with the Mind of Enlightenment he is Vajrasattva who empowers the mantras and mudrā-s. He adheres to the glorious practice of the Bodhisattvas. He identifies with *nātha* Acala or with Trailokyavijaya (conqueror of the three worlds)—where the 'three worlds' according to the Sino-Japanese ritual appendix are the three poisons of greed (=lust), hatred, and delusion.

4. BUDDHAGUHYA'S COMMENTARY ON THE V-A-T

Buddhaguhya belongs to the middle eighth century, A.D. This is shown by his letter, preserved in the Tibetan Tanjur, dispatched to the Tibetan king Khri-sroṅ lde-'u-btsan, whose reign began 755 A.D. Not much is known of the lineages carried by this eminent author, except that he was a direct disciple of Buddha (śrī) jñāna, responsible for one of the two main commentarial cycles on the *Guhyasamājatantra*, the one called Ye-śes źabs, and who took Prajñāpāramitā scriptures as the basis for Tantra.

Because Buddhaguhya came to Tibet and worked with the Tibetan translators, probably all his main works (originally composed in the Sanskrit language) have been translated into the Tibetan language. Thus, besides his concise commentary on the meaning of the *Vairocanābhisambodhi-tantra* (V-A-T) and the large commentary on the chapters of this scripture, he has similarly written two commentaries on the *Subāhuparipṛcchā-tantra.* He has also written a commentary on the meaning of the *Tattvasaṃgraha-tantra* called *Tantrārthāvatāra;* and an attributed commentary in the composition order of the *Sarvadurgatipariśodhana-tantra.* He has also written commentaries on the brief but important *Dhyānottara* and *Vajravidāraṇā-dhāraṇi.* Almost all of his translated works are included in the tantric section of the Tibetan canon called Tanjur, the V-A-T commentaries as well, since the scripture is counted as a Tantra in the Tibetan canon, although a Sūtra in the Chinese-Japanese tradition of this scripture.

Of all his works, though, his two main commentaries on the V-A-T can be considered the high point of his career as an author. This is because this scripture is highly sophisticated in its explicit expression with about a thousand verses, and a rich prose; and takes much for granted of its readers in its broad coverage of doctrinal matters, its delineation of ritual movement, its depiction of many deities. I believe it strained Buddhaguhya's commentarial power to its utmost. Fortunately, Buddhaguhya, as I learned from some of his other commentaries, is encyclopedic in knowledge, which he is willing to share with the reader.

I shall refer to his commentary on the chapters of the V-A-T as 'B-comm.' The title is reconstructed as *Vairocanābhisambodhi-tantravṛtti* (the word *vṛtti* meaning 'commentary'). There is no record of the translators, but presumably Buddhaguhya himself directed the translation in Tibet, circa 760-70 A.D. near the end of his life. As far as is known there has been only one translation into Tibetan, although there is a later version of the B-comm. by Gźon-nu dpal. Accordingly, there is the terminology 'unedited' for the original translation and 'edited' for Gźon-nu dpal's modified version of the one translation.[75]

I shall refer to Buddhaguhya's work on the concise meaning (piṇḍārtha) of the V-A-T as 'Concise-comm.' With title catalogued as *Vairocanābhisaṃbodhitantrapiṇḍārtha,* it is translated into Tibetan by the same pair, Śīlendrabodhi and Dpal-brtsegs rakṣita, who translated the V-A-T itself into Tibetan. This occurred in the last quarter of the 8th century, but in the generation after Buddhaguhya's lifetime.

Before treating the B-comm. it appears necessary to point out the main problems involved. These are that the order of chapters differs in the Tibetan scripture (V-A-T) and the Chinese scripture (V-A-S); and that the B-comm. ('unedited version') has a different order of chapters from the Tibetan scripture on which it comments, as far as the Tibetan renditions are concerned. It is also a fact that none of Buddhaguhya's works are extant in the original Sanskrit, and so for considerations about the B-comm. and the Concise-comm. we are limited to inspecting their Tibetan renditions.

For the present work I have utilized throughout the old version of B-comm. ('unedited'), and so the text numbers are to this version in the Peking Kanjur-Tanjur (PTI), which also has the later version ('edited') (while the Derge edition of the Tanjur has only the 'edited' version). During the Orientalist meeting in Japan in early September 1983, Professor Shinjō Kawasaki of Tsukuba University endorsed my employment of the 'unedited' B-comm.(suggesting that Japanese researches had cast doubt on the standard of the 'edited' version). However, I have had to consult the 'edited' version; and even the 'unedited' version must have endured a later attempt to touch it up. For example, when analyzing the *homa* chapter (including in this work) I noticed among numerous names in B-comm. that some had corruptions identical with the corruptions of those names in the V-A-T chapter. Besides, in a few cases chapter numbers were entered at the ends of chapters of B-comm., but I had to disregard them because they did not work out. Thus, at B-comm. 206-4-7, the no. "24" is given for chapter just ended, while in fact it is B-comm.'s no. 22 of the text as presently extant. Much earlier, at 176-4-6, the no. "11" is given, while it is no. 9. The numbers given are few and do not even agree with the numbers of the V-A-T chapters, so they appear as clumsy attempts, whereas the original B-comm. probably had no chapter numbers at all. Perhaps this kind of re-touching occurred when correcting the early orthography, as was generally necessary for the early canonical works.

Gźon-nu dpal's version ('edited') is much more drastic in its modifications. To give an indication of his method, I shall mention five sensitive points that commanded his attention (probably there were others), and afterwards will give his solutions along with my evaluations of them.

(1) B-comm. comments on the brief chapters, "Samādhi of the Gods", "Samādhi without Signs", and "Mundane and Supramundane Recitation" as its chapters in my numbering, nos. 26, 27, 28, whereas V-A-T has these chapters as nos. VII, VIII, IX.

(2) B-comm. at 209-1-1 has a virtual duplication of its chapter "Eight Secret Mudrā-s" (Just preceding its comments on "Samādhi of the Gods") that came earlier at 188-2-6, no. 12 in my numbering.

(3) B-comm. apparently has no commentary on V-A-T, Chap. V ('Working for Mundane Siddhi'), or on V-A-T, Chap. XXV ('Mantra Rite of the Hundred Syllables').

(4) For the chapters V-A-T, XVIII ('Reality of the *ācārya*') and XIX ('Array of Letters') there is an apparent B-comm. 193-4-8 to 195-3-6, but where does Chap. XIX begin?

(5) V-A-T, Chap. XIII ('Secret Maṇḍala') has at 246-3-3, 4: he dwells in the three pure places (Tib *gnas gsum la ni 'dug pa*). On this B-comm. 186-3-5 explains that he dwells in "the wind circle" following this by the word 'two' (*gñis*) and in "the fire circle" following this by the word 'three' (*gsum*). How is the commentary to be corrected?

Now for Gźon-nu d pal's solutions:

(1) He moved the three chapters of B-comm. to the earlier places in agreement with their order in the V-A-T, Tibetan version in the Kanjur. However, the Chinese version of the scripture has those three chapters toward the end approximately in agreement with the places of commenting in B-comm.'s plan of organizing the commentary.

(2) He .dropped out the duplication of the "Eight Secret Mudrā-s" chapter. This was certainly proper to do.

(3) No commentary was found for V-A-T, Chap. V, or Chap. XXV. This shows that Gźon-nu dpal had no further version, did not have access to an original Sanskrit manuscript of the work; and it shows why the 'edited' version is unable to assign chapter numbers.

(4) He kept the mention of chapter ending for 'Reality of the *ācārya*' along with repetition of the incorrect chapter no. "16", but correctly moved it up higher by a line to precede the words "*ka ni lkog mar śes b ya*" to inaugurate a mere summary reference to the content of V-A-T Chap. XIX ('Array of syllables') which assigns places in the body for the 32 syllables, Ka, etc. Then he made up a new indication of chapter ending for 'Array of Letters' (where there was no such indication in the 'unedited' version) just preceding the next chapter 'Method of Instructing the Bodhisattvas'. One should concede that Gźon-nu dpal acted properly in this solution.

(5). For the thorny problem of the "three pure places", Gźon-nu dpal left the 'two' after the "the wind circle" but changed the 'three' after "the fire circle" to a 'one' *(gcig)*, the 'two' and the 'one' totalling 'three'. He thus interpreted B-comm. to mean: "two of the wind circle" and "one of the circle". My own solution differs: I assume that *gñis* should be *gñis pa* ('second') and *gsum* should be read *gsum pa* ('third'), meaning that B-comm. text had lost the indication of the 'first' pure place which I went on to suppose (see my n. 58 to chap. II translation in this work) is the 'water circle'.

The 'unedited' version of the B-comm. is my source of references in this work, not Gźon-nu dpal's 'edited' version; and we must appreciate that the Peking canon has included both versions.

Before presenting the list of chapters in B-comm. it will be necessary to speak about the lost commentary on Chap. V. The 'Concise'-comm. at 107-2-3, generously cites the brief chapter of fifteen verses. B-comm. 212-1-2, on Chap. IX ('Mundane and Supramundane Recitation') states: "When involved with the 'impure deity' (i.e. attended with images), one is equipped with the four members of muttering (Tib. *bzlas pa' i yan lag bźir idan pa*), which were previously explained *(snar yan bśad zin te)*." Looking back in the B-comm., at 194-4-2, the outset of the commentary on V-A-T, Chap. XXI ('Origin of the hundred letters') there is this significant remark: "The initial exposition of the inner and outer four members of muttering was in the section on reciting mantras according to the empowerment in this diamond-ornament circle of the Bhagavat Vairocana's Inexhaustible Body, and so on. Later on, there was the exposition of the inner four members of muttering in the section on heart (mantras) of the Tathāgatas. And later than that, there was the exposition of the inner three members of muttering in the section on the heart (mantras) of the great hero. Those places (of V-A-T) state the definite service in terms of amount and times for the recitation." B-comm. certainly points to the importance of the topic. Indeed, we must conclude that B-comm. commented upon V-A-T. Chap. V exactly in its position, on which Tibetan and Chinese agree, namely, among the five chapters devoted to the heading Maṇḍala of the Lord's Inexhaustible Body, the chapters II through VI. That V-A-T, Chap. V, teaches the four members of muttering will be shown in my chapter "chapter V, and the preliminary service", so this is what B-comm. means as the "initial exposition". The second exposition is in V-A-T, Chap VI, as discussed at length in B-comm. 162-1-2, ff: and the mention (B-comm. 162-1-5) of a previous exposition *(snar bśad pa)* clearly points to V-A-T, Chap. V and commentary thereon. The third exposition is apparently that of V-A-T, Chap. XVII ('Observations of the *vidyā-vrata')* which emphasizes the times in terms of months; and the reference to hero is there, because after Vajrapāṇi asks the Buddha to explain the *vidyā-vrata,* the Buddha begins the answer (V-A-T, text, 266-3-5) by remarking, "Vajrapāṇi, great being (mahāsattva) of great status *(mahānubhāva),* hero ! It is good *(sādhu)*".

Using Buddhaguhya's own comments at different places of B-comm., I am able to group his commentarial chapters. Of great importance is the grouping for the chapters on the 'inexhaustible body', 'inexhaustible speech', and inexhaustible mind'. B-comm. is careful to clearly indicate these. Thus B-comm. 170-2-7, concluding the commentary on Chap. VI, states: "From among the empowerments of the three *maṇḍala-s*, the circles of Body, Speech and Mind of the Vairocanābhisambodhi, (now concluded) is the elucidation of the empowerment of the Body circle, the *maṇḍala* of *mahākaruṇā*". Then B-comm. 170-2-8, states: "I shall elucidate here (Chap. X) 'Turning the Wheel of Syllables', the empowerment of the Speech circle". Then B-comm. 170-2-6, beginning its commentary on Chap. XIII (Secret Maṇḍala) mentions that there are those three empowerments of Body, Speech, Mind and that the elucidation of the first two having just concluded, "now will be expounded the empowerment of the Dharmakāya, the *maṇḍala* of inexhaustible Mind."

In the following, besides the beginning numbers of chapters in the commentary ('unedited' version), using the Peking canon, I shall present the beginning numbers for the corresponding V-A-T chapters, order in the Tibetan canon, giving the Peking photo edition (PTT) reference in terms of page, folio side and line numbers.

Commentary chapters		*V-A-T chapters*	
MAHĀYĀNA INTRODUCTION			
1. 111-2-7	Different Minds	I.	240-5-1
MAṆḌALA OF THE LORD'S INEXHAUSTIBLE BODY			
2. 129-5-2	Access to the Maṇḍala	II.	243-5-6
3. 157-3-4	Suppression of Demons	III.	250-2-5
4. 159-4-3	(Introduction to) Treasury of General Mantras	IV.	250-4-8
5. —	Working for the Mundane siddhi (missing)	V.	252-1-4
6. 159-5-2	Reality of Fulfilling Siddhi		
MAṆḌALA OF THE LORD'S INEXHAUSTIBLE SPEECH			
7. 170-2-7	Wheel of Syllables	X.	256-3-3
8. 174-1-2	The Mudrā	XI.	258-1-6
9. 175-5-6	Setting into Motion the Dharma Syllables	XII.	261-3-4

MAṆḌALA OF THE LORD'S INEXHAUSTIBLE MIND			
10. 176-4-6	The Secret Maṇḍala	XIII.	261-4-8
11. 187-4-2	Entering the Secret Maṇḍala	XIV.	265-2-7
12. 188-2-6	Eight Secret Mudrā-s	XV.	265-3-3
13. 189-1-8	Guidance in the Secret Maṇḍala	XVI.	265-5-3
OBSERVANCES FOR ALL THREE MAṆḌALAS			
14. 191-5-4	Observances of the Vidyā-vrata	XVII.	266-3-1
15. 193-4-8	Reality of the Ācārya	XVIII.	266-5-2
16. 195-3-3	Array of Letters	XIX.	267-2-1
17. 195-3-7	Method of Instructing the Bodhisattvas	XX.	267-2-7
THE HUNDRED SYLLABLES			
18. 197-4-2	Origin of the Hundred Syllables	XXI.	268-4-1
19. 199-2-1	Fruitional Praxis	XXIII.	268-4-8
20. 201-4-7	Fruit of Placing the Hundred Syllables	XXIII.	269-1-4
21. 205-1-1	Self Goal	XXIV.	269-4-1
22.—	Mantra Rite of the Hundred Syllables (missing)	XXV.	270-2-3
FRUITION			
23. 206-2-6	Nature of Complete Enlightenment	XXVI.	270-2-8
24. 206-4-7	Practice of the three Samaya	XXVII.	270-3-6
25. 208-2-6	The Tathāgata	XXVIII.	270-5-3
— 209-1-1	(duplication of Chap. 12)		
TANTRA GENERALITIES			
26. 210-1-6	Samādhi of the Gods	VII.	255-5-2
27. 210-5-6	Samādhi without Signs	VIII.	256-1-4
28. 211-5-8	Mundane and Supramundane Recitation	IX.	256-2-6
FOUNDATION OF HOMA			
29. 212-3-8	Mantra Practice of the Bodhisattva	XXIX.	271-1-1

The order of Buddhaguhya's commentarial chapters is quite close to the chapter order of the Sino-Japanese V-A-S. This supports a conclusion that this is the basic order. In short, the early position in the Tibetan canonical version of the three chapters it places as VII, VIII and IX, might be a peculiarity of the manuscript that was at the disposal of the translators of the version preserved in the Tibetan canon, or might reflect an alternate textual tradition.

B-comm. is only on the scripture itself, not on the seven chapters of Continuation Tantra, namely XXX-XXXVI. There is no reason to doubt that Buddhaguhya had for commentarial purposes a manuscript of the V-A-T amounting to what is in the Tibetan canon (irrespective of chapter order), to wit, the V-A-T with twenty-nine chapters of the basic scripture, plus the seven appendix chapters. The commentary at 189-2-6 on XVI ('Guidance in the Secret Maṇḍala') refers to the *maṇḍala* of the ('Continuation Tantra' in a manner agreeing with the content of the last appendix chapter (XXXIV). Buddhaguhya's commentary on the *Subhāhuparipṛcchā-tantra,* the "tshig gi don bśad" (Derge Rgyud ǵrel, Vol. Thu, f. 60a-3-4), when commenting upon the expression meaning "having the heart (mantra) of *pratityasamuṭpāda*", cites from the *Vairocanābhīsambodhi-tantra* the famous verse found in the Continuation Tantra, Chap. XXXIV, "Whatever natures have arisen, ..."

NOTES

1. See part 4 of these textual studies for description of Buddhaguhya's commentary.
2. I give here only the main details of Buddhaguhya's commentary on the title Japanese photo ed. of Tibetan Peking canon (PTT). Vol. 77, 111-3, 4.
3. For the two senses of 'tathāgata', cf. Etienne Lamotte. *Le traité de la Grande Vertu de Sagesse* (Bureaux du *Muśeon*, Louvain, 1944), Tome l, p. 126.
4. See Alex Wayman, "Three Tanjur Commentators—Buddhaguhya, Ratnākaraśānti, and smṛtijñānakīrti". *The Tibet Journal,* VIII, 3 Autumn 1983, pp. 26-27, while citing Buddhaguhya's explanation from his 'Concise commentary' on the *Vairocanābhisambodhi-vikurvitādhiṣṭhāna* of the four bodies of the Buddha.
5. Cf. Udānavarga (ed. Franz Bernhard, Götingen, 1968) XXII, 12: ye rūpeṇa praminṿanti mām ghoṣenānuyānti ca / chandarāgavaśopetā na mām janānti te janāḥ// "Whoever estimate me by form, and follow after me by sound, those persons, controlled as the are by sensuous lust, do not know me."
6. Wayman "Three Tanjur. . ." (n. 4, above), pp. 27-28.
7. Wayman "Three Tanjur. . ." p. 27.
8. PTT, Vol. 5, p. 256-4-5.
9 PTT. Vol. 77, p. 102-5-2, ff. Buddhaguhya also refers to the 'First Eon' when commenting on the V-A-T, Homa chapter (see our Study this chapter, beginning).
10. Cf. *Mkhas-grub-rje's Fundamentals of the Buddhist Tantras,* tr. by F.D. Lessing and A. Wayman (The Hague, 1968), pp. 27-35, for the theory of the five Abhisaṃbodhi.

11. PTT, Vol. 77 p. 88-4, 5. There appears to be a slight bit of corruption in this passage. The text's "six pāramitā-s" is impossible because the extant Sanskrit citation uses the expression *upāya*, which in Mahāyāna Buddhism is the first five 'perfections' (*pāramitā*); and the sixth, *prajña-pāramitā*, would be included in the 'omniscient wisdom'. Likewise, the text uses the expression (Tibetan) *rgyu* for all three causes, to wit *Jug pa' i rgyu, ñe bar len pa'i rgyu. lhan cig byed pa'i rgyu*; but in the Mahāyāna period there would be one *hetu* (T. *rgyu*), the rest *pratyaya* (T. *rkyen*). Since *bodhicitta* is termed *hetuka*, this should be the only *hetu* of the three.
12. PTT, Vol. 77, p. 111-4-7: / raṅ bźin gyi dkyil 'khor 'di ni rgyud 'di'i rgyud yin no/.
13. For an argument about this theory, see Y. Karunadasa, *Buddhist Analysis of Matter* (The Department of Cultural Affairs, Colombo, 1967), p. 34.
14. Motohiro Yoritomi, "Kongosattā zuzō obegaki (Part I)", *Mikkyō zuzō Gakkai,* Vol. I, 1982, pp. 37(b)-38(a).
15. Cf. Ninkaku Takata, "The Relation between Esoterism and the Tathāgatagarbha Theory as seen in the Shou-hu-kuo-chieh-chudharaṇī-ching", *Journal of Indian and Buddhist Studies* (Indogaku Bukkyōgaku Kenkyū), Vol. IX No. 2 (March, 1961), pp. 725-30.
16. Shunkyo Katsumata, in his essay (in Japanese), "The Tradition of the Thought Concerning the Development of Bodhicitta", *Journal of Indian and Buddhist Studies*, Vol. IX, No. 1 (January 1961), pp. 1-7.
17. Cf.N. Takata, "The Relations. . ." (n. 15, above), p. 36, where he mentions as found in the tantric scripture 'compassion as a root' amounting to sixteen great compassions, and 'the means as a conclusion' amounting to thirty-two actions. However, neither the Chinese commentary on the V-A-S nor the Tibetan commentary on the V-A-T in the respective canons, when coming to the place of the scripture's Chap. I, where this formula is given, show any knowledge of the 'sixteen great compassions' or 'thirty-two actions'.
18. Jisshu Oshika, *Tibetan Text of Ārya-Acala-Mahākrodharaja-kalpa,* 1978, *Acta Indologica IV* (Naritasan Shinshoji, 1976/9).
19. Oshika, *Tibetan Text*, p. 310.8-13.
20. See A. Wayman's Received Teaching of Tibet and Analysis of the Tantric Canon, reprinted in *The Buddhist Tantras; Light on Indo-Tibetan Esotericism* (Samuel Weiser, New York, 1973), p. 237, using number of the Tohoku catalog of the Derge Kanjur-Tanjur, where the V-A-T has no. 494, the *Acala-kalpa,* no. 495, and the commentarial cycle 2662-2669 (V-A-T exegesis, nos. 2662-2665; exegesis of *krodha* form of Mañjuśrī, nos. 2666-2669).
21. Oshika, *Tibetan Text,* p. 204.30-31.
22. For the list of ten *vaśitā* going with the Eighth Stage, and the list of ten Bodhisattva powers called *bala* prevalent on the Ninth Stage, cf. Alex and Hideko Wayman, *The Lion's Roar of Queen Śrīmālā* (Columbia University Press, New York, 1974), pp. 82-3.
23. From *Mahāyānasaṃgraha,* II, 14B; cf. Nagao Gajin, *Shōdaijō-ron,* Part I (Tokyo, 1972), pp. 72-3 (Sanskrit-Tibetan part, prepared with the help of N. Aramaki).
24. See Ariane Macdonald, *Le maṇḍala du Mañjuśrīmūlakalpa* (Adrien-Maisonneuve, Paris, 1962), p. 29; and also, Marcelle Lalou, *Iconographie des Étoffes Peintes (Paṭa) dans le Mañjuśrīmūlakalpa,* Planche I and Planche II.

25. Debala Mitra's *Ajanta* (Department of Archeology, India, no date), p. 4; and *Buddhist Monuments* (Sahitya Samsad, Calcutta, 1971), p. 181.
26. M.K. Dhavalikar, "The Origin of Tārā", *Bulletin of the Deccan College Research Institute,* XXIV, 1963-64, p. 18. In D. C. Sirkar (editor), *The Śakti Cult and Tārā* (University of Calcutta, 1967), recording a seminar held there in 1965, R. S. Gupta (p. 180) took a position agreeing, in effect, with Dhavalikar; While D. C. Sirkar (109) argued for the East India origin of Tārā, appealing to the *Tārāstotra* by Candragomin, whom he identifies with the grammarian of fifth or sixth century who lived in Candradvīpa in Southern Bengal. The trouble with Sircar's position is that there are probably three Buddhist authors named Candragomin, the grammarian being the earliest; a second placed in the seventh century by Mark Tatz ("The Life of Candragomin in Tibetan Historical Tradition", *The Tibet Journal*, VII:3, 1982, pp. 1-22); and a third which I place in the late eighth century, who wrote praises and ritual of Tārā, and is probably the one who wrote a commentary on the *Mañjuśrī-nāma-saṃgīti*.
27. M. Winternitz, *A History of Indian Literature,* Vol. 1 (part 1 & 2) (University of Calcutta, 1962), p. 485.
28. See information with notes 15-17, above. Also, N. Takata (n. 15, above) mentions p. 730, that the two translators of this tantric scripture, namely Prajña and Muniśrī entrusted it to Kūkai, hence in the latter eighth century. This does not explain when this particular scripture was composed, except that it follows the *Vairocanābhisaṃbodhi* and precedes its translation into Chinese.
29. Hajime Nakamura, "A Critical Survey of Mahāyāna and Esoteric Buddhism Chiefly based upon Japanese Studies", *Acta Asiatica* (Bulletin of the Institute of Eastern Culture), 7 (the Toho Gakkai, Tokyo, 1964), "The Second Chapter: Esoteric Buddhism", p. 76, mentions that some Japanese scholars opined that V-A-S was composed in North India about 500 A.D., while another opinion puts the composition about 650. My own conclusion therefore sets the date between these limits.
30. J. N. Banerjea, *Paurānic and Tantric Religion* (University of Calcutta, 1966), p. 147.
31. See entry 'Skanda' in Sures Chandra Banerji, *Kālidāsa-kośa* (Chowkhamba Sanskrit Series Office, Varanasi, 1968), p. 59.
32. Cf. Marcelle Lalou, *Iconographie des etoffes peintes (paṭa) dans le Mañjuśrīmūlakalpa* (Paul Geuthner, Paris, 1930), pp. 68-69.
33. Sylvain Lévi, *Sanskrit Texts from Bāli* (Oriental Institute, Baroda, 1933), p. 77.18.
34. I treat this matter later in this very section under 'Orissa'.
35. Cf. Moti Chandra, *Trade and Trade Routes in Ancient India* (Abhinav Publications, New Delhi, 1977), p. 23.
36. D. Mitra, *Buddhist Monuments* (cited above), pp. 149-189.
37. R. Sen Gupta, *A Guide to the Buddhist Caves of Elura* (Bhulabhai Memorial Institute, Bombay, 1958), p. 24.
38. Sen Gupta, *A Guide,* pp. 29-30.
39. D. Mitra, *Buddhist Monuments*, pp. 163-4.
40. D. Mitra, *Buddhist Monuments*, p. 164.
41. Cf. Amita Ray's article "Sculptures in Aurangabad", *Marg,* XVI,3, June 1963.

42. Debala Mitra, *Bronzes from Achutrajpur, Orissa* (Agam Kala Prakashan, Delhi, 1975), p.10.
43. D. Mitra, *Bronzes,* pp. 7-8.
44. D. Mitra, *Bronzes,* p. 8.
45. Motohiro Yoritomi, "Indo Mikkyō chōsa chūkan hōkoku (1)", *Mikkyōgaku,* No.18, 1982, pp. 51-81. On the occasion of the First International Conference on Buddhism and National Cultures, New Delhi, Oct. 10-15, 1984, Dr. Debala Mitra told me that she disagrees with the identification of these Orissa images as Vairocana ones, in particular saying they do not have the Vairocana *mudrā* as I depicted it to her (cf. my Intro. to V-A-T, Chap. II, 'Description of Mahāvairocana'); but from the photos which Yoritomi supplied me, it is difficult to decide; the one with the V-A-T, Chap. VI mantra on the back side presumably should be accepted as Mahāvairocana; a third image with eight Boddhisattvas definitely has the *samādhi-mudrā,* which is not Vairocana's. As to this last mentioned image, Debala Mitra, *Ratnagiri (1958-61)* (Archaeological Survey of India, New Delhi, 1983), Vol. II, pp. 314-5, and pl. CCLX, depicts and describes it as possibly a Dharmasankha-samādhi-Mañjuśrī. Granted that it does have features in common with this variety of Mañjuśrī (cf. Mari-Therese de Mallmann, *Etude iconographique sur Mañjuśrī* Paris, 1964, Pl. VI, depicting this variety), but this form of Mañjuśri has a differing headdress. Since Mañjuśrī is one of the eight Bodhisattvas, he would not reasonably be also the central deity. See *Mkhas grub rje's Fundamentals of the Buddhist Tantras,* tr. by Lessing and Wayman, p. 105 and p. 121. Here we learn that the lord of the Tathāgata family is Bhagavat Śākyamuni, and that here are also the eight great Bodhisattvas. Hence, the deity surrounded by eight Bodhisattvas may be this form of Śākyamuni in the pure abode (*śuddhāvāsa*), said to be seated on a lion throne formed by the Bodhisattvas of the tenth stage who had magically transformed themselves into lions.
46. By reference to our Introduction to Chap. II, V-A-T, 'comparison with the *Taizo genzu maṇḍala*', of the three traditions there expounded, Yoritomi, "Indo Mikkyō", says that this image which he identifies as Vairocana is the (1) 'Taizō zuzō, namely, agreeing with the description is Śubhakarasiṃha's commentary in Chinese (Taishō 1796) on the *Mahāvairocana-sūtra*. It is without ornamentation.
47. Yoritomi, "Indo Mikkyō", says that this Vairocana image is the (2) 'Taizō Kyū zuyo', namely, agreeing with the Tibetan version, which I call V-A-T. It is ornamented.
48. For this story my summary has two sources: (1) Chou Yi-liang, "Tantrism in China", *Harvard Journal of Asiatic Studies,* Vol. 8, nos. 3-4, March, 1945, pp. 241-332, in particular pp. 251-72. (2) Ryūjo Kambayashi, introduction to the *Kokuyaku Issaikyō* series version of the Sino-Japanese *Mahāvairocana-sūtra* called in Japanese *Dainichikyō* (as read by my wife Hideko).
49. Rajendralala Mitra, *The Antiquities of Orissa,* Vol. I (reprint by Indian Studies Past & Present, Calcutta, 1961), p. vi.
50. Biswarup Das, *The Bhauma-karas-Buddhist Kings of Orissa and Their Times* (Oriental Publishers, New Delhi, 1978), Chap. 2.
51. Chou Yi-liang (n. 48, above),p. 254.
52. Leon Hurvitz, tr. *Scripture of the Lotus Blossom of the Fine Dharma* (Columbia University Press, New York, 1976).

53. It is curious that Mañjuśrī should come up at this point; but observe M. Lalou (n. 32, above), p. 68 Mañjuśrī is a spiritual son of the Buddha Saṃkusumita.
54. R. Kambayashi (n. 48, above), Intro., p. 2.
55. Chou Yi-liang (n. 48, above), p. 254.
56. R. Mitra (n. 49, above) mentions (pp. xiv-xv) that when the pilgrim Hsüan-tsang was at the port Tāmralipta in Bengal planning to go to Ceylon he was advised that it would be a dangerous course to try to get there from this port; rather one should proceed to south-east India, take in the sacred monuments of Orissa, and use a southern port, in which case one could arrive in Ceylon within three days. This would naturally be the Orissa port.
57. My interpretation that he decided to go to China years after his study with Dharmagupta—going against the story as preserved in the Chinese chronicle—is because it makes no sense that Śubhakarasiṃha learned his Tantra as an old man, and then suddenly upon going to China is able to give an oral commentary on the profound, sophisticated *Mahāvairocana-sūtra.* Indeed, his decision to go to China implies he was invited (he was already renowned for his command of the topic).
58. In Tajima's *Study of the Mahāvairocana-sūtra.*
59. Cho Yi-liang (n. 48, above), pp. 262-263.
60. Binayendra Nath Chaudhury, *Buddhist Centres in Ancient India* (Sanskrit College, Calcutta, 1969), pp. 189-191.
61. C. Collin Davies, *An Historical Atlas of the Indian Peninsula* (Oxford University Press, London, 2nd ed. 1959), pp. 20-21.
62. Moti Chandra (n. 35, above), p. 200.
63. D. Mitra, *Buddhist Monuments* (n. 25, above), pp. 143-144.
64. Cf. A. Wayman, "Three Tanjur Commentators" (n. 4, above), p. 30, for Śāntipa's statement that Mahāyāna *per se* is not a speedy means, but that the four Tantra Classes are; and through their position of transforming defilement, i.e. that one does not get rid of poison; one detoxicates it, as the tantric procedure.
65. According to *Mkhas grub rje's Fundamentals of the Buddhist Tantras,* tr. by F. D. Lessing and A. Wayman (2nd ed. *Introduction to the Buddhist Tantric Systems*, Motilal Banaridass, Delhi, 1980; Samuel Weiser, Inc., New York, 1980), pp. 157, ff., this speeding up process involves contemplation of oneself as a god, contemplation of a god in front from the sphere of the void, introduction of the 'wisdom' (*jñāna*) beings into oneself; and this may involve *prāṇāyāma* (breath and mind control). In the case of the V-A-T, this is discussed by the terminology 'four members of muttering' (see our explanation of V-A-T, Chap. V).
66. See below 'Sanskrit citations' for the original Sanskrit of this passage.
67. PTT, Vol. 77, p. 116-5-3, 4.
68. W.K. Müller (n. 21 above), facsimile edition, p. 89.
69. Y. S. Hakeda (n. 21 above).
70. Alex Wayman, "The Mahāvairocanasūtra and the Kriyā-Saṃgraha", *Kōbōdaishi to Gendai* [The Chizan-Ha's volume for 1150th anniversary of Kōbōdaishi] (Chikuma Shobō, Tokyo, 1984), pp. 23-34 (English section).
71. Cf. J. W. de Jong, "Note on the Sources and the Text of the Sang Hyang Kamahāyānan Mantranaya", *Bijdragen; Tot de Taal-, Land- en Volkenkunde,* Deel 130 (Martinus Nijhoff, 'S-Gravenhage, 1974), pp. 465-82.

72. Cf. Alex Wayman, *Yoga of* (no. 8 above), p. 41 (for the Sanskrit citation), pp. 49-50 (for the translation).

73. *Kokuyaku Issaikyō, Mikkyōbu,* Vol. 1, Daibiroshana-Jobutsu-Jinpen-Kaji-kyō (= Mahāvairocana-abhisaṃbodhi-Vikurvitādhiṣṭhāna-sūtra), J. Kambayashi's Introduction, p. 36.

74. The Rev. Shorei Nakayama (of the Naritasan, Japan) has kindly called my attention to the article by SAKAI Shirō on Sino-Tibetan comparison, "Dainichikyō kuyohō wayaku (Japanese translation of ritual method)" in *Shinko* (special issue), No. 3, 1936, pp. 101-112, and No. 5, 1938, pp. 1-36, published at Naritasan. Rev. Nakayama not only supplied a copy of this article (in its two parts), but also the Tibetan text from the Tanjur, both the Peking and Derge versions. I have used only the Peking edition for my summary of the five chapters. The equivalent Sino-Japanese of the ritual appendix was consulted by my wife Hideko from the volume of n. 73 above, p. 141, f. (the chapter "7", Pūja Chap., Section 3).

75. For the terminology of 'unedited' and two 'edited' for the editions of Buddhaguhya's commentary in the chapter order, cf. Shin'ichi Tsuda "A Critical Tantrism", *Memoirs of the Research Department of the Toyo Bunko,* No. 36, 1978, p. 185, n. 20.

PART II

DOCTRINAL POSITION OF THE SCRIPTURE

5. BEINGS AND THEIR MINDS

The scripture-composer faces up to an issue that commanded the attention of Buddhism from its inception: how to raise beings and their minds from the mundane situation to the supramundane status? And after they have been so raised, are they now heroes of the system, to be called 'Bodhisattvas', 'Buddhas', and the like? Yes and no, according to the message of this scripture. To follow up on this topic is not a matter of named beings, such as the celebrated disciples of the Buddha, named Bodhisattvas like Vajrapāṇi, or a named Buddha like Vairocana; or the 'Bodies' of the Buddha (Dharmakāya, etc.). Of the 'sentient realm' (*sattvaloka*) and the 'receptacle realm' (*bhājanaloka*), I shall deal here mainly with the 'sentient realm'.

My present topics are: Mundane and supramundane minds; ācāryas and disciples; the praiseworthy and the heroes; V-A-T on the Bodhisattva; V-A-T on the Tathāgata; V-A-T on Buddha; V-A-T on Saṃbuddha; Vajrasattva, liberation from *karma*. The scripture-composer was keenly aware of these topics in their ramifications and profundity. His Chap. I was addressed to Mahāyānists in general. His Chap. II assumes a disciple of Tantra. More is in Tajima's translation of Chap. I and my translation of Chap. II, along with the further studies herein.

Mundane and supramundane minds. V-A-T, Chap. I, introduces the theory of mind as 'mundane' (*laukika*) and 'supramundane' (*lokottara*), and the 'mundane' is characterized as having apprehension outward (*dmigs pa can*). This chapter has a list of sixty minds, that I call 'atomic', which contribute to one-hundred-sixty mundane 'streams of consciousness' (*cittasaṃtāna*) that I call 'molecular'. The theory seems patterned after the old Buddhist *dharma* theory, where atomic *dharmas* combine into molecules of *dharmas* by which ordinary thinking takes place. B-comm. 121-3-1, mentions that these sixty minds are of four kinds: defiled (*kliṣṭa*), virtuous (*kuśala*), unvirtuous (*akuśala*), and indeterminate (*avyākṛta*). Now, the scripture list lacks one item, and Buddhaguhya's solution is to add 'slush' as no. 46, while the commentary in Chinese adds 'monkey' as no. 60. The scripture itself, V-A-T and V-A-S, Chap. I, only gave the first five factors of 60 for combining into molecules; Tib. 243-1-2: "Master of the secret ones, accordingly one divides by 1, 2, 3, 4, 5;..."[1] Buddhaguhya's 'Concise-comm.' 84-4-6, ff. indicates a solution: (starting with) 60 minds; divided by two, 30; divided by three, 20; by four, 15; by five, 12; then ten, seven, six. By the number 'seven' (which does not divide 60 evenly) he evidently means either 3, 4; or 5, 2, which respectively add up to 'seven', but surely here the solution demands the 3, 4. The following should clarify how the no. 160 is arrived at:

No. of atomic minds combined		Resultant no. of molecular minds
1	—	60
2	—	30
3	—	20
4	—	15
5	—	12
6	—	10
10	—	6
15	—	4
20	—	3
		Total 160

The meaning seems to be that some persons repeat just one of the sixty in their stream of consciousness, thus making molecular minds out of a single atomic mind; there are 60 possibilities. Some persons combine pairs, taken successively from the list. Thus, they might take together no. 1, a mind of 'desire' attached to impure natures, and no. 2, a mind of 'aversion' attached to pure natures. So also in Buddhaguhya's list, they might take no. 45. 'mud', which smears another with one's own faults, together with no. 46. 'slush', which smears itself with another's faults. This way of combining results in 30 molecular minds. When there are pairs in that manner, the two atomic minds are of equal force. As soon as one goes to a set of three atomic minds, there will be a predominance. Thus, if one takes the first three of the list, no. 1 'desire', no. 2 'aversion', no. 3 'hatred', there is a predominance of 'defiled' natures (nos. 1 and 3). Again, taking 4. 'love', 5. 'delusion', and 6. insight', there is a predominance of 'virtuous' natures. According to this solution, the largest set of atomic minds that one mundane person could have amounts to 20, which suggest that the list divides into three sets of 20 each. This does indeed seem to be the case; thus taking the V-A-T list, for which I have studied Buddhaguhya's commentary, here is the first twenty: 1. desire (*rāga*), 2. aversion (*virāga*), 3. hatred (*dveṣa*), 4. love (*maitrī*), 5. delusion (*moha*), 6. insight (*prajñā*), 7. decision (*nirṇaya*), 8. doubt (*vicikitsā*), 9. darkness (*andhakāra*), 10. light (*āloka*), 11. condensing (*saṃgraha*), 12. strife (*kalaha*), 13. disputation (*vivāda*), 14. non-disputation (*nirvivāda*), 15. deity (*deva*), 16. demi-god (*asura*), 17. serpent (*nāga*), 18. man (*nara*), 19. woman (*strī*), 20. lord (*īśvara*). These are definitely items that are frequently mentioned in Buddhist texts of all periods, either with praise or blame. This is the next twenty: 21. merchant (*vāṇija*), 22. farmer (*kraṣika*), 23. river (*nadī*), 24. pool (*vilva*), 25. well (*kūpa*), 26. protection (*parirakṣita*), 27. avarice (*mātsarya*), 28. cat (*mārjara*), 29. dog (*kukkura*), 30. garuḍa bird (*garuḍa*), 31. mouse (*mūṣa*), 32. song (*gīta*), 33. dance (*nṛtya*), 34. drumming (*tūrya*), 35. house (*gṛha*), 36. lion (*siṃha*), 37. owl (*ulūka*), 38. crow (*kāka*), 39. demon (*rākṣasa*), 40. thorn (*kaṇṭaka*). These items all appear to be similes. Thus, 28. he has a mind like a cat, which tends to move with stealth; 29. he has a mind like a dog, which getting little, is satisfied with it. This is the last twenty: 41. abyss (*nāgaloka*), 42. wind (*vāyu*), 43. water (*jala*), 44. fire (*anala*), 45. mud (*paṅka*), 46. slush (*āvila*), 47. chameleon (*varṇarūpa*), 48. wooden board (*phalaka*), 49. contrariety (*viparyāsa*), 50. poison (*viṣa*), 51. noose (*pāśa*), 52. shackles (*nigaḍa*), 53. cloud (*megha*), 54. field (*kṣetra*), 55. salt (*lavaṇa*), 56. razor (*kṣura*), 57. Mt. Sumeru, 58. ocean (*samudra*), 59. hole (*chidra*), 60. recurrence (*upapatti*). This final set is of mainly items involving the four elements, an important topic in the V-A-T. Thus 41. 'abyss' suggests earth as the underworld; then 42-44 name the elements wind, water, and fire. 45-46, 'mud' and 'slush' are combinations of earth and water. 47. 'chameleon' means the colors of all the elements. If the foregoing analysis be acceptable, it appears that Buddhaguhya's replacement for the missing scripture item as 'slush' is preferable to the Chinese one, 'monkey'.

The V-A-T, Tib. 243-1-2, continues, "one transcends the three eons of the 160 mundane minds by arousing the supramundane mind." It explains this kind of mind by the one that observes non-self in the personal aggregates, rejecting an agent, and so on. B-comm. on Chap. I, at 121-3, says that in general there are two kinds of praxis (*caryā*) through the "gate of *mantra*", namely 'accomplished' (*siddha*) and 'pledged' (having *samaya*). The 'accomplished' kind belongs to the nature of mind and of body of persons on the Adhimukti-caryā-bhūmi (see our section "Theory of Stages") and of those on advanced stages (of the Bodhisattva *bhūmis*). The 'pledged' kind is again of two kinds, with dull faculty and with keen faculty. Ones with dull faculty focus on mundane voidness, and advance to non-self of personality (*pudgala-nairātmya*), but mistakenly conceive the personal aggregates (*skandha*) as existing, even for three eons (*kalpa*). (Eventually) they realize the non-self of *dharmas* where the *skandhas*, etc. are like illusions and mirages, and attain the Adhimukti-caryā-bhūmi. The one of keen faculties from the outset realizes the non-self of both *pudgala* and *dharmas*, and enters upon the Adhimukti-caryā-bhūmi (i.e. the supramundane mind of 'constructed morality').

The scripture agrees with this explanation of 'mundane and supramundane mind' in its treatment of 'mundane and supermundane recitation, (Chap. IX) (see my explanation of V-A-T, Chap. V, near end); but the heroes of the system are described differently.

Ācāryas and disciples. B-comm., explaining the prose passage in Chap. II between verses 14 and 15 alluding to stellar omens, states at 133-3-2 that there are two kinds of living beings—those who cling to realia (*vastu*) or who cling to non-realia (*avastu*); for the former the Buddha explains in terms of lunar days, of time and place; while for the latter it is the reverse (hence presumably such teachings as the non-arising of *dharmas,* and so on). V-A-T, Chap. VIII ('Samādhi Without Signs') teaches (text 256-2-3), "Master of the secret ones, furthermore, the minds of the childish ordinary persons (*pṛthagjana*) imagine along with signs (*sa-nimitta*). There is an expression for this: 'imagination of what does not really happen' (*abhūtaparikalpa*). They do not recognize that it does not really happen, i.e. is a non-production."

So also, B-comm. 179-2-8 (on 'The Secret Maṇḍala'), there are two kinds of ācāryas: (1) 'profound and broad'; (2) 'apprehending outwardly' (*dmigs pa can*). By 'profound' they are convinced of voidness and non-apprehension. It is difficult to know their mind. By 'broad' they have comprehended that all *dharmas,* in the absolute sense, are void like the sky; in the conventional sense, knowing that they are like illusions and mirages, practice broadly offerings etc. Those who apprehend outwardly are initiated only in the *maṇḍala* of external powdered colors, etc. but are not initiated in the mental *maṇḍala* (which is the 'Secret Maṇḍala'). Also B-comm. on Chap. II, at 152-2- to -3, discusses two kinds of offerings—apparently, when the performer is 'profound' or 'with apprehension outward'.

V-A-T (the 'Secret Maṇḍala') at 262-5-2 mentions "by way of 'a time' and 'no time' there are four kinds of disciples". B-comm. 179-4-3 explains this, but I should preface with a few remarks to clarify the matter. This is an explanation that among the persons who attend an initiation (*abhiṣeka*) and witness the *maṇḍala*, there are four kinds, two that 'pass' with 'a time', and two that 'fail' with 'no time'. What is meant by passing (as in school, getting the "A" or the "B") is that some persons can listen intently and understand what they hear and also have the Mind of Enlightenment, and when they go through the motions of the initiation, they accomplish something (such as purification of mind, and so on) and are initiated; and this happens at 'a time'. Some other persons do not have those sterling qualities of mind, so at 'no time' do they accomplish anything worthwhile by going through the motions, nor are they really 'initiated'. In the passage now to be translated, the expression 'tantra of mantras' apparently refers to the *maṇḍala* called Mahākaruṇāgarbhodbhava set forth in V-A-T, Chap. II, and to the subsequent *maṇḍala* called 'Wheel of Dharma Syllables' because both of these are required for the introduction to the 'Secret Maṇḍala', for which this material is given. This is B-comm.'s explanation:

(1) Some disciples have heard and comprehended the 'tantra of mantras' and have cultivated the Mind of Enlightenment; at a time they are introduced into the *maṇḍala* they 'accomplish' and are initiated.

(2) But if (while having heard and comprehended), they do not have the Mind of Enlightenment, while being characterized like the *ācāryas* who apprehend outwardly, should they be initiated as *ācārya,* they do not 'accomplish' anything at a time they are introduced into the *maṇḍala*; but they should be taught the means of cultivating the Mind of Enlightenment. If they do cultivate the Mind, subsequently they will both 'accomplish' and be initiated.

(3) and (4) Some have not heard or comprehended the 'tantra (of mantras)' and so on; or have not cultivated the Mind of Enlightenment; in both these cases, they may be introduced to the *maṇḍala*; but at no time is there either 'accomplishment' or initiation.

Chap. II verse 2, apparently speaking of the candidates for the 'tantra of mantras' states: "And he observes the beings that are proper vessels, free from faults, have faith and steadfast conviction, who delight in another's benefit."

The praiseworthy and the heroes. B-comm. 104-5-5, ff. on Chap. XIX ('Array of Letters') mentions four to praise: (1) supramundane deities, who are the Tathāgatas, Complete Buddhas, and so on. (2) mundane deities, who are Brahmā, Maheśvara, and so on. (3) supramundane men, who are *bhikṣus*, illustrious persons whose fluxes (*āsrava*) are exhausted. (4) mundane men, who are brahmins, brahmacārins. One notices about this terminology that 'mundane' and 'supramundane' do not necessarily agree with the previous usages of 'mundane and supramundane minds'. This is because 'supramundane deities' are beyond the 'supramundane minds'; whether 'mundane deities' apprehend outwardly is not certain; and 'supramundane men' might not have supramundane minds.[2]

As to the deities, B-comm. 181-5-7 (on 'Secret Maṇḍala') states that deities have three kinds of form (*rūpa*): (1) form, i.e. body, of maturation (*vipāka*), which is produced from one's own *karma* and merit; (2) form of transformation *in situs*, which is the body produced by praxis; (3) materialization (*nirmita*), which is by dint of *saṁādhis,* imagined by one-(pointed) mind. The second of these, 'form of transformation *in situs*', is explained by B-comm. 163-1-5, ff. (on Chap. VI 'Reality of Fulfilling Siddhi'): in general for transformation into the body of a deity, there are three (degrees): (1) those forms of deities by *mudrā* and *mantra,* and the form only amounts to one's faith as imagined. (2) by dint of continually practicing (those *mudrā* and *mantra*) (one's body) appears vividly in the form of a deity without doubt. (3) by dint of the praxis there is an exchange of one's body for a divine body.

The heroes of the system are called Bodhisattva, Tathāgata, Buddha, Saṃbuddha, and Vajrasattva. Verse definitions of each, except for Vajrasattva, are found in V-A-T, Chap. XXVIII ('The Tathāgata') and are repeated in the last chapter of the 'continuation tantra' ('Empowering the great maṇḍala "arising of Tathāgata" ').

V-A-T on the Bodhisattva. Speaking of Bodhisattvas in the sense of this tradition, B-comm. 134-5-8 (on Chap. II), says there are two kinds of Bodhisattva, who practice through the Pāramitā gate, and who practice through the Mantra gate. B-comm. adds that this is said by way of emphasis, since the former kind may also practice through the Mantra gate; and the latter kind may also practice through the Pāramitā gate; thus each kind practices through a gate predominantly and through the other gate incidentally. (Usually, the Pāramitā gate consists of taking the 'means', the *upāya,* as the first five *pāramitā* of giving, morality, forbearance, striving, and meditation; while the Mantra gate consists of taking the 'means' as the *maṇḍala* deities.)

The V-A-T devotes its Chap. XX to 'Instructing the Bodhisattvas', so contains some basic information. B-comm. 195-4-2,3 (on XX) defines the term: *bodhi* means 'thusness' (*tathatā*); the one desiring to realize it, (so) aspiring, is the *bodhisattva.* A *'mahāsattva'*(*sems dpa' chen po*) ('great being') has the explanation (B-comm. 195-4-3 to -5, apparently taking this from other sources and adding that the explanation applies to the present case): one who is aware of all *dharmas* as illusions, and that the *pudgala* (person) is unsubstantial, but because he seeks to rescue the sentient beings, understands (the *dharmas* in the conventional sense (*saṃvṛtas*) by way of cause and effect, and (understands) (the *pudgala)* in the conventional sense by way of 'practical efficiency' (*arthakriyā;* Tib. *don byed*) illusion.

V-A-T, Chap. XX, 268-2-8, mentions that there are two kinds of Bodhisattvas—those who stay at home (*gṛhastha*) and those who leave home for the religious life (*pravrajita*). For those who stay at home, the scripture says (268-3-1) that they are subject to the *śikṣāpada* (moral commandments) which are (268-3-3,4) the five layman vows, i.e. desisting from taking life, taking what was not given, sexual impropriety, telling lies, and false views (Tib. *log par blta ba*) [the fifth one substituting for the usual 'indulging in intoxicating liquors']. Since the person is a Bodhisattva, the scripture (268-3-5) says he must practice the 'constructed morality' (*saṃskṛtaśīla*), which is controlled by the 'means' (*upāya*) and 'insight' (*prajñā*), and must avoid the four transgressions: (1) to abandon the illustrious doctrine; (2) to renounce the Mind of Enlightenment; (3) to be greedy (or, envious); (4) to harm sentient beings—because these four are a reassertion of defilement (*kleśa*) that causes loss of the 'means' and 'insight'. (As to the 'Mind of

Enlightenment', B-comm. 121-2-6, on Chap. I, says that the Mind of Enlightenment arises through transcending the 160 streams of consciousness.) The scripture (268-3-1,2) says that because the (beginning) Bodhisattva is in the dominion of space and time, (the Tathāgatas) teach him with expedient methods (*upāya-kauśalya*) to open his eyes wide and induce him to desire to attain the 'omniscient wisdom' (*sarvajña-jñāna*).

As to the 'unconstructed morality *(asaṃskṛta-śīla*), the scripture (268-3-7,8) says that when one is controlled by the 'means' and 'insight' and practices with this control, by this kind of morality he attains the incomparable enlightenment (*anuttara-bodhi*). Apparently, this is the meaning of the 'great being' (*mahāsattva*), as was explained above from B-comm.

The explanation of 'Bodhisattva' in the 'Tathāgata' chapter of V-A-T is taking the term not in this beginning sense, but as the hero who has attained the eighth, ninth, or tenth Stage of the Ten Stages of the Bodhisattva. So the verse in that chapter:

> Who has eliminated all constructed thought (*kalpanā*) and wishes to realize the enlightenment with the character of the sky—he is the Bodhisattva.

B-comm. 208-5-6, the Bodhisattvas like Samantabhadra are in Nirvāṇa with remainder. (Usually, 'with remainder' means remainder of the personal aggregates, the *skandha*). B-comm. 113-5-7 (on Chap. I) the Bodhisattvas Samantabhadra, etc. have attained the Tenth and other Stages (i.e. the Eighth and Ninth). B-comm. 146-3-5, ff. (on Chap. II) calls 'Buddha-*samādhi*' that of Tenth Stage Bodhisattvas who are called 'Buddhas', whose *samādhi* of voidness is that the *dharmas* of personal aggregates *(skandha*), realms (*dhātu*), and sense bases (*āyatana*), even their tiniest particles, immemorially are not to arise and have not, and whose mind does not shift from that kind of *samādhi*. Such a *samādhi* is not possible for Bodhisattvas between the First and the Seventh Stages, because they still have the hindrance of the knowable (i.e. are involved with eliminating defilement). Since starting from the eighth (Stage) there is elimination of the knowable hindrance, the Buddha-*samādhi* also applies to the Eighth and Ninth Stages and is brought to consummation in the Tenth Stage.

V-A-T on the Tathāgata:

> Because he has eliminated even names (*saṃjña*),
> who introspects with vision the true nature (*svarūpa*)
> that cannot be explained—he is the Tathāgata.

B-comm. 208-5-7,8: the description of Tathāgata amounts to

Nirvāṇa without remainder. (Usually, 'without remainder' means without remainder of the personal aggregates, the *skandha*). B-comm. 111-3-3 (on Chap. I), explains 'manifest enlightenment' (*abhisaṃbodhi*) as rightly understanding one's own mind as it is.

The theory that the Tathāgata has the inexhaustible Body, Speech, and Mind is found in the discussion about the 'arising of the Tathāgata'. Buddhaguhya in 'Concise-comm.', 90-3-8, ff. cites a passage from V-A-T , Chap. I, and then a passage from the "Arising of the Tathāgata" chapter of the *Avataṃsaka-sūtra* to show the agreement of scripture. Here is the passage from V-A-T, Chap. I:

> Then those Bodhisattvas, Samantabhadra, and so on; and those Vajradharas, Master of the secret ones (=Vajrapāṇi), and so on, were empowered by the Bhagavat Vairocana to be amidst this array of Body-equality, the lion-stretching of inexhaustible treasure; to be amidst this array of Speech-equality and Mind-equality, the lion-stretching of inexhaustible treasure.

This is the citation from "Arising of the Tathāgata" chapter of *Avataṃsaka:*

> Son of the family, the Tathāgatas, having become Complete Buddhas, equipoised themselves in the *samādhi*, 'Buddha and Complete Buddha'. No sooner had they so equipoised, than the multitude of sentient beings, no matter how many, were amidst their Body. As many as were the bodies, they were amidst their Speech. As many as were the bodies and speech, they were amidst their Mind.

Buddhaguhya, 'Concise-comm.' at this place asserts that both scriptures teach this theory of the inexhaustible Body, Speech, and Mind. B-comm. on V-A-T, Chap. I, discusses the matter at 113-4-1, ff. He explains the 'equality' of 'Body-equality', and so on, as equality with the sentient realm. The Bhagavat (notice that this title is used interchangeably with 'Tathāgata') performs the aim of sentient beings through the inexhaustible circles of Body, Speech and Mind. Besides, through the circle of Body, the Bhagavat also performs the deeds of the Speech and Mind. Through the circle of Speech, also performs the deeds of Body and Mind. Through the circle of Mind, also performs the deeds of Body and Speech. B-comm. at 113-4-5: "equality since it is a single taste (*ekarasa*)". (This important explanation also clarifies the role of the Garbha-maṇḍala of V-A-T, Chap. II which, though classified as 'inexhaustible Body' also alludes to the Mind and Speech).

V-A-T on Buddha:

Who having accomplished the Tenth Stage, realizes the ten powers; comprehends the *dharmas* as void and illusory; omniscient in this life, while knowing the mundane rules—he is called 'Buddha'.

B-comm. 208-4-5,6. A Buddha has realized the voidness and illusoriness of characters, whether conventional or absolute. B-comm. 207-4-8, ff. 'Buddha' here means the Nirmāṇakāya displayed by the Saṃbuddha and going through the 'Buddha acts', such as birth as son of Śuddhodana, etc. Besides, it was mentioned above that Bodhisattvas of the Tenth Stage are called 'Buddhas'.

V-A-T on Saṃbuddha:

Who has awakened to the *dharmas* as the character of the sky; not two, one characteristic; and is equipped with the ten powers—that is the Saṃbuddha.

B-comm. 208-5-3,4. A Saṃbuddha (Complete Buddha) has realized that whether it be the voidness of any of the five personal aggregates, all *dharmas* have the character of the sky, as non-two; and has fully accomplished the ten powers as a single characteristic. B-comm. 146-3-8, mentions the Saṃbuddha-samādhi: It avoids the apprehending and apprehensible, and also avoids the idea (*saṃjñā*) of voidness, the two kinds of avoiding being called 'great void', prevalent on the Eleventh Stage, called Samantabhadra. This is called 'omniscience' (*sarvajña-jñāna*) and called 'voidness of voidness'. V-A-T, Chapter XXVII 'Practice of the Three Samaya' says at 270-4-4,5, "Besides, what are the three *samaya*? As follows: the (Saṃbuddha's) first 'mind' is Buddha (in the historical sense, Śākyamuni); the second is the Dharma to be known; (the third), mind born together with it, is the Saṃgha. B-comm. 207-4-8, ff. The Dharma taught by the Saṃbuddha by way of inexhaustible Speech is the twelve groups of scriptures (*pravacana*). It is also the Dharma of the three vehicles, for *śrāvakas,* i.e. that the *pudgala* is selfless; for *pratyekabuddhas,* i.e. that Dharma arise dependently; for Mahāyānists, i.e. that both *pudgala* and *dharma* are selfless. 'Saṃgha' means the eight kinds of followers. (Since the Saṃgha is the 'mind' born together with the Dharma, the Saṃgha can be referred to as 'Speech born').

The Vajrasattva (Diamond Being). B-comm. 15-3-3 (on Chap. II) defines the name Vajrasattva this way: who has a mind firm like *vajra* that cannot be overcome; also whose body exhibits the circle of moonlight; or who contemplates on the moon in his heart the five-pronged *vajra* that is the nature of the five wisdoms. Earlier, B-comm. 153-1-2, speaks of the *ācārya* who has emerged from his *ācārya-samādhi* and initiates the disciple as a 'karma-vajrasattva' (see Chap. II, verse 205). The preceptor himself (the *ācārya*) is called 'Vajrasattva' when he turns the wheel of the Dharma (Chap. II, n. 123). Thus, B-comm. 174-5-3, explains: "Having empowered the DD, so as to turn the Wheel of the Dharma, one is empowered as Vajrasattva. 'Glorious supreme' means Vajrasattva himself. The glorious Vajrasattva turns the Wheel of Dharma-s, of the 'school' and of 'attainment'. Having become Vajrasattva by means of that seal (*Mudrā*), the Bodhisattva lords of the world, turn the Wheel of the Dharma." This shows that the title 'Vajrasattva' can be used in several ways.

Vajravarman's commentary on the *Sarvadurgatipariśodhana-tantra* cites the "Vairocana-tantra" for four diamond beings (Vajrasattva), with a verse that does not appear to be in the V-A-T but seems to be consistent with this scripture. The Bhagavat is reported to say:

> There are four Diamond Beings (Vajrasattva) by way of cause, condition, path, and fruit, because (respectively) free from constructive thought, bright, unbreakable, and all-conquering.[3]

Vajravarman explains: (1) the causal Diamond Being has the non-two Wisdom free from constructive thought, by benefiting all the sentient beings. (2) the conditional Diamond Being has the bright mind by generating the incomparable Mind of Enlightenment. (3) the Diamond Being of the Path has the unbreakable Mahāmudrā contemplation of the deity. (4) the fruitional Diamond Being is the all-conquering Dharmakāya. Of these four, it appears that the disciple who has been initiated as 'karma-vajrasattva' is no. 2 with the bright mind, while the *ācārya* who goes through the three *ācārya-samādhi-s* (See the essay on "Reality of the *ācārya*") is no. 3, with the unbreakable Mahāmudrā contemplation.

Liberation from karma. This has to do with the theory of getting the fruits of the praxis in the present life, a well-known claim of the Tantras. V-A-T ('Secret Maṇḍala' chapter), 263-5-2 (end), ff., has two verses that are also cited in alternate translation by Bu-ston, second Tantra survey (Works, Ba, no. f. 13, Delhi):

> As to maturation in this life, the fruit of *karma* matures. At the time *siddhi* ('success', 'occult talent') is attained, it is then that the *karmas* are warded off. Because the mind is not

self-existent, because causes and effects are abandoned, one is liberated from *karma* and āyus (life motivation). Life is like the sky.

B-comm. 183-3-3. At that time, both one's *āyus* and past merits (*puṇya*) become fulfilled in this very life. B-comm. 183-3-4,5: One is (re)born in the family of *vajra*, and so on; one achieves birth as a Vidyādhara, and so on. As to the scripture, "Life is like the sky", B-comm. 183-3-6,7, states that one is skilled in such craft as walking in the sky; such magical powers are attributed to the Vidyādhara.

This topic deserves more discussion than the above. In the limited space, I shall refer to a scripture which our Introduction pointed out as important to the background of the V-A-T, namely, the *Tathāgata-guhya*, for which I refer to its Chap. XVII (Derge ed., Ka, 169a-1, ff.). The Bodhisatta Śāntamati asked Vajrapāṇi about prophecy. After being told there is no prophecy for a sentient being, for personal aggregates, etc., for one with sin or without sin, one in *saṃsāra*, one in Nirvāṇa; and then told there is prophecy for one who does not analyze into two-Śāntamati wondered what is the prophecy and to whom. The response gave the prophecy as 'the liberation of Tathāgata'; and to whom—those who have attained sameness (*samatā*), explained as 'dwelling in the (non-two) limit', i.e. the 'limit of sentient being' (**sattvānta*), or 'limit of self' (**ātmānta*).

6. THE DHARMADHĀTU

The numerous instances of the word *dharmadhātu* (DD) in the V-A-T deserve a special treatment. Buddhaguhya's commentary on V-A-T, VI, at his 162-3-4,5, states that when the term is for including all the DD, then it means both the 'receptacle realm' (*bhājana-loka*) and the 'sentient realm' (*sattva-loka*). The 'sentient realm' includes all beings, men, gods, hell beings etc.; and the 'receptacle realm' means the ancient Buddhist cosmology—the continents, rivers, heavens and hells—the support world. However, there are remarkable implications of the *dharmadhātu*, enough to make up a whole book. Rahula mentions a Dharmadhātu book, referred to as a Vaitulya *sūtra*, brought to Ceylon from Benares in the 10th year of Silākāla (525-537 A.D.), hence 534 A.D.[4] Although he reports a theory that it dealt with the three bodies of the Buddha, he says there is no certainty of its contents; hence the work no longer exists under this name. The Dharmadhātu book is certainly not the V-A-T, whose title and our dating are different. The V-A-T, which was composed soon afterwards, presents the term *dharmadhātu* so frequently in important contexts as to suggest that this topic was much discussed in Mahāyānist circles of those times, and that the scripture composer, whether or not that 'Dharmadhātu book' was known to him, definitely intends to solve problems about this matter in the course of the scripture chapters.

The Dharmadhātu has a suggestion of intermediate-space implication in Vedic tradition, and even with Tantra. Let me simply cite *Ṛg-veda,* IV, 52, 7 (from the hymn to Uṣas, the Dawn Goddess): ā dyāṃ tánoṣi raśmibhir āmtarikṣam uru priyam / uṣáḥ śukreṇa śociśā / "Uṣas, you stretch (*tánoṣi*) with beams the broad, favorite intermediate space to the sky, along with your bright radiance." Thus, the Dawn Goddess is mystically credited with stretching between sky and earth the lengthwise threads (the 'beams') called the warf (*tantu*) of the loom—as the intermediate space—which warf the present scripture will refer to as the Dharmadhātu; and then is credited with being a kind of shuttle that puts in the crosswise colorful threads (the 'bright radiance') called the woof, which the present scripture will term the 'elements' (*dhātu*) (see our Introduction to the Chapter II, section on "Difference between the two parts of V-A-T, Chapter II"). The Dawn Goddess is attributed the function of stretching per the Verb *tan-*, which is the root of *tantu*, the warf, as it is of the word *tantra* itself.

The manifold implication of the Dharmadhātu are here treated by these groupings of topics: (a) Theory introduction: 1. the DD as an object of the mind; 2. connection with the DD; 3. pervading the DD. (b) Foundation of praxis; 4. *dharmatā,* two kinds of DD, Nirvāṇa; 5. *dharmatā* a continuum; 6 the pure DD. (c) Praxis: 7. power of the DD; 8.letter of the DD; 9.*mudrā* of the DD. (d) Comparative essay: 10. DD and Vajradhātu.

(a) THEORY INTRODUCTION

1. ***The DD as an object of the mind.*** V-A-T, Chap. VI at 235-5-4,5, states that the DD is the inconceivable realm; but its Chap.XIII at 263-5-5 mentions "understanding the DD"—so the expression 'inconceivable' perhaps means only so to the ordinary mind. The Buddhist Abhidharma doctrines teach that the DD is the object of the 'mental perception' (*manovijñāna*).[5] Further, in Buddhist meditation theory, as in Asaṅga's *Śrāvakabhūmi*, when a person is confused about 'cause' *(hetu)* he is given the meditative object 'skill regarding realms' (*dhātu-kauśalya*).[6] The Mahāyāna scripture *Akṣayamatinirdeśa* in its section on

the eight objects of 'insight' (*prajñā*) devotes its first three objects to 'personal aggregates' (*skandha*), 'realms' (*dhātu*), and 'sense bases' (*āyatana*). For its object of 'realms' it expounds only the DD, stating first that skill in it is wisdom (*jñāna*) that understands the DD. The further discussion in this Sūtra shows that the DD is constituted by twenty-two realms, which are the four elements, six sense organs, six perceptions based on the sense organs, six sense objects; hence the DD in this usage is both the 'sentient realm' (*sattva-loka*) and the 'receptacle realm' (*bhājana-loka*). But the Sūtra insists that in no case does the DD have any character (*lakṣaṇa*) amounting to a function of these realms, or elements. It states that the DD has the elements of earth, but does not have the character of hardness; has the element of water, but not the character of moistening; has the element of fire, but not the character of cooking; has the elements of wind, but not the character of swaying (anything). It says the same about the sense organs: the DD has the realm of eye, but not the character of seeing; (down to:) the DD has the realm of mind, but not the character of representation (*vijñapti*). It says the same about the six perceptions: the DD has the realm of perception based on the eye, but not the character of discriminating form; (down to:) the DD has the realm of perception based on the mind (*manas*), but not the character of discriminating *dharmas*. It says the same about the sense objects: the DD has the realm of form, but not the character of what, is represented by eye-perception; (down to:) the DD has the realm of *dharma* (*dharmadhātu*), but not the character of what is represented by the perception based on *manas*. The scripture then repeats the sense objects, in this way: the DD has the realm of form, but not the character of representation as form; (down to:) the DD has the realm of *dharma*, but not the character of representations as *dharma*.[7] This Sūtra series clarifies the frequent expression 'void *dharmadhātu*', apparently meaning by the word 'void' — 'void of every function or character'; and it clarifies the frequent remark in Mahāyāna literature that 'perfection of insight' (*prajñāpāramitā*) has 'voidness' as object, apparently meaning by the word 'voidness'—the 'void *dharmadhātu*'. This represents the void *dharmadhātu* as an ideal world, minus action (*karma*).

2. ***Connection with the DD.*** V-A-T, VI at 235-5-6, has the expression "non-separation from the DD" (T. *chos kyi dbyins dbyer med pa*), in Vajrapāṇi's appeal to the Lord, "Pray explain how one may be not in conflict with the Dharmadhātu!" The

advice is to recite the syllable "A". Buddhaguhya, 'Concise-comm.' 100-1-2-3, discusses the depositing of this "Syllable of the DD" in the disciple's heart as an act of faith in 'thusness' (*tathatā*). Ratnākaraśānti in his "*Ratnāvalī*" commentary says that the ordinary body is not distinct from the DD, and suggests that thereby is the 'means' (*upāya*) for speeding up the attainment of enlightenment.[8] Vajravarman's commentary on *Sarvadurgatipariśodhana* holds it would be Vajrapāṇi who represents the body connected with the DD:[9]

> (Of the three bodies), Bhagavat Vairocana displays the Wisdom Body (*jñāna-kāya*); Bhagavat Śākyamuni displays the Symbolic Body (*samaya-kāya*); Bhagavat Vajrapāṇi displays the Karma Body (*Karma-kāya*). Among them, the Wisdom Body is the perfect (*pariniṣpanna*) body, without beginning or end arisen from the Dharmadhātu, and free from the constructive thought (*kalpanā*) of living sentient beings; with activity of the mind that is intrinsically bright. The Symbolic Body has realized the Manifest Enlightenments by way of five Wisdoms and is arisen from the Incomparable Mind of Enlightenment; it acts automatically to perfect the aims of all the living sentient beings. The Karma Body, while arisen from the twelve members of dependent origination (*pratītya-samutpāda*), has severed the conscious stream (*saṁtāna*) of suffering, and operates without clinging to the joys of the five 'strands of desire' (i.e. the five sense objects).

This comment on Vajrapāṇi shows that he does not cling to the functions of the world that lack in the DD, according to Sūtra information previously given (from the *Akṣayamatinirdeśa*); and in this sense in "not in conflict with the DD".

Padmavajra's commentary (the *Vyākhyāṇa*) on Buddhaguhya's *Tantrārthāvatāra* raises the question: "What is this expression 'connection with the DD' (*chos kyi dbyins daṅ 'brel pa*)?" And answers:[10]

> Granted that it is pure, that is to say, purified by some persons who understand it—in the manner any performers display the signs of *mahāmudrā* and so on, (arisen) from the Dharmadhātu, and end the entire host of obscurations though intensely contemplating how be the distinctive marks and meaning; or comprehending the Dharmadhātu attain liberation as fruit; or at the time there being desires to perfect the aims of oneself and others, there occurs the skill of ability

of how to make the principles (for doing it)—that is called 'connection with the absolute (*paramārtha*)'.

Padmavajra presents three explanations for 'connection with the DD': (1) concerns contemplating the 'distinctive marks' in the meaning of *mudrā*, for which see the section below "Mudrā and the DD"; (2) on comprehending the Dharmadhātu is the topic of the preceding section "The DD as an object of the mind", and the information now given that this comprehension leads to liberation, appears to implicate the above citation about Bhagavat Vajrapāṇi's Karma Body, which is liberated from suffering; (3) on compassion and skilful means is the topic of the section below "Pervading the DD".

There is also the terminology, "entering the DD" B-comm., 200-1-5, on Chap.XXII: " 'The pure gate' is the means of entering the pure DD." And the V-A-T, Chap. XVI ('Guidance in the Secret Maṇḍala'), at 266-1-1, uses the word 'immersed' (*gźol ba*), "In its middle, the Body of the Tathāgata is immersed in the Dharmadhātu."

3. ***Pervading the DD.*** V-A-T, Chap. II, translated in this Study, has towards its end, "all the Tathāgatas emitted sounds pervading the Dharmadhātu and protecting all the sentient realms". This theory of pervading the DD by the 'jewel circle of Speech' (among the three circles of Body, Speech and Mind) is illustrated also in V-A-T, Chap. VI ('Reality of Fulfilling Siddhi'), 253-1-1,2 (Mantra corrected), states: "Then (the Lord) uttered this mantra, pervading all the Dharmadhātu, occurring equally throughout space—

> Namaḥ Sarvatathāgatebhyo viśvamukhebhyaḥ sarvathā A Ā AṂ AḤ. Homage to all the Tathāgatas with multiple faces, altogether A Ā AṂ AḤ.

No sooner had those heart(-mantras) of the Complete Buddhas been uttered, than through the pure gate of resounding throughout the DD, the sounds of the heart(-mantras) of the Complete Buddhas were expressed in sequential sound of the realm that informs with signs. The Bodhisattvas, hearing it, opened their eyes in amazement." As to the four heart mantras, they are explained in Buddhaguhya's 'Concise' commentary, 105-5-4, ff. and extensively in B-comm. on Chap. VI. Speaking briefly they are: "A" goes with enlightenment (*bodhi*); understanding the non-arising like a non-burning fire. "Ā" is the 'career' (*caryā*) of the two Buddha bodies, the Sambhogakāya and the Nirmāṇakāya, to perform the aim of sentient beings. "AṂ" is the Complete Buddha, with the

Inexhaustible Body, Speech, and Mind. "AḤ" is Nirvāṇa, the phase of comprehending voidness.

A further illustration of the pervasion of DD by the 'Circle of Speech' is in B-comm., 200-1-2,ff, on Chap. XXII: "Those materializations (*nirmita*) of Śākyamuni from the 'Circle of Speech' fill up every bit of space of the world realm. Since they display the acts of a Buddha, they are called 'far extended'. What is called 'pervading all the world' is associated with 'teaching the Dharmadhātu'; i.e. it is the Nirmāṇakāya, teaching all the sentient beings while pervading the mundane realm with words and meanings of the Dharmadhātu; and it is solely the pure gate." B-comm. goes on (200-2-3, ff) to point out that these bodies of Śākyamuni teach the sentient beings according to their potentialities, but that sentient beings do not realize that these teachings originate in the 'Circle of Speech', that is, unless these beings are Bodhisattvas emerging from the practice of Samantabhadra.

(b) FOUNDATION OF PRAXIS

4. *Dharmatā, two kinds of DD, and Nirvāṇa.* The term *dharmatā* is sometimes equivalent to *dharmadhātu* and has occasioned some hot disputes. In the present literature the term *dharmatā* means a continuum.

What incensed such writers in the Pāli tradition as Jayatilleke and Rahula was the theory that *dhammatā* (the Pāli equivalent to *dharmatā*) could produce something.[11] Their denial is shared by Nāgārjuna, who using the term *svabhāva* rather than the connotation-overlapping *dharmatā*, denies *svabhāva* as a source while not denying *svabhāva* or the fact of arising.[12] But B-comm. 177-4-4, on V-A-T, Chap. XIII ('The Secret Maṇḍala') speaks about the productive character of *dharmatā*:

> "In short, the character of '*dharmatā* of the *dharmas*' is the arising of natures (*dharma*) or the arising of places (*sthāna*) from the Dharmadhātu thusness for Buddhas, Śrāvakas, Bodhisattvas, Complete Buddhas, (in) the sentient realm (*sattvaloka*) or (in the receptacle realm (*bhājanaloka*), insofar as they are always in possession of 'insight' (*prajñā*) and the 'means' (*upāya*)."

The V-A-T uses the term *dharmadhātu* to mean a source, at least of some priviledged natures. Thus, V-A-T, Chap. XIII, 261-5-4, 5, "The bodies generated by the Dharmadhātu come forth", and (261-58), "Tathāgata bodies arisen from the Dharmadhātu"; also (263-1-5, 6) "many clouds arisen from the Dharmadhātu". On this

Chap., B.-Comm., 177-1-5, states: what arises from the DD is called "Treasure of the Dharmadhātu". Besides, in our translation of V-A-T, Chap. II, the *samādhi* "having the treasure womb of the Dharmadhātu", and "the mantra whose source is the Dharmadhātu"; and Chap. II, v. 202 "*mudrā*-s arising from the Dharmadhātu".

Those natures in the sentient realm and places in the receptacle realm, mentioned above, are illustrated in B-comm., 157-5-8 (on Chap. II): "The DD has two aspects—profound and far-extended. The 'profound' has the nature of *bodhimaṇḍa* (precincts of enlightenment): the 'far-extended' is the circles of inexhaustible Body, etc. which are adorned with diamond." What is here called the inexhaustible Body, Speech, and Mind of the Tathāgata is the 'far-extended', and in the sentient realm. The *bodhimaṇḍa*, the 'profound', is a privileged place in the receptacle realm and is also referred to as the 'Tree of Enlightenment'.

Besides, the V-A-T lists places where the *maṇḍala* may be drawn; these are sanctified places in the receptacle realm. Also, B-comm. at 162-5-4, on V-A-T, Chap. VI ('Reality of Fulfilling Siddhi') states: "A cave (*guhā*) is a place for isolation (*viveka*) of the body. A monastery (*vihāra*) is a place for isolation of the mind; it is not an isolation of body, but when there is isolation of mind, it is better." V-A-T, Chap. III ('Suppression of Demons') deals with countering the demons of the four elements—earth, water, fire, wind; and where they are countered becomes a privileged place in the receptacle realm.

The above information clarifies the DD and *dharmatā* sources. They are not productive of everything, which would include rocks, etc. The theory limits the production to privileged natures and places for the heroes of the system, the Buddhas, and so on. However, this may not be just a peculiar feature of the V-A-T, but perhaps has an antecedant in early Buddhism. Thus in the Pāli canon, the *Anguttara-nikāya*, Book of Tens, 2d *sutta* called *Cetanākaraṇīya* ('[no] need for thinking-volition') seems to agree. The first paragraph runs: "Monks, for one who is moral, perfect in morality, there is no need for the thinking-volition, 'May lack of regret arise in me'. There is a *dhammatā* (continuum) that for the one who is moral, perfect in morality, lack of regret arises." The following paragraphs are of the same type, with the preceding attainment constituting the background for the next one, making ten in all: 1. morality 2. lack of regret, 3. gladness, 4. rapture, 5. bodily appeasement, 6. happiness, 7. mental equipoise, 8. knowing and seeing as things really are, 9. world disgust and dispassion, 10. knowledge and vision of liberation. The *sutta* goes on to describe each preceding member of the series as the place (P. *thāna*) and the advantage (P. *ānisamsa*) for the subsequent one; so this is a causal relation, although not using such terms as *hetu* ('cause') or P. *paccaya* ('condition'). And the *sutta* summarizes the passage in the remark: "Thus you should know, monks, the *dhammas* flow into *dhamma*' the *dhammas* are fulfilled in *dhamma*—for going from the not-beyond to the beyond." Hence the *sutta* regards each of the ten as a *dhamma*. The point of using the term *dhammatā* is to indicate a non-volitional continuum of seemingly disparate natures. Each preceding nature has the advantage, is privileged to precede the next one. In a realistic sense a person goes from one place to another; but this *sutta* claims it is a train, so to say, of *dhammas* that are along the same track, with first stop called 'morality', second stop 'lack of regret,' and so on. But now, suppose we grant the causal nature of the series, can we not say each is the result of its position, i.e. that the train first stops at the place where morality is growing out of the *dhammatā* (S. *dharmatā*) then stops at the place where lack of regret is growing? The previous citations suggest an affirmative response to the question.

In illustration of B-comm., as cited above for the arising from *dharmatā* and for the case of an arising of a place from the Dharmadhātu thusness of a Buddha, it may well be relevant to take the passage about the seven steps in the Buddha's biography, the *Lalitavistāra* (Lefmann ed., p. 86.1, f.):

> yadā ca bodhisattvo jātamātraḥ saptapadāni prakrānto 'bhūt/...mahāvīry[o] mahāsthān[o] dharmatāpratilambhena tasmin samaye daśadiglokadhātusthitā buddhā bhagavantas tam pṛthivīpradeśam vajramayam adhitiṣṭhanti sma/ yena mahāṛthivī tasmin pradeśe nāvatīryata...
>
> At the time when the Bodhisattva had just been born he stepped forth seven steps, with great striving, with great energy, by receipt from the *dharmatā*. At that time the Buddha lords dwelling in the world-realms of the ten directions empowered that spot of earth to be made of diamond, so that the great earth would not be broken up at that spot.

The *Madhyāntavibhāga,* I, 14-15, in the Yogācāra class of texts, refers to the Dharmadhātu in consistent terms:

Thusness (*tathatā*), True Limit (*bhūtakoṭi*), the Attributeless (*animitta*), Absolute State (*paramārthatā*), Dharmadhātu, are the terms in short for Voidness (*śūnyatā*). The meanings of those terms in the given order are: not otherwise, not opposite, cessation of those (attributes), range of the noble ones, and cause (*hetutva*) of the noble *dharmas*.

As to Dharmadhātu being explained as "cause of the noble dharmas", Vasubandhu's commentary on the verse states that the noble *dharmas* arise having it as support (*āryadharmānāṃ tadālambanaprabhavatvāt*), because here the meaning of 'cause' (*hetu*) is the meaning of '*dhātu*' (*hetvartho hy atra dhāvarthaḥ*).[13] And in the Tanjur commentary on the three large *Prajñāpāramitā* scriptures, the 100,000, the 25,000, and the 18,000 versions, PTT, Vol. 93 p. 306-4-6, it states: " 'Dharmadhātu' is said to be the character of arising place ('byuṅ gnas), namely, of *dharmas*: the ten powers, confidence, and the unshared Buddha dharmas."

Asaṅga's *Mahāyānasaṃgraha* cites from the lost Mahāyānist *Abhidharmasūtra* a passage that refers to the receptacle-realm kind of DD in the widest sense:[14]

anādikāliko dhātuḥ sarvadharmasamāśrayaḥ/
tasmin sati gatiḥ sarvā nirvāṇādhigamo 'pi ca//
The realm without beginning is the base of all the
dharmas: it being so, there is every destiny, as well
as the attainment of Nirvāṇa

The V-A-T, Chap. X ('Wheel of Syllables') uses the term *dharmatā* as the place of Nirvāṇa in this important verse:

/ 'di yis byin brlabs saṅs rgyas daṅ /
/ byaṅ chub sims dpa' grags chen rnams /
/gaṅ du sdug bsṅal 'gag 'gyur ba'i/
/chos ñid chags med thob par 'gyur//

The Buddhas and famous Bodhisattvas who are empowered by that [queenly charm (*vidyārājñī*)] attain the dispassionate *dharmatā* (continuum) wherein suffering is extinguished.

B-comm. 170-5-4, states that the expresssion 'Buddhas' here does not mean Complete Buddhas, but rather the Bodhisattvas on the Tenth Stage (of our previous essay "Beings and their Minds", under 'V-A-T on Buddha') and that the expression 'Bodhisattvas' means ones other than the Tenth Stage ones, but who have 'noble dwellings' ('phags pa'i gnas pa rnams) (presumably those on the Eighth and Ninth Bodhisattva Stages). So empowered *(adhiṣṭhita)*, they attain the beginningless dispassionate *dharmatā* wherein suffering is extinguished.

V-A-T, Chap. I, states: "Those who do not understand voidness, do not understand Nirvāṇa." Just prior to this, the scripture clarified what is meant by not understanding voidness. "Voidness is neither existent nor non-existent." Hence, those who take it as a present thing or an absent thing do not understand it. B-comm. 121-2-4 adds: "Hence, even those in the quiescent Nirvāṇa of the DD cannot understand it." The implication of this remark is that when *dharmatā* is taught to be the place of Nirvāṇa, it is the quiescent Nirvāṇa that is meant. However, the Nirvāṇa going with the voidness that is neither existent nor non-existent would be the 'Nirvāṇa of no fixed abode' (*apratiṣṭhita-nirvāṇa*), which avoids the one-sidedness of the quiescent nirvāṇa and the turbulent saṃsāra.

5.***Dharmatā, a continuum.*** The preceding section has introduced *Dharmatā* as a continuum. Here the consideration is its nature of a continuum in comparison with the possible arising of the Tathāgata to express it. There is a well-known passage, found in the Pāli canon as well as in Mahāyāna scriptures, including the V-A-T, Chap. II, and which runs in one version like this:

"Whether Tathāgatas arise or do not arise, there remains this *dharmatā* (continuum) of *dharmas*."

Then V-A-T, Chap. II (B. The Various Means) states that the *dharmatā* of dharmas is the *mantra*-character of *mantras*, and that this *mantra*-character was not made by any of the Buddhas.[15] B. comm. 210-4-1, refers to this *mantra*-character when commenting upon V-A-T, Chap. VII ('Samādhi of the Deities'), its statement that there are three kinds of form of divinity—letter (*akṣara*), seal (*mudrā*), and form (*rūpa*); that 'letter' is of two kinds—sound and *bodhicitta*. Now, B-comm. points out, 'sound' is the letters of the *mantra* (*sṅags kyi yig 'bru*). According to Chap. V, v.1-2, this sound is added to the unchanging, which is the Mind of Enlightenment (*bodhicitta*): B-comm. 210-4-1, 'unchanging' because not changing to a different nature. Then, "there remains this *dharmatā* of *dharmas*" because it is the *dharmatā* of the *mantra*. B-comm. 210-3-8, by that 'sound' the conventional and absolute deities teach liberation. (Hence the Tathāgata, a *paramārtha*-deity, expresses the *bodhicitta* by adding the 'sound', i.e. the *mantra,* to it.)

The *Laṅkāvatāra-sūtra* (text, pp. 143-144) deserves to be cited in this regard, in my translation:

(The Bhagavat spoke:) "Here, what is the 'continuum'

(*dharmatā*) anciently abiding? As follows: Through the abiding anciently of the Dharmadhātu, Mahāmati, this 'continuum' is like a mine of gold, silver, or pearl. And whether Tathāgatas arise or do not arise, there abides the continuum of dharmas. There is the abiding of dharmas and the order of dharmas, like the road in an ancient city. Thus, suppose a man walking in a forest should observe an ancient city, and should enter that city through a faultless entrance road. And having entered it, and going back and forth in the city, should enjoy the activities and pleasures of the city. What do you think, Mahāmati? Did this person make the road by which he entered the city, and the various things of the city?" (Mahāmati) replied, "No, Bhagavat." The Bhagavat spoke: "Just so, Mahāmati, what was realized by me and by those Tathāgatas is this abiding 'continuum', the abiding of dharmas, the order of dharmas, thusness (*tathatā*), reality (*bhūtatā*), truth (*satyatā*). Thus, for that reason, Mahāmati, I have stated that from the night in which the Tathāgata was manifestly enlightened up to the night in which he will enter Parinirvāṇa, the Tathāgata has not uttered even a single syllable (*akṣara*), nor will he utter one."

This last remark agrees with the V-A-T explanation of 'Tathāgata' (cf. the previous section, "Beings and their Minds") and with the Tibetan tradition, following Buddhaguhya, that the Tathāgata as Dharmakāya does not speak. This is the interpretation of 'Tathāgata' as *tathā-gata* ('who has understood the same way'). But notice that the Bhagavat speaks this ("I have stated"). Here the Bhagavat is the 'Saṃbuddha' as explained in V-A-T (cf. the section, "Beings and their Minds"); and is the 'Tathāgata in the interpretation *tathā-gata* ('who has come the same way', i.e. teaches accordingly as he learned). Therefore, this is the Tathāgata who expresses the unchanging by adding the sound, i.e. the *mantra* to it.

6. ***The pure DD.*** There are various passages about the purity of the DD, which amounts to the 'single-taste' DD. V-A-T. Chap.II, explains the DD as 'single-taste' while suggesting why sentient beings usually do not want to purify the DD: they prefer diversity, the variegated colors, so do not try to obtain the single-taste DD. These remarks also use the term *dharmatā*. A commentary on the *Sarvadurgati-pariśodhana-tantra* of unknown authorship (PTT, Vol. 76, p. 206-4-4) states: "By way of *dharmatā* (continuum) in

that way is the single-taste" (*chos ñid kyis de bźin du ro gcig pa' o*). And B-comm. 145-4-6,7; having gained joyfully the purity of the sentient realm, it is the single-taste DD.

B-comm. 138-5-2 states that the DD becomes pure by the sequence of the four Wisdoms (*jñāna*). The first rank of the M-K-G maṇḍala represents this purification of the DD, since B-comm. 138-1-7, ff. identifies the Sameness Wisdom (*samatā-jñāna*) with the Bhagavat Vairocana in the middle; the Mirror-like Wisdom (*ādarśa-j.*) with the seal (*mudrā*) of the Dharmakāya in the East (i.e. the flaming triangle); the Discriminative Wisdom (*pratyavekṣaṇā-j.*) with Avalokiteśvara in the North; and Procedure-of-Duty Wisdom (*kṛtyānuṣṭhāna-j.*) with Vajrapāṇi in the South. As to the sequence, Buddhaguhya's 'Concise-comm.', 88-4-1, states that the Sameness Wisdom is the first instant of complete Enlightenment; and at 88-3 7, that the other three Wisdoms follow as forms of omniscience (*sarvajña-jñāna*), apparently in the above given order, namely, Mirror-like Wisdom, Discriminative Wisdom, and Procedure-of-duty Wisdom.

Padmavajra's commentary on Buddhaguhya's *Tantrārthāvatāra* has a discussion about *mantra* power, which we have noticed as due to the DD and being independent of the Tathāgatas who can use it.[16] Padmavajra brings up the question: Do mantras, by virtue of just being pronounced, have a productive power by their own nature? He answers: Indeed so, provided that the DD is pure, free from adventitious defilements, for then it is productive of all virtues. He cites a well-known *mantra* about the inseparateness of oneself from the Dharmadhātu:

OṂ SVABHĀVAŚUDDHĀḤ SARVADHARMĀḤ SVABHĀVAŚUDDHO' HAM

Oṃ. All dharmas are intrinsically pure. I am intrinsically pure. But it follows that this inseparateness from the DD is the case if one—in the sentient realm—has purified himself.

When it comes to purifying the receptacle kind of DD, this appears to take place in spots. Thus, V-A-T Chap. XIII ('Secret Maṇḍala') remarks: "he dwells in the three pure places." In my note 58 to translation of V-A-T, Chap.II, I have discussed B-comm. on this passage, which said, "second, in the wind-*maṇḍala*; third in fire-*maṇḍala*", advancing my theory that the first pure place is water. Notice in the Abhidharma theory of *saṃvartakalpa* (destruction of the lower planes of the 'receptacle realm') the destructions by fire, wind, and water, but not by earth.[17] That same n. 58 refers to B-comm. on Chap. III ('Suppression of Demons') that the water *maṇḍala* is white, the fire one is red, and the wind-*maṇḍala* is black. This triad of colors can represent the three psychological 'poisons.'[18] Elsewhere I have cited a commentary of Ratnākaraśānti's for a quotation of the *Vairocanābhisambodhi-tantra* of a verse that is not in either the present Tibetan or Chinese versions:[19]

> Lust, hatred, and delusion, are the three great poisons in the world.

By destroying the poison itself, one makes it into non-poison. This represents a detoxification, rather than elimination: the personal poisons of a being in the sentient realm are converted into non-poisons. So also the purification of the DD in the sense of the receptacle realm is not the elimination of any part of it, but the realization of it in pure form; thus the demons are converted to non-demons.

(c) PRAXIS

7. ***Power of the DD.*** V-A-T, Chap. VI, 253-2-7, refers to the power of the DD by the word in Tibetan *stobs*, Sanskrit *bala*, when it says:

> Sentient beings can be benefited by the power of one's merit, by the gift power of the Tathāgata, or by the power of the Dharmadhātu.

B-comm. 162-3-8, when commenting on this verse, mentions that the power of the DD is incomparable.

The V-A-T frequently uses the term *adhiṣṭhāna,* which I render 'empowerment'. This in Buddhist Tantra generally requires the performer's *anuṣṭhāna,* the laid-down procedure, otherwise called the 'means' (*upāya*). The V-A-T also stresses the word *samaya* in its meaning of 'pledge' but it is also used sometimes as 'linkage', namely of the human performer with the divine world; and the term then also means 'symbolic' as the human in his person symbolizes the deity.

V-A-T, Chap. XVI ('Guidance in the Secret Maṇḍala') has a passage, 266-1-6,ff. about empowerment of the body. The Buddha says to Vajrapāṇi: "Son of the family, listen about the inner maṇḍala! Master of the secret ones, what be the 'earth-spot' (*sa gźi*) of the body, this will be empowered by the empowerment of *mantra* and *mudrā* belonging to the nature of the DD, because it is pure by nature. Then oneself is empowered as the *karma*-Vajrasattva, free from all dust..." (Referring to the four kinds of

Vajrasattva set forth at the end of the foregoing essay "Beings and their Minds", this is the second kind, the one with the mind of enlightenment getting the initiation, who has the ('bright mind'). B-comm. 190-3-8, ff. commenting upon this V-A-T passage, mentions for *mantras* at 190-4-3, the 'general heart' (*spyi'i sñin po*)—apparently the four set forth previously as A, Ā, AṂ, AḤ—and the sequence of inner and outer worship; especially the *mudrā* of diamond armor, that the kind of *mudrā* involved is the *samaya-mudrā*; and that the rite is done in the evening (Tib. *nub mo*). After realizing voidness, one imagines (in the body) the wind-*maṇḍala*, then the water-*maṇḍala*, then the 'golden-*maṇḍala*' (i.e. that of earth). One imagines beneath one's navel the 'golden-*maṇḍala*' as a square; and imagines upon it a lotus, with stem, that reaches up to the heart. Then, in its middle, the Lord Vairocana seated; on the Eastern petal, the Tathāgata Śri-Ratna (i.e. Ratnasaṃbhava); on the Southern petal, the Tathāgata Kusumitendra; on the Western petal, Amitābha; on the Northern petal, Dundubhinirghoṣa. One imagines on the S.E. petal Samantabhadra; N.E. petal Avalokiteśvara; S.W. Mañjuśrī Kumārabhūta; on the N.W. petal, the Bodhisattva Maitreya. There is much more to it; and the sequence of ritual and imagination, besides illustrating the role of 'empowerment' due to the Dharmadhātu, shows the difference of this Secret maṇḍala from the *Mahākaruṇāgarbhodbhāva-maṇḍala* presented in V-A-T, Chap. II. This M-K-G-maṇḍala is what Buddhaguhya calls the inexhaustible Body Maṇḍala. The Secret Maṇḍala sketched above is called the inexhaustible Mind Maṇḍala.

8. ***Letters of the DD.*** A problem about these passages is that the term *akṣara* was translated into Tibetan both as 'letter' (*yi ge*) and 'unchanging' (*mi 'gyur*), suggesting that in some contexts the term *akṣara* was employed with this double meaning. Thus, Buddhaguhya's 'Concise-comm.' 99-5 to 100-1 and -2, discusses the V-A-T passage of Chap. XIV ('Entering the Secret maṇḍala'), including, "By the letter (*akṣara*), the unchanging (*akṣara*) burns it up" (*yi ge yis ni mi 'gyur bsreg*). The scripture had just mentioned that the disciple's sin is burnt up. The commentary, at 100-1-1, 2, explains that 'sin' here means the 'habit-energy' (*vāsanā*) of 'undispersed *karma*' (*mi 'doṅ ba'i las)* that leads to bad destiny (*durgatī*). 'Burning it up' means 'dispelling it from the disciple's stream of consciousness (*saṃtāna*)'. 'By the letter' is explained at 100-2-1 as 'by the RAṂ that dwells in the fire-*maṇḍala*'. There, 'the

unchanging burns it up' means: 'the unchanging, since it does not change from true nature (**svarūpa*), rightly burns it up.'

B-comm. on Chap. II, at p. 155-5-6, speaks of the letter RAṂ of the DD, colored white, and called 'form of the DD', that is placed on the center of the lotus. B-comm. on Chap. VI, at 170-1-3, ff. speaks of placing an extremely white "A" at the top of the head as the nature of Dharmakāya, while one imagines an extremely white RA(Ṃ) between the two eyes as a letter of the DD. And B-comm. on Chap. II, at 153-1-6, mentions the part of the ritual where one imagines the white letter RAṂ of the DD at the crown of the head, there creating a heat.

Previously ('Connection with the DD') the syllable "A" was shown to be a 'syllable of the DD'. Also, B-comm. on Chap. II, at 158-1-2, ff. explains the expression 'Treasure of the DD' to mean that the *samaya* and other *mantras* arise from it. It is the source of the 'heart' mantras (of which four were presented above, 'Pervading the DD'), and mantras when empowered are held to arise from it.

9. ***Mudrā of the DD.*** V-A-T, Chapt. VII, mentions that there are two kinds of *mudrā*-form; according to B-comm. 210-4-3, 4, 'similar' and 'dissimilar'. The 'similar form' are seals such as *padma* and *utpala* which are the captivity (*pratimukti*) of deities (and called 'emblems'). The 'dissimilar form' are padmo and other seals converted to hand gestures. Later *sādhanas* (deity evocations) refer to emblems as *hasta-cihna* ('hand signs'). The lineage of the *Tattvasaṃgraha-tantra* uses the terminology '*samaya-mudrā*' (symbolic seal) for the emblem, which can be divorced from the hand, appearing, for example, along with others in the *maṇḍala* of just these emblems.

V-A-T, Chap. XI ('The Mudrā'), mentions near its beginning (258-1-7), "*mudrā* as the mark of comprehending the DD". B-comm. at 174-2-4, explains 'mark' as the *mudrā* such as curved blade, *vajra*, and so on, with which the Bodhisattvas are decorated. Previously, B-comm. at 174-1-7, points out that *mudrā* such as the curved blade and *vajra* are virtues (*guṇa*) of the Body; *mudrā* such as the conch are virtues of the Speech; and *mudrā* such as the *uṣṇīṣa* are virtues of the Mind.

V-A-T Chap. XXII ('The Mudrā') several times uses the expression '*mahāmudrā*' (great seal), sometimes adding "of all the Buddha protectors" or "which purifies the DD". Hence the term '*mahāmudrā*' does not stand for a particular gesture. It rather means one which a Buddha might exhibit. The very first one

(258-2-6) appears to be the one which Vairocana of the Garbha-maṇḍala exhibits (See 'Description of Mahāvairocana' in our Introduction to Chap. II); this like a number of others is called "*mahāmudrā* of all the Buddha-protectors", so is not the true name of the seal. However, when the scripture presents (258-2-6) the seal of Dharmacakra (wheel of the Dharma) it is called "seal that is glorious (*śrīmati*)". What is important is that a seal usually is associated with a *mantra* to be recited.

There is a later chapter (V-A-T, XV) on the "Eight Secret Mudrā-s". where 265-3-6, the eight are said to create one's "yoga of the deity". B-comm. 188-3-2, explains that there are two aspects to perfecting the body of a deity—to perfect the place, and to perfect the body. Among them, to perfect the place are two *mudrā* 'unbreakable vajra' and 'lotus treasure'. (Hence, according to my later treatment of Chap. V, they perfect the earth and water *maṇḍalas*.) The remaining six are to perfect the body; and are divided into those that perfect the Body, the Speech, or the Mind. To perfect the Body are the mudrā 'arising of all members' and the *mudrā* of 'light'. The *mudrā* of form (*rūpa*) and 'devotion to Dharma' perfect the mind. The *mudrā* 'many speech ornaments of the Buddha' perfects Speech, while the *mudrā* of great praxis perfects the praxis of *samādhi*.

One may notice of the above details that in this V-A-T lineage, the term *mudrā* indicates 'seals' that perfect the body, speech, and mind. They, along with their designated *mantrās*, create privileged places in the sentient and receptacle realms.

(d) COMPARATIVE ESSAY

10. ***DD and Vajradhātu.*** The term *dharmadhātu* is found in other tantric texts, especially in contrast to the term *vajradhātu*. A comparison of the two terms may further clarify the V-A-T usage. Also, the *maṇḍala* described in V-A-T, Chap. II, called the 'M-K-G-maṇḍala', may well be the *Dharmadhātu-maṇḍala*, also called "Palace of the Dharmadhātu", of other tantric literature.

Thus, a Dharmadhātu-Vāgīśvara-maṇḍala is described in the *Niṣpannayogāvalī*,[20] with a central deity Mañjughoṣa having four faces and eight arms carrying hand symbols, along with a large number of deities, including Hindu deities—as is also the case with the V-A-T 'M-K-G-maṇḍala.' The *Niṣpannayogāvalī* version reflects a situation in later Indian tantrism when the *maṇḍala* became more elaborated and when Mañjughoṣa as 'primordial Buddha' (Ādi-Buddha) was made the central deity. The *Niṣpanna-yogāvalī* also contains a Vajradhātu-maṇḍala, stemming from the

Tattvasaṃgrahatantra. This has basically thirty-seven deities in a quite symmetrical pattern, outside of which is added the sixteen Bodhisattvas.[21] The situation is quite different from the 'M-K-G-maṇḍala', where the great Bodhisattvas Avalokiteśvara and Vajrapāṇi are admitted to the first rank along with the fierce deity Acala.

A more interesting comparison can be made with a tantric text very popular among the Tibetan sects called *Mañjuśri-nāmasaṃgīti,* to which I have devoted a separate work.[22] Following the lead of the commentator Smṛtijñānakīrti, I assigned seven *maṇḍalas* respectively to seven chapters of this text; and in this solution assigned the Dharmadhātu-Vāgīśvara-maṇḍala to its brief chapter "Net of Illusion". This text has a chapter devoted to the Vajra-dhātu-maṇḍala, followed by five chapters going with the five 'wisdoms' (*jñāna*), starting with the *Dharmadhātu-jñāna*. The content of this "Dharmadhātu Wisdom" chapter appears to have much in common with the V-A-T "Secret Maṇḍala", which is described in Buddhaguhya's lineage as the 'inexhaustible Mind' and the *maṇḍala* in which there is arising of the Tathāgata. This Mind-*maṇḍala* of the V-A-T especially exemplifies the descriptions made above by citations from the scripture and B-comm., of DD as a source, namely, as cited from V-A-T, Chap. XIII ('The Secret Maṇḍala'), "The bodies generated by the Dharmadhātu come forth", and "Tathāgata bodies arisen from the Dharmadhātu." Therefore, this chapter of the V-A-T has affinity with the Tathāgatagarbha theory, as does that chapter of the *Mañjuśrī-nāma-saṃgīti*. Three verses of that chapter are particularly relevant:

(1) mahāvairocano buddho mahāmauni mahāmuniḥ /
mahāmantranayodbhūto mahāmantranayātmakaḥ //
Buddha Mahāvairocana,[23] possessed of great silence, the Mahāmuni, arisen from the great *mantra* method, identical with the great *mantra* method.

(19) janakaḥ sarvabuddhānāṃ buddhaputraḥ paro varaḥ /
prajñābhavodbhavo yonir dharmayonir bhavāntakṛt //
Progenitor of all the Buddhas; most excellent son of the Buddhas; womb-source for the gestation by insight; *dharma*-womb making an end to phenomenal life.[24]

(21) vairocano mahādīptir jñānajyotir virocanaḥ /
jagatpradīpo jñānolko mahātejāḥ prabhāsvaraḥ //
Vairocana the great light is the light of knowledge, shining

upon, the torch of Knowledge that is the lamp for the world, the great brilliance, the clear light.

It may even be possible to match up the four great Bodhisattvas of the V-A-T "Secret Maṇḍala" with the four statements in the above verse no. 19. As I translated above under "7. *Power of the DD*", "One imagines on the S.E. petal Samantabhadra; N.E. petal Avalokiteśvara; S.W. Mañjuśrī Kumārabhūta; on the N.W. petal, the Bodhisattva Maitreya." Samantabhadra, representing the Mind of Enlightenment, would be "progenitor of all the Buddhas". Avalokiteśvara as the son of the mind (personification of the Buddha's gaze) would be "most excellent son of the Buddhas". Mañjuśrī the Youth, because of his insight into all the dharmas, would be "womb source for the gestation by insight". Finally, Maitreya, the future Buddha, would be "*Dharma*-womb making an end to phenomenal life".

A comparison can be made to the *Sarvadurgatipariśodhana-tantra* since elsewhere I abstracted from Buddhaguhya's ascribed commentary the "reflected-image *maṇḍala*".[25] Here, the commentator employs the term *'dharmadhātu'* a number of times e.g. "sixteen golden flasks which show the seal *mudrā)* of the *dharmadhātu*"; other references that show that the DD applies to Body, Speech, or Mind when these are being symbolized. And he makes no mention there of "diamond realm" (vajrạdhātu).

Even though we can notice much to contrast between the Vajradhātu-maṇḍala and the Dharmadhātu-maṇḍala,[26] the author Padmavajra in his commetary on Buddhaguhya's *Tantrāvatāra* attempts to make them compatible: "As to the phrase 'wisdom beings *(jñānasattva)* who comprehend the Vajradhātu", beings arising from comprehending the Dharmadhātu by means of diamond-like unconstructed wisdom (*asamskṛta-jñāna*) are called 'wisdom beings".[27] This commentator treats the Vajradhātu as a special case of Dharmadhātu, which does not appear to be the prevalent viewpoint of the Shingon sect. But we should grant that in the Japanese Shingon there is a view that the two *maṇḍala* realms—the Garbha and the Vajra—are ultimately not two, which presumably amounts to Padmavajra's statement. This commentator's point seems to be that the 'Vajradhātu' is not an existent realm; rather, when one comprehends the DD a certain way ('diamond-like...') at that time the DD is made of *vajra*. What does exist is the DD. Indeed, the V-A-T appears to accept wholesale the ancient Buddhist ontology of worlds, as well as the theory of early and later Buddhist scriptures which teach that the mind is intrinsically pure; or that the Dharmadhātu is primordially pure, i.e. without functions or *karma* (act) which 'defile' it. I suppose followers of the Mādhyamika or Yogācāra might find philosophical traces of their respective positions in the V-A-T, but in fact this Mahāyāna scripture does not uphold a particular philosophy against others. The scripture-composer is keen to promote the Mahāyāna ideal of compassion and Bodhisattva practice, along with artistic representation; and prefers that the appeal be along these lines.

7. THEORY OF STAGES

The V-A-T takes for granted the developed theory of stages *(bhūmi)* and has various allusions to it. The commentaries, such as Buddhaguhya's on Chap. I, bring in the well-known list of ten Bodhisattva Stages. The preceding introduction section on 'Beings' has various references to Stages, principally from the commentary. But the V-A-T itself is cited for identifying the Tenth Stage as the Buddha-bhūmi, which implies an Eleventh Stage for the Complete Buddha (Saṃbuddha). And it implies as well the traditional ten Stages of Mahāyāna texts, pre-eminently known from the *Daśabhūmika-sūtra*. V-A-T II, verse 15, mentions Stages (*bhūmi*) and perfections (*pāramitā*), but without listing the individual names. However, there are definitely some features of the Stages that are peculiar to this scripture. This section's solution of the ten will be presented at the end.

Noteworthy is the special treatment of the Stage called Adhimukticaryā, which for the time being I shall leave untranslated. The V-A-T, i.e. the Tibetan version of Chap. I (243-2-8), has this passage:[28]

> "Master of the Secret Ones, moreover, the Stage of Adhimukticaryā is cultivation of the three kinds of Mind. Because it is the practice of the Perfections and the four Persuasions the Stage of Adhimukti is incomparable, unfathomable, inconceivable, the source of immeasurable gnosis and attained to by ten kinds of Mind. I shall mention briefly that all [Stages] are attained thereby. Therefore, the omniscient knowledge is called '*adhimukti*'."

B-comm. starts the topic at 126-5-8 and continues for several folio sides. At 127-1-2 it explains the 'cultivation of the three kinds of Mind' as the Minds of 'starting' (*jug pa,* S. *prasthāna)*, 'abiding' (*gnas pa,* S. *avasthāna)* and 'rising' (*ldaṅ ba,* S. *utthāna*), thus differing from the Chinese commentary.[29] These are stages of the Mind of Enlightenment (*bodhicitta*), clarified at 126-3-4, 5, where the striking passage "the omniscient knowledge is called '*adhimukti*' " is explained by the cause (*hetu*) being referred to as the result (*phala*). Now, the cause of the omniscient knowledge is the Mind of Enlightenment *(Bodhicitta)* as the V-A-T itself has stated earlier in its Chap. I. The B-comm., at 127-3-1, explains the ten kinds of Mind as the sequence of Mind (*citta*) of practicing the ten Perfections that go with the ten bodhisattva Stages, as though the Mind of Enlightenment goes upward by way of ten Perfections until reaching its goal. Without disagreeing with B-comm.'s explanation, one should also keep an open mind for what the scripture may have additionally intended by 'ten kinds of Mind', and below I shall offer an alternate interpretation, namely, that the ten represent stages in penetrating the Dharmadhātu.

The 'Stage of Adhimukticaryā' is a term of the Adhidharma texts and of the early Mahāyāna.[30] It is held to be the four degrees 'conducive to penetration' (*nirvedha-bhāgīya*), called 'warmth', 'summits', 'forbearance', and 'supreme mundane natures'. Of the several diverse explanations, presumably applicable here is the Prajñāpāramitā manner of detailing them.[31] When a Bodhisattva dimly realizes that there is no self but only the consciousness apprehending externals, he is in the state of warmth. Continuing, as his understanding increases and the image of the external fades, he is in summits. When the reality of the external world disappears, with 'consciousness only' remaining, he is in forbearance and is now liberated from rebirth in the three evil destinies. Finally, when the Bodhisattva realizes the unreality of the perceiving consciousness as well, he is in the supreme mundane natures and not yet a saint, but this *samādhi* conducts him without interruption to the state where he can contemplate the supramundane natures whereby he will be a saint. In the classical accounts, he is thus ushered into the First Bodhisattva Stage, called Pramuditā; in agreement, B-Comm. (127-4-1) says that this Stage is the effect of the Adhimukti-caryābhūmi.[32] But the V-A-T, Chap. I (243-3-2) puts it this way in a verse:

/ blo Idan bskal pa gcig gis ni /
/sa las yaṅ dag 'da 'bar 'gyur/
/'di yi yaṅ ni bzi cha yis/
/mos pa las kyaṅ 'da 'bar 'gyur//

A wise person, in a single eon (*Kalpa*), will rightly transcend the (respective) Stages. And by its fourth part, he will also transcend the Adhimukti.

In contrast to the classical accounts that take the Adhimukti-caryā-bhūmi as a Stage to be surmounted for the Bodhisattva to start his career of the Ten Stages, the V-A-T appears to regard the Adhimukti-caryā-bhūmi as continuing through each of the Stages, and to be itself surmountable by the fourth part of the eon. This is also what we must conclude from the scripture's immediately preceding remark, cited above, which includes the practice of the Perfections and the Persuasions in the Adhimukti-caryā-bhūmi.

To support our contention that the V-A-T remarks about the Adhimukti-caryā-bhūmi implicate stages of penetrating the Dharmadhātu, one may refer to a celebrated treatise that in China was attributed to Nāgārjuna, the *Mahāprajñāpāṛamitāśāstra*. In the French translation, we note that the treatise cites the *Viśeṣacinti-brahmaparipṛcchā,* where we find the DD referred to as 'without measure' (*apramāṇa*) and 'unseizable' (i.e. incomprehensible) *(anadhigamya)*, reminding us that the V-A-T describes the Adhimukti-caryā-bhūmi as 'incomparable', 'unfathomable', 'inconceivable', and 'the source of immeasurable gnosis'.[33] To comment on these terms in the manner that I notice comments by Buddhaguhya and others elsewhere—it is 'incomparable' in the beginning (the first Mind), 'unfathomable' in the middle (the second Mind), 'inconceivable' in the end (the third Mind); and finally it brings about the 'immeasurable gnosis' of the 'omniscient knowledge' (*sarvajña-jñāna*) (="the fourth part of the eon").

Now it is possible to translate the expression *'adhimukti-caryā'*. The term is understood as 'zealous application, or inclination' in Edgerton's *Buddhist Hybrid Sanskrit Dictionary*. This rendition accords rather well with the V-A-T usage. However, the V-A-T appears to employ the term close to its literal value, i.e. *adhi* ('above') and *mukti* ('liberation')—the 'liberation at the head'—as though *adhimukti-caryā* signifies 'the practice with liberation ahead'. In short, it intends the 'career upward' as a life commitment.[34]

As to the penetration of the Dharmadhātu, it has been pointed out from 'Vijñānavāda' texts that in successive *bhūmis* the Bodhisattva realizes (or rather, penetrates, *pratividhyate)* successive meanings of the Dharmadhātu.[35] However, once one admits this serial penetration, there is the possibility of differing solutions of what this penetration amounts to. As an indication of such difference, observe that the 'Vijñānavāda' penetration on the Sixth Bodhisattva Bhūmi is that the Bodhisattva realizes that the DD is neither afflicted not purified.[36] But Abhayākaragupta's *Munimatālaṃkāra* explains that at the Sixth Bodhisattva Stage the DD means no separation of consciousness-streams (*saṃtāna*), making it difficult to know whether the 'facing' (Abhimukhī, title of the Sixth Bhūmi) is the facing toward Nirvāṇa or Saṃsāra.[37] It is of interest in the light of V-A-T's position of associating the Adhimukti-caryā-bhūmi with all ten Minds, that the verb *pratividhyate* is from the same root *vyadh-* as is the *nirvedha* in the term *nirvedha-bhagīya* ('conducive to penetration'), the four degrees in the usual formulation of the Adhimukti-caryā-bhūmi.

It has been observed that the Stage called 'Adhimukti-caryā' is not a part of the *Daśabhūmika-sūtra*; but is found in Asaṅga's *Bodhisattvabhūmi*, among other texts (mentioned previously).[38] Also, not all Mahāyāna by the term 'stages' (*bhūmi*) necessarily intends the standard ten as found in and popularized by the *Daśabhūmika-sūtra*. Thus, the lineage that came into Tibet with the celebrated teacher Atīśa, namely, the combined schools of Nāgārjuna and Asaṅga, resulted in the large compendium by Tsoṅkha-pa, called the *Lam rim chen mo*. The Bodhisattva section of this native Tibetan work presents the Perfections as the ancient Mahāyāna set of six—Giving (*dāna*), Morality (*śīla*), Forbearance (*kṣānti*), Striving (*vīrya*), Meditation (*dhyāna*), and Insight (*prajñā*). After the presentation of these, the text goes into the four Persuasions (*saṃgraha-vastūni*)—Giving (*dāna*), Pleasant Speech (*privākhyāna*), Aim Inducement (*arthacaryā*), Common Pursuits (*samārthatā*). Indeed, in this whole large section the only mention of a standard name among the ten Stages is of the Eighth one.[39] The set of six Perfections is given in various Mahāyāna scriptures.[40]

Now, it cannot escape notice that the V-A-T mention of the Perfections and the four Persuasions amounts to a total of ten. But this does not conflict with adding four more Perfections to the old list of six, as is standard for the *Daśabhūmika-sūtra* list of ten Perfections going with the ten Stages. There is no reason to think that the V-A-T intends by its 'ten kinds of Mind' the set of six Perfections and four Persuasions. Rather, according to the *Daśabhūmika-sūtra*, one should associate the four persuasions respectively with the first four Bodhisattva Stages, since giving—the first persuasion—is prevalent on the first stage of the Bodhisattva; although this seems a rather forced solution.

If the 'ten kinds of Mind' are susceptible of being accorded ten standard names of stages (in whatever system of Stages), it does seem that the V-A-T insists that the first six be the six Perfections, or Stages that agree with them. Now, these six Perfections themselves divide into the first five, called 'means' (*upāya),* and the sixth, simply 'Perfection of Insight'. The scripture uses this vocabulary, as was pointed out in the preceding section devoted to "Beings and their Minds", namely, the teaching from the Chapter on instructing the Bodhisattvas that 'constructed morality' *(saṃskṛta-śīla)* is controlled by the 'means' and 'insight'. This 'constructed morality' therefore must also apply to the first seven Bodhisattva Stages. The suggestion of the scripture is that the 'unconstructed morality' (*asaṃskṛta-śīla)* would apply to the last three Bodhisattva Stages.

It is feasible that a passage in V-A-T Chapter VI, as commented upon by Buddhaguhya, refers to the Stages. The scripture passage (254-2-6, 7) is this one: "Then the Bhagavat Vairocana equipoised himself in the Vajravikrīḍitasamādhi (samādhi of making easy work with a *vajra*) that defeats Māra, and expressed these diamond syllables that are victorious over the four Māras, liberates from the six destinies (T. *rgyud drug*), and achieves the omniscient knowledge, to wit: Homage to all the Buddhas; A VĪRA HŪṂ KHAṂ". But B-comm. 165-1-3 to -8, makes four perfections (*sampat*) out of scriptural passage. It says that defeating the four Māras is 'perfection of elimination' (*prahāṇa-sampat*); that the ability like a *vajra* to manifest without impediment is 'perfection of strength' (*bala-sampat*); that liberating from the six destinies is 'perfection of others' aim' (*parārtha-sampat*); that the perfection of onmiscient knowledge *(sarvajña-jñāna)* is 'perfection of knowledge' (*jñāna-sampat*). In the theory of the Bodhisattva Stages, a Bodhisattva could enter Nirvāṇa through the Seventh Stage,[42] which suggests that 'perfection of elimination' is then completed, whereby the defeat of the four Māras is an achievement of the first seven Bodhisattva Stages. In fact, strength or powers (*bala*) can be associated with the Eighth Stage, but likewise associated with the Ninth Stage.[43] Then the 'perfection of others' aim' presumably goes with the Tenth Stage, when the Bodhisattva is a Buddha though not a Complete Buddha; and when the Bodhisattva is able to rescue sentient beings from *saṃsāra.* Finally, 'perfection of knowledge' would be the theoretical Eleventh Stage of the Complete Buddha. The *Daśabhūmika-sūtra* in its Eighth

Stage section denies that the Bodhisattva in the Eighth Stage can have the Buddha's enlightenment.[44] However, in the tradition of the *Mahāvastu* and the Tathāgatagarbha manual *Ratnagotravibhāga* (known in Tibet as the *Uttaratantra*), starting with the Eighth Stage a Bodhisattva is to be honored as a Buddha, and that the Eighth Stage has a conventional representation of the Buddha sitting under the Tree of Enlightenment.[45] Previously in the section "Beings and their Minds" and in the part devoted to 'V-A-T on the Bodhisattva' it was pointed out that the great Bodhisattvas like Samantabhadra are in the Tenth and other Stages, meaning the Eighth and Ninth. Since Bodhisattvas in the last three Stages are called 'non-regressing' (or, irreversible), it follows that starting with the Eighth Stage the Bodhisattva has a kind of Buddha-samādhi that is brought to consummation at the Tenth Stage. Of course, it does not follow that if the V-A-T agrees in part with the Tathāgatagarbha-type scriptures on this matter of Stages, that it necessarily accepts other tenets of such scriptures, such as the special theory of the Tathāgatagarbha itself.

But that still leaves the problem of how the 'three Minds' apply to the 'ten Minds'. I propose that these three are the three 'bodies made of mind' (*manomaya-kāya*) of the *Laṇkāvatāra-sūtra.*[46] It would follow that the first of the three Minds (the 'incomparable') would be the 'means' (*upāya*) of the first five Perfections. The second of the three (the 'unfathomable') would be the sixth Perfection of Insight and the Seventh of Skilful Means.[47] The third of the three Minds (the 'inconceivable') would then be the last three Bodhisattva Stages. Such a solution by no means disagrees with B-comm.'s explanations of the three as respectively 'starting out', 'abiding', and 'rising'. Then I suppose that the stages of penetrating the Dharmadhātu are in terms of those three Minds, hence three successive penetrations into the mystery of the DD. And it is well also to notice that the Sanskrit term I have offered for the 'rising', i.e. *utthāna,* indeed means 'rising for leaving', hence suggesting the Bodhisattva's return to the world, thus with the 'Nirvāṇa of no-fixed abode' *(apratiṣṭhita-nirvāna)*.[48]

So far it has been taken for granted that the ten kinds of mind go with the ten Bodhisattva stages, as B-comm. maintains, with the further qualification that they represent also 'penetrations' of the Dharmadhātu. I have consulted various lists of tens, of which there are many in the *Daśabhūmika-sūtra*;[49] also the ten 'abodes'[50] and the ten 'mysteries'[51] in the *Avataṃsaka-sūtra* tradition. But there appears no reason to doubt that the ten Bodhisattva stages are accepted in the V-A-T. Before going to my solution in terms of these, it is worth considering Kūkai's description of the sequential ten as followed in the Shingon:[52]

1. The mind of the 'buck' (male animal). This person seeks only to fulfill the desires of stomach and sex.
2. The mind of the 'stupid child' (*bala*). This person has learned social restraints. The level of Confucianism.
3. The mind of 'no fear of nursing the infant'. This person has become dissatisfied with the mundane world and does not fear to nurse the infant of spiritual life. This is the level of Brahmanism and Taoism.
4. The mind of existence of the personal aggregates, but non-self. This is the Buddhist state of the Śrāvaka who realizes non-self of the five personal aggregates (*skandha*) while living in the five aggregates.
5. The mind which extirpates the *karma*-seed of dependent origination. This is the buddhist state of arhat, i.e. Pratyekabuddha, who eliminates nescience (*avidyā*) by comprehending dependent origination (*pratītya-samutpāda*).
6. The mind of the great vehicle (*mahāyāna*). This is the Bodhisattva's mind (*citta*), directed to enlightenment while having compassion (*karuṇā*) for others. Yogācāra (or 'Mind-only') is the philosophical level here.
7. The mind which realizes the immemorial non-arising of the mind. This is the position of the Mādhyamika school.
8. The mind of the unique path of non-action. This is the comprehension of reality found in the Japanese Tendai sect and in the *Saddharmapuṇḍarīka-sūtra*.
9. The mind of non-self-nature. This is the realization found in the *Avataṃsaka-sūtra* (Japanese: Kegon) of the *dharmatā*-continuum, as is well expressed by the English poet William Blake's *Auguries of Innocence:*

   To see a World in a Grain of Sand
   And a Heaven in a Wild Flower,
   Hold Infinity in the palm of your hand
   And Eternity in an hour.

10. The mind decorated with the mysteries. This is the mind of the Shingon person who affiliates his body, speech, and mind with the three 'Mysteries' of the Buddha.

The foregoing solution, apart from the association with named persons and sects, does appear to echo the scripture itself with faithfulness. The first three minds are mundane, and so agree with the sixty minds of V-A-T , Chap. I (that grow to 160). By referring to my breakdown of the sixty into three groups of twenty (see the preceding section "Beings and their Minds"), it seems that the first three 'minds' in Kūkai's solution go in the given order with the three groups of twenty in order. Then, when the scripture itself in Chap. I (see our "Beings and their Minds") says that one transcends the mundane minds by the kind of mind that observes non-self in the personal aggregates, this agrees with Kūkai's mind no. 4. It is proper to allot another number, no. 5, for the arhat, i.e. Pratyekabuddha. The last five 'minds' go with the adhimukti-caryā-bhūmi, in this scripture's use of the term. Of course, the expected criticism of Kūkai's solution is from persons who are accorded lower levels of their respective minds than they are willing to acknowledge.

If we wish to dovetail the foregoing system of ten 'minds' with the ten Bodhisattva Stages, only the last five 'minds' apply. Indeed, the 'mind' no. 6 would cover all the first seven Bodhisattva Stages. This is because 'mind' no. 7, "which realizes the immemorial non-arising of the mind" goes with the Eighth Stage which is described with 'forbearance of the non-originated *dharmas*' (*anutpattika-dharmakṣānti*).[53] Hence, the last four 'minds' in Kūkai's description constitute realization of the last three Bodhisattva Stages (the Eighth, Ninth and Tenth).

Finally, here is my solution with the three minds and the ten Bodhisattva Stages, employing two previous essays of mine.[54]

A. ***The first mind*** ('incomparable'):

First Stage is joyful (Pramuditā) through giving (*dāna*)—like the earth.

Second Stage is pure (Vimalā) through morality (*śīla*)—like the moon.

Third Stage is luminous (Prabhākari) through forbearance (*kṣānti*)—like the sun.

Fourth Stage in radiant (Arciṣmatī) through striving (*vīrya*)—like fire.

Fifth Stage solves difficulties (Sudurjayā) through meditation (*dhyāna*)—like a king.

B. ***The Second Mind*** ('unfathomable'):

Sixth Stage is facing (Abhimukhī) through insight (*prajñā*)—like the ocean.

Seventh Stage is far-going (Dūraṅgamā) through great means (the *upāya-kauśalya*)—like a great road.

C. ***The third mind*** ('inconceivable'):

Eighth Stage is motionless (Acalā) through power (*bala*)—like a mountain.

Ninth Stage is good-minded (Sādhumatī) through aspiration (*praṇidhāna*)—like a fountain.

Tenth Stage is a Cloud of Doctrine (Dharma-meghā) through wisdom (*jñāna*)—like a cloud.

The foregoing is a brief exposition of Stages—a topic that has a rich literature in Mahāyāna Buddhist texts.

NOTES

1. According to the Tibetan, namely: de ltar na gcig gñiṣ gsum bźi lṅa gñissu lesgyur ba byas pas/, we would expect "multiplied by two" (*gñis su bsgvur ba byas pas*), instead of "divided". I render it as division by authority of Buddhaguhya's commentary on this matter in his 'Concise-comm.' He apparently understood the scripture's advice that appears to be a kind of multiplication to be in fact a way of working with the basic list of 60 minds to get to the number 160 in a manner amounting to a kind of division. He was forced to this kind of solution because the scripture before this remark had just finished expounding the list of 60 minds. It is of interest to see what the Chinese commentary did with the same problem. The doctoral dissertation of Wilhelm Kuno Muller at the University of California, Los Angeles, an annotated translation of Śubhākarasiṃha and I-Hsing's commentary to the Mahāvairocana-Sūtra, Chap. One entitled "Shingon Mysticism", 1976 (available by Xerox University Microfilms, Ann Arbor, Mich.) states (p.196), "If one multiplies these five basic kleśas for the first time by two, then they make ten; multiply a second time by two, and they become twenty; multiply a third time by two, and they become forty; multiply a fourth time by two, and they become eighty; multiply a fifth time by two, and they become one hundred and sixty minds." This solution does respect the scripture's sentence with the verbal element "multiplied by two". The trouble is that the scripture says nothing about increasing five kleśas to one hundred sixty; in fact, does not at this point even mention five *kleśas*.
2. This is the implication of Tsoṅ-kha-pa's comment on the 2-1/2 verses from V-A-T, Chap. IX ('Reality of Mundane and Supramundane Recitation'), which he cites in *Sṅags rim chen mo,* Peking block print, f. 86b-6 (and which I translate in the essay on Chap. V, near end), *'di'i 'jug rten las 'das pa yaṅ 'phags pa 'i rgyud kyi zag med la mi byed kyi bdag med pa'i rnam pa can daṅ des zin pa'i rnal 'byor yin no/*. I translate this: "The supramundane of this

passage does not mean the non-flux (*anāsrava*) of a noble person's stream of consciousness, but is his selflessness character and the *yoga* comprised by it." B-comm., as cited, mentions that supramundane men include those who have exhausted their fluxes (*āsrava*). Hence, the 'supramundane mind' of this tradition might constitute a higher attainment than is indicated by the terminology 'supramundane men'.

3. The passage is in the Peking canon, PTT, Vol. 76, p. 192-4-7 (the verse only):/ rgyu rkyen lam daṅ 'bras bu yis/ rdo rje sems dpa'bzir'gyur ziṅ/ rtog daṅ bral żiṅ 'od gsal daṅ/ gżig par mi nus kun 'joms phyir/.
4. Walpola Rahula, *History of Buddhism in Ceylon* (M.D. Gunasena & Co., Colombo, 1956), p. 102.
5. Louis de la Vallée Poussin, I *Abhidharmakośa de Vasubandhu,* premier et deuxiéme chapitres (Paul Geuthner, Paris, 1923), i.p. 30, 100.
6. A. Wayman, *Analysis of the Śrāvakabhūmi Manuscript* (University of California, Berkeley, 1961), pp. 86-87.
7. From the translation of this *sūtra* passage in Alex Wayman, "Some Accords with the Sāmkhya Theory of Tanmātra", in *A Corpus of Indian Studies*; essays in honour of professor Gaurinath Sastri (Sanskrit Pustak Bhandar, Calcutta, 1980). pp. 118-119.
8. Cf. Alex Wayman, "Three Tanjur Commentators—Buddhaguhya, Ratnākaraśānti, and Smṛtijānakīrti", *The Tibet Journal*, VIII, 3, Autumn 1983, p. 30.
9. The passage is in the Peking canon, PTT, Vol.76, p. 145-5-8, ff.
10. In PPT. Vol. 70, p. 90-1-6, ff.
11. Cf. K.N. Jaytilleke, *Early Buddhist Theory of Knowledge* (London, 1963), starting at pp. 420-421; Walpola Rahula, "Wrong Notions of Dhammatā (Dharmatā)," *Buddhist Studies in Honour of I.B. Horner* (Dordrecht, 1974), pp. 182,185, 186; and the discussion by A. Wayman, "The Mahāsāṃghika and the Tathāgatagarbha (Buddhist Doctrinal History, Study I)". *The Journal of the International Association of Buddhist Studies,* 1 : 1, 1978, pp.43-47.
12. This is a topic more of Nāgārjuna's *Madhyamaka-kārikā,* Chap. 10 on fire and the fuel, than of its Chap. 15 on *svabhāva.*
13. Gadjin M. Nagao. ed., *Madhyāntavibhāga-bhāṣya* (Suzuki Research Foundation, Tokyo, 1964).
14. See David Seyfort Ruegg, *La theorie du Tathāgatagarbha et du Gotra* (École Française d'Extrême Orient, Paris, 1969), pp. 94-95.
15. The Chinese commentary, i.e. Śubhakarasiṃha's, on V-A-S, Chap. II, namely, on this very passage, is cited in a work by Kūkai; cf. Dale Todaro, "An Annotated, English Translation of the Tenth Stage of Kūkai's *Jūjūshinron,*" *Mikkyō Bunka* No. 147, Sept. 15, 1983, p. 80: "... True natures as such are not fashioned or formed ...If a nature is created then it can be destroyed ... Accordingly, Buddha himself did not make this nor did he cause others to make It... Thus,... whether Buddhas appear in the world or not, whether they preach in the past, future or present, natures abide in the state of natures... " And Kūkai himself says (Todaro's translation. p. 79), "The Buddha, sitting under the Bodhi tree, realized this teaching. He realized all worlds are fundamentally the constant Dharmadhātu."
16. In PPT, Vol. 70, p. 150-4 and -5; the *mantra* at 105-4-6; and *mantra* power and no purity at 105-4-8 to -5-1,2.

17. Louis de La Vallée Poussin, *L' Abhidharmakośa de Vasubandhu*, troisiéme chapitre (Paris, 1926) p. 184.
18. However, for this type of correspondence, admittedly I must go to the *Guhyasamāja* tradition, where the three-headed deity (or three-faced) has the colors attributed to the three of black, red, and white (as kinds of light) with their domains of purification as lust (white), hatred (red), and delusion (black); cf. Alex Wayman, *Yoga of the Guhyasamājatantra* (Motilal Banarsidass, Delhi, 1977), pp. 125 and 249.
19. Wayman, "Three Tanjur Commentators" (n. 8, above), p. 31.
20. See Benoytosh Bhattacharyya, ed., *Niṣpannayogāvalī* of Mahāpaṇḍita Abhayakaragupta (Oriental Institute, Baroda, 1949), *maṇḍala* no. 21, described in the introduction, pp. 60-68.
21. B. Bhattacharyya, *Niṣpannayogāvalī, maṇḍala* no. 19, introduction, pp. 54-57.
22. Under the title *Chanting the Names of Mañjuśrī*, Shambhala Publications, Inc., Boston, 1985.
23. Smṛtijñānakīrti, whose commentary title is Sanskritized as *Mañjuśrī-nāmasamgīti-lakṣa-bhāṣya*, in PTT, Vol. 75, p. 43-3-2, explains that the name 'Mahāvairocana' here means the Dharmakāya, 'all-knowing' (*sarvavit*) of sentient beings, the three Tathāgatagarbha. These three Tathāgatagarbha implicate three meanings of the word *garbha* as alluded to in a passage of the *Śrī-mālādevīstiṃhanāda-sūtra*; cf. the translation by Alex Wayman and Hideko Wayman *The Lion's Roar of Queen Śrīmālā* (New York, 1974), p. 106; 1. the illustrious Dharmadhātu womb, 2. the Dharmakāya embryo, 3. the essential of supramundane *dharma* and the essential of the intrinsically pure *dharma*. I have discussed the three meanings in "The Title and Textual Affiliation of the Guhyagarbhatantra", within *Daijō Bukkyō kara Mikkyōe* (Shunjūsha, Tokyo, 1981), p. 1331.
24. According to the three meanings of Tathāgatagarbha (n. 23, above), 'progenitor' is the Dharmadhātu womb; 'son' is the Dharmakāya embryo; 'womb-source' and '*dharma*-womb'—two qualifications of *dharma*—are the third kind.
25. Cf. Alex Wayman, *The Buddhist Tantras; Light on Indo-Tibetan Esotericism* (Samuel Weiser, Inc., New York, 1973), pp. 93-97.
26. One may consult Ryūjun Tajima, *Les deus grande maṇḍalas et la doctrine de Esoterisme Shingon* (Maison Franco-Japanaise, Tōkyō, 1969) for the contrasts and similarities.
27. In PTT, Vol. 70, p. 84-2-5, 6: /rdo rje dbyiṅs rtogs pa'i ye śes kyi sems dpa' źes pa ni/rdo rje ltar 'dus ma byas pa'i ye śes kyis chos kyi dbyiṅs rtogs pa las byuṅ ba'i sems dpa' rnams la ye śes kyi sems dpa' rnams źes brjod do/.
28. /gsaṅ ba ba'i bdag po gzam yaṅ/mos pa yis ni spyod pa'i sa/sems gsum rnam par bsgom pa ste/pha rol phyin rnams spyod pa daṅ/bsdu ba dag ni bźi po yis/mos pa'i sa ni mtshuṅs pa med/dpag tu med ciṅ bsam mi khyab/dpag med ye śes 'byuṅ ba ni/sems bcu dag gis 'thob par'gyur/ṅas kyaṅ cuṅ brjod pa ni/thams cad 'di yis 'thob par 'gyur/de phyir thams cad mkhyen pa yis/mos pa źes hi bya bar bśad/.
29. The Chinese solution is reported in Tajima, *A Study*, last page of the doctrinal analysis of the first chapter, showing *bodhicitta* for First Stage,

mahākaruṇā for Second through Seventh Stages, and *upāya* for Eight through Tenth Stages. The Bodhisattva Stages are the ten standard ones of the *Daśabhūmika-sūtra*.

30. There is a good treatment of the topic in E. Obermiller, "The Doctrine of Prajñā-pāramitā as exposed in the Abhisamayālaṃkāra of Maitreya, "*Acta Orientalia*, Vol. XI (1932), where the Adhimutkicaryā-bhūmi is identified with the *prayoga-mārga* (Path of Training), under which terms there are different explanations for the Śrāvaka, the Pratyekabuddha, and Bodhisattva. In this terminology, the Path of Training is succeeded by the Path of Vision (*darśana-mārga*).
31. Cf. Alex Wayman, "Buddhism", in *Historia Religionum* II (E.J. Brill, Leiden, 1971), pp. 437-8, giving there the explanation (1) according to Vasubandhu's *Abhidarmakośa*; (2) that of the Prajñāpāramitā of '25,000' and its *Abhisamayālaṃkāra* summmarization; (3) Sthiramati's in his commentary on Chap. XIV of the *Sutrātaṃkāra*. The second of these is presented now.
32. Cf. Har Dayal, *The Bodhisattva Doctrine in Buddhist Sanskrit Literature* (Kegan Paul, London, 1932), p. 278, for the Adhimukti-caryā-bhūmi as immediately preceding the *pramudita-vihāra* in *Bodhisattvabhūmi* terminology, or the Pramuditā Bhūmi in *Daśabhūmika-sūtra* terminology, the prevalent view that the Bodhisattva in the Adhimukti-caryā-bhūmi is an ordinary being who has not yet entered the 1st *bhūmi* is the one which Gadjin M.Nagao presents in "The Bodhisattva Returns to this World," in *The Bodhisattva Doctrine in Buddhism*, ed. by L.S. Kawamura (Wilfrid Laurier University Press, Waterloo, Ontario), p. 69.
33. Cf. Etienne Lamotte, *Le Traité de la Grande Vertu de Sagesse*, Tome IV (Université de Louvain, 1976), p. 1850.
34. Yenshu Kurumiya, "Adhimukti in the Saddharmapuṇḍarīkasūtra" (*Indological and Buddhist Studies*, Canberra, 1982, pp. 337-351), reports the view that the words *śraddhā, adhimukti* and *prasāda* all imply 'faith'; and his conclusion (p. 351) that *adhimukti* can mean "assuring or convincing oneself through penetration" agrees with our present findings.
35. Cf. Noritoshi Aramaki, "Paratantrasvabhāva (I)", *Journal of Indian and Buddhist Studies* (Japan), Vol. XVI, No. 2, March 1968, pp. (37)-(38).
36. Aramaki, *op. cit.*, p. (38).
37. As shown in Alex Wayman, "The Interlineary-type Commentary in Tibetan", *Tibetan and Buddhist Studies*, edited by Louis Ligeti (Akadémiai Kiadó, Budapest, 1984), pp. 368-9.
38. Dayal, *The Bodhisattva Doctrine*, p. 283.
39. The foregoing remarks are based on A. Wayman's MS translation of Tsoṅ-kha-pa's Bodhisattva section in the *Lam rim chen mo*.
40. For example, both the *Bodhisattvapiṭaka-sūtra* and the *Akṣayamatinirdeśa-sūtra* present the six Pāramitā as topics in themselves, independent of Bodhisattva *bhūmis*; cf. A. Wayman, "A Report on the Akṣayamatinirdeśa-sūtra", in *Studies in Indo-Asian Art and Culture,* Vol. 6, ed. by Lokesh Chandra (International Academy of Indian Culture, New Delhi, Oct. 1980), p. 216 and pp. 218-9.
41. Dayal, *The Bodhisattva Doctrine*, pp. 285-88.
42. Dayal, *The Bodhisattva Doctrine*, p. 271.

43. According to the *Daśabhūmika-sūtra* (Dayal, *The Bodhisattva Doctrine*, pp. 290-1), aspiration (*praṇidhāna*) is associated with the Eighth Stage, and strength (*bala*) with the Ninth; but the *Sarvarahasyatantra* (used in the solution at the end of this section) makes the reverse associations. As to the powers (*bala*) associated with the Ninth Stage, see A. and H. Wayman, *The Lion's Roar*, pp. 82-3, n. The Eighth Stage also has ten powers, called *vaśitā* (Dayal, p. 290).
44. This is in the passage of the Eighth Stage cited in the Bodhisattva section, *Lam rim chen mo* (referred to above).
45. See A. and H. Wayman, *The Lion's Roar,* pp. 33-4.
46. For the following solution of the three Minds and the ten Bodhisattva Stages, see A. and H. Wayman, *The Lion's Roar*, p. 31, the theory reported in the Chinese Chi-tsang commentary.
47. See A. and H. Wayman, *The Lion's Roar*, pp. 32-3, for the argument that in the Sixth and Seventh Stages the Bodhisattva, though superior by reason of his vow, shares the second 'body made of mind' with the Arhats and Pratyekabuddhas.
48. See Nagao's article, "The Bodhisattva Returns to this World" (cited above).
49. *The Daśabhūmika-sūtra* was translated into English by Megumu Honda, *Studies in South, East and Central Asia* (International Academy of Indian Culture, New Delhi, 1968).
50. Leon Hurvitz, *Chih-I, Melanges chinois et bouddhiques*, Bruzelles, 1962, pp. 363-4.
51. Garma C.C. Chang, *The Buddhist Teaching of Totality* (Pennsylvania State University Press, 1971), pp. 155-167.
52. Tajima, *Les deux grande maṇḍalas*, pp. 220-227, presents a reasonably lengthy treatment of the ten stages of mind according to Kūkai. I have severely reduced the discussion and added some touches of my own.
53. Dayal, *The Bodhisattva Doctrine,* p. 290.
54. A. Wayman, "The Samādhi lists of the *Akṣayamatinirdeśasūtra* and the *Mahāvyutpatti*", *Acta Orienta Huṅ g.*, Tomus XXXIV, Fasc. 1-3, 1980, pp. 314-7; A. Wayman, "The Sarvarahasyatantra", *Studies in Mysticism in Honor of the 1150th Anniversary of Kōbō Daishi's Nirvāṇam, Acta Indologica*, 1984, p. 535.

PART III

ANNOTATED TRANSLATION OF THE FIRST CHAPTER OF THE DAINICHIKYŌ

8. INTRODUCTION TO CHAPTER TWO, V-A-T

Here there are the topics: (1) Vajrapāṇi, the interlocutor of the V-A-T; (2) Introduction to the three *maṇḍalas* of the V-A-T; (3) Triadic world conception of the M-K-G-maṇḍala; (4) Synopsis of the Speech-maṇḍala deities; (7) Synopsis of the Mind-*maṇḍala* deities; (8) Contrast between the M-K-G-maṇḍala in the scripture and the Taizō genzu maṇḍala of Japan; (9) The M-K-G-maṇḍala and the Caryātantra class; (10) Description of Mahāvairocana; (11) The feminine deities; (12) Difference between the two parts of V-A-T, Chap. Two.

(1) ***Vajrapāṇi, the interlocutor of the V-A-T.*** Since Vajrapāṇi is the constant interlocutor of the V-A-T, and appears in the first rank of the M-K-G-maṇḍala, it is necessary to speak about this deity. The manuscript remains of Professor Ferdinand D. Lessing include his summary of Shōun Toganoo's treatment of this deity in his *Rishukyō no kenkyū,* p. 485 ff. This work by the eminent Japanese scholar is on a tantric *prajñāpāramitā* scripture called *Adhyardhaśatikā.* I have further reduced and edited Lessing's summary.

Vajrapāṇi ('thunderbolt-handed') can be traced back to the Ṛgvedic god Indra, slayer of the dragon Vṛtra, and bestower of rain. Indra had many epithets. As the leader of the gods, he was called Śakra; and as war god, was called Vajrapāṇi.

When adopted by Buddhism, Indra was regarded either as king of the gods, or (later in Mahāyāna Buddhism) as Vajrapāṇi among the Eight Great Bodhisattvas;[1] or as the minor deity Vajrapāṇi, ruler of the 'secret ones' (*guhyaka*).[2] This latter form as Vajrapāṇi is represented on the railing of Barhut, whereby we may presume he was adopted by Buddhism already in pre-Aśokan times. According to Toganoo the original motive for his adoption as a Buddhist deity was to have him protect the Buddha against hostile elements or dangers, called 'dragons'. Gandhāran art proves that Vajrapāṇi finally became a permanent attendant of the Buddha.

The weapon in the hand of Vajrapāṇi, namely the *vajra* ('thunderbolt'), developed into various forms[3] A number of *vajra*-holding deities arose, for whom Vajrapāṇi is the prototype. These *vajra*-holding deities in time came to be interlocutors of the Buddha, putting all sorts of problems and questions to the master. As such an interlocutor and as ruler of the 'secret ones' (also called *yakṣa*), Vajrapāṇi was supposed to be familiar with a host of secrets (not exposed to mortals). On this account, there are legends of scriptures being secreted, for example, in the Iron Stupa (or Tower) of South India.

The notes drawn from Toganoo turn to the *Mahāvairocanasūtra*. This has seemingly two Vajrapāṇi, indeed, in Chap. Two, Vajrapāṇi the external interlocutor and Vajrapāṇi the internal *bodhisattva* in the first rank of the M-K-G-maṇḍala. But suppose the two are identical. In such a case, Vajrapāṇi asking the searching questions is the 'diamond being' (Vajrasattva) of this scripture, namely, the activity of the yogin striving with the Mind of Enlightenment, so also with the vows of Samantabhadra; and so when the two Vajrapāṇi are identified, we can say that the Vajrapāṇi in the first rank is identified with Samantabhadra.[4]

Those remarks based on Toganoo's Japanese work are very helpful. The name Samantabhadra is not mentioned in the M-K-G-maṇḍala, although it is, in the subsidiary *maṇḍala* of V-A-T, Chap. Two as well as in the 'Secret Maṇḍala' of a later chapter. It makes sense if Vajrapāṇi is identified with Samantabhadra that their names do not both occur in the same *maṇḍala*. As to the identification with Vajrasattva, B-comm. on Chap. X, at 173-2-6,7, states that there are the *karma*-Vajrasattva, etc., and that Vajrapāṇi is identified with Vajrasattva, only in the phases of the *ācārya-samādhi* (see my treatment of "Reality of the *ācāryā*") where Vajrasattva is generated by the "A" syllable, the seed of enlightenment. The scripture-composer may have preferred the name Vajrapāṇi in the M-K-G-maṇḍala, the Body-maṇḍala, because Vajrapāṇi like his predecessor Indra has a body emphasis; and Samantabhadra in the 'Secret Maṇḍala', the Mind-*maṇḍala,* since elsewhere I have shown that Samantabhadra stands for the Mind of Enlightenment (*Bodhicitta*).[5] Taking Vajrapāṇi as striving with this Mind, we may appreciate the V-A-T description of Vajrapāṇi in Chap. II, verses 89-91: "famed during the great eon as 'wish-granting gem *mudrā*' among protective bodhisattvas, who bring about all hopes". Here, the role of Vajrapāṇi as having in his care the hidden treasures while himself being the corporeal representative of the 'Mind of Enlightenment' putting questions to the Buddha to learn how to pursue the wished-for end, can be called the 'wish-granting gem *mudrā*'.

However, the V-A-T no longer uses Vajrapāṇi in the old Indra role of fighting with the demons. This old function of the "*vajra*-holder" is now allotted to Acala and Trailokyavijaya, who are placed in the first rank, and in the West, of the M-K-G-maṇḍala. Besides, the old fight, frequently mentioned in the Hindu books, between the gods and the asuras,[6] seems in the V-A-T to have moved to the mind as the battleground. Thus for V-A-T, Chap. III ('Suppression of Demons'), B-comm. (158-4-4) says: "The demons arise from our own mind". Hence, Acala ('non-moving') suggests the one-pointedness of *samādhi* that is unassailable; this could be what B-comm. (158-4-3) calls the 'signless' (*animitta*) method, while recitation of Acala's syllable HAṂ would be the method 'with signs' (*sa-nimitta*) to counter the 'demons'.

(2) ***Introduction to the three maṇḍalas of the V-A-T.*** The *maṇḍala* of the Lord's inexhaustible body is the *Mahākaruṇāgarbhodbhava-maṇḍala* (M-K-G-maṇḍala) in three ranks, drawn in two dimensions but imagined in three dimensions. The name does not mean *maṇḍala* in which great compassion arises, but *maṇḍala* that is the 'upsurge, i.e. *garbha,* of great compassion' (of the Bhagavat's *samādhi*), i.e. directed to sentient beings with the Bhagavat's compassion.

The *maṇḍala* of the Lord's inexhaustible Speech has a germ syllable for each deity that must be combined with a gesture *(mudrā)*, and also is drawn externally.

The *maṇḍala* of the Lord's inexhaustible Mind must be prepared for by a *samādhi* on the M-K-G-maṇḍala in terms of element colors. It has only nine deities and is usually called the 'Secret Maṇḍala'. The scripture provides only a sketch for drawing it externally, called the 'reflected image' (*pratibimba) maṇḍala* in B-comm. 189-2-2-5, ff.

The 'master' (*ācārya*) is initiated into these *maṇḍalas* in the sequence of Body-*maṇḍala*, Speech-*maṇḍala*, and Mind-*maṇḍala*, with continually higher realization, because the Mind-*maṇḍala* is the arising of the Tathāgata.

As to initiation (*abhiṣeka*) in these *maṇḍala,* there is a passage in the V-A-T, 'Secret Maṇḍala' chapter, 263-2-7, treated at length in B-comm. 182-2-4,ff., and cited in Bu-ston's second Tantra survey (Works, Ba, no.f. 47, Delhi ed.):

> Know that there are three initiations: so listen attentively! By which seal (*mudrā*) someone is initiated, while avoiding rite (*karma*) and ritual acts (*kriyā*)—that is the initiation of the Protectors; that best one is first. I rightly explain the second one as made to work by rite and ritual acts. The third one is to be known by the mind; it avoids space and time.

B-comm. 182-2-6,7, explains that what is here called 'first' means the M-K-G-maṇḍala and the 'Speech-maṇḍala', i.e. Wheel-of-Syllables, but not depending on pots, constructed maṇḍalas, conchshells, etc. The further commentary shows that by the second one is meant initiation of the *ācārya* and his disciples, requiring rite and ritual acts, in the M-K-G-maṇḍala and the 'Speech-*maṇḍala*'. B-comm. 182-3-1, on the third one, "it occurs in the lower 'earth' then operating" (*dṅos kyi sa 'og nas 'byuṅ ba 'o*). This remark is consistent with the passage in V-A-T, Chap. VI (cited in my essay Chap. V), including: "the *mantrin* should stay in the middle of the *maṇḍala,* dwelling in the *samādhi* of the complete Buddha of shining yellow color and hair tied up with jewel crown—called the 'ground' of earth (*maṇḍala*)." And it is consistent with the first of the twelve fires in the study of Homa Chapter, called 'Fire of Wisdom' (*jñānāgni*), which the scripture calls Mahendra (a name of earth), colored golden.

(3) ***The triadic-world conception of the M-K-G-maṇḍala.*** The M-K-G-maṇḍala, set forth in V-A-T, Chap. II, consists of three ranks. The scripture has various indications that the three go with the ancient Indian theory of three worlds, which in the Vedic terminology are Dyaus (the sky), Antarikṣa (intermediate space), and Pṛthivī (earth and below). These three ranks go in that order as first, second, and third. As 'tiers' they would go in reverse order, with the third rank the first tier, and so on to first rank the third tier. Hence, I use the word 'rank' with the understanding that each of these amounts to an enclosure, and in two-dimensional representation the enclosures would be demarcated in square fashion.

First rank. On the center lotus is Vairocana in the middle surrounded by four Buddhas on four of the eight petals (the other four vacant)—the five Buddhas constituting the 'intrinsic *maṇḍala*'. In the square around the lotus is the hall in the East of the flaming triangle and Mother of the Buddhas; Avalokiteśvara's hall in the

North; Vajrapāṇi's hall in the South; Acala's hall in the West. V-A-T, Chap. II, verse 23, declares: "My Dharma is fully enlightened. It arises from the sky. Foolish beings, who range in wayward imagination, do not know it." Chap. II, tr., n.43, cites V-A-T, Chap. X, that Bhagavatī Mother of Buddhas is called 'Space Eye' (here 'space' renders *ākāśa* in the meaning of 'sky'). Notice also Chap. II, tr., n.15, citing B-comm., that superior omens, those of the devas, come from the sky. Also, Chap.II, tr., n.19, citing B-comm., that one imagines the five Buddhas in the sky; and that they are called the 'intrinsic *maṇḍala*' (**svabhāva-maṇḍala)*.

Notice that the first rank can be interpreted by the well-known formula of V-A-T, Chap. I, namely, that 'omniscient wisdom' (*sarvajñajñānam*) (= the flaming triangle) has Great Compassion (*mahākaruṇā*) (=Avalokiteśvara) as a root (*mūla*) which nourishes (the *vikurvitādhiṣṭhāna*); has the Mind of Enlightenment (*bodhicitta*) (=Vajrapāṇi, for Samantabhadra) as a (primary) cause (hetuka) (of *Vairocanābhisambodhi)* like a sprouting seed that grows in the manner of a lotus; has the means (*upāya*) (= the five Buddhas) as the conclusion (*paryavasāna*) amounting to the fully opened lotus flower. The fierce deity Acala ('non-moving') is the protector of the gate—in the West—of the first rank. For the first rank's having only one gate, cf. V-A-T, Chap. II, verse 71 and n.39.

Second rank. The *Sūtra*'s second rank belongs to Śākyamuni in the East. The others taken as his retinue go with the old Buddhist doctrine that the Buddha is the teacher of gods and men. See Chap. II, verse 104-105 Śākyamuni is given the role of explaining the Dharma. In three-dimensional conception of the ranks, Śākyamuni is directly under the flaming triangle in the East in the first rank, which is the source of the Dharma. Śākyamuni according to the verse 106-126 has in his retinue the deities of the ten directions of space, including the moon (and the asterisms); and see Chap. II, n.67: he teaches his Dharma in all the mundane realms extended in space. Now, in the ancient conceptions of India the directions of space, including the path of the moon through the asterisms (*nakṣatra*), is the middle realms (*antarikṣa*). Macdonell call the deities here "the atmospheric gods"—headed by Indra.[7] Here is also the Vedic Agni (fire god), the cosmic waters, and so on. Chap. II, n.15, good omens are middling when they come from intermediate space. Śākyamuni's hall has two gateways (as stated in Chap. II, verse 125), which must be the East and West, place of the rising and setting sun—in the reverse order for defeat of Māra and for complete enlightenment.

(When teaching men, the teacher sits on a higher seat, thus corresponding to the intermediate realm).

Third rank. The third rank is thus the 'bottom' one, on earth. It has Mañjuśrī in the East; in the So. Sarvanivaraṇaviṣkambhin; in the No. Kṣitigarbha; in the West Ākāśagarbha. Chap. II, n.39 mentions four gates in the third rank. Chap. II, n.15, good omens are inferior when coming from the earth. Notice that in three-dimensional format, Mañjuśrī in the East would be directly under Śākyamuni, who is in the second rank in the East; this is consistent with Mañjuśrī being the 'insight' (*prajñā*) Bodhisattva. Chap. II, n.68 points out that the great Bodhisattvas in this rank are seated in the manner of listening to the Dharma.

As to the halls of the three ranks, V-A-T, Chap. II, verses 34-36, specifies the first six of the list; the first hall is Vairocana's, the second of the other four Buddhas (called the 'protectors'), the third of the Mother (who is 'equal' to the Buddhas), the fourth of Avalokiteśvara, the fifth for Vajrapāṇi, the sixth for Acala (gate guardian of the first rank). Others are named in the V-A-T, Chap. II, without ascribing numbers. In the order in which the remainder are named, they are seventh for Śākyamuni, eighth for Mañjuśrī, ninth for Kṣitigarbha, tenth for Sarvanīvaraṇaviṣkambhin, eleventh for Ākāśagarbha. Śākyamuni's second rank has only his own group in the East, and Aparājita, etc. in the West. Chap. II, verse 126, allows for drawing other beings that are trained by the Nirmāṇakāya Śākyamuni (see verse 126, n.67); hence such beings, whether bodhisattvas, śrāvakas, or pratyekabuddhas, would be placed in the North and South of the second rank, since the West is normally reserved for the gate guardians of the rank. It should be noted that a hall for the mundane gods, the Ṛṣi-s, etc., is necessarily in two-dimensional drawing placed outside the third rank; but is imagined as being exterior to the second rank, because it is in the 'intermediate space' surrounding Śākyamuni's second rank.

The lotus seats are referred to in the Secret Maṇḍala Chapter, 263-1-1; B-comm. 180-4-5, ff.

/ Saṅs rgyas rnams ni thams chad daṅ / de sras blo can rnams kyi gdan
/ pad mad yid las byuṅ ba'i mchog/ bkra śis 'jig rten rnams kyi (s) (b) sṅags
/ raṅ rgyal daṅ ni dgra bcom pa / phyogs cig ces par gaṅ grags pa
/ de dag stạn du śes bya ba / pad ma las byuṅ 'dab ma'o//

The seat of all the Buddhas and of their wise sons is the splendid [white] lotus, best of those arisen in mind [when at the time of the four members of muttering, in the heart] that is praised by the worldlings.

Since the Pratyekabuddhas and Arhats are recognized to be one-sided, their seat is a [single] petal of the [white] lotus.

V-A-T goes on to describe the seat of the mundane gods such as Brahmā as the red lotus, and as royal [B-comm. 180-5-1,2: attended with passion]. Finally, minor deities, like one's guru, have lower seats.

(4) ***Synopsis of the Body-maṇḍala deities.*** The Body-*maṇḍala* in this scripture means the three-ranked *maṇḍala* and the deities that reside therein. The three ranks were delineated in the foregoing. Now I shall list the deities according to V-A-T, Chap. II.

First rank. On the central eight-petalled lotus, in the middle is Vairocana. E. Ratnaketu (= **Ratnasaṃbhava**); S. Saṃkusumita (= Amoghasiddhi); N. Akṣobhya; W. Amitābha. (So the five Buddhas; petals in the intermediate directions vacant). To the East, the triangle (*mudrā* of all the Buddhas); to its right ('north') the Mother (=Prajñāpāramitā).

To the North, Avalokiteśvara (and seven others): at his right, Tārā; at his left, Bhṛkuṭī; near her, Mahāsthamaprāpta; near him, Yaśodharā. In the near retinue of Tārā is Paṇḍuravāsinī; after her, the *vidyārāja* Mahābala, and Hayagrīva.

To the South, Vajrapāṇi (and a large group): at his right, Māmakī; below, Vajrasūcī (with a host of messengers), at his left, Vajraśṛṅkhalā (surrounded by messengers); below, *vajradhara* called Gaganāmalavajra and others (12 in no.).

To the South-west, Ārya-Acala.

To the North-west, Trailokyavijaya.

Second rank. In the East, Śākyamuni (and fifteen others): at his right, Buddhalocanā; at her right, Vidyorṇā; at his left, these five Uṣṇīṣa deities: Sitātapatroṣṇīṣa, Jayoṣṇīṣa, Vijayoṣṇīṣa, Tejorāśyuṣṇīṣa, Vikiraṇoṣṇīṣa. to the right of Vidyorṇā, these three: Mahoṣṇīṣa, Mahodgatoṣṇīṣa, Anantasvaraghoṣoṣṇīṣa, at his North [*sic.* for South], these (five) Pure Abode deities (Sanskrit reconstructed):

*Īśvara, *Saṃpuṣpaka, *Prabhāmālaka, *Manojavana, *Prakīrtita. Around Śākyamuni is the mundane circle, imagined at this time but not invited within the *maṇḍala*: S.E. (fire corner)—Ṛṣi-s. S. Yama (on buffalo), surrounded by 'mothers, Kālarātrī-s, and Mṛtyu-s. S.W. Nirṛti. N. Devendra (=Indra) on Mt. Meru, surrounded by the gods. E. Varuṇa; to his East, chariot of the sun; to his right and left, Jaya and Vijaya; to his (i.e. Varuṇa's) right, Brahmā, 4-faced. W. Pṛthivī (Earth Goddess), Sarasvatī, Viṣṇu, Skanda (Tib. *skem byed*), Vāyu, Śaṃkara (= Śiva), Chandra. (Besides) to the West (i.e. opposite Śākyamuni in the East), the *mahākrodha* called Aparājita and Aparājitā, and Kṣitipati (field protector), facing Śākyamuni's two doorways, the *mahānāga* called Nandin and Upananda.

Third rank. To the Earth, hall of Mañjuśrī (and eight others named): at his North, Jālinīprabhā, with two followers, Ratnamukuṭa and Vimalaprabhā. At his left, the five female messengers possessed of his discrimination: Keśinī, Upakeśinī, Citrā, Vasumatī, Ākarṣaṇī; these five each have one attendant, not named.

To the North, hall of Kṣitigarbha (and five others): Ratnākara, Ratnapāṇi, Dhāraṇīprāpta, Ratnamudrāhasta, Dṛḍhādhyāśaya.

To the South, hall of Sarvanivāraṇaviṣkambhin (and seven heroes): Abhayaṃdada, Sarvāpayajaha, Paritrāṇāśayamati, Karuṇāmṛditamati, Maitryabhyudgata, Sarvadāhapraśamita, Acintyamati.

To the West, hall of Ākāśagarbha (and five others): Gaganāmala, Gaganāmati, Viśuddhimati, Caritamati, Sthirabodhi.

Besides, two gate protectors, Durdānta (Tib. 'Dul dka') and Abhimukha (Tib. Mṅon phyogs), are mentioned in V-A-T, Chap. IV (Mantra chap.) at 251-3-7,8; and in V-A-T, Chap. VI ('Reality of Fulfilling Siddhi') at 253-3-4. But neither place clarifies their location. B-comm. omitted commentary on the bulk of the Mantra chapter, and B-comm. for this portion of Chap. VI is missing. Since the gatekeepers for the first rank are already established with Acala and Trailokyavijaya; and those for the second rank are presumably the *mahākrodha* Aparājita and Aparājitā; while no gatekeepers were mentioned for the third rank—it follows that these two gatekeepers—Durdānta and Abhimukha—are reasonably to be assigned to the third rank, but since the third rank has four gates we would expect four gatekeepers.

(5) ***Subsidiary maṇḍala.*** The M-K-G-maṇḍala goes with what a later chapter of V-A-T will call the first *ācārya-samādhi* (see my later treatment of the 'Reality of the Ācārya' and 'Array of Letters' chapters). The three *maṇḍalas* of Body, Speech, and Mind each have their stipulated '*ācārya-samādhi*'. The person so established as a 'master' (*ācārya*) can confer initiation (*abhiṣeka*) on disciples. V-A-T, Chap. II, is in two parts—(A) The Single Means, and (B) The

Various Means. The M-K-G-maṇḍala is presented in the first part (A), and a subsidiary *maṇḍala* meant for disciples is presented in the second part (B), starting at 249-2-4. As a preliminary for initiation, the disciple's Buddha family must be determined by the throwing of a flower. For this subsidiary *maṇḍala* there is also an eight-petalled lotus.

In the center: the inconceivable form of the Dharmadhātu. B.comm. explains that the letter 'R' (or syllable RA), colored white, is meant; and we note that previously the *ācārya* had imagined this on the crown of the disciple's head (V-A-T, Chap. II, verse 205).

In the middle on four petals, these Bodhisattvas: 1. Dhāraṇīśvara-rāja, 2. Smṛtiprajanyin, 3. Hitādhyāśayin, 4. Kārunya. On the other four petals, their retinue: 1. *Cittaviśeṣacarita, 2. *Kāmaniṣpatti, 3. *Asakta, 4. *Vimukti. Four *vajradhara* at corners of the *maṇḍala* (which has no door): 1. Niṣprapañcavihārin, 2. Gaganāmala, 3. Vimalanetra, 4. Citravāsadhṛk. Of these four *vajradhara,* three are in the list of *vajradhara* in V-A-T, Chap. I, in the assembly as the Bhagavat proclaims the Teaching; and the one not mentioned, Gaganāmala(-vajra), is a *vajradhara* in Vajrapāṇi's hall in the first rank. The eight on the lotus petals are not provided names that are important for this scripture, and this may be purposeful to stress the virtues indicated by their respective names; thus the names of the four Bodhisattvas in order: 1. "king who is lord of memory (or, ritual formulas)"; 2. "who is mindful and aware"; 3. "who aspires to the benefit (of sentient beings)" 4. "who is compassionate". And their retinue: 1. "who behaves with distinguished mind"; 2. "the fulfilment of desire"; 3. "who is unclinging"; 4. "liberation". The meaning of the four *vajradhara* names in order: 1. "who dwells in non-elaboration"; 2. "pure sky"; 3. "pure eyes"; 4. "who wears multi-colored clothes".

For the sprinkling, there are four jewel pitchers, empowered by Samantabhadra, Maitreya, Sarvanivāraṇaviṣkambhin, and Sarvāpaya-jaha. Three of these—Samantabhadra, Maitreya, and Sarvanivāraṇ-aviṣkambhin—were in the assembly of V-A-T, Chap. I. Two—Samantabhadra and Maitreya—are among the four Bodhisattvas in 'Secret Maṇḍala'—that of Mind. Since the other two are in the M-K-G-maṇḍala—that of Body—the intention is to have representation of Mind and Body for empowering the pitchers. The fact that there are four suggests that this tantric tradition recognizes four 'initiations' for the flask.[8] This chapter of the scripture states that the pitchers are used to sprinkle the heads of the disciples. Of course, the *ācārya* does the sprinkling; it is imagined that those four Bodhisattvas empower the pitchers.

(6) ***Synopsis of the Speech-maṇḍala deities.*** Like the Body-*maṇḍala* (the M-K-G-maṇḍala), the Speech-*maṇḍala* is represented externally. This goes with the second *ācārya-samādhi*. The deities of the *maṇḍala* are presented in V-A-T, Chap. X. For the *ācārya* to realize this Speech-*maṇḍala,* he must combine the syllables of the deities with the gestures (*mudrā*) that are given in the next chapter, V-A-T, Chap. XI. As in the Body-*maṇḍala,* the Speech-*maṇḍala* has three ranks. Chap. X provides the germ syllable for each deity. Each letter can be sounded because possessed of the 'A'.

The first rank is the 'inner *maṇḍala*':

		Germ syllable
	In center, Vairocana, golden-colored[9]	A
E	Dharmakāya of all Buddhas (=triangle)[10]	AM
N.E.	Mother of all Buddhas	GA
S.E.	Wish-granting gem (*cintāmaṇi*), which is the *mudrā* of the Buddhas	KA
N.	Padmapāṇi, with retinue of bodhisattvas having one more life	SA
S.	Vajrapāṇi	BA
W.	Vajrapāṇi Vajradhara-s	HŪṂ
S.W.	Acala seated on boulder	HAṂ
N.W.	Trailokyavijaya (very fearsome)	HA

In the four quarters are placed four female guardians who were not mentioned in the M-K-G-maṇḍala:

E.	"She who is fearless" (Abhaya), gold-colored, dressed in white, face angry only in mind, holding a staff (or, club)	CA
N.	"She who nullifies fear" (Sarvabhaya-bhāvā), white-colored, dressed in white fiery clothes, holding a curved sword	PA
W.	"She who is hard to tame" (Durdantā), like the color of the red Aśoka flower, dressed in red, smiling face gazing at the entire *maṇḍala* retinue	SA
S.	"She who tames by *vajra* the untamed" (Adāntavajradamanī), black and dressed in black lower garment, brows wrinkled, hair bound up and having crown, having	

the entire mundane realm as her blaze,
who renders visible, carries a staff with
gesture that negates the great obstacles
(or, demons) KṢA

In the second rank as expected is Śākyamuni,
exhibiting the thirty-two characteristics, with the
gesture of giving confidence (*abhaya-mudrā*) to
all sentient beings; his syllable BHA
In the third rank, in the East is Mañjuśrī MĀṂ
To his right is Jālinīprabha CA
S. Sarvanivāraṇaviṣkambhin Ā
N. Kṣitigarbha I
W. Ākāśagarbha Ī

(7) ***Synopsis of the Mind-maṇḍala deities.*** As was shown in the treatment of Buddhaguhya's commentary on the V-A-T, the "Maṇḍala of the Lord's Inexhaustible Mind" covers the four chapters, V-A-T, XIII, XIV, XV, and XVI. The first of these, "The Secret Maṇḍala", reviews the M-K-G-maṇḍala (the Body-*maṇḍala*) by way of the five *samādhi*-s (which I explain later when treating V-A-T, Chap. V), namely on the five elements. For example, it starts with the lord Vairocana of golden color situated in the square earth-*maṇḍala*. The second one (Chap. XIV) briefly refers to twelve letters as "Entering the Secret Maṇḍala". The third one (Chap. XV) is on the "Eight Secret Mudrā-s". Finally (Chap. XVI), "Guidance in the Secret Maṇḍala", actually gives the Secret Maṇḍala by the deities on an eight-petalled lotus:

Center—Mahāvairocana (his mind on voidness)
E. Ratnaketu (=Ratnasaṃbhava)
S. Saṃkusumitarāja (= Amoghasiddhi)
W. Amitābha
N. Divyadundhimeghanirghoṣa (= Akṣobhya)
S.E. Samantabhadra
S.W. Mañjuśrī
N.W. Avalokiteśvara
N.E. Maitreya

It should be pointed out that Buddhaguhya explains in his commentary (182-3-1) that initiation (*abhiṣeka*) in the 'Secret *maṇḍala*' is by the mind. It will be noted that the 'Secret Maṇḍala' in contrast to the two previous ones—the Body and Speech maṇḍalas—does not consist of three ranks. It is the only one of the three that has four Buddhas and four Bodhisattvas on the eight petals. In contrast, the M-K-G-maṇḍala has the four Buddhas but leaves the other four petals of the lotus unoccupied. The 'Speech-maṇḍala' does not represent separately the four Buddhas, only their *mudrā*—the *cintāmaṇi*.

(8) ***Contrast between the M-K-G-maṇḍala in the scripture and the Taizō genzu maṇḍala of Japan.*** While there are a number of Garbha (ja. Taizō) *maṇḍalas* preserved in Japan, they are all included in three traditions of iconography from China to Japan.[11]

1. *Taizō zuzō*. Here *zuzō* means 'drawing' or 'iconography', but the term *Taizō zuzō* means the one by Śubhakarasiṃha, made in 724 A.D. When he was translating the *Mahāvairocana-sūtra*. Enchin, a Japanese monk, copied it in 855 and brought it back to Japan. This original copy is lost, but three copies of it are kept in Nara Museum, Nara, Japan. There are various points of difference between this drawing and the other two traditions to be mentioned, but I wish to signal the striking alteration in this drawing of interchanging the two ranks—that of Śākyamuni and the one with Mañjuśrī in the East, and of making a fourth for the mundane deities, Indra, Varuṇa, etc. Also, that this drawing was more appreciated, i.e. followed, in China, than the other two.

2. *Taizō kyū zuyō*. Here *kyū* means 'old'; *zuyō* style of 'drawing', but the term *Taizō kyū zuyō* means the one in the tradition of Amoghavajra. Enchin and his disciple Hōchi made a copy of it in China in 854. This original copy is lost, but its exact copy was found by S. Ōmura at the Maṇḍala Hall, Shiga Prefecture. This tradition is more faithful to the scripture and to Buddhaguhya's commentary (preserved in Tibetan) than is the case of the other two traditions. Thus, it keeps the second and third ranks as the scripture sets them forth.

3. *Taizō genzu*. Here *genzu* means 'present iconography (or, drawing)', but the term *Taizō genzu* is also used for a tradition following Amoghavajra. It was brought back to Japan by Kūkai, by Enchin, also by Sōci. It seems that Kūkai's copy was a presentation to him by this teacher when he departed from China. The mundane gods, Indra, etc. are put in fourth rank outside the three ranks stated in the scripture. For purposes of symmetry another hall, called Susiddhi, is added to the third rank. Like the preceding Amoghavajra tradition the number of deities drawn is considerably increased over the scripture's number. The *Taizō genzu maṇḍala* is the prevalent one in Japan nowadays.

Naturally there must be some rationalization to justify these departures from the scriptural text. It is reported that Śubhakarasiṃha concluded that there is a "disorder on purpose" in the scripture itself.[12] The two Amoghavajra traditions apparently do not accept this interpretation, but conclude rather that the scripture has some gaps or omissions of essential data; and that this justifies a filling in with deities or theories from elsewhere. The scripture itself allows filling in only for Śākyamuni's hall (II,126).

Since the *Taizō genzu maṇḍala* is the main one copied now, and is the one described by Tajima in his work on the two *maṇḍalas* of the Shingon, my further comparisons will be to this particular *maṇḍala* tradition.

Ryūjun Tajima in his work *Les deux grands maṇḍalas et la doctrine de l'esoterisme Shingon*[13] may easily bewilder the reader by the multitude of deities in the various 'quarters' or 'halls' in both the Garbha-maṇḍala and the vajra-maṇḍala. In both, there is a principle operating of filling up all the space, as though abhoring a vacuum. Doubtless, both *maṇḍalas* are a triumph of religious decorative art, impressive to the devotees.

When filling up spaces in the Garbha-maṇḍala (the M-K-G-maṇḍala), the four empty petals on the lotus of the first rank were filled with the four Bodhisattvas (Samantabhadra, Mañjuśrī, Avalokiteśvara, and Maitreya) that are in the intermediate directions of the eight-petalled lotus of the Mind-*maṇḍala* (the 'Secret maṇḍala'). It would be awkward to justify this theologically, because Avalokiteśvara is already in the first rank of the M-K-G-maṇḍala to the North; and Mañjuśrī is already in the third rank of the M-K-G-maṇḍala, to the East; and, as we saw by the explanation of Vajrapāṇi above, Samantabhadra is already present in the M-K-G-maṇḍala by Vajrapāṇi (his corporeal equivalent) in the first rank in the South. This kind of filling up creates a revaluation about the nature of Vairocana in the M-K-G-maṇḍala. This is because in the Mind-maṇḍala, Vairocana is understood as the Dharmakāya. In the Body-*maṇḍala* (the M-K-G-maṇḍala), Vairocana according to Buddhaguhya must be the Saṃbhogakāya; the flaming triangle to the East in the first rank represents the Dharmakāya. By shifting the four Bodhisattvas from the 'Secret maṇḍala' to the M-K-G-maṇḍala, the lotus center of the M-K-G-maṇḍala takes on the same appearances as the principal part of the "Secret Maṇḍala". So Vairocana could be called Dharmakāya in the M-K-G-*maṇḍala* (and in fact was). It must be noted that the scripture-composer did not define *maṇḍala* with Buddha bodies on a respective basis, so it is up to the commentary lineages to decide such matters. It follows that the principal value of filling up the four empty petals in the M-K-G-maṇḍala, first rank is as part of the general plan of filling all the spots to present to the faithful an impressive temple hanging, with all deities colorfully executed by master painters, the whole evoking a sense of mystery and beauty.

Since the comparisons could be interminable, and a thoroughgoing comparison is out of the question for our present purposes, I shall now follow a limited course of comparing in terms of Tajima's diagram (his Fig. 1) of the Garbha-maṇḍala, which I reproduce here with translation of titles:[14]

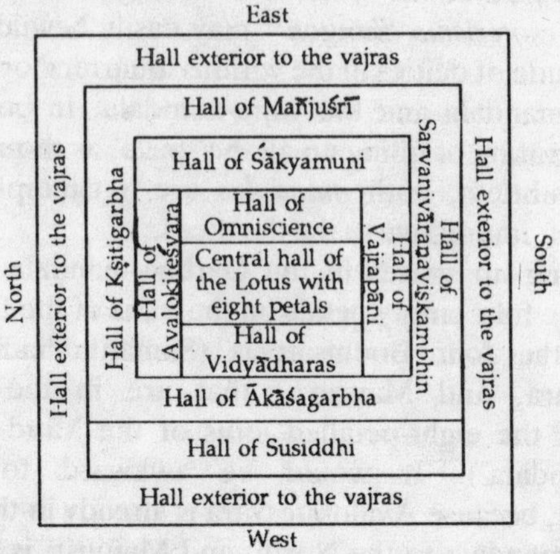

It is necessary to distinguish the diagram *per se* from the deities entered in the various halls. One may notice immediately that the diagram takes no account of the scriptural information that Śākyamuni's hall has two gates (necessarily East and West), that while the scripture allotted Śākyamuni the entire second rank, the diagram allots him only an eastern area. Furthermore, the diagram includes a hall of Susiddhi that is not mentioned at all in the scripture. On the other hand, that the mundane deities, starting with the Ṛṣi-s, should be placed in an exterior hall is quite reasonable from the scriptural evidence, since these in three-dimensional conception would constitute a kind of bulge around the second rank—Śākyamuni's; and since these deities are not admitted to the *maṇḍala,* in two dimensional representation it is reasonable to place them exactly where the diagram does place them ('Hall exterior to the vajras'). It may also be noted that the scripture does not use the expression 'hall of vidyādharas' where it places only Acala and Trilokyavijaya. Of course, when one considers not just the diagram but the deities entered therein, one must acknowledge that the *Taizō genzu maṇḍala* includes many deities that are not mentioned in the V-A-T, the scripture itself. Apparently some deities were borrowed from the other chief *maṇḍala*—the Vajra-maṇḍala, but this is also outside our objective of discussion. The conclusion is as previously: it would not have served the interests of an impressive religious temple hanging to have tried to represent in awkward fashion merely the scripture's deities and its main halls, with attendant gaps and lack of symmetry.

One should recall that at the time and place when the *Vairocanābhisaṃbodhi* was composed (my work claims mid-sixth century), such temple hangings were not apparently made. The scripture addresses itself to a religious practice that amounts to a kind of yoga, where one must master three *ācārya-samādhis* in terms of three *maṇḍalas* (of Body, Speech, and Mind); and there were sculptural representations of individual deities, or small groups of them. V-A-T, Chap. II, specifies various places where the *maṇḍala* may be drawn, namely in verses 12-14. V-A-T, Chap. II, v.157-59 indicates that powdered colors were used; and this is a practice continued to modern times. The emphasis in various verses on preparation of the soil suggests that this was the predominant method of *maṇḍala* construction. The scripture itself provides no directions for constructing a temple hanging.

(9) ***The M-K-G-maṇḍala and the Caryā-tantra class.*** The Tibetan classification of the Tantra translations into that language (the Kanjur, Rgyud 'bum) has four main categories—Kriyā, Caryā, Yoga and Anuttarayoga Tantra. The V-A-T is taken as the chief Tantra of the Caryā Tantra Class. There are traditional explanations for the four Tantra categories, but for our present purposes we need not go into them. Suffice for the present discussion that the Tantras included in the Caryā Tantra group were associated with the premise that there is some consistency between them to justify being so put together.

For a revealing conclusion about the works in the Caryā Tantra class, I shall allude to Bu-ston's work on the *maṇḍalas* of the Caryā Tantra (in his Vol. Tsa, the work *Spyod pa'i rgyud kyi dkyil'khor gyi bkod pa*).[15] I shall make reference below to the inhabitants of the first rank of the M-K-G-maṇḍala, as were detailed above.

Bu-ston begins naturally with the V-A-T, *maṇḍala*, i.e. the M-K-G-maṇḍala of Chap. II, which he exposes generously. Then he proceeds briefly to a Yamāntaka *maṇḍala* from a *Krodha-vijayatantra,* whose central deity is six-faced and six armed; admitting that its inclusion is challengeable. (No doubt, since neither the Peking nor the Derge Kanjur Caryā-tantra sections include it!) Then he presents extensively the *maṇḍala* of the *Āryācalamahākrodharājasya....* which in both Peking and Derge editions immediately follows the V-A-T. Finally he treats extensively the *maṇḍala* of the *Vajrapāṇy-abhiṣeka-tantra,* which in the Derge immediately follows the Acala Tantra, but in the Peking edition follows two other Vajrapāṇi Tantras. The Peking and Derge editions have the same texts in the Caryā-tantra section (the V-A-T, the Acala Tantra, and the set of Vajrapāṇi Tantras), except that the Derge edition places right after the *Vajrapāṇy-abhiṣeka-tantra* the brief *Ārya-Aṣṭadevī-dhāraṇī,* missing at that place in the Peking edition. Of these works only the *Vairocanābhisaṃbodhi* was also translated into Chinese. As to why some other work that would feasibly belong to the *Caryā-tantra* is missing. Bu-ston points out that no Tantra of the 'lotus' (Padma) family belonging to this class of Tantra was translated into Tibetan; and since Avalokiteśvara or also Tārā belongs to the 'lotus' family this explains why there is no Tantra of his or hers in this section. The fact that Bu-ston tried to include a Yamāntaka *maṇḍala* suggests that he thought that the Caryā-tantra Acala can be interpreted as a kind of Yamāntaka.

That some Kriyā-tantra or Yoga-tantra scripture might be somewhat affiliated with the *Vairocanābhisaṃbodhi-tantra* (officially classified as *Caryā-tantra*), is supported by observations of S.Tsuda, in an article "Classification of Tantra in dPal brtseg's lTa *baḥi rim pa bśad pa* and Its Problems", *Journal of Indian and Buddhist Studies,*XXX:1 Jan 1965, p. 400, or (44), pointing out that Buddhaguhya's *Shorter Commentary* on the *Vairocanā-bhisaṃbodhi-tantra* classifies tantra as either *Kriyā* or *Yoga* and that the *Vairocana* is a *Kriyā* kind; and that in his *Longer Commentary* on the words of the *Vairocana* he again classifies tantras as either *Kriyā* or *Yoga*, but here says that the *Vairocana* is either of the two, or "*ubhaya-tantra*" *(gñis ka'i rgyud*).

We may therefore conclude that the kind of Tantra placeable in the Caryā-tantra class would be, beside the Acala Tantra and the Vajrapāṇi Tantra, a Tantra of Prajñāpāramitā (as Mother of the

Buddhas) and an appropriate Tantra of Avalokiteśvara or also Tarā. As to a possible *Prajñāpāramitā* Scripture, I immediately think of the one already mentioned, that is very important to the Shingon sect in Japan by its name *Rishukyō,* of which six translations are extant in the Chinese Buddhist canon, and which in the Tibetan canon is entered in the Yogatantra section of the Kanjur under the title *Ārya-Prajñāpāramitānayaśatapañcaśatikā*, but which in the Chinese version is accorded the Sanskrit title *Adhyardhaśatikā Prājñāpāramitā.*[16] The most important version of the Chinese ones is the Amoghavajra text, which contains a set of verses cited in the Javanese work *Sang Hyang Kamahāyānan Mantranaya* soon after a set of verses taken from V-A-T, Chap. II. The Amoghavajra version in the Chinese canon is probably the best candidate to go with the Prajñāpāramitā goddess in the Eastern hall of the first rank of the M-K-G-maṇḍala, and the usual version would also serve the purpose.

As to a possible Avalokiteśvara Tantra for the Caryā-tantra section, it should be mentioned that the Khasarpaṇa form of Avalokiteśvara appears to be the nearest to the V-A-T description in terms of companions, by having four companions, Tārā, Sudhanakumāra, Bhṛkuṭī, and Hayagrīva.[17] Tārā, here is described as green and Bhṛkuṭī three-eyed as in the V-A-T description. Sudhanakumāra is not included in the V-A-T group. The name Khasarpaṇa (Tib. *mkha 'spyod*) means "who moves (softly) in the sky"; and this agrees with the 'sky' situation of the M-K-G-maṇḍala first rank, as was previously discussed. The Sādhana of this Avalokiteśvara form in the collection "Rin lhan",[18] ka, 261b-5, puts an Amitābha on his head, as in the V-A-T description. His color 'pure moon' is close to the V-A-T "like conch and the Autumn moon".

There is a possible Tārā Tantra as a companion to that Avalokiteśvara one. This is the *Ūrdhvajaṭāmahākalpa* (now in the Kriyā-tantra of the Kanjur *Rgyud 'bum,* starting in Vol. Tsa and ending in Vol. Tsha of the Derge edition). This is because I have noticed in its second chapter devoted to *maṇḍala* as happens with the V-A-T itself, a description of Śākyamuni on a par with the prominent role in the M-K-G-maṇḍala's second rank, which is reserved for Śākyamuni and his entourage; and that Tārā Tantra also includes in his entourage the mundane deities. However, this inclusion is speculative.

It is not possible here to show an extensive amount of Bu-ston's coverage of *maṇḍalas* in the Caryā-tantra section. A sample should suffice; in fact, on the treatment of the Mañjuśrī group in the third rank. According to the V-A-T, Chap. II, and notes, the group is as follows:

(a) *V-A-T on the Mañjuśrī group.* Mañjuśrī, like a young boy, five locks on his head; in his left hand a blue lotus having a *vajra* upon it; has lower garment of silk and cotton, upper garment of satin; is seated on a white-lotus seat; has a pronounced smile; is surrounded by light rays; and is in the East. To his right is the youth Jālinīprabha; his hand holding a jewel net or a hook; his mudrā is the hook (*aṅkuśa*); adorned with various jewels, is seated on a red-lotus seat, gazing at Mañjuśrī; apparently has as retinue the youth Ratnamukūṭa, his *mudrā* a *ratna* (jewel), and the youth Vimalaprabha, his *mudrā* an unopened lotus. To his left, the five female messengers, who are: keśinī, Upakeśinī, Citrā, Vasumatī, Ākarṣaṇī—who are the female messengers possessed of (Mañjuśrī's) discrimination; they have five attendants, not named. Bu-ston, Tsa, *Spyod rgyud dkyil 'khor,* f.15a-6, adds from the *Sūtra* the information that Keśinī's *mudrā* is a curved blade; Upakeśinī's a trident; Citrā's a staff; Vasumatī's a banner; Ākarṣaṇī's a hook. All five *mudrā* have the mark of 'blue lotus'. Their five attendants each have as *mudrā* a sword-blade (*khaḍgārita*), which is like a curved blade.

(b) *The Acala Tantra on Mañjuśrī.* Bu-ston's work at 20a-5, reports: Mañjuśrī in East, reddish-yellow; in his right hand the curved blade standing for wisdom *(jñāna)*; in his left hand the blue lotus (*utpala*). At 22b-7, in the West draw Keśinī whose curved blade is marked with an utpala; upakeśinī's trident; Citrā's staff; Vasumatī's banner; Ākarṣaṇī's book—all *mudrā* of the female messengers marked with an *utpala*. Their five attendants have a curved blade. (I did not notice an inclusion of the youth Jālinīprabha; and a number of *maṇḍala* features differ from the V-A-T *maṇḍala*. While the description of the five female messengers is virtually the same as in the V-A-T, the group appears to be separated from Mañjuśrī and said to be among the male and female messengers, hence of the main deity Acala.)

(c) *The Vajrapāṇy-abhiṣeka-tantra on Mañjuśrī.* At f. 27a-4, Bu-ston starts the treatment of the *maṇḍala* called Mahāvajra-maṇḍala, and the Mañjuśrī group included turns out to be precisely as in the V-A-T, Chap. II, and Bu-ston makes a remark to that effect, but with minimal information. Subsequently, at fol. 30b-2, he has enlarged remarks about the same *maṇḍala,* with a special section on the Mañjuśrī group. At 30b-7, Mañjuśrī has his legs in the crossed-leg position, on his right side wears a calm-looking *sñiṅ-po* (probably meaning, a flower), dwells amidst a languid blaze of fire tongue. His right hand shows the gift-giving (*varada*) gesture, his left hand shows a *vajra,* wears white garments. From the tip of his 'gift-giving' gesture five streams of water descend. There follows the same list of five female messengers.

One gets the impression that both the *Acala Tantra* and the *Vajrapāṇy-abhiṣeka* are compositions that follow closely the V-A-T in time.

(10) ***Description of Mahāvairocana.*** The given descriptions of the central deity in various spots of the scripture are closely consistent. The deity is sometimes called 'supreme Jina', 'lord' (*nātha*); in Chap. X ('Wheel of Syllables') is called Mahāvairocana. As to the name 'Vairocana', see *Studies in Indo-Asian Art and Culture,* Vol. 6, edited by Lokesh Chandra, Oct. 1980, "Vairocana in the Japanese Tradition" a translation from Mochizuki, *Bukkyodaijiten* (without translator's name) pp. 165-177, rendered 'brilliant everywhere', and so on.

His hairdress is uniformly described; thus V-A-T II, verses 28 and 76, his hair is bound up and wearing a jewel in the crown (or jewel crown), so also V-A-T, Chap. VI, and the 'Wheel of Syllables' chapter. The commentator Buddhaguhya explains this hair description as indicating a deity of the Akaniṣṭha Heaven (highest of the Pure Abodes, *śuddhāvāsa*). Those two verses of Chap. II are in the first part, devoted to 'Single Means', hence point to 'Sameness Wisdom', *samatā jñāna*). Buddhaguhya, Chap. II, n.41, explains the jewel in the crown as meaning 'King of the Dharma'. Shuyu Kanaoka, "Vairocana in Tathāgata form," *Journal of Indian and Buddhist Studies* (Tokyo), XIII:2, March 1965, cites the Chinese commentary on the *Mahāvairocana-sūtra* to the effect that this is the form of the Bodhisattva, and adds that it is possible to find other Vairocana images in Complete Buddha form, and so concludes that there are two Vairocanas.

The color of body is agreed to be golden or shining yellow. The 'Wheel of Syllables' chapter says he is clothed with lower garment of silk or cotton, and upper garment of silk. He is said to be surrounded by various colored rays; and 'Wheel of Syllables' chapter says those are burning rays. He is always on a white lotus.

As to his hand gesture, it seems to be the first one described in the

V-A-T, Mudrā chapter, Tib. 258-2-5,6: the two empty palms are added, with the thumbs touching in an upward point. This appears to be the *mudrā* described in E. Dale Saunders, *Mudrā* (London, 1960), pp. 85, ff., especially his Type B, where the fingers of the right hand are placed on the fingers of the left hand, and the thumbs make an upward point. Saunders calls it a *dhyānamudrā* or *samādhimudrā,* which is not corroborated by the V-A-T scripture; and further goes astray, trying to make it the "Body of Fire". The scripture itself explains: "not transgressing the three Dharma Paths, and having fulfilled the (ten) Stages and the (six) Perfections." B-comm. on this, 174-4-5,ff., the 'three Dharma Paths' are the three inexhaustible streams of Body, Speech, and Mind; or the three Bodies; and not transgressing means preserving their pledges. And at 175-5-2, calls it the 'seal of Dharmadhātu voidness' (Tib. *chos kyi dbyings stong pa nyid phyag rgya*). In the above description of the Mind-*maṇḍala,* Mahāvairocana was described as contemplating voidness (*śūnyatā*). Now, voidness goes with the element 'space' (*akāśa*); and later in my chapter "Chapter V and the preliminary service" the five geometric forms of the elements forming the human body as a stūpa show the top one, namely 'space', in the shape indicated by this *mudrā* 'seal of Dharmadhātu voidness'. For a sculptural representation of this Mahāvairocana, see Saunders, *Mudrā*, plate XVI, "Dainichi Nyorai, Japan", which he attributes to the Tenryaku era, 947-956, and describes as made of cryptomeria wood, 9 ft. 8 in. tall (Providence Museum, Rhode Island School of Design). The fingers of one hand laid upon the other, with the two thumbs touching in a point, do not form a triangle. Since the base of the two hands in the lap have a rounded appearance, the whole amounts to the form used to represent space (*ākāśa*). The V-A-T lineage, insofar as Buddhaguhya conveys it, does not supply a term to represent this form.[19] However, a Śaivite work, *Śivasvarodaya,* when presenting forms of the five elements, assigns *bindu* to space (*ākāśa*). This word *bindu* means 'drop' (as of water); and this shape appears to fit the *mudrā* of Vairocana perfectly.[20] Since the glyph for space goes with the top of the head, the symbolism of the *mudrā* must involve a correlation between the hands in the lap and the top of head.

Besides, I have noticed this *mudrā* on an important sculpture that was wrongly described in T.K. Biswas, "A note on Six Gandharan Sculptures," *Studies in Indology* (D.C. Sircar Felicitation Volume)

(Sundeep Prakashan, New Delhi, 1983). These Gandharan sculptures are at the Bharat Kala Bhavan of Banaras Hindu University, and Biswas assigns a theoretical terminal date of A.D. 450. Pl. 52 going with his article is captioned "Bodhisattva in Dhyāna-Mudra". However, it is surely Vairocana with the 'space' mudrā. On the crown of this figure is a solar disk representing the sun in the sky. If Biswas' terminal dating holds up, this would imply that the 'space' gesture precedes its employment in the V-A-T as Vairocana's gesture. Moreover, among my present holdings is a photograph of 'H 315' (meaning that number in the Sven Hedin collection in Stockholm), wrongly identified as Amitāyus but again depicting Vairocana's 'space' *mudrā* (while *sādhanas* of Amitāyus agree on the Samāpatti mudrā=the Dhyāna *mudrā*, with the two hands laid upon the other, palms up, in flat manner). This 'H 315' shows on top of the head a headdress consisting of the five Buddhas, suggesting that the figure is the Saṃbhogakāya Vairocana with the headdress of the five Buddhas of the 'sky'.

(11) ***The feminine deities.*** Because of the likelihood, mentioned already in my introduction ('Composition and Influence'), that the earliest Tārā artistic representations were made in the Mahārashtra area in the 6th-7th centuries, it is well to consider the role of the female divinities in the V-A-T since I have assigned this text to this area and in the mid-sixth century. There is indeed a considerable number of these goddesses, suggesting either an innovation by the scripture-composer or a concession to a powerful movement. I shall first simply list them by their appearance in the Chap. II in the ranks. First rank: (in the Buddha group) the Mother Prajñāpāramitā; (in the Avalokiteśvara group) Tārā, Bhṛkuṭī, Yaśodharā, and Pāṇḍaravāsinī; (in the Vajrapāṇi group) Māmakī, Vajrasūcī, and Vajraśṛṅkhalā. Second rank: (in the Śākyamuni group) Buddha-locanā, Vidyorṇā and Aparājitā; (and in Śākyamuni's mundane group) Kālarātri, Nirṛti, Pṛthivī, and Sarasvatī. Third rank: (in the Mañjuśrī group) the five messengers, Keśinī, Upakeśinī, Citrā, Vasumatī, Ākarṣaṇī. This amounts to a total of twenty female divinities.

Most of our individual discussion will be about divinities in the first rank. The Mother Prajñāpāramitā, i.e. Mother of the Buddhas, is a teaching of the Prajñāpāramitā scriptures, e.g. *Aṣṭasāhasrikā Prajñāpāramitā,* Chap. 12. But notice that in the second rank Buddhalocanā is commented upon as the mother of Śākyamuni. Hence, in the V-A-T, Buddhalocanā is a specialization of the goddess Prajnāpāramitā. This character of Buddhalocanā, as well as of the (green) Tārā, Pāṇḍaravāsinī, and Māmakī of the first rank, indicates the early nature of the V-A-T female divinities, since the fully developed Buddhist tantra makes these four goddesses the companions of four of the five Buddhas; and this is not the case in the V-A-T.

The Avalokiteśvara group of feminine deities can all be referred to as 'Tārā-s'. It is quite reasonable that the worship of Tārā originally developed from a star cult, since *tāra* and *tāraka* do mean 'star' (as well as other things), and the stars did guide traders,[21] so also those who departed from the West coast, probably visible from the Kanheri cave where the Tārā goddess is found represented. This V-A-T group, as was mentioned, consists of Tārā (green), Bhṛkuṭī (white), Yaśodharā (golden), and Pāṇḍaravāsinī ('white dressed', but red).

The green Tārā apparently developed into the twenty-one forms of the Green Tārā. It is presumably the prototype of various green goddesses that are referred to as Tārās, to wit, the popular Khadiravaṇī Tārā, the Vaśyatārā (called also Āryatārā), and perhaps the green Parṇaśabarī. I have not noticed any convincing tracing of this green Tārā to an earlier Indian goddess; it may well be an origination of the Buddhists.[22] It is otherwise with the next three of the Avalokiteśvara group.

For the three, Bhṛkuṭī, whose white color goes with appeasing rites (*śāntika*); Yaśodharā, whose golden color goes with prosperity rites (*pauṣṭika*); and Pāṇḍaravāsinī, whose red color goes with dominating rites (*vaśīkara*).[23] I may suggest the remote ancestry of a Vedic triad of goddesses, Sarasvatī, Iḍā, and Bhāratī. Since the ancient text *Vājasaneyi-Saṃhitā,* among others, associates this goddess triad of three sacrificial fires with the three regions of the world, (respectively, intermediate space, earth, and sky) modern writers have repeated these associations;[24] and to my mind as well they appear reasonable in terms of the evidence I shall marshall in rather curtailed fashion.

The easiest identification is taking Īḍa (the earth goddess) as the prototype of the golden Yaśodharā, because Lal's chapter on Iḍā[25] shows this goddess in the predominant role of creating prosperity in terms of food, and so on. Lal could only think of a successor goddess as the minor one Annapūrṇā; but certainly the important successor and supplantor is the goddess Lakṣmī, generally yellow. The equivalent Buddhist goddess Vasudhārā is also yellow and like Yaśodharā carries an ear of corn.[26] So also, Yaśodharā should be accepted as V-A-T's nickname for the well-knwon goddess Vasudhārā.

The Vedic Sarasvatī (the goddess of the intermediate space) in her role of promoting *dhi*[27] goes with the 'appeasing rite' by the suggestion that perfect comprehension of the *śāstras* and supernormal faculty (*abhijñā*) are successes (*siddhi*) of the 'appeasing rite';[28] and this is consistent with Bhṛkuṭī's third among her three eyes, namely the one in the middle of the forehead. Also the white color of Bhṛkuṭī agrees with the prevalent color attributed to Sarasvatī, namely white. I presume that the white Bhṛkuṭī has a prototype in Sarasvatī and in turn gives rise to the popular white Tārā and then in time was differentiated from the latter by changed color, multiple arms, etc.

Bhāratī is the most obscure of the triad. The indication supplied by Lal that the three goddesses feed Apām Napāt (= Agni) means that Bhāratī feeds the form of Agni in the sky, which is the sun.[29] This shows the Bhāratī is a promotional aspect of the sun. This provides a clue to the speedy disappearance of the goddess Bhāratī as the old Vedic period came to an end. This is because the well-known goddess of dawn, Uṣas, herself brings on the sun. Uṣas, I am confident, is the prototype of the red goddesses, such as Pāṇḍaravāsinī. This Pāṇḍaravāsinī may be said to have the remote ancestor Bhāratī, but more recognizably Uṣas, who could also be said to be 'white-dressed' but red. Pāṇḍaravāsinī in turn may be taken as the ancestor of the red domination (*vaśīkara*) goddesses such as the later popular Kurukullā.

In short, of the four goddesses in Avalokiteśvara's group, one, the green Tārā, is presumably a Buddhist conception; and the remaining three are theoretically Buddhist recastings of an old Vedic triad of goddesses.

The Vajrapāṇi group of goddesses is also of much interest; it consists of Māmakī, Vajrasūcī, and Vajraśṛṅkhalā. Of these, the blue Māmakī destroys demons, using a 'fury illusion'.[30] As such, she bears comparison with the Hindu Durgā. This Durgā evidently descends from the Vedic Rātri, "shining like the petals of a blue lotus", who kills the two demons Śumbha and Niśumbha, as Durgā is credited with doing; and who is the Yoga-nidrā (cosmic sleep), also the Viṣṇumāyā (Viṣṇu's illusion).[31] According to Buddhaguhya (the Chap. II, n.53), the *vajra* which Māmakī holds means that she threatens the would-be evil-doer, "Don't do it, don't do it!"

Vajrasūcī is not entered by name in B. Bhattacharyya's *The Buddhist Iconography*. Since the name means "She the Diamond

Needle", the scripture-composer evidently employs this as a nickname for Mārīcī, who carries needle and thread, with which she is said to sew up the eyes and ears of the wicked.[32] This form of Mārīcī is called Āryā Mārīcī. Her complexion is of molten gold; and this goddess is evidently a form of the sunrise. Hence, this goddess, mentioned subsequent to Māmakī, is in the symbolism immediately subsequent to Māmakī in fact. Buddhaguhya's comment (the Chap. II, n. 54) implies that she imparts fear of retribution.

Vajraśṛṅkhalā is a goddess whose name means "She (carrying) a chain (*śṛṅkhalā*) (marked) with a Vajra". A *sādhana* of her in the *Sādhana-mālā* allots her the green color and depicts her with three faces, the first one gently smiling, the right one 'brown with brown eyes', the left one red and terrible by brow-contortions and bared fangs.[33] Therefore, when Buddhaguhya comments (on Chap.II, n.55) that she pulls the sentient beings onto the Noble Path of Buddhism, the suggestion of the iconography is that she does this by alternately threatening, gazing placidly, and then smiling; and pulls the beings on to the Path with her chain. It may be the intention to have this activity as a practical third in the sequence of the three goddesses.

In the second rank there is only Śākyamuni and his close group and the mundane group. Here there is Buddhalocanā, whose vision, i.e. insight (*prajñā*), is Śākyamuni's 'mother'. Vidyorṇā is evidently a personification of the *ūrṇakośa,* the Buddha characteristic in the middle of the forehead, comparable to a third eye which experiences the three clear visions (*vidyā*) of the night of enlightenment. Aparājitā is a fierce deity, yellow in color, who holds a parasol and destroys wicked beings.[34] The mundane group of feminine deities needs only a few comments. Lal treats Nirṛti as the goddess of malice, bringing disorder into the world; and Kālarātrī keeps up the phenomenal world (*saṃsārasthitikāriṇī*).[35] In contrast, Pṛthivī and Sarasvatī are good goddesses.

In the third rank only Mañjuśrī has goddesses in his group, the five, Keśinī, etc., who share his discrimination; but the meaning of their being 'messengers' is not clarified. Since Mañjuśrī is a Bodhisattva who emphasizes 'insight' (*prajñā*), the implication is that this is of five kinds; and indeed 'wisdom' (*jñāna*) is in Mahāyāna Buddhism of five kinds. So the five goddesses may possibly be the 'insight' side of the five 'wisdoms'.[36]

The foregoing concludes our cursory treatment of the goddesses in the M-K-G-maṇḍala. Besides, the Speech Maṇḍala has a set of four goddesses as doorkeepers. We find other Tantras in which the *maṇḍalas* have female divinities as doorkeepers.[37] However, there may be an ancient misplacement of the passage, as though for the first rank, since here is also found Acala and Trailokyavijaya (both in West) who serve as door guardians in the West in the M-K-G-maṇḍala; and so there is an excess of door guardians for the first rank. The four colors of these four feminine divinities go with the four elements, so these doorkeepers are evidently those who counter the demons of the four elements.[38] These four added to the previous twenty goddesses bring the total to twenty-four. Besides, the five female divinities in the Mañjuśrī retinue have each an attendant (not named), and these attendants can feasibly increase the total to twenty-nine.

(12) ***Difference between the two parts of V-A-T, Chap. Two.*** The incentive to write this introductory section was due to a native Tibetan work by the celebrated Sa-pan (more fully, Sa-skya Pandita), founder of the Sa-skya-pa, a well-known sect of Tibetan Buddhism. His work in question is called *Sdom gsum* (on the three vows, the Prātimokṣa, the Bodhisattva, and the Tantric ones). This work translated[39] as a doctoral dissertation, and which I have sponsored, contains a reference in its large treatment of the Tantric vow, verses 367-68, to a dispute over a passage in the *Vaircanā-bhisaṃbodhi.* Sa-pan disagrees with certain teachers who pointed to the V-A-T to justify a theory of a 'single means' of voidness for attaining enlightenment.[40] In fact, such an attributed theory could only have been made by a hasty look at the V-A-T, Chap. Two, which does indeed devote its first part to the 'single means' and its second part to the 'various means'. But the fact that such an attribution was made does indicate the authoritativeness of the V-A-T, in particular its Chap. Two, and probably also suggests the difficulty which many readers experienced in deciding upon the V-A-T's message. It is therefore worthwhile to discuss these matters by showing the difference between the two parts of V-A-T, Chap. Two. May I state now in brief what appears to be this difference, and then discuss it in greater detail. In short, the first part sets forth the Mahākaruṇāgarbhodbhava-maṇḍala; and 'single means' signifies that there is no difference in terms of persons to witness this *maṇḍala.* The second part does make a difference in persons, thus the terminology 'various means'; and reserves the initiation (*abhiṣeka*) into the *maṇḍala* to certain persons.

V-A-T, Chap. Two, A. The Single Means, has this passage:

> Now the Bhagavat Vairocana had formerly taken a vow to accomplish the purport-inexhaustible Dharmadhātu and to rescue the realm of sentient beings. Rightly consulting about the single means with all the Tathāgatas, he equipoised himself in the samādhi (called) Mahākaruṇāgarbhodbhava.

This *samādhi* is therefore on the M-K-G-maṇḍala. As the scripture continues, it introduces the *ācārya* (master) who will find the proper spot of ground for drawing the *maṇḍala*. It is this master that the scripture has in mind when it describes the actual *maṇḍala,* first the drawing of it, then the imagination of the deities placed in its three ranks. (Cf. the above two sections "Triadic world conception of the M-K-G-maṇḍala" and "Synopsis of the Body-maṇḍala deities"). After this description, the V-A-T speaks of the benefit of beholding such a *maṇḍala,* including verse 148:

> "For them destroyed is evil destiny and the sources of all suffering, for whom in this best practice the mind does not shift to something else."

This rite of the M-K-G-maṇḍala, to be viewed without exclusion of any persons, is therefore what is referred to as the 'single means'.

But then Vajrapāṇi asked about the coloring material for the *maṇḍala*. The reply includes the remarkable verse 157:

> "The Buddhas formerly stated that sentient beings crave 'realms' (*dhātu*), and that this Dharmadhātu is a (single) 'taste' (*rasa*)." For that reason, there is 'coloring material' (i.e. the *dhātu*).

This depicts the *maṇḍala* as a kind of loom, in which the warp, namely the length-wise threads, stands for the white or void Dharmadhātu.[41] The warp is crossed by the woof, the colored threads, standing for the *dhātu*, the realms or elements, which the sentient beings crave. The first part of Chap. Two concludes with these two verses (nos. 163-164):

> "Great being, listen single-mindedly in a special way! The *samādhi* of all the Buddhas is called by the Jina 'voidness' (*śūnyatā*). When the mind has fully experienced *that,* there is nothing else to gain.
>
> 'Complete Buddha' is explained as avoiding the two. 'Great void' is the fulfilment of omniscient knowledge. Hence, in all images, always remember voidness."

The teachers with whom Sa-pan disagrees evidently interpreted these concluding verses of the first part as indicating the fruit(s) of the 'single means' as though the M-K-G-maṇḍala should be looked upon as void and with this realization one would be a Buddha. But according to Sa-pan, this 'voidness' amounts only to realizing the Dharmadhātu, the colorless warp of the loom; hence the realization is only the Śrāvaka's 'cessation' (*nirodha*). It takes no account of the sentient-being realm, the colors of the woof. Thus, the V-A-T, in speaking of 'single means' does not imply voidness, because the *maṇḍala* rite requires both the theory of the void Dharmadhātu as the warp, and the colored sentient-being realm as the woof.

Hence it is important to explain the remark of V-A-T, Chap. Two, verse 156: "The best rules of mantra practice arise as the fruit of Mahāyāna." In the second part of V-A-T, Chap. Two, verses 176-177 allude back to the single means.

> "There is the method of samādhi which is the method of rite for mantra praxis whether the one based therein be a Buddha, a Pratyekabuddha, protective Bodhisattva, or Śrāvaka—who are celebrated for having destroyed sin—or a mundane god. O hero, with desire for benefit to the sentient beings, I explained it at that time."

These verses show that while the 'single means' issues from the Mahāyāna, the V-A-T position does not exclude Śrāvakas or Pratyekabuddhas from participating in it, i.e. viewing the M-K-G-maṇḍala.

Then, V-A-T, Chap. Two, B. The Various Means, at its outset shows that by 'various means' is intended the *samādhis* that differ for the Śrāvakas, Pratyekabuddhas, and Bodhisattvas. It then distinguishes the Bodhisattvas 'limited to only one more life' and who abide in the Buddhabhūmi, i.e. are on the Tenth Stage, from the Bodhisattvas who are 'lords of the Eighth Bodhisattva Stage'. It refers to the method of *samādhi* of the Śrāvakas that avoids the extremes of nihilism and eternalism; the method of *samādhi* of the Pratyekabuddhas that dwells in the inexpressible Dharma, i.e. that is silent. Then it mentions the *samādhi* of worldlings who believe in (realistic) cause and effect, and imagine being in the power of others (i.e. created by a Lord, etc.). In contrast to the 'single means' there is the theory of mantra, and the actual syllables of mantra; and the initiation of the disciple in the *maṇḍala* (Cf. section 5 above, "Subsidiary *maṇḍala*"), which does not occur in the 'single means'. There follows the mention of benefits, and the pledges (*samaya*); and the second part concludes with the 'treasure of mantras'. It follows that the 'single means' is non-exclusive, since all who wish to view the *maṇḍala* are allowed to do so. The 'various means' does amount to kinds of exclusion, since it appears that the actual initiation is for Mahāyānists, who have taken the Bodhisattva vow, and so forth. Therefore, the Śrāvakas and Pratyekabuddhas as defined in this tradition are not eligible for the initiation.

The foregoing distinctions are also referred to in cited scripture. Notice the text known in Tibetan translation as the *Uttaratantra*, but now known by Johnston's Sanskrit edition as the *Ratnagotravibhāga,* its I, 92:

> lekhakā ye tadākārā dānaśīlakṣmādayaḥ/
> sarvākāravaropetā śūnyatā paratimocyate//
> The painters, i.e. giving, morality, forbearance, and the rest. are its aspects (= images); and the voidness possessing the best of all aspects—is the 'framer' [i.e. the bare canvas].[42]

And Tson-kha-pa, soon after citing this in the Bodhisattva section of his *Lam rim chen mo,* cites a passage (taken from Śāntideva's *Śikṣāsamuccaya*) of the *Sarvadharmavaipulyasaṃgraha-sūtra*, concluding: "These men of delusion will speak thus: 'Only by one rule is there enlightenment, to wit, by the rule of voidness.' Now, will they be pure in conduct? [Of course not!]." Those passages allude to the 'single means' as the *maṇḍala* rite that requires both voidness (*śūnyatā*) and the means which assists the sentient-being realm; and acknowledge that deluded persons claim that a realization of the bare canvas is enlightenment!

In that same place of his *Sdom gsµm,* Sa-Pan cites the *Sūtralaṃkāra*, IX, 35 (for which Sylvain Lévi's edition, while correct, is helped by the Tibeṭan for interpretation):

> yathā pāṃśuvaśād vastre rangacitrā vicitratā/
> tathā 'vedhavaśān muktau jñānavitrā vicitratā//
> Just as it is by dint of knotting that there is brightness of color, or no color, in a cloth; so it is by dint of impetus (= aspiration) that there is brightness of knowledge, or no color, in the liberation.

This goes with the 'various means' of the second part, V-A-T, Chap. Two, namely, that the Śrāvakas and Pratyekabuddhas, by reason of their kinds of aspiration, have no color in their liberation, amounting to the passive Nirvāṇa of the void Dharmadhātu. The Bodhisattva, by reason of his different kind of aspiration, has a colorful knowledge in the liberation, i.e. the voidness possessing the best of aspects.

NOTES TO THE INTRODUCTION, CHAP. TWO

1. The list of eight Bodhisattvas in Abhayākaragupta's *Niṣpannayogāvalī*, ed. by B. Bhattacharyya (Oriental Institute, Baroda, 1949, 2. Akṣobhya Maṇḍala, is as follows: Maitreya, Kṣitigarbha, Vajrapāṇi, Khagarbha (= Ākāśagarbha), Lokeśara (= Avalokiteśvara), Mañjughoṣa (= Mañjuśrī) Sarvanīvaraṇa-viṣkambhin, Samantabhadra.
2. According to Ananda K. Coomaraswamy, *Yakṣas,* part I (edition in Delhi, 1971), p. 31, this Vajrapāṇi is independent of Indra and is himself a Yakṣa, in this role called "benevolent Lord of the Guhyakas, vajra in hand."
3. Four kinds of *vajra* are associated with the retinue of Kṣitigarbha for which see Chap. II, n.76. The *vajra* in this tradition is associated with the earth-*maṇḍala,* which is consistent with the name Kṣitigarbha (Earth-womb).
4. Cf. Tadeusz Skorupski, ed. and tr., *The Sarvadurgatipariśodhana Tantra* (Motilal Banarsidass, Delhi, 1983), p. 74, for this Tantra's Maṇḍala of Cakravartin, where the center deity is permitted to be Vajrapāṇi, or Vajrasattva or Samantabhadra.
5. Ferdinand D. Lessing and Alex Wayman, *Mkhas grub rje's Fundamental of the Buddhist Tantras* (The Hague, 1968), pp. 30-1.
6. I included this paragraph after my wife acquainted me with Shigen Takagi, "Taizo Maṇḍala ni miru Indo no Kamigami", in *Maṇḍala—Iro to Katachi no imisuru mono,* ed. by Yūkei Matsunaga (Asahi Culture Books 10, Osaka, 1983) dealing with the directional placement of the Indian deities in the Garbha-maṇḍala of the V-A-S and the Indian background for the gods-and-demons battle.
7. A. A. Macdonell, *The Vedic Mythology* (Indological Book House, Varanasi, 1963), pp. 54, ff.
8. According to Mkhas-grub-rje's treatise (n.5, above), pp. 141-2, the *vajra,* bell, and name initiations are conferred in the Caryā-tantra (of which according to the Tibetan canon, the V-A-T is the chief Tantra) and the Hierophant's Initiation would make a fourth. However, as far as the evidence of the V-A-T itself is concerned, the hierophant (*ācārya*) is initiated in the three *maṇḍalas* (Body, Speech, and Mind), and the disciple is initiated in a subsidiary *maṇḍala* of the Body-*maṇḍala*, by way of the mirror initiation.
9. According to our essay herein, "The dharmadhātu", section 3. 'Pervading the DD', "A" goes with enlightenment (*bodhi*); hence here Vairocana represents the enlightenment body.
10. According to the same essay (n.9, above), "AṂ" is the Complete Buddha, with the inexhaustible Body, Speech, and Mind. Hence here the triangle stands for Body, Speech, and Mind.
11. The following summaries of the three iconography traditions have been abstracted for me by my wife Hideko from the one-volume tantric dictionary in Japanese by R. Sawa, *Mikkyō Jiten* (Kyōto, 1975), pp. 469-471.
12. Cf. for this remark, Chikyō Yamamoto, *Introduction to the Maṇḍala* (Dohosha, 1980), p. 6.
13. This work was published posthumously in 1959 by the Maison Franco Japonaise, Tokyo; and the Presses Universitaires de France, Paris.
14. Tajima, *Les deux grands maṇḍalas.....,*p. 63.
15. From the collected works of Bu-ston, published by the International Academy of Indian Culture, New Delhi.

16. See Yukio Hatta, *Index to the Ārya-Prajñā-pāramitā-naya-śatikā* (Heirakuji-Shoten, Kyoto, 1971), Introduction (pp. ix-xiii).
17. See Benoytosh Bhattacharyya, *The Indian Buddhist Iconography* (Firma K. L. Mukhopadhyay, Calcutta, 1958), pp. 128-130.
18. This is in the collection published under the title *Sādhana-mālā of the Panchen Lama*, 2 vols., by Lokesh Chandra, International Academy of Indian Culture, New Delhi, 1974.
19. This is attributed the form of a gem in Hisao Inagaki, "Kūkai's Principle of Attaining Buddhahood with the Present Body," Ryukoku Translation Pamphlet Series 4 (Ryukoku Translation Center, Ryukoku University, Kyoto, 1975), p. 33.
20. Cf. *Shiva Svarodaya,* text with English translation by Ram Kumar Rai (Prachya Prakashan, Varanasi, 1980), verse 153 (p. 26), where *bindu* is mistranslated as 'dotted'. An earlier rendition by Rama Prasad in *Nature's Finer Forces* (Theosophical Publishing House, Adyar, Madras, 1889; with a number of later editions), his verse 149 (p. 229), mistranslates it as 'spotted'.
21. Cf. D. C. Sircar, *The Śakti Cult and Tārā* (University of Calcutta, 1967), p. 111.
22. But cf. A. Wayman, "The twenty-one Praises of Tārā, a Syncretism of Śaivism and Buddhism", now reprinted in *Buddhist Insight; Essays by Alex Wayman,* ed. by George R. Elder (Motilal Banarsidass, Delhi, 1984).
23. For correlation of colors and the type of magical rite, see now Alex Wayman. The *Sarvarahasyatantra* (*Acta Indologica,* Japan, Vol. VI, 1984), p. 531, verses 37-38.
24. See Shyam Kishore Lal, *Female Divinities in Hindu Mythology and Ritual* (University of Poona, 1980), p. 39 and n.123, for references to the ancient works.
25. Lal, *Female Divinities,* pp. 31-40.
26. Cf. Niranjan Ghosh, *Concept and Iconography of the Goddess of Abundance and Fortune in Three Religions of India* (University of Burdwan, 1979), p. 53 and elsewhere. See the handsome image of Vasudhārā holding the corn, in Debala Mitra, *Ratnagiri 1958-61*), Vol. 1 (New Delhi, 1981), Plate CXXXVII.
27. But cf. Raghunath Airi, *Concept of Sarasvati* (Munshiram Manoharlal, Delhi, 1977,) pp. 64-66.
28. *Mkhas grub rje's Fundamentals of the Buddhist Tantras,* tr. by F.D. Lessing and A. Wayman, p. 201.
29. Lal, *Female Divinities*, p. 187.
30. *Sarvarahaṣyatantra* (n. 23, above), v. 188 and commentary.
31. Lal, *Female Divinities,* pp. 144-147. See also V. Raghavan, "Rātri and Ratri Sūkta", *Hindutva,* Vol. X. No. 4, July, 1979, pp.15-21, for his arguments on behalf of deriving Durgā from Rātri.
32. However, B. Bhattacharyya, *The Buddhist Iconography* (2d ed., 1958), pp. 210-211, explains this use of the needle and thread only for the form Mārīcīpicuvā.
33. Bhattacharyya, *The Buddhist Iconography,* p. 235.
34. Bhattacharyya, *The Buddhist Iconography*, p. 246.
35. Lal, *Female Divinities,* pp. 109, ff. and p. 145.
36. The five 'wisdoms' or 'knowledges' are the 'mirror-like' (*ādarsa-jñāna*) 'sameness' (*samatā-j.*), 'discriminative, (*pratyavekṣaṇā. j.)*, 'procedure-of

duty' (*kṛtyānuṣṭhāna-j*), and 'natural realm' (*dharmadhātu-j*). For more information on their role in the Buddhist Tantras, ef. *Mkhas grub rje's Fundamentals of the Buddhist Tantras,* Index, under 'knowledge': and see V-A-T, the Chap. II, n. 19.

37. Cf Bhattacharyya, *The Buddhist Iconography,* pp. 297-298, for one set of doorkeepers and pp. 316-317, for another set of such. In both cases, the doorkeepers are described in terms of what they carry in hand.
38. Cf. n.23 above; and V-A-T, the chap. II, n. 58.
39. By Jared Rhoton.
40. To deny that voidness can be a 'means', Sa-pan cites three verses from the *Vajrapañjarā,* namely the first three of the four which I present from *Tson-khapa's Snags rim chen mo* in *The Buddhist Tantras; Light on Indo-Tibetan Esotericism* (Samuel Weiser, New York, 1973), pp. 4-5.
41. Notice Acharyya Jogesh Chandra Ray, *Ancient Indian Life* (Calcutta, 1948), p. 137: "A spindle (Tarku) was used to spin yarn, and the weaver (*Vāya*) had his loom (*Veman*) from which the warp *(Tantu)* was stretched by a wooden peg (*Mayūkha*), while lead was employed to extend it. A shuttle (*Tasara*) was used in weaving." This suggests that the void Dharmadhātu as the 'warp' (*tantu*) is the basis of Tantra.
42. My present translation of the Sanskrit word *pratimā* as 'framer' is justified: (a) Since the perfections of giving, etc. are referred to by an agent word, 'painters', one may expect voidness to be referred to by an agent word, i.e. 'framer'. (b) The rendition 'framer' is found for *Pratimā* in the Monier-Williams Sanskrit-English Dictionary. Just as 'painters' is metaphoric language for the five perfections, to wit, giving, morality, forbearance, striving, and meditation; so also we may reasonably accept 'framer' as metaphoric language for the bare canvas. Still, we cannot object to the translation of *pratimā* as 'picture', the rendition which both E. Obermiller and Jikido Takasaki employ—the former, when translating from the Tibetan when the Sanskrit was still not available *(The sublime Science of the Great Vehicle to Salvation*, 1931, p. 209); and the latter, when translating from E.H. Johnston's edition of the Sanskrit (*A Study on the Ratnagotravibhāga,* Roma, 1966, p. 264). The present writer also rendered it as 'picture' when citing this verse in an article "The Role of Art among the Buddhist Religieux", now reprinted in *Buddhist Insight; Essays by Alex Wayman,* p. 302. The rendition 'picture' is an alternate solution in the present context, as though some persons thought that the M-K-G-maṇḍala is a picture to be regarded as void—to which one cannot object, as long as these persons do not go on to say that it is a 'single means', i.e. by itself can achieve the goal of Buddhahood.

9. VAIROCANĀBHISAMBODHI, CHAPTER TWO
(A. The Single Means)

Then Vajrapāṇi, Master of the Secret Ones,[1] spoke to the Bhagavat in these words: "How wondrous it is that the very Bhagavat who transcended the stage of (160) minds[2] and in the inconceivable Dharmadhātu[3] became a Complete Buddha,[4] should be the Bhagavat who teaches the sentient beings, in accordance with their aspirations and faith, with a multitude of means and methods. Would the Bhagavat also explain how to make the great king of maṇḍalas,[5] the Mahākaruṇāgarbh [odbhava], with the manner of practicing the mantras? It would serve many future sentient beings with benefit and happiness."

Then the Bhagavat surveyed Vairocana's maṇḍala along with all its circles of deities and proclaimed as follows to Vajrapāṇi, Master of the Secret Ones: "Vajrapāṇi, listen to the dharma manner that teaches the method of maṇḍala-practice, that brings to fulfilment the omniscient knowledge."

Now the Bhagavat Vairocana had formerly taken a vow to accomplish the purport-inexhaustible Dharmadhātu and to rescue the realm of sentient beings. Rightly consulting about the single means with all the Tathāgatas, he equipoised himself in the samādhi (called) Mahākaruṇāgarbhodbhava. No sooner had the Bhagavat equipoised, than from all his limbs there (emanated) the Tathāgata bodies that he had honored since his first Thought of Enlightenment, and that had performed acts for the benefit of sentient beings up to the Tenth Stage. And when those (bodies) emerged they circled the ten directions; and returning, re-entered the spots of the Bhagavat's body.[6] Then the Bhagavat announced to the Bodhisattva Vajrapāṇi: "Vajrapāṇi, listen to the maṇḍala-arrangement. First of all,[7] there should be an *ācārya,* who has taken the Mind of Enlightenment, insightful, steadfast, compassionate, and skilled in the special methods; being always proficient in the rule of Prajñāpāramitā,[8] knows the difference of the three Vehicles;[9] is skilled in the (various) meanings of the reality of mantra,[10] and knows the mental make-up (of beings);[11] should have faith in the Buddhas and Bodhisattvas; has asked for the maṇḍala, and being allowed to perform the rites, has been initiated (in the maṇḍala)."

Rely on the Bodhisattva who practices the mantras of the noble families (*kula*); endeavoring, and established in them;

is skilled in the praxis and is capable in *yoga*.(1)

"Vajrapāṇi, such an *ācārya* is a son of the Buddha, is extolled by the Buddhas and Bodhisattvas. Vajrapāṇi, the other one (i.e. the disciple) may beseech that *ācārya*."

And he observes the beings that are proper vessels, free from faults, have faith and steadfast conviction, who delight in another's benefit. Having recognized such a disciple, the *ācārya* himself, even if not beseeched, should call him, and with desire to benefit him, should say this: 'You are a vessel for the great work. Son, come here. I shall properly teach you how to practice the mantras by way of the Mahāyāna.' (2-4)

Whether the Complete Buddhas are of the past, the future, or the present, these lords are engaged for the benefit of living beings.(5)

All of them learned this excellent, best rite of mantras and as heroes acquired the signless omniscience at the Bodhi-tree.(6)

The protector, Lion of the Śākyas, employed that unequalled praxis of mantra[12] to utterly destroy the Māra group together with its vast army.(7)

Hence, my son, you must turn your mind to the attaining of omniscience. You must frequently enhance your mind with compassion. (8)

Having recognized the steadfast disciple, you should well examine the spot of ground, site of the pure and pleasing water, which yields the flowers and fruit.(9)

All the Buddhas praise the acts of drawing the maṇḍala, where many streams descend, adorned by water-birds like swans. There a wise mantrin should draw the maṇḍala which gives rise to compassion.(10)

The Muni (i.e. Buddha) always praises those Buddhas, Pratyekabuddhas, or disciples of a Jina[13] who gain a (hallowed) spot of ground.(11)

Desirous of benefitting the disciples, one may also assiduously draw the maṇḍala in a number of other places, such as pleasing and good monasteries, a house with a high roof, by lotus ponds and in parks, in *caitya* halls, junctions where cows gather, shrine of a god, by waterfalls, all temples, and in empty rooms as well as in any pleasing spot. (12-14)

"Master of the Secret Ones, one should thoroughly purify the spot of ground, getting rid of stones, lumps, potsherds, rocks; hair, straw, charcoal, ashes, thorns, bones, rotting tree (parts)—all such 'pains'. The gods recognize a place that lacks ants, worms, and insects, and is rid of all faults.[14] All the Tathāgatas salute it when it has good marks according to lunar day, asterisms, planets, astrological diagram (*byed pa*), and moment; or is marked with good omens[15] at the early morning period of the sun. One should praise with two verses delivered to the earth goddess:"

> Goddess, you have been empowered by all the Buddha protectors in the Stages (*bhūmi*) and in the perfections (*pāramitā*) which are (respectively) the rules of praxis and the distinguished (features.)[16] (15)
>
> Just as the protector, the Lion of the Śākyas, destroyed the Māra army, so may I be victorious over the Māra army, and draw the maṇḍala. (16)
>
> Having planted both knees upon the earth with hands on it, and having spoken many times that way, one should make offering with flowers and perfume.(17)
>
> The mantrin having made offering, then should salute the Tathāgatas. Thus a wise person with these rites will purify the spot.(18)

At this point Vajrapāṇi bowed his head to the feet of the Bhagavat, and said to the Bhagavat:

> "The Buddha is dissociated from signs (*nimitta*); he abides in the Dharmakāya,[17] resorting to the Dharma that is signless, unconstructed, and unequalled.(19)
>
> "O great hero, for what purpose do you announce this praxis of mantras, a ritual associated with signs, which is not the rule of true nature *(dharmatā)*?" (20)
>
> So asked, the Bhagavat Mahāvairocana at that time told Vajrapāṇi to listen to this character of Dharma. (21)
>
> "The Dharma is free from (mundane) analysis, rejects all constructive thought, avoids the constructions of thought (*citta*) and mentals (*caitta.)*(22)
>
> My Dharma[18] is fully enlightened. It arises from the sky.
>
> Foolish beings, who range in wayward imagination, do not know it.(23)

Persons obscured by darkness believe in time, spatial objects, and signs. So as to help them, this means is expressed. (24)
Spatial object is not, time is not; there is neither deed nor agent. None of the natures *(dharma)* is real. The *dharmas* are only ephemeral.(25)
However, Master of the Secret ones, the beings of feeble intellect, deluded by activity-alone, crave concrete entities and in future time will be reborn.(26)
Because ignorant of this kind of method they are attracted to the fruits of delusion by the virtuous and unvirtuous signs from spatial objects, time, and activity. So they may become great beings, this rite is expressed.(27)

"Master of the Secret Ones, given an appropriate place as was already indicated, one should belabor the hard spot of ground, applying it with cowdung fallen on the road, and mixed with cow urine. Then one should make offering with this purifying mantra."
Namaḥ samantabuddhānām apratisame gaganasamtānugate / Prakritiviśuddhe dharmadhātuviśodhani svāhā/
"Thereupon the mantrin should imagine me."[19]

Having arisen, in its middle (i.e. of the maṇḍala) dwelling on seat of white lotus, hair bound up and wearing a head ornament, (28)
completely surrounded by the various colored rays.
Then the avowed person should imagine the four complete Buddhas in the quarters.(29)
Imagine the Tathāgata Ratnaketu, like a rising sun (i.e in the East); and in the South, the King of Jinas, called Saṃkusumita, with blazing golden color, dwelling in the samādhi that destroys faults. In the northern quarter Akṣobhya, staying in the samādhi that frees from pain. (30-31)
In the western quarter Amitābha. Having imagined these five Jinas, then by mantras of the great lord Acala or of Trailokyavijaya, [20] i.e. with mantras that accomplish all aims, one should take hold of the spot,—(32-33) and do it with auspicious maṇḍala offerings, sandlewood, etc., in the middle. [Imagining the maṇḍala compartments:] (34A)
The first is my own; the second is of all the protectors(=the four Buddhas). (34B)
The third is of the Mother, doubtless equal to them; the

fourth of the lotus-handed one (=Avalokiteśvara); the fifth for Vajrapāṇi; (35)

the sixth, of Acalanātha; and one should continue for the remainder.[21] Remembering the Tathāgatas, one should offer flowers, perfumed water, etc. (36)

Having equipoised onself, one should speak words in devotional terms: 'May all the Lords of compassionate heart, pray listen to me! May ye, together with your sons (i.e. the Bodhisattvas), tomorrow allow me to keep the spot (of ground)! And having said that, he should speak this mantra:(37-38)

Namaḥ samantabuddhānāṃ sarvatathāgatādhiṣṭhānādhiṣṭhite/ acale/ vimale/ saraṇe/ prakṛtipariśuddhe svāhā/

Then the mantrin having arisen, his mind become compassionate, stands facing in the western direction (i.e., the setting sun), while being pure within. (39)

He puts his mind on the Bodhicitta, and in that (state of mind) is to sleep. Then the mantrin should examine his dream(s), as to whether a Bodhisattva of great fame, or a Buddha Bhagavat (Speaks:) 'For benefit to sentient beings, you should endeavour with all devices in the acts of drawing the maṇḍala'. (40-41)

And these words may come to him: 'O great being, you are an excellent son. Quickly draw the maṇḍala!' They encourage enthusiasm (for the drawing). (42)

Then some other day you should examine whether the disciple has faith, and a noble family; has faith in the Three Jewels, profound insight, enthusiastically follows the moral rules, is forbearing and free of jealousy, is courageous and of steadfast vow. Whether he has ten (of those characteristics), or eight, or seven, or five; and if he has one, two, four or more, you should accept him without further requirement. (43-44)

Thereupon Vajrapāṇi asked the Bhagavat: "Bhagavat, what is the name of this maṇḍala? What is a 'maṇḍala'?" The Bhagavat responded, "Master of the Secret Ones, as to 'maṇḍala', the *maṇḍa* of the *maṇḍala* is the arising of Buddha; the *-la* is the Complete, its higher (hence: a 'Complete Buddha'); what is *maṇḍala* is not otherwise; hence the term 'maṇḍala'. Master of the Secret Ones, however, this enlarged maṇḍala is called 'Mahākaruṇāgarbhodbhava' ('arising in the womb of great compassion), because it rescues the uncertainty of the sentient realm. It is the empowerment by the Tathāgatas for uncountable eons of the right procedure of the incomparable right perfected enlightenment (*bodhi*). Master of the Secret Ones, that being the case, with this (procedure), you, like the Tathāgatas, should not become manifestly awakened to enlightenment on behalf of one sentient being, not on behalf of two, not on behalf of three. Rather, controlled by great compassion, you should become manifestly awakened to enlightenment so as to promote the entire sentient realm. By way of these (right procedures), fully according with the multi-formed aspirations of the sentient realm, you should acquaint the sentient beings while teaching the Dharma. Master of the Secret Ones, those who have not repeatedly practiced in the Great Vehicle, even if they have heard or seen the manner of practicing the mantras, neither experience joy in mind or surge of faith. Master of the Secret Ones, those who have repeatedly practiced in the past the Great Vehicle and have engaged by many gates the manner of practicing the mantras, are called 'diamond beings' (*vajrasattva*). It is precisely for them that these extensive (instructions) are made. However, the ācārya possessed of great compassion need only take a vow to rescue the entire sentient realm; since it will motivate the Bodhicitta, he will benefit immeasurable sentient beings. Then, calling them, he should enact the refuge (formula) three times. He should direct them to not commit sins. Then he confers on them perfumed water, flowers, etc. He makes them take the vow of knowledge unhindered in the three times.[22]

> Making them take (the vow), with mantras he also gives them the sticks (Tib. *so śiṅ*). They are sharpened to a point and made even, to be thrown facing East or North. (45)
>
> The sticks to be displayed are of auspicious Udumbara or Aśvattha wood, rubbed with flowers, perfume, etc., and protected (by mantra). From the throwing one determines whether it is a good or bad disciple ('vessel').[23] (46)
>
> Then, while oneself concentrates the mind, one should properly tie on the (disciple's) left arm a cord with three knots. (47)
>
> When the faultless disciples have been so attended to, so as to firm their aspiration their enthusiasm should be promoted in this manner: (48)
>
> 'Today you great-souled ones have gained the incomparable gain. You sirs have gained it by way of all the Jinas and their sons, and by their teaching in this life. For this reason, you will be well born into the Mahāyāna, all assisted when you great souls are reborn'. (49-50)

One should examine his dreams and assess them as auspicious when in dreams there occur monasteries, parks, superb buildings, the dome of a residence; a sword, wish-granting gem, umbrella, assorted flowers, good women dressed in white, pleasant relatives and children; books, brahmins, Buddhas, Pratyekabuddhas, disciples of a Jina, eminent Bodhisattvas; gain of fruit, seeing a crossing of lakes and oceans; from the sky auspicious entrancing words that mention the desired fruit as arising. And a wise person knows that their reverse is a bad dream.[24] (51-55)

You should explain the Dharma to the disciples after counselling them with the words, 'You (sirs) with the goodly avowed practice must report to me all that is within.'[25] (56)

'This glorious supreme path[26] is the great source of the Mahāyāna, proceeding by which you sirs will become Tathāgatas; self-arisen, of great shares (*mahābhāga*) reverenced by the whole world; transcendent of existence and non-existence, like the pure sky. (57-58)

'Staying in this means, you will reach the profound mind-base (*manālaya*)[27] that cannot be reasoned by any reasons, that is free of all verbal elaborations and is elaborated by verbal elaborations; (will reach) this supreme best vehicle that is free from rite and ritual acts and is rightly based on the two truths. (50-60)

Then Vajradhara Niṣprapañcavihārin ('Dweller in non-elaboration') requested the Bhagavat as follows: "Bhagavat, please explain, to please the Buddhas and Bodhisattvas, the vow of knowledge that is free from the hindrances of the three times and on which the Bodhisattvas stand." When he had been so asked, the Bhagavat announced to Vajradhara Niṣprapañcavihārin: "Son of the family, listen to what is the vow in which body, speech, and mind operate as one, in which all dharmas neither begin nor act! It is the votive offering of one's body to the Buddhas and Bodhisattvas.[28] Why so? Anyone who abandons his body, renounces three given things. And what are the three given things renounced? As follows: (the ordinary) body, speech, and mind. Son of the family, that being so, the Boddhisattva should avow the vow of the three—(the ordinary) body, speech, and mind. Why so? The Bodhisattvas who do not abandon the (ordinary) body, speech, and mind, do not act to retain the instruction."

Later that day, Trailokyavijaya, having saluted the Bhagavat

Vairocana, praised him while himself filling a pot with perfumed water for blessing the 'diamond beings'; so having placed it in the first gate a wise person will make secret offering with it to all persons (who are 'diamond beings').[29] Thus, to purify the mind, one offers pure water with perfume (in it).[30]

Then Vajrapāṇi inquired of the Bhagavat in these words:

"At what time should the ācāryas of the maṇḍala, endeavoring in the exercise of mantras, bless the great beings in the maṇḍala? O may the best of speakers, omniscient of time and due measure, proclaim it!" And having been asked, the Bhagavat proclaimed to the Vajra-holder, "When oriented to the goal of maṇḍala, one should always draw it in the evening."[31] (61-62)

"Vajrapāṇi, when that ācārya has saluted all the Buddhas, he should carry thread of diverse colors. Himself empowered as the Bhagavat Vairocana,—[32]

He should 'draw' the (colored) thread[33] in the East. Taking it straight upward at the 'nave', he should 'seize' the intermediate space; then proceeding to the southern quarter, should 'draw' it in the North.[34] (63)

Now taking a second thread, remembering the Tathāgata in that very (thread), looking toward the East he should draw.[35] (64)

Then proceeding to the southern quarter, he should draw in the North. The wise person, then reversing himself, situated in the S.W. quarter (*nirṛti*), should draw in the northern direction.(65)

Then he should change to the right; and having changed, should stay right there, and draw in the southern direction.[36] (66)

Then giving up that place,[37] he should be in the 'fire' quarter (i.e. S.E.) (where) the mantrin should dwell in the rite of mantra. In the East he should draw the colored thread. (67)

Thereupon proceeding to the Īśāna direction (N.E.) he should look to the West. Then he should draw in the northern direction up to the 'wind' quarter (N.W.). (68)

In that way the mantrin has to make it an exact square. Then, going to the center, at that time he marks in threefold manner. (69)

In all the various areas he should mark three parts; and in each of these, three parts.[38] (70)

One goes around one rank with a one-part 'perimeter'. The two remaining ranks belong to the deities. One should be certain about the location (i.e. which rank).[39](71)

A wise person vigorously following his vow should put the chief deities in the four directions and put the doorways according to ranks with their various directions.[40] (72)

Having done all those (steps), i.e. having segmented sequentially in that manner, a supreme white lotus is in the center and called the *'garbha'*. (73)

There is all the maṇḍala 'Karuṇodbhava' when it is supplied the *'garbha'*, its measure up to sixteen 'fingers' (*aṅguli*). (74)

One puts in eight petals, possessed of excellent filaments (*kesara*), and draws vajras all around the petals. (75)

In the middle of the *garbha* is the master, the supreme Jina, of golden color, blazing, his hair bound up and wearing a jewel in the crown, and completely surrounded by rays of light.[41] (76)

To draw the lord (*nātha*) one should be free from illness and be stationed in *samādhi*. To his East, the wise one will draw in condensed manner the 'seal' (*mudrā*) of the Buddhas, the triangle all whitish green on a lotus and surrounded by white rays.[42] (77-78)

To its North, wise persons, while in a *samādhi*, will draw the mother of all the protectors (= Buddhas), with golden color and fiery, wearing white clothes, shining all about.[43] (79)

To the North of the Lord (*nātha*) one draws Avalokiteśvara, seated on a white lotus, like conch and the autumn moon, his face faintly smiling; and Amitābha seated on his head.[44] (80)

To his right is the goddess Tārā of great fame, virtuous, dispeller of fear, green in color, of many forms.[45] (81)

One draws her with measure of a young woman; palms together holding the *utpala* flower, surrounded by light rays; and wearing white clothes. (82)

To his left is the goddess Bhṛkuṭī (She of Wrinkled Brows). One draws her with a mantra-garland suspended from her hand, 3-eyed, hair bound up, of white color, surrounded by white, yellow, and red light rays.[46] (83)

Near Bhṛkuṭī is Mahāsthāmaprāpta whom one draws as carrying a lotus, of great kindness, wearing white clothes, a hero surrounded by light rays. His lotus is unopened.[47] (84)

Close by him the insightful person will draw the Vidyā-devī Yaśodharā, appearing with golden color, adorned with all ornaments, with left hand holding a delightful saffron-colored (*priyaṅgu*) ear of corn.[48] (85)

In the near retinue of Tārā, the discriminating one should draw Pāṇḍuravāsinī, her hair bound up, wearing white clothes, holding a lotus in hand.[49] (86)

After her (*or,* beneath her) the mantrin should draw the Vidyārāja Mahābala, color like the rising sun, adorned with a white lotus;[50] and Hayagrīva, his hair a blazing garland of disagreeable light, seated like a lion, having the mind of Avalokiteśvara.[51] (87-88)

To the South of the Buddhas one should draw him (i.e. Vajrapāṇi) famed during the great eon as 'wish-granting gem *mudrā*' among protective Bodhisattvas, who brings about all hopes, seated on a white lotus. Draw him, the vajra holder, to the South of *nātha* Mahāvairocana, as protecting all hopes, his body saffron-colored (*priyaṅgu*), or yellow-green like an emerald (*marakaṭa*), the 'green lord' having on his head a jewel, adorned with all the adornments of a great Bodhisattva, holding the great vajra of boundless range, surrounded by light rays.[52] (89-91)

To his right draw the goddess named Māmakī, adorned with diamond jewels, holding in hand a vajra.[53] (92)

After her one draws Vajrasūcī of great strength, encircled by female messengers (*dūtī*), face with faint smile.[54] (93)

To his left the mantrin draws Vajraśṛṅkhalā, in her hand a chain of vajras (*vajraśṛṅkhala*), surrounded by female messengers, greenish-yellow like saffron, well marked with diamond marks.[55] (94)

Lower than Vajrapāṇi is Krodhacandratilaka, pacifier of the great demon enemies, the Krodha celebrated in the three worlds. Draw him with three eyes, four tusks, color like a rain cloud of summer; uttering sounds of savage laughter, adorned with vajra adornments, (and imagine him) surrounded by a multitudinous retinue of Krodha lords, whose myriad arms hold and brandish diverse weapons, who resemble the great Krodha.[56] (95-97)

To his West, draw a group of Vajradhara-s, holding diverse weapons in hand, of various colors, of great power, surrounded by light rays, who perform the aim of all sentient beings. (98)

In the lower direction (i.e. South-West) to the master of mantras, in the S.W. (Nirṛti) quarter, is Acala. Draw him as wielding the sword and noose, head locks inclined to left, ornamented, one crooked eye, living within his own light (*svābha*), furiously seated on a boulder, his face with menacing wrinkled brows, with shape of a lad, somewhat rough.[57] (99-100)

Having drawn that, the person in the know will energetically draw in the 'wind' direction (i.e. N.W.) the Bhagavat's Krodha, Trailokyavijaya, with inexhaustive blazing garland, ornamented as Vajrapāṇi's top servant, seated like receiving the (Lord's) promulgations, his color as during the Pralaya (i.e. without sun or moon, pitch-black darkness).[58] (101-102)

Having drawn the inner part in that manner, now for the enlarged explanation the mantrin retreats to the certainty of the second rank. (103)

In the eastern direction, the rank is divided into two.[59] On the inner part from the (eastern) doorway, the mantrin should draw the Jina Śākyamuni, of blazing golden color, possessed of the best thirty-two characteristics, *nātha* who wears the orange robe, pervading lord who performs the teaching aim, seated on a white-lotus seat, and seated in the manner of explaining the Dharma.[60] (104-105)

To his right is the Devī called Buddhalocanā. Draw her with slightly smiling face, with a full-fathom length of light disk, her matchless body pure. She is Śākyamuni's 'mother' (*yum*).[61] (106)

At her right is the goddess famed as Vidyorṇā. Draw her, seated on a lotus, with color like the conch or moon-light, holding in her hand the wish-granting gem, which fulfills all hopes.[62] (107)

Then the mantrin should draw on the left side of the protector Śākyasiṃha his five uṣṇīṣa-s that are fiery and of great energy, namely, Sitātapatroṣṇīṣa, Jayoṣṇīṣa, Vijayoṣṇīṣa, Tejorāśyuṣṇīṣa, and Vikiraṇoṣṇīṣa.[63] (108-09)

Draw these five powerful uṣṇīṣa-s of Śākyaketu in five spots in compressed manner. (110)

To his North, one should draw all these Pure Abode deities, nemely, *Īśvara, *Saṃpuṣpaka, *Prabhāmālaka, *Manojavana, *Prakīrtita.[64] (111)

To the right of Vidyorṇā one should draw in compressed manner the triad of uṣṇīṣas, namely Mahoṣṇīṣa, Abhyudgatoṣṇīṣa, Anantasvaraghoṣoṣṇīṣa. (112)

The five powerful uṣṇīṣas are colored either white, yellow, or yellowish-white. The other three are white, yellow, and red. They are (all) completely radiant, ornamented with all ornaments; and as the great power of aspiration they fulfil all hopes. (113-14)

Then the mantrin should draw in the 'fire' corner (S.E.) a fire accompanied by the great ṛṣi-s, standing in the fire, marked (on their foreheads) with three lines of ash. All these heroes are intensely red, hearts marked by a *triveṇi* (road fork). They stand in the middle of blazing tongues of flame, all carrying *akṣamālā* (rosary). (115-116)

Then one draws in the southern quarter the master Yama, holding in hand a club and riding a buffalo, color like a summer rain cloud, surrounded by 'mothers' (*mātṛkā*), Kālarātrī-s, and Mṛtyu-s. In the 'Truthless' corner (Nirṛti) (S.W.) draw Nirṛti, the curved sword in hand, and terrifying. (117-118)

Now the discriminating one, proceeding quickly to the northern quarter, draws Devendra (=Indra), staying on Mt. Meru, surrounded by the gods, with *vajra* (thunderbolt) in hand and crowned, adorned with all adornments. (119)

Then, at his East one draws Varuṇa, holding the noose. Also at his East one draws the Sun riding in a chariot. At his right and left, draw Jayā and Vijayā. (120)

At his right draw Brahmā, four-faced, hair bound up, pronouncing OṂ, seated on haṃsa and lotus. (121)

At his West, draw these: Pṛthivī (earth goddess), Sarasvatī, Viṣṇu, Skanda (Tib. *skem byed*), Vāyu, Śaṃkara (=Śiva), Chandra. (122)

While the mantrin thus stays in the West, he should draw with dedication. So drawing he will be undeluded in mind. (123)

In the lower area of the Mantra Lord (= Śākyamuni), draw devotedly the Mahākrodha called Aparājitā and the goddess Aparājitā; also Kṣitipati (field protector) holding in hand a pot.[65] (124)

And one should draw the Mahānāga(s) called Nandin and Upananda, facing the two doorways of the protector Śākyasiṃha; and in compressed style.[66] (125)

Moreover, Śākyamuni explains mantra and mudrā in the maṇḍala according to all streams of consciousness (*saṃtati*). A wise person will draw them also.[67] (126)

The mantrin retreats to certainty of the third rank. The one with 'gift of sublimed vajra' (resting on his lotus) is colored like Marigold (i.e. deep yellow).[68] (127)

The mantrin should draw him whose head has five locks (i.e. Mañjuśrī), with the form of a young boy, who holds in his left hand a blue lotus (*utpala*) having a vajra, and is seated on a white-lotus seat; with pronounced smile, and completely surrounded by goodly character of light rays.[69] (128-29)

To his North is the youth Jālinīprabha. Draw him with hand holding a jewel net, adorned with various jewels, seated on a red-lotus seat, gazing at the son of the Jina.[70] (130)

At the left of him with 'gift of the sublime vajra' draw the five female messengers (*dūtī*), Keśinī (She the Hairy One), Upakeśinī (Adjacent Hairy One), Citrā (Variegated), Vasumatī (Holding Treasure), Ākarṣaṇī (Summoning), who are the female messengers possessed of (Mañjuśrī's) discrimination (*buddhi*).[71] (131)

Below also draw two retinues, the five attendants (*parivāra*) of those (five messengers), and another of the youth Jālinīprabha.[72] (132)

Then in the southern quarter the mantrin should draw the famous great Bodhisattva Sarvanīvaraṇaviṣkaṃbhin, holding a cintāmaṇi.[73] (133)

Using up two parts of his (quarter) the wise one will draw his eight heroes: Āścarya (vajra), Abhayaṃdada (giving non-fear to all beings), Sarvāpayajaha, Paritrāṇāśayamati, Karuṇāmṛdita-mati (mind overcome by compassion), Maitryabhyudgata, Sarvadāhapraśamita, and Acintyamati.[74] (134-35)

Proceeding to the northern quarter, draw Kṣitigarbha, fiery, full of forbearance and certainty. Since his seat is endowed as universal source, a wise one will decorate it with all jewels. One should contemplate him, seated on the delightful lotus possessed of jewels (of colors) four; and should draw him, the famous great Bodhisattva, upon it.[75] (136-38)

His retinue, an uncountable multitude, is chief in merits. Among it, draw these famous great Bodhisattvas: Ratnākara, Ratnapāṇi, Dharaṇīṃdhara, Ratnamudrāhasta, and Dṛdhādhyāśaya.[76] (139-40)

Likewise, the mantrin should draw in the western quarter the hero Ākāśagarbha, contemplating him as gloriously shining, dressed in white clothes, holding in hand the curved sword, the son of the Jina well seated on lotus seat.[77] (141)

Among the retinue of that great soul, draw the famous ones. The great heroes of his retinue are Gaganāmala, Gaganāmati. Viśuddhimati, Caritamati, and Sthirabodhi. Draw them in compressed style, and always contemplate oneself together with these heroes in the given order.[78] (142-43)

Then Master of the Secret Ones Vajrapāṇi surveyed all the members of the retinue, and gazed for a long time without winking at Bhagavat Vairocana. Thereupon he spoke in joyous tones this joyful utterance:

Like the flower of the Uduṃbara, there is hardly ever an appearance anywhere in the world of the omniscient ones.[79] (144)

So it is also rare to gain the means of mantra praxis whereby there is unhindered ability to perform the incomparable aim of sentient beings. (145)

All of that sin committed in the past for myriads of eons is dissipated when one sees a maṇḍala like this! (146)

Why speak of the boundless fame when one stays in the method of mantra praxis? Or when one stays in the incomparable rank, reciting the mantras of the protectors? (147)

For them destroyed is evil destiny and the sources of all suffering, for whom in this best practice the mind does not shift to something else. (148)

At that time those Vajra-holders and the entire retinue members spoke in unison these words:

"Very well, very well, hero, that you have come to control the mantra practice! Whatever your mind wishes, do ask the incomparable omniscient one! (149)

May the other Bodhisattvas who know with understanding the

mantra lineage, and those who are in the fruit of mantra practice, empower all of us!" (150)

Thereupon, Vajrapāṇi asked the Bhagavat the following:

'What is coloring material? Why is there coloring material? How divide the coloring material! What should be used first? What is the measure of the arch-ways (*toraṇa*) and of the gate-enternaces, and of what kind the door measure? May the Lord kindly explain! (151-152)

Pray tell extensively the food offering to the gods, the flowers, anointment, perfumed water, and flasks. Pray tell me how to assist the disciple, how to initiate him, the offering to the guru, the place for the *homa*. What are the characteristics of a mantra, what claimed as a samādhi?" (153-154)

Having been so asked, the Bhagavat replied to Vajrapāṇi by his lordly capability in all the Dharma: "Listen to me single mindedly! (155)

The best rules of mantra practice arise as the fruit of Mahāyāna. What you, great being, have asked, I shall explain. (156)

The Buddhas formerly stated that sentient beings crave 'realms' (*dhātu*); and that this Dharmadhātu is a (single) 'Taste' (*rasa*). For that reason, there is 'coloring material' (i.e. the *dhātu*).[80] (157)

Coloring material is to be divided internally; not to be divided externally. The first to be used is white. After that, red. Then one should use yellow. After that, use green. The completely internal (requires) black. In that way is explained the rite of coloring material.[81] (158-159)

The measure of the arch-ways is equal to the middle of the maṇḍala (the *garbha* taken as the *padma*). The gates also equal it. The lotus (*padma*) is explained to have 16 *aṅguli*. (160)

The first door is equal (in measure) to the garbha of the maṇḍala. In the sequence of the 'fearless ones', one increases (by four *aṅguli*) successively.[82] (161)

One should place door-keepers in the respective doors.[83] Samādhi is explained in short as the right ecstasy of the mind. (162)

Great being, listen single mindedly in a special way! The samādhi of all the Buddhas is called by the Jina 'voidness' (*śūnyatā*). When the mind has fully experienced that, there is nothing else to gain. (163)

'Complete Buddha' is explained as avoiding the two. 'Great void' is the fulfilment of omniscient knowledge. Hence, in all images, always remember voidness."[84] (164)

VAIROCANĀBHISAMBODHI, CHAPTER TWO

(B. The Various Means)

Then the Bhagavat Vairocana, having aroused conviction in the single means by way of all the Buddhas, announced the various means of samādhi for the Śrāvakas, Pratyekabuddhas, and Bodhisattvas. On that occasion he equipoised himself in the samādhi called "the impetus by dint of a single stream of consciousness with all the Buddhas." Thereupon, the Bhagavat spoke to the Bodhisattva Vajrapāṇi:

"Brahmā and the rest of the gods call 'Great Hero' the one who was seated at the *bodhimaṇḍa* (terrace of enlightenment) and destroyed the four Māras.[85] (165)

Later I am the hero gladly pronouncing the words that annul all fear, and am called 'Great Hero'. (166)

I have comprehended 'non-arising', have dropped off the domain of speech, negated all fault, and lack cause and conditions.[86] (167)

I have the knowledge of voidness, like space. I am freed from all darkness. How does this occur only immaculate? It (arises) from that (reality).[87] (168)

Dwelling in the manner of only omniscience, is the character of the omniscient Buddha. This very sublimity of mine illumines the world. (169)

By dint of empowerment, and on account of compassion, I explain everything in teachings that use words." (170)

Then the glorious vajra holder, his eyes wide open in astonishment, bowing his head to the omniscient one spoke these words: (171)

"The means (*upāya*) and insight (*prajñā*) of all the Buddhas is wondrous. The self-originated ones have understood the Dharma free from all elaboration.[88] (172)

They show the fulfilment of all hopes of the entire world. Their character of mantra is based on the two truths. When that is recognized by any sentient being, they become the offering place as universal basis."[89] (173)

Thereupon, Vajrapāṇi, Master of the Secret Ones, having offered those diamond verses, gazed without winking at Bhagavat Vairocana and remained speechless.

At that time the Bhagavat announced to Vajrapāṇi, Master of the Secret Ones, "Master of the Secret Ones, besides, there is the method of samādhi of those Bodhisattvas who are 'limited to only one more life' (*ekajātipratibuddha*) and who abide in the Buddhabhūmi, namely:

Those who free from fear know the character of the world and are located in the state of stipulation—are located in the Buddhabhūmi.[90] (174)

"Master of the Secret Ones, besides, there is the method of samādhi of the lords of the Eighth Bodhisattva Stage:

The worldling who does not apprehend any nature (*dharma*), and having recognized that the world is like an illusion, rejects gestation and rebirth—I hold to be a master of the world. (175)

"Master of the Secret Ones, besides, there is the method of *samādhi* of the Śrāvakas. Those dwelling in the stage attended with the Śrāvaka kind of apprehension, having comprehended arising and passing away, destroy the two extremes [i.e. avoid nihilism because of the arising, and avoid eternalism because of the passing away]; but because they do not apprehend the cause (*hetu*) do not practice (pursuant to) the knowledge of complete absence (*abhāva*).

"Master of the Secret Ones, there is the method of *samādhi* of the Pratyekabuddhas. The pratyekabuddhas, having destroyed the cause and result, dwell in the method of the inexpressible *dharma*, i.e. have gained the knowledge 'all *dharmas* are inexpressible'; have contacted the samādhi 'complete cessation of speech'.

"Master of the Secret Ones, besides, there is the method of samādhi of worldlings. The worldlings engender a samādhi of voidness, whereby they imagine a result from a cause, the arising of dissolution from (previous) *karma*, and (imagine) being in the power of others.

"Master of the Secret Ones:

There is the method of the samādhi which is the method of rite for mantra praxis whether the one based therein be a Buddha, a Pratyekabuddha, protective Bodhisattva, or Śrāvaka—who are celebrated for having destroyed sin—or a mundane god. O hero, with desire for benefit to the sentient beings, I explained it at that time."[91] (176-177)

Then the Bhagavat proclaimed to Vajrapāṇi, Master of the Secret Ones: "Master of the Secret Ones, listen to the mantra-character of the mantras!" "May the Bhagavat expound it", he asked; and gave full attention to the Bhagavat. The Bhagavat spoke thus to the Master of the Secret Ones:

"The mantras of the Complete Buddhas are characterized by syllables, names, and words. When those syllables are empowered, the mantras accomplish all aims.[92] (178)

Some (mantra deities) have syllables of exhortation; some their own name given at the beginning. The ones having Hūṃ and Phaṭ accomplish what is (in the province) of the (eight) uṣṇīṣas.[93] (179)

Zun(s) ('Remember!'), zo ('Consume!'), chom śig ('Conquer!'), snun ('Stab!'), sod ('Kill!'), drol cig ('Tear to pieces!')—the leader has stated to be mantras of the attendants and the Krodhas. Those having 'namaḥ' and 'svāhā' are characterized by samādhi-comprehension.[94] (180)

The pure letters of quiescence and the mantras that fulfil all hopes are of all the Buddhas and the protective Bodhisattvas. (181)

The mantras of Śrāvakas are isolated, based on themselves;[95] those of Pratyekabuddhas are like them, but are specialized—the purification of *karma* and life-energy through special samādhis. (182)

"Master of the Secret Ones, besides, the mantra-character was not made, nor arranged to be made, nor rejoiced in, by any of the Buddhas. Why so? It is like this: There is this continuum (*dharmatā*) of natures (*dharma*) whether a Tathāgata arises or does not arise. The continuum of dharmas remains immemorially. And this is the mantra-character of mantras.[96] Master of the Secret Ones, in that regard, at whatever time the Complete Buddha, omniscient, all-seeing, appears in the world, at that time, by reason of the diverse methods and diverse purports of the continuum (*dharmatā*), he empowers (chosen) understanding persons in diverse words, diverse letters, diverse assured verbalizations of sense objects, and in diverse tones, towards sentient beings of diverse aspiration; and he (the Buddha) expounds the mantra-method." (Vajrapāṇi inquired:) "How are the Tathāgatas able to empower the letters in the mantra-method?" "Master of the Secret Ones, in this regard, the Tathāgatas for myriads of eons have engaged in the words of truth, the four noble truths, the four stations of mindfulness, the four bases of magical power, the ten powers of a Tathāgata, the six perfections *(pāramitā)*, the seven precious limbs of enlightenment, the four sublime abodes, and the eighteen unshared Buddha natures. And, Master of the Secret Ones, in short, whatever the omniscient knowledge of the Tathāgatas, there is the power of merit and knowledge belonging to all the Tathāgatas, their power to recall a former vow, their power of spiritual support of the Dharmadhātu, by which (powers) lending spiritual support they rightly teach the rite of mantra to sentient beings exactly as is their allotted fortune.

"And what are the syllables of mantra? Because immemorially unborn (*anutpanna*), 'A' is a gate of all dharmas hereafter: G-A-D[97]. Because free from result (*kārya*), 'KA' is a G-A-D. Because like the sky (*kha*) offering no apprehension, 'KHA' is a G-A-D.[98] Because all 'goings' (*gati*) lack apprehension, 'GA' is a G-A-D.[99] Because the amassed (*ghana*) lacks apprehension, 'GHA' is a G-A-D.[100] Because free from all death and passing on (*cyuti*), 'CA' is a G-A-D. Because the same as all shades (*chada*), 'CHA' is a G-A-D.[101] Because there is no apprehension of birth (*jāti*), 'JA' is a G-A-D. Because the rubbed off dirt (*jhamara*) lacks apprehension, 'JHA' is a G-A-D.[102] Because pride (**ṭaṃkāra*) lacks apprehension, 'ṬA' is a G-A-D.[103] Because an arousal (**viṭhara*) lacks apprehension, 'ṬHA'. is a G-A-D.[104] Because commotion (*ḍamara*) is without apprehension, 'ḌA' is a G-A-D. Because free from all infection (**ḍhakka*), 'ḌHA' is a G-A-D.[105] Because thusness (*tathatā*) is without apprehension, 'TA' is a G-A-D. Because a place (*sthāna*) is without apprehension, 'THA' is a G-A-D.[106] Because taming (*damana*) is without apprehension, 'DA' is a G-A-D. Because a realm (*dhātu*) is without apprehension, 'DHA' is a G-A-D.[107] Because absolute truth (*paramārtha-satya*) is without apprehension, 'PA' is a G-A-D. Because without pith like foam (*phena*) 'PHA' is a G-A-D.[108] Because free from the path of speech (*vāk-patha*), 'BA' is a G-A-D.[109] Because gestation (*bhava*) is entirely without apprehension, 'BHA' is a G-A-D.[110] Because death (*maraṇa*) is without apprehension, 'MA' is a G-A-D.[111] Because a vehicle (*yāna*) is without apprehension, 'YA' is a G-A-D.[113] Because a character (*lakṣaṇa*) is without apprehension, 'LA' is a G-A-D.[114] Because naturally quiescent (*śānta*), 'ŚA' is a G-A-D. Because naturally unintelligent (*jhaṣa*), 'SA' is a G-A-D.[115] Because all truth (*satya*) is without apprehension, 'SA' is a G-A-D.[116] Because a cause (*hetu*) is without apprehension, 'HA' is a G-A-D. Master of the Secret Ones,ṄA, ÑA, ṆA, NA, and MA (the nasals) control all samādhis; and being all powerful, they speedily effectuate the needed aims.[117]

"Master of the Secret Ones, these samādhi gates, which are the method of mantra, fulfil all hopes. All the Tathāgatas are an inconceivable maturation fruit; have the best of all aspects; and their certainty meaning, namely, the reality of mantra, has transcended the three times."

Like the pure sky, they dwell in the stage of lofty mind. Their after-attainment in the stage of practice arising from *karma* and deeds confers the lofty fruit.[118] (183)

This is the sublime reality taught by the Buddhas. Having understood this rite of mantra, the mantrin may acquire the *siddhi*. (184)

'Speech' is the best reality when it is the name of mantras which mantras have. When the mantrin realizes it in his mind, he attains the place where there is no death and passing on. (185)

Thereupon Vajrapāṇi, Master of the Secret Ones, petitioned the Bhagavat: "The Bhagavat has taught the 'inconceivable' dharma-manner, namely, the method of mantra-characteristic. Bhagavat, it is a wonder. It is not shared with any Śrāvakas or Pratyekabuddhas. Bhagavat, the sentient beings with faith in this mantra method will derive unshared merits (*guṇa*). Bhagavat, besides, please expound the rite of maṇḍala requisites."[119] The Bhagavat responded to Vajrapāṇi as follows:

"Now the mantrin should eagerly offer to the gods pleasing flowers yellow, white, and red.[120] (186)

A wise mantrin should eagerly offer red lotus (*padma*) or blue lotus (*utpala*) Nāgakeśara 'bu nag' (black son), Campa (ka), Aśoka, Tilaka, Pāṭala, Sāla, as feasible; or other flowers that are pleasing (in fragrance), good looking and auspicious. (187-188)

He should offer various pleasing and excellent incenses, i.e.

candana (Sandlewood), *tagara* (Powder), Spṛkkā, *kuṅkuma* (Saffron), *ruvuka* (Castor-oil), as feasible. (189)

The mantrin should also offer ritually to the gods various pleasing perfumes celebrated in the world and auspicious to wit, *agaru* (the Aloe wood), *dīpavṛkṣa* (the yew-leaf fir), *karpūra* (Camphor), *candana* (Sandlewood), auspicious Sāla resin, or *sirīśa* (Acacia). (190-191)

Besides, O great being, listen now to the rite of food offering to the gods. One should offer: *pāyasa* (milk product), *odana* (cooked rice), *dadhi* (coagulated milk), *maitreya* (kind of intoxicating drink), *yava* (barley), *mūla* (radish), *maṇḍa* (cream), pleasing *garmoṭikā* (a kind of bean or rice), fine drink of *khaḍa* (spiced buttermilk), *pūraka* (ball of meal), *gāritra* (grain), *mada* (wine), *śira* (kind of root), *phenaka* (boiled ground rice), *śāka-vartula* (vegetables and peas), *barbaṭa* (a kind of grain). (192-193)

Those and other foods one should offer extensively, including various fruits of trees, sugared medicine, medicinal sugars, molasses, honey, butter; and various drinks such as milk and curdled milk. (194)

One should offer various lamps, vessels filled with clean and fine grains that are fragrant. (195)

One should offer aloft in the directional quarters umbrellas and banners of various colors, and excellent arches (*toraṇa*) along with bells. Besides, one should generate eagerly all the mental offerings. (196)

One takes eight pots—or extensively sixteen—filled up with herbs and jewels, (or) filled with perfumed water, their mouths adorned with stalked plants, (or) their mouths filled with fruit, (or) excellently adorned with fragrant flowers. Thus one creates protection. (197-198)

A wise person, having tied their necks with cloth, will put them in their places, and will offer cloth in each corner to the chief gods. (199)

O great being, it is laid down that in the case of pairs of 'minor' (Tib. *phal pa*) deities (of the maṇḍala), one makes offering to one of the two. When one has offered in the foregoing manner, he should bring the disciple near to the maṇḍala.[121] (200)

The mantrin burns incense along with (use of purifying) water. He gives perfume and flowers. He induces (the disciple) to remember the Tathāgatas and take the Mind of Enlightenment. (201)

(Informs him) that he will be born in all the virtue of the Jina's family. And ties the seals (*mudrā*) that arise from the Dharmadhātu.[122] (202)

Having also tied the Dharmacakra (kind of *mudrā*) he is empowered by Vajrasattva.[123] Then in furtherance of the pledges (*samaya*) and vows (*samvara*), he ties (the *mudrā* of) all the Buddhas.[124] (203)

At that time, according to the mantra rite, he should incant the cloths three times. With a mind becoming compassionate, he confidently incants them. (204)

Having recited the pledge (*samaya*) three times, he imagines that the syllable RA on the crown of the (disciple's) head, shining along with the head circle that radiates in blazing-garland form; has white color, like a rising (full) moon.[125] (205)

In the presence of all the protectors he then induces (the disciple) to throw the flower. Where the flower falls, the mantrin will give (the disciple) to it (i.e. the Buddha family of that place).[126] (206)

Near the gate of the first maṇḍala, he will assist the disciple between two gates of the maṇḍala. For him there, he will perform in proper sequence all the rites.[127] (207)

Having in that manner well installed the disciple who is free from sin, so as to appease those (gods) he should ritually perform a *homa* (burnt offering).[128] (208)

In front of the garbha-maṇḍala, with back to the second maṇḍala, in the middle part of the maṇḍala with non-wavering mind he should perform it (i.e. the *homa*).[129] (209)

An exact measure in cubits (*khru*) for the hearth is stipulated. The 'mouth' (*kha*) should be exactly four *anguli* (*sor*). In the middle he 'sizes' the *vajra*. (210)

Then the *mantrin* places the accessories for the *homa* at his right side. He leisurely introduces the disciple into the circle on his left side. And avowed himself stays on a kuśa-grass seat at that spot. (211)

Besides, the mantrin, having taken some fine quality red paint, paints all the places of fire at the connecting points. (212)

All the perimeter circle is to be strewn with kuśa grass by way of the right, strewn while circling many times; and one should purify it with perfumed water. (213)

Then the goodly avowed one, while imagining the inner hearth which benefits all sentient beings, should present a fine ladle (*dgaṅ blugs*) together with this mantra:[130]

Namaḥ samantabuddhānām agnaye svāhā.

Then the wise one, with his left hand holding the (right-hand) thumb of each disciple (in succession), should make the burnt offering, while being in equipoise. (215)

While his mind is in equipoise, ritually reciting mantras for each burnt offering (*bsreg lugs*), he should make the twenty-one burnt offerings.[131] (216)

Namaḥ samantabuddhānām Āḥ mahāśāntigata śāntikara praśāmadharmanirjāta /
Abhāvasvabhāvadharmasamatā-pravata svāhā /

After the burnt offering, the mantrin makes sacrificial offering to the disciples. Thereupon, the disciples, by their devotion and faith having aroused an ecstasy in their mind, offer to the guru gold, silver, or jewels; a horse, elephant, camel, cow, or buffalo; cloth or some other item as feasible. And, in any event, that guru will be very pleased. (217-218)

When that is done, he should guard himself. Calling the disciple(s), he instructs him, "This is the field of merit (*puṇyaksetra*) for the sake of all sentient beings. The protectors have all stated: 'To the Saṃgha which has pure and vast good qualities, one gives by way of all (presentation); an offering to the Saṃgha has great fruit.' (219-220)

'Whatever wise persons will make offerings to the Saṃgha, they will derive inexhaustible great pleasure (*mahābhoga*) and be well-regarded in the world.' Hence, one should joyfully put one's mind in a consistent frame; and should show honor, as one is able, to the Saṃgha that was so praised by the Buddha." (221-222)

Then Bhagavat Vairocana proclaimed to Bodhisattva great being Vajrapāṇi:

"Great being! The previous Buddhas have explained who is initiated (*abhiṣikta*).[132] It will be explained. Listen well, your mind in single attention." (223)

Master of the Secret Ones! In this connection, the ācārya should draw in front of the basic maṇḍala at an outer place a distance of a cubit a second maṇḍala with four corners and one door; and should place four Vajradhara-s in the four corners. Which four? As follows: —Niṣprapañcavihārin, Gaganāmala, Vimalanetra, Nānavāsadhṛk.[133] In the middle he should put a great lotus with eight petals and having stamens. On four petals he should draw four famous Bodhisattvas, having the power of their former aspiration, as follows: Dhāraṇīśvararāja, Smṛtiprajanyin, Hitādhyāśayin, and Kāruṇya.[134] On the other petals, their four attendants, as follows: * Cittaviśeṣacarita, * Kāmaniṣpatti, * Asakta, and * Vimukti.[135] In the center he should place the 'inconceivable' form of the Dharmadhātu.[136] Then he should fill four precious pots with jewels and herbs.[137] They will be empowered by Samantabhadra, Maitreya, Sarvanivāraṇaviṣkambhin, and Sarvāpayajaha. And with them he will sprinkle[138] on the (disciples') heads.[139]

The mantrin will say: 'On that petalled lotus I have placed (Bodhisattvas and their attendants); and will honor (them) with incense and flowers, will delight (them) with lamps and other offerings; pleasing and auspicious umbrellas, flags and banners, and sounding drums, along with words that are heard far-off. In the presence of the protectors (saying), 'having taken care in that (needful) may there be initiation'. With excellent incense and flowers, I shall honor them.' (224-227)

Then taking a golden 'probe' (*śalākā*), standing in front (of the disciple), he should speak in these words appealing to the disciple's heart: (228)

'Just as the kings of healing with their probe removed the eye-caul of men, so may I (or, the Jinas) remove your film of ignorance, my son.[140] (229)

Then taking a mirror he should explain the character of the dharmas:

'The dharmas are like reflected images, clear and pure, without turbulence: ungraspable, inexpressible, arisen from cause (*hetu*) and action (*karma*).

In that way, one should explain their character. (230-231)

'Having understood the dharmas that way, as without own-nature and without a location, may you perform the aim of sentient beings that is without equal, and be heart-born of the protectors!' (232)

Then he should put the Dharmacakra between his legs, and with his hand give an excellent conch shell. (233)

'From this day on may you set in motion the wheel of the Dharma for the world, filling throughout with the supreme conch of the Dharma.' (234)

'Act not with hesitation, but with a non-doubting mind. Always preach in the world the rule which is the means of mantra praxis.' (235)

'Knowing what is right that way, is called being useful to the Buddhas. And all those Vajradhara-s will protect you in every way!' (236)

Then bidding the disciple to rise, the mantrin, his mind compassionate, drawing him inside (the maṇḍala) should teach him the pledges (*samaya*): (237)

'From this day on you must not abandon the Illustrious Dharma and the Mind of Enlightenment, even for your life. You must not have envy, or do harm to sentient beings. O well avowed one, these pledges are given to you by the Buddha. In the same way as you would guard your life, so you must guard these.' (238-239)

The disciple, having bowed to the feet of the guru with faith and devotion and with his mind up, takes all those (pledges). (240)

Then Vajrapāṇi, Master of the Secret Ones, requested the Bhagavat: "Bhagavat, when any son of the family or daughter of the family is introduced to the pledges of this great king of maṇḍala-s, the 'Mahākaruṇodbhava', may he know what merit would be collected from doing so?" The Bhagavat responded to the question by speaking as follows to Vajrapāṇi, Master of the Secret Ones: "After initially generating the Mind (of Enlightenment), and adhering to it, as much as be the merits collected that arise from the Tathāgata, one may know that this much be the merit collected by that son of the family or daughter of the family. Master of the Secret Ones, while it is in this manner, you should also regard it as follows: Those sons of the family and daughters of the family are children born from the mouth and heart of the Tathāgata.[141] In whatever direction that son of the family or daughter of the family stays, the Tathāgata does not need to be involved greatly.[142] Master of the Secret Ones, accordingly, the son of the family or daughter of the family who wishes to honor the Tathāgata, should honor those (of the retinue who act on behalf of sentient beings). Who wishes to see the Tathāgata, should see those!" Then those Vajradhara-s, Vajrapāṇi, etc., and those Bodhisattva great beings, Samantabhadra, etc., spoke in unison: "Bhagavat, from now on those sons of the family and daughters of the family will honor and be devoted to those (of the retinue who act on behalf of sentient beings). But, Bhagavat, why should those sons of the family or daughters of the family be led to see the Buddha Bhagavats?" Thereupon, the Bhagavat Vairocana surveyed that entire retinue, and spoke to Vajrapāṇi, Master of the Secret Ones, as well as the Vajradhara-s and the rest of the retinue: "O, sons of the family, the the mantra-sounds of the Tathāgata fulfil all hopes like the gem of diverse form[143] in the large entrance to the enormous maṇḍala whose circle-perimeter is made of speech. They stay in the unfathomable and immemorial erection of the merit collection. They possess the unclinging power of the three times." When that was spoken, Vajrapāṇi, Master of the Secret Ones, as well as the Vajradhara-s, and the retinue, spoke in unison: "The Bhagavat has come at the right time. The Sugata has come at the right occasion."

Now the Bhagavat, at this time having with his (glorious) tongue organ fully manifested all the desired (information), covered over the all-possessing Buddha realm and equipoised himself in the *Samādhi*, 'Viewing the pure[144] peak of the wide banner of Dharma.' No sooner had the Bhagavat (so) equipoised, than, in agreement, all the Tathāgatas emitted sounds pervading the

Dharmadhātu and protecting all the sentient realms, namely, expressed this great protection, the Vidyārajñī of great power.[145] Namaḥ sarvatathā-gatebhyaḥ sarvabhayavigatebhyo viśvasukhebhyaḥ sarvathā Haṃ Khaṃ rakṣa mahābale sarvatathāgatapuṇye nirjāte Hūṃ Hūṃ Traṭa Traṭa apratihate svāhā.

While all the wise Buddhas were pronouncing this charm (*vidyā*), this Buddha realm quaked in six manners.(241).

All those Bodhisattvas, their eyes wide open in amazement, attendants of all the Buddhas, expressed words of delight.(242)

'Ah! All the Buddhas have expressed this protection of great power as a secret (device) to protect and save all sentient beings. (243)

'In whose hearts this protection dwells, they fearless, remembering the mantra of great power, will destroy all the hindrances and evil spirits, and all the fearfully formed rākṣasas.'(244)

Then the Bhagavat, having empowered the far-extended Dharmadhātu, at the time equipoised himself in the samādhi 'Having the treasure womb of the Dharmadhātu.' No sooner had the Bhagavat (so) equipoised, then there was emitted a charm (*vidyā*) to incite the pledge (*samaya*), as follows: Namaḥ samantabuddhānām asame trisame samaye svāhā. Immediately thereupon, all the Buddha realm, and all the maṇḍala of Bodhisattva attendants, having heard this sound of the charm to incite the pledge, pledged that they would not transgress any of the Dharma of the wise ones.[146] Then the Bhagavat stated the mantra whose source is the Dharmadhātu: Namaḥ samantabuddhānām/ dharmadhātu-svabhāva ātmako 'ham/. This empowers the Dharmadhātu.[147] Namaḥ samantavajrānām/ vajra ātmako 'ham/. This empowers Vajrasattva.[148] Namaḥ samantavajrānām/ vajrakavaca Hūṃ/. The diamond armor.[149] Namaḥ samantavajrānām/ tathāgatacakṣur vyavalokaya svāhā. The Tathāgata's eye.[150] Namaḥ samantabudhānām/ viśuddhagandhodbhava svāhā. Mantra of the perfume.[151] Namaḥ samantabuddhānām/mahāmaitryabhyudbhūta. Mantra of the flowers.[152] Namaḥ samantabuddhānām/dharmadhātvanugate svāhā. Mantra of the incense.[153] Namaḥ samantabuddhānām/sarvatathāgatārcispharaṇe 'vabhāsa-gaganocarebhya svāhā. Mantra of the lamp.[154] Namaḥ samantabuddhānām/ gagana-samāsama svāhā. Mantra of the votive offering (*argha*, Tib. *mchod yon*).[155] Namaḥ samantabuddhānām/ gaganānantaspharaṇa-viśuddhadharma-nirjāta svāhā. Mantra of the Uṣṇīṣa.[156]

Namaḥ samantabuddhānām/ pracaṇḍa-vajrajvāla-visphura Hūṃ. The Tathāgata's armor.[157] Namaḥ samantabuddhānām/jvāla-mālini tathāgatārci svāhā. The encircling blaze.[158] Namaḥ samanta-buddhānām/mahātathāgata-jīhvasya dharma-pratiṣṭhita svāhā. Mantra of the Tathāgata's tongue.[159] So the treasury of mantras for the arrangement in the maṇḍala.[160]

NOTES TO THE TRANSLATION

1. In Sanskrit Guhyakādhipati, the *guhyaka* being the family of yakṣa; see Edgerton, *Buddhist Hybrid Sanskrit Dictionary*, p. 214A.
2. The Sūtra portrays the mundane minds in Chap. I translated and annotated in Tajima's Study of the Mahāvairocana-Sūtra. See also our doctrinal section 'Beings and their Minds.'
3. For the V-A-T position on the Dharmadhātu, see our "Doctrinal Positions of the Scripture".
4. For the V-A-T position on a 'Complete Buddha', see our doctrinal section 'Beings and their Minds'.
5. The V-A-T gives its own explanation of the word 'maṇḍala' in this Chap. II; for other explanations and varieties, see A. Wayman, "Reflections on the Theory of Barabuḍur as a Maṇḍala", in *Barabudur; History and Significance of a Buddhist Monument* (Berkeley Studies Series, Berkeley, 1981), pp. 139-172.
6. Buddhaguhya's commentary (old version) on the V-A-T and using the Peking Tanjur edition (hereafter: B-comm.), states at 129-5-4: this is called the 'jewel wheel of the inexhaustible Body'. The Sūtra emphasizes the Mahākaruṇāgar-bhodbhava-maṇḍala as the Body kind among the three maṇḍala of the Sūtra. B-comm. at 138-2-1,2 mentions the three as (1) Mahākaruṇāgarbha-maṇḍala, called also *padmavat* ('lotus endowed') *maṇḍala;* (2) syllable maṇḍala, or circle of syllables; (3) secret maṇḍala (of the five elements). B-comm., 157-2-1, ff. gives the three kinds as (1) Mahākaruṇā-maṇḍala; (2) maṇḍala of whirling the circle of syllables; (3) secret maṇḍala; going respectively with the Tathāgata's signs (*nimitta*) of Body, Speech, and Mind.
7. B-comm., 131-1-7, there are three (in sequence): 'cause' (*hetu*)—the *ācārya* (the hierophant); 'main part' (*svabhāva*)—the *maṇḍala*-rite; 'result' (*kārya*)—initiation (*abhiṣeka*) of the disciple.
8. B-comm. 131-2-7: 'rule of Prajñāpāramitā' means in the absolute sense, contemplation of voidness (*śūnyatā*); in the conventional sense, practice of the perfections (*pāramitā*) of giving (*dāna*), etc.
9. B-comm. 131-3-2: The Śrāvaka vehicle comprehends voidness of *pudgala* (ordinary person); impermanence of personal aggregates (*skandha*), realms (*dhātu*), and so on; the varieties of suffering (*duḥkha*). The Pratyekabuddha vehicle comprehends the dependent arising (*pratītyasamutpāda*) of the personal aggregates, and so on. The Great Vehicle (*mahāyāna*) comprehends the immemorial non-arising of the *dharma*-s. (Hence the second and third vehicles do not negate the previous, but add a higher attainment.)
10. B-comm. 131-3-5: skilled in the syllables of mantras for the various deities; in the associated *mudrā*-s, and in the *samādhi*-s required for the maṇḍalas of earth, water, and so on.

11. B-comm. 131-4-1: 'mental make-up' means he knows their suitability for service to calm or angry deities, and their faculty, whether inferior, middling, or superior for the 'work' (*grub pa*). In Buddhist meditation theory this is supernormal faculty (*abhijñā*) called 'knowledge of the state of others' minds' (*paracittajñāna*). From Pāli sources, see the discussion in P. Vajiranana, *Buddhist Meditation in Theory and Practice* (Colombo, 1962), pp. 445-447, where the commentary shows it must be preceded by the supernormal faculty called 'divine vision' (*divyacakṣus*), and that a less progressed person on the path cannot possibly apply this faculty to the mind of someone more progressed.
12. While B-comm. at 132-3-4, treating this verse, does not explain the somewhat surprising claim, the Sūtra statement does seem to agree with traditional accounts. For example, Edward J. Thomas, *The Life of Buddha* (New York, 1952), p. 73, cites, the *Lalitavistāra,* "at these words Māra the evil one pained, dejected, and sorrowful vanished from thence." This shows that the words Gautama used vanquished Māra; and it is these words that are being referred to as 'mantra'.
13. Edgerton, *Buddhist Hybrid Sanskrit Dictionary,* p. 243A, says the expression *jina-śrāvaka* might mean: pupil of the founder of a sect. Here, it appears to mean simply the group of śrāvakas.
14. B-comm. 132-5-3: 'rid of all faults' means rid of all outer faults such as rocks, etc.
15. B-comm. 132-5-6: 'good omens' are of three kinds—(1) superior, namely, those from the devas, sounds coming from the sky. (2) middling, namely, auspicious words from intermediate space; meeting a (pure) brahmin, etc. (3) inferior, namely, from the earth, such as seeing a conch, etc. on the ground.
16. B-comm. 139-2-7,8: mentions that the number 16 for the *aṅguli* measure, stands for the ten Stages and the six Perfections. Also, B-comm. 171-3-5, the form of causal praxis is the Stages and the Perfections; just before this, stating that the fruitional praxis is the circle-practice of Body, Speech, and Mind.
17. B-comm. 176-5-2, ff. (on Tib. Chap. XIII, 'The Secret Maṇḍala'): The Dharmakāya transcendent of signs and devoid of materiality—thus cannot be shown—has these virtues (*guṇa*): not astray, non-changing consummate nature, avoiding all constructive thought, free from all defilement, able to do anything. Accordingly, these virtues empower the element-maṇḍalas. One of them empowers the vajra-maṇḍala of earth *(mahendra)* because earth is non-changing and firm, with consummate nature like *vajra*. The nature of avoiding all constructive thought empowers the water-maṇḍala, because water purifies everything by washing. The one free from all defilement empowers the fire-maṇḍala, because the nature of fire is to burn up, and because the syllable RA shows that all dharmas are free from dust. The ability to do anything empowers the wind-maṇḍala, because wind goes everywhere and separates everything.

    B-comm. here does not mention the space-element, because the four element-maṇḍalas when so empowered are employed to overcome the four Māras, in the order stated later; see notes 85-86 below. However, the *Sūtra* does have the *ākāśa*-element; and 'not astray' appears to agree with it.
18. B-comm. 171-5-7: 'my Dharma' means there are three kinds of Dharma—(1) incomparable Dharma, (2) Dharma quiescent from the outset, (3) supreme Dharma, which are respectively inception (*'jug pa*), praxis (*sbyor ba*), and fruit (*'bras bu*). (1) is the ten virtues and the virtuous *dharmas* of giving, etc. (i.e. the

Perfections), called 'incomparable' because the *dharma* of outsiders does not compare. (2) is the stages of the praxis toward Buddhahood, 'quiescent from the outset' because all *dharmas* are generated by cause and condition. (3) is the fruit of the 'inception' and 'praxis' kinds, and expresses the Nirvāṇa of no fixed abode.

Hence the three agree with the old formula, 'good in the beginning, good in the middle, good in the end'. The three kinds of Dharma are in the scripture itself, Tib. Chap. X (Wheel of Syllables', text 256-4-5): "I am called Lord of the World, am first of the world, and teach the Dharma that is supreme, quiescent from the outset, and incomparable." The Tibetan for this: / ṅa ni 'jig rten daṅ po yin / 'jig rten mgon źes bsgrags pa yin / bla med gzod nas źi ba ni / mñam pa med pa'i chos bśad do /.

19. B-comm. 133-4-6: 'imagine me', in the sky (*nam mkha)*, in the middle of the *maṇḍala.* B-comm. 133-4-8, one imagines the five Buddhas in the sky; and here calls this the 'intrinsic *maṇḍala*' (raṅ bzin gyi dkyil 'khor). And B-comm. 133-4-7, while imagining them, one ties the seal (*mudrā*) of the three *samaya*. B-comm. when stating associations of the four or five wisdoms (*jñāna*), i.e.at 138-4,5, their directions and order of arising: at 139-1, the four going with the first rank of the M-K-G-maṇḍala, and at 173-5, their five colors, does not bring in the five Buddhas. The V-A-T and B-comm. seem not inclined to associate the five Buddhas with the five wisdoms. While V-A-T, Chap. II, verses 30 and so on, assigns directions to the Complete Buddhas, this does not warrant our going ahead and trying to force those directions of the five wisdoms to go with the five Buddhas.
20. The mantras are presented in Chap. IV, Mantra of Acala at 251-3-3: Namaḥ samantavajrānāṃ caṇḍamahāroṣaṇa sphoṭaya Hūṃ Trak Hāṃ (Māṃ). Mantra of Trailokyavijaya at 251-3-3,4: Namaḥ samantavajrānāṃ ha ha ha vismaya sarvatathāgata-viṣaya-saṃbhāva trailokyavijaya Hūṃ Jaḥ Svāhā.
21. The list of six amounts to the compartments in rank one (the top one) of the three-ranked Mahākaruṇāgarbhodbhava-maṇḍala, with individual 'belonging' ("The first is my own", etc.). These six define the inner realm, called *garbha.* Verse 71, below, mentions that the two remaining ranks belong to the deities (and for these, see 'Beings and their Minds", 'the praiseworthy and the heroes').
22. B-comm. 135-2-8: There are nine steps, namely, (1) confessions of sins, (2) taking of refuge, (3) making them take the vow of knowledge unhindered in the three times, (4) giving of perfumed water and flowers, (5) making them prepare the sticks, (6) tying the arm with cord, (7) generating the guarding and enthusiasm, (8) having them examine their dreams, (9) explaining the dharma to them. The Sūtra deals below with most of these, but does not explicitly list them as nine.
23. B-comm. 135-5-3,ff., when the stick is thrown, the direction in which the point of the stick lies, amounts to a portent of whether or not the disciple is a fit vessel. (When thrown facing East:) If it is pointed East, the disciple is a fit vessel for best *siddhi* and for the rite of prosperity (*pauṣṭika*). If it is pointed South, one is fitted to accomplish the fierce rite (*abhicāruka*). If it is pointed West, one can succeed at the domineering the rite (*vaśīkāra*). When thrown facing North, and it falls directed tò oneself, one is able to achieve speedily a middling success. If it is directed North, one is fit for the rite of appeasing (*śāntika*). If it is directed to the N.E. corner, one can succeed at both the appeasing and prosperity rites. Directed to the S.E. corner, one does the fierce rite. Directed to the S.W. one is fit to

magically frighten or dessicate. Directed to the N.W. one can command the *yakṣa*-s, etc. When it plants itself at a spot, and is pointed to the intermediate space, the disciple can achieve the intermediate space. In such case, when pointed upward, he can achieve such siddhis as *vidyādhara*. Likewise, when pointed downward, he is a fit vessel for achieving the *siddhis* of the underworld (*pātāla*). B-comm. then says that Tantras like the *Guhya-tantra* go into these matters in detail.

24. B-comm. 136-3-3, the dream portents are classified by origin, whether sky, intermediate space, and ground, accordingly, superior, middling, or inferior, respectively. And each of those three are themselves superior, middling, or inferior. Thus, 'monastery' down to 'dome' is counted as inferior kind of 'ground' source. Sword, wish-granting gem, are superior ones of 'ground'. Umbrella, and so on, down to brahmins, are middling omens of the 'ground'. Buddhas are the superior kind of omen among 'āryas'; Bodhisattvas who have attained power, and Pratyekabuddhas, are the middling kind of 'ārya'; śrāvakas are the inferior kind of 'ārya'. Gain of fruit is the inferior kind of omen from the intermediate space; seeing the crossing of lakes and oceans is the middling kind from the intermediate space; and the auspicious words from space occurring in dreams that mention the desired fruit, are superior kinds of portents from intermediate space. [Therefore, the Sūtra did not illustrate here any omens from the sky.]
25. This means that the disciples must report the dream to the preceptor.
26. B-comm. 136-4-5, this signifies the *mantra*-path.
27. Notice v. 183, below, "Like the pure sky they dwell in the stage of lofty mind."
28. The renunciation of body is described in the scripture translated as *The Lion's Roar of Queen Śrīmālā* (tr. by Alex and Hideko Wayman, New York, 1974). p. 75: "Lord, the good son of the family or good daughter of the family by renouncing his body, thus obtaining the body of a Buddha, is equal to the outermost limit of *saṃsāra;* thus obtaining freedom from old age, sickness, and death, is indestructible; thus being permanent, steadfast, calm, and eternal, is free from [ordinary] passing away and is endowed with boundless inconceivable merits; reaching the Dharmakāya of the Tahtāgata."
29. Trailokyavijaya, when placed in the Mahākaruṇāgarbhodbhava-maṇḍala, is nearby Acala in the first rank, which has one gate, called here 'the first gate'. B-comm. 137-2-8, "having saluted the Bhagavat" means he does it mentally (*yid la bya*), by tying the *mudrā* of the three *samaya,* called 'seal of the Dharmadhātu'; tying the seal of the Dharmacakra, one is empowered as Vajrasattva. [The secret offering is mental.]
30. B-comm. 137-3-4, one makes the offering with the mantra of Trailokyavijaya to dispel the demons. One recites the basic mantra (given above, n. 20) 21 times; and if an abbreviated form is used, called the *hṛdaya* (sñin po), it is recited 108 times. [The *hṛdaya* form is found in Chap. X ('Wheel of Syllables', text 257-3-5) as HA.]
31. Notice v. 16, above: The Māra host appeared at dusk; having defeated this army, i.e. purified the mind, one draws the maṇḍala hence draws it in the evening. Besides, one does not eat in the evening in which one draws it; and this is the right time to honor the maṇḍala Bodhisattvas. B-comm. 137-4-1, imagination of eating food is in violation of mantras. B-comm. 137-5-5, the Bodhisattvas gather together in the evening.
32. B-comm. 138-1-4, for drawing the maṇḍala, there are six topics: (1) the samādhi of 'drawing' the thread of the maṇḍala; (2) 'drawing' the thread; (3) measurement of the maṇḍala; (4) variegation of the 'strip' (*paṭa*) series; (5) variegation of the door

and gateways; (6) determining the location of the deties. B-comm., 138-2-1, the hierophant is empowered as Vairocana for the Mahākaruṇāgarbhodbhava-maṇḍala.

33. B-comm. 138-2-4: the thread is of five colors (twisted together), considered as the five wisdoms (*jñāna*), and considered as the five Buddhas.

34. B-comm. 138-2-6, first the performer is on the Western side looking toward the East, then stands up. He ,imagines, by the manner of non-apprehending, the 'intrinsic maṇḍala' in the sky (see note 19, above), the Body, etc. of Bhagavat Vairocana along with the inexhaustible jewel wheels. Then in the southern direction, facing North, he should extend the thread, while imagining the 'intrinsic maṇḍala' in the sky. The subsequent drawing of the maṇḍala on the ground should be understood as the reflected image of that 'intrinsic maṇḍala'. It is because one imagines that 'intrinsic maṇḍala' that one can 'draw' it on the ground.

35. B-comm. 138-3-2, ff. The meaning is that this is the next (square) maṇḍala. [A square is drawn around the original square in order to make a place for the 'second rank'.] Again the thread is five-colored. For this phase it is necessary to put a peg (*phur bu*) in the middle of the maṇḍala, and then set four pegs for the corners of this second square. [He remembers the Tathāgata, because, noticing verses 104-105, below, Śākyamuni is assigned to the second rank, and in the East.]

36. B-comm. 138-3-8, the preceptor had been sitting in the S.W. corner, looking to the North, so shifting to the right means shifting in the direction of East.

37. "Giving up that place" apparently means going outside the second square to make a third square, since it is the third time the Sūtra mentions drawing in the East. This requires a further rite of mantra to rid this extended area of demons, and this area will become the third rank.

38. B-comm. 138-5-4: There parts means division in the 'strips' (*paṭa*) [This is necessary to mark off places for the doorways; and each in three parts because later subordinate deities are placed to the right and left of main ones.]

39. B-comm. 138-5-2 (end), ff.: the rank with one-part perimeter (is so because this rank has only one gate, namely in the West); 'one-part perimeter' is the character of the dharmadhātu. [The second rank has two gates per v. 125, below, namely, East and West, so two strips are necessary for the perimeter. The third rank with four gates, namely in E, S, W, N, requires four strips.] The second and third ranks belong to the deities there depicted.

40. B-comm. 139-1-2, ff.: Each side has nine segments (per v. 70, above). In the inner *maṇḍala,* in the East one should place the seal of the dharmakāya (i.e. the triangle) (and so on).

41. Chap. X ('Wheel of Syllables' adds some more details at 257-2-6: Bhagavat Mahāvairocana has a lower garment of silk and cotton, and an upper garment of satin. His (germ) syllable is 'A'. B-comm. 139-4-4, says of 'hair bound up, that this is characteristic of all deities of Akaniṣṭha; and that it shows him to be the Vairocana of Akaniṣṭha. It says of 'wearing a jewel in crown' that this means 'king of Dharma'.

42. B-comm. 139-5-3 the triangle means the three doors to liberation, namely. voidness (*śūnyatā*), signless (*ānimitta*), and wishless (*apraṇihita*). [Above (n. 40), it is the seal (*mudrā*) of the Dharmakāya. Since the Dharmakāya is so represented in the East, it is an indication of why the Vairocana in the center of the lotus is identified as the Sambhoga-kāya.] B-comm. 139-5-1, it symbolizes all

the Tathāgatas of the past who became manifestly enlightened. The direction in which it is placed, i.e. the East, is in Sanskrit *pūrva*, which also means 'past' or 'former'.

43. B-comm. 139-5-8: Bhagavatī, Mother or Buddhas, is called 'Eyes of Space (or sky)'. Prajñāpāramitā is the Mother of all the Buddhas, since the Buddha Bhagavat-s arise from that Prajñā. 'golden color' stands for the blaze that burns up the hindrances of the knowable and defilement.
44. B-comm. 140-1-4, 'like conch and autumn moon' means the color of his body. Amitābha seated on his head indicates the discriminative wisdom (*pratyavekṣaṇa-jñāna*), with which he views (*gzigs*) the pure dharmadhātu.
45. B-comm. 140-2-5, ff., green covers all colors, hence she has the character of all three *homa* rites (i.e. for appeasing, prosperity, and fierce acts); 'for many forms' means sometimes as a male, sometimes as a female. [The comments show that this green Tārā gave rise to the 21-Tārā cult in later centuries that was very popular in North India.]
46. B-comm. 140-4-5, her third eye represents *krodha* (fury); 'hair bound up'—the character of Akaniṣṭha deities.
47. B-comm. 140-5-1, the unopened lotus is his 'seal' (*mudrā*), and shows his difference from Avalokiteśvara.
48. B-comm. 140-5-4, her golden color signifies the character of prosperity (*pauṣṭika*). The saffron-colored ear of corn is her *mudrā*.
49. B-comm. 140-5-8, 'hair bound up'—same meaning as above (notes 41, 46).
50. B.comm. 141-1-2,ff. Mahābala is the Vidyārāja of the Lotus Family; 'color of rising sun'—red.
51. B-comm. 141-1-6, the name Hayagrīva ('horse neck') signifies that his wisdom to penetrate the Dharma is speedy like a horse; and that his aid to sentient beings is speedy like a horse.
52. Since Vajrapāṇi is called 'green lord' he succeeds in all *homa* rites (see n.45, above); this is confirmed by B-comm. 185-5-4.
53. B-comm. 141-3-4, with her *vajra* threatens those who would do evil things: "Don't do it; don't do it!"
54. B-comm. 141-3-8, has the character that inspires fear toward the continuum (*dharmatā*).
55. B-comm. 141-4-3. She has the nature of the Noble Path, because she pulls the sentient beings onto that path.
56. B-comm. 141-5-2: 'four tusks' signifies the four doors to liberation, voidness, signless, wishless, and (mind) naturally radiant (*prakṛtiprabhāsvara*).
57. B-comm. 142-1-4: 'one crooked eye' means the unimpeded path (*ānantarya-mārga*). [For this term, see E. Obermiller, "The doctrine of Prajñāpāramitā as exposed in the Abhisamayālaṃkāra of Maitreya", *Acta Orientalia,* Vol. XI, p. 106: generally, the knowledge which directly removes the defiling forces.]
58. Chap. X ('Wheel of Syllables') at 257-3-4, has more information, explaining the name as 'destroying the great obstacles (=demons)'; his form like the dreadful world-destroying fire; holding in hand a *vajra* radiating light, which is his *mudrā*.

    (As to the name which seems to mean 'Victorious over the three worlds'), Chap. XIII ('Secret Maṇḍala') at 264-3-3,4: he dwells in the three pure places; B-comm. 186-3-5: second, in the wind circle; third, in the fire circle. [This explanation agrees with V-A-T, Chap. III, 'Suppression of Demons', where the demons as gods go with element *maṇḍalas* according to their colors; thus these are demons of earth, water, fire, and wind. According to the Buddhist Abhidharma theory of world destruction by the elements, there is destruction by water, fire, and wind. This suggests that there is a textual omission in B-comm. on the 'first' pure place which should be water. One interpretation is that the name of this deity stands for purification of the three 'poisons', of lust, hatred, and delusion. In the *Vimalaprabhā* exegesis of the *Kālacakra* (see A. Wayman, "Studies in Yama and Māra", *Indo-Iranian Journal,* III, 1949, pp. 128-29), there are the expressions 'fire of hatred' and 'water of lust'. Adding 'wind of delusion', we can understand the 'three pure places' as detoxification of the three poisons, alternatively referred to as destroying the demons of three elements.]

59. Concerning the rank divided into two, notice v. 125, below, the two doorways. This means that the entrance doorway in the East, and the exit doorway in the West cause a break in the 'Strips' (*haṭa*), thus two fo them. Sūtra's on the inner part should place Śākyamuni—in three-dimensional conception—right under the triangle in the first rank in the East.

60. B-comm. 142-2-7: in the name Śākyamuni ('*muni* of the Śākya clan'), *muni* means who is 'muted' in body, speech, and mind. [Since this goes with representing the Enlightenment Body at the Tree of Enlightenment, and since this is toward dawn, he is placed in the East.] For explaining the Dharma, B-comm. 198-4-5,ff. (on Chap. XXI, 'Origin of the Hundred Syllables'), states of the name 'Lord of all the Dharmas' (*sarvadharmeśvara*) that it means two kinds of Dharma, which like the rising sun negate all the dark ignorance, namely, 'installation' (T. *chud pa;* S. *praveśa*) Dharma, and 'central' (T. *gzuṅ*) Dharma, both of which eliminate hindrance, but in the conventional (*saṃvṛti*) and absolute (*paramārtha*) manner, so the perfection of elimination and the perfection of knowledge. The conventional installation involves elimination while objects are taken realistically. When omniscience rises like a sun, one can see all the entities clearly as they are. [See also n. 18, above, where 'my Dharma' is explained as three kinds of Dharma.]

61. B-comm. 142-3-7: She is his 'mother' because Buddha Śākyamuni has arisen from *prajñā*; and she is called 'insight' (*prajñā*) because Buddhalocanā (She the Buddha Eye) has the nature of vision. (*saṅs rgyas śākya thub pa śes rab de las byuṅ ba 'i phyir / saṅs rgyas kyi yum zes bya 'o / saṅs rgyas kyi spyan źes pa ni gzigs pa' i raṅ bzin pas śex rab la bya' o/*) [I include the Tibetan for this, because various Western translators of Buddhist literature have adopted renditions for *prajñā* (Pāli, *paññā;* Tib. *śes rab*) that take no account of the visionary implication of this word.]

62. B-comm. 142-4-3, the goddess (personification) of the *ūrṇa-koṣa* [the Buddha characteristic in middle of forehead]. [The addition of the term *vidyā* suggests a position that this forehead characteristic is responsible for the three *vidyā* (clear visions) which Gautama experienced during the night of the enlightenment. This may also be the implication of v. 112, below, associating three *uṣṇīsas* with this place.]

63. The Japanese Buddhist dictionary *Bukkyō daijiten* by Mochizuki Shinkō has at Vol. 1, p. 177c (under Ingei "mudrā") a set of correspondences to these five *uṣṇīṣa,* including the five personal aggregates (*skandha*), five sense organs (*indriya*), five germ syllables, and five elements. The correspondences are repeated with the five fingers of each hand. The two hands differ in that the right hand goes with the values, 'outer', 'sun', 'compassion' (*karuṇā*), 'discernment' (*vipaśyanā*), 'insight' (*prajñā*), and 'omniscience' (*sarvajña*); while the left hand

goes with the values, 'inner', 'moon', 'love' (*maitrī*), 'calming' (*śamatha*), 'meditation' (*dhyāna*), and 'principle' (Chin. *li*). One may compare with E. Dale Saunders, *Mudrā* (London, 1960), pp. 32-33. Two of the five *uṣṇīṣa* are personified in well-known, popular goddesses, the White Umbrella Lady (Sitātapatrā) and Uṣṇīṣavijayā.

64. B-comm. 142-5-1, takes the text's remark "to his North" to be a slip (or corruption) for "to his South", i.e. they should be put next to the five *uṣṇīṣa*. [There is an implication that the five *uṣṇīṣa* correspond—besides what is mentioned in n. 63, above—to the five Pure Abodes that in Buddhist cosmogony surmount the 'Realm of Form'.]

65. The remark "in the lower area" must mean to separate off these deities from the immediately preceding group of mundane deities that are in the plane of the second rank (in 3-dimensional conception) but outside the *maṇḍala* proper. Hence, these deities, Aparajita, Aparajitā, and Kṣitipati, are reasonably to be assigned inside the second rank and in the West (where the V-A-T normally puts gate protectors).

66. Nandin and Upananda come in Buddhist legend as the two serpent kings who washed the new-born Siddhārtha. They are depicted in one of the *toraṇa*-s of Sanchi. B-comm. 143-3-5: They are drawn yonder and hither, outside the doors. (*chab sgo ba* ≡ *phyi sgo ba*). [Hence, they face the East and West doorways.] They are also on two sides of Śākyamuni in Marcelle Lalou, *Icnographie des Etoffes peintes* (*paṭa*) *dans le Mañjuśrīmūlakalpa* (Paris, 1930), Planche I.

67. B-comm. 200-1-7,ff. (on Chap. XXII, 'Fruitional Praxis'): The Buddha teaches śrāvakas, pratyekabuddhas, Indra, Brahmā, and so on as follows—Śākyamuni teaches his Dharma in all the mundane realms extended in space. There is not just one body of Śākyamuni, or two; rather Śākyamuni's bodies fill all the mundane realms, as many as there be in space, teaching all the sentient beings according to their expectation; maturing as many as be the fit vessels among the sentient beings; and delivering those who are matured. Those bodies are materializations (*nirmita*) from the 'speech circle'. And, explaining the remark "a wise person will draw them also". B-comm. 148-3-4: Bodhisattvas and so on, i.e. bodhisattvas, śrāvakas, and pratyekabuddhas, that are not specifically mentioned, may be included among those to be trained by the Nirmāṇakāya. [Presumably, they are in the North and South wings of the 2nd rank.]

68. The third rank description starts with the East where Manjuśrī is located. B-comm. 143-3-8, the great Bodhisattvas in this rank (i.e. Mañjuśrī, and so on) are drawn seated in the manner of listening to the Dharma. Listening to the Dharma is of two kinds: Dharma of the school (*lugs kyi chos*) and Dharma of attainment (*thob pa'i chos*). The Dharma of the school means those (teachings) stated after one has slept. The Dharma of attainment is the jewel circle of the inexhaustible Body. These great Bodhisattvas listen to the latter. [Presumably they listen to this kind of Dharma whether they are asleep or awake; in the retinue of the Saṃbhoga-kāya.]

69. Chap. X, at 257-4-6,7, has some further description: with his left hand holds a blue lotus upon which is a *vajra;* has lower garment of silk and cotton, upper garment of satin.

70. B-comm. 144-2-4, explains the name Jālinīprabha ('netted light') as having continuous rays connected one to one in 'netted' fashion. Chap. X at 257-4-8, he holds in hand either a jewel net or a hook (*aṅkuśa*); while Chap. XIII at 264-5-8, his *mudrā* is the hook.

71. Chap. XIII at 265-1-1: The seal of Keśinī is the curved sword. That of Upakeśinī is the trident. That of Citrā is a staff. That of Vasumatī is a banner. That of Ākarṣaṇī is a hook.
72. Apparently the retinue of Jālinīprabha is that of Chap. XIII at 264-5-8: the youth Ratnamukuṭa, his *mudrā* Ratna; the youth Vimalaprabha, his *mudrā* an unopened lotus. See Raoul Birnbaum, *Studies on the Mysteries of Mañjuśrī* (Society for the Study of Chinese Religions, Monograph No. 2, 1983), p. 79, for the eight 'youths' placed in the directions, Ākarṣiṇī, and so on, beginning with South; with Vimalaprabha found in the East.
73. Chap. X at 257-5-1, adds more detail: hair bound up with golden color and having a crown; Chap. XIII at 265-1-3: he sits in a fire circle.
74. Chap. XIII at 256-1-4: The *mudrā* of Āścarya is a pot which is a one-pointed vajra.That of Abhayaṃdada is hand with 'confidence-giving' gesture. Sarvapayajaha's hand is as though with a fire pulled upwards. Paritrāṇāśayamati's hand is held at chest. Maitryabhyudgata's hand holds a flower. Karuṇāmṛditamati has his hand at his heart with middle finger inwards. Sarvadāhapraśamita's hand shows the *varada* gesture, and from his fingers drips a stream of water. Acintyamati holds a cintāmaṇi in his hand.
75. B-comm. 143-5-2, reads instead of *ṅes pa* ('certainty'), *dga'ba* ('delight'), namely, in his gate of liberation. His 'forbearance' of three kinds: of the profound Dharma, of suffering, of harm (toward himself) inflicted by other. The 'jewels' (four) are the forbearances and the 'delight'. Chap. X at 257-5-2, adds description: the color of his body is green (*ljaṅ-ku*); hand holds a lotus; he is decorated with all adornments. Chap. XIII at 265-1-7 adds that he dwells in the earth-*maṇḍala*; on top of his seat is a large lotus; his seat has all colors and is warm; surmounting it is a large banner, at the top of which one places a great jewel.
76. Chap. XIII at 265-2-1: Ratnākara's *mudrā* is a trident. Ratnapāṇi has a one-pointed vajra. Dhāraṇīṃdhara has a two-mouthed vajra. Ratnamudrāhasta's *mudrā* is a five-pointed vajra. Dṛdhādhyāśaya has crossed-vajra. Each one of them is seated individually on a jewel.
77. V-A-T, Chap. XIII ('The Secret Maṇḍala') at 265-2-3 adds: "He is seated on a large white-lotus seat in the water-*maṇḍala*; and has excellent sharp teeth". The placement of deities in elements according to their color shows that Ākāśagarbḥa is white in color to be situated in the white water-circle. But his retinue (see n. 78, below) is located in the wind-*maṇḍala*! Perhaps the *'garbha'* of Ākāśagarbha is a 'womb' of the winds.
78. Chap. XIII at 265-2-4, on the seals (*mudrā*) of the retinue: Gaganāmala, in the wind-*maṇḍala,* has a wheel with marks. Gaganamati in the middle of that *maṇḍala* has a conch. Viśuddhimati has a white lotus and sits in the middle of the wind-*maṇḍala*. Caritamati in the midst of the wind-*maṇḍala* has a conch upon which is a blue lotus (*utpala*). Sthirabodhi has a vajra and is seated on a lotus.
79. Once my Sanskrit teacher at the University of California, Professor Murray B. Emeneau explained to me that this fig has its flowers inside, where they are not visible, except (metaphorically) to the (six-footed) wasp that crawls inside through the tiny aperture.
80. The apparent logic of the verse is that sentient beings do not crave the Dharmadhātu, which is of a 'single taste' because they crave diversity, called here 'realms' or 'colors'. Besides, it is a fact that when the sun rises, the world is filled with color. B-comm. 145-5-3, suggests that this very color when employed ritually

can serve as a way to restore the state of unity, and needs for the purpose the empowerment by the syllables, 'A', etc.

81. B-comm. 145-5-6: 'first, white'—white is the nature of the Dharmadhātu 'after that, red'—the compassion to aid sentient beings is red. 'then yellow'—expanding their aim is yellow. 'after that, green'—capability in everything is green. 'Completely internal, black'—harsh rites to tame the demonic; black is said to be completely internal because esoteric.
82. B-comm. 146-1-6, provides the information that the successive increase is by four *aṅguli*.
83. The topic of doorkeepers has some difficulties. B-comm. 146-1-7 says that the doorkeepers for Śākyamuni's hall were already mentioned, These must be the *mahākrodhas* Aparājita and Aparajitā (n. 65, above). Acala and Trailokyavijaya are doubtless doorkeepers of the first rank. Chap. IV names Durdānta and Abhimukha in their *mantras,* and at 251-3-7, 8, calls them doorkeeper (*sgo sruns*). Chap. VI, at 253-3-4, describes them: One should energetically draw them in the *grva* (corners) with furious red eyes, angry threatening gestures: (holding) a trident. However, the text does not specify their direction or rank.
84. B-comm. 146-3-6: 'avoiding the two' means, avoiding apprehension (*grāhaka*) and apprehensible (*grāhya*). 'Great void' is avoiding even the idea that something is void.
85. The four Māras are frequently mentioned in Buddhist literature, and their defeat variously stated. They are (in the order to be treated in this scripture): 'personal-aggregate Māra' (*skandha-māra*), 'son-of-the gods Māra' (*devaputra-m*), 'defilement Māra' (*kleśa-m*), and 'death Māra' (*maraṇa-m*).
86. B-comm. 147-1-1,ff. Having become awakened (*sans*) to the non-arising of dharmas, and so having no apprehension of the personal aggregates, he destroyed the 'personal-aggregate Māra'. Having dropped off the domain of speech, i.e. having dropped off the domain of discursive thought, thus transcending the domain of discursive thought he concretely destroyed the 'son-of-the-gods Māra'. Having negated all fault, thus liberated from defilement, he concretely destroyed the 'defilement Māra'. Lacking cause and conditions—and given that when there is no cause or condition there is no arising, and so no death—he concretely defeated the 'death Māra'. (For more information, see the later section "Chapter V and the preliminary service").
87. B-comm. 147-1-1,ff. Having become awakened (*sans*) to the non-arising of pure reality, i.e. having eliminated the hindrances of the knowable (*jñeya*) and defilement (*kleśa*).
88. For the remark 'free from all elaboration', see verses 59-60, above.
89. B-comm. 147-3-6. The two truths, namely, *paramārtha-satya,* whose nature is voidness; and *saṃvṛti-satya,* the best *siddhi*-s, and the performance of the *homa*-s *śāntika,* etc.
90. B-comm. 147-4-1,ff. This is the Tenth Bodhisattva Stage, called 'Stage of the Prince Regent of the Dharma'. It is called 'Buddhabhūmi' because having the adornments of a 'Buddha land' (*buddhakṣetra*). B-comm. 148-3-3. The chief of the fulfilled bodhisattvas, such as Ārya-Mañjuśrī and others of the Tenth Stage, dwelling in the last (i.e. third) maṇḍala, are Buddhas.
91. The remark "I explained it at that time" refers to the first part of Chapter II, namely, 'The Single Means'.
92. B-comm. 148-4-4, illustrates 'mantras of the Complete Buddhas' by such as *Jinajik.* B-comm. 157-5-3 (on Chap. III): for protection of the sentient realm, the

Bhagavat is called Vidyārāja and uses mantras with the power of Vidyārajñī, to protect, i.e. beings from minor demons; to cover, i.e. from medium demons; and to rescue, i.e. from great demons.

93. B-comm. 148-5-1, points out that other Tantras apply HŪṂ and PHAṬ to other deities than *uṣṇīṣa* ones, so this application to the eight *uṣṇīṣa* is a peculiarity of this Tantra.

94. B-comm. 148-5-6, says that the examples zuṅ(s) ('remember!') and chom zig ('conquer!') are 'quiescent' (hence mantras of the attendants), not fierce, as preseumably are the second group ('stab', kill', and 'tear to pieces') (hence mantras of the Krodha deities).

95. B-comm. 148-5-7, the Śrāvaka mantras are isolated, because they are not related to body places, such as crown of head, i.e. are not imagined in the eye, throat etc.

96. B-comm. 149-2-4, ff. If the Tathāgata had made the mantra-power, then for the sake of sentient beings, he would say, 'Let them be good' or 'Let them be rescued' and all mankind would be good or rescued. But this is not so. The meaning of a mantra comes merely from its pronunciation [i.e. the meaning is the goal (*artha*) of its pronunciation]. For example, we pronounce the word 'fire' when there is the nature of fire that burns, and the mouth does not get burned. Thus, the power of mantras is independent of the Tathāgata. [The idea appears to be that the mantra power of the syllables is independent of persons, but some persons master the syllables, learn to use them for magical purposes. Hence, the Sūtra emphasizes that certain persons, the fit vessels, are empowered by the Tathāgata. Also, this theory of mantra seems opposed to idealistic philosophy, since it accepts the objectivity of the mantra-power, as a real world independent of the person.]

97. B-comm. 150-2-5,ff. Indeed, 'A' suffices to show voidness. But the other syllables are necessary for (constructing) mantras, and they also show voidness. That is why each syllable is a gate of all dharmas, associated with a voidness *samādhi*. There are thirty-two such syllables, beginning with KA. Among them, some teach voidness of all dharmas; some teach voidness of a single area; some teach the way of entering the void.

98. B-comm. 150-3-8, points out that in the Indian language, KHAṂ is said to be *khasama* ('like the sky').

99. B-comm. 150-4-3, *gati* means the six destinies (which are men, gods, etc.), and also the going in the various directions, East, West, etc.

100. B-comm. 150-4-5, atoms are 'amassed' in one entity, and so cannot be (individually) apprehended.

101. B-comm. 150-4-8, 'shade' means 'shadow'. It is not different from the body; in the absence of a body, there is no shadow.

102. B-comm. 150-5-3, 4, in transcription, *jhamara*.

103. B-comm. 150-5-4, in transcription, *ṭakara*.

104. B-comm. 150-5-5, in transcription, *bhiṭhava*.

105. B-comm. 150-5-7,8, in transcription, *ḍhanga*.

106. B-comm. 151-1-2, place means 'receptacle realm' (*bhājana-loka*); and the dharmas have momentary character.

107. B-comm. 151-1-5, realm means the three, realm of desire, realm of form, formless realm.

108. B-comm. 151-1-7, the personal aggregates (*skandha*), and so on, are like foam.

109. B-comm. 151-2-8, (commenting on 'VA' instead of 'BA'), one expresses in words after pondering wordlessly.

110. B-comm. 151-1-8, gestation means in the three realms; and means the five personal aggregates. [This is the tenth member of Dependent Origination.]
111. B-comm. 151-2-2, since the dharmas do not arise, one cannot apprehend their death.
112. B-comm. 151-2-3, 4, having abandoned the dharmas like a boat (or, raft), i.e. having comprehended dharmas as void, one enters a vehicle, and that vehicle also is not apprehended.
113. B-comm. 151-2-5, 'dust' means defilement.
114. B-comm. 151-2-6, 'character' means constructed (*saṃskṛta*) and unconstructed (*asaṃskṛta*) characters.
115. B-comm. 151-3-3, the sense organs are naturally dull (i.e. thoughtless, unintelligent). [But how the word *jhaṣa* ('fish', and so on) comes to mean 'sense' organs is a mystery.]
116. B-comm. 151-3-5, 'truth' is both conventional (*saṃvṛti*) and absolute (*paramārtha*).
117. B-comm.151-3-7, regarding the five nasals: the nasal *ṅa* controls the set of syllables KA, etc. *ña* controls the set of GA, etc. *na* controls the set of TA, etc. Since they (the five nasals) control the *samādhis* of the (32) syllables taken in sets, they are said to control all *samādhis*.
118. B-comm. 151-5-4: After *samādhi* there is the 'after-attainment' (*pṛṣṭhalabdha*), the fruit, to benefit sentient beings.
119. B-comm. 152-2-1, ff. mentions the topics that go under the heading of 'maṇḍala requisites': *Samādhi* of offering, namely, 1. offering with folded hands, 2. offering with love (*maitrī*), or 3. compassion (*karuṇā*); 4. the perfume, flowers, etc. going with mundane offering—which are the V-A-T's (Secret Maṇḍala, 263-1-3) four kinds of offering; protection of the maṇḍala, installing the deities of the maṇḍala. Hence, Vajrapāṇi had asked for information on all these topics. B-comm. then states that some of this information is presented in the present chapter, some in the chapter on turning the wheel of syllables, some in the chapter on the secret maṇḍala. And that the reader should add the explanations of the latter two chapters to the present explanations.
120. B-comm. 152-3-2. The hierophant (*ācārya*) of the deep and broad conviction may chiefly offer with his mind. The disciples who are *'dmigs pa can'*(apprehend outwardly), so as to fix them in their mind, will make external offerings.
121. B-comm. 152-5-7,8 treats this verse, but does not clarify the meaning of being a 'minor' (*phal pa*) deity, so we may conclude that such a deity is in the retinue of a chief deity.
122. B-comm. 152-2-8,ff., these are the seals of the three 'linkages' (*samaya*) the 'inception mind of enlightenment','continuation mind (of enlightenment)', and 'rising mind', which respectively go with the fruitional inexhaustible Body, inexhaustible Speech, and Inexhaustible Mind of the Bhagavat, as explained in B-comm. 206-4-7,8 on V-A-T, Chap. XXVII ('practice of the three Samaya').
123. B-comm. 174-5-2,3 (on V-A-T, Chap. XI, 'The Mudrā'): the *mudrā* of the void Dharmadhātu is called Dharmacakra. When turning it, Vajrasattva empowers it, so Vajrasattva is called 'Illustrious Supreme' (*śri-parama, T. dpal mchog*). For making the *mudrā* of turning the wheel of the Dharma, see E.Dale Saunders, *Mudrā* (London, 1960), pp. 94-95.

124. B-comm. 175-1-5,6: '*mudrā* of all the Buddhas' is called 'Mahāmudrā of Uṣṇīṣa'. Tying it is an identification with the Body of a Buddha. This *mudrā* appears to be the one described in the *Trisamayarājasādhanam (Sādhanamālā,* Vol. I, p. 9): "Then he should bind the 'Uṣṇīṣa of lustre all around' which encompasses all *mudrā*-s: With both hands open (*uttāna*) and extended equally, the two ring fingers turned toward the middle of the hands, their two fingernails alongside, one should bend the two thumbs with their tips at the two fingernails."

125. B-comm. 153-3-7,8: Having recited the pledges, and tied the seals, by their empowerment, the 'eye of knowledge' (*jñānacakṣus*) arises, by which he sees the disciple's head shining (in the manner of the verse).

126. A. Wayman's article, "The Ritual in Tantric Buddhism of the Disciple's Entrance into the Maṇḍala", *Studia Missionalia,* Vol. XXII, 1974, pp. 41-57, cites various sources about the throwing of the flower along with the implication of where it falls, and attendant symbolism.

127. B-comm. 153-5-4,5, explains that 'first maṇḍala means the third maṇḍala (i.e. third rank— 'first' encountered); and that the preceptor places the disciple in the doorway (which must be the Eastern one, since direction is not mentioned); so 'between two gates' must mean: between the two sides of the doorway.

128. B-comm. 154-1-3. He performs the 'appeasing' *homa*(called *śāntika).*

129. The terminology garbha-maṇḍala is used for the inner maṇḍala, or the first rank.

130. For 'inner hearth' see our subsequent chapter, Study of the Homa Chapter, part on the 'inner *homa*'.

131. B-comm. 154-2-2, 'twenty-one' means repeating the formulas 21 times. [See n. 30, above, regarding recitation 21 or 108 times. Also, there is the conclusion of the *Vajravidāraṇa-nāma-dhāraṇī* (basic Kriyā Tantra scripture of Vajrapāṇi in the Tibetan Kanjur, Tantra section); "Oh king, ever cleanse yourself by reciting the Vajravidāraṇa either 21 times, or 108 times!"]

132. B-comm. 154-4-2, ff., mentions that there are three topics: (1) what is the name of the one initiated? (2) to whom is the initiation conferred? (3) why is one initiated? (1) It is called the *ācārya's* initiation. (2) It is conferred only on the superior disciples who have taken the necessary pledges, who have learned the mantras and mudrā-s, who are practiced in the rites of *śantika*, etc. to dispel demons, who are mature in asking appropriate questions about the maṇḍala, etc.; and the initiation is conferred to their bodies. (3) One is initiated so the person's *dharma*-eye does not toss about (i.e. is firmed). B-comm. 182-2-4, ff. (on Chap. XIII,'The Secret Maṇḍala') enlarges the discussion to initiation in the three kinds of maṇḍala (cf. n. 6, above). Initiation in both the Mahākaruṇāgarbhodbhava-maṇḍala (i.e. body) and the maṇḍala of whirling the wheel of syllables (i.e. speech) requires the *ācārya* and the disciple, along with mudrā and rites. Initiation in the Secret Maṇḍala is conferred by the mind.

133. B-comm. 155-3-8 (end) ff., as to the four Vajradhara in the corners, they are the Tathāgata's merits (*guṇa*): Gaganāmala—the range of voidness like the sky, which has eliminated the hindrances of knowable and defilement. Vimalanetra—wise in avoiding the apprehending and apprehensible, and the hindrances of knowable and defilement. Citravāsadhṛk—has shame of, because covered with garment, refrains from anything shameful, and practices with propriety. [B-comm. omits Niṣprapañcavihārin ('who dwells in non-elaboration'), but see verses 59-60 for the Sūtra's description.]

134. B-comm. 155-4-5 (mid), ff., these Bodhisattvas are the merits (*guṇa*) of thusness (*tathatā*), and possess either the aim for oneself or for others; and by dint of

aspiration have the initiation 'King of the Dharma'. Dhāraṇiśvararāja—King of Insight (*Prajñā*). *Smṛtiprajanyin*—that *prajñā* having the nature of Nirvāṇa without fixed abode, and which is uninterruptedly in sentient beings. Hitādhyāśayin—the wish to benefit sentient beings by dint of compassion. Kāruṇya—the wish to benefit sentient beings. The first two are the perfection of one's own aim; the last two the perfection of others' aim.

135. B-comm. 155-5-2 (end), ff., the attendants are also the merits of Thusness: *Cittaviśeṣacarita—whose nature is knowing the minds of others [the supernormal faculty called 'knowing the make-up of others' minds']. *Kāmaniṣpati—who fulfills the hopes of sentient beings. *Asakta and *Vimukti—having the nature of voidness and (respectively) unattached and liberation; both being merits of the result (*phala*). The first two are the nature of cause (*hetu*).

136. B-comm. 155-5-5,'inconceivable form of the Dharmadhātu': the syllable RA of the Dharmadhātu, colored white and placed in the *garbha* of the lotus.

137. B-comm. 155-5-6: The pots are of gold, silver, ruby, emerald, and are decorated with gold and silver.

138. B-comm. 156-1-3, at first one employs the mantra of Sarvāpayajaha and sprinkles, so that they may avoid evil destiny. Next, with the mantra of Sarvanīvaraṇaviṣkambin, so that they may become free of the knowable and defilement hindrances. Third, with the mantra of Samantabhadra, so that they may attain the rank of Samantabhadra. Fourth, with the mantra of Maitreya, so that they may become prince regents. [As to the mantras, I have employed the V-A-S, Peking Kanjur, 250-5,4,5,7; Bu-ston, Vol. Pha, *Rnam snaṅ mṅon byaṅ gi dkyil chog,* f. 23b-5,f. 28a-6,7,f. 28.b-1; and the *kokuyaku Issaikyo, Mikkyōbu* p. 87; as follows: Sarvāpayajaha's mantra—Namaḥ samantabuddhānām Āḥ buddharasatva dhātum svāhā. Sarvanīvaraṇaviṣkambin's mantra—Namaḥ samantabuddhānām Āḥ sattvahitābhyudgata traṃ traṃ raṃ raṃ svāhā. Samantabhadra's mantra—Namaḥ Samantabuddhānāṃ samantānugata viraja dharma-nirjāta mahāṃaha svāhā. Maitreya's mantra—Namaḥ samantabuddhānām ajitaṃjaya sarvasattvāśayānugata svāhā.]

139. B-comm. 155-2-2, says that now, although the Sūtra does not mention it, the preceptor should bless the disciple with *mudrā*-s and *mantra*-s of the Tathāgata's *uṣṇīṣa*, eye, tongue, and armor. [These mantras are included at the end of V-A-S, II. The *mudrā*-s are illustrated in the work *Si-do-in dzou,* tr. from Japanese into French, first published in the old series of *Musee Guimet, Annales,* Tome huitième 1899; and reprinted with title *Japanese Mudras* (New Delhi, 1973): the invisible *Uṣṇīṣa* (no. 68, p. 40); the eyes of compassion (no.73, p. 44); the tongue (no. 81, p. 48); the armor (no. 80, p.48).]

140. This popular verse is available in Sanskrit, included among the eighteen edited from a Nepalese work that cites them (without source mentioned) from this Chap. II; I present them above in my introductory chapter on composition of the V-A-S and its influence. As the verse is employed in the *Guhyasmāja* initiations 'of the flask', it occurs in the 'initiation of the mirror', for which one may refer to A.Wayman, *The Buddhist Tantras* (New York, 1973), pp. 68-70. As cited in that tradition, the verse has the option of 'the Jinas' (i.e. the Buddhas) as agent to remove the 'film of ignorance': while the verse as I edited it has 'I' (the preceptor speaking) as the agent.

141. B-comm. 157-3-1. Those born from the mouth, enter by way of the Tathāgata, namely, on the stage of 'action by faith', and so on. Those born from the heart (*lhums* 'womb'), practice in conformity with the Tathāgata.

142. B-comm. 157-3-2,3. The Tathāgata need not be involved, because the Tathāgata's retinue acts on behalf of sentient beings.
143. B-comm. 157-3-8, says this gem is the *cintāmaṇi* (wish-granting gem).
144. B-comm. 157-4-8, says that 'pure' here means free from the knowable and defilement hindrances.
145. See n. 92, above, for data on this Vidyārajñī.
146. The four basic transgressions are in verses 238-239, above, namely: (1) to reject the Illustrious Dharma; (2) to abandon the Mind of Enlightenment; (3) to have envy; (4) to harm sentient beings. B-comm. 158-2-2, however, says 'Dharma of the wise ones' is of two kinds, the 'Dharma of the school' (*lugs kyi chos*) and the 'Dharma of attainment' (*thob pa 'i chos*) (for which see n. 68, above). To not transgress the one of the 'school' is not to reject the Illustrious Dharma and not to violate the pledges (*samaya*). To not transgress the one of 'attainment' is not to abandon the mental orientation toward the 'intrinsic maṇḍala'. (For this maṇḍala, see n. 19, above.)
147. B-comm. 158-2-3,4, says this is the 'entrance' (*jug pa*), and involves voidness (*śūnyatā*).
148. B-comm. 148-2-4, this is the 'dwelling' (*gnas pa)*, namely, in the five wisdoms or as the body of Vajrasattva.
149. B-comm. 158-2-5, attired in the armor of 'great love' (*mahāmaitrī*) that all sentient beings should be happy.
150. B-comm. 158-2-5, to remove the bandage over the disciple's eye, so he may enter to see the maṇḍala.
151. B-comm. 158-2-6, which arises from the purity of the Tathāgata's morality (*śīla*).
152. B-comm. 158-2-6,7, which arise from the merits of Mahāmaitrī.
153. B-comm. 158-2-7, which arises from the merits of Wisdom, consistent with the Dharmadhātu, that burns up defilement.
154. B-comm. 158-2-8, which arises from the blazing light of Tathāgata wisdom that spreads far in the sky.
155. B-comm. 158-2-8, arises from being equal and unequal to the sky of the pure Dharmadhātu.
156. B-comm. 158-3-1, which is invisible on top of the Tathāgata's head, and arises from the limitless like the sky.
157. B-comm. 158-3-2, which arises from the burning up of the defilement and knowable hindrances by the blazing Wisdom (*jñāna*) of the path that attains Thusness.
158. B-comm. 158-3-3, which arises from the burning up of those two hindrances by the blazing Insight (*prajñā*) of the same path.
159. B-comm. 158-3-4, which arises from abiding in the Dharma of true words.
160. B-comm. 158-3-4, points out that the *mantras* for the Tathāgata's eye, *uṣṇīṣa,* etc. occur in the Mudrā chapter along with *mudrā*-s. After the disciple is sprinkled during the initiation, he is to combine these *mantras with mudrā*-s.

PART IV

MEDITATION AND RITUAL

10. CHAPTER V AND THE PRELIMINARY SERVICE

My earlier section "Buddhaguhya's commentary on the V-A-T" pointed out that the extant version of B-comm. in Tibetan translation lacks commentary on V-A-T, Chap. V, which has an importance far exceeding its few verses, fifteen. B-comm.'s exposition of this chapter is presumed to have been present in the original Sanskrit, but lost in the Tibetan version due to vicissitudes of textual transmission from the early period of Tibetan Buddhism. However, I pointed out from B-comm. that the theory of the four members of muttering are initially presented in Chap. V, that a further treatment is in Chap. VI (on fulfilment of *siddhi*), and a still further one in Chap. XVII (on the *vidyā-vrata*). Therefore, materials in those two later chapters can be employed to help explain Chap. V. Before proceeding to these additional materials, it is well to point out that Chap. V presents the theory for mundane magical success, such as prosperity; while Chap. VI goes into the theory of supramundane success, i.e. enlightenment. Besides, the theory of six months of preliminary service, first expounded in Chap. V, is a theory of service that precedes the initiation in any one of the three *maṇḍalas,* namely of Body, of Speech, and of Mind. Clearly, the preliminary service for the initiation into the *maṇḍala* of Mind (the Secret *maṇḍala*) requires the supramundane interpretation of the six elements, among which the first five are correlated with five syllables, A, VA, RA, HA, KHA. Therefore, it should be understood that in the following whenever there is mention of these five syllables, there is implication of supramundane purpose. As long as this is kept in mind, the materials help to explain Chap. V in the light that B-comm.'s commentary is unfortunately lacking. Hence, I now draw from the extensive B-comm. on Chap. VI's *mantra* A VĪRA HUṂ KHAṂ, which stands for defeating the four Māras and attaining enlightenment. B-comm. relates the five syllables A, VA, RA, HA, KHA to the five elements, first at B-comm. 163-3-8 for defeat of the Māras, and next at B-comm. 163-5-1 as a general statement of the correlation. I shall reverse the order.

Here, then, is the general statement, useful for relating the five elements to the first five months of a six-month drill, B-comm. 163-5-1,ff: The personal aggregates (*skandha*), being dense, can carry a burden,[1] and earth, being dense, can also carry it; from 'A'[2] is the earth-*maṇḍala.* Now, imagination, and so on, is a kind of dirt, and water washes this, so from 'VA' is the water-*maṇḍala.*[3] Fire burns away everything, so from 'RA' which negates all the defilement powder,[4] comes the fire *maṇḍala*. The syllable 'HA' being the *samādhi* that all *dharmas* lack a cause; and the wind dispersing (or, scattering) and [thus eliminating the concatenation of causes],[5] and destroying—from 'HA' is the wind-*maṇḍala*. Finally, from 'KHA' comes the space-*maṇḍala*, and this is the general meaning of the foregoing four (i.e. pervades them).

Here is the special interpretation going with the Māras. B-comm. 163-3-8 presents the syllables for overcoming the four Māras: 'A' being the *samādhi* realizing that all *dharmas* are immemorially non-arising; and 'all *dharmas*' being the personal aggregates (*skandha*), realms (*dhātu)*, and sense bases (*āyatana*)—it follows that non-apprehending destroys the 'personal aggregate Māra'; 'VA' being the *samādhi* that all *dharmas* have dropped off the 'path of speech'; and 'path of speech' being discursive thought (*vikalpa*)—it follows that the realization of non-discursive thought and not imagining time, destroys the 'son-of-the-gods Māra'. 'RA' being the fire negating defilements (*kleśa*), and realizing that all *dharmas* are like powder (specks), i.e. defiled—it follows that burning the powder (specks) destroys the 'defilement Māra'. 'HA' being the *samādhi* realizing the cause and result of all *dharmas,* namely, that *karma* and life (*āyus*) arise in what is defiled, it follows that when defilement does not arise, neither does *karma* or *āyus;* and by lacking *āyus* death does not occur. So realizing, one destroys the 'death Māra'. 'KHA' being the *samādhi* that all dharmas are like the sky (or, space), it makes the foregoing four syllables equivalent to realizing voidness (*śūnyatā*).

The V-A-T in Chap. V alludes to a tantric practice on the highest level of importance in these cults. It has to do with imagining a spot or 'ground' (Tib. *gzhi*) in the performer and then imagining a comparable 'ground' in the deity. Chap. V alludes to the praxis called 'preliminary service' which is generally held to take six months. It implies a Buddhist doctrine that man is composed of six elements, earth, water, fire, wind, space and *vijñāna*(meaning: 'understanding').[6] The 'preliminary service' involves the recitation of '100 syllables' in a strenuous practice called in V-A-T, Chap. XVII, the '*vidyā-vrata*' conducted at the *samādhis*—sunrise, sunset, etc. Now, 'preliminary service' means the preliminary to each one of three *maṇḍalas*—of Body, Speech, and Mind; and so the focus of the 'preliminary service', necessarily changes in accordance with which one of the three *maṇḍalas* it is the preliminary. For the difference, see the comment cited below just prior to V-A-T, Chap. V, verse 4cd; in brief, it has to do with what one imagines on the moon-disk in one's heart: in the case of body-preliminary, one imagines there the body of one of the Tathāgatas; in the case of the Speech-preliminary, one imagines there the syllable (of that deity); in the case of the Mind-preliminary, one imagines the gnosis body there as the Dharmakāya. After the 'preliminary service' one proceeds to realizing one or other of the Body, Speech, or Mind *maṇḍalas*, but these must be realized in the given sequence of those three, Body, and so on, because the Mind-*maṇḍala* is the highest attainment.

The preceding *samādhis* using the five syllables, 'A', etc., take care of five months of 'preliminary service', but there are actually six *samādhis*, the sixth one being by the element of man called *vijñāna* (understanding).[7] The six *samādhis* are intimated in V-A-T. Chap. II, v. 167-168ab, by six statements:[8]

"I have comprehended 'non-arising'":	Ist month, *samādhi* on earth;
"have dropped off the domain of speech":	2nd month, *samādhi* on water;
"negated all fault":	3rd month, *samādhi* on fire;
"lack cause and conditions":	4th month, *samādhi* on wind;
"have the knowledge of voidness":	5th month, *samādhi* on space;
"and freed from all darkness":	6th month, *samādhi* by vijñāna.

The five elements are first mentioned in V-A-T, Chap. I, where each of these elements serves as a simile for omniscience (*sarvajñajñānam)*. Thus, omniscience, like space, does not imagine, neither inquires nor deliberates. Like earth, it sustains worldly beings, along with gods, men, and demi-gods. Like fire, it is unwearied by burning all the ignorant fuel. Like wind, it dispels all the ignorant powder specks. Like water, it refreshes the world along with the gods. In Chap. I, however, it is 'omniscience' which is being pointed to, and the elements do not appear with the import they have in subsequent Chapters of V-A-T.

Here I shall present a translation of Chap. V. Besides information drawn from B-comm. on Chap. VI, and V-A-T, Chap. XVII, I shall also have comments drawn from a brief Tantra called *Dhyānottarapaṭalakrama,* which enjoys a generously long commentary by Buddhaguhya. The *Dhyānottarapaṭalakrama* (abbreviated D-P-K), in the lost Sanskrit original probably only three Sanskrit folios, is located in the Tibetan Kanjur in the generalities section of the Kriyā-tantra.[9] It has verses and topics overlapping V-A-T, Chap. V, verses 1-5, as Buddhaguhya explicitly notices in his commentary, which I call 'D-P-K- comm.'[10] On that account, we might speculate that it should be considered as a 'continuation Tantra' (Uttaratantra) for the V-A-T, since the last of the admitted 'continuation Tantra' chapters of the V-A-T has verses in common with the V-A-T, 'Tathāgata' chapter. Besides, the words '*paṭalakrama*' in the D-P-K title is how the chapters of V-A-T are called. However, Tibetan textual tradition did not admit the D-P-K as a 'continuation Tantra' for the V-A-T, because D-P-K-comm., 73-2-5,6, refers to the lost **Vajroṣṇīṣa-tantra* and the *Dhyānottara* in a manner as though the D-P-K is either a part of or a continuation of, that Tantra; and explains the *uttara* part of the D-P-K title as the *prāṇāyāma*.

In the following translation of V-A-T, Chap. V, I shall italicize this throughout to distinguish it from other cited materials.

> *Then the Bhagavat announced to the Bodhisattva Vajrapāṇi: "Master of the secret ones, listen to how mantras are worked upon, and to what be the fruit of being worked upon."*
>
> 1. *The letter (akṣara) is added to the unchanging (a-kṣara).*[11] *Likewise, from the ground (gži) to the ground. For controlling the mind, one should recite (the syllable) a hundred thousand times.*
>
> 2. *The unchanging (a-kṣara) is the Mind of Enlightenment. The second one (i.e. the letter) is the sound. The 'ground' is the depositing of one's presiding deity, enacted in a place of one's body.*
>
> 3ab. *The second 'ground' is the Complete Buddha, known as best of the two-footed ones.*

D-P-K, 53-3-4,5:

The unchanging *(a-kṣara)* possesses the syllable *(akṣara)*. From the ground, in like manner, to the ground. Who surveys for one's own *mantra*, should imagine the purity of the mind.

D-P-K, 53-3-4:

Immerse yourself in the sound, the mind, and the ground! Place the *mantra* in the unchanging ground! Recite the *Mantra* without loss of the (four) members. When tired, take rest in yourself!

D-P-K-comm. 73-3-1,ff. refers to the above verse 2 of V-A-T, Chap. V, to explain what are the four members which are (1) the first ground, oneself identified with the deity; (2) the second ground, the Tathāgata; (3) the mind which is the Mind of Enlightenment; (4) the sound, which is the letter. Ibid., 73-4-8, the 'sound' is the garland of *mantra*-letters. Ibid., 73-5-6, as to the 'ground', there is the 'ground of thought (*citta*) and mentals (*caitta*) of oneself and of the other being; there is the 'ground' by way of sense object and basis; or the 'ground' for dawning of recognition of the form of male, etc. Ibid., 74-1-7,8: When one imagines the body of maturation (one's physical body) with the appearance of illusion, mirage, and so on, this is referred to with the words "take rest in yourself."

3cd-4ab. *The mantrin should contemplate a pure moon disk placed therein. One well arranges in its middle according to the sequence of the letters.*

D-P-K, 53-4-2,3:

The subtlety placed in the heart is a pure moon-disk. Upon it, very quiet, is the good light of a fire-tongue. Having placed it there on the unchanging ground, one dwells happily contemplating the sound; or placing the letter in the unchanging, one should imagine only the letter itself.

D-P-K-comm., 74-3-7: There are two kinds of mental purity, viz. (1) non-arising of the defiled impurities of lust, etc. attended with mental wandering; (2) in the phase of the moon-disk, the conventionally immaculate appearance. Ibid., 74-1-6, as to the moon-disk, one imagines thereon the body of one of the Tathāgatas; or imagines thereon the body of one's presiding deity; or imagines thereon the letter of that (deity); or imagines there the sound of that (letter); or imagines in its sound the gnosis body of the deity; or the imagining of the gnosis body is the imagining of it as the Dharmakāya; and that is called the 'non-apprehending self-reality'.

4cd. *One should restrain by way of repeated words, and should purify the prāṇa and āyāma.*

5. *Prāṇa is explained as 'wind'; āyāma is 'stretching unto' (in mind). Having restrained both of them, one should well perform the preliminary service.*

D-P-K, 53-3-5:

Drawing back by reiteration (Tib. *slar sdud*), the mind restrains the *prāṇa* and *āyāma*. The one who knows the *mantra* should multiply the *mantra*, and should start the mental muttering.

D-P-K-comm. 74-5-2,3: The person who is not yet equipoised (*samāhita*), by reiteration (of the *mantra*) draws back the mind from outer objects. Ibid., 73-1-3: "*Prāṇa* is the wind (*vāyu*) characterized as issuing from, and entering, the eyes, ears, nostrils, mouth, navel, male and female sex organs, the unclean orifice, the pores of head hair and body hair." "Restraining it means in the present context, preventing the ingress and exit." Ibid., 73-1-1: re the *āyāma* (the stretching of the mind unto external objects), its restraint is by the 'one-pointedness' of mind, also called *samādhi*; and *samādhi* restrains both *prāṇa* and *āyāma*. Ibid., 74-5-7: It is 'mental muttering' because expressed by the mind and discursive thought (*kalpanā*). Ibid., 74-5-7: Or (as authorized by D-P-K) the *mantra* may be whispered.

6ab. *Then the mantrin should restrain for a month, while performing the recitation.*

V-A-T, Chap. XVII, 266-4-1,2:

Dwelling in the earth-*maṇḍala* by the given-thing of earth (*mahendra*), he makes the seal (*mudrā*) of *vajrin*, and continually drinks milk as food. Restraining the *prāṇa* and *āyāma*, the mantrin recites for a month.

6cd. *The preliminary praxis of mantras is from one's ground to enter another one.*

7. *All the renowned Buddhas have explained the preliminary praxis. Later, one offers a bit of flowers, incense, etc.*

8. *So as to attain Buddhahood, at that time one should offer (himself) to enlightenment. The mantrin, fearless, of such type, should recite for a second month.*

V-A-T, Chap. XVII, 266-4-2,3:

Occupied with water-*maṇḍala*, while making the mudrā of lotus, during that time he drinks water as food.

B-comm. 193-2-8, ff. (abbreviated): In the first month the *mantrin* is occupied with the earth-*maṇḍala* in the lower part of his body. In the second month is occupied with the water-*maṇḍala* above that. In succeeding months is occupied with the next higher element, fire, then the next higher one, wind.

V-A-T, Chap. XVII, 266-4-3:

Then in the third month he immerses himself in the area of fire. He subsists on food that is not taken. Exhibiting the *mudrā* of sword, he burns up all the sins that arise from body, speech, and mind.

V-A-T, Chap. XVII, 266-4-3,4:

In the fourth (month) he is occupied with wind, and continually feeds on wind for food. Meanwhile he ties the *mudrā* of wheel; and while equipoised, recites the *mantra*.

V-A-T, Chap. XVII, 266-4-4,5:

Then in the fifth month he rejects receipt and non-receipt; and the illustrious one, devoid of any clinging at all, is like a Complete Buddha.

V-A-T, Chap. XVII, 266-5-1,2:

Having completed six months he attains as fruit the desired *siddhi* (occult power or success); and thereafter is a continual benefit to himself and others.

B-comm. 197-5-6,7, introducing the five chapters on '100 syllables' shows that five nasals govern five sets of letters used in the 'preliminary service'. The following tabulation clarifies the distribution in the five months of service:[12]

	(Earth)	(Water)	(Fire)	(Wind)	(Space)
Velar series	K	KH	G	GH	Ṅ
Palatal series	C	CH	J	JH	Ñ
Retroflex series	Ṭ	ṬH	Ḍ	ḌH	Ṇ
Dental series	T	TH	D	DH	N
Labial Series	P	PH	B	BH	M

These of course amount to 25. They are multiplied by four (A, Ā, AṂ, AḤ) to make one hundred. So presumably for first month, involved with earth, KA, KĀ, KAṂ, KAḤ; and so on, to make a set of twenty; and those under the four elements are also '*dharma* gates', as in V-A-T, Chap. II, each with its reason as a gate. Since this service accounts for just the first five months, the sixth month is left over to manifest clearly whatever be the praxis fruits to go with the scriptural phrase "am freed from all darkness". The contemplation during the first five months is interiorized, while the fruit in the form of *siddhi* in the sixth month is exteriorized, as is mentioned in part in V-A-T, Secret maṇḍala Chap., p. 262-1-4,5:

/daṅ por sṅags pas dkyil 'khor de /
/raṅ gi lus la dgod byas te /
/rkaṅ ba nas ni chu so la /
/thug gi bar du sa yir bsam //

At the outset the *mantrin* should arrange the *maṇḍala* in his own body. He should imagine the earth (*maṇḍala*) from the feet up to the belly (*chu so*).

/ de nas goṅ du sñiṅ ka'i bar /
/ sdom brtson can gyis chu yir bsam /
/ chu/yi yan chad me ru ste /
/ me yi yan chad rluṅ yin no //

Next the devoted one should imagine the water (*maṇḍala*) up to the heart. What is beyond the water *(maṇḍala)* is with fire. Beyond fire is wind.

/ bsams nas de nas mkhas pa yis /
/ sa la gzugs brñan bzag par bya //

Having so contemplated [in *samādhi*], the wise one will dispose a reflected image on the ground.

B-comm. on this, p. 178-1-7, points out that each of the elements is marked with the associated syllable, starting with "A" for earth. (speaking of the interiorized series), B-comm., 178-2-3, mentions that the syllable HŪṂ is placed between the eyebrows, thus going

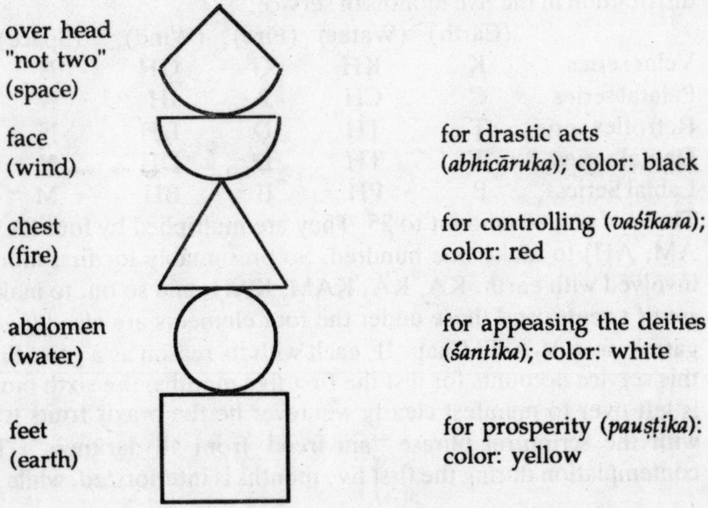

with wind (as in the 'Reality of the Ācārya' Chap.) (leading us to suppose that the syllable HA for wind is reserved for the exterior case). Each of these *maṇḍalas* is associated with a geometrical form used for the 'burnt offering', whether interior or exterior. Since these are four in number, this must be the reason that the scripture mentions only the four element *maṇḍala* as placed within the body, and then to be reflected outwards in the outer 'burnt offering' (*homa*); and does not mention the fifth one, 'space' (*ākāśa*), which is not reflected outwards. These traditional associations of geometrical forms with the elements are preserved in manuals of the Shingon school of Japan, namely, earth—square; water—circle; Fire—triangle; wind—half-moon (or bow); space—bowl with surmounting triangle vertices; all five representing the body as a *stūpa:*[13]

B-comm. 159-2-6,ff. on Chap. III, gods of yellow color go with the earth-*maṇḍala:* of white color with the water-*maṇḍala;* of red color with the fire-*maṇḍala*; of blue or black color with the wind-*maṇḍala*. Some gods, like the Green Tārā, have all colors. V-A-T, Chap.II has: "Master of the secret ones, ṄA, ÑA, ṆA, NA, and MA control all *samādhis*; and being all powerful, they speedily effectuate the needed aims." By their means, in the sixth month, per V-A-T, reflecting the element *maṇḍalas* outward on the ground, one succeeds in prosperity, etç. This show that the title of Chap. V, "Working for the mundane *siddhi*" is correct.

The *siddhis* (magical talents) are expounded in V-A-T, Chap. VI; from its considerable information, there is space here to mention the association with element centers. Thus, V-A-T,VI, 254-3-8,ff:

> So as to accomplish attainments of self, using just his body of 'increasing' (i.e. prosperity), the *mantrin* should stay in the middle of the *maṇḍala,* dwelling in the *samādhi* of the Complete Buddha of shining yellow color and hair tied up with jewel crown—called the 'ground' of earth (*maṇḍala*). These substances, *vajra,* lotus, and sword—likewise explained as 'pure'—whether yellow, master of soil (*kṣitipati*), 'wish-granting gem' (*cintāmaṇi*), and so on, are contemplated and accomplished in the earth (*maṇḍala*).

B-comm. 165-4-5: the earth-*maṇḍala* has the character of '*vajra*'. (This shows that V-A-T alludes to *vajrin,* diamond character, for earth center; lotus for the water one; sword for the fire one; intending also wheel for the wind one.) B-comm. 163-4: five syllables go with the five elements: A—earth; VA—water; RA—fire; HA—wind; KHA—space. B-comm. 165-4-7, the "A" (for the earth center) is of golden color. B-comm. 165-5-3, ff. sets forth the remarkable theory that one can combine these elements, with one in charge, as indicated by its syllable (whether A, VA, RA, HA). Thus, for curing the illness of another, the performer imagines that his "A" using wind (i.e. breath) passes from his body into the body of the other person. In particular, he imagines that his breath and the breath of the other person mingle and become unified. Or he imagines that the "A" coming from the feet pervades the series of eye and other sense organs. (It appears that for various curative methods assumed for the system, one uses this "A" along with the 'water', 'fire', or 'wind'. 'Master of soil' and 'wish-granting gem' are here terms for *siddhis* stemming from the earth-*maṇḍala*).

As to the various types of magical talents (*siddhi*, success), V-A-T, Chap. VI, p. 255-4-7,8, summarizes:

> If one wishes to attain the great waves of wisdom, or else the *siddhis* of the five supernormal faculties *(abhijñā)* or of *vidyādhara,* or of long life and youthfulness, as long as he does not perform the (preliminary) service, for that long he does not attain them.

This means that if one has not done the preliminary service during the five-month period, it will not be possible to obtain the 'success', i.e. the occult powers, that are attributed to the sixth month.

Also, V-A-T, Chap. IX (the brief chapter entitled "Reality of Mundane and Supramundane Recitation") has this summary (256-2-7 to -3-1):

> I have explained the four members (i.e. the ground, the second ground, the letter, the non-changing) by outward and inward praxis. Besides, one should restrain by way of repeated words the incomparable mundane one possessed (of outward object). I teach that the mind which is consistent with the deity has the best whispered recitation, and is possessed of apprehension (of the deity object), (so is) called the "Supramundane mind". (The inward praxis) avoids the repetition, and so on; acts as one with the deity and does not conceive a difference. The indissoluble nature is to be made by the mind. There is no other way to make it.[14]

According to B-comm. on this chapter, 212-1-2, the inward praxis is the signless kind, i.e. is free of the subject-object duality, the apprehension of object (in Tibetan, *dmigs pa can*). The signless praxis is the pure kind. Both the mundane and the supramundane recitation with subject-object duality are the impure kind of praxis. Since Chap. V is devoted to the theory of mundane *siddhi* it sets forth the praxis with subject-object duality, and so in this terminology can be called the 'impure praxis'; but, after all, it portrays the 'preliminary service' of six months. Later, the Reality of the Ācārya chapter will set forth the inward praxis.

9-10. *Then at the time of the full moon, that man should enter upon the 'work'. He should energetically draw the maṇḍala on a mountain peak, place with tracks of cows, temple of the gods, where a waterfall merges with the plain, at a crossroads, secluded room, place of the ma-mo type of goddesses, or a quiet place. And should make all the maṇḍala into a diamond residence.*

V-A-T, Chap. VI, 253-3-2, when making the same statement, has 'solitary tree' (*ekavṛkṣa*) instead of 'secluded room'. The ma-mo goddesses are mentioned in V-A-T, Chap. VI, 253-5-3; and B-comm. 161-3-4, calls them the 'seven mothers (*mātṛkā*)'. V-A-T, Chap. VI, 253-3-3, instead of "should make all the *maṇḍala* into a diamond residence" has "the *maṇḍala* which deranges all the demons", so the 'diamond residence' must be one that repulses all the demons.

11. *Having there performed the protection of the place, he should energetically proceed with the 'work' there at midnight, or else at the time of sunrise.*

According to *Mkhas grub rje's Fundamentals of the Buddhist Tantras*, p. 193, midnight is the time for drastic rites, including the cemetary rituals, while in other periods one performs the appeasing, etc. rites.

12-13. *When he gets omens for such as this ('work'), the wise should recognize it, namely the syllable HŪṂ, sound of a drum, earthquake, gratifying words, as the case may be; or when there is sound from the sky, because of those pure signs, he should recognize mentally the subsequent success.*

14. *The Buddhas, best of the two-footed ones, have rightly proclaimed its fruit. The one who in that way is based in the method of mantra, will certainly become a Buddha.*

15. *Hence, you should remember always the mantra itself in all its aspects. The powerful former Buddhas have also explained that one should remember it.*

11. MANTRA EFFICACY PER V-A-T, CHAP. VI

Chapter VI is one of the most remarkable chapters of the entire V-A-T; and B-comm. is lavish in commentary to bring out the full implications of this chapter to the best of Buddhaguhya's erudition and ability. I have already cited this chapter in the treatment of Chap. V, thereon B-comm.'s explanation of five syllables, including the four about defeating the four Māras. I have pointed out that B-comm.'s commentary on Chap. V is missing. In fact, there are two missing portions of the commentary on Chap. VI;[15] but fortunately B-comm.'s precious comments on mantra efficacy are preserved in the extant version of the Tibetan translation. V-A-T, Chap. VI, goes in the PTI edition from 252-2-6 to 255-5-2, while B-comm.'s, unrevised version in this edition goes from 159-5-2 to 170-2-8. The Chinese version starts its Chap. 7 near the end of the (Tibetan) V-A-T, Chap. VI. In V-A-T, the Chinese Chap. 7 starts at 255-3-3, *de nas dpal ldan rdo rje 'dsin* ("Then the *śrīmat* Vajra-holder"); B-comm. at 169-1-2, *de nas dpal rdo rje 'dsin ces pa nas*.

The previous section on V-A-T, Chap. V, showed that both that chapter and Chap. VI assign the time of the full moon for entering upon such activities as drawing the *maṇḍala*. Why the full moon time? Below, an explanation will be proposed. It has to do with the effect of mantras, which is one of the four features of mantras which B-comm. on Chap. VI mentions at 160-4-6, and following. The four features are their 1. cause (*rgyu,* S. *hetu*), 2. nature (*raṅ bźin,* S. *svabhāva*), 3. power (*mthu,* S. *bala*), and 4. effect or purpose (*'bras bu,* S. *kārya*). Of these, B-comm. says the 'cause' and the 'nature' are always included within the syllables. The 'power' of mantras is here the 'means (*upāya*), with three degrees of ranking: 1. The superior ranking is the power of the 'sons of the gods' in the family of the great lord of the Kāmadhātu (Realm of Desire), and the power arising in the family 'Manojava' (with the speed of mind) among the sons of the great lord of the Rūpadhātu (Realm of Form). The scripture, 252-4-8, states the first kind, in the Kāmadhātu, as the deities around the Paranirmitavaśavartin ('who dominates others by magical manifestations'). B-comm., 161-1-5,6 re the magical faculty *manojavā* (T. *yid mgyogs*): since it accomplishes the aim of sentient beings just by expecting it (*bsam pa tsam gyis sems can gyi doṅ du bya ba*) and confers instantaneously those situations exactly as they are desired, it is called *manojavā* ('the speed of mind'). 2. The middling ranking is the power of mantras that creates hallucinations of the sense organs;

and the illusion-craft (*māyā*) of the Asura-mantras. B-comm. 161-2-4: by 'hallucinatory mantras' is meant those that cause appearances to men, etc. of fine parks, streams, and waterfalls—explained to be the power of Indra's mantras. B-comm., 101-2-7,8 by 'illusion-craft of the Asura-mantras' is meant the illusion-craft of materializing innumerable asuras, and asuras of Rāhu form to scare the devas. 3. The inferior ranking is the power of mantras that creates poison, fever, death, due to the 'mothers' (*mātṛkā*). B-comm., 161-3-5,6: by 'mothers' is meant the seven mothers, going with Indra, Brahmā, etc.[16] They drink the blood (of demons) falling (before the blood meets the earth) caused to issue by reason of sword, and pacify the demonic asuras.[17]

The B-comm. goes to the 'effect' of mantra, saying this at 161-3-7:

> / lha dan lha ma yin du 'thab pa'i tshe / 'jig rten na sems can rnams dge ba spyod pa man źin / bsod nams che na / lha rnams rgyal bar 'gyur / dge ba spyad pa ñuṅ źiṅ mthu chuṅ na / lha ma yin rgyal bar 'gyur te / de la lha rnams rgyal bar-'gyur na / gaṅ zla ba daṅ / spyaṅ kis zin pa' i dṅos grub kyaṅ thob / lha ma rnams rgyal na / sems can gyi khams su / sems can rnams bciṅ bar byed pa'i rims nad rnams kyi sṅags kyi mthu las 'byuṅ bar byad pa' o /. At the time when the gods and not-gods (i.e. demons) are fighting, if the sentient beings of the world have much virtuous practice, are great in merit, the gods win; if their virtuous practice is meager, the (moral) strength low, the demons win. And when the gods are winning, (mantras) gain the success in the dominion of 'moon' and 'wolf'. And when the demons are winning, mantras result within the realm of sentient beings in bondage and severe illness.

As to 'moon' and 'wolf', the moon rules by night when the wolf mainly hunts,[18] so the reference must be to certain lunar phases mainly observed at night. I have been informed[19] that according to Tibetan traditions, the gods and demons fight at the critical moon phases, such as full moon and dark of moon. In India there are a total of eight of these days called 'non-study' (*an-adhyāya*). Of these the dark of the moon (*amāvasyā*), the 'fourteenth' (first day of full moon), and the 'eighth' in the increasing and decreasing phases of the moon are especially pointed to as harassing ('killing') the teacher, the student, or the subject matter. There is some disagreement over which phase harasses which of the three, except for the fourteenth day's disqualification of the pupil, which is agreed upon by the *Manusmṛti* (IV, 114) and by the 'grammarian's tradition'.[20] This theory has enormous significance, because it disallows imparting instruction to the disciple during the three days associated with the full moon. But the *ācārya* is not hindered from drawing the *maṇḍala* on the full-moon day according to the V-A-T. This finding agrees with V-A-T, Chap. II, the first part dealing with the 'single means' which is the drawing of the Mahākaruṇāgarbhodbhava-maṇḍala, having no mention of imparting this information to the disciple; then with the second part, the 'several means' including what is meant to the later initiation of the disciple, the giving of pledges, etc. The theory agrees with the prevalent assignment of Indian festivals to the 'non-study' days; and so by fasting and other practices to help the gods 'win' on those occasions, there is also the prospect of the mantra's success.

Then V-A-T, 252-5-3, states that by power of mantra, one can make fire lose its heat and become cold. And that by such an example, one should derive trusting faith in the power of mantras. V-A-T, 252-5-4, continues:

> / gsaṅ snags kyi mthu de yaṅ gaṅ źe na / gsaṅ sṅags rnams las byuṅ ba ba yan ma yin / rdsas las 'jug pa yaṅ ma yin / sbyor ba po las dmigs pa yaṅ ma yin mod kyi rigs kyi bu dag 'on kyaṅ gsaṅ sṅags kyi byin brlabs kyi chos ñid 'byuṅ ba las 'da' bar yaṅ mi 'gyur te / dus gsum las 'das pa'i phyir daṅ rten ciṅ 'brel bar 'byuṅ ba zab m̄o bsam gyiṣ mi khyab pa las mṅon par grub pa'i phyir ro /.
>
> From what comes the power of mantras? It does not arise from the mantras (themselves). And is not aroused from substances. It is not obtained from the pronouncer. O sons of the family, the *dharmatā* of mantra empowerment is not transcendable, because it transcends the three times; and because it is accomplished through profound, inconceivable dependent origination (*pratitya-samutpāda*).

B-comm. 161-4-6: Since the power of the Buddha is obtained from mantra, neither is it acquired by stealing a book of mantras, nor is it burnt by fire. Hence, the power of mantra does not arise from itself. It is not aroused through substances, such as sword, wheel, or pills........ It has been explained that whether Tathāgatas arise or do not arise, the *dharmatā* of mantras exists and remains. B-comm. 161- 5-5,ff. 'through profound, inconceivable dependent origination', i.e. the empowerment by the *dharmatā* of mantras, there is obtained the 'power' of mantras with three degrees, superior, middling, and inferior.

It was shown in the introductory section on the Dharmadhātu that mantra power is the power of the Dharmadhātu. It was shown above that it works properly if sentient beings of the world have much virtuous practice. Hence, it works if the mantra pronouncer is in a community referred to by the scripture as 'sons of the family'. 'Family' is here the *kula*, the community that empowers the DD.[21] Thus the 'community' is tantamount to a group soul. This position insists that a pronouncer of a mantra cannot succeed by himself, because the scripture states: "It is not obtained from the pronouncer."

V-A-T, Chap. VI, then proceeds to give two important sets of formulas which were presented above in the introductory section on Dharmadhātu (3. Pervading the DD). First, at V-A-T, 253-1-1,2 it gives the four 'heart mantras', A, Ā, AṂ, AḤ. These were explained in brief, that 'A' is enlightenment (*bodhi*), 'Ā' the career (*caryā*), 'AṂ' is the Complete Buddha, and AḤ is Nirvāṇa. B-comm. 162-1-2,ff. has much information about 'A', including at 162-1-8: in an absolute sense, 'A' is thusness (*tathatā*); in a conventional sense, it is the thirty-two characteristics of the great person,........ and the thirty-two syllables of a later chapter can so be regarded. Then, at V-A-T, 254-2-8, there is the important formula A VĪRA HŪṂ ḲHAṂ. B-comm. 163-2-8, starts a lengthy treatment of this mantra, saying, "Now, to explain the performance and stages of the five-syllabled heart-mantra of the great hero—" But curiously the syllables are changed into A, VA, RA, HA, KHA for the explanation in terms of elements and defeat of the four Māras, as I have previously presented them. This form of the five syllables is given by the scripture itself, so B-comm. must follow suit.

The question arises as to the role of the syllables themselves in regard to the identifications, admitting, as was already pointed out, that mantra power does not arise from the mantra itself. According to B-comm. 163-1-1, by 'heart mantras' is meant that one of them, as appropriate, is contemplated on the moon disk imagined in the heart. They are known as 'seed-syllables' (*bīja*). When one contemplates the 'A' on the moon disk, one should be equipoised in voidness, engaged that all *dharmas* are immemorially unborn, and that one's five personal aggregates have never arisen, so that the moon disk and the 'A' dissolve in non-apprehension. Then, aroused from that *samādhi*, by dint of compassion, one (again) contemplates the 'A' in the heart as though it is an illusion. Thereupon, that 'A' radiates, and by bringing back the radiation, one transforms oneself into the form of a deity (the three stages of this were given previously in the section 'Beings and their Minds'). One now imagines that through the 'A' the moon-disk is transformed into the 'seal of-bodhicitta' like a mirror, imagined as clear and vivid. Then one imagines that the 'A' in its middle changes into the body of the Bhagavat Vairocana. According to the scripture, V-A-T, 253-1-8, this is followed by imagining the 'second ground' (*gźi gñis*), i.e. a second Vairocana in front, and in his heart on a mirror-like moon disk the great lotus-king seated—thus one is equipoised in the *samādhi* "like being seated in a cave".[22] On that (second) moon disk one imagines the syllables of the *dhāraṇī* to be recited. (All this) will produce benefit to innumerable sentient beings. Those instructions of the scripture and of B-comm. show that the syllables like 'A' do not in themselves produce what they are identified with (e.g. 'A' is enlightenment), but that they go with a procedure of *samādhi* which if properly pursued will lead to the intended results.

Then V-A-T, Chap. VI, treats at length, with B-comm. generously expanding, the praxis based on the four elements as corporeal centers to obtain the respective occult results (*siddhi*). This practice has been stated with the main ideas, although with brevity, in the preceding treatment of Chap. V, with important citations of this Chap. VI. The section begins in the scripture at 254-2-8; in B-comm. at 165-2-2. While an extended treatment of this material would not further the present object of explicating mantra efficacy, it is well to mention that B-comm. near the beginning of these comments, at 165-2-8, appears to allude to the incident of the Buddha's life called the 'Miracle of the Pairs', first performed at Sāvatthī, when as the Buddha rose in the air, flames issued from the upper part of his body, and streams of water from the lower part.[23] This kind of practice is formulated in the V-A-T in terms of the four- element centers.

Passing to the part of V-A-T, Chap. VI that corresponds to the Chinese V-A-S, Chap. 7, we observe this as concerned with the supramundane beings, in particular the Bhagavat with the commentarial explanation of the three Buddha Bodies. The scripture, V-A-T, 255-3-5, repeats a praise of the Bhagavat: "You are the abode of all dharmas, like the ocean is of all streams" (khyod ni ci ltar chu rnams kyi/rgya mtsho bźin chos kun gyi gnas /). This depicts the dharmas as the content, the Bhagavat as the container. The scripture continues, 255-3-6, with the Bhagavat responding to the Bodhisattva Vajrapāṇi with verses:

/ sems dpa' chen po dkyil 'khor gyi / gnas ni yid ces bśad pa yin /

/ sñin ni gsaṅ sṅags gnas yin par / śes na 'bras bu 'thob par 'gyur / /
/ dkar po ser po dmar po gaṅ / yid kyis sems par byed pa ste /
/ de la yoṅs su gcod pa gaṅ / de ni sems kyi byed pa yin / /

Great being! The abode of the *maṇḍala* is explained as 'mind'. The heart is the place of the mantras, knowing which, one attains the fruit. Whether white, yellow, or red, one creates it in thought with the mind. Whoever discriminates those, he is the creator in mind.

B-comm. 169-2-7,ff. 'Mind' refers to *maṇḍalas*; the place of mantras is the mind. 'Knowing which' means realizing it through the previously described process of imagining the moon-disk (*candra-maṇḍala*) with the seed mantra thereon. Whether the yellow earth-*maṇḍala,* the white water-*maṇḍala,* the red fire-*maṇḍala* (or the blue-black wind-*maṇḍala*), one creates it in mind for the respective fruit (*siddhi* of the rite). Whoever discriminates those, i.e. contemplates the appropriate one of them, creates it in mind.

The scripture, 255-3-8, passes to verses about the eight-petalled lotus of the heart, the mirror of the heart, as though the moon in the waters; and imagining there the 'A' like crystal and the full moon. B-comm. 169-5-2, ff. treats this as pointing to three Bodies of the Buddha, to wit, the 'A' represents the Dharmakāya; being surrounded by the blazing garland, etc. is the nature of Saṃbhogakāya; like the moon in the waters is the nature of Nirmāṇakāya. Hence, this is the ultimate efficacy of mantra.

12.'REALITY OF THE ĀCĀRYA' AND 'ARRAY OF LETTERS' CHAPTERS

The praxis of V-A-T cannot be appreciated without knowing the role of the master (*ācārya*). Whatever be the 'preliminary service' (initially six months) before *maṇḍala* ritual, he places thirty-two letters in his body for initiation in the three *maṇḍalas*—the M-K-G-maṇḍala, the Wheel of Syllables, and the Secret *Maṇḍala.* Then he is the hierophant who confers initiation upon suitable candidates. B-comm. has a number of comments on the 'Reality of the Ācārya' chapter. Coming to the 'Array of Letters' chapter, B-comm. does not comment on what is just a list of letters with attributed spots of the body, but does have a valuable statement placing the three *ācārya-samādhis* with the three *maṇḍalas*. I shall first translate the *ācārya* chapter with interspersed comments from B-comm.

Then Vajrapāṇi asked the Bhagavat about the 'womb' (*garbha*) of the *mantras* and the *maṇḍalas*: "What is the 'womb' of all *mantras*? Partaking of which, does one become an *ācārya*? Having been so appealed to, Mahāvairocana at that time announced to Vajradhara: "Mahāsattva, very well. I shall explain to you, my son, what is more secret than the secret gnosis—the arising of the great gnosis of *mantra*. Listen with non-swerving mind."

B-comm. 193-5-6: 'more secret' because not to be taught to those who are not good vessels or are without pledges.

1. It is rightly explained that "A" is the womb of all *mantras*. Countless are the *mantras* that arise therefrom. It gives rise to all the gnosis when all elaboration is appeased.

B-comm. 194-1-2: 'womb' (T. *sñiṅ po*) means 'place of arising'. Now there are two kinds of 'place of arising'—conventional and absolute. Since K and all the other (mute) letters cannot be spoken in the absence of "A", it is said that they all arise from "A"; and that is the conventional place of arising. As to the 'absolute' kind, the arising of gnosis from "A" that all natures (*dharma*) are immemorially not arising—this is the absolute place.

"Master of the secret ones, as to how 'A' is the womb of all the *mantras*":—

2. The Complete Buddha, best of the two-footed ones, has declared "A" to be the life (*āyuḥ*). Hence, all these letters have ("A") in each case, when placed in all the limbs.

B-comm. 194-2-2,ff. (to show that "A" is the 'life') says the explanation requires A, AṂ, I, and U. The *anusvara* of Aṃ is the self-existence (*svabhāva*) of the five nasals. The five respectively assemble the velar, palatal, retroflex, dental, and labial series of 'mutes' (see the preceding section on Chap. V), (i.e. is their respective pervading 'space'). [Y is included in I; V is included in U]. R is included in Ṛ and Ṝ.L is included in Ḷ and Ḹ. Ś, Ṣ, S, H are included under the pair of letters. (The remark is obscure; in fact, Ś is a palatal like I; Ṣ is retroflex like Ṛ; S is dental like Ḷ; and the aspirate H probably under A).

B-comm. 194-2-6: 'Best of the two-footed ones' since "A" is the life of both the conventional and the absolute [Note that the syllable "A" goes with earth, which in man is the feet, as is shown in the section on Chap. V]; i.e. in the conventional sense, is the life of the letters by expressing them; and in the absolute sense, is the life of the knowledge that the *dharmas* are unborn.

3. You must always fully understand what are the rules for the limbs. They are all pervaded by the letters. And all the letters are pervaded by it ("A").

B-comm. 194-2-2, 'all the letters' means K, etc.

4. The vocalization of the letters occurs part after part. Therefore, all of them occur in all the diverse body (parts).

B-comm. 194-3-6. All those letter entities, K, etc., are also the seeds (*bīja*) of deities; and so one may represent the group of letters by those deities. (B-comm. does not here or elsewhere detail the deities that would go respectively with the germ syllables; and the *Sūtra* itself gives little information—it does give germ syllables for some of the deities, but for example, in its Chap. IV, SA for Padmapāṇi, i.e. Avalokiteśvara, is not a letter ["s"] included among the thirty-two letters). (van Gulik, *Siddham,*[24] gives the germ syllables for the deities in the Japanese Garbha-mandara, but this has considerably more deities than in the M-K-G-maṇḍala, and has so many repetitions of syllables as to make one conclude they were used for calligraphy practice rather than for evocation purposes.)

5. I shall explain the right way to dispose them. Pay heed with awareness to the 'womb'. Having placed the 'womb' in the heart, one places the 'limbs' in the limbs.

B-comm. 194-4-1: the 'womb' is alone the "A".

6. The wise yogin takes his seat, (and thinks), I shall do all of this. (Thus,) I shall make my body into the Body of a Complete Buddha, and remember the Tathāgatas.

7-8-9. Who has comprehended through the rite the wide gnosis, at that time the powerful Buddhas explain him to be an *ācārya*. Hence, he is called 'Tathāgata'. He is called 'Complete Buddha'. And he is called Buddha, Bodhisattva, Brahmā, Viṣṇu, Maheśvara, Sun, Moon, Varuṇa, Indra, Prajāpati, Kāla, Yama, Pṛthivī, Sarasvatī, Brahmin, snātaka, brahmacārin, bhikṣu, śrīmat, *kṣīṇāsrava* (who has destroyed the fluxes), holder of all secrets, sarvavit, sarvadarśin, sarvadharmeśvara, foremost.

B-comm. 194-5-4: The *ācārya,* when on the stage of action in faith, (*adhimukti-caryā*), is not (at that time) a Tathāgata. Since that constitutes the cause for being (later) a Tathāgata, and so on, one should understand (those praises) to associate the fruit with the cause. (This points to the difference between the first two *ācārya-samādhis* on the Body ad Speech *maṇḍalas*—here referred to as 'cause'—and the third *ācārya-samādhi* on the Mind-*maṇḍala* —here referred to as 'fruit').

10. The one who fortifies the Mind of Enlightenment, and knows the sounds, that industrious one, not clinging to any *dharma*, should know all the aspects (*ākāra*).

11. Whoever places the Wheel of syllables in his body, he is the mantrin, holder of *mantras*, Śrīmat-mantrarāja, Vajradhāra.

B-comm. 195-1-3. This (i.e. verses 10-11) is the first Ācārya-samādhi.

12. The syllable HŪṂ between his brows is the 'ground' (*gzhi*) of the vajrin. The syllable SA at the collarbone midpoint is called 'ground' of Padmapāṇi.

B-comm. 195-1-7: HŪṂ between the brows belongs to Vajrapāṇi; SA at the collarbone midpoint belongs to Avalokiteśvara.

13. I dwell in the heart, master of all, Īśvara, pervading all the host of moving and non-moving (entities).

B-comm. 195-2-1: 'I dwell', viz. the syllable "A".

B-comm. 195-1-5: This (i.e. verses 12-13) is the second Ācārya samādhi.

14-15-16. "A" is the best of 'life', "VA" is the 'Word' (*vāk*). "RA" is called 'fire'. "HŪṂ" is the *krodha* fierce deity). "KHA" is space (*ākāśa*). The *anusvara* ('*klad kor*') is best of voids. Who knows (those) is called the *ācārya*. This is the genuine sublimity. Therefore, the one who continually strives in this mantra of the Complete Buddha in all the aspects, attains the level (or, 'rank') without death or transference.

B-comm. 195-2-2,3: This (i.e. verses 14-15-16) represents the third Ācārya-samādhi.

B-comm. 195-2-3,ff.: "A" he imagines going far down from above. VA in his mouth. RA as 'fire' together with the 'intrinsic *maṇḍala*' and imagined as a 'light *maṇḍala*' (*prabhā-maṇḍala*). HŪṂ imagined between his brows. KHA—all *dharmas* have a character like the sky. The *anusvara*, the void beyond void.

Next is the chapter 'Array of Letters'. Since each of the thirty-two letters is 'pervaded' by "A", they can be referred to as syllables.

B-comm. 195-3-5: The thirty-two letters apply to the thirty-two characteristics (*lakṣaṇa*) of the Great Person (*mahāpuruṣa*).

B-comm. 195-3-6,7: While keeping the letters deposited in his body, the first Ācārya-samādhi is at the time of the M-K-G-maṇḍala; the second Ācārya-samādhi at the time of the Wheel of Syllables *maṇḍala*; the third Ācārya-samādhi at the time of the Secret Maṇḍala.

The chapter begins:

> The Complete Buddha has rightly taught how to dispose the syllables. Hence, give complete hearing.

It continues, telling where to place each syllable (in sets of four):

1. KA in larynx
2. KHA in palate
3. GA in neck
4. GHA in throat
5. CA in beginning of tongue
6. CHA in middle of tongue
7. JA in tip of tongue
8. JHA in root of tongue
9. TA in calf of the leg
10. THA in thigh
11. ḌA in hip
12. ḌHA in the two feet
13. TA in urinary passageway
14. THA in navel
15. DA in both armpits
16. DHA in both ribs
17. PA in the (top) back
18. PHA in the sternum
19. BA in both shoulders
20. BHA in both hands
21. MA in place of the mind (= heart)
22. YA in sex organ
23. RA on crown of head[25]
24. LA on forehead ('broad place')

25-26. I Ī in the two eyes
27-28. U, Ū in the two lips
29-30. E, AI in the two ears
31-32. O, AU on the two cheeks

The chapter continues:

> AṂ in the seat (*āspada*) of the Complete Buddha; AḤ in Nirvāṇa.

> Having understood this according to the rite, create a Buddha by supreme *vrata!*

And concludes:

> The treasure-store of omniscience,
> when always located in someone's heart,
> completely knows in the world,
> certainly according to omniscience.

The V-A-T itself in its Chapter XII ('Setting into motion all the Dharma-syllables'), 261-4-1,ff., has explanatory phrases about what constitutes perfection of skill in the method of the 'Wheel of Dharma-syllables'. B-comm. 176-2-1, ff., classifies these scriptural phrases (*chos kyi rnam grans*) under the headings, 'perfection of self-presence (**svabhāva*)', 'perfection of empowerment (*adhiṣṭhāna*)', 'perfection of enforcement (**anubhava*)', and perfection of rite (*karma*)'. The 'perfection of self-presence' is indicated by the phrase "skill in the method of the syllables". The 'perfection of empowerment' is indicated by the phrases "at the time one pronounces the syllable-mantras", "cultivation of *samādhi*", "when operating in the form of a deity", "empowerment by the Tathāgatas". The 'perfection of enforcement' is indicated by the phrase "It is expounded by past, present, and future Buddhas". The 'perfection of rite' is indicated by the phrase "rite based in the method of *mantra*"; and also shown to be of four kinds, as indicated by the phrases "praxis of *mantras*", "change into the form of a deity", "praxis of *samādhi*", "playful practice of the Bodhisattvas". Among these, the praxis of mantras was already indicated by the phrase "rite based in the method of *mantra*", which amounts to making *mantras* out of the letter-syllables. "Change into the form of a deity" goes with the phrase "appropriating the form" and means praxis in the form of a deity while using the relevant syllables. "Praxis of *samādhi*" goes with the phrase "skill in the method of the Tathāgatas" and means praxis in the Dharmakāya, which is the true nature of voidness, while using the letter-syllables. "Playful practice of the Bodhisattvas" means the practices of the rites *śāntika, pauṣṭika,* and so on (see "A Study of the Homa Chapter") and the practices with attainments superior, middling (and inferior).

13. 'FRUIT OF PLACING THE HUNDRED LETTERS' CHAPTER

There are five chapters, each rather small, in the V-A-T on the 'hundred letters' (*śatākṣara*). What the hundred are, has already been exposed in our treatment of Chapter V.[26] Since these hundred letters are mandatory in the 'preliminary praxis' for each of the three *maṇḍala* initiations *(abhiṣeka)* in the sequence of Body-Speech and Mind-*maṇḍalas,* it follows that this is an extremely important topic of the V-A-T. B-comm., as was shown in our section in the "Textual Studies", is extant on all these five chapters, except for the last one, 'Mantra Rite of the Hundred Letters'. The chapter chosen for translation, with extracts from B-comm.'s generously expansive explanations, is Chap. XXIII in the V-A-T Tibetan scripture in the Kanjur, but was Chapter 20 in B-comm. on the scriptural chapter. I shall indent the translation of the scripture chapter, with verse numbering that may not agree with the presumed original Sanskrit, and cite the commentary as 'B-comm.'

Then Vajrapāṇi, master of the secret ones, appealed to the Bhagavat as follows:

> "1. Bhagavat, this explanation by the Lord of mantras as to the mantra meaning of mantras is a marvel!

B-comm., 201-4-8: The merit and potency of the 100 letters, as previously explained, is a marvel.

> "2. O Mahāmuni, pray tell me where, whereby, and how the mantras arise. O Lord of mantras, best of speakers, pray explain all of this to me."

> 3. Having been so asked, the Bhagavat, Dharmeśvara, Mahāmuni, omniscient one, the lord Vairocana, then proclaimed in gentle words that filled all the world-realms:

> "4. Vajrapāṇi, mighty one (*mahābala*), great being (*mahāsattva*), very well, very well. I shall explain to you all the highest secret of the Buddhas, the great marvel which is secret, which cannot be understood through any logic.

B-comm. 202-1-5: 'secret' means having a subtle character arisen from mind.

"5-6. whoever are initiated in this *Karuṇodbhava-maṇḍala* of the Mahāyāna (Great Vehicle), who are free from deceit or hostility, ever compassionate, rightly awakened, and do not observe in terms of externals (*dmigs pa can*), their potency is the understanding as 'great souls' (*mahātman*).

B-comm. 202-1-8: Generally speaking, they have both calming (*śamatha*) of mind and discerning (*vipaśyanā*) of the real.[27] Thus, 'free from deceit or hostility' is consistent with *samādhi,* hence there is 'calming'. The terms 'compassionate' and 'do not observe in terms of externals' show 'discerning'. The *śamatha* and *vipaśyanā* together are 'the 'potency'. The verses implicate initiation in the two conventional (*saṃvṛti*) maṇḍalas, that of Body—the M-K-G-*maṇḍala;* and the Speech *maṇḍala.* However, here the term 'great souls' is reserved for the absolute (*paramārtha) maṇḍala* of Mind, the Secret Maṇḍala, where the candidate has taken the five pledges (*samaya*).[28]

"7. Where the guidance dwells—its place is the heart, beautified by the eight petals of the mind-arisen lotus.

B-comm. 202-3-6: This answers the question, 'where'. A white lotus is imagined in one's own heart.

"8. On the lunar *maṇḍala*, and on what is like a spotless mirror, ever dwells the powerful Mantra-Lord.

B-comm. 202-3-8: One imagines on the eight-petalled lotus a wind-disk and in the middle of it, 'AṂ', the hundred-lettered Bhagavat. As to 'ever dwells': dwells both with *paramārtha*-body, non-changing; and with *saṃvṛti*-body—the inexhaustible jewel—up to the end of *saṃsāra*.

"9. Of golden color and blazing (at) the place of sinless *samādhi*; hard to look at, like the sun; whereby all these living beings, 'inner' as well as 'outer', are pervaded with empowerment (adhiṣṭhāna).

B-comm. 202-5-2: Also the performer must stay with non-swerving *samādhi* at the heart place until successful in imagining the golden syllable which is luminous. B-comm. 203-1-4, ff: As to 'inner' and 'outer', the 'inner', i.e. the five personal aggregates (*skandha*), is empowered at the moon-*maṇḍala* of the heart. The 'outer' body becomes Saṃbuddha. Also, 'all these beings' can be interpreted as the *mantra*-deities of Mañjuśrī, Avalokiteśvara, and so forth, as 'outer'; and 'inner' the syllable 'A', etc. on the moon-*maṇḍala* of their hearts.

"10. Be aware of the mirror itself! And with the eye of insight! When the *mantrin* uses the eye of insight to look at the mirror, his own bodily form is the Saṃbuddha.

B-comm. 203-2-2: One should be convinced that in the heart is a mirror.

B-comm. 203-2-5: The mirror is of the mind itself. When the *mantrin* gazes with this eye of insight, at the next instant his bodily form is that of the Saṃbuddha.

[This appears to answer the question, 'whereby', i.e., by the eye of insight.]

"11. At the time he sees the characteristic(s) as calm, the body is the form of Body, the Mind is mind-produced, pure and beautiful, arisen from his own act.

B-comm. 203-2-7, ff: His body is then seen to have the characteristics of a Saṃbuddha. The Mind is the heart-syllable of the moon-*maṇḍala*, produced by his mind (i.e. his own act).

B-comm. 203-3-4: The 'outer' is pure and beautiful. The 'inner' mind, i.e. the letter-syllable, is vivid and pure.

"12. Then, by its rays the *mantrin* performs all the acts of a Buddha. That being so, one is Vairocana.

B-comm. 203-4-2: The rays of that heart-*mantra* arouse the series of letter-syllables, namely, of *mantra*-deities such as Ārya Mañjuśrī. This sequence is shown in the next chapter ("Self Goal").[29]

13. Likewise, even though one views or speaks with a pure self, he must (that way) contemplate in his mind to be all-doing."

B-comm. 203-4-4: When one views that way, with the Body of Saṃbuddha, he is a Vidyādhara (Holder of Clear Vision). The Vidyādhara should think, "May the sentient beings become such-and-such a way," and "May their aim be effected". He should recognize that sentient beings have such potentiality through their collection of merit. [The foregoing appears to answer the question, 'how', i.e. how to be 'all-doing'.]

"Master of the Secret ones! Besides, the Bodhisattva who is engaging in Bodhisattva practice by way of *mantras* must in this way generate his body into the bodily form. Otherwise, it is impossible for him to be a Rightly Complete Buddha. In the manner one's eye, ear, nose, tongue, corporal touching sense, and mind belong within the four great elements, they are void of intrinsic nature, incorporated (therein) just by name; are like the sky ungraspable, arisen from cause (*hetu*) and action (*karma*), and are like a reflected image.

B-comm. 203-5-6: When one generates the Body of Saṃbuddha, it is the form in an absolute sense (*paramārtha-tas*). However, while the sense organs are incorporated within the four great elements in a conventional sense (*saṃvṛti-tas*), arisen from *hetu* and *karma*, and while the Buddha Bhagavats have realized them to be void, they do appear to arise; thus, it is not they do not exist, for the scripture says, they "are like a reflected image".

"Accordingly have the Tathāgatas manifestly realized them. And those are mutually, uninterruptedly dependently arising. Whatever arises dependently, that is like a reflected image. Thus, because they mutually arise dependently, whatever the deity, it is a master; whatever the master, it is a deity. Accordingly, by body one generates the bodily form into the body of a deity.

B-comm. 204-2-8: The *dharmas* arise dependently in a conventional sense. Thus, in conventional appearance, a deity is generated, having oneself as condition; and oneself is generated, having a deity as condition. When one generates the deity, the 'self' is the letter-syllable AṂ, which is the nature of the hundred letters; because these arise from their contemplation when (AṂ) is situated in the heart. Accordingly, one generates the form of self into the Body of Saṃbuddha.

"Master of the Secret ones! In dependence on *dharmas,* there is understanding. In dependence on understanding, one notices *dharma*-arising. And because both are void of intrinsic nature, one should refrain from positing them as mutually the agent and the action.

B-comm. 204-3-5: The '*dharma*' is the letter AṂ; 'understanding' is the Saṃbuddha. Each arises having the other as condition. [Hence, one should not take 'understanding' as the 'agent' of '*dharma*-arising' as the 'action'; or '*dharma*-arising' as an agent, 'understanding' as its action.]

"Master of the Secret ones, how does the mind generate the mind-born form? Master of the Secret ones, like this: Whether the mind takes it as white, yellow, or red, it is that mind's clinging to a perception. Hence, when there is such a requirement, one should attend to it just that way.

B-comm. 204-4-1: This concerns firming the *mantra*-letter placed on the moon-*maṇḍala* in the mind. The three colors are of the water- circle, earth-circle, and fire-circle; having contemplated any of these, the mind becomes that way.

> "Master of the Secret ones, it is like this: When a person happens to be feverish, there is no doubt that by contemplating a *maṇḍala* in his mind he would be rid of the fever. Lacking mind, there is no *maṇḍala*; lacking *maṇḍala* there is no mind. Why so? It is because a *maṇḍala* is the same as a characteristic (*lakṣaṇa*).

B-comm. 204-4-6: When the head is feverish, a water-*maṇḍala* is prescribed for the top of it. One must think of a flask with mouth turned downwards, from which comes an ambrosial fluid, imagined to enter the head and continue further downward. In the case of an illness to the face, there is no doubt that it is alleviated by imagining an earth-*maṇḍala* there. When one is afflicted with a chill and shivering, one should imagine the fire-*maṇḍala*. As in the other cases, one should imagine that the element-circle pervades the entire body. The *maṇḍala* is the same as an element characteristic, e.g. of fire. The mind and the element-*maṇḍala* must be inseparable.

> "Master of the Secret ones, it is like this: Suppose a magician transforms an illusory man into another man. Master of the Secret ones, what do you suppose? Is there a difference between those (persons)?" Having been so asked, Vajrapāṇi, Master of the Secret ones, said to the Bhagavat: "There is no difference between those two men. Why so? Because those two men did not really arise, and illusions are void of intrinsic nature." "Master of the Secret ones, it is the same with the mind-arisen entity and the mind, because both are designations, and because (both are) void of intrinsic nature".

B-comm. 204-5-7: In short, when one generates the moon-*maṇḍala* and the heart-syllable in the mind, in an absolute sense they are void of intrinsic nature; still, in a conventional sense, one performs as necessary with cause (*hetu*) and condition (*pratyaya*), thus earnestly placing the moon-*maṇḍala* in the mind with attendant contemplation.

So ends this chapter.

APPENDIX TO PART IV. MEDITATION AND RITUAL YOGA OF THE DEITY

From Buddhaguhya, *Concise Commentary,* PTT, Vol. 77, p. 90-3-1,ff.

/ raṅ gi lha'i rnal 'byor kun rdsob pa'i go rims kyaṅ 'di las rnam pa gñis su bstan te /
Moreover, there is the conventional sequence of *yoga* of one's deity.
Here two aspects are taught.
/ de la gcig ni raṅ gi sems kyi rnam pa snaṅ ba thams cad kyis dben pa zla ba'i dkyil 'khor la sogs pa'i rnam par bsgyur bas bdag ñid ltar snaṅ ba bsgrubs pa yin no /
Among them, one is the aspect of one's own mind secluded from all appearances; then by transformation of the moon-disk, and so on, the accomplishment of an appearance like oneself.
/ de las gzan pa ni snaṅ las dben pa'i sems las laṅs te / bdag daṅ raṅ gi lha sgyu ma lta bur mñam pa ñid du mos pa sṅon du 'gro la chos ñid mñam par gcig tu mos pas bdag nid lha'i gzugs su mos par byas te / bdag gi rnam par smin pa'i gzugs kyi rnam pa kho na raṅ gi lha ñid du ṅa rgyal bya ba ni'di lta ste /
The other one is when one emerges from the mind secluded from appearances. First, one should be convinced that oneself and one's deity are alike in being illusory; and being convinced that they are alike in true nature (*dharmatā*) one is made convinced that oneself has the form (or, body) of the deity. That one's own maturation body has this sole aspect is the pride of being one's deity.
/ raṅ gi lha'i rnal 'byor kun rdsob pa gñis yin no /
These are the two conventionalities of *yoga* of one's deity.

NOTES

1. Recalls the 'Burden scripture'; cf. *Saṃyutta-nikāya,* iii, 25. The first line of the two verses: "Surely the five personal aggregates are burdens, and the bearing of burden is the person (*pudgala*)." But here the five aggregates are themselves the burden-bearers, and so likened to earth.
2. Here, the association of the "A" syllable with earth, the bearer, implicates this syllable's role in making all the letters 'sound', so to say, carrying them.
3. Here there is a premise that thought is basically non-verbal but dirtied by discursive element; and "VA", the unintelligent speech, can do the washing.
4. This takes 'defilment' as adventitious (i.e. the mind is intrinsically pure), and the adventitious can serve as a fuel for fire.
5. This appears to be the reversal of dependent origination (*pratītya-samutpāda*), arriving at the original nescience (*avidyā*).
6. For a good treatment of the six elements, see Ryūjun Tajima, *Les deux grands maṇḍalas et la doctrine de l' esoterisme Shingon* (Tokyo, 1959), pp. 233-244.
7. According to the table in Tajima, *Les deux grands,* p. 242, the sixth syllable going with *vijñāna,* is HŪṂ, but at pp. 236-237 Tajima admits that Kūkai identified HŪṂ with wind. The pure *vijñāna* ("freed from darkness") does not

need to destroy demons with HŪṂ. Cf. Alex Wayman, The Sarvarahasyatantra, in *Studies of Mysticism in Honor of the 1150th Anniversary of Kōbō-Daishi's Nirvāṇam*, Acta Indologica, Vol. VI 1984 (Naritasan Shinshoji, Japan): p. 537, in verse 66: "If he desires the highest *siddhi*, he has no pride, he has no HŪṂ." because there are no demons (to chase away).

8. The correlation of the six scriptural statements with the elements is due to the Japanese savant Kūkai Kōbō-daishi; see Tajima, *Les deux grands*, p. 235.
9. In the Japanese photographic edition of Tib. canons (PTI), Vol. 9, p. 53-1-1 to p. 54-1-8.
10. In PTT, Vol. 78, p. 65-1-1 to p. 83-2-7.
11. The Tibetan translated the a-*kṣara* as though it were *akṣara*. i.e. *yi gi* in both cases.
12. I was greatly hepled in making the distribution in terms of elements by Tsoṅ-kha-pa's *Sṅags rim chen mo,* Peking blockprint, f. 381b-6,ff. which shows a system of including the letters in five elements.
13. See H. Smidt, *Eine populare Darstellung der Shingon-Lehre* (Berlin, 1918), p. 203; and Tajima, *Lex deux grands,* table, 242.
14. For the difference between the 'outward' and the 'inward' praxis in terms 'with signs (or images)' and 'without signs (or images)', see *Mkhas grub rje's Fundamentals of the Buddhist Tantras,* tr. by F.D. Lessing and A. Wayman, pp. 209-211.
15. After B-comm. 160-4-4, it omits comments for Chap. VI, 252-3-2, *de nas*, down to 252-4-6, *sgrub la śes.* The commentary continues down to where Chap. VI, 253-2-2, has *sems can rnams la rnam maṅ po'i;* and the commentary, 163-2-8, has *sems can la ni rnam pa maṅ du śes pa ni,* indicating that comments will follow dealing with this scripture remark. However, instead of such comments B-comm. at 163-2-8, starts the lengthy treatment of the mantra A VĪRA HŪṂ KHAṂ. Thus, commentary is missing for Chap. VI, 253-2-2, *phan pa ñe ber sgrub byed cin,* down through 254-1-6, first two words *du ġyur*.
16. B-comm. probably means the group of seven, Aindrī, Brāhmī, Vaiṣṇavī, Kaumārī, Raudrī, Vārāhī and Cāmuṇḍā. However, the last three, considered as three mothers, or wives, of Śiva, have variant names in the lists.
17. B-comm. apparently accepts the legend that all seven of the *mātṛkā* were allotted the function of fighting the demons and making sure that their spilled blood did not fall upon the earth. However, the legends usually allot this role just to Śiva's consort in the angry form, whether Kālī or Durgā. The iconography of the goddess Chinnamastā (See Janārdana Miśra, *Bhāratiya Pratīk-Vidyā,* Patna, 1959, illustrations 73 and 74) apparently depicts three 'mothers' drinking the streams of blood due to the decapitated head of the central 'mother' (whose head is also drinking the blood). That the 'mothers' do not allow a drop of blood to fall upon the ground, points to an ancient prohibition of letting menstrual blood do this. It could be construed as soiling the goddess. This is because in Bengal, earth is also said to menstruate for three days at the first falling of the rains, in June-July, when all farm work must cease (William Crooke, *Religion and Folklore,* p. 49). The same idea is found in Orissa, where the name Raja is used for a leading women's festival starting one day before the first solar day of mithuna and continuing for three days, when one cannot dig, etc. the earth, which is then 'menstruating' (Kunjabehari Das, *A Study of Orissan Folk-lore,* p. 104).

18. The Tibetan term *spyaṅ-ki* means 'wolf', but the *Amarakoṣa* (Sanskrit-Tibetan edition) does not give the rendition *spyaṅ-ki* for any of its three 'wolf' words, *vṛka, koka,* and *īhāmṛga.* Of these words, the *īhā-mṛga* is understood to mean 'who pursues the deer'. B-comm.'s reference to 'moon' and 'wolf' is susceptible of various interpretations. The wolves hunt in a pack, so they might symbolize the family (*kula*) of sentient beings with single purpose. Then, since this is when the gods are winning, there is the path leading to the gods mentioned in the *Chāndogya Upaniṣad,* V, 10, 2: "from the moon to the lightning. At that place is a non-human person; he leads those persons to Brahmā." This non-human person (*amānava-puruṣa*) is a kind of psychopomp; according to the French *Dictionnaire des symboles* (four volumes), under the word *loup* ('wolf'), a wolf can be a psychopomp, but this role is not attributed to South-Asia, so it is not necessarily what B-comm. has in mind.
19. Oral information from Ven. Lozang Jamspal, November, 1984, at New York City.
20. *Mkhas grub rje's Fundamentals of the Buddhist Tantras,* tr. by Lessing and Wayman, pp. 74-5.
21. Cf. Noritoshi Aramaki, "Paratantrasvabhāva (I)", *Journal of Indian and Buddhist Studies*, XVI: 2, March 1968, p. 36, where he speaks of the 'supreme community', namely, of Buddhas, Bodhisattvas, and other advanced sentient beings.
22. *Mkhas grub rje's Fundamentals of Buddhist Tantras,* p. 209, may be consulted for more details about this.
23. Cf. Edward J. Thomas, The Life of Buddha as Legend and History (New York, 1952), pp. 98-99,n. and Plate III.
24. R.H. van Gulik, *Siddham* (International Academy of Indian Culture, Nagpur, 1956), pp. 85-90.
25. The Tibetan reading *nam mtshod* is not really corrupt. The term *mtshod* is rare, but the Tibetan syllable dictionary by Jampa Chogyal, *A Tibetan Dictionary* (Delhi, 1969) has it in the compound *dur mtshod*, apparently: "place where corpses are taken." The suggestion of *mtshod* as a kind of place is borne out in Bu-ston (Works, Vol. Pha. *Mṅon byaṅ dkyil chog*, f.5-1ff.) where he gives the list, and for the placement of RA, says naṅ tshoms su (apparently: "in the inner courtyard"). Here *naṅ* ('inner') is a corruption of *nam* which should be taken here as *gnam* ('sky'), while Bu-ston's word *tshoms* was his replacement of the rare, virtually obsolete term *mtshod.* So the compound *nam mtshod* means "hall or courtyard of the sky". (The Sino-Japanese translation, 'visual faculty', as read by my wife Hideko, does not help). The conclusion is that the place is the crown of the head, from which emerges the *uṣṇīṣa.* In agreement, we note that the V-A-T, Chap. II, v. 205 shows the hierophant imagining a RA on the crown of the disciple. Besides, the crown of the head was about the only spot left, the other main places having been mentioned in the list.
26. There are two *Śatākṣara-vidhi* treatises in the Tanjur, tantric section; in Ja. Photo ed., Vol. 77, pp. 56 and 57, neither of which details the hundred letters, so takes them for granted. The first of these, by Padmavajrāṅkuśa, gives examples of when the term *akṣara* intends recitation and when drawing: thus, at p. 56-1-7: "When one is struck by severe illness, plague, enemies, and fights; by mischief, harm, and shadows (generally), one should recite the hundred syllables. When there are the deeds of Māra, one draws the hundred letters; having applied them to a banner, one whirls (it) in all directions." The

difference appears to go with troubles due to human agency (*puruṇakāra*) to be countered by recitation, and troubles due to spirits or divinities (*daiva*) to be countered by inscribed letters.

27. For more information, see A. Wayman, *Calming the Mind and Discerning the Real; Buddhist Meditation and the Middle View;* from the *Lam rim chen mo* of Tsoṅ-kha-pa (New York, 1978).

28. B-comm. on V-A-T, Chap. XIII ('The Secret Maṇḍala') at 182-3-6, goes into the theory of five *samaya* ('pledge'). Previously (n. 122 to V-A-T, Chap. II. translation) I have given the information of three *samaya,* 'inception mind', 'continuation mind', and 'rising mind' going with the three *maṇḍala*. Here, B-comm. comments on the expression *samayin* (Tib. *dam tshig can*). Explaining the first one, 'inception mind', he mentions that for entering the Secret Maṇḍala, some disciples enter on account of their desire to be *samayin* (possessed of the *samaya* 'pledge', 'linkage'), in which case they may disregard the other two *maṇḍalas.* Some enter for the purpose of accomplishing (the *maṇḍala*); and some enter on account of their desire to be masters (*ācārya*); in both of which cases the other two *maṇḍalas* are required. B-comm. 182-4-4, concludes that the other two of the five *samaya* are the use of *mudrā* and *mantra* while seeing the *maṇḍala.* B-comm. on V-A-T, Chap. XIV ('Entering the Secret Maṇḍala') at 188-2-3, mentions that the 'inception mind' is the initial 'burning' for entrance into voidness (*śūnyatā*). The 'continuation mind' is the unchanging, thus the repeated fostering. The 'rising mind' is the conversion into the Body of the Bhagavat. For more information, see our treatment of the three minds in our previous section "Theory of Stages", V-A-T, Chap. XXIV ('Self Goal') has a further treatment; and B-comm. 205-4-4 states that the 'inception mind' is the *samādhi* which accomplishes the knowledge of voidness. The 'continuation mind' is called "inconceivable", with enlightenment mind like the sky, when *dharmas* are not apprehended. The 'rising mind' is called "returning", because through compassion one re-enters the world.

29. The discussion in B-comm. 205-2-2 (on the 'Self Goal' chapter) indicates what was previously given in the 'Reality of the Ācārya' chapter, B-comm. on its verse 2, namely, the letter-syllables A, AṂ, I and U, which generate the rest of them.

PART V

HOMA

14. A STUDY OF THE HOMA CHAPTER

This is a study of the V-A-T, Chap. XXIX of the Tibetan version, commented upon by Buddhaguhya's Chap. 29. Basic reference works for this research have been *Vāyu-Purāṇa,* Chap. 28; *Gṛhyasaṃgraha-pariśiṣṭa*; M. Winternitz, *Sacred Books of the East, A General Index, Amarakoṣa* (Sanskrit-Tibetan edition); *Trikāṇḍaśeṣa*. Besides, such works as A.A. Macdonell, *The Vedic Mythology*; E. Washburn Hopkins, *Epic Mythology*; have been very helpful. The bibliography at the end of this study will present all the works utilized for explaining this Homa chapter.

The V-A-T begins this chapter by saying that the bodhisattva doing his bodhisattva practice once was dwelling in the realm of Brahmā, and Great Brahmā asked him about the kinds of fire. The response first gives a traditional genealogy of fire (Agni):

> Abhimānin (Tib. *ṅa rgyal can)* was *Svayambhu* ('self-arisen') but later called 'son of Brahmā'. From him was born Pāvaka, the first mundane fire. The son of the latter was Brahmodana ('food of Brahmā'), and of him Bharata; and of him Vaiśvānara, the Havana and Havyavah, Saharakṣa [fire of the Asuras], called son of the Atharvan and celebrated in the (puṣkara) Ocean; and the fire called Māruta at the time of entering the womb.

Buddhaguhya's commentary (p. 212-5-1) points out that Abhimānin was self-arisen, since this refers to the first eon before the worlds developed. Later, beings in the realm of Brahmā imagined themselves 'sons of Brahmā'. The mention that the fire is called Māruta ('wind-fire') when entering the womb is consistent with a Mahāyāna Buddhist scripture (in the Tibetan canon in a larger and a smaller version) called *Nandagarbhāvakrānti-nirdeśa,* which gives the intrauterine development by a 'wind of *Karma*' with a different name for each week.

Now, besides Abhimānin's son Pāvaka, according to the *Vāyu-P.*, Chap. 28, verses 1-4, he had two others called Pavamāna and

Śuci, thus the three brother fires. Pāvaka is the lightning or flash, Vaidyuta fire; Pavamāna is excited by friction, Nirmathya; Śuci is solar, Saura fire. Pāvaka was the parent of the Asura fire; Pavamāna the parent of the Pitṛ fire; Śuci of the Deva fire. This information helps to understand the Sūtra continuation, which now turns to Pavamāna, mentioned in transcription:

> (He had these sons:) Maṇgala, the fire for the (*saṃskāra*) 'parting of the hair' (*simāntonnayana*) (observed by women in a late month of pregnancy). Pragalbha for the rite of the newly born (*jātakarman*). Pārthiva for the rite of name-conferral (*nāmadheya*). Śuci at the first feeding (*prāśana*). Sabhya (corrupted in the text to *śadvī*) at the time of the tonsure rite (*cūḍā-karaṇa*). Samudbhava at the second-birth initiation (*vratādeśa)*. Sūrya when giving the cow (go-*dāna*) (at the final tonsure, *keśānta*).

Since the Sūtra fails to make division for the sons of Śuci, I appeal to the Hindu work *Sandhya Vandhana, Darsa Tarpana and Notes on 'Gayathri'*. English part, p. 3, which states that the first series of *saṃskāra* involves "physical, mental, moral, intellectual and spiritual development", while the second series, beginning with 'marriage' (*vivāha*), involves public service. Hence, now begin the sons of Śuci:

> Yojaka at the wedding (*vivāha*). Āgneya when going to the husband's residence, and the same fire 'bending' for auspice (*Upanāmaka*). Pāvaka when offering to the miscellaneous gods. Brahmā for the Gārhapatya (transmittal from father to son). Śiva for burnt offerings (*homa*). [Both the Brahmā and Śiva fires are in the southern direction, *dakṣiṇa*.]

The remainder of the Sūtra list probably shows descendants of all three brother fires (of Pāvaka, Pavamāna, and Śuci).

> Anikavat ('having a face') when tying the sacrificial animal. Vivici ('The discerning') in the case of a transgression (*āpatti*). Sāhasa ('strong') when prescribing a remedy. Havis ('oblation') at *sandhi* rites. Nidhi ('treasure') at lunar phases. Mātariśvan (who bring down the hidden fire) at an image casting. Varada ('fulfilling entreaties') at the rite for appeasing the deities (*śāntika*). Yama ('lord of the dead') at funeral ceremonies. Balada ('strength giving') at prosperity rites (*pauṣṭika*). Krodha ('furious') for overcoming enemies (*abhicāraka*). Kāmada ('granting desires') for dominating (*vaśīkara*). Dūtaka ('envoy') for burning the forest. Jathara ('which digests the food') as the internal fire. Kravyāda ('consuming flesh') for eating (the

corpse). Vaḍabā-mukha ('mare's mouth') in the ocean. Saṃvartaka ('world destroying'), the alarm at the time of dissolution.

The Sūtra appends these remarks:

> Hero! I have explained these fires to you with brevity. On that occasion I told the forty-four sons of Brahmā because practicing the word as it was heard. Master of the secret ones! [I said:] Whoever practice the *homa* and do not know the nature of those fires, I declare it a non-*homa* and not actually done. Nor is there any fruit to their activity.

Curiously, the number 'forty-four' is given for the fires, yet counting from Abhimānin down to Saṃvartaka, the total appears to be thirty-six. The Sūtra continues:

> When I become fully awakened to enlightenment, I taught twelve fires. And what are they? —

The remark acknowledges that the previous list of fires comes from non-Buddhist sources, and that the list of twelve fires is a Buddhist contribution to the topic. The contrast is also consistent with a frequent remark in the old Buddhist canon when the Buddha would clarify for the monks the difference between pre-Enlightenment and post-Enlightenment realizations, usually starting with "Monks, before my awakening, when being a Bodhisattva I was not completely enlightened..."

(1) Fire of wisdom *(jñānāgni)*.

> (*Sūtra:*) It is called Mahendra; colored golden; confers (good) complexion, Prosperity, and power, The *samādhi* of great blazing garland, is called 'completer of wisdom'.

Mahendra is a name of Indra, located in the East; and Mahendra is in the Buddhist Tantras a word meaning 'earth'—colored yellow. As Shendge, *The Civilized Demons,* p. 348, cites *Ṛgveda,* X, 88, 6: "Of nights Agni is head of the earth; out of him is born in the morning the rising sun. (See) still this piece of craft (*māyā*) of the sacrifice worthy god, that he begins his work punctually, the knower of path." As to the "(good) complexion", in the *Lalitavistāra* (the Mahāyāna life of the Buddha) version of the First Sermon, when the recently enlightened Gautama Buddha approached the "fortunate band of five" in the Deer Park, their resolution not to greet him broken, their seats as though with a fire underneath, they springing up, welcomed the Bhagavat, and said, "Clear are your senses, Gautama, pure is your complexion. Have you realized something special of the truly noble wisdom and vision, surpassing human nature?" (*viprasannāni te.. Gautamendriyāni pariśuddhaś chavivarṇa iti... asti te kaścid uttarimanuṣyadharmād alamāryajñānadarśanaviśeṣaḥ sākṣātkṛtaḥ* (Lefmann ed., p. 409.2-5). Since the 'fire of wisdom" constitutes the 'inner *homa*' our previous citations (Alex Wayman, "Studies in Yama and Māra", pp. 121-122) are relevant: First the *Taittirīya Saṃhitā*, in Keith's translation (HOS 18, p. 261), "Yama is agani, Yamī is this (earth); the sacrificer becomes under a debt to Yama in that he strews the altar with plants; if he were to go away without burning (them), they would drag him about bound by the neck in yonder world." So one must burn the 'plants' —in Buddhism the five personal aggregates (*skandha*); and this is how Buddhaguhya describes the manner in his commentary on the *Vairocanābhisaṃbodhi* (edition of the Derge Tanjur) (commenting on the Sūtra's passage on the 'inner *homa*' near the end of the Homa chapter, translated below):

> Moreover, one destroys the five *ātmaka-skandha* in voidness (*śūnyatā*), and also destroys the forms of sense objects (*viśaya*), such as the external 'hearth' (*agnikuṇḍa*), in voidness. In the same way one individually destroys the issuances of six-doored preception (*vijñāna*) (five outer-directed, and one on a mental object); and when they do not issue and are stopped, in the same way the 'thought of enlightenment' (*bodhicitta*) which destroys and stops those is itself stopped by the non-issuing insight (*prajñā*); and that abiding in the non-discursive (*avikalpa*) *samādhi* is the inner burnt offering (*homa*). Hence, one stops the 'fire of wind' by the non-issuing insight, and 'makes the burnt offering to fire with the mind'. 'Stops the fire-wind' means 'restrains the *prāṇa* and *āyāma*' (*prāṇāyāma,* dvandva interpretation). 'Makes the burnt offering to fire with the mind' means 'burns thought immobile (*aniñjya*)'.

The *samādhi* which the Sūtra describes as "great blazing garland" may well be the one described near the end of Tsoṅ-kha-pa's *Lam rim chen mo,* in our translation *Calming the Mind and Discerning the Real* of the last part, p. 418. It is said to be the arising of 'noble wisdom' (*ārya-jñāna*) in a *samādhi* with four characteristics: (1) non-reflection (=nondiscursive thought) (*nirvikalpa*); (2) it is bright (*vyakta*); (3) clear (*accha*); (4) subtle, as thought fragmenting a tip of hair. The description of noble insight (*ārya-prajñā*) destroying defilement in the manner of a fire, agrees with the legendary or mythic beginnings of the Fire genealogy, naming Pāvaka as the first born of the three brother fires. This is because Pāvaka is usually explained by commentary as 'purifying' (*śodhaka*); see in this connection the translation by Eggeling of the *Śatapatha-Brāhmaṇa* (Part 1), p. 305 (11,2,1,10-12), that Agni Pāvaka is the purifying (*pāvaka*) according to the *Vāyu P.*, in a flash of lightning; that Agni Pavamāna is the blowing (*pavamāna*)—likewise, the fire excited by friction and blown into flame; that Agni Śuci is the brightness (*śuci*)—likewise, the solar invigoration. The *Vāyu P.* legend that Pāvaka gave rise to the Asura fire goes back to the *Ṛgveda,* V,12.1, where, as Shendge, *The Civilized Demons,* p. 349, points out, Agni is identified with Asura. This cannot be in the later meaning of *asura,* to wit, *a-sura* ('not god'; opponent of the gods), but in the original meaning *asu-ra* ('holder of the *asu*' where) *asu* has the meaning 'life of the spiritual world' (Monier-Williams Sanskrit Dictionary, referring to *Ṛgveda,* X, 15.1).

(2) Preserving Fire (*dhāraṇāgni).*

> *(Sūtra:)* Like the light of the autumn moon; attired in a white, glorious garment, carrying the rosary and a gourd bottle.

Buddhaguhya, commentary, 213-5-6,7, "the "*homa* fire for appeasing (*śāntika*)". According to Lessing, *Yung-Ho-Kung,* p. 151, the appeasing or propitiation of various deities to remove evil (in the form of disease, etc.) has the color white and a circle for shape of the *homa* altar. The *Sūtra's* Chap. XXX ('Rite of homa for Appeasing') has at 273-2-3 a description of this Agni: Like the color of conch and the moon; with matted hair, three-eyes, four arms; in his hands the rosary, a gourd bottle, a club, and the confidence giving gesture (*abhaya-mudrā*); attired in white garment; holding white thread in his half-open mouth; at his heart the fork design (probably a form of the *śrīvatsa*); (forehead) marked with the letter 'RA'; emanating a white tongue of flame. The rosary and gourd bottle agree with Banerjea, *The Development of Hindu Iconography,* p. 524, two images, one seated on an animal mount (goat or ram), the other standing, but both carry the rosary in the right hand and a water vessel in the left. Both images show flames issuing from the body; in the case of the seated one, a beard and angry stare. However, the *Sūtra* description goes against the "beard and angry stare", so the standing option is preferable.

(3) Wind-fire (*māruta*).

(*Sūtra:*) Colored black, and a gust.

Buddhaguhya (214-2-5): "kindling Fire" (i.e. fire of friction). Hence this is the Agni brother called Pavamāna, involved with blowing. The *Sūtra* previously associated this Fire (the Māruta) with entering the womb; hence it is the first light in the darkness. Many Agni names go with this initial production; found in Macdonell, *The Vedic Mythology,* Hopkins, *Epic Mythology,* and other reference works. Agni is called Tanū-napāt ('son of himself'), kṛpītayoni ('water-born' according to *Amarakoṣa* Tibetan translation and commentary) and (see *The Vedic Mythology*, pp. 69-70) Apām napāt ('son of the waters') and said to be hidden there and in plants. More comprehensible birthplaces yield names like Skandhāgni ('fire made from thick logs'), Kukula and Tuṣāgni ('fire made of chaff'), Chāgaṇa and Kariṣa ('fire of dried cow dung'). Agni is Uṣar-budh ('early waking'), meaning the Agni kindled early in the morning. *The Vedic Mythology,* p. 90-91, shows that kindled he opens the gates of darkness, and is the 'youngest' (*yaviṣṭha*), and having grown old is again born as a youth. The *Sūtra* reference to black color accounts for a name Asitārcis ('black flame'); and *The Vedic Mythology,* p. 90, "driven by the wind he rushes through the wood", while "his steeds make black furrows". Here should be mentioned the place where Agni is deposited in the sacrifice; in Vedic ritual it is the excavated altar or *vedī;* also *The Vedic Mythology,* p. 92: "the gods made Agni the 'navel' or center of immortality. The *Vedī* later in the Buddhist Tantra *maṇḍala* became the five colored bands running inside next to the palace wall and representing the five Buddhas, so this place of Agni may account for his name—of course in pre-Buddhist literature—Pāñcajanya ('relating to the five races'); while the 'navel' would be the center of the *maṇḍala*. Also (*Epic Mythology*, 98), Agni may divide into five *prāṇa*-s

(4) Red fire (*rohitāgni*).

(*Sūtra:*) Like a red cord of the Western Region.

Buddhaguhya comments (213-5-8), "the *homa* fire for controlling (*vaśīkara*), like a series of disjoined lights." Lessing, *Yung-Ho-Kung,* p. 151, subduing demons, i.e. to attain power over the beings inhabiting the three worlds; goes with the color red; our Chap. V treatment: fire's triangle. V-A-T, Chap. XXXII ('Rite of Homa for Controlling'), gives at 274-5-8, this description: One imagines the form of fire arising from the syllable 'RA'; as difficult to tame as the rising sun; three-eyed, brownish matted hair, four handed; in his hands holding a club, a noose, a rosary, and a pitcher; attired in red garments; holding red thread in his half-open mouth; marked with the letter 'RA'; emanating red light and tongues of flame. "Red cord of the Western Region" evidently refers to the setting sun; and Buddhaguhya's comment apparently refers to the festival of lights called Dīvāli. This custom is associated with a belief that light and fire can drive away demons, as discussed in Crooke, *Religion & Folklore of Northern India,* p. 206, alluding to Agni's name Rakshohan, 'destroyer of the Rakṣas goblins'. *The Vedic Mythology*, p. 95, mentions that this name Rakṣohan is found in Ṛgveda 10,87, and that this is probably the oldest cult of fire. Presumably a similar result would be believed for carrying of fire round the house (see Crooke, *Religion & Folklore,* p. 341). A torch or firebrand (Agni Saṃkila in *Trikāṇḍaśeṣa*) trailing sparks (agnikaṇa) could be carried running round the house for the purpose.

(5) Benevolent Fire (*mṛḍāgni*).

(*Sūtra:*) Yellow hair, with long and brilliant neck; named 'kindly to all'.

Buddhaguhya comments (214-1-1), "the *homa* fire for prosperity (*pauṣṭika*)"; Lessing's *Yung-Ho-Kung,* p. 151, assigns yellow color and square altar. Buddhaguhya there adds "like Rāhu" (*sgra gcan de bzin*). Rāhu is only a head and neck; and perhaps this is meant for the form of Agni here. There is considerable emphasis on Agni's face (see *The Vedic Mythology,* p. 89). The *Sūtra,* Chap. XXXI ('Rite of Homa for Prosperity'), has this description at 247-2-5: One imagines that from the syllable 'YA' arises a hearth and in it an Agni, with matted hair like gold, three-eyed, four-faced; holding a rosary and the gourd pitcher; attired in yellow garment; holding thread in his half-open mouth; (forehead) applied with three 'finger' design; and (heart area) marked with a fork design. Winternitz, *A General Index,* in his valuable, detailed entry on Agni, alphabetical sub-section '*l*' "A. as a kind and helpful god", mentions many passages where Agni is invoked for personal prosperity, especially health and wealth.

(6) Wrath Fire (*krodhāgni*).

(*Sūtra:*) Bulging red eyes; hair standing-up, with adjacent hair hardly left; with four 'tusks'; powerful.

Buddhaguhya (214-1-2): "the *homa* for drastic acts (*abhicāruka;* sometimes *raudrakarman*)"; according to our previous Chap. V treatment, it goes with black or dark blue wind and the bow

V-A-T, Chap XXXIII ('Rite of Homa for Drastic Act'), gives at 275-4-6 this description: One imagines that from the letter 'HŪṂ' arises this form of Agni; with a very unpleasant black color; three-eyed, four-handed; hard to look at; with brownish matted hair; smoky; with rays like a dark-blue rain-cloud; with large belly; wearing dark-blue garment; holding dark-blue thread in his half-open mouth; from his mouth-opening four tusks menacing angrily; holding in his hands the sword, the noose, the club, and the gourd pitcher; his heart marked with the fork design; (forehead) marked with the letter 'RA'; brow with fury wrinkles. *Epic Mythology* (p. 98) provides the imagery for the Wrath Fire: "flames burst from his orifices, together with smoke, sparks, and fire, 'as if from the holes of a burning tree'." Thus, the four 'tusks' may refer to fire issuing from four such holes. Dowson, *A Classical Dictionary of Hindu Mythology,* p. 7, from *Harivaṃśa:* "four hands". It might also be the appearance of fire when underneath a pot it comes up along the sides with four tongues=hands=tusks=horns. Banerjea, the *Development of Hindu Iconography*, p. 542, refers to *Viṣṇudharmottara* Bk. III, ch. 56, vv. 1-10) for an elaborate description, in which Agni is depicted as "bearded, four-armed, four-tusked, three-eyed, riding a chariot with smoke standard drawn by four parrots and driven by wind, having his consort Svāhā on his left lap, holding flames, trident and rosary in his hands."

(7) Belly Fire (*audāryāgni*).

(*Sūtra:*) Having speedy iridescence (*rnol kha dog kun daṅ ldan*).

Buddhaguhya's commentary gives no help for this and following ones. *Epic Mythology*, p. 98: this is the fire of hunger, extinguished by food. The *Sūtra*, as cited previously, mentions Agani Jaṭhara as the internal fire which digests food. Bhagwan Dash, *Concept of Agni in Āyurveda*, works out the whole theory of Agni as *pitta*, the power to break down and restructure; at pp. 24-25, cites *Suśruta* "hence *pitta* is known as *antarāgnī*" Presumably it is this internal fire which *yogis* learn to evoke as the *siddhi* (magical power) of heat.

(8) Transient Fire (*kṣayāgni*).

(*Sūtra:*) Like rays of lightning.

The equivalence of Tibetan *żad pa* to Skt. *kṣaya* is standard; and here is justified by the Sino-Japanese transcription. *The Vedic Mythology,* p. 94, mentions the transient nature of Agni Vaidyuta. Therefore, it concerns such names as Tṛṇa-agni ('grass fire') or Taratsama ('conflagration of chaff'), meaning the fire that flares up and quickly dies down, the name Kṛśānu ('the archer' said to be armed with the lightning), is rendered in the Tibetan version of *Amarakoṣa* as though from the verb *kṛś-*, so 'making lean' but this might refer to the 'lean' character of lightning. The *Vāyu P.* associates Agni Pāvaka with the lightning; and Pāvaka cannot mean here 'purifying' (in the spiritual sense, as was mentioned), but perhaps Agni Mātariśvan who brings down the fire, as was suggested, for casting, somewhat in the manner of Hephaestus, the Greek god of fire and of metal-working.

(9) Mental Fire (*mānasāgni*).

(*Sūtra:*) Multiformed; very powerful.

The *Sūtra* remark implicated the Agni name Citrabhānu ('of variegated lustre', 'shining with light'), hence also the third of the three Agni brothers, Śuci. The 'mental fire' is treated in Knipe, *In the Image of Fire,* 93, ff. He calls this the "fire in the head", namely mind and speech. 'Mental fire' in his explanation (p. 96) is proved by the ṛṣi's fiery 'halo' or *nimbus,* perhaps what is meant by the name Citrabhānu. Knipe says it arises "from inspiration (*manīṣā*), from the cultivation of meditation techniques, or from the heat of soma-intoxication and ecstasy." Our own article, "The Significance of Mantras", cites a passage from the *Śatapathabrāhmaṇa* (from 8.6.3.22) that speech and mind are the two parents to be made young again as two fires that lead to the gods. And cites Arthur Beriedale Keith, *The Aitareya Āraṇyaka* (1969 reprint) (from 2.4.1): 'From the mouth came speech, from speech fire.' Agni is himself a mouth, explicitly stated in the name Vaiśvānaramukha, as the name is given in *Vāyu P.* Chap. 28.

(10) [Householder's Fire (*gārhapatyāgni*), in Sino-Japanese text, missing in Peking Tibetan Kanjur]

(*Sūtra:*) World- protector [Sino-Japanese: reddish-black].

This is Āgneya, the protector in the south-eastern corner. Our article, "Studies in Yama and Māra", (*op. cit.*), p. 59, shows that the directional regent Agni is symbolized by the hearth (*agnikuṇḍa*) and has a retinue of the seers (*ṛṣi*). It is in this sense (cf. *The Vedic Mythology,* 95-96) that Agni is called a 'guest' (*atithi*), has the epithet *viśpati* ('lord of settlers'), and also has the name vītihotra ('invited to a feast'). The commentary attributed to Buddhaguhya on the *Durgati-pariśodhana-tantra* called the *Artha-vyañjana-vṛtti* in the Tibetan canon (Peking Tanjur, photo ed., Vol. 76, p. 32-2-2) says one should examine the Vītihotra (Tib. *byin za*). Through this examination of the offering fire, one may observe signs of good and bad auspice. First the six of good

auspice: tongue of fire turning to right (*me lce g'yas su 'khyil ba*)—
turning away from *Saṃsāra;* of shining appearance (*dkar la 'tsher
ba lta bu*)—ending of habit-energy (*vāsanā*); tongue of flame
blazing straight (up) (*me lce draṅ por 'bar ba*)—reaching heaven;
fire which continually does not spread (*me rtag mi 'phro ba*)
—good luck to the sponsor (*ñe gzi*); tongue of fire which blazes
without scattering upward (*me lce gyen du mi 'thor bar 'bar
ba*)—averting sins from the sponsor; tongue of flame that is firm and
blazes clear and bright like lightning (*me lce brtan la glog bzin du dri
ma med la gsal bar 'bar ba*)—increasing wealth. There are five of bad
auspice: with yellow color and blaze not clear (*kha dog kham la mi
gsal bar 'bar ba*)—not averting the hindrance of habit-energy; a kind
of green flame turning to left (*sno la bslon la me g'yon du 'khyil
ba*)—no heaven or liberation; tongue of fire that tosses about
downward, mixed with smoke (*me lce thur 'tshub ciṅ du ba daṅ 'dres
nas 'bar ba*)—forecasts bad luck for the sponsor; tongue of fire that
scatters with mixed blue (*me lce 'phro zin sñon gdu 'bar ba*)—no
getting of wealth or animals; flame that tosses about, or is blown by
the wind toward the south (*me 'tshub ciṅ rluṅ gis lho phyogs su gsad
[sic. for 'bud]*)—one will get an infectious disease or be victim to
an epidemic. From a different tantric tradition, cf. Tsuda, *The
saṃvarodaya-tantra; Selected Chapters,* pp. 309-311, for a different
classification of fire signs for good and bad auspice.

(11) Flesh-eating Fire (*piśācāgni*).

(*Sūtra:*) (Eats) anything other than it.

This demonic fire eats everything that is 'other' than itself. Since
among the four elements, wind, water, and earth are counted as
'other', this fire can also be the submarine 'Mare's mouth'
(Vaḍabāmukha), which drinking ocean water causes the dreaded
whirlpool. This Mare's fire is also called Kākadhvaja ('with crow
banner') as well as Vāṇija ('born from the loom'), according to the
Trikāṇḍaśeṣa lexicon. The *Sūtra* remark reminds us of the mythic
beginnings of the world in *Bṛhad-āraṇyaka Upaniṣad* (1.2.1) "In
the beginning there was nothing at all here. By death alone was this
covered, or by hunger, for hunger is death." Hence this hunger
called the world into being as an 'other' to be 'eaten'.

(12) Delusive Fire (*saṃmohanāgni*).

(*Sūtra:*) Which deludes all sentient beings.

Taking the *Sūtra* remark at value, it points to the fascination of
fire, getting hypnotized by staring at it. This is especially a
Buddhist category according to our article, "Similes for the four

elements from Buddhist Literature", p. 398. Early Buddhism has the Fire Sermon, teaching that all constituents of the world, the eye, and so forth, are on fire. So the later *Dharmasamuccaya*, Chap. VII, Kāmajugupsāvarga, v. 134: "just as someone through fear of fire uses that very fire, so also one confused by sense objects takes recourse to the sense objects" (*yathā vahnibhayāt kaścit vahnim evopasevate / tathā viṣayasaṃmūḍho viṣayān upasevate*). On the other hand, see Goudriaan, *Māyā Divine and Human*, p. 243, citation of *Atharva Veda* 3.2.2. *Agnir...amūmuhat* which I render "agni has just been deluded". Presumably the practice of fire-walks (cf. Crooke, *Religion & Folklore,* p. 340), as though the performer is immune from being burnt, is construed by some as having fooled the fire. However, the information in *Epic Mythology,* p. 99, that Jātavedas "spares the houses of the good", shows the Fire of ordeals to be Jātavedas as the Fire that knows the just deserts, in which case it was not the Fire that was fooled.

The Sūtra goes on to show the difference between an "outer *homa*" and an "inner *homa*".

> Accordingly, the form of fire empowers. Its own (respective) form and the fuel-substance creates its nature. This is the 'outer *homa*'. Those desiring the (respective) *siddhi* (occult success) should make a *homa*.
>
> An inner nature possessed of three (self, fire, fuel), by the method of taking the three together (in voidness), is the 'inner *homa*'.

The Sūtra then explains more for the two types, starting with the 'outer homa':

> A person possessing great love and great compassion belongs to (can do) the *śāntika* (appeasing the deities), the one possessing sympathetic joy (can do) the *pauṣṭika* (prosperity *homa*). With the wrath-fire one may practice *abhicāruka* (dreadful magic). Having made the wrath mighty, one should place its 'name' between the ṬA and the MA (i.e. in the middle of the forehead); place the reflected image in a *krodha maṇḍala*; and do it by taming the wrath. One should place the 'wind-fire' in the middle.

Since an 'outer *homa*' is rather expensive in terms of wood, and so on, the performer may need a patron; so the Sūtra remarks:

> Master of the Secret Ones! According as this and those places have been described; according as it is proper and according

as one possesses (the wherewithal), one should make the Homa (burnt offering).

Then Vajrapāṇi asked the Bhagavat for directions on making the fire pit, purifying the offering, arranging the *kuśa* reeds, and the mental conception.

The Bhagavat responded:

Among them, make the fire pit a measure of exactly a *hasta* all around, and make the altar exactly four *aṅguli*— marked with *vajra* marks. One should arrange wet *Kuśa* reeds on the right side of the fire pit, tied at their tips and base. With the *kuśa* one encircles by the right side the offering to be purified. One should offer it to the 'benevolent fire' (*mṛdāgni*) along with perfumes and fragrant flowers. In that engaged fire pit, the *mantrin* firm in vows should conceive his own form as the single flower (offered) to the 'benevolent fire'. A wise person should make offering to it (that fire) with a ladle and its individual mantras. Then he should make either a *śāntika-homa* or a *pauṣṭika-homa*. These mundane *homa* are designated 'outer'.

The Bhagavat went immediately to the 'inner *homa*':

Moreover, as to the 'inner *homa*', one 'stops' the *karma* and life-force (T. *tshe*; S. *āyus*). One abandons (sense objects) form, sound, etc. One imagines the eye, ear, nostril, tongue, and corporeal (sense organs) to be born from the mind and to be located in the mind-king—generated by discursive thought *(kalpanā)*. The mind-of-enlightenment, sense objects, sense organs of eye, etc., and also the fire-wind, are stopped by 'insight' (*prajñā*) to not issue forth; and are to be offered to the fire of the mind. This is the 'inner *homa*'.

This distinction of 'inner' and 'outer' *homa* clarifies that of the twelve fires described previously some are both 'fires' and *homa*, and a number are not *homa*. Specifically, the 'inner *homa*' is only fire no. 1; and the four 'outer *homa*' are fire nos. 2, 4, 5, 6. Among the fires that are not involved in *homa* are the three Agni brothers, nos. 3, 8, 9. As to why the remaining fires are included—they seem to involve features of Buddhist practice. Thus the 'belly fire' (no. 7) would concern the fasting cults. 'World protector' (no. 10) includes the fire signs, or omens, good or bad, and concerns discrimination. 'Flesh eating fire' (no. 11) is the bad fire; thus stands for the various Buddhist avoidances, such as the five layman vows. Finally, 'delusive fire' (no. 12) may stand for illusion generally, symbolized by the whirling fire-brand, and so on—which is to be recognized by 'insight' (*prajñā*).

After clarifying the difference between 'inner' and 'outer' *homa*, the Bhagavat told his fortunate audience to listen and be heedful.

> Which (instructions) are not to be conferred on others—except my 'sons' (=disciples)—their characteristics I shall explain. Remembering the kindness of the Solar-Race Descendent and of Abhimānin, one should crave the Dharma, learn the Dharma, and endeavor in the Dharma.
>
> They are all my sons who are colored greenish blue, with handsome face, with high sharp-tipped nose, pleasing head and forehead; and who ponder the meaning of the Teaching.
>
> It (the Teaching) should always be earnestly given to them.

Then the retinue, delighted with the discourse, bowed to the Tathāgata and asked him for a protective formula so this Dharma-rule may long last in the world. This is the formula which the Bhagavat gave them on this occasion:

> Namaḥ samantabuddhānām / sarvathā / śiṃ śiṃ traṃ traṃ dharaṃ dharaṃ sthāpaya buddhaṣatyavāg dharmasatyavāg saṃghasatyavāg hūṃ hūṃ vidi vidi svāhā.

And this concluded the chapter, which could be called from the contents 'Discriminating the *homa*- from non-*homa*-fires'.

So far, there has been no comment on the difficulty of figuring out the Agni names in the foregoing translation and explanations. One may get an idea of trying to read this chapter with just one version, say the Tibetan or the Chinese, by consulting Michel Strickmann's essay, "Homa in East Asia." In the present study it was found out that even employing both the Tibetan and the Sino-Japanese versions is insufficient for this chapter; hence, the variety of reference works employed.

While the homa chapter has clearly differentiated between the 'inner' and the 'outer' Homa, it will be useful to notice the treatment in V-A-T, Chap. XIII ('The Secret Maṇḍala'), 263-1-8,ff.:

> There are two kinds of *homa* by distinction of inner and outer. I explain the inner *homa* as free from *karma* and *āyus*.
>
> One makes the burnt offering with desire for the rite (*karma*) while reverting to the 'seed'. The best mundane *homa* possesses the outer three, places three with three places, accomplishes the *karma* of three *karmas*.

B-comm. 184-1-2, explains for the 'inner *homa*' that one again changes into the form of a deity from one's own seed (i.e. from inner resources, and offerings to the inner 'fire'). This 'inner *homa*' is free of the three 'faults' (or, poisons), lust, hatred, and delusion. The 'outer *homa*' according to this tradition goes with threes. According to B-comm. 181-4-4,5 the three *karmas*, or rites for *siddhis* are *śāntika*, *pauṣṭika*, *abhicāruka*, going respectively with three geometrical hearths (circle, square, and triangle), which may be an older system than the four already alluded to, which include the *karma* called *vaśīkara* (and so require a fourth geometrical hearth, as already explained). T. Skorupski's essay, "Tibetan Homa Rites", gives further information on visualizing the four hearths.

B-comm. at 184-2-7, treats the two kinds of *homa* in terms of the *samādhis* lacking signs (*nimitta*) or possessing them. The Buddha's lacks signs and uses the Syllables "A", and so on. The *mantrin-s* have the *samādhi* wherein the deities have 'signs', and use the *mantra-mālā* ('garland of mantras'), i.e. the sentence type called *dhāraṇi,* from which result powers, fearlessness, and so on. B-comm. 184-3-3,ff, points out that the Bhagavat may emerge from his 'absolute' *samādhi* which realizes that all *dharmas* are immemorially non-arising, and then teach the retinue by means of his 'inexhaustible Body' (*sku mi zad pa*), teaching them as is done in Chap. II with depictions of deities in terms of 'signs'. Thus, this scripture has numerous iconographical descriptions of deities with 'signs', but they are stipulated as imaginations of the performer, as are the depictions of Agni in this Homa chapter; so they are bound to be impermanent, hence not lasting realities. When the expression 'heretical', i.e. non-Buddhist, is employed for the *samādhi* of mundane gods, it then means a one-sidedness of such a *samādhi* exclusively, whereby deities are attributed signs of color, shape etc. as lasting realities (*dravya*).

So far, only the V-A-T was used as the scripture source—then annotated from a number of other sources. It might be worthwhile to consider a verse from the *Mañjuśrī-mūla-tantra,* p. 125 in its Chap. 13, since this chapter is on *homa*:

> kuryāt pāvakakarmāṇi nisiddhā jinavair iha /
> nirmale cāmbhaso śuddhe kṛmibhir vārjite sadā //
> He should always perform the acts of the Pāvaka (fire) that in this world are prohibited by the best of Jinas; when what was abandoned by the worms of the celestial waters is stainless and pure.

This verse seems to mean by "acts of the pāvaka (fire)" the old Brahmanical rituals that Buddhism rejected. (John K. Locke, *Karunāmaya,* p.103, states that the Brahmans expanded the simple vedic ritual with later forms of ritual, that the tantric Buddhists adopted this rather elaborate *homa*, and then adapted it in accordance with the *Vajrayāna*). The verse seems to defend the Buddhist *homa* as though it is a pure form of the Brahmanical ritual. But it couches this defense in mysterious terms. What was 'abandoned', i.e. left behind, must still be there. Then what or who are the "worms of the celestial waters"? According to the commentary on V-A-T, this is the Puṣkara Ocean, so the 'worms' are a reference to the "sons of the Atharvan". They evolved into lower forms of fire, but the original realm is still there. By purification through 'inner *homa*' one may ascend to that.

It was already observed that the list of fire genealogy is drawn from non-Buddhist sources. This points to a time when there was mutual influence between the Hindus and Buddhists, which could happen at many different times. It is the position of this work that the contents of this Homa chapter of the V-A-T and other chapters of the Sūtra are reasonably placed in the sixth century, A.D. It was at that time that a brahmin convert to Buddhism gave a hint of his background when writing this last chapter of his remarkable Sūtra. He first gave a genealogy of fire like that of the *Vāyu-purāna,* Chap. 28; and continued with names of fires going with the Hindu *Saṃskāra* rites like the correlation in the *Gṛhyasaṃgraha-pariśiṣṭa*. Having shown his mastery over this Brahmanical lore, which he certainly did not despise, he went on to give a list of twelve fires more useful to his Buddhist readers.

This Homa Chapter is brief and trenchant. The numerous names of the fires were frequently presented in transcription, both in the Tibetan and in the Chinese (continued in the Japanese). The two Brahmanical sources just mentioned helped to correct corruptions in the Asian transcription, and besides my wife Hideko read my draft translation along with the Japanese version in the *Kokuyaku Issaikyō,* suggesting some further corrections. Below is a bibliography of the works consulted for the translation and annotation of the 'Homa Chapter'.

Amarakoṣaḥ with Tibetan version. Ed. by Satis Chandra Vidyābhūṣaṇa. The Asiatic Society, Calcutta, 1911. (Also, *Amara-ṭīkā Kāmadhenuḥ*; same ed. and Publ., [first part only of Tibetan version]).

Banerjea, Jitendrea Nath. *The Development of Hindu Iconography*. University of Calcutta, 1956. Rept. Motilal Banarsidass, Delhi, 1985.

Bṛhad-āraṇyaka Upaniṣad. In *Eighteen Principal Upaniṣds*, Vol. 1. Ed. by V.P. Limaye and R.D. Vadekar. Vaidika Samśodhana Maṇḍala, Poona, 1958.

Buddhaguhya attribution *Durgatipariśodhanārtha-vyañjana-vṛtti*. PTT edition, Vol. 76.

Buddhaguhya. *Vairocanābhisambodhi-vikurvitādhiṣṭhāna-mahā-tantra-bhāṣya*, PTI edition, Vol. 77.

Crooke, William, *Religion & Folklore of Northen India*, S. Chand & Co., New Delhi, 1925.

Dash, Vd. Bhagwan. *Concept of Agni in Āyurveda*. Chowkhamba Sanskrit Series Office, Varanasi, 1971.

Dharma-samuccaya, 2d partie (chapitres VI a XII). Ed. and tr. by Lin Li-kouang, revised by A. Bareaus, J. W. de Jong and P. Demiéville. Adrien Maisonneuve, Paris, 1969.

Dowson, John. *A Classical Dictionary of Hindu Mythology and Religion*. Routledge & Kegan Paul, London, 1950.

Goudriaan, Teun. *Māyā Divine and Human*. Motilal Banarsidass, Delhi, 1978.

Grihyasangraha; an appendix to the Gobhila Brihyasūtra. Ed. by Chandrakānta Tarkālankāra. The Asiatic Society, Calcutta, 1910.

Hopkins, E. Wasbhurn. *Epic Mythology*, Motilal Banarsidass, Delhi, 1974.

Knipe, David M. *In the Image of Fire*; Vedic Experiences of Heat. Motilal Banarsidass, Delhi, 1975.

Kokuyaku Issaikyō; Mikkyōbu, Vol. 63, Intro. by Ryūjo Kambayashi, Tokyo.

Lalita Vistāra, text Ed. by Dr. S. Lefmann. Halle, 1902.

Lessing, F.D. *Yung-Ho Kung*; an Iconography of the Lamaist Cathedral in Peking, Vol. One. the Sino-Swedish Expedition. Publication 18, Stockholm, 1942.

Locke, John K. *Karunamaya; the Cult of Avalokitesvara-Matsyendranath in the Valley of Nepal* (Sahayogi Prakashan, Kathmandu, 1980).

Macdonell, A.A. *The Vedic Mythology,* Indological Book House, Varanasi, 1963.

Mahāvyutpatti, Ed. Ryōzaburō Sakaki, 2 Vols. Tokyo, 1962.

Mañjuśrimūlakalpa, Part 1. Ed. by T. Gaṇapati Sāstrī. Trivandrum

Sanskrit Series No. LXX, Trivandrum, 1920.
Nandagarbhāvakrānti-nirdeśa-sūtra. [In a modern summary based on the Tibetan version, Publ. at Dharmasala, H.P. India, n.d.] ***Mdo dkon mchog brtsegs pa ga pa'i naṅ tshan dga 'bo mṅal 'jug*** *gi mdo nas legs par btus pa.* [booklet].
Sandhya Vandhana, Darsa Tarpana and Notes on 'Gayathri'; Deva-nagari and English, Ed. by M.V. Harihara Aiyar. Publ. by Ed., Madras, 1962. [booklet].
Śatapatha-Brāhmaṇa. Tr. by Julius Eggeling, Part I, *Sacred Books of the East.* Motilal Banarsidass, Delhi, 1963.
Shendge, Malati J. *The Civilized Demons: The Hārappans in Ṛgveda.* Abhinav Publications, New Delhi, 1977.
Skorupski, Tedeusz. "Tibetan Homa Rites", *Agni; the Vedic Ritual of the Fire Altar,* ed. by Frits Staal (Asian Humanities Press, Berkeley, 1983), Vol. II.
Strickmann, Michel. "Homa in East Asia", *Agni,* Vol. II.
Trikāṇḍaśeṣa by Sri Purushottamadeva. Venkateshwara Press, Bombay, 1916.
Tsuda, Shinīchi. *The Samvarodaya-tantra,* Selected Chapters. The Hokuseido Press, Tokyo, 1974.
Vāyu-Purāṇa, Part One. Saṃskṛti Saṃsthān, Barelī.
Wayman, Alex. *Calming the Mind and Discerning the Real.* Columbia University, New York, 1978.
Wayman, Alex. "The Significance of Mantras, from the Veda Down to Buddhist Tantric Practice", *The Adyar Library Bulletin,* Vol. XXXIX, 1975.
Wayman, Alex. "Similes for the four Elements from Buddhist Literature", *Indologica Taurinensia,* Vol. VII, 1979, Part One.
Wayman, Alex. "Studies in Yama and Māra", *Indo-Iranian Journal,* Vol. III, 1959 Nrs. 1 & 2.
Winternitz, M. *A General Index to the Sacred Books of the East,* Motilal Banarsidass, Delhi, 1969.

Subhakarasimha

Further explanation :

This drawing is claimed by Japanese authorities to be the authentic version which Enchin (814-891) copied from the original in China and brought back to Japan in 858 A.D. Under the drawing, there is the legend, "This Dharma belongs to ācārya Subhakarasimha". Here, he is depicted with right hand holding the handle of an incense burner; and with left hand, palm upward, tightly clasping a rosary, making a kind of Vajrasattva *samaya* gesture. Reproduction, courtesy of the Onjōji temple.

BOOK II

STUDY OF THE MAHĀVAIROCANA-SŪTRA (DAINICHIKYŌ)

With an annotated translation of
the first chapter by

R. TAJIMA

English translation edited with
an appendix by

ALEX WAYMAN

EDITOR'S PREFACE

Ryūjun Tajima's *study* that is here presented in English translation, first appeared in French with the title *Étude sur le Mahāvairocana-sūtra* (Paris, 1936). Adhir Chakravarti's translation into English is faithful to the French, and prepared with care. Even so, because of the many technicalities, the present writer has had to edit the translation with frequent consultation of the original French, preparing a new copy for the publisher. Since there are many Japanese words in Tajima's *Study*, my wife Hideko (who is Japanese) kindly checked all these expressions to make sure no errors crept in.

Since his *Study* is being published as a companion to my own *Study*, it is well to state at the outset that in my own work I scarcely used this work of Tajima's. The two studies are completely independent. It is true that there are some usages of Japanese scholarly sources for my own study, but these were supplied independently and especially utilized by my wife, as was testified to in my own *Study*. This independence of study was necessary to preserve the integrity of the two approaches, my own stressing the Indo-Tibetan traditions; and Tajima's stressing the Sino-Japanese traditions. In an appendix, I shall treat certain issues raised by Tajima's explanations.

Tajima herein presents a translation of the scripture's Chapter One with elaborate comments drawn from Śubhakarasimha's Chinese commentary. He then summarizes all the remaining chapters with depictions influenced by that Chinese commentary. His felicitous introductions show the place of this scripture in the Japanese Shingon sect, itself inspired by an esoteric current of China. The Shingon sect was established by the Japanese savant Kūkai (774-835) after his studies in China. He is also called Kōbō daishi, the posthumous title by imperial order of 921 A.D. He is approximately contemporary with the construction in Java of the great monument Barabudur; and the commentator Buddhaguhya, a contemporary of Śāntarakṣita, belongs to Kūkai's immediately preceding generation.

Since the time of Kūkai, there has been much study of this

scripture in Japan, and in modern times a steady output of scholarly researches in the Japanese background of Tajima's *Study*.

Dr. Ryūjun Tajima has a remarkable life record. He was born in 1893 (Jan. 9) in Tengamachi, Tochigi-ken, Japan. At the age of 13 he was ordained at Manpukuji Temple, Tochigi. In 1919 he graduated from Busan University, where he studied Tibetan under Ekai Kawaguchi. His graduation thesis was on the Sino-Tibetan *Dainichikyō* (the *Mahāvairocana-sūtra*). In 1923 he became a Lecturer at Busan University. The next year he took a trip to Manchuria, Mongolia, and North China in search of the Tibetan Tripitaka. In 1928 he was appointed Professor at Taishō University in Tokyo. Then in 1931 with a grant from the Busan Educational Foundation he went to Paris to study Sanskrit, Tibetan, and Kuchean under Sylvain Lévi—also under A. Foucher—at the Sorbonne. In March 1934 he organized the 1100th centenary celebration of Kōbō daishi, along with numerous lectures, at the Institute of Indian Culture, University of Paris. He was awarded the Ph.D. in July, 1935, for his French work, *Étude sur le Mahāvairocana-sūtra.* Then he began work on a book Tantric Doctrine, and another one on the two Mandaras (*maṇḍala*)—both in French—which he finished years later in Japan in 1955. In 1936 (August) he returned to Japan after 4 years and 10 months abroad. In April 1937 he resumed teaching at Taishō University. During over 20 years of teaching, among others he held the post of head Librarian, Chairman of the Department of Literature, and later the Chairmanship of the Department of Buddhism. He succeeded Dr. Ryūjo Kambayashi as the second Director of the Shingon Study Center, Taishō University—a well-established joint research center of the Busan and the Chisan sects of the Shingon school. Dr. Tajima was involved in politics. In 1941 he travelled around the U.S.A. with a peace mission, hopefully to avert the danger of a Pacific war, in company of parliament member K. Takami, and a Christian scholar, Prof. Fugii. After the war ended in 1949, he was appointed Sugamo Prison's chaplain for the "War Criminals" who were high-ranking military officers, politicians, including General Tojo. In 1951 he had a stroke brought on by overwork in spite of which he kept up his teaching at the Taishō University, and his position as chaplain. In June 1955 he finished the drafts of the two books in French (the two Mandaras book was published posthumously in 1959). In 1955 he received the highest honorary title Daisōjō (Grand Abbot of Busan sect, Shingon school). While proof-reading his books he died in 1958 at the age of 65. A statue to honor him, named Rūjin Jizō-son, was erected at Shōshinji Temple, Tochigi-ken.[1]

As to the present work, Tajima has succeeded in expressing the essential facts of this difficult scripture in a manner so clear and felicitous that a rank outsider could get a good idea of what it is all about by reading his work. It is honor for the present writer to have his own *Study* published together with this striking presentation by the Grand Abbot of the Busan sect.

1. This summary of Tajima's life is prepared from a Japanese publication on the directors of the Shingon Study Center at Taishō University, Tokyo, furnished us by Rev. Shorei Nakayama, of the Naritasan Institute of Buddhist Studies, at Narita, Japan. Hideko Wayman abstracted the data from this publication.

TAJIMA'S FOREWORD

It is with a sense of profound regret that at the very beginning of this modest work it must be to the memory of my venerable teacher Sylvain Lévi. I pay tribute of gratitude which will be forever living in my heart. It was he who at the end of one of his classes at the College de France remarked to me how much the *Mahāvairocana-sūtra,* the fundamental text of Buddhist esoterism, was poorly known to Western specialists. Since then he did not cease to encourage me to undertake a translation of this text along with an exposition of the essential doctrines of the Shingon sect to which I belong and for which the work constitutes the principal scriptural authority.

In the preparation of this work, Mr. Foucher, President of the Institute of Indian Civilization at the Sorbonne, has shown me no little kindness. Mr. Honorat, President of the Institute of Japanese Studies of the University of Paris, as also Dr. Satsuma, Administrator of the Cite Universitaire, has very kindly taken an interest in my work. Thanks to the kind agency of the Japanese Embassy in Paris, a financial grant was accorded to me by the Japanese Society for the Development of International Cultural Relations (Kokusai Bunka Shinko kai). I have tried to make myself worthy of all these manifestations of interest and goodwill, without which this little work could not have been published and which bind me with a deep debt of gratitude. In fine, I must thank particularly Mr. Demieville and Mr. Haguenauer, both Professors at the Ecole des Langues Orientales Vivantes, since without their help I could not have been able to successfully complete the work. Thanks are equally due to my dear friend Mr. Buhort who has rendered me constant and most devoted assistance.

For a long time Western scholars have been studying Buddhism. France particularly has honored herself by giving birth to a great number of specialist savants like Eugene Burnouf, Stanislas Julien, Ph. E. Foucaux, Léon Feer, Emile Senart, Louis Finot, Sylvain Lévi—to name only a few among the dead—and in the present generation she alone has a brilliant galaxy of such scholars. After their researches, their editions and translations of the texts, the works of travellers and collectors, it may seem that the subject is completely explored. However, insofar as esoteric Buddhism is concerned, it may be observed that the rare texts which have been so far published in Europe chiefly belong to what is called in Japan "mixed esoterism". But the sacred texts, commentaries and treatises of pure esoterism remain practically unknown in the Western world. The *Dainichikyō* is the most representative of all these.

In 1934 the whole of Japan celebrated the eleventh centenary of Kōbō daishi, the great monk who founded the Shingon sect and also exercised considerable influence on the progress of culture in Japan. Even in Paris on March 21 a commemorative was arranged at the Musée Guimet under the auspices of the French Association of the Friends of the Orient, where numerous orientalists assembled on this occasion. I was entrusted to introduce the work of Kōbō daishi to the Western public. Then I outlined the project of the work which is now presented.

All the doctrine of Kōbō daishi may be deduced from the *Dainichikyō*. It is the first text to know. Along with the system of Shingon, we had the plan of studying the doctrinal principles of the two great *maṇḍalas*. But circumstances beyond our control have not permitted us to publish the two parts of our work simultaneously. However, we hope that our study of the *maṇḍalas* will see the light of day in the near future.

The author regrets his inability, especially in a foreign language, to describe in a worthy manner the principles of esoteric Buddhism which has known so many great masters. But he will be satisfied if the readers find here some general notions of the beautiful doctrine.

Paris, TAJIMA RYŪJUN
17 June 1936

PART I

INTRODUCTION

ANTECEDENTS OF ESOTERIC BUDDHISM

The origins of esoteric thought go back to ancient times of India. As is known, magical formulas and charms are found in the *Atharva-veda*, one of the four Vedas. Afterwards, this predilection for magic develops more and more in Brāhmaṇas. Prior to the rise of Buddhism it adopts a religious form and occupies an important place in popular belief. Once it was incorporated into Buddhism, it acquired its full maturity and its full development.

In early Buddhism, however, one notices that the Buddha forbids the use of the *dhāraṇī* and the charms. Likewise, it is out of the question for *mantras* and *dhāraṇīs* to be in the Hīnayāna *sūtras*. It is no less true that in the Vinaya books the Buddha has often repeated his prohibition, from which it may be inferred that it was often violated.

On the other hand, *mantras* and *dhāraṇīs* are recommended in the Mahāyāna books, even in their most representative ones, like the *Saddharmapuṇḍarīka-sūtra*, the *Avatamsaka-sūtra* and the *Prajñāpāramitā-sūtra*. In other *sūtras* they are mentioned in large number. It may be shown that esoteric thought always rose to the surface in Buddhist currents.

At the very time when Mahāyāna Buddhism was developing, Brāhmanism was transforming itself into Hinduism. At that time Buddhism came under the latter's influence, and a new ferment of ideas brought great changes in it.

At about the sixth century was born what would come to be esoteric Buddhism. It grew quickly, thanks to the labors of the church masters. In spite of their fundamental unity, their ideas, however, failed to constitute the doctrinal body of a single sect. With regard to their differences, Matsumoto Bunzaburo wrote:[1] "In India esotericism has never been able to unify itself. It was only twenty years after Yi-tsing had returned from India (695 A.D.) that Śubhakarasimha and Vajrabodhi visited China. In his *Nan hai ki kouei tchouan* (Vol. I, Taishō No. 2125) he has reviewed the Mahāyāna schools of India. It is clear that these could be reduced in brief to two schools, the Mādhyamika and the Yogā(cāra). Certainly it is at this precise time that the esoteric movement begins to develop in India. And since Yi-tsing had travelled for about twenty years, from South India up to the East and the Middle part of the Peninsula, doubtless he had some knowledge of it (i.e. esoteric Buddhism). In fact, esotericism in India formed an integral part of each school with varying nuances and in these circumstances it could not unify itself. It was still not represented by a single school that could attract an observer's attention. Some twenty years later Śubhakarasimha and Vajrabodhi came to China at about the same time and each of them was ignorant of the other's doctrine: it was inevitable."

After the heights it had attained in the eighth century with Śubhakarasimha and Vajrabodhi, esoteric Buddhism slowly decomposed in India and fell so much in decadence as to lose itself finally in Hindu beliefs.[2]

In contrast, the correct tradition of esoteric Buddhism was planted in China during the T'ang dynasty with the arrival of Śubhakarasimha in 716, of Vajrabodhi and Amoghavajra in 720. However, the sacred books of a mixed esotericism had been translated long before, between 223 and 253 by Tche-k'ien[3] of the Wou dynasty; and many other translators anterior to the T'ang dynasty are also known: Śrīmitra[4] of Kucha who worked in China between 317 and 322; Buddhabhadra,[5] an inhabitant of Central India, from 408 to 429; Kumārajīva[6] who also hailed from Kucha, from 401 to 413; Bodhiruci[7] from Central India between 508 and 535; Jñānagupta[8] of Gandhāra from 560 to 600, and so on.

According to the summation table arranged by Omura Seigai in his *Mikkyō hattatsu-shi* (The Development of Esotericism), before the works of Śubhakarasimha there had already been translated into Chinese 96 esoteric *sūtras*, 35 *sūtras* containing *dhāraṇīs*, and 4 commentaries.[9] The translators were perhaps not all adepts in esoteric Buddhism. They kept themselves engaged in translating the *sūtras* of the Mahāyāna and the Hīnayāna. One may even suppose that the monks hailing from different parts of India and Central Asia had the prime consideration of spreading the Buddhist doctrines as fast as possible.

In China, esoteric Buddhism was perhaps never so flourishing as during the T'ang period when Śubhakarasimha and Vajrabodhi were among its exponents. The Taishō Issaikyō, in its section properly called esoteric Buddhism, includes 612 numbers in 961 'volumes' (*kwan*); but then in other sections one finds a vast number of works connected with esoterism. Nearly all these works were translated into Chinese before the middle of the T'ang dynasty.

On their arrival in China, all these great translators, Śubhakarasimha (Zemmui), Vajrabodhi (Kongōchi), and Amoghavajra (Fukū) were admitted to the audience of the emperors. It is under their patronage that they could successfully complete their translations. Also, esoteric Buddhism witnessed an era of great prosperity and spread itself throughout the empire. Although it co-existed with the different sects already established in China, esoteric Buddhism could not organize itself into one single school. After the middle of the T'ang period its decline was getting near. At the beginning of the Song period some of its books were still being translated, but it was decaying. In China it no longer possessed vitality, nor did it have the interest that it experienced in a very different form, that of Lamaism.

THE SHINGON ESOTERISM

The founder of Shingon esoterism of Japan, Kōbō daishi (Kūkai, 447-835) in 804 went to China in search of the Dharma. At this time Chinese esoterism had already completed the translation of the *sūtras* and the commentaries; and from the doctrinal point of view, it was sufficiently mature. Kōbō daishi, at Tsing-long-sseu, received the complete initiation from the mouth of the *upādhyāya* Houei-kouo (Keikwa, 746-805) who was the most brilliant disciple of Amoghavajra, the great master of esoterism. In 806 he returned to Japan. His visit to China coincided with the apogee of esoterism in China. He was able to assimilate its quintessence and was the first to succeed in unifying solidly the sects of esoteric Buddhism into a single school. One may recall that in the distant past it was born in India; and in the course of centuries it had slowly gathered force, and was transplanted in China. There it bloomed fully, but it was in Japan that it was destined to bear fruit. Even today, eleven centuries after Kōbō daishi, it remains very prosperous there.

If we were to make a history of it, how many have been the transformations of Buddhist esoteirc thought before it crystalized into Japanese Shingon? It is evident that it is completely different from the esoterism known in India. It is for this reason that we reserve the appellation of Shingon for the esoteric Buddhism of

Japan, disregarding the intermediate aspect which it had assumed in China.

Indian esoterism had among others two important centers—the monastery of Nālandā and that of Vikramaśīla; and as such it divided itself into two schools of tradition. The first was a development of Mahāyānist thought. It was an orthodox esoterism based on the Vinaya. The second consisted in a more popular form toward the close of the VIIIth century, and before long it degraded itself into esoterism of the left (SADŌMIKKYŌ).

It (i.e. the Vikramaśīla tradition) did not inspire the Japanese Shingon. As a matter of fact, the patriarch from whom it claims its origin, viz. Śubhakarasimha, had himself been the disciple of Dharmagupta at Nālandā; and it is at Nālandā again that Vajrabodhi adopted the life of religion (680) for studying grammar from Śāntijñāna. At the age of twenty he received the *upasampadā* (GUSOKU-KAI) and in six years he learned all the doctrines of the two vehicles. These facts peremptorily show that the Shingon belongs to the most orthodox tradition.

From the point of view of chronology, the esoterism of Tibet was introduced in that country later than the foundation of Chinese esoterism. With regard to its affiliation, we have historical proofs that it was derived chiefly from the Vikramaśīla center. On the other hand, researches on the Tibetan versions of the scriptures are in themselves important for the texts. But it may be stated that the strange esoterism of Lamaism is in fact far removed from the teachings of the Buddha. It must not, therefore, be forgotten for a moment that there exists considerable difference between Chinese esoterism, to which the Japanese Shingon in its entirety goes back, and the Tibetan esoterism.

What is then the esoterism of the Shingon (SHINGON MIKKYŌ)? One may say that it represents the summit of Mahāyānist Buddhism. It directly exposes the essential thought of the Buddha. Kōbō daishi calls popular Buddhism (KENGYŌ) the doctrine disclosed by Śākyamuni in his Nirmāṇakāya. He conceives it as a simple expedient of salvation. From this he concludes that the Shingon, the true domain of the internal experience of the Tathāgata is the veritable Buddhism which Mahāvairocana reveals in Dharmakāya. Again, these truths obtained through the enlightenment of the Tathāgata are profound and full of mysteries which are difficult to be grasped by ordinary people listening to them. This is why they are called the *Guhyayāna* (HIMITSU-JŌ), the secret vehicle or simply esoteric Buddhism. If they have something which is secret or recondite, it is not that the Buddha wanted to hide it, but that mankind is not able to understand it.

The Buddhists distinguish two kinds of esoterism: (1) pure esoterism (JUMMITSU) which is the teaching of Vairocana in his Dharmakāya and of which the scriptures par excellence are the *Dainichikyō* (the *Mahāvairocana-sūtra*) and the *Kongōchōgyō* (the *Tattvasamgraha*); and (2) mixed esoterism (ZŌMITSU) which comprises the other esoteric schools and which mixes up the teachings of Vairocana with that of popular Buddhism in such a way that esoteric books other than the *Dainichikyō* and the *Kongōchōgyō* belong to the ZŌMITSU.

In the esoteric scriptures, there are on the one hand those things which belong to the supramundane realm and directly tend to stir up the Thought of Bodhi. On the other hand, there are also those things which teach us how to get satisfaction of mundane desires like security, well-being, etc. It is evident that the true goal of esoterism is of a supramundane nature and that the other tendencies may be regarded as expedients to lead the common man to the Buddha's doctrine. This is why the books of pure esoterism deal entirely with the supramundane level. The *Dainichikyō*, the *Kongōchōgyō*, and their commentaries speak of strange divinities of original Buddhism. These are again devices to attract mankind and testify to the generosity of esoterism which is inclined to admit the infidels into its bosom. It is in the same spirit that it has taken recourse to non-Buddhist rites so as to make its true thought understood. Thus the Buddhist *homa* (GOMA) bears the same name as the Brahmanical ceremony but its significance is completely different. The *homa* of esoteric Buddhism is the first phase of contemplation. It signifies the destruction of our passions by fire, and the fire is the insight and compassion of the Tathāgata. The twigs and the offerings which feed the fire are only the symbols of our passions. Purely symbolic, the Buddhist *homa* has nothing in common with Brahmanical *homa*. He who does not know the true esoteric thought must not take it as a simple external rite or interpret it in a superficial way.

The method of esoterism has something direct and positive. Popular Buddhism states that our defilements (*kleśa*) are the principal obstacles to Bodhi; and consequently it is necessary to suppress them completely. On the contrary, esoteric Buddhism declares that the defilements are of the same nature as Bodhi. It proceeds in the same way as a physician who derives the healing remedies from the most deadly poisons. Just as it is dangerous to give a child an unsheathed sword as a plaything, so also to reveal the esoteric thought to people who are incapable of understanding it, would lead them to error and in the end would be injurious to them. At all times esoterism has condemned individual study among the non-initiates, and has insisted on the importance of the oral transmissal from the master to the disciple. If the subject is not fit to receive the instruction, it is forbidden to give it to him.

THE DAINICHIKYŌ AND ITS PLACE AMONG ESOTERIC TEXTS

What is the exact place of the *Dainichikyō* among the esoteric scriptures of India? We are not able to know this. In China, it had an important position because each of eight religieux (NITTŌ HAKKE)[10] who in the beginning of the Heian period went to China to study esoteric Buddhism brought with them a copy of this Sūtra. It resulted in the fact that no sooner was the *Dainichikyō* introduced to Japan than it easily occupied a premier position among Mahāyāna texts.

Japanese esoterism is divided into two schools, namely, the Shingon founded by Kōbō daishi, and the Tendai introduced to Japan by Dengyō daishi, Jikaku and others, in accordance with the study they had (respectively) made of it in China. The first one had as its principal home the Toji ("Temple of the East")—this is how the Kyōōgokokuji of Heian (Kyōto) was called—from which has come the name Tōmitsu for this branch of esoterism. The second school, by opposition, is called Taimitsu because it is connected with the sect known as Tendai (Chinese T'ien-t'ai). Its point of view is opposed to that of the *Dainichikyō* and the *Kongōchōgyō*. In the Tōmitsu, the fundamental principle which inspires the *Dainichikyō* is RI, the innate Reason, and what inspires the *Kongōchōgyō* is CHI, Knowledge. These two principles are as much inseparable from each other as are the one side and the other side of the very same fabric (RICHI FUNI). Consequently, the two Sūtras contain but one and the same doctrine. But in the Taimitsu, as long as the two principles remain matters of teaching they are regarded as mutually independent; and the unity of the two Sūtras is realized only in third, the *Soshitsujikyō* (the *Susiddhikaramahātantra*). What value do the masters of the Taimitsu attach to the *Dainichikyō* in relation to the

Hokekyō (*Saddharmapuṇḍarīka-Sūtra*), which is the fundamental text of the Tendai? They view it as a work which explains how to put into practice the precepts of the *Hokekyō*. Chisō daishi (Enchin) of the Tendai sect puts it as follows in his *Daibirushanakyō, shiki* (Taishō No. 2212): "Upon reflecting on it, one finds that this discipline of *Samādhi* is obtained only in esoterism. Nothing is said of it in any other *sūtras*. This is why in the Mahāyāna (this Sūtra) has the position of primacy; and in esoterism it is the most esoteric of all. Even the *Hokekyō*—to say nothing of the other *sūtras*—does not come up to its height."[11] The masters of the other schools are of the same opinion. We have thus seen the place the *Dainichikyō* occupies in Japanese Buddhism.

PLAN OF THE DAINICHIKYŌ

The *Dainichikyō* in Chinese comprises in all 36 chapters in seven 'volumes' (KWAN), but only the chapters I-XXXI, constituting the first six 'volumes', represent the original work. The five chapters of the seventh 'volume', added under the title *Kuyōbō* ("The Offering Rites") are nothing else than the *Daibirushana* yōryaku nenjukyō[12] ("A Sūtra Resume of the Recitations of Mahāvairocana") which was translated by Vajrabodhi. Originally, it was an independent work. Śubhakarasimha also translated it into Chinese, and appended it to his own translation of the *Mahāvairocana-sūtras* as the seventh 'volume'. At present, the fact is well known. This is why the Tibetan editions of the *Dainichikyō* never contain this appendix of the 'Seventh volume'. Our discussion will therefore be confined exclusively to the first six KWAN.

The Chinese commentaries on the *Dainichikyō* are of two categories. The first is represented by the *Dainichikyōsho* in twenty 'volumes'.[13] It was taught by Śubhakarasimha (Zemmui Sanzō) in the Year 13 of K'ai-yuan (725) to his Chinese disciple Yi-hing (Ichigyō) who took dictation from him of the first six 'volumes'. After the death of Ichigyō (727) two other monks, Tche-yen (Chigon) and Wen-kou (Onko) re-arranged them in fourteen volumes under the title *Dainichikyōgishaku*.[14] The Tōmitsu uses the first version, the Taimitsu the second. As to the seventh 'volume' of the Chinese *Dainichikyō*, a disciple of Śubhakarasimha, viz. the monk Fukashigi (Pou-K'o-sseu-yi) of the Reimyōji (Ling-miao-sseu) in Shiragi (Korea) wrote a commentary on it in two 'volumes' under the title *Daibirushanakyō Kuyōshidaibōsho* (abbreviation: *Dainichikyō kuyōbōsho*),[15] more simply called "the Commentary of Fushigi".

The *Dainichikyō* consists of two parts, one doctrinal, i.e. the first chapter; and the other devoted to practice, i.e. the second and later chapters. One may say that the first part is a general introduction which suffices to explain the essentials of the doctrine. The second and successive chapters deal with the application of the principle contained in the first (chapter), in particular with the mode of establishing a *maṇḍala* and initiating a disciple. This initiation (KWANJŌ) is the ancient *abhiṣeka* ceremony of India, a ceremony celebrated for the accession of sovereigns, but to which esoterism has given a more profound significance. The head of the prince was sprinkled with water collected from the four oceans to symbolize his universal domination.[16] In the ceremony of esoteric Buddhism, the master sprays on the head of the disciple water from five vessels to symbolize the Five Wisdoms of the Tathāgata so that he may continue the lineage of the Buddhas.

As has been already stated, the first chapter of the *Dainichikyō* explains the principles of the doctrine which any listener may come to understand; but from the second chapter onward the text needs to be elucidated by the oral tradition which only the master can transmit to his disciple and he is not permitted to do this for someone who has not yet received the initiation (*abhiṣeka*). The same prohibition applies also with regard to the commentaries of all this part.

In the present work we propose to study principally the first chapter. Besides, it enables us to give a general idea of the totality of the Sūtra.

THE ESSENTIAL IDEAS OF THE DAINICHIKYŌ

How can the directional thought of the *Dainichikyō* be summed up? It has been sufficiently expressed by the maxim contained in the text itself: "Know the truth your own heart" (JITSU NO GOTOKU JISHIN WO SHIRE). The common goal of all the schools of Buddhism is to arouse this understanding in man who goes astray. Unlike the other texts of the Mahāyāna, the *Dainichikyō* has not taken recourse to learned expositions. It does not stop to take the round-about way of the dialectic or of the myths. It goes straight towards its goal. It declares once for all that the unenlightened is Buddha.

Esoterism calls our heart "the Pure Heart of Bodhi"; and at each instant this definition is recalled. This Pure Heart[17] of Bodhi (JŌ BODHI SHIN=*Śuddhabodhicitta*) is not anything else than the JISHŌ SHŌJŌSHIN (*svabhāvaśuddhacitta*), the "Heart pure in itself by nature" of Buddhism in general. It shines in the depth of our soul; it is our original nature. Its unlimited and eternal function is knowledge or what we call Bodhi. The person who has been able to master it has become a buddha.

The Buddha asks: ....Master of Mysteries! What is the Bodhi? He says: "It is to know one's own heart as it is".[18]

The Buddha asks: "For what reason do you say, not to seek the Bodhi and the omniscient knowledge anywhere else than in one's own heart"? He says: "Because its original nature is pure".[19]

"A treasure of Omniscience exists eternally in our heart (Tib. *snying=hṛdaya*[20]); man calls it *sarvajñāna,* Omniscience."[21]

These brief quotations may furnish an idea of the whole of the *Dainichikyō*. This, moreover, presents a particular characteristic. It defines the true nature of our heart and also the true nature of all *dharmas*. By *dharmas* Buddhism understands material as well as spiritual things; in short, all the forces of existence. In the second chapter which deals with the practice, objects or actions of this world are taken for comparison in order to inculcate in us the necessity of understanding well the true nature of all the *dharmas*. During the ceremony of initiation (*abhiṣeka*) the Master also explains the Dharma to his disciple by presenting to him diverse objects: "He takes a clear mirror and shows him the *dharmas* without characteristic signs. He tells him these marvellous *gāthā*-s [cf. II,230-32, in Wayman's translation]: 'The *dharmas* have neither any form nor any characteristic sign. They are pure and unblemished, imperceptible, and ineffable. They are born of causal actions only. To know them as such, without blemish so far as their true nature is concerned, is an incomparable advantage for the world. Thou art born of the 'Heart of the Buddhas.' "[22]

The image which the disciple sees in the mirror appears because of the mirror and is not 'spontaneous'. The Master explains that in the same way the *dharmas* arising in the causal chain are not spontaneous.

"All these *dharmas* as *dharmas* remain the same, whether or not a Tathāgata appears."[23] [cf. the prose immediately following 11,182, in Wayman's translation.]

"The *dharmas* (as) the Buddha (teaches them) are devoid of all characteristic signs; they simply exist in the state of *dharmas.*"[24]

The essential principles have been commented upon many times. But to understand the true nature of the *dharmas* is to understand the true nature of our heart. Subjectively seen, the true nature of our heart is the true nature of the *dharmas*. From the objective point of view, the true nature of the *dharmas* is the true nature of our heart. The *Dainichikyō* discusses this truth under the symbol of the *a* syllable: "What is the doctrine of the Shingon? It is that all *dharmas* are primordially unborn (HOMPUSHŌ, *adyānutpāda*); it is the discipline of the syllable *a*."[25]

"The syllable *a* is at the base of all the doctrines. As soon as somebody opens his mouth, all the sounds bear the vowel *a*. Without the *a* there would have been no language. This is why it is called 'mother of all the sounds'. The speeches of the three worlds all depend on the name, but the name depends on the syllable. That is why the virtue (SHITTAN, *siddham*) of the syllable *a* is the mother of all the syllables. It is important to know that such is the true meaning of *a*; and this sense extends itself to all the *dharmas*. How is it that there is no *dharma* which is not the effect of a cause? Things arising from a cause all have a beginning, an origin. But if we consider the causes which give birth to them, we find that they are themselves born of other causes. It is always the same circle. Where then shall we look for the origin? Thus if we ponder over it seriously, we shall come to recognize the truth about the original non-production. It is the origin of the ten thousand *dharmas*. Just as when listening to some speeches, we hear the sound *a,* so also when we consider the production of the *dharmas* we see their original nonproduction. The one who realizes their original non-production knows his own heart as it really is; and the one who knows his own heart as it is possesses omniscient knowledge. . . According to the principle of original non-production, whether there is a Buddha or not, the *dharmas* remain *dharmas* as such. What would be their creator?"[26]

In the last analysis, since the *dharmas* are not born of a first cause, it may be deduced that the *dharmas* in essence are neither born, nor can they perish. The object of the *Dainichikyō* is to reveal the absolute value of things.

THE DAINICHIKYŌ IN EUROPE

The first fragments of the *Dainichikyō* reaching Europe formed part of a lot of manuscripts sent by the Russians from the ruins of Ablaikit near the source of the Irtych. These were presented by Peter the Great to the French Academy. In 1723 the Abbot of Bignon was able to tell the Czar that these fragments were written in Tibetan. Abbot Fourmont even made an attempt to translate these. This translation was corrected by Müller (*Commentatio de Scriptis*

Tanguticis in Siberia repertis, Petropoli, 1747), and then by the Augustine monk Georgi who published the fragment in his *Alphabetum Tibetanum,* II, appendice III, *Tabula Tibetana e voluminibus non longe a fontibus Irtis repertis excerpta,* Rome, 1762.

Finally, Csoma de Körösi made a new translation of the same fragment in English (*Journal of the Asiatic Society of Bengal,* I, p. 270).

In his *Analyse du kandjour* (Annales du Musee Guimet, II, 1881), Léon Feer characterized the Sūtra as follows: "(Folios 300-412) Grand Treatise (or Sūtra) containing many religious articles and *mantras.* Pronounced by Vairocana, the most perfect Bodhisattva on the request of Vajrapāṇi. . . It is the volume or the work, a fragment of which in Tibetan characters was published in Europe in 1722 at Leipzig in *Actes des savants.* . . . The fragment, folios 337-39 (published by Georgi) consists chiefly of the *bījamantras* pronounced (with the blessing or benevolence of Bhagavat Vairocana) by many Bodhisattvas, gods and goddesses, and addressed to the saintly Buddhas (*samantabuddhānām*)."

The Kanjur (*bka' 'gyur*) which Léon Feer had before his eyes was the edition of Narthang (Snar-thang). The fragment in question, as may be verified by comparing with the Chinese version was from the end of Chapter III ("On the suppression of obstacles") to the beginning of Chapter IV ("The store of current *mantras*"). In the *Taishō lssaikyō,* Vol. XVIII, it goes from pp. 13c-28 to 14b-23.

THE SHINGON AND ITS CANON

It was necessary to give a name to the new sect founded in Japan. Kōbō daishi called it the Shingon sect. Shingon, "true speech", has the sense of "an exact *mantra* which reveals the truth of the *dharmas.*"[27] It is the word of the Tathāgata in Dharmakāya. The *Dainichikyō* uses sometimes the name SHINGON MON ("discipline of the Shingon"), sometimes SHINGON HŌKYŌ ("teaching of the Dharma by the Shingon"). Amoghavajra, in his preface to his translation of the *Ryakujutsu kongōchō yuga fumbetsu shoi shushō hōmon,*[28] writes: "The SHINGON DARANI SHU is the secret and profound doctrine of all the Tathāgatas. It is the discipline which causes one to bear witness to the Dharma by spontaneous awakening."[29]

The catalog prepared by Kōbō daishi of the *sūtras, vinayas,* and *śāstras* which the Shingon sect may study (*Shingonshū shogaku kyo ritsu ron mokuroku*[30]) is very long (188 works in 468 kwan). The most important (to these) are:

(1) *Daibirushana jōbutsu jimben kaji kyō* (called in abbreviation *Dainichikyō*), 7 kwan, Chinese translation by Śubhakarasimha.[31]

(2) *Kongōchō issai nyorai shinjitsushō daijō genshō daikyōōgyō* (called in abbreviation Kongōchōgyō), 3 kwan, translated by Amoghavajra.[32]

(3) *Kongōchō yugachū ryakushitsu nenju kyō (Ryakushitsu nenjukyō)*, 4 kwan, translated by Vajrabodhi.[33]

(4) *Soshitsuji kara kyō,* 3 kwan translated by Subhakarasimha.[34]

(5) *Kongōburokaku issai yuga yugi kyō* (*Yugikyo*), 2· kwan, translated by Vajrabodhi.[35]

(6) *Kongōchō yugachū hotsu anokutara sammyaku sambodhaishin ron* (*Bodaishinron*), 1 kwan, translated by Amoghavajra.[36]

(7) *Shaku makaen ron,* 10 kwan, translated by Batsudaimata (Vṛddhimata? cf. *Hōbōgirin,* fascicule annexe, p. 128b).[37]

Among these books, Nos.1 and 2, i.e. the *Dainichikyō* and the *kongōchōgyō,* are the sacred scriptures par excellence of the Shingon esoterism. They are called the Grand Sūtras of the two BU (RYŌBU DAIKYŌ), namely, the TAIZŌ BU which summarizes the topics of the *Dainichikyō*, and the KONGŌCHŌ BU which does it for the topics of the *kongōchōgyō*.

It is fit to say here a few words about the origins of the *Kongōchōgyō*. The Sanskrit original contained ten myriad of *gāthā* collected in eighteen 'assemblies'; and we have an analysis of these in the *Jūhachieshiki* (analysis of this work), which Amoghavajra translated (Taishō, No. 869). But what we actually possess nowadays is only a part of this work, i.e. 3000 *gāthā*. However, No. 3 of the above list (*Ryakushitsu nenjukyō*) contains a resume of the first 'assembly' and is considered as important as No. 2, i.e. *Kongōchōgyō*. It makes only a few allusions to the other seventeen 'assemblies'. This summary of the first assembly is divided into four sections, the first of which has six chapters. The first chapter is entitled *Kongōkaimandara kōdai giki hon* ("On the Grand Rite of the Vajradhātu-maṇḍala"). During the Song epoch, Che-hou (Sego, Dānapāla?) translated all the chapters of the first assembly. This is the *Bussetsu issai nyorai shinjutsushō daijō genshō sammai daikyōōgyō,* 30 kwan (called by abbreviation *Sōyaku kyōōgyō* or else *Sanjikkwan no Kyōōgyō*).[38] But since this translation took place later than Kōbō daishi's foundation of the sect, this work is not considered as fundamental. Speaking simply, it is the treatise No. 2 that pre-eminently is designated *Kongōchōgyō*.

THE TWO GREAT MAṆḌALAS

The Shingon esoterism has two great *maṇḍalas* (RYŌBU MANDARA), respectively called Vajradhātu (KONGŌKAI) and Mahākaruṇāgarbha (DAIHITAIZŌ, abbreviated to TAIZŌ for Garbha), which set forth graphically the ideas of the Shingon doctrine. The two fundamental principles are, as we have stated, the innate Reason (RI) and Knowledge (CHI). The first is explained in the *Dainichikyō*, the second in the *Kongōchōgyō*. Buddhism uses the term *rūpa* for material objects, and the term *citta* for spiritual objects. The RI and CHI of esoterism correspond to these two categories. According to Kōbō daishi the nature of all things may be ascribed to six elements, viz. earth, water, fire, wind, space, and idea. Now, the first five elements spring from RI and the last one from CHI. If things are contemplated in an objective manner, their Thusness (SHINNYO=*tathatā*) is revealed and their identity becomes apparent. It is the RI. Examining them subjectively, though they are innumerable, they differ only according to the diversity of the merits of our hearts. This is the CHI. Thus the Garbhamaṇḍala graphically describes the aspect of the RI, the identity or fundamental quality (*samatā*) of all the *dharmas*. The Vajradhātu-maṇḍala shows how the CHI looks at the diversity of hearts which can train the RI. But the RI and the CHI are nothing but two faces of one and the same thing, to wit, RICHI FUNI—the most important of the Shingon principles, which states, "The RI and the CHI are non-two." The Garbhamaṇḍala presents the *dharmas* in their original nature. The Vajradhatu-maṇḍala indicates the domain of the Buddha's knowledge permeated with the RI. Although these two *maṇḍalas* make one pair and are complementary, they are the ideal center, the unique and indivisible principle of Mahāvairocana's RI-CHI. We ordinary, even unenlightened, human beings, possess all the virtue of the indivisible RI-CHI and this the esoteric doctrine boldly affirms. That is why the RYŌBU MANDARA, *maṇḍala* of the two principles, is in reality the image of our original and potential nature.

TRADITIONS REGARDING THE PATRIARCHS OF THE SHINGON

Considered from the doctrinal point of view, the Shingon is not an Indian import from China. Its doctrine has been formulated by Kōbō daishi alone. What he has inherited from India are the secret rites of unction (*abhiṣeka)*, for example, transferring water from one pitcher to another. The patriarchs of the Shingon are also divided categories, viz. those who associate themselves with the propagation of the doctrine, and those who have transmitted the secret rites. On each side there are eight but certain personages occur in both these lists.

The eight partriarchs of the ritual tradition (FUHŌ NO HASSO) are: (1) Dainichi Nyorai, (2) Kongōsatta (3) Ryumyō Basatsu, (4) Ryūchi Bosatsu, (5) Kongōchi Sanzō, (6) Fukū Sanzō (7) Keikwa Ajari, and (8) Kōbō daishi.

The eight patriarchs known for the propagation of the doctrine (DENJU NO HASSO) are: (1) Ryūmyō Bosatsu, (2) Ryūchi Bosatsu, (3) Kongōchi Sanzō, (4) Zemmui Sanzō, (5) Fukū Sanzō, (6) Ichgyō Ajari, (7) Keikwa Ajari, and (8) Kōbō daishi.

Dainichi Nyorai (Mahāvairocana): He is the Buddha in Dharmakāya and promulgates the two grand Sūtras.

Kongōsatta (Vajrasattva): He received the doctrine from the mouth of the Tathāgata and by his orders wrote it down and deposited the same in the Stūpa of Iron, situated in South India (NANTEN NO TETTŌ ; *infra*). He awaits its being revealed to men deserving of receiving it.

Mahāvairocana is a deification of Śākyamuni (*infra*), and Vajrasattva represents the humanity which aspires to develop the Heart of Bodhi.

Ryūmyo (Nāgārjuna): He flourished in South India eight hundred years[39] after the passing away of the Buddha. With the blessings of Mahāvairocana he opened the Stūpa of Iron and found himself face to face with Vajrasattva. He received the *abhiṣeka*, collected the "grand Sūtra of the two BU" and was finally able to spread it in the world.

Ryūchi (Nāgabodhi):[40] He was a great disciple of Nāgārjuna.[41] His virtues were well known in South India. Perhaps he went to the Land of the Lions (Simhala=Ceylon) to preach esoterism. He is the same person who under the name of Dharmagupta lived in the monastery of Nālandā[42] and under the name of Fugen Ajari (Samanta-bhadra-ācārya?) visited Ceylon.[43] During his long life extending for many centuries he spread the secret doctrine in a large measure.[44]

Kongōchi Sanzō (Vajrabodhi, 671-741): He was Iśānavarman, the third son of a princely family of Central India. Some say that he (Vajrabodhi) was descended from a Brāhmaṇa family of Malaya (Malabar) in South India. At the age of ten years he became a monk in the monastery of Nālandā. When he was twenty-eight years old he proceeded to Kapilavastu and in three years learned from Srībhadra the *Yugaron (Yoga[ācārabhūmi]śāstra), Yuishikiron Vijñaptimātrasiddhi-śastra*), and the *Benchūbenron (Madhyāntavibhāgaṭikā)*. At 31 he visited South India. There he met Nāgabodhi and stayed with him as his disciple for seven years. (From him) he studied the *sūtras* of Vajrayoga (*Kongōchōyugakyō*), the doctrines of the *dhāraṇī* of Vairocana (*Birushanasōjidaranimon), the sūtras* of Mahāyāna, and the Sāstra of the Five Vidyās (*Gomyōron*). Having received the unctions of the five clans (BU), he learned the deep meaning of esoterism. Thereafter he returned to Central India and made pilgrimage to the Eight Holy Places.

Avalokiteśvara of Potalaka (South India) asked him to go to China. He went to Ceylon and worshipped the tooth-relic of the Buddha at the monastery of Abhayarāja (present Anurādhapura). He climbed up the Ryōgasan (Lanka, Adam's Peak). Once again he stayed in India for some time and then returned to Ceylon. From the port of P'o-Iche-li he embarked on a merchant ship which formed part of a fleet of thirty five Persian ships and after one month arrived at Śrivijaya (whose capital at that time was Palembang in the island of Sumatra; cf. Coedès, B.E.F.E.O, XXX, p. 33f.). Here one certain Chizo (Jñānagarbha? later called Amoghavajra), aged 14, associated himself with him as a *śrāmaṇera* (novice).

After a stay of five months he recommenced his journey towards China. A terrible tempest destroyed thirty other ships (of the fleet). The ship carrying him reached China toward the close of the year 7 of K'ai-yuan (719). In the following year he arrived at Lo-yang. Hiuan-song was the reigning king at that time. From the year 11 to the year 29 of K'ai-yuan (723-41) he resided at Ts'eu-cheng sseu and ta-fou-tsien sseu, and made (various) translations.[45] On the eve of returning to India he died, in A.D. 741.

Fukū Sanzō (Amoghavajra, 705-44) was a Ceylonese. He accompanied his master Vajrabodhi and arrived at Lo-yang in the year 8 of K'ai-yuan (A.D. 720). At that time he was only aged 16. During the following twenty years till the death of Vajrabodhi, he did not leave his master and helped him in translating the *Sūtras* and the commentaries. Being ordered by his master, he paid a visit to Ceylon in 743 in search of *śūtras* and *śastras*. In Ceylon he met Ryūchi (Nāgabodhi, Fugen Ajari) and received from him the esoteric doctrine. Then he travelled all over India. In 746 he returned to China, bringing with him a large number of works. Emperor

Hiuan-tsong ordered an altar to be raised in his palace and himself received the unction (*abhiṣeka*). Following him, all classes of society adopted this cult. This was the most prosperous epoch of esoteric Buddhism in China. The number of translations rendered by Amoghavajra is enormous—one hundred and odd works in more than two hundred 'volumes'.[46] He was one of the four great translators of Chinese Buddhism.

Zemmui Sanzō (Śubhakarasiṃha, 637-35): He was born in a family of Magadha. In accordance with the last wishes of his father, he ascended the throne (then thirteen years old), but immediately afterwards he abdicated the throne so as to become a monk. At Nālandā he learned esoterism from Dharmagupta. Being asked by him, he visited China to spread the doctrine there. He went to Kashmir, the country of the Tou-kiue and many other regions and (finally) arrived in China via Tibet. He brought with him many books in Sanskrit and reached Tch'ang-ngan in the year 4 of K'ai-yuan (716). At that time he was 80 years old. The next year he presented a translation of the first part of the *Kokūzōgumojihō* (Taishō, No. 1145). He translated 21 works[47] and died at the age of 98 years.

Ichigyō (Yi-hing, 683-727): He embraced the monastic life as the disciple of a Dhyāna master P'ou-tai. In the year 5 (717) of K'ai-yuan, he studied on the mount T'ien-t'ai. He became the religious guide of Emperor Hiuan-tsong. After Śubhakarasiṃha and Vajrabodhi had arrived in China, he became their disciple and helped them in their works of translation. Not only did he write down by dictation the *Dainichikyō* and its commentary, but was besides the author of many works.[48] He was proficient in astronomy and in calendric details. He died at the age of 44.

Keikwa Ajari (Houei-kouo, 746-805): He came from Tchao-ying near Tch'ang-ngan. He was the most brilliant disciple of Amoghavajra and as such was the venerable master of three emperors, viz. T'ai-tsong, Tö-tsong, and Chouen-tsong. He had many famous disciples. The *Juhachi keiin* (Taishō, No. 900) is his principal work.

Kōbō daishi (Kūkai,744-835): At the foot of the eastern pagoda of Kumedara in Yamato, a manuscript of the *Dainichikyō* was discovered, but the text was difficult to understand. Kōbō daishi conceived the idea of going to China. In 804 he left in the company of the Japanese ambassador to Tch'ang-ngan. On his arrival in this city he resided in (the monastery of) Tsing-long sseu. There he received the *abhiṣeka* of the Vajradhātu and the Garbhadharma from the *upādhyāya* Houei-kouo. When his disciple learned the doctrine completely, he died. After two years he (Kōbō daishi) returned to Japan (806) and gave for the first time an exposition of the principles of the Shingon sect. He was patronized by the Emperors Heizei, Sanga, and Junna, and thus was able to propagate his faith in the court at the same time as he was spreading it among the people. He was the initiator of a new movement in the history of Japanese thought. In 616 he founded the monastery of Kōyasan (90 kilometers south of Kyōto). In 823 Emperor Saga entrusted to him a temple of the capital, viz. the Tōji, which was consecrated for the safety of the nation. Emperor Daigo conferred on him the posthumous name of Kōbō daishi.

LATER DEVELOPMENTS OF THE SHINGON SECT: ITS TWO BRANCHES—THE KOGI AND THE SHINGI

About three hundred years after the establishment of the Shingon by Kōbō daishi, the discipline of the sect had become somewhat relaxed. Kakuban Shōnin (Kogyō daishi, 1095-1134) gained the favor of the ex-emperor toba. In 1132 he established at the Kōyasan the Daidenbō-in where he advocated some reform. Two years later he was made abbot of the Kongōbuji. But the reactionary and narrow-minded elements were opposed to his innovations. In pursuance of their intrigues, the Shōnin gave up the high office he held and soon afterwards retired to the Negorosan. Nevertheless, partisans of the reform became more and more numerous and at the Daidenbō-in a savant named Raiyu Sōjō (1226-1304) gave some new interpretations. His adversaries were entrenched in the Kongōbuji and the Tōji. As a result, there followed frequent clashes between them. In 1288 Raiyu removed the Daidenbō-in, as also his disciples, to the Negorosan (at a distance of ten leagues). Thus took place the secession between the Shingi and the Kogi.

The main point of dispute between the two sects relates to the identity of the personage who is supposed to have disclosed the *Dainichikyō*. He is the Buddha in Svabhāvadharmakāya (JISHŌ HOSSHIN), but the Shingi school distinguishes in it the HONJISHIN, the fundamental body which is in the absolute and the KAJISHIN, the *adhiṣṭhānakāya*, which is conditioned. The Shingi claims that the former cannot take part in preaching, but that this role is taken by the *Adhiṣṭhānakāya.* The Kogi, on the contrary, attributes the preaching to the HONJISHIN.

The big temples (DAIHONZAN) of the Kogi are those of the Kōyasan, the Ninnaji (Omuro), the Daigakuji, the Daigoji, the Tōji, the Sennyūji, the Zuishin-in, and the Kwanjuji.

The Shingi predominates in the Chishaku-in (Chisan), the Hasedera (Busan, Chōkokuji) and in many other temples which comprise about sixty per cent of some 12,000 temples of the Shingon cult.

Laymen sometimes have the impression that Shingon Buddhism is just another form of the strange Tibetan Buddhism. Some represent it as a pure ritualism based on foolish beliefs. To others, it is a mystic interpretation of a mythology. But, on the contrary, orthodox Mikkyō takes pains to consider realities in a positive spirit.

If anybody studies in detail the profound thought of the *Dainichikyō*, he will notice that it is permeated with ideas known from the principal treatises of the Mahāyāna, viz. the *Saddharma-puṇḍarika-sūtra, the Avatamsaka-sūtra*, and the *Prajñāpāramitā-sūtra. The Dainichikyō* is the culmination of a religious movement of which those famous *sūtras* constitute the earlier stages.

NOTES

1. *Shingon mikkyō no okoru made,* "Up to the development of the Shingon Esoterism", p.65.
2. M. Kawaguchi Ekai has studied the antecedents of Indian esoterism in *Mikkyō Kenkyu,* II, l, p. 75.
3. Translator of the Sūtras: Taishō Nos. 1011, 1300, 1351, 1356 (cf. *Hōbōgirin,* fascicule annexe, *Table des auteurs et traducteurs*).
4. *Ibid,* Nos. 986, 987, 1331.
5. *Ibid,* No. 1012.
6. *Ibid,* No. 988.
7. *Ibid,* No. 1028 (a).
8. *Ibid,* Nos. 1017, 1093, 1334, 1337, 1340, 1341, 1345, 1348, 1353, 1354.
9. See the work cited, Vol. V, appendix.
10. These are (1) Saicho (Dengyō) who lived in China from 804 to 805; (2) Kūkai (Kōbō), 804 to 806; (3) Jōgyō, 838-39; (4) Engyō, 838-39; (5) Ennin (Jikaku), 838-47; (6) Eun, 842-47; (7) Enchin (Chishō), 853-58; (8) Shūei, 862-63. Among them, two schools may be distinguished: the monks numbered 2, 6, 8, belong to the esoterism of the Shingon, the Tōmitsu; the other belong to the Tendai (Taimitsu). See below.
11. Taishō, Vol. LVIII, p. $19b^{22}$.
12. Taishō, No. 849. Vol. XVIII.
13. Taishō, No. 1796, Vol. XXXIX; cf. *infra* "Bibliography", note.
14. *Dainihon Zokuzōkyō* ("Supplement of Kyōto") leaf XXXVI, fascicules 3-4.
15. Taishō, No. 1797, Vol. XXXIX.
16. Cf. the Commentary, Taishō, No. 1796, Vol. XXXIX, p. $736b^{2}$.

17. 'Heart' for Japanese SHIN but this term renders the Sanskrit word *citta* which is gererally translated as 'mind'. We have, however, preferred to translate it by 'heart'.
18. Taishō, Vol. XVIII, p. 1c[1].
19. *Ibid,* p. 1c[7].
20. For the Tibetan, see Hattori, *Zobun Dainichikyō,* p. 357[9].
21. Taishō, Vol. XVIII, p. 38c[20].
22. Taishō. Vol. XVIII, p. 12a[15], cf summary of Chap. II etc. with note 9.
23. *Ibid,* p. 10a[12].
24. *Ibid*, p. 4c[13].
25. Taishō, Vol. XXXIX, p. 10a[24].
26. Commentary of *Dainichikyō,* Taishō, Vol. XXXIX, pp. 651c[4]-632a[7].
27. See p. 91.
28. Taishō, No. 870, Nanjo, No. 1433.
29. Taishō, Vol. XVIII, p. 287c[18].
30. Kōbō Daishi zenshū, Vol. I.
31. According to the Tibetan Version: *Mahāvairocanābhisambodhivikurvitādhiṣṭhānavaipulyasūtrarājendrarājanāmadharmaparyāya.* Taishō, No. 848; Nanjō, No. 530; Ōtani, No. 126; Tohoku, No. 494.
32. According to the Tibetan version: *Sarvatathāgatatatattvasamgrahanāmamahāyānasūtra.* Taishō, No. 865; Nanjō, No. 1020; Ōtani, No. 112; Tōhoku, No. 479.
33. Taishō, No. 866; Nanjō No. 534.
34. According to the Tibetan version: *Susiddhikaramahātantrasādhanopāyikapaṭala.* Taishō, No., 893; Nanjō, No. 533; Ōtani, No. 431; Tōhoku, No. 807.
35. Taishō, No. 867: Nanjō, No 1039.
36. Taishō, No. 1665; Nanjō, No. 1319.
37. Taishō, No. 1668.
38. Taishō, No. 882; Nanjō, No. 1017; Ōtani, No. 112; Tōhoku, No. 479.
39. According to Kōbō daishi, *Fuhōden* (ed. *Dainihon bukkyō zensho,* p. 3).
40. On the basis of Chinese texts Omura Seigai doubts whether Nāgabodhi ever existed (*Mikkyōhattatsushi,* p. 581). In Tibetan texts he is mentioned many times. In Tāranātha and the *Pag sam jon zang,* Nāgabodhi (Klu'i byang chub) or Nāgabuddhi (klu'i blo) is met with. See *Pag sam jon zang,* Calcutta edition, p. 90, and Index, p. 12; Tāranātha, ed. Schiefner, p. 87, or the translation by Teramoto (Tōkyō, 1928), p. 141.
41. In the same work (Tāranātha, *Pag sam jon zang*).
42. In the *Ryaku Fuhōden* (ed. Dainihon bukkyō, p. 28a), a work belonging to the Taimitsu, the article on Sramaṇa Śubhakarasimha states: "He was also a disciple of Ryūchi Bosatsu (Nāgabodhi), as was Kongōchi Sanzō (Vajrabodhi). In that case, the identity of Nāgabodhi and Dharmagupta may be accepted, but in the Taimitsu they are regarded as two distinct personages."
43. *Kō Fuhōden* (ed. Dainihon bukkyō zensho, p. 24b): "The fourth patriarch is called Ryūchi Bosatsu. He is also given the name Fugen Ajari."
44. If he was a disciple of Nāgārjuna, he flourished toward the end of the third century, A.D. If (on the other hand), he was the master of Vajrabodhi he was still alive in the beginning of the 8th century, A.D., thus leaving an interval of four hundred years. For a long time different solutions to this enigma have been proposed (see *Mikkyō daijiten,* p. 2248, Ryūchi). The *Kongōchi sanzō gyōjo* (Taishō, Vol. LV, 875c[10]) makes him live for 700 years. On the funerary stele of Zemmui Sanzō (Śubhakarasimha) the following is written: "The face (of

Dharmagupta) was (like) that of a man of 40 years; he was already 800 years old" (Taishō, Vol. L, p. 260c13). See also J. Hackin, *Guide-Catalogue du Guimet,* pp. 100-01 Nāgabodhi.

45. His translations: Taishō. Nos. 241, 849, 866, 867, 876, 904, 923, 932, 980, 1061, 1062(a), 1075, 1087, 1112, 1149, 1166, 1173, 1202, 1208, 1220, 1223, 1251, 1269, 1293, 1303.

46. His translations: Taishō, Nos. 243, 246, 297, 319, 326, 404, 413, 469, 521, 667, 682, 710, 789, 856, 857, 861, 865, 869, 870, 871, 873, 874, 878, 879, 880, 897, 902, 903, 908, 909, 915, 921, 924(a)(b), 930, 931, 944(a), 948, 950, 953, 954(a), 955, 957, 958, 961, 962, 963, 972, 974(a), 982, 983(a), 989, 990, 994, 995, 996, 1000(a), 1001, 1002, 1003, 1004, 1005(a), 1008, 1009, 1010, 1019, 1020, 1022(a)(b), 1030, 1031, 1032, 1033, 1037, 1039, 1040, 1041, 1042, 1056, 1064, 1066, 1067, 1069, 1072(a), 1076, 1085, 1086, 1091, 1098, 1100, 1101, 1102, 1110, 1111, 1113(b), 1119, 1120(a), 1122, 1123, 1124, 1125, 1132, 1133m, 1134(a)(b), 1135, 1136, 1146, 1150, 1151, 1153, 1155, 1163, 1167, 1171, 1172, 1174, 1175, 1176, 1177(a), 1195, 1200, 1201, 1204, 1205, 1209, 1210, 1211, 1214, 1215, 1216, 1222, 1225, 1244, 1247, 1248, 1249, 1250, 1252, 1253, 1254, 1255, 1258, 1260, 1261, 1263, 1264, 1266, 1271, 1273, 1276, 1277, 1289, 1290, 1291, 1294, 1297, 1299, 1306, 1313, 1315, 1318, 1319, 1320, 1323, 1324, 1653, 1665, 1798.

47. His translations: Taishō, Nos. 848, 850, 851, 877, 893, 894, 895, 905, 906, 907, 917, 973, 1068, 1075, 1079, 1141, 1145, 1158, 1239, 1270, 1286.

48. His works: Taishō, Nos. 848, 922, 1219, 1304, 1309, 1310, 1311, 1796.

PART II

GENERAL STUDY OF THE DAINICHIKYŌ

A. THE TITLE DAINICHIKYŌ

The titles of Sūtras are often given in Chinese by either translation or transcription, in an abridged form, of the original Sanskrit title. These abbreviations are particularly frequent in the case of esoteric texts, the original titles of which are often long and complicated. For example, No. 893 of the *Taishō Issaikyō* [a Japanese edition of the Chinese Buddhist canon] carried, to believe the Tibetan canon, the title *Susiddhikaramahātantrasādhanopāyikapaṭala.*[1] The Chinese title is simply *Susiddhikara.*

With regard to the *Dainichikyō*, the Tibetan version as also the indications contained in the Chinese commentaries permit us to reconstruct the title of the original Sanskrit text which is no longer extant. As a matter of fact, the Tibetan title always bore the Sanskrit title above it. For our Sūtra, the title is given as follows: *Mahāvairocanābhismbodhivikurvitādhiṣṭhānavaipulyasutrendrāja-nāmadharmaparyāya,*[2] "topic of the Dharma called King Indra of the large Sūtras with the marvellous Transformations of Mahāvairocana as a blessed basis."[3]

The Chinese commentary states: "According to the original Sanskrit text, the complete title would have to be, *Ta kouang po king yin-t'o-lo wang* (Sūtra of great development Indra-King). King Indra is Devendra Śakra. That is to say, this Sūtra, the storehouse of all the secrets of the Tathāgatas is of particular prestige, commanding respect among all the Mahāyāna teachings, just as the thousand-eyed (SEMMOKU=Daśaśatanayana, epithet of Indra). Śakra is the sovereign of all the gods (Śakra-Devendra). To avoid the great length of the title, the whole of it has not been conserved."[4]

As a matter of fact, the complete Chinese title as it appears in the Chinese canon is [read in the Japanese manner] *Daibirushana-jōbutsu-jimben-kaji-kyō.* This would correspond to a Sanskrit title *Mahāvairocana-[abhi]sambodhivikurvita-adhiṣṭhāna-sūtra,* including neither the terms *vaipulya* and *dharmaparyāya* nor the epithet Indrarāja.

Beside, the complete Chinese title is itself usually abridged into [Japanese pronunciation] *Dainichikyō,* i.e. *Mahāvairocana-sūtra.* This abbreviation is found even in the text of the Sūtra itself,[5] and in the Śubhakarasimha Commentary.[6] The present work employs throughout this abbreviated form.

B. THREE ALLEGED SOURCES OF THE DAINICHIKYŌ

According to one ancient tradition, the *Dainichikyō* is derived from three sources, viz. the HŌNI-JŌGŌ-NO-HON (the eternal specimen which is in accordance with the Dharma); the BUNRU-NO-KŌHON (the developed copy for diffusion); and BUNRU-NO-RYAKUHON (the abridged copy for diffusion). It is last mentioned text comprising more than three thousand *gāthā* that constitutes our actual *Dainichikyō.*

In this connection, Kōbō daishi, in his introduction (KAIDAI) to *Dainichikyō,* writes as follows: "In all, the Sūtra is represented by three texts. The first (of these), the HŌNI-JŌGŌ-NO-HON is the *dharma-maṇḍala* of all the Buddhas. The second the BUNRU-NO-KŌHON, is that which was probably recited and transmitted by Nāgārjuna. It is the Sūtra of one hundred thousand stanzas. The third (text) is the RYAKUHON consisting of more than three thousand verses. While it comprises only three thousand verses in seven 'volumes', it nevertheless gives a resume of the whole KŌHON (the developed copy). With an economy of words it expresses very many things. One single letter of it has infinite significance, and one single point *(anusvāra,* etc.) innumerable arguments. This is all the more reason that an *akṣaracakra* (wheel of one hundred letters) contains the substance of the book. How many arguments are (then) not revealed in its three thousand *gāthā*? The developed specimen and the abridged specimen, though distinct, are identical as far as the doctrine is concerned."[7]

As to the first source, the HŌNI-JŌGŌ-NO-HON, this is an exposition of the doctrine which is the thought of the Buddhas. It is identical with the teaching perpetually preached by the omnipresent Mahāvairocana in his Dharmakāyas. It goes without saying that it has no material existence. Neither the Chinese text of the Sūtra nor the Commentary makes any allusion to this source. One finds here an original creation of Kōbō daishi.

The second source, that is to say the BUNRU-NO-KŌHON, and the third, "the resume in three thousand verses" are defined in the Commentary, where we read: "...However, in the Sanskrit text of this Sūtra, a general introduction is lacking. The *ācārya* (Śubhakarasimha, the translator of the Sūtra) says: The big copy [of the Sutra] of Vairocana comprises a hundred thousand verses. Being so voluminous, it is difficult to retain. The "Saints who transmit the Dharma" gathered its essential by reducing its bulk to three thousand and odd *gāthā*. Although it furnishes a thorough summary of the doctrine and practice of the Shingon, it is not the grand original work. That is why one does not find any introduction on the first page......"[8] A little later he writes, "The Sūtra [in its original text] contained nearly one hundred thousand verses for diffusion in Jambudvīpa."[9]

Besides, Śubhakarasimha's Commentary makes frequent references to the 'grand text' (or such expression as) "in terms of the grand text". Moreover, Amoghavajra in his TOBU-DARANI-MOKA (Taishō, No. 903) says as follows: "According to the *Birushana-jōdō-kyō* (Sūtra of the Bodhi of Vairocana), the grand copy consisted of a hundred thousand *gāthā* which would have made three hundred 'volumes' (in Chinese translation). When it was translated in the country of the T'ang, it was only a summary in seven 'volumes'."[10]

This original (version) in one hundred thousand *gāthā* was never brought to China but the belief in its existence was introduced there by the Indian translator-monks.

C. THE LEGENDARY ORIGINS OF THE DAINICHIKYŌ

There are two traditions which explain the origins of the *Dainichikyō*. According to the first one, Nāgārjuna found the book in the Stūpa of Iron of South India (NANTEN NO TETTŌ) and then made it known. This tradition is accepted in the Tomitsu, one of the two branches of the esoteric school of Japan. According to the other one, monkeys in a forest of North India gave the book to a wood-cutter. This legend is adopted in the Taimitsu.

With regard to the legend of the Stūpa of Iron, Kōbō daishi states the following in his *Fuhōden*: "So says Vajrabodhi: After the passing away of the Tathāgata there was a man of great virtue (*bhadanta*) named Nāgārjuna. Already he practised the *mantras* of Mahāvairocana. The Buddha Vairocana manifested his infinite body, and from above, the wind revealed his doctrine and his compositions. Later, when Nāgārjuna had taken them down, he disappeared. This text is the first volume (KWAN) of *Birushana-nenju-hōyō*.[11] Then the *bhadanta* Nāgārjuna memorized it, recited it and put it into practice. In South India he arrived before the 'Stūpa-warehouse' of the great Bodhisattvas and prayed for the opening of the door. All the time reciting, he moved round the *stūpa* for seven days. He empowered grains of white mustard and knocked at the door. On the seventh day the door opened. In the *stūpa* all the divinities of Vajra were there. In a fit of rage, they refused him entry. But in the interior he saw lamps with perfumed oil casting flames at a distance of ten or twenty feet, and a large number of ornamented and precious canopies, hanging. And he heard voices (singing) praises. Then this Bodhisattva (Nāgārjuna) confessed and repented with all his heart. He uttered the grand vow and all the divinities of Vajra came out and asked him, 'What is thy business?' He replied, 'After the passing away of the Tathāgata, the forests of heresy have become dense. The Mahāyāna is in the course of becoming lost. I have heard said that all the doctrines of the Tathāgatas of the three ages (past, present, and future) are conserved in this *stūpa*. I want to receive them for the redemption of all sentient beings.' The Vajra-wielders bade him enter. As soon as he had entered, the *stūpa* closed down again. Looking at the interior, the palace of Dharmadhātu was the *stūpa* where Vairocana, all the Buddhas of the three worlds, all the great Bodhisattvas—Samantabhadra, Mañjuśrī, and all others, revealed themselves. They lived there. Then he received the unction (*abhiṣeka*) and the empowerment (*adhiṣṭhāna*) of Vajrasattva and others. He recited and committed to memory all the different esoteric formulas (*dharmaparyāya*) and spread them among mankind."[12]

This legend was orally transmitted by Vajrabodhi to Amoghavajra, who put it into writing. It formed part of the text entitled *Kongōchō-giketsu,*[13] from which Kōbō daishi took it with few changes. But this does not mention the name of the man 'of great virtue'. It is Kōbō daishi who according to the prophecy (*vyākaraṇa*) of the Ryōgakyō (*Laṅkāvatāra-sūtra*) shows that Nāgārjuna is meant.[14]

The Tōmitsu and the Taimitsu agree in recognizing Nāgārjuna as one of the patriarchs of esoteric Buddhism. On the other hand, according to the *Kongōchō-giketsu*, the *Kongōchōgyo* is also pretended to be a text found in the Stūpa of Iron. But according to the tradition of the Taimitsu, the *Dainichikyō* does not come from the Stūpa. However, there are many variants of this tradition of the Taimitsu.[15] The generally accepted version contained in the

Dainichikyō Indroduction[16] by Ts'ouei-mou (Saimoku) is as follows: "In North India there is a small country called P'o-lou-lo (Jap. Borora). To the north of the capital of this country, a great rocky mountain stands above the clouds; its cliffs are a hundred thousand feet high. On its summit there is a cave where the secret Dharma is preserved. Every year on the seventh day of the seventh month, all the saints assemble there. Thousands of monkeys take out the sūtras for airing them. On a clear day, one can barely distinguish them. There is no staircase to climb there and it is said that there were wild birds in the thick clouds. Suddenly there arose a gust of wind which caused a volume in Sanskrit to fall. A wood-cutter picked it up and seeing that it was a marvellous book, he brought it to the king. The king accepted it. He had never seen such a thing. The same day in the evening a big monkey came to demand its return. 'If you do not give it back to me, I will have to kill myself.' The king, employing skilful means of persuasion, politely told him thrice: 'I shall return the Sūtra to you, but I want to make a copy of it'. Considering the instant zeal of the king, the monkey at last gave his consent: 'In three days I shall come back to take it'. The king assigned the task to a multitude of scribes, had a copy prepared, and on the expiry of the time limit, returned the text (to the monkey). (This text) the king communicated only to the crown-prince. The prince inherited it but did not spread it in the world. In recent times, a Yogācāra from Central India undertook a long voyage across the mountains and rivers in search of the secret treasure. Observing the extraordinary merit of this *ācārya*, the king gladly handed over the Sūtra to him."

This detailed story seems to narrate real facts; and still there is nothing authentic in it. One does not know where to locate the country of P'o-lou-lo. It may be asked if this country exists at all.[17] The story does not specify either the name of the king or of the *ācārya*. The sequel to this introduction of Ts'ouei-mou suggests that Śubhakarasiṃha is meant and that the *Mahāvairocana-sūtra* translated by Śubhakarasiṃha was a text which he had brought with him (from India).

But the facts do not confirm this legend, and rather point to the contrary. The text which Śubhakarasiṃha brought with him was only the seventh *kwan* or the Sūtra, the first six having been already collected by Wou-hing (see the next section). This is why there is no reason to take into consideration the legend of the monkeys.

The wise men of the Tōmitsu admit that the *Dainichikyō* was found in the Stūpa of Iron exactly in the same way as the *Kongō-*

chōgyō. When Vajrabodhi was in South India, he could very well have been given the *Kongōchōgyō* and the *Dainichikyō* by Nāgabodhi, the disciple of Nāgārjuna. Precisely this is declared by Fei-si in his inscription of the commemorative stele of Amoghavajra,[18] by Tchao Ts'ien in his biography of the same (Amoghavajra) (Fukū-gyōjō),[19] and finally in the *Catalogue of the Tripiṭaka* or the Tchegō-Yuan era.[20] These documents have an historical value equal to that of the *Kongōchō-giketsu.*[21]

But what is really this Stūpa of Iron? For centuries, some have accepted it as a real *stūpa*; others have seen in it an ideal *stūpa.* Kōbō daishi said: "Thus Stūpa is not the work of human strength. It was constructed by the divine prowess of the Tathāgata."[22] Kōgyō daishi adds that "If one likes to explain it in the profound esoteric sense, the Stūpa of Iron would appear as nothing else than our own body. As a matter of fact, our body contains the ten thousand dharmas and unites all the 'qualities' (*guṇa*). This is why the tradition says that the Stūpa of Iron symbolizes the body of the believer."[23]

(Thus) it appears that there is nothing which can compel us to represent the Stūpa of Iron as a real edifice. The *Dainichikyō* Commentary does not speak of it, but significantly states: "Thy heart is a *stūpa* of the Buddha". From the point of view of the esoteric doctrine there is no contradiction if we understand the original grand *stūpa* of the heart to be the Stūpa of Iron of South India, the doors of which opened for Nāgārjuna.

D. THE CHINESE TRANSLATIONS OF THE DAINICHIKYŌ

The Sanskrit *Mahāvairocana-sūtra*, which was translated into Chinese, was included among the manuscripts collected in India by the Chinese monk Won-hing (Mugyō), who had left for India during the reign of the emperor Kao-tsong of the T'ang dynasty in the year 2 of the era of K'ien-fong (667). He worked zealously during the entire period of his stay there. In the first year of Chang-yuan (674) at the time when he was about to return to China, he fell ill and died in North India.[24] By order of the emperor, the manuscripts he had collected were brought to China and preserved at the Houa-yen sseu of Tch'ang-ngan. From this collection the translator Śubhakarasiṃha (Zemmui) chose the *Dainichikyō* [Japanese pronunciation]; and upon imperial order, he worked in collaboration with Yi-hing on its translation at the Ta-fou-sien Temple (sseu) of Lo-yang during the years 12 and 13 of K'ai-yuan (724-25). The "Buddhist Catalogue of the Era of K'ai-yuan", *K'ai-yuan che kiao lou,* states the following:[25] "In olden days the monk Won-hing made study tour in the West, in India. He announced (his intention) to return to China, but unfortunately when he reached North India, he died. There was an imperial order to look for the Sanskrit books he had with him, and to bring them (to China). These were deposited at, and preserved in the Houa-yen Temple of the western capital. [Chan]-wou-wei (Śubhakarasiṃha) along with the *śramaṇa* Yi-hing was able to choose from this collection many Sanskrit manuscripts all belonging to esoterism (literally: to the sublime category of the *dhāraṇīs*) and which had not been translated. In the year 12 he followed the (imperial) retinue and came to Lo-yang. He established himself at the Ta-fou-sien Temple and at last translated the *Mahāvairocana-sūtra* for the monk Yi-hing. The complete Sanskrit text of the Sūtra contains one hundred thousand *gāthā* (each of 32 characters). The translation we have in hand is only a resume of this work. The monk Pao-yue orally translated it and the monk Yi-hing took it down with the brush, received the explanations and finalized the expressions and ideas."

E. THE TIBETAN VERSION OF THE DAINIÇHIKYŌ

The *Mahāvairocana-sūtra* was translated into Tibetan by the Indian savant Śīlendrabodhi and the Tibetan translator Dpal-brtsegs-rakṣita. If the introduction to the catalogue of the Kanjur in the edition of Narthang is to be believed,[26] king Ral-pa-can invited Śīlendrabodhi, Jinamitra, and other *paṇḍitas* to come from India.[27] The exact dates of the Ral-pa-can reign are very much contested. In any case his reign has to be placed in the first half of the ninth century A.D.[28] The Tibetan translation is therefore posterior to the Chinese translation by about one hundred years.

The Tibetan version contained in the "rgyud sde" of the Kanjur[29] is divided into two sections, the first of which has received in the Catalogue of the Kanjur of Narthang the epithet 'internal'. The first comprises seven parts and 29 chapters. For the first section, the concordance between the Tibetan and Chinese versions may be established as follows:

	Tibetan version		*Chinese version*[30]
1.	Sems kyi khyad par rim par phye ba	1.	Jou tchen yen men tchou sin p'in (1)
2.	Dkyil 'khor du dgod pa'i gsang snags kyi mdzod	2.	Jou men-t'ou-lo kiu yuan tchen yen p'in(1-2)

3.	Bgegs shi bar bya ba rim par phye	3.	Si tchang p'in (2)
4.	Spyi'i gsang sngags kyi mdzod rim par phye ba rgyas pa	4.	P'ou t'ong tchen yen tsang p'in (2)
5.	'Jig rten pa'i dngos grub sgrub pa'i rim par phye ba	5.	Che kien tch'eng tsieou p'in (3)
6.	Dngos grub sgrub pa'i de kho na nyid rim par phye ba rgyas pa.	6.	Si-ti tch'ou hien p'in (3)
		7.	Tch'eng tsieou si ti p'in (3)
7.	Lha'i ting nge 'dsin gtan la dbab pa rim phye ba	28.	Chouo pen ts' ouen san-mei (6)
8.	Mtshan ma med pa'i ting nge 'dsin rim par phye ba	29.	Chouo wou siang san-mei p'in (6)
9.	'Jig rten pa dang 'jig rten las das pa'i bzlas brjod kyi de kho na nyid rim par phye ba	30.	Che tch'ou che tch'e song p'in (6)
10.	Yi ge'i 'khor lo rim par phye ba	8.	Tchouan tseu louen man t'ou-lo hing p'in (3)
11.	Phyag rgya rim par phye ba rgyas pa	9.	Mi yin p'in (4)
12.	Rnam pa thams cad du 'jug pa pa'i sgo chos kyi yi ge'i tshul rim par phye ba	10.	Tseu louen p'in (5)
13.	Gsang ba'i dkyil 'khor rim par phye ba rgyas pa	11.	Pi mi man-t'o-lo=p'in (5)
14.	Gsang ba'i dkyil 'khor du 'jug pa rim par phye ba	12.	Ju pi mi man 't'ou-lo fa p'in (5)
15.	Gsang ba'i phyag rgya brgyad rim par phye ba	14.	Pi mi pa yin p'in (5)
16.	Gsang ba'i dkyil 'khor du gzud pa la 'jug pa rim par phye ba rgyas pa	13.	Ju pi mi man-t'ou-lo wei p'in (5)
17.	Rig sngags kyi brtul shugs rim par phye ba rgyas pa	15.	Tch'e ming kin kiai p'in (5)
18.	Slob dpon gyi de kho na nyid ces pa rim par phye ba	16.	A-chö-li tchen che tche p'in (5)
19.	Yi ge dgod pa rim par phye ba	17.	Pou tsen p'in (5)
20.	Byang chub sems dpa'i bslab pa thams cad dang ldan pa rim par phye ba	18.	Cheou fang pien hio tch'ou p'in (6) p'in (6)
21.	Yi ge brgya 'byung ba bstan rim par phye ba rgyas pa	19.	Shuo po tseu cheng p'in (6)
22.	'Bras bu'i bsyor ba bstan pa rim par phye ba	20.	Po tseu wei tch' eng p' in (6)
23.	yi ge brgya pa rnam par dgod pa sgrub pa rim par phye ba	21.	Po tseu kouo siang ying p'in (6)
24.	Bdag nyid sgrub pa'i rim par phye ba	22.	Po tseu tch' eng tsieou tch'e song p'in (6)
25.	Yi ge brgya pa'i snags kyi cho ga rim par phye ba	23.	Po tseu tchen yen fa p'in (6)
26.	Rdsogs par byang chub pa'i ngo bo nyid bstan pa'i rim par phye ba	24.	Shuo p'ou-t'i sing p'in (6)
27.	Dam tshig gsum spyad pa rim par phye ba	25.	San san-mei-ye p'in (6)

28. De bzhin gshegs pa bstan pa rim par phye ba	26. Chouo jou lai p'in (6)
29. Gsang sngags kyi sgo nas byang chub sems dpa'i spyad pa spyod pa' i cho ga ji snyed par rim par phye ba[31]	27. Che tch'ou che hou-mo fa p'in (6) 31. Tchou lei p'in (6)

This first section with 29 chapters is nearly identical with the contents of the 31 chapters which form the first six 'volumes' (KWAN) of the Chinese version. The difference in the number of chapters is due to the fact that the Tibetan chapter 6 contains the Chinese chapters 6 and 7, while the Tibetan chapter 29 contains the Chinese chapters 27 and 31. Besides, the order of the chapters is not the same. To the chapters 7, 8 and 9 of the Tibetan version correspond the chapters 28, 29 and 30 of the Chinese. And the Tibetan chapter order 14, 15 and 16 agrees respectively with the Chinese order 12, 14, 13, showing a disagreement in sequence.

We have already published a Japanese translation of the first chapter of the Tibetan version along with a comparative study of the two versions as a whole. In this study we have considered in particular the facts which the Chinese commentary of Śubhakarasiṃha and Yi-hing present.[32]

In the 'external' part of the Tibetan text, [the 'continuation tantra'] chapters 1, 2, 3 and 4, describe the four kinds of rite (Tib. *cho ga = vidhi*), viz. those of appeasement (Tib. *shi ba = śāntika*), of prosperity (Tib. *rgyas pa = pauṣṭika*), of dominance (Tib. *dbang du bya ba = vaśīkaraṇa*), and of dreadfulness (Tib. *drag shul spyad pa = ābhicārika*). Consequently, they are excluded from the Sūtra part, which is supposed to be spoken by the Buddha. The most important chapter of this ('external') part is No. 7, where a resume of the 'internal' part is believed to be found. We have published an analysis of it in the journal *Taishō Daigaku Gakuhō,* No. 2 (1928).

In any case this part 'external' remains, as has been pointed out in the Catalogue of Narthang organically unrelated and incomplete.[33]

To the Tibetan version are attached three [sic. for 'two'] commentaries by Buddhaguhya. These are incorporated in the Tanjur (see the *Catalogue* of Cordier, pp. 290-91).

F. THE PERSONAGE SUPPOSED TO HAVE PREACHED THE DAINICHIKYŌ

Mahāyāna doctrine distinguishes three bodies of the Buddha: (1) The Nirmāṇakāya is the historical Buddha who lived in

Magadha in India about 2500 years ago. At the age of 35 he attained enlightenment and for the next 45 years he preached (the Dharma) and converted numerous persons. At the age of 80 he entered into Nirvāṇa. For the benefit of laymen as well as the *śrāvakas* and *pratyekabuddhas,* he revealed the Hīnayāna; and for the benefit of Bodhisattvas on the lower stages (he revealed) the Mahāyāna. (2) The Saṃbhogakāya is an idealization of the same historical Buddha. It is an unlimited and eternal body. It is this Buddha who is supposed to have preached the Ekayānavāda [theory of 'one' vehicle] described in the *Saddharmapuṇḍarīka-sūtra* and the *Avataṃsakasūtra.* (3) Finally, the Dharmakāya is identical with reality itself, devoid of beginning or end.

From the temporal point of view, the Nirmāṇakāya, body of metamorphosis belongs to the historical Buddha, and has a beginning and an end. The Saṃbhogakāya, the body obtained by the Buddha as a result of his past acts, has a beginning but no end. The Dharmakāya is a body which has neither beginning nor end.

According to the doctrine of popular or exoteric Buddhism (KENGYŌ), the Dharmakāya otherwise described as the reality of the eternal and unconditioned Buddha, does not preach the Dharma; but according to the esoteric doctrine the Dharmakāya itself, possessing form and act, explains the Dharma. Kōbō daishi insists on this difference in his *Ben-kemmitsu-nikyō-ron* (Treatise on the distinction between the two doctrines, exoteric and esoteric).[34] Exoteric Buddhism, says he, is preached by the Saṃbhogakāya and the Nirmāṇakāya; the esoteric Buddhism has been taught by the Dharmakāya. Then he explains in detail the difference between the two doctrines. His thesis may be thus summed up: The exoteric Buddhism is a collection of superficial doctrines which Śākyamuni has revealed with the purpose of converting all beings, just as different medicines are administered to different patients. It is, as it were, an expedient which does not contain the profound thought of the Tathāgata. For this reason it is called the doctrine of "the thought which follows others" (that is to say, the beings). On the contrary, the esoteric doctrine is the veritable secret of the Tathāgata. The Dharmakāya of the Tathāgata Vairocana himself realizes this secret and teaches it to the retinue (*parivāra*) emanating from him in order to enable the *parivāra* to share the joy which he himself has derived from it. This doctrine is of the domain of the Buddhas alone. Hence, there is no necessity of introducing 'expedients'. Thus, it is also called the doctrine of "the thought which follows itself", that is to say, which conforms only to the thought of the Buddha himself.

In this respect, the *Ben-kemmitsu-nikyō-ron* states: "The Buddhas of the *svabhāva (kāya)* and the *saṃbhoga (kāya),*[35] in order to experience themselves the joy of the Dharma, each with their retinue, preach the rubric (*paryāya*) of the Triple Mystery (Body, Speech, and Mind). This is what is called the esoteric doctrine and this rubric of the Triple Mystery is known as the domain of the knowledge realized internally by the Tathāgatas. The [Bodhisattvas of the] Ten Earths [and those who have attained the degree called] TŌGAKU [Equal Awakening, Saṃbodhi, the degree which immediately follows the Ten Earths], cannot enter into the chamber of the mystery. How much less is there reason to think that those of the two vehicles [of the Hīnayāna: Śrāvaka and Pratyekabuddha], or the profane, could mount to the Place?"[36]

In that text, the term "Buddha of *svabhāva*" refers to the Dharmakāya of 'reason' [or 'principle' or 'ingrained element'] (RIHOSSHIN) of Mahāvairocana who preaches the *Dainichikyō*. The term "Buddha of *saṃbhoga*" refers to the Dharmakāya of 'knowledge' (CHIHOSSHIN) which preaches the *Kongōchōgyō,* which along with the *Dainichikyō* constitutes the scriptural authority for the Shingon esoterism.

The *Dainichikyō* Commentary reports that the term 'Bhagavat' employed in the Sūtra's beginning applies to the fundamental Dharmakāya of Vairocana.[37]

Kōbō daishi, in his *Dainichikyō-kaidai* (Summary of the *D.-kyō*), explains this as follows: "The *Dainichikyō* is the grand secret of all the Buddhas; it is the great marvel of all the beings. All the Buddhas in Saṃbhogakāya protect it and do not discuss anything of it; the Tathāgatas in Nirmāṇkāya keep silent and do not respond".[38]

These passages clearly show that Vairocana in his Svabhāva-dharmakāya is the one who preaches this Sūtra.

G. THE PLACE OF PREACHING

It is common knowledge that in Buddhism the preaching of the Sūtras generally took place in different localities of an earthly area; for example, on top of the Gṛdhrakūṭa mountain, at Jetavana, and so on. But the *Dainichikyō*, according to its text, is regarded to have been revealed in "the vast Palace of the Vajradharmadhātu where the Tathāgata gives his marvellous blessings (*adhiṣṭhāna*)". The Commentary affirms that "this Palace is the place where the earlier Buddhas received *Bodhi*; it is said that it is the celestial Palace of Maheśvara".[39]

The Shingon sect has two sacred books, viz. the *Dainichikyō* and the *Kongōchōgyō*; and the place where the latter was preached is also the Palace of Maheśvara and is the palace of the Akaniṣṭha heaven. It is located on top of the Rūpadhātu (Realm of Form). However, as the body of Mahāvairocana in Dharmakāya is omnipresent, it is inevitable that Mahāvairocana is everywhere and does not stay confined to a particular locality. The Commentary expresses this idea as follows: "The interpretation actually given in the tradition is that it is the residence of the Mind of the Buddha with sovereign blessings (*īśvara-adhiṣṭhāna*); and for this reason it is called the royal palace of Īśvaradeva. Whatever be the localities where the Tathāgata manifests himself for furthering his work, these can be nothing else than this palace which cannot be located anywhere in the three worlds (*kāmadhātu, rūpadhātu, arūpadhātu*).[40]

Besides, the Commentary explains the esoteric significance of the Palace of the Vajradharmadhātu as follows: "The Dharmadhātu is the vast body of the knowledge of *vajra* which is called the body of the true knowledge of the Tathāgata. By dint of his empowerment, it is a place adorned with real merits. It is called a palace because it is a transcendental residence and the capital of the King of the Heart (*Cittarāja*, Mahāvairocana)."[41] From this it follows that we must understand that the Tathāgata disclosed this Sūtra while it was in his body called that of real knowledge.

Furthermore, it is generally explained that the seat of the Tathāgata is the siṃhāsana, the throne held by lions. The Buddha is called 'lion among men' since he has vanquished 96 different kinds of heretics (*tīrthika*). But the Commentary gives us an additional explanation for it: "According to the true interpretation of the tradition, the lion is the heroic Heart of Bodhi. Since at the outset he has adopted the resolution of becoming a Buddha, he has acquired a great striving (*vīrya*) and courage and does not know what fear is. In every way he is like a lion who having seized his prey does never let it go. The significance (the Lion's seat) therefore lies in the fact that the Buddha supremely accomplished the safety of humanity so that his effort can never be in vain."[42]

Thus the esoteric doctrine offers an interpretation of spiritual nature for each detail and each circumstance.

H. CIRCUMSTANCES OF THE TEACHING

The Tathāgata Mahāvairocana in Dharmakāya is omnipresent and eternal in the three times, past, present, and future. Consequently, the exact time of the teaching of the Sūtra cannot be told with the temporal categories of the world of mortals. Its time can only be regarded as eternal, being as much present as past or future. Besides, the text of the *Dainichikyō* deals with the transcendent over the three modes of time, to wit, the teaching of the formula of the equality of Body, Speech, and Mind realized by the marvellous grace of the Sun who is the Tathāgata.[43]

The Commentary defines the Sun of the Tathāgata as follows: "Past, present, and future are the divisions of time in this world. There are all sorts of different measures, long and short, of 'eon' (*kalpa*). For example, as the sun traverses the four worlds, day and night both have a beginning, a middle, and an end. Again, the thirty 'hours' (*muhūrta*) and other divisions do not remain fixed even for a moment. They succeed and push one another. If anybody contemplates this with a pure vision, the characteristic signs of the three modes of time appear completely inconceivable. Without any end or beginning, without a past or a future, it is the true Sun, spherical and shining, eternally stable, limpid and calm as space. The differences of length, such as the shortness of the time divisions, do not exist. Thanks to his divine power, the Buddha makes for him who practices the *yoga* that an immeasurable *kalpa* be equal to a moment, or that a moment be (equal to) an immeasurable *kalpa,* free to contract or to spread himself so as to be adapted to the necessities of all the beings. Because it is indeterminate, it is called the Sun of the Tathāgata."[44]

Again the Sūtra declares: "All the acts of the Body of Vairocana, all the acts of his Speech, all the acts of his Mind, are the Teachings of the Dharma in terms of the formulas of the Shingon path, in the world of living beings, at all times and all places."[45]

Thus Vairocana in his Dharmakāya is eternally occupied with the Teaching of the Dharma. But we do not see him nor do we hear him, just as a blind man does not see the clear light of day or as the roaring of the thunder does not reach the ear of the deaf. We can see our face (reflected) in the clear mirror of tranquil water, but the face cannot be seen when the water is troubled. In the same way, we see the Buddha in Dharmakāya and hear his teaching more or less clearly according as our heart is more or less pure.[46]

I. SIGNIFICANCE OF THE NAME DAINICHI (MAHĀVAIROCANA)

Dainichi translates Mahāvairocana, the great illuminator. Regarding this appellation, the Commentary says that it always has had three significances:

(1) Mahāvairocana disperses darkness and spreads light (JOANHEMMYŌ) in all directions.

(2) He fulfils all the functions (SHŪMUJŌBEN).

(3) He shines with an eternal splendour (KŌMUSHŌMETSU). The commentary says: "In Sanskrit Vairocana is one of the names of the sun, and it really does dissipate darkness and spread light everywhere. However, the worldly sun is limited. While able to illuminate the exterior, it cannot penetrate the interior. When it spreads its light on one side, the other side remains in darkness. Besides, it shines only during day time and does not give light during the night. But, as regards the solar light of the Tathāgata's Insight (*prajñā*), it is not that way. It spreads itself in all places and produces a universal enlightenment. In the interior as in the exterior (of human hearts), in all places and (at all times) in day or night, it is not different. Furthermore, when the sun traverses jambudvīpa, plants and trees, shrubs and forests grow according to their respective nature; and thanks to him, all the functions of the world can be performed. In the same way, the radiance of the Tathāgata's Sun which illuminates the *dharmadhātu,* makes it possible for all the innumerable beings to produce equally good roots of all sorts; and nothing of excellence within or outside of this world can be achieved without it. Again, the sun may be obscured by a thick black cloud, but is not destroyed; and when a strong wind chases away the cloud, the sun shines radiantly once more. One cannot, however, say that he is born for the first time. In the same way, the Sun of the Buddha's Heart, even when overcast with and obstructed by the thick clouds of ignorance (*avidyā*), defilement (*kleśa*) and futile discussions (*prapañca*), has nothing subtracted from it; and even in the unlimited plenitude of the definitive *samaya* [read: *samādhi*] of the truth of all the dharmas, nothing is added to it. These are some of the reasons why Vairocana is compared with the sun of this world but since the former resembles him very little, the qualifying word 'great' (*mahā*) is added to his name and he is called Mahāvairocana."[47]

From another point of view, the first significance of the name Mahāvairocana is the boundlessness of the splendour of the

Tathāgata's Insight; the second significance, the infinity of his compassion; and the third, the immutability and permanence of his nature.

Or again, the fundamental idea explained in the *Sūtra* is that we must realize our identity with Mahāvairocana. From this point of view, the threefold significance of Mahāvairocana is the distinction between the three aspects or merits (*guṇa*) of the Pure Heart of Bodhi which is in us. The first is that the Pure Heart of Bodhi breaks the passions of ignorance; the second is that it ripens into the fruit of Bodhi; and the third is that it remains unmoved aimlessly. This threefold significance of the name Dainichi sums up the essence of the Shingon's doctrine.

J. THE RELATION BETWEEN ŚĀKYAMUNI AND MAHĀVAIROCANA

Kōbō Daishi's critique of the Buddhist doctrines has as its pivot the distinction between exoteric and esoteric Buddhism, the representative Buddhas for which being Śākyamuni and Dainichi. It is evident that Buddhism is the doctrine of Śākyamuni. As to esoterism, if it is not doctrine of Śākyamuni, it could not be included in Buddhism. But, as a matter of fact, we believe that esoteric doctrine is not only Buddhist, but also occupies quite an eminent place in Buddhism as a whole. What then is the precise relation between Śākyamuni and Mahāvairocana? Let us state our conclusion immediately. In the *Fuhōden* of Kōbō daishi we read: "The three Bodies of Dharma, Saṃbhoga, and Nirmāṇa are the different functions (YŪ) of the same substance (TAI)."[48] Thus Śākyamuni in Nirmāṇakāya and Vairocana in Dharmakāya are identical. Vairocana without Śākyamuni cannot exist.

We can consider Śākyamuni from two points of view: as historical person and as the enlightened Buddha. He was a human being and acquired Enlightenment as a consequence of his conviction in the truth of the Dharma. The Dharma which he learned under the tree of Bodhi is the absolute reality (*tathatā*) which is sovereign and unchangeable, and lies even outside the *bodhi* of Śākyamuni. This is what the *Dainichikyō* expressed in the following terms: "Whether Tathāgatas appear or not, the dharmas always remain such (NYOZE), according to their true nature (HŌNI)."[49]

The Dharmakāya is the body of the Dharma of eternal reality which Śākyamuni took hold of at the time of his Enlightenment. To explain this body of the Dharma according to the esoteric doctrine, three formulas are appealed to:

(1) It is the Enlightenment of the Buddhas by one and another and belongs exclusively to the domain of the Buddhas.

(2) The body of the Dharma being eternal, it is Mahāvairocana, himself eternal, who explains this Dharma.

(3) According to the *Dainichikyō* and the *Kongōchōgyō*, the explanation of the Dharma is recorded in "the eternal copy which exists in the dharma-manner (HŌNI-JŌGŌ-NO-HON)."[50]

In short, Mahāvairocana is the historical Buddha idealized in Dharmakāya "which neither is born nor dies."

NOTES

1. Cf. *Ōtani Catalogue,* No. 431; *Tōhoku Catalogue,* No. 807.
2. Such is the title given in the Narthang edition; the Peking edition has *-vikurvati-;* the Sde-dge edition [also] has *-vikurvati-.* Cf. Hattori, *Zōbun Dainichikyō,* p. 1; *Ōtani Catalogue,* No. 126; *Tōhoku Catalogue,* No. 494.
3. French translation by Mr. Sylvain Levi.
4. Taishō, No. 1796, Vol. XXXIX, p. 579b[12].
5. Taishō, No. 848, chap. vii, Vol. XVIII, p. 45a[7].
6. Taishō, No. 1796, chap. ii; Vol. XXXIX, p. 605b[8].
7. Taishō, No. 2211, Vol. LVIII, p. 1.
8. Taishō, No. 1796, Vol. XXXIX, p. 597c[9].
9. Taisihō, Vol. XXXIX, p. 582c[29].
10. Taishō, Vol. XVIII, p. 899a.[13]
11. Identical with *Yōraku-nenju-kyō,* Taisho, No. 849.
12. *Fuhoden,* ed. *Dainihon bukkyo zensho,* pp. 21a[4]-21b[2].
13. Taishō, No. 1798, Vol. XXXIX, p. 808a-b. According to the oral teachings of Vajrabodhi, the work was compiled in China in the 7th century by Amoghavajra. It is a sort of introduction of the *sūtra* No. 866 of Taishō. Cf. our Introduction, n. 34. This text precisely states that the *stūpa* had an iron door-leaf sealed with an iron lock.
14. *Dainihon bukkyō zensho.,* p. 21b.[2]
15. See *Mikkyōdaijiten.* 1501, article "Tettō sōjō".
16. "*Dainichikyō jo",* a text dated in the 16th year of K'ai-yuan (728); in *Dainihon zokuyōkō* (Trip. of Kyoto, Supplement), XXXVI, fascicule I; cited also in the *Dainihon bukkyō zensho,* Vol. 106, p. 87.
17. Cf. Kambayashi, *Dainichikyō kaidai* (Introduction to the D.) in *kokuyaku Issaikyō,* Mikkyō bu, 1. p. 9. P'o-lou-lo is evidently Bolor, that is to say, in the Gilgit Valley; cf. B.E.F.E.O. III, p. 406, n. 7. This identification does not in the least clash with the rest of the legendary character of the story.
18. Taishō, No. 2120, Vol. LII, p. 848, date A.D. 744.
19. Taishō, No. 2056, Vol. L, p. 292; circa 776-79.
20. Taishō, No. 2157, Vol. LV, p. 875b, A.D. 799-800.
21. Cf. Kambayashi, *Kongōchō-ryakushitsukyō kaidai* (Introdution to the K.) in *Kokuyaku Issaikyō,* Mikkyō-bu, I, p. 214c.
22. Fuhōden, ed. *Dainihon bukkyō zensho,* p. 22a[16].

23. Quoted in *Kongōchō-ryakushitsukyō kaidai* (Introduction to the K.), in *Kokuyaku Issaikyō,* Mikkyō-bu, I, p. 214. Cf. also the similar interpretation of Shōken (1037-92) in Taishō, No. 2538, Vol. LXXXIX, pp. 606-607.
24. Cf. Yi-tsing (translation by Chavannes, *Mémoire sur les religieux eminents...* Sec. 52); Taishō, No. 2066. Vol. LI, p. 9a[21], and Kambayashi, *Dainichikyō kaidai (Kokuyaku Issaikyō,* Mikkyō-bu, I, p. 12b).
25. Taishō, No. 2154. chap. IX, Vol. LV, p.572a[15]; cf. *Tcheng-yuan sin ting che kiao mou lou,* Taishō, No. 2157, Vol. LV, p. 874c.
26. See *Narthang-ban Tibet daizōkyō Kanjur Makouroku,* "Catalogue of the Kanjur of the Narthang edition" (translated into Japanese by Kawaguchi Ekai, edited by Munekawa Sōman with Tibetan characters, Tokyo, 1928), p. 7. In the Catalogue the name of the king is given as Mnga' khri Ral.
27. Surendrabodhi, Dānaśīla, Bodhimitra, etc.
28. E. Schlagintwit, *Die Konige von Tibet:* 806-42; A.H. Francke, *Antiquities of Indian Tibet,* p. 92, "about 810-20"; Rockhill, *The Life of the Buddha*, pp. 223-25, "816-38"; Teramoto Engo, *Ōtani Gakuho, XI, 3, pp. 27-28: "816-99"; Matsumoto Bunzaburō, op. cit.,* pp. 10-12 "817-38"; Tada Tōkan, *Shūkyō Kenkyū,* III, 2, p. 109: "866-901"; Sarat Chandra Das, *Tibetan-English Dictionary,* p. 361: "towards the close of the 9th century. A.D.."
29. Editions: Narthang, Ta, 301a-455a; Sde-dge, Tha, 151b-260a; Peking, Tha, 115b-260a; No. 126 of the *Ōtani Catalogue;* No. 949 of the *Tōhoku Catalogue.*
30. The Arabic numerals given in brackets refer to the 'volumes' (KWAN) of the Chinese version.
31. As we have shown on p. 94, ff. of our work mentioned below (n. 31, following), the Tibetan chapter XXIX, in spite of the title differences, corresponds well in terms of its content to the Chinese chapters XXVII and XXXI.
32. *Zō-kan taiyaku Dainichikyō jūshimbon narabi ni Dainchikyō zō-kan ryōyaku* ***kenkyū gaikwan.*** Tōkyō, 1927.
33. See the catalogue by Kawaguchi and Munekawa (mentioned above, n. 26), p. 144; my work already cited (n. 31, above), p. 61.
34. Taishō, No. 2427, Vol. LXXVII.
35. The Sambhogakāya "for one's own self' (JIJUYŪSHIN) as distinct from the Sambhogakāya "for others" (TAJUYŪSHIN) is meant here. The former tastes the joy of the Dharma himself while the latter makes the Bodhisattvas of the Stages (*bhūmi*) relish it. Cf. the *Hōbōgirin,* p. 183.
36. *Loc. cit.,* p. 375a[2]. The "place" symbolizes the domain of esoterism.
37. Taishō, No. 1796, Vol. XXXIX, p. 580a[12].
38. Taishō, No. 2211, Vol. LVII. p. 3c[3].
39. Taishō, No. 1796, Vol. XXXIX, p. 580a[29].
40. *Ibid.,* p. 580b[3].
41. *Ibid.,* p. 580a[26]2.
42. *Ibid.,* p. 580a[2].
43. Taishō, No. 848, Vol. XVIII, p. la[21].
44. Taishō, Vol. XXXIX, p. 538a[3].
45. Taishō, Vol. XVIII, p. la[28].
46. Cf. *Mahāprajñāparamitāśāstra,* chap. IX, quoted by Kōbō daishi in Taishō, No. 2427, Vol. LXXVII, p. 38la[13].
47. Taishō, No. 1796 Vol. XXXIX, p. 579a[4-19]
48. Fuhōden, ed. *Dainihon bukkyō zensho,* p. 2a[8].
49. Taishō, No. 848, chap. II, Vol. XVIII, p. 10a[12].
50. See above, "B. Three Alleged Sources of the Dainichikyō".

PART III

ANNOTATED TRANSLATION OF THE FIRST CHAPTER OF THE DAINICHIKYŌ

Translation of the first chapter of the Sūtra (concerning) the Advent of Mahāvairocana to the State of Buddha, his supernatural Transformations and his Miraculous Graces[1] (Which was) translated into Chinese in the T'ang period by the master of the Tripiṭaka Śubhakarasiṃha of India (in collaboration) with the *śramaṇa* Yi-hing (Ichigyō)

CHAPTER I ACCESS TO THE DISCIPLINE OF THE SHINGON[2] WHICH INSTALLS (THE BEING) IN THE HEART (OF BODHI)[3]

Thus have I[4] heard: Once the Blessed One[5] was staying in the vast Palace of Vajra-Dharmadhātu[6] (where) the Tathāgata creates his miraculous graces.

All the 'wielders of Vajra'[7] were present with no exception. The precious royal edifice (in the form of) a great pavillion, which the Tathāgata had created by miraculous transformation and by a display[8] of his fervent conviction,[9] was aloft (and infinite) with no center or limits.[10] Splendid treasures of all sorts adorned it in different manners. The body of the Bodhisattva occupied the throne made of lions.[11]

THE RETINUE

The names of Vajra-wielders were: the vajra-wielder 'Purity of Space',[12] the vajra-wielder 'Who traverses space',[13] the vajra-wielder 'Born of space',[14] the vajra-wielder 'Clothed in multi-colored dress',[15] the vajra-wielder 'Who moves around in an excellent manner',[16] the vajra-wielder 'Who dwells in the sameness of all the dharmas',[17] the vajra-wielder 'Who is compassionate toward the world of innumerable living beings',[18] the vajra-wielder 'Vigor of Nārāyaṇa',[19] the vajra-wielder 'Vigor of Mahānārāyaṇa',[20] the vajra-wielder 'Sublime',[21] the vajra-wielder 'Who moves with great speed',[22] the vajra-wielder 'Immaculate',[23] the vajra-wielder 'Quickly cutting',[24] the vajra-wielder 'Shield of the Tathāgata',[25] the vajra-wielder 'Born of the Tathāgata's rank',[26] the vajra-wielder 'Who dwells where there are no vain discussions',[27] the vajra-wielder 'Born of the ten forces of the Tathāgata',[28] the vajra-wielder 'Immaculate Eye',[29] and Vajrapāṇi,[30] 'Master of the Mysteries'[31].

With such chiefs in front, the assembly of vajra-wielders numerically equal to the atoms of the ten domains of the Buddha,[32] as also Bodhisattva Samantabhadra,[33] Bodhisattva Maitreya,[34] Bodhisattva Mañjuśrī,[35] Bodhisattva Sarvanīvaraṇaviṣkambhin,[36] and all the other great Bodhisattvas in front and back, encircled Mahāvairocana.

THE PREACHING VAIROCANA

He preached to them the Dharma, to wit, the formula[37] of the Equality of Body, Speech, and Mind,[38] realized by the miraculous grace of the Tathāgata Sun, which is transcendent in relation to the three (modalities) of time.[39]

Then,[40] by the miraculous grace of Mahāvairocana Tathāgata, upon making Samantabhadra as the chief of the Bodhisattvas, and making the Master of Mysteries as the chief of the many kinds of vajra-wielders, there appeared with the speed (of a bounding lion)[41] the magnificent and inexhaustible Treasures[42] of the Equality of Speech and of Mind. (These Treasures) are not born of either the Body, or the Speech, or the Mind of the Buddha Vairocana; (like him) they appear and disappear in all places and do not admit of any limit either in time or in space.[43] All the acts of the Body of Vairocana, all the acts of his Speech, and all the acts of his Mind are the preaching of the Dharma of the formulas of the Shingon path[44] in all places and at all times in the world of beings. And he manifests himself also in the form of Vajra-wielder,[45] or Bodhisattva Samantabhadra,[46] or Bodhisattva Padmapāṇi,[47] and so on,[48] for the propagation (in this way) of the Dharma of the pure[49] formulas of the Shingon path, universally and in all directions (so as to generate) the initial Thought (of Enlightenment), then to give access to the Ten Stages,[50] and to gradually cause attainment of Plenitude (that is to say, the state of Buddha) in this life.[51] (Next) are extirpated the (bad) seeds (*bīja*) of life force[52] due to *karma* among those belonging to living beings, whose births (and rebirths), conditioned by *karma*, grow (that is to say, take place continuously in the cycle of transmigration);[53] and there are also (good) seeds that arise anew.[54]

VAJRAPĀṆI'S QUESTIONS

Then[55] vajra-wielder 'Master of Mysteries', seated in the said assembly, spoke to the Buddha: "World Honored One,[56] how has the Tathāgata-Arhat-Samyaksambuddha[57] attained omniscient knowledge? How is it that, having attained omniscient knowledge,[58] he preaches it widely and reveals it clearly to innumerable beings? How does he teach the omniscient knowledge by all sorts of methods,[59] (namely) ways of liberation,[60] adapting them to the diverse destinies[61] and inclinations (of each of these beings)—the method of the Śrāvaka vehicle,[62] the method of the Pratyekabuddha,[63] the method of the Great Vehicle,[64] the method of the five supernormal faculties?[65] How does he explain the Dharma (per each being's desire) which corresponds to the desire to be born in heaven (among the devas) or among human beings or among the nāgas, the yakṣas, the gandharvas, and so on,[66] up to (the desire) to be born among the Mahoraga? (If) a living being has to be rescued by the Buddha, how is it that the Buddha reveals to him, as the case may be, either a body of Buddha or a body of Śrāvaka or a body of Pratyekabuddha or a body of Bodhisattva or a body of Brahmā or Nārāyaṇa, or a body of Vaiśravaṇa, and so on, up to (a body of) Mahoraga, a human body, a non-human body,[67] etc.? How does he employ (for each being) the appropriate language[68] and adopt varied attitudes[69] (and how) do these methods of omniscient knowledge all have nevertheless, a single taste, viz. the taste of the Tathāgata's liberation?"[70]

OMNISCIENT KNOWLEDGE

"(Thus,) O World Honored One, to take recourse to comparisons,[71] the omniscient knowledge (of the Buddha) which is free from all particularization[72] is at the same time without particularization[73] and not without particularization just as space is both without particularization and not without particularization.

"World Honored One, to take (another) comparison, the omniscient knowledge supports[74] (the manifestations of diverse bodies such as the body of a deva, of human beings, of asuras, as the earth supports the totality of living beings.

"World Honored One, the omniscient knowledge insatiably consumes the combustible ignorance in the same way as the element fire insatiably consumes everything combustible.

"World Honored One, the omniscient knowledge removes all the 'dust' of passions[75] just as the element wind removes all dust.

"World Honored One, the omniscient knowledge brings profit and joy to all the devas and human beings in the same way as water serves the pleasure of living beings.

"World Honored One, for such a knowledge [i.e. omniscient], what is the cause?[76] what the root?[77] what the fulfilment?[78]

When the Master of Mysteries had finished speaking thus, the Buddha Vairocana told him: "Excellent, excellent,[79] Vajra-wielder! Excellent, Vajrapāṇi! You have asked me to explain the significance of all this. Listen carefully. Be attentive. Now I shall explain it." Vajrapāṇi replied, "So be it, World Honored One, I desire to hear it."[80]

The Buddha declared: "The Bodhi-heart[81] is its cause. Great Compassion[82] is its root. The Means[83] are its fulfilment. What is Bodhi, Master of Mysteries? It is to know one's heart (*citta*) as it is.[84] Master of the Mysteries, the least part[85] of this Anuttarasamyak-sambodhi (Incomparable Right Complete Enlightenment)[86] and even of these dharmas[87] cannot be attained (by understanding). How is it that Bodhi is (endowed with) the character[88] of space; is neither knowable nor comprehensible; nothing but it casts light (in the beings)?[89] The reason that Bodhi lacks character, and that the dharmas (also) lack character[90]—that is why Bodhi is said to have the character of space."

Then Vajrapāṇi spoke again to the Buddha: "O World Honored One, who seeks the omniscient knowledge? Who becomes a Sambuddha by dint of Bodhi? What produces this omniscient knowledge?"[91]

The Buddha declared: "Master of the Mysteries, Bodhi and the omniscient knowledge must be sought (by each being) in his own Heart. Why so? Because (our) original nature[92] is pure.[93] The Heart is neither inside nor outside (the beings); nor is it to be found between these two. Master of the Mysteries, the Tathāgata-Arhat-Samyak-sambuddha[94] is neither blue, not yellow, nor red, nor white, nor purple, nor crystalline, nor long, nor short, nor round, nor square, nor clear, nor dark, nor male, nor female, nor sexless. Master of Mysteries, the Heart has nothing in common with the realm of desire,[95] or with the realm of form,[96] or with the formless realm;[97] it has nothing in common with (any) destiny[98] of either the Deva, Nāga, Yakṣa, Gandharva, Asura, Garuḍa, Kimnara, Mahoraga, or beings human non-human.[99] Master of Mysteries, the Heart is not in the realm[100] (perceptible) to the eye, nor in those (perceptible) to the ear, nose, tongue, body, or mind.[101] It is neither a view nor a manifestation.[102] Why so? Because the Heart, which has the character of space, is transcendent to all particularization and non-particularization.[103] Since there is identity of nature, the character of space is similar to that of the Heart; and if its nature is identical with that of the Heart, it is identical (also with that of Bodhi. It is thus, Master of Mysteries, that the Heart, the realm of space, and Bodhi—these three—amount to one thing.[104] They have compassion for a root[105] and have the perfection of means[106] for a fulfilment.[107] Master of Mysteries, the reason for my explaining thus the dharmas is so that all these assemblies of Bodhisattvas may adopt[108] the attitude for purification of the Bodhi Heart (their true heart). Master of Mysteries, if men of good birth, or women of good birth,[109] desire to have the knowledge of Bodhi, they must (at the outset) adopt the attitude in this way toward their own heart.[110] Master of Mysteries, how can they adopt the attitude by themselves toward the (true) Heart? One cannot find it, if one seeks it in (this world of) fragments,[111] colors,[112] shapes,[113] and (external sense) objects;[114] or in (material) forms,[115] feelings,[116] conceptions,[117] motivations,[118] and perceptions;[119] or else in the self[120] or in the attachment to one's own;[121] or else in the apprehending[122] or the apprehended;[123] or else in purity,[124] or in the realms,[125] in the bases,[126] and so forth, namely, in anything that is fragmented.[127]

"Master of Mysteries, this rubric of the pure Bodhi Heart of the Bodhisattvas bears the name of Path (along which) one begins to be clear about the dharmas.[128] If the Bodhisattvas devote themselves to its exercises and to its study, without long ascetic practices, they will easily obtain the *samādhi* which removes all obstacles.[129] He who attains this *samādhi* will occupy the same rank as the Buddhas and the Bodhisattvas. He will possess the five supernormal faculties;[130] acquire the languages,[131] the sounds,[132] and the innumerable *dhāraṇīs*; come to know the mental conduct[133] of all the sentient beings; benefit from the protection of all the Buddhas; be exempt from passionate attachment,[134] even toward birth and death,[135] will not spare himself any pain for sentient beings in respect to the *dharm-dhātu*;[136] reach unconstructed morality[137] and maintain himself there; reject erroneous views[138] and arrive at correct ones.[139] Furthermore, Master of Mysteries, the Bodhisattva who possesses the *samādhi*[140] that casts off all obstacles, will, thanks to the force of his fervent conviction,[141] accomplish all the Buddha natures, and do it without long religious exercises. In short, Master of Mysteries, this man (or this woman) of good (birth)[142] may realize (each by oneself) all the innumerable merits[143] (of the Buddha)."

GENERATION OF BODHI

The Vajra-wielder Master of Mysteries then put new questions to the Buddha in the form of *gāthā*:[144]

"How does the World Honored One explain[145] the generation of Bodhi in the heart,[146] and the character to recognize that the Bodhi Heart has been generated?[147]

"I beseech thee, pray explain the birth of the *vijñāna-citta*[148] or Heart of the supreme, autonomous[149] knowledge (*jñāna*).

"Great hero![150] After how many (stages) in succession is the Heart at last born?[151]

"O Buddha, I wish that you would explain in an elaborate manner the characteristics of the Heart (still particularized and impure)[152] and the period of time (necessary for achieving Bodhi).[153]

"As also the totality of merits[154] (which the Heart of Bodhi involves) as well as the observance of the practices;[155] also the Heart (the ***vipākavijñānacitta*** among beings in general)[156] and the special features of the Heart (of the ascetic practising *yoga*).[157]

"O great Muni,[158] pray explain all these matters."

When the Vajra-wielder had finished speaking that way, the World Honored One Mahāvairocana responded to him:

"Very good,[159] O true son of the Buddha!

"The grandeur and amplitude of (thy) Heart will benefit the beings.

"The successive characters of the Heart[160] from the lofty standpoint[161] of the Great Vehicle (*mahāyāna*) are the grand secrets of the Buddhas. Heretic doctrines[162] cannot comprehend them.[163]

"Now I shall expose them in full. Listen carefully with all thy Heart.

"(Once anyone) transcends the one hundred and sixty (types) of (defiled) Heart,[164] then are born (in him) immense merits.[165]

"The birth of Bodhi is recognized by its eternally firm nature. It is immeasurable like space,[166] immaculate and eternally stable. The dharmas cannot disturb it. From the moment of its origin it is calm and characterless. (In it) one may realize immeasurable knowledge; and (in it) Samyaksambodhi may manifest itself. The observances of offering practices[167] proceed from this initial arousal of the Heart (of Bodhi)."

THE HERESIES OF ORDINARY PERSONS

"Master of Mysteries, ordinary persons,[168] stupid as infants,[169] dwelling in the beginningless circle of life and death,[170] remain always attached to the terms of self[171] and what belongs to self.[172] They operate through distinctions among innumerable facets of 'self'.[173] Master of Mysteries, if they do not properly assess the true nature[174] of 'self',[175] it happens that 'self' and 'self-ownership'[176] arise in them. Some[177] claim that the ultimate principle is Time,[178] or the transformations of earth and the other (elements),[179] or the Self of *yoga*;[180] either established and pure,[181] or not established and impure;[182] or the Īśvara, or the (primordial) Outflow,[183] or (a kind of) Time;[184] the Respected One (Nārāyaṇa),[185] or Spontaneity,[186] an Inner Self,[187] or the Person of variable size,[188] the Pervader (Viṣṇu),[189] or Long Life,[190] the Personality (*pudgala*),[191] or Consciousness (*vijñāna*),[192] or the Store (*ālaya*), or the Knower,[193] or the Seer;[194] the apprehender[195] or the apprehended;[196] introspection,[197] or outer-directed perception;[198] or the Jñātvan (a kind of knower),[199] the Manuja (born of Manu),[200] or the Mānava (descendant of Manu),[201] or (the Self) born in an eternal and determined way;[202] (divine) Word,[203] (divine) Silence.[204] Thus, Master of the Mysteries, people have sought liberation of the yogin[205] for ever so long by these partial (views) [about the Ātman] that are associated with particularization."

EIGHT STAGES OF THE GOOD MAN

"Master of the Mysteries, ordinary person, stupid (as) infants,[206] are also like sheep.[207] By chance there may be an occasion when they have an idea[208] of *dharma* (duty, or, the good), namely, to observe abstinence.[209] Should they stay on this modicum, finding therein a source of joy; and give themselves up to this practice many times. Master of Mysteries, that is the initial seed[210] from which good action (*karman*) is born. Should they continue on that basis, and on six (lunar) days of abstinence,[211] make gifts to their father, mother, and to male and female relatives, this would be the second stage, that of the sprout.[212] Should they then make gifts to persons who are not relatives (and are not acquaintances), this would be the third stage, that of the trunk.[213] If subsequently they make gifts to persons of expertise and of high merit, this is the fourth (stage), that of growing leaves.[214] Then, should they out of joy make gifts to artists, musicians, and the like; and also make respectful presentations to venerable and aged persons, this is the fifth (stage), that of flowering.[215] When they do the same out of affection or love this is the sixth (stage), that of the fruit.[216] Master of Mysteries, should they then observe morality (*śīla*)[217] so as to be reborn in heaven,[218] this is the seventh (stage), utilization of the grain.[219]

"Then, Master of Mysteries, should they preserve in the course of transmigrations[220] this spirit (of giving and morality), they will come to hear said in the company of good friends (or, spiritual guides),[221] 'Heaven, great heaven, that is what confers (on us) every pleasure. All the prayers are heard if one observes the practices of offering with piety and sincerity. Taken notice of by Īśvara,[222] Brahmā,[223] Nārāyaṇa,[224] Śaṅkara,[225] Rudra,[226] Son of Īśvara (= Skanda),[227] Sūrya,[228] Candra,[229] Varuṇa,[230] and others; as well as by Kubera,[231] Vaiśravaṇa,[232] Śakra,[233] Virupākṣa,[234] Viśvakarman,[235] Yama[236] and consort, Brahmā's wife, Agni who is worshipped in the world, the god son of Garuḍa,[237] Īśvara's consort;[238] by (the Nāgas) Padma, Takṣaka,[239] Vāsuki,[240] Śaṅkha,[241] Karkoṭaka, Mahāpadma,[242] Kulika,[243] Mahāphaṇaka,[244] Ādideva,[245] Sadānanda,[246] and so on; the divine Ṛṣis[247] and the great Veda[248] masters—those practices of offering being taken notice of in each case, may you supply well!' Upon hearing these words, (people) nourish in their heart a splendid joy, and with piety and respect they attend to the (offering) practices in (a spirit of) submission. That is what, O Master of Mysteries is called the fearless[249] support of worldly people, the ignorant infants, while they stray in the course[250] of births and deaths;[251] and this is the eighth stage, the heart of a child.[252]

"(But) Master of Mysteries, there are practices superior (to those stages). When one conforms to the most elevated parts of the teaching by these (good friends, spiritual guides), one may get installed in a superior (stage). That is, one arouses the knowledge (by which) one seeks liberation, namely, (the knowledge relating) to the Void (whether considered to be) eternal (or considered to be) non-eternal;[253] and one conforms submissively to this teaching.

(However), Master of Mysteries, such a one[254] understands neither the Void nor the non-Void;[255] and (becomes a partisan of) eternalism,[256] nihilism,[257] of non-existence[258] or of existence.[259] He assumes constructive thought[260] in the case without constructive thought.[261] How could one use constructive thought for the Void? If one does not know all (kinds of) the Void,[262] one cannot reach the knowledge of Nirvāṇa. That is why it is necessary to recognize that the Void is dissociated from annihilation and eternalism."

THE SIXTY (ERRANT) HEARTS

Vajrapāṇi now addressed a new question to the Buddha: "Would the World Honored One kindly explain the (errant) hearts?"[263] The Buddha spoke to Vajrapāṇi, Master of Mysteries, along these lines: "Master of Mysteries, listen carefully! The characteristic signs of hearts[264] are these: the heart of greed,[265] that of non-greed,[266] of hatred,[267] of love,[268] of delusion,[269] of insight,[270] or resolution,[271] of doubt,[272] of darkening,[273] of making clear,[274] of reduction,[275] of contention,[276] of inward struggle,[277] without inward struggle,[278] of deity,[279] of demi-god,[280] of serpent,[281] of man,[282] of woman,[283] of a lord,[284] of a merchant,[285] of a farmer,[286] of river,[287] of a pool,[288] of a well,[289] of protection,[290] of avarice,[291] of a dog,[292] of a cat,[293] of a garuḍa-bird,[294] of a mouse,[295] of a song,[296] of a dance,[297] of drumming,[298] of a house,[299] of a lion,[300] of an owl,[301] of a crow,[302] of a demon,[303] of a thorn,[304] of a cave,[305] of the wind,[306] of water,[307] of fire,[308] of mud,[309] of chameleon,[310] of wooden board,[311] of contrariety,[312] of poison,[313] of a noose,[314] of shackles,[315] of a cloud,[316] of a field,[317] of salt,[318] of a razor,[319] of Mt. Sumeru,[320] of the ocean,[321] of a hole,[322] of recurrence.[323] Master of Mysteries:

1. What is the heart of greed? It is that which attaches itself to tainted (impure) dharmas.[324]
2. What is the heart of non-greed? It is that which attaches itself to unsullied dharmas.
3. What is the heart of hatred? It is that which conforms to the dharmas of anger.
4. What is the heart of love? It is that which conforms to the dharma of love (with partiality).
5. What is the heart of delusion? That which conforms to the dharma of non-reflection.
6. What is the heart of insight? That which seeks profit and gain.

7. What is the heart of resolution? That which follows to the letter the respected master's instruction.[325]
8. What is the heart of doubt? That which remains in a state of indecision.
9. What is the heart of darkening? Which doubts in the case without any doubt.
10. What is the heart of making clear? What does not doubt, while one should be apprehensive that there is no doubt.
11. What is the heart of reduction? That which makes a unity out of the immeasurable.[326]
12. What is the heart of contention? Which contends on issues of right or wrong.
13. What is the heart of inward struggle? Which is troubled by right or wrong for itself.
14. What is the heart without inward struggle? That which abandons any argument over right or wrong.
15. What is the heart of deity? That which believes everything will happen exactly as planned.
16. What is the heart of demi-god? That which desires to remain in *samsāra*.[327]
17. What is the heart of serpent? That which dwells on acquiring immense fortune.
18. What is the heart of man? That which is pre-occupied with interests of other things.[328]
19. What is the heart of woman? That which follows the dharmas of lust.
20. What is the heart of lord? That which believes everything will be exactly as one wishes.
21. What is the heart of a merchant? That which takes first, to sell later on.[329]
22. What is the heart of a farmer? Which extensively listens first (to the farming advice) to harvest later.
23. What is the heart of river? Which leans on both sides.[330]
24. What is the heart of pool? Which satisfies thirst without ever having enough.
25. What is the heart of well? Which deliberates as deep and profoundly.[331]
26. What is the heart of defense? Which believes only itself true, the others not.
27. What is the heart of avarice? Which thinks only of oneself, but not giving anything to another.[332]

28. What is the heart of a cat? Which proceeds stealthily.
29. What is the heart of a dog? Which is satisfied with the little that is received.
30. What is the heart of a garuḍa-bird? Which leans on the wing of the group-companion.
31. What is the heart of mouse? Which thinks only of gnawing away its bonds.
32. What is the heart of song? [Which deceives others.][333]
33. What is the heart of dance? That which believes that by exercising, one achieves supernormal powers.
34. What is the heart of drumming? Which believes that by exercising, one is beating the drum of the Dharma.
35. What is the heart of house? Which takes pains to protect its own body.
36. What is the heart of a lion? That which acts without any timidity.
37. What is the heart of an owl? That which thinks in night's darkness.[334]
38. What is the heart of a crow? That has feelings of dread in all circumstances.
39. What is the heart of a demon? That would arouse evil in the good.
40. What is the heart of a thorn? Which would arouse evil action in all circumstances.[335]
41. What is the heart of a cave? One that is led to withdraw into a cave.[336]
42. What is the heart of wind? That has a nature of circulating everywhere and of self-raising.
43. What is the heart of water? That would wash away all impurities.[337]
44. What is the heart of fire? Whose nature is to burn intensely and to blaze with heat.[338]
45. What is the heart of mud? [Which soils others with its own faults.][339]
46. What is the heart of chameleon? Whose nature conforms to the color.[340]
47. What is the heart of wooden board? It is that which accepts dharmas if they fall within the (square) dimensions, but not good extra ones if they fall outside.[341]
48. What is the heart of contrariety? Which adopts and thinks in disaccord with itself.[342]

49. What is the heart of poison? That which succumbs with no wish to revive.[343]
50. What is the heart of a noose? That has the nature leading to be tied up by its self.
51. What is the heart of shackles? That is prone to have the two feet immobilized.
52. What is the heart of a cloud? Which is constantly preoccupied with rain.[344]
53. What is the heart of a field? Which devotes all its concern to its own body.
54. What is the heart of salt? One adding thoughts to thoughts [as bits of salt continually added produce a pile-up of salt].[345]
55. What is the heart of a razor? That thinks it suffices to be shaved and goes no further.[346]
56. What is the heart of Mt. Sumeru? That is prone to raise itself ever higher.[347]
57. What is the heart of the ocean? Which would utilize everything for its own advantage.[348]
58. What is the heart of a hole? Which tends to fall back from resolutions already made.[349]
59. What is the heart of rebirth? That which accepts all acts as causes of rebirth.[350]
60. ... (not listed).

Thus, the characteristics of heart are the same as are above mentioned.

THE THREE KALPAS

"Master of Mysteries, one hundred and sixty hearts [are obtained] by multiplying by two [the five basic defilements, *kleśa*], once, twice, thrice, four times, and five times.[351] If one transcends the three errant mundane attachments (*laukikakalpa*),[352] then the supramundane heart is born.[353]

"That is to say, in that one understands that (he) is only the five aggregates (*skandha*), with no self (*ātman*) therein,[354] while remaining immersed in the activities of the (six) sense organs,[355] their (six) objects,[356] and the (six) spheres (of perception),[357] it is then[358] that one extirpates the stump[359] and trunk of *karman* and *kleśa*, as well as the seed of nescience (*avidyā*), generator of the twelve links.[360] One abandons the schools of the established (*dharmas*),[361] and the others (that are heretic),[362] because none of the heretic schools can take hold of such a plenitude of calm.[363] The former

Buddhas have said that it (i.e. the heart) is (then) liberated from all faults. Master of Mysteries, from the supramundane heart[364] which remains in the personal aggregates (*skandha*) is born the insight[365] as follows: To shake off the attachment for the *skandhas,*[366] it is necessary to consider them with the nature of froth and scum,[367] of floating bubbles,[368] of the (pithless) banana tree,[369] of mirages,[370] or illusion,[371] and so on. Thus, one arrives at the liberation[372] (from the realistic positing of the skandhas). This is because personal aggregates, sense bases,[373] and realms;[374] appropriator[375] and the appropriated,[376] are all far from the true nature (*dharmatā*).[377] To have an experience of (absolute) calm[378] as such, is what is known as the supramundane heart.[379] Master of Mysteries, the one who avoids the streams of consciousness (*saṃtāna*) of eight deviant[380] or non-deviant hearts,[381] as also, who avoids the snares of *karma* and *kleśa*, may with the practice of yoga,[382] cross the first of the three *kalpas*.[383]

"Then, Master of Mysteries, by the practice of the Great Vehicle, one arouses the heart which has no object,[384] and realizes the non-self of dharmas. Why so? It is because in ancient times such practitioners examined the *ālaya* (store) of the personal aggregates (*skandha*)[385] and discovered that their true nature is similar to an illusion, the mirage, the reflected image, an echo, the fire wheel (of a rotating torch), the castle of gandharvas.[386] Master of Mysteries, the non-self having been rejected, the heart becomes sovereign and independent,[387] understands that the heart itself is without production primordially;[388] because, O Master of Mysteries, neither the anterior nor the posterior limit can be (intellectually) reached.[389] He who thus grasps the true nature of his heart, may with practice of yoga, cross the second of the three *kalpas*.

THIRD KALPA AND ADHIMUKTICARYĀ

"And then, O Master of Mysteries, all the Bodhisattvas who cultivate Bodhisattva practices in the discipline of the Shingon,[390] completely realize the wisdom[391] (backed) by innumerable merits[392] accumulated in the course of myriads of *koṭi*[393] and *nayuta* of eons (*kalpa*); they realize also the means[394] of the immeasurable wisdom. They are an object of devotion by the devas and the worldlings.[395] They surpass the stages of all the *śrāvakas* and *pratyekabuddhas*, while Śakra-Devendra and other gods approach them to render them veneration.

"What is called 'voidness'[396] pertains neither to the sense organs nor their objects; has neither characteristic[397] nor objective scope;[398] this 'voidness' transcends all vain discussions,[399] and is limitless like space. While based in this voidness, the Buddha's teachings are delivered serially.[400] It therefore transcends the constructed[401] and the unconstructed[402] spheres, all artificiality,[403] (the sense organs) sight, hearing, smell, taste, the body (surface), and the mind (*manas*).[404] So is born the heart that is completely void of an own-nature.[405] Master of Mysteries, it is this initial heart[406] that the Buddha has declared to be the cause of Buddhahood (eventually).[407] Thanks to it, while leaning on *karma* and *kleśa* one may be delivered from these.[408] The world will devote to him a cult and constantly present offerings.

"And then, O Master of Mysteries, one gains the Stage of Adhimukticaryā,[409] one examines deeply the three kinds of hearts,[410] and with the immeasurable wisdom of the Perfections (*pāramitā*)[411] meditates on the (four) means of persuading (sentient beings).[412] The Stage of Adhimukticaryā is absolute, immeasurable, inconceivable.[413] Therein the ten hearts[414] are established, and it gives rise to the omniscient knowledge. All that I teach, one receives through it. A wise man should also reflect upon this Ạdhimukticaryā as (directed toward) omniscience. (Having so meditated) he transcends the (third) *kalpa*, being elevated to this stage[415] (the fourth) among the four divisions, which (even) transcends the Adhimukticaryā."[416]

THE SIX NON-FEARS

The Vajra-Holder, Master of Mysteries, then addressed the Buddha as follows: "Respected venerable of the world, savior of the world, I implore you to explain the characteristics[417] of the heart. How many kinds of non-fear[418] are feasible up to the Bodhisattvas?" Having so asked, the Vajra-Holder was addressed by Vairocana. world-honored one, in these terms: "Listen attentively and ponder over it, O Master of Mysteries. Lay people, of child-like immaturity, by performing virtuous acts, and desisting from unvirtuous acts, may obtain the non-fear called 'moral' (strength). When one knows oneself as it really is, he may obtain the non-fear called 'corporeal'. When the body is viewed as a 'pile-up' (*skandha*) and its visual image is rejected, one obtains the 'non-self' kind of non-fear. When belief in the *skandhas* has been destroyed, but one still reifies the dharmas, one should seek the 'dharma' kind of non-fear. When one has negated dharma[419] and refrains from objectifying them,[420] one obtains the non-fear called 'non-self of dharmas'. Given that all the *skandhas*,[421] realms,[422] and sense bases,[423] the appropriator[424] and the appropriated;[425] the self,[426] life power,[427] and so on; as also the dharmas and non-production;[428] are void, their own-nature consisting of non-own-nature—if the knowledge of this void arises, one obtains the non-fear called 'sameness of own-nature of all dharmas'."

THE TEN SIMILES

"Master of Mysteries, all the Bodhisattvas, while cultivating the exercises of the Bodhisattvas who practice the Shingon disciple, will examine thoroughly the ten similes for arising due to dependence.[429] They will then thoroughly penetrate the practice of the Shingon and prove it in themselves.

"What are these ten (similes)? These are the illusion,[430] mirage,[431] dream,[432] reflection,[433] castle of gandharvas,[434] echo,[435] the moon in the waters,[436] floating bubbles,[437] the flower in space,[438] and the whirling fire wheel.[439] Master of Mysteries, all the Bodhisattvas who cultivate the exercises of the Bodhisattvas who practice the Shingon discipline must consider the following:

"What is illusion? It is like the visual images[440] of all sorts which are created by the (two) means, art of incantations and power of drugs, These illusions deceive our eyes, and that is why we perceive extraordinary things mutually promoting each other, but which neither come nor go in the ten directions. Why so? The own nature, (of illusion) is pure,[441] and so such phantasmagorias are all only products[442] of the *mantra* recitation and of the realization (*siddhi*) of the three mysteries. "Furthermore, Master of Mysteries, mirage is also void of own-being. People apply a verbal convention due to their erroneous notion; and this verbal convention becomes the topic of discussion. Likewise, the imaginations (produced as one practises) *mantras*.[443] They are nothing but borrowed names.[444]

"Furthermore, Master of Mysteries, when one is dreaming, what is seen therein may last for a day, a *muhūrta,* a moment, a year, and so on; but nothing visible, whether agreeable or painful, remains of it after awakening. Likewise, the practice of mantras is comparable to a dream.[445]

"And then, Master of Mysteries, the reflection analogy shows that if the *siddhi*-occurrence[446] can be due to *mantra* practice, it is like the facial reflection needing mirror.[447] The *siddhi* of mantra is just like that.[448]

"Next, Master of Mysteries, the perfection-site of the evocation is like the castle of the gandharvas [in the sky].[449]

"Then, Master of Mysteries, the sound of the mantra is like an echo. An echo arises in dependence on a sound; and one should understand the mantra-method to be just like that.[450]

"Then, Master of Mysteries, when the moon rises and people see its reflections in the pure waters, they speak of the 'moon in the waters'. The holders of mantra-science[451] must thereby understand the comparison of the *mantra* with the moon (reflected) in the waters.[452]

"Furthermore, Master of Mysteries, water bubbles are produced in the event of falling rain. The diverse transformations of the mantra (i.e. miraculous evidences of the *siddhi*) are like that.[453]

"Again, Master of Mysteries, while there are no sentient beings[454] or life[455] or their creator,[456] in space, our straying and troubled heart creates mistaken views (like the flowers of space).[457]

"And, Master of Mysteries, it is like a person holding a torch[458] in hand and rotating it, creating the form of a wheel in space."[459]

THE SIX PADA

"Master of Mysteries, it is in this way that one must know[460] the Word (*pada*) of the Great Vehicle,[461] the Word of the (true) heart,[462] the Word of being equal to the unequalled,[463] the Word of certainty,[464] the Word of Right Complete Enlightenment,[465] the Word of progressive access to the Great Vehicle.[466] One may thus possess the richness of the Dharma[467] which gives rise in great measure to the diversity of knowledge, and rightly and exactly knows all the distinctions of the heart."[468]

NOTES

1. For the original Sanskrit title see our previous chapter General Study of the Dainichikyō, "A. The Title Dainichikyō". The expression "miraculous graces" translates the Sino-Japanese term KAJI= *adhiṣṭhāna,* Tib. *byin gyis brlabs pa.* The *Hōbōgirin* translates it by "benediction". Kōbō daishi gives the following explanations of this term: "It expresses the great compassion of the Tathāgatas and the belief of all the beings: KA (= *adhi*) means the penetration of the Buddha's light in the water of all the beings; and JI (=*ṣṭhāna*), the power of absorption of the Buddha's light, which this water, the Heart of all beings, possesses" (*Sokushin Jobutsu gi,* Taishō, No. 2428, Vol. LXXXVII, p. 383b[25]).

In the Tibetan version, the title is followed by the formula: "respectfully offered to the Master of Speech (Vāgīśvara = Mañjughoṣa or Mañjuśrī), venerated in the world". This is a pious addition of the translator.

2. For the meaning of the word Shingon, see our next chapter Doctrinal Analysis, "A. The title of this chapter".
3. For the meaning of the title of this chapter, see our next chapter, "A. The title of this chapter". SHIN=*citta*=*śuddha-bodhicitta,* the "pure Heart of Bodhi" which is innate in us.
4. It refers to Vajrasattva, to whom the transmission of the sermons of the Buddha has been confided (*saṃgītikāra*).
5. *Bhagavat* is an epithet of the Buddha Vairocana considered as Dharmakāya of Reason (LI) and as preacher. See the preceding chapter, "I. Significance of the Name Dainichi (Mahāvairocana)".
6. This expression designates the Palace of Maheśvaradeva at the summit of the *rūpadhātu.* According to the Chinese Commentary of Subhakarasimha and Yi-hing ("*Dainichikyōsho*". Taishō, No. 1796, abr. *Cm.*), *vajra* symbolizes knowledge, the veritable attribute of the buddha. The complete expression is applied to this same knowledge which has the three virtualities of the *vajra* (diamond, thunder). Like the *vajra*, it is firm and cannot be swayed (by the passions, *kleśa*); it is the most precious of all treasures; it is also the supreme weapon (Taishō, Vol XXXIX, p. 580a[21]).
7. 'Vajra-wielder': Each one of them symbolizes a faculty of knowledge (the totality) constituting omniscience, the Buddha's attribute. They use a *vajra* for the destruction of the passions. The *Cm.* notes that the early translations use mostly the expression SHŪKONGŌ while the more recent ones prefer the expression JIKONGŌ. The present Sūtra, however, uses the two expressions indiscriminately (*ibid.*, p. 580b[9]).
8. According to the *Cm,* these two terms correspond to the *vikurvita* (*ibid.*, p. 580c[4]).
9. *Śraddhādhimukti.*
10 The Tibetan text reads: "(extremely) elevated at its summit". What must be understood is a building which by virtue of the omnipresence of the Buddha is as vast as the universe and the dimensions of which cannot be calculated.
11. *Simhāsana.* The fiery lion is not afraid of anything. He stands for the Heart of Bodhi (*bodhicitta*) of the Buddha who being endowed with supreme power has nothing to fear from the passions and destroys the erroneous doctrines with the ardor of a lion (*ibid.*, 581a[2]).
12. Tib. *rdo rje 'dsin nam mkha' dri ma med pa,* Vimalākāśavajradhara (?). The number of the Vajra-wielders is as unlimited as that of the knowledges (*jñāna*) of the Buddha. Of these the text mentions only nineteen, which correspond to the NAIKENZOKU (*parivāra,* retinue [of the palace]) who possess the *vajra-jñāna-mudrā* of the Buddha Mahāvairocana and who are supposed to represent the multitude of the vajra-wielders. According to the *Cm.* the name of the first of these bears an allusion to the essential purity of the Heart of Bodhi which by nature is also immaculate and undiversified. The space is free from all obstacles and darkening [caused by obstructions] (*timira*) (*ibid.*, p. 581a[21]).
13. Tib. *nam mkha 'la rnam par 'gro ba,* Ākāśavicaraṇavajradhara (?) symbolizes another virtuality of the *bodhicitta* to be in continual movement, progressing in the pursuit of attaining Bodhi (*ibid.*, p. 581a[25]).
14. Tib. *nam mkha' 'byung ba,* Ākāśasambhavavajradhara (?). Unless there is

some obstruction from the soil, after germination (of the seed) a plant grows according to the four great seasons. In the same way, the *bodhicitta* with all the practices as conditions is born to truth, that is to say, to [the knowledge of] the Great Void (*mahāsūnyatā*) (*ibid.*, p. 581b[1]).

15. Tib. *gos sna tshogs gyon pa*. This imagery suggests the multiplicity and variety of virtues (merits or virtualities, *guṇa*) which Bodhi produces in the course of revealing itself in full (*ibid*, p. 581b[5]).
16. Tib. *sna tshogs su rgyu ba*, ZENGYŌBU, *Vicitracaraṇavajradhara* (?). According to the *Cm*, ZEN, 'excellent', corresponds here to *vicitra*, the great compassion of the Buddha who exerts himself at all times, in all places and circumstances, to lead the beings on the way to liberation (*ibid.*, p. 581c[10]).
17. Tib. *chos thams cad mnyam pa nyid la gnas pa*, Sarvadharmasamatāsthita-vajradhara (?). The name alludes to the reciprocal equality of each of the five phases of the process with which the above-mentioned names are related; namely: (1) production of the *bodhicitta*; (2) practice for the attainment of Bodhi; (3) obtainment of Bodhi;(4) entry into Nirvāṇa; (5) application of the proper means to lead the beings to enlightenment. Each of the five phases is a manifestation of one of the virtualities of the Buddha (cf. our chapter Doctrinal Analysis of the First Chapter, no.7, and in that chapter the section "The Triple Formula", the table with five stages).
18. Tib. *sems can gyi khams mtha' yas pa yongs su skyob pa'i rdo rje*, Apramāṇasattvadhātvanukampanavajradhara (?). Allusion is here to the infinite compassion of the Buddha who sympathizes with innumerable beings. He identifies himself according to the principle of sameness, *samatā* (Taishō, Vol. XXXIX, p. 581c[19]).
19. Tib. *sred med kyi bu'i stobs can*, Nārāyaṇabalavajradhara, the divine athlete. This epithet is applied to the energy that the Buddha deploys for the relief of the beings (*ibid.*, p. 581c[24]); cf. this chapter, n.224.
20. Tib. *sred med kyi bu chen po'i stobs can*, Mahānārāyaṇabalavajradhara. This expression qualifies the force of the supernormal faculty (*abhijñā*) of the Buddha which enables him to help even the *icchantika* (persons condemned by predestination), a power which the Bodhisattvas do not possess in the least.
21. Tib. *rdo rje bzang*, Suvajradhara. This expression indicates the plenitude and unsurpassable perfection of the virtualities (*guṇa*) of the Buddha (*ibid.*, p. 581c[4]).
22. Tib. *rdo rje mchog gi shugs can*, Paramavegavajradhara. This expression suggests the rapidity with which the Buddha can lead the beings to Bodhi.
23. Tib. *dri ma med pa'i rdo rje*, Vimalavajradhara. The *bodhicitta* is free from all blemishes and is liberated from all the obstacles caused by the defilements (*kleśa*).
24. Tib. *rdo rje mchog 'chang*, Paramavajradhara (?). The *Cm.* shows that the Chinese term is the rendering of a Sanskrit word signifying "the highest wrath, extreme sharpness". The Buddha's Knowledge is so sharp that it can cut out the defilements (*kleśa*) incisively (*ibid.*, p. 581c[15]).
25. Tib. *de bzhin gshegs pa'i go cha*, Tathāgatavarmavajradhara (?). This coat of armor is compassion. Thanks to this ornament, the Buddha can protect the beings and, under its invincible and non-attackable shelter, accomplish his task against the attacks of the defilements (*kleśa*) (*ibid.*, p. 381c[18]).
26. Tib. *de bzhin gshegs pa'i go 'phang du 'byung ba*, Tathāgatapadodbhavavajradhara (?). The *Cm.* observes that KU (which generally translates *pada* in the sense of

'foot' of a stanza, hemistiche, clause) signfies here the place of support and designates the "Grand Void", that is to say, the letter *a*, the symbol of the uncreated (*ibid.*, p. 581c[21]).

27. Tib. *spros pa med pa la gnas pa,* Niḥprapañcapratiṣṭhavajradhara. The Buddha resides in the insight (*prajñā*) of the Void where all relative statements and differentiations are abolished (*idib.*, p. 58c[24]).
28. Tib. *de bzhin gshegs pa'i stobs bcu las nges par skyes pa,* Tathāgatadaśabalodbhava. The knowledge born of the Tathāgata's Knowledge is the knowledge from which springs forth the appropriate means by which the Buddha leads the beings to liberation (*ibid.*, p. 581c[27]), *Daśatathāgatabalāni,* cf. *Mahāvyutpatti* (abbr. *Mvtp.*). ed. Sakaki, Nos. 120-29.
29. Tib. *dri ma med pa'i mig,* Vimalanetra. Allusion is to the five eyes, viz. (1) *māmsa-cakṣus,* (2) *divya-c.,* (3) *prajñā-c.,* (4) *dharma-c.,* (5) *buddha-c.* These enable him to catch hold of the dharmas exactly and without obstruction.
30. Tib. *phyag na rdo rje,* Vajrapāṇi, synonym of Vajra-wielder (Vajradhara) who stands here as the chief of the group of 18 vajra-wielders mentioned earlier. It is he who in the course of the Sūtra will be the interlocutor of the Buddha. He is none else than Vajrasattva.
31. Tib. *gsang ba pa'i bdag po,* "Master of the Mysteries" is the honorific appellation of Vajrapāṇi who represents the threefold mystery (*triguhya*) of Vairocana (cf. n.37, below).
32. *Buddhakṣetra:* Each of the ten domains represents one of the Tathāgata's ten Knowledges (*jñāna*).
33. This Bodhisattva is one of the four "grand acolytes" (*mahāparivāra,* DAIKENZOKU) who are the symbols of the Buddha's virtualities and aid him in rescuing the beings with the help of compassion. Samantabhadra represents all the merits contained in the immanent *bodhicitta.*
34. He is another *mahāparivāra,* that is to say, the four infinite Hearts (SHIMURYŌSHIN, see Summary of the Chapters starting with the Second, n.48) which are born only after one has awakened oneself to the *bodhicitta* and has realized it in one's own self.
35. As *mahāparivāra,* he represents the merit which consists in teaching the Dharma with a view to removing all doubts. This virtue is born of the Grand Compassion.
36. Sarvanīvaraṇaviṣkambhin, the fourth *mahāparivāra,* represents the virtuality for the destruction of all the obstacles which obstruct Bodhi, that is to say, all the *kleśa.* This virtuality is in consequence of the preaching (which precedes).
37. KU = *pada;* the Tibetan version has *gzhi.*
38. The three Mysteries (*triguhya*), said to be of the Body, the Speech, and the Mind (*kāya, vāc, manas*), are omnipresent but in fact form one and the same thing and are equal to one another.
39. Past, present, and future. The Buddha Vairocana, the eternal sun, preaches the Dharma constantly and for all times.
40. Before explaining the equality of the Body, Speech, and Mind, the Buddha displays miracles so as to catch the attention of his listeners, to show them his strength and (thus) increase their faith in him.
41. The Buddha preaches (the Dharma) with the ardor of a jumping lion (*simhavijṛmbhita*).
42. Tib. *bkod pa mi zad pa'i mdzod,* Akṣayavyūhagañja.
43. It is not necessary to believe that the Buddha displays for the first time here the

three supernormal manifestations of his person. Unlike other creatures, the Buddha is not subject to the laws of time and space, and can make these manifestations appear at will. These are inherent in the Buddha, and like him they are infinite and eternal.

44. Tib. *gsang sngags kyi tshul gyi tshig gis chos, mantra-mārga-pada-dharma* (?). By nature the Buddha is without birth or death. If he manifests himself before the living beings, it is with the desire of assuring their liberation.

45. The *Mahāvairocana-sūtra* distinguishes between the three clans (BU = *kula*) represented in the Mahākaruṇāgarbha-maṇḍala (DAIHI TAIZŌ), to wit, (1) that of the Buddhas, (2) that of the Lotus (*padma* or *abja*), (3) that of the Vajra. To each of these correspond respectively appropriate religious rites. (1) The rites called Appeasing (*śāntika*) are related to the Buddhas. They drive away misfortune. (2) The Prosperity (*pauṣṭika*) rites refer to the Padma. They "cause growth of" or augment good fortune. (3) The Destructive (*ābhicāruka*) rites are connected with the Vajra. They "exorcise", destroy the evil. The *Cm.* explains that the Vajra-wielder corresponds to the rites of *ābhicāruka* (GŌBUKU) (Taishō, Vol. XXXIX, p. 584a[9]).

46. The *Cm.* explains that this manifestation relates to the *śāntika* rites (JAKUSAI).

47. RENGESHU, another name of Avalokiteśvara who holds a lotus in his hand. According to the *Cm.*, this manifestation corresponds to the *pauṣṭika* rites (SŌYAKU).

48. Besides these three divisions or 'clans' (see n. 45, above) of the *maṇḍala*, there is a fourth clan, to wit, "the division external to the vajra", which brings under its fold the diverse divinities which are not specifically Buddhist; as, for example, the *nāgas* and the *devas*. The text makes allusion to these.

49. This epithet qualifies the absolute purity of omniscient knowledge (*sarvajñā-jñāna,* ISSAI-CHICHI).

50. *Daśabhūmi:* cf. infra, n. 409, and in Doctrinal Analysis of the First Chapter, section F. The ten earths (*daśabhūmi*). Mahāyāna Buddhism generally distinguishes 52 stages which must be traversed before one attains awakening. But the Shingon knows only 'Ten Earths' and does not interpret these the same as do other sects. It regards the 52 stages as unnecessary steps since the state of awakening is of sudden occurrence for the being who has conceived the desire of becoming a Buddha. As to the Ten Earths, it interprets them as a symbolic whole of regions each of which corresponds to one of the Buddha's merits. There can exist no more distinction, whether of importance or of degree, between these "Earths" than there is between the merits of the Buddha.

51. Contrary to the doctrines which require the believer in initiation to follow it by long practices, esoteric Buddhism teaches the possibility of getting a 'sudden' revelation of the Buddha's merits; and, consequently, the certainty of understanding the truth, that is to say, of becoming a Buddha in the present life, not just in a future life.

52. JU, *āyus*?

53. The *Cm.* explains that the births and rebirths in the six *gati* which drag the living beings in the ever widening cycle of *samsāra* and of suffering are due to evil acts which in their turn have ignorance and desire as cause or condition (*ibid.*, p. 584b[11]).

54. The defilements (*kleśa*) have not been able to smother the good 'seeds' innate in each being which will enable him to become a Buddha. Once the defilements are removed, these 'seeds' re-emerge.

55. The preceding paragraphs serve as the introduction. The word 'then' acts as the connecting link between this introduction and the veritable development. The topic now really begins.
56. SESON = *bhagavat* (or lokajyeṣṭha).
57. These epithets are applied here to the Buddha Vairocana.
58. ISSAI-CHICHI, according to the *Cm. sarva(jñā)-jñāna,* Tib. *thams cad mkhyen pa'i ye shes.* When providing the original Sanskrit term *sarvajñāna* in transcription, the *Cm.*, p. 585a, explains that the Chinese translation CHICHI signifies "the Knowledge of Knowledges", that is to say, knowledge *par excellence.*
59. DŌ, literally 'way'; according to the Tibetan text, *tshul (naya).*
60. *Upāya;* Tib. *thabs.*
61. *Gati.*
62. Per the Tibetan version, it is *śrāvakayāna-naya.* They listen to the teaching of the Buddha, hold the four noble Truths (*catvāryārya-satyāni*) and obtain the fruit of Arhat.
63. Per the Tibetan version, it is *pratyekabudhayāna-naya*, the category of Buddhas who by themselves attain enlightenment. They understand the chain of the twelve causes (*pratītyasamutpāda*) and obtain the fruit of Pratyekabuddha.
64. Per the Tibetan version, it is the *mahāyāna-naya.* In the Mahāyāna one does not seek only one's own liberation—as is the case in the Lesser Vehicle—but at the same time that of others as well. With this object in mind, one practises the six perfections (*pāramitā*) in order to become a Buddha.
65. *Abhijñā* (Tib. *mngon par shes pa*), which enable one to help the beings.
66. The text says, "and so on" because the Asuras, Garuḍas, and Kimnaras, included in the Tibetan text, are omitted in the enumeration in the Chinese text.
67. See n. 99, below.
68. That is to say, varied, different languages.
69. *Īryāpatha.*
70. The *Cm.* recalls the identity between our fundamental nature and that of the Buddhas. This is why when a being attains Bodhi, it is not due to a cause external to himself, but indeed something of his own nature, so of himself and in himself. The Buddha plays only the role of the provocator and guide who reminds all beings of the possibilities of their own nature. For this reason, the Buddha, after having obtained Bodhi, casts away the principle of Equality (*samatā*) and deploys his virtualities in the form of *maṇḍalas* so as to bring beings to the realization of their veritable nature. Thus, the commentary says that the different embodiments of the Buddha are similar to how the sea water, whether calm or agitated, retains always the same bitter taste (*ibid.*, p. 585b[28]).
71. With a view to expressing his admiration of the Buddha's virtualities, the Vajra-wielder compares them with the five elements (*mahābhūta*) which are generally enumerated in the following order: earth (*pṛthivīdhāthu*), water (*ābdhātu*), fire (*tejodhātu*), wind (*vāyudhātu*), and space (*ākāśadhātu*). Here the last is mentioned first, because it characterizes the absolutely pure nature of the Buddha's Knowledge.
72. RI-FUNBETSU, *nirvikalpa* (cf. *Mvtp.*, ed. Wohihara, CCXLV, 1,044).
73. MU-FUNBETSU, *avikalpa* (cf. *ibid.*, CCXLV, 1,045). The *Cm.* has KOPPA (*kalpa*) in place of FUNBETSU, and KOPPAYATEI (*kalpayati ?*) for MU-FUNBETSU (Taishō, Vol. XXXIX, p. 585c[16]).
74. The Tibetan version has *gsos pa (poṣaka, poṣika).*

75. BONNŌ = *kleśa*. The Tibetan version lacks the word.
76. IN = *hetu,* Tib. *rgyu,* that is to say, it is the first cause of enlightenment.
77. KON = *mūla,* Tib. *rtsa ba*. That is to say, what religious practices have to be observed after the appearance of the Thought of Enlightenment (*bodhicitta*)?
78. KUKYŌ =*niṣṭha,* Tib. *mthar thug pa* or *mur thug pa* (cf. *Mvpt*. ed.Sakaki, No. 372). To put it otherwise: What is the ultimate objective that a follower of the teaching of the Shingon must propose to attain? This last, and the two preceding points (notes 76 and 77), constitute what is called the SANKU (*tripada*) or Threefold Formula containing the essential summary of the doctrine propounded in the *Dainichikyō*. See the section "The Triple Formula" in the next chapter.
79. *Sādhu, sādhu*; Tib. *legs so legs so*.
80. *Bhagavataḥ pratiśrutya*.
81. *Bodhicitta*. The Hōbōgirin translates: the Mind of Enlightenment, that is to say, the pure nature of the Buddha which is innate in all beings.
82. *Mahākaruṇā*. In the manner of the plant, whose stem can grow only by its root pushing further in the soil, it is by cultivating Great Compassion and other good practices of Body, Speech, and Mind (SAMMITSU) that a being can bring the *bodhicitta* to the fullest development.
83. *Upāya*. When one has reached the stage of Buddha, the final objective is to put into action all the proper means to guide other beings in the path of liberation and to help them to become Buddhas also.
84. NYOJITSU = *yathābhūta;* Tib. *yang dag pa ji lta ba bzhin*.
85. The *Cm*. gives ANOKU *(aṇu)*: "molecule composed of seven other smaller (particles)" (*ibid*., 587b[27]).
86. The *Hōbōgirin* translates: "enlightenment which is complete, correct, and which has no superior".
87. According to the *Cm*. what is meant is the totality of the dharmas of which there is not a single one which is not comprised in the *bodhicitta* (*ibid*., p. 587b[30]).
88. *Lakṣaṇa*: Tib. *mtshan,* 'character', 'characteristic sign'.
89. This is an essential passage. Bodhi has an absolute and transcendental character because its existence does not depend on the subject who conceives it as object. It is also not born of the action of an external agent. It cannot be seized either by the senses or by understanding. Moreover, it is innate. (That is to say:) religious practices cannot provoke its presence in the being. From the subjective as well as the objective point of view, it pre-exists all experiences.
90. To put otherwise; their universal and absolute character denies to them *a priori* all individual and limited characteristics.
91. The phrase, "Who (or what) produces this omniscient knowledge?" does not occur in the Tibetan version.
92. HONSHŌ = *svabhāva*; Tib. *rang bzhin*. Our innate nature contains in itself all the virtues of the Buddha.
93. *Pariśuddha*: Tib. *yongs su dag pa*.
94. Cf. n.57, above. Here it signifies the Heart. The *Cm*. explains it as something which is "without any color or form, because, contrary to what certain heterodox doctrines pretend, one cannot come to know its likeness" (Taishō, Vol. XXXIX, p. 588b[9]).
95. *Kāmadhātu*; Tib. *'dod pa 'i khams* it is also directed against heterodox teachings.
96. *Rūpadhātu*; Tib. *gzugs kyi khams*.

97. *Ārūpyadhātu*; Tib. *gzugs med pa'i khams.*
98. *Gati.*
99. Cf. n.67, above. NIN-HI-NIN is always interpreted as Kimnara (Tib.*mi'am ci*) but the Kimnaras are explicitly mentioned before; and according to the Tibetan version, it must be understood literally as *manuṣya amānuṣa* (*mi dang mi ma yin*).
100. KAI = *dhātu.* The word does not occur in the Tibetan version.
101. *Ṣaḍdhātavaḥ: cakṣurdhātu, śrotradh., ghrāṇadh., jihvādh., kāyadh., manodh.*
102. Tibetan version lacks this sentence.
103. Cf. notes 72 and 73, above.
104. Here ends the explanation of the first of the three essential points of the Threefold Formula (cf. note 76, above).
105. The second point (cf. note 77, above).
106. The third and the last point (cf. note 78, above).
107. MANZOKU; the Tibetan text has *yongs su bzung ba* (*parigrāha*).
108. The Tibetan text has *yongs su shes pa* (parijñā).
109. *Kulaputra*; Tib. *rigs kyi bu. Kuladuhiter;* Tib. *rigs kyi bu mo.*
110. This passage serves for both conclusion and transition.
111. Tib. *rnam pa.* According to the *Cm.*, it is the general epithet of all the *pratītya-samutpāda-dharma;* that is to say, the personal aggregates *(skandha)* (Taishō, Vol. XXXIX, p. 589c[16]).
112. KENJIKI = *varṇarūpa*; Tib. *kha dog gi gzugs* (cf.*Mvtp.*ed. Wogihara, CI, 28).
113. GYŌJIKI = *samsthānarūpa;* Tib. *dbyibs kyi gzugs* (cf. ibid., CI, No. 4; and *Mvtp.*, ed. Sakaki, No. 1, 877).
114. KYŌGAI = *viṣaya;* Tib. *yul: rūpa, śabda, gandha, rasa, spruṣṭavya, dharma*— that is to say, the objects of sense perception.
115. *Rūpa*; Tib. *gzugs.*
116. Vedanā; Tib. *tshor ba.*
117. Samjñā; Tib. *'du shes.*
118. Samskāra; Tib. *'du byed.*
119. Vijñāna; Tib. *rnam par shes pa* = SHIKI.
120. Ātman; Tib.. *bdag nyid.*
121. Ātmīya; Tib. *bdag gi yin.*
122. *Grāhaka;* Tib. *'dzin pa= NŌSHŪ.*
123. *Grāhya;* Tib. *gzung ba* = SHOSHŪ. *Hōbōgirin:* The taker (*grāhaka*) is he who appropriates; and what is appropriated (*grāhya*) is taken.
124. The *Cm.* explains that what is meant is *nirvāṇa* considered as purity *par excellence* in some heterodox doctrines (Taishō, Vol. XXXIX, p. 589c[9]). The Tibetan version adds the word *ma dag pa* ("impurity").
125. Dhātu, "are precisely the 18 spheres, *aṣṭādaśadhātavaḥ*".
126. *Āyatana*—the twelve place, *dvādaśāyatanāni.*
127. See note 111, above.
128. SHOHŌ-MUŌDŌ; *prathamadharmālokamukha,* Tib. *chos snang ba'i sgo dang po* (cf.*Mvtp.*,ed.Sakaki, No. 6973) designates what precedes the moment before one enters into the stage Pramuditā, the first of the ten Earths. Then only the true Heart is perceived clearly. Each of the Ten Earths is divided into three stages or regions, viz. (1) entrance, (2) residence, and (3) exit. Exceptionally, in the case of the first Earth the Pramuditā, two moments (*kṣaṇa*) are distinguished, to wit, a prior moment, referred to as the *prathamadharmāloka-mukha;* and a later moment.

129. JO-ISSAI-GAISHŪ-ZAMMAI = Sarvanīvaraṇaviṣkambhīsamādhi. It is obtained in the later moment, posterior to entry into the Pramuditā Stage. The *Cm.* recognizes five kinds of obstacles, to wit, *kleśāvaraṇa* (hindrance of defilement), *karmāvaraṇa* (hindrance of act), *jātyāvaraṇa* (hindrance of class), *dharmāvaraṇa* (hindrance of nature), and *jñeyāvaraṇa* (hindrance of the knowable) (Taishō, Vol. XXXIX, p. 590a[26]). With the attainment of the mentioned *samādhi,* there is total and immediate liberation from these obstacles.
130. Cf. note 65, above.
131. *Bhāṣa*; *Tib. skad.*
132. *Śabda*; Tib. *sgra.* Tibetan adds *dbyangs* (*svara*).
133. *Cittacarita.*
134. *Saṃkliṣṭasaṅga.* He will be free from defilement (*kleśa*), that is to say, the impurities or faults caused by the *kleśa.*
135. That is to say, even in the world of *Samsāra.*
136. *Dharmadhātu.* Tibetan version lacks this term.
137. *Asamskṛtaśīla,* Tib. *'dus ma byas kyi tshul khrims.* It is the innate morality, indestructible as diamond and inhérent in the pure Bodhicitta which is in us, and not what one receives from a master (cf. the *Cm., ibid.,* p. 590c[25]).
138. *Mithyādṛṣṭi*; Tib. *log par lta ba.*
139. *Samyagdṛṣṭi*; Tib. *yang dag par lta ba.*
140. *Samādhi*: Tib. *ting nge 'dsin,* added in the Tibetan version.
141. *Adhimuktibala*; Tib. *mos pa'i stobs.*
142. See note 109, above.
143. *Guṇa*; Tib. *yon tan.*
144. (The words) "in the form of *gāṭhā*" are not found in the Tibetan text.
145. Given below is a series of nine questions. The *Cm.* calls them, "KUKU: nine formulas". They serve the purpose of clarifying the explanations of the Threefold Formulas (SANKU) (see notes 75-77, above). Beginning from here to the end Sūtra, only answers to these questions are given. However, the Buddha in his replies does not follow the order in which the questions were put. The Buddha's replies are given in the order he thinks profitable for teaching his doctrines.
146. First question: How is the *bodhicitta*—which pre-exists in us—to be considered the result of practices born the nature of that *bodhicitta*?
147. Second question: *Bodhicittotpāda.* The *Hobogirin* translates it as "production of the spirit of awakening".
148. The Heart as it is known by itself.
149. That of the Buddhas which is eternal and which is precisely experience of the Heart by the Heart itself without the help of others.
150. *Mahāvira.* The *Cm.* says that up to this passage of the text questions relating to the virtualities found in the Buddhas are given (*ibid.,* p. 591b[12]).
151. Third question: At the end of how many successive stages does the Heart of Bodhi reveal itself?
152. Fourth question: What types of errors are opposed to the Heart of Bodhi?
153. Fifth question: The time necessary for the attainment of Bodhi from the moment of arousing the Heart of Bodhi.
154. Sixth question: What are the merits attributed to the Heart of Bodhi?
155. Seventh question: What is to be done for the attainment of superior *siddhi*?
156. Eighth question: That is to say, the *ālayavijñāna.*

157. Ninth question.
158. *Mahāmuni*; Tib. *thub pa chen po*; Buddha.
159. *Sādhu*; Tib. *legs so.*
160. This is the 'brief' answer to the third question.
161. KU = *pada*; the Tibetan version has *go 'phang* ('position').
162. *Tīrthika* (Tib. *mu stegs can*); the Tibetan text, however, has *tog ge pa*(*tārkika*).
163. All teachings lying outside the esoteric doctrine are meant.
164. Hearts blemished with *kleśa* have been grouped into one hundred and sixty categories; see note 351, below.
165. What follows is a 'brief' answer to the first question.
166. What follows is a 'brief' answer to the second question.
167. What follows is a 'brief' answer to the seventh question. The *Cm.* says that there are two kinds of offering-practices, to wit, external and internal (Taishō, Vol. XXXIX, p. 592b[12]). By external offering-practices are understood material offerings such as flowers, incense, lamp. By practices of internal offerings are designated moral or symbolic offerings. According to the esoteric doctrine there are three types of such offering, namely, corporeal, verbal, and mental.
168. BOMBU = *pṛthagjana*; Tib. *so' i skye bo.*
169. *Bāla*; Tib. *byis pa.* GUDŌ, stupid child.
170. *Samsāra*; Tib. *'khor ba,* transmigration.
171. *Ātman.*
172. *Ātmīya.*
173. From this passage onward begins the developed answer to the third of the nine questions. It refers to the ascension of the Heart towards the perfection of Buddha. To bring into focus this ascension, the passage in question presents it in opposition to the heterodox doctrines. These are referred to as "the thirty kinds of heterodoxy". The Sūtra enumerates only 29 of these, while the translator commentator divides the 28th (heterodoxy) into two parts, viz. (1) SHŌKEN and (2) SHŌSHŌ. See note 203, below.
174. *Svabhāva*; Tib. *ngo bo nyid.*
175. The first heretics do not know that all the dharmas have for origin the *pratītyasamutpāda;* that is to say, the causal relation which produces all the dharmas—and these do not possess a nature of their own.
176. *Mamakāra*; Tib. *bdag gir 'dzin pa.*
177. The thirty heterodox schools do not possess at all the right notion of the self. All these schools are found deeply plunged into error, due to not taking cognizance of *pratītyasamutpāda.* They are prisoners of individualistic ideas.
178. This school accords to Time the power of governing everything in this world (*Cm.*, Taishō, Vol. XXXIX, p. 592c[21]).
179. Another school attributes to the earth, water, fire, wind, and space, the origin of all things (*Cm. ibid.*, p. 592c[27]).
180. According to this school, the object of mystic contemplation (*yoga*) is a Self considered as true. It sees in it an invariable and permanent principle which enables one to attain deliverance (*Cm.*, *ibid.*, p. 593a[5]).
181. The pantheistic school or the school of immanence professes to see the Puruṣa (SHINGA) in the dharmas which it institutes; and, according to this school, to be able to realize the Puruṣa it is necessary to cultivate exercises and practices (rites) based on these dharmas and that are pure in as much as they enable one to rediscover the pure Puruṣa in these dharmas purified by the exercise of the practices (*Cm. ibid.*, p. 593a[8]).

182. The transcendentalist school according to which the dharmas are not the absolute reality. According to this school, the Puruṣa is an *asamskṛta* ('uncreate'), transcendental to the dharmas. In this sense it "does not institute the dharmas" (as absolute realities); and (this school) considers that the pure Puruṣa is entirely distinct from the dharmas taken as impure. Consequently, the exercises and practices do not consist in purifying the dharmas (*Cm. ibid.*, p. 593a[21]).

183. It is almost the same doctrine exposed in note 181, above. It is the Spirit which serves as the basis of all reality. Here this basis is compared with the hand of the potter; and all the dharmas flow from a first principle in the same way as the pots come out of the hands of the potter (*Cm. ibid.*, p. 593a[21]).

184. A very slight difference separates this school from the school mentioned in note 178, above. As is the case there, here also the doctrine rests on Īśvara (*Cm., ibid.*, p. 593a[24]).

185. SONKI, i.e. Nārāyaṇadeva, Tib. *sred med bu.* According to this school, this god is eternal and unmovable. The divinities who serve him create all things. Thus a governor counts on his subordinates for the administration of the country. The master, therefore, does not work but assigns to each of his servants his specific duty (*Cm., ibid.*, 593b[4]).

186. JINEN. They are the adepts of the spontaneous generating. They affirm that the universe and all that is enclosed in it have no creator. For example, the lotus flower blooms naturally with all its beautiful colors. Nobody has given it these colors (*Cm. ibid.*, p. 593b[15]).

187. Tib. *nang gi bdag.* Reference is to those who pretend to possess in their body, (and) outside the Spirit, a Self of a particular nature to which they attribute all their movements and acts (*Cm. ibid.*, p. 593b[22]).

188. Puruṣa (*skyes bu*), according to the Tibetan version. According to this school, the Puruṣa is proportionate to the size of the human body. If the latter is small, Puruṣa is also small; if the body is big, Puruṣa is also equally big (*Cm., ibid.*, p. 593b[26]).

189. HENGON: Viṣṇu, Tib. *khyab bdag.* The Puruṣa creates everything. He has the faculty of ubiquity (*Cm. ibid.*, p. 593c[4]).

190. According to the Tibetan version, Jīva (*srog;* cf. *Mvtp.* ed. Sakaki, No. 4670). The principle of life resides in all the beings. If one cuts a plant or a tree, they grow again, and if they grow afresh, it is because they use this principle of life (*Cm., ibid.*, p. 593c[9]).

191. Tib. *gang zag.* This school pretends that even if one is reborn many times, the "I" does not change at all. It is the same "I" that is reborn in the different *gati*-s (*Cm., ibid.*, p. 593c[16]).

192. Tib. *rnam par shes pa.* The *vijñāna* is everywhere. The earth, water, fire, wind, and space, are all imbued with it (*Cm., ibid.*, p. 593c[24]).

192a. Tib. *kun gzhi.* Here, the *ālaya* which maintains our body is meant. If it tightens itself up, there will be no longer anything. If it extends itself, it fills the world and gives rise to all the phenomena. This *ālaya* is different from the *ālayavijñāna* of Buddhism (*Cm., ibid.*, p. 593c[29]).

193. *Jānaka*; Tib. *shes pa po* (*cf. Mvtp.* ed. Sakaki, No. 4680).

194. *Paśyaka*: Tib. *mthong ba po* (cf. *ibid.*, No. 4681), which in our interior knows and sees everything, particularly pain, pleasure, etc. (*Cm.* p. 594a[6]).

195. *Grāhaka*; Tib. *'dsin pa.* According to this school, apart from our consciousness,

there is an appropriator which directs all our action, speech, and thought. It is the Puruṣa (*Cm. ibid.*, p. 594a[12]).

196. *Grāhya*: Tib. *gzung ba.* The appropriator is precisely our consciousness. The domain to which our consciousness is attached is called the Puruṣa (*Cm., ibid.*, p. 594a[15]).

197-98. According to the *Cm.*, these are other names of the 'Knower' (see above, note 193). For true *ātman,* some take a principle in us which "makes its presence felt internally" (NAISHO) or one which is capable of knowing the external sense objects (*ibid.*, p. 594a[19]).

199. Jñātvan. Cf. Kambayashi, Japanese translation of the *Dainichikyō,* note 29 (*Kokuyaku Issaikyō,* Mikkyō bu, i, p. 55). The Tibetan version gives *shes par bya ba = jñeya.* The *Cm.* says that it is almost the knower (see above, note 193); the difference lies chiefly in the fact that it pertains to another school (*ibid.*, p. 594a[19]).

200. Tib. *shed las skyes pa,* "what is born of Manu". The *Cm.* explains that it is necessary to translate it as "the birth of man". A school analogous to that of Īśvaradeva is referred to here. It believes that man is born of man (Manu is the ancestor of man). (*ibid.*, p. 594a[24]).

201. Tib. *shed bu,* "son of Manu; man". The *Cm.* says: "This is school similar to that of Viṣṇudeva. If one likes to translate it exactly, it will be necessary to say "Supreme I", that is to say, that the "I" is supreme in body and spirit. It believes that in the spirit there is an *ātman* which is as big as a thumb or more (*ibid.*, p. 594a[27]).

202. JŌJŌSHŌ. The *Cm.* adds: "This school believes that the Self (GA) is eternal and indestructible and that it is always 'born'; that is to say, it exists spontaneously without being subject to new births (*ibid.*, p. 594b[5]).

203. This school believes that the substance of the voice (*vāc*) is an eternal substance which manifests (SHOKEN) itself as a result of occasional causes. Further, according to another branch of the school, the voice while making itself heard is 'born' due to some occasion. Once 'born' (SHŌSHŌ) it persists endlessly (*Cm.*, *ibid.*, p. 594b[7]).

204. This school on the contrary holds that nothing persists of the spoken word (*Cm.*, *ibid.*, p. 594b[11]).

205. *Yogin* is translated by JUNRI, "what conforms to reasoning"; the term *yogin* is given by the *Cm.* (*ibid.*, p. 594b[25]) and the Tibetan text.

206. See above, notes 168 and 169.

207. According to the *Cm.*, what precedes is related to hearts which are "contrary to reason". The text now defines "the eight successive stages of the mundane Heart" which are initial and "reasonable" hearts (*ibid.*, p. 594c[1]). A revolution takes place in those who, unable to discern the good from the bad, continue to act in the wrong way while a good thought is born and develops little by little. It is this (revolution) which is here indicated. The *Cm.* says: "Amongst animals the sheep has the vilest nature. It thinks only about eating grass and giving free rein to its sexual instinct. Moreover, according to the Western (i.e. Indian) style of speech, it signifies a stupid fellow who is incapable of discriminating between good and bad (*ibid.*, p. 159c[6]). The Tibetan text does not specifically mention the sheep, but some domestic animal, i.e. *phyugs= paśu.* The Sarat Chandra Das *Dicitionary* (p. 789) shows that *phyugs ma = lug = eḍakā* = sheep.

208. Tib. *'du shes = samjñā.*

209. JISAI; Tib. *bsnyung ba; upoṣadha* or *upavasatha;* cf. *Mvtp.* ed. Sakaki, No. 7137.

210. *Bīja*; Tib. *sa bon;* SHUJI. This is the first of the eight stages of the Heart.
211. The six days of abstinence are the 8th, 14th, 15th, 23th, 29th and 30th days of the month. It is believed that particularly on these days demonical beings try to take the lives of man.
212. 2nd Heart GESHU; Tib. *myu gu; pravāla.*
213. 3rd Heart HŌSHU: Tib. *sdong bu; daṇḍa.*
214. 4th Heart YOSHU; Tib. *lo ma; parṇa*
215. 5th Heart FUKE; Tib. *me tog; puṣpa.*
216. 6th Heart JOKA; Tib. *'bras bu (r bcas pa); phalaprasūti.*
217. Tib. *tshul khrims.*
218. The Tibetan version has *mtho ris* (*svarga*).
219. 7th Heart JUYŌ; Tib. *longs spyod; bhoga.* The *Cm.* writes: "From one single grain many grains can be had, and from these other grains again considerable quantities of grains are derived. (In this way) the quantity of grains goes on increasing until it becomes incommensurable. This is so because the first grain has been utilised to produce other grains and these, in their turn, have been utilized in the same fashion. This is why the expression 'exploitation of the grain' has been used" (Taishō, Vol. XXXIX, p. 595a[21]).
220. *Samsāra*; Tib. *'khor ba.*
221. Kalyāṇamitra; Tib. *dge ba'i bshes gnyen.*
222. Tib. *dbang phyug.*
223. *Tshangs pa.*
224. This is an incarnation of Viṣṇu (The Tibetan version has *khyab 'jug* [= Viṣṇu]. He is a very powerful divinity. It is said that an elephant in rut (*gandhahastin*) is sixty times more powerful than an (ordinary) elephant. (But) Nārāyaṇa is more powerful than sixty *gandhahastin* (*Cm. ibid.*, p. 581b[23]). Cf. above. Introduction, note 7.
225. Tib. *bde byed.* This is another name of Maheśvara (*Cm. ibid.*, 595b[11]).
226. Tib. *drag po.* He is a satellite of Īśvara (*Cm., ibid.*, p. 595b[12]).
227. One of the Chinese editions mentions only Īśvara (see Taishō, Vol. XVIII, p. 2, note 4) but earlier Īśvara himself has already been mentioned. The *Cm.* does not give any explanation of the son of Īśvara. The Tibetan text gives the name as *skem byed.* This is the name of the demon of thirst, of drought (cf. Sarat Chandra Das *Dictionary,* p. 93).
228. Tib. *nyi ma,* sun.
229. Tib. *zla ba,* moon.
230. RYŪSON. In the Tibetan text, *Çhu lha* (Varuṇa Nāgarāja; cf. *Mvtp.* ed. Sakaki, No. 3225). The *Cm.* says that it refers to a dragon (*ibid.*, p. 595b[13]).
231. The Tibetan text has *lus ngan pa,* the villain body. This is another name of Vaiśravaṇa (cf. Sarat Chandra Das, *Dictionary,* p. 217). According to the *Mvtp.* ed. Sakaki (No. 3159), *lus ngan pa* = Kuvera.
232. The Tibetan text has *nor sbyin,* Dhanada. This is another name of kuvera (cf. *Mvtp.* ed. Sakaki, No. 3166).
233. The Tibetan text has *brgya byin* = Śatakratu = Śakra. These are other names of Śakra-devendra (cf. *Mvtp.* ed. Sakaki, Nos. 3114 and 3143).
234. Tib. *mig mi bzang.*
235. Tib. *las sna tshogs can* or *bzo sna tshogs can.* The Tibetan version has *sna tshogs 'byung.* He is the divinity of the arts.
236. Tib. *gshin rje.*
237. The Tibetan text has *rnam par 'dud pa'i bu.*

238. Umā. The Tibetan text has *lha mo dka' thub bzlog.* According to the *Mvtp.* ed. Sakaki (No.=3172), the consort of Īsvara (Umā) = *Dka'zlog.*
239. Tib. *'jog po.*
240. Tib. *nor rgyas* or *nor ldan.*
241. Tib. *dung.*
242. Tib. *padma-chen po.*
243. Tib. *rigs ldan* or *rigs can.*
244. Tib. *gdengs ka chen po* or *dgengs ka mang.*
245. Tib. *thog ma'i lha.*
246. Tib. *rtag tu mtha' yas.*
247. Tib. *drang srong.*
248. Tib. *rig byed.*
249. *Nirbhaya.* The Tibetan text has *dbugs 'byin* (*āśvāsa*).
250. *Paribhramate*; *paribhrāmaka*; Tib. *kun tu 'khyams pa* (cf. *Mvtp. ed.* Sakaki, No. 5114; see Sarat Chandra Das *Dictionary,* p. 21).
251. *Samsāra*; Tib. *'khor ba.*
252. Just as the child lets itself be taken care of by the mother and without any fear, the believer at this stage looks unto the gods for support and relies completely on them. The *Cm.* says, "Thought at this stage a person has not yet heard of the Buddha's Dharma, still he knows that all these divinities have obtained their *dharmas* by virtue of their good practices. If then he hears someone speaking of this supreme marvel which is the doctrine of the Buddha, he will be definitely in the state of taking refuge there, and will receive it with faith. Those are therefore the most elevated worldly hearts outside Buddhism" (Taishō, Vol. XXXIX, p. 595b[4]).
253. According to the *Cm.*, the Void on which rests knowledge at this stage is not yet exempt from the two views of perpetuity and discontinuity; one still considers the reality either as permanent (*śāśvata*) or as impermanent (*uccheda*) (*ibid.*, p. 595c[2]).
254. Those who believe in the divinities enumerated above and in the worldly doctrines concerning them.
255. According to the Buddhist doctrine, the true vacuity; it is the causal connection which produces all the *dharmas.*
256. *Śāśvata.* The eternalist heresy consists in the belief that men are always men, animals always animals and that the rich and the poor have their destiny fixed at the time they come in this world.
257. *Uccheda.* Heterodoxy consisting in the belief that when men die, nothing subsists of them. They disappear forever.
258. *Śūnyatā,* the void.
259. *Bhava.*
260. FUMBETSU = *vikalpa*; Tib. *rnam par rtog pa.*
261. MUFUMBETSU = *avikalpa*; Tib. *rnam par mi rtog pa.*
262. The species of the void; the void of Buddhism and the void in other philosophies.
263. This is the answer to the fourth of the nine questions (cf. above, note 145 and note 152). This is related to the impure characters of the 'Heart'.
264. There are one hundred and sixty (different types of) worldly hearts (see below, note 351) which may arise in the heart of someone practising *yoga* (*yogācāra*). Of these hundred and sixty (types) mention is here made of sixty, or more precisely, fifty nine (types). The *Cm.* adds the heart of monkey with a view to making the number perfect and declares that the omission existed in the original Sanskrit text

(cf. below, note 350). In the Tibetan text reference is made to sixty hearts, the enumeration of which is complete. However, there is no allusion in it to the heart of monkey. For the 60 (types of) hearts, cf. the *Hōbōgirin* (pp. 130-131), article "BONNŌ".

265. Ist heart, Tib. *'dod chags = rāga.*
266. 2nd heart, Tib. *'dod chags dang bral ba=virāga.*
267. 3rd heart, Tib. *zhe sdang = dveṣa.*
268. 4th heart, Tib. *byams pa = maitrī.*
269. 5th heart, Tib. *gti mug = moha.*
270. 6th heart, Tib. *shes rab = prajñā.*
271. 7th heart, Tib. *gtan la dbab pa = nirṇaya.*
272. 8th heart, Tib. *the tshom = saṃśaya.*
273. 9th heart, Tib. *mun pa = andhakāra.*
274. 10th heart, Tib. *snang ba = āloka.*
275. 11th heart, Tib. *sdud pa = sañcaya.*
276. 12th heart, Tib. *'thab pa = kalaha.*
277. 13th heart, Tib. *rtsod pa = vivāda.*
278. 14th heart, Tib. *mi rtsod pa = nirvivāda.*
279. 15th heart, Tib. *lha = deva.*
280. 16th heart, Tib. *lha ma yin = asura.*
281. 17th heart, Tib. *klu = nāga.*
282. 18th heart, Tib. *mi = nara.*
283. 19th heart, Tib. *bud med = nārī.*
284. 20th heart, Tib. *dbang phyug = īśvara.*
285. 21st heart, Tib. *tshong pa = vāṇija.*
286. 22nd heart, Tib. *zhing pa = karmāntika.*
287. 23rd heart, Tib. *chu bo = nadī.*
288. 24th heart, Tib. *'ten ka = vilva.*
289. 25th heart, Tib. *khron pa = kūpa.*
290. 26th heart, Tib. *kun tu srung ba = parirakṣita.*
291. 27th heart, Tib. *ser sna = mātsara.*
292. 28th heart, Tib. *khyi = kukkura.*
293. 29th heart, Tib. *byi la = viḍala; mārjāra.*
294. 30th heart, Tib. *nam mkha'i ldan = garuḍa.*
295. 31st heart, Tib. *byi ba = mūṣa; mūṣika.*
296. 32nd heart, Tib. *glu = gīta.*
297. 33rd heart, Tib. *gar = nṛtya.*
298. 34th heart, Tib. *dundubhi*; Tib, has *sil ngan = tūrya; vādya.*
299. 35th heart, Tib. *khyim = gṛha.*
300. 36th heart, Tib. *sng ge = simha.*
301. 37th heart, Tib. *'ug pa = ulūka; divābhīta.*
302. 38th heart, Tib. *bya rog = droṇa; kāka.*
303. 39th heart, Tib. *srin po = rākṣasa.*
304. 40th heart, Tib. *tsher ma = kaṇṭaka.*
305. 41st heart, Tib. *sa 'og = nāgaloka.*
306. 42nd heart, Tib. *rlung = anila; vāyu; mārut.*
307. 43rd heart, Tib. *chu = jala.*
308. 44th heart, Tib. *me = anala; dahana.*
309. 45th heart, Tib. *'dam = panka*; Tib. adds *rnyog pa = āvila* (impurity).
310. 46th heart, Tib. *varṇarūpa*; Tib. gives *tshon rtsi* (colors).

311. 47th heart, Tib. *shing leb* = *phalaka*.
312. 48th heart, Tib. *nor ba* = *bhrānti*.
313. 49th heart, Tib. *dug* = *viṣa*.
314. 50th heart, Tib. *zhags pa* = *pāśa*.
315. 51st heart, Tib. *lcags sgrog* = *nigaḍa*.
316. 52nd heart, Tib. *sprin* = *megha*.
317. 53rd heart, Tib. *zhing* = *kṣetra*.
318. 54th heart, Tib. *lan tshva* = *lavaṇa*.
319. 55th heart, Tib. *spu gri* = *kṣura*.
320. 56th heart, Tib. *ri rab* = *sumeru*.
321. 57th heart, Tib. *rgya mtsho* = *samudra*.
322. 58th heart, Tib. *phug* = *guhā*.
323. 59th heart, Tib. *skye bar 'gyur pa*.
324. The figures represent the ordering number of the sixty hearts and indicate proper means to counter them. In the following notes, whenever there is an occasion, we have given explanations following the *Cm*.
325. Consists in conducting oneself by the literal observance — and lacking critical examination—of a Master's teaching (Taishō, Vol. XXXIX, p. 595c[17]).
326. This is the case when after having studied a doctrine, someone is carried away by the belief that all the other doctrines are similar to that which he has studied thoroughly (*ibid.*, p. 597a[5]).
327. This is to know the advantages of deliverance, but to remain incapable of making progress (towards it), because one is exclusively attached to the pleasures obtained as recompense in this world of transmigration. In the same way the *asuras* (whose name is taken to signify 'not gods') enjoy the fruits of recompense similar to those of the gods, although their *karman* and situation are not all the same (*ibid.*, p. 597b[16]).
328. The insignificant things of this world absorb him so completely that he is not the least preoccupied in perfecting within the Dharma (*ibid.*, p. 527b[15]).
329. The merchant thinks of amassing goods so as to sell them later at a profit. In the same way, this heart draws to itself all the teachings so as to derive from them, later on, some personal gain, which is blameworthy (*ibid.*, p. 579c[2]).
330. This heart hesitates perpetually between the two extremes (eternalism and nihilism), or between orthodoxy and heterodoxy, just as an object carried away in the current of a river incessantly swings between the two banks (*ibid.*, p. 597c[17]).
331. This is the heart of one who never ceases to make his thought more and more profound in the same way as a man examines the depth of a well. In the zeal of becoming profound, he makes it impossible for others to judge what he has in him good or bad, and even his neighbors and companions do not know what is going on in his spirit (*ibid.*, p. 597c[28]).
332. (For Nos. 28-29). The comments for the two similes are switched in the text.
333. According to the *Cm.*, the Sanskrit text omits an explanation for the heart of song. According to the Tibetan text, this consists in an attempt of inveigling the beings by the charm of the voice and attracting them to itself selfishly. The *Cm.* states that just as music charms all beings, this heart in embellishing the teachings seeks only to charm the beings (*ibid.*, p. 598b[13]).
334. This is to take rest by daytime and to think of business, or to practice meditation only during the night. It is in total ignorance that this heart meditates (*ibid.*, p. 598c[14]).

335. This is the heart of one who is constantly tormented with remorse for having taken action (*ibid.*, p. 599a[3]).
336. The terrestrial caves or the depths of the sea are the place where the Nāgas and the Asuras live. There they find the herbs giving long life as also beautiful women. It is the heart which seeks longevity and sensual pleasures (*ibid.*, p. 599a[9]).
337. This is a mistake of believing that water has the virtuality of purifying us from all our blemishes (*ibid.*, p. 599a[23]).
338. At first the fire burns with ardor, but its intensity diminishes little by little (*ibid.*, p. 599a[29]).
339. The *Cm.* says: "The explanation of this heart is lacking in the original Sanskrit". The *ācārya* (i.e. Śubhakarasimha) explains: "This is the heart which is completely devoid of science (nescience, *avidyā*). It is incapable of distinguishing and recalling objects that are found at arm's length." The Tibetan text explains it as follows: "To do wrong to others by one's ignorance, by one's own faults. The Tibetan text here mentions the "heart of impurity" which is tainted with all the external impurities (*ibid.*, p. 399b[5]).
340. Just as silk assumes the color with which it is dyed, this heart feels the impact of all influences, good, bad, or indeterminate (*avyākṛta*), as the case may be (*ibid.*, p. 599b[11]).
341. The plank floating on water carries objects that may be placed upon it, but it sinks if they become too heavy. In the same way, this heart is incapable of progressing beyond easy practices (*ibid.*, p. 599b[17]).
342. This is the heart which is incapable of realizing what it has decided to accomplish (*ibid.*, p. 599b[29]).
343. Just as under the action of poison the body becomes inert.
344. During the rainy season in India the spirit sinks, vacillating between joy and sorrow. (As such) it is incapable of holding elevated and generous thoughts. It is the same with this heart (*ibid.*, p. 599c[18]).
345. Salt lends an agreeable taste to food. The more one uses it, the more one's taste gets accustomed to it. By accumulation of diverse errors, one after another, this heart reinforces its liking for the bad (*ibid.*, p. 599c[28]).
346. To become a Buddhist monk, one has to get hairs and beard shaved, but this is truly a minor initiation (*ibid.*, p. 600a[7]).
347. This proud heart is inclined to think that all living beings stand below it (and) even refuses to respect those to whom it has an obligation to show respect, namely, masters, parents, and so on (*ibid.*, p. 600a[13]).
348. Just as the sea absorbs all the rivers (*ibid.*, p. 600a[19]).
349. If a basket is pierced, all its contents fall through the hole. Likewise this heart, at first inclined to observance of the Doctrine, one day slips through a hole produced by the non-observance (*ibid.*, p. 600a[27]).
350. The one which takes action, without even taking the pain of examining what is good and what is bad. In the *Cm.*, it concerns the 60th heart. In fact, (the following) is found there. Heart No. 60 does not occur in the Sanskrit text; the *ācārya* (i.e. Śubhakarasimha) says that this is the heart of a monkey (*markaṭa*), which is missing (cf. above, note 264). The heart which is like that of a monkey's cannot remain tranquil even for a moment and is continually distracted (*ibid.*, 600b[5]).
351. *Rāga* (TON, covetousness), *pratigha* (SHIN, anger), *moha* or *mūḍha* (CHI, stupidity), *māna* (MAN, Pride, Conceit), *vicikitsa* (GI, doubt). The five

fundamental defilements (*mūlakleśa* = KOMPON BONNŌ) five times multiplied by two (5×2^5) = 160 defiled hearts. These five fundamental *kleśas* arise from *avidyā* (MUMYŌ, nescience), says the *Cm.* (*ibid.*, p. 600b[25]).

352. *Laukikakalpa; laukika (pari) kalpa (naparāmarśa)*. The text has MŌJŪ which corresponds to Sanskrit *kalpa*. The Tibetan translation is *bskal pa*. The *Cm.* explains that the Sanskrit word *kalpa* signifies two things: (1) period of time (JIBUN) and (2) erroneous attachment (MŌJŪ = *parikalpana-parāmarśa*). In the usual Buddhist translation, the term is applied to the three "incalculable periods" which have to be traversed before arriving at the stage of a Buddha. But these three *kalpa* (SAMMŌJŪ) referred to here bear the names of (a) *sthūla* (gross), (b) *sūkṣma* (subtle), and (c) *prasūkṣma* (very subtle). The esoteric doctrine, abandoning popular Buddhism on this point, interprets *kalpa* in the sense of erroneous attachment. This is an interpretation which is peculiar to the Tantra; and which admits of the possibility of becoming a Buddha quickly and in course of this present life (*ibid.*, p. 600c[21]). See section C in "Doctrinal Analysis of the First Chapter".
353. *Lokottaracitta*; Tib. *'jig rten las 'das pa'i sems*. The *Cm.* says: "The Supramundane heart is the Pure Heart of Budhi" (*ibid.*, p. 600c[20]).
354. It is conceived that personality has no proper reality, this being nothing else than the product of the assemblage of the five aggregates (*skandha*) which alone are real. This is the truth (known as) the *pudgala-śūnyatā-nairātmya* (NINGU-MUGA) which the Śrāvakas conceive when they attain the stage of Arhat.
355. *Indriya*; Tib. *dbang pa*.
356. *Viṣaya*; Tib. *yul*.
357. (*Vijñāna*)-*dhātu*; [but] Tib.(*ye shes pa'i*) *khams*.
358. The duration of the Śrāvaka practices is very long. They require at least three lives and sometimes as many as sixty *kalpa*.
359. CHŪKOTSU. The dry stumps and roots of nescience (*avidyā*) are the original cause of delusion (*moha*) and action (*karma*). To abolish the *avidyā* is to destroy the seeds of the five fundamental *kleśa*.
360. *Nidāna*.
361. See above, note 181. The Tibetan version has *byed po* = *kāraka*.
362. That is to say, the thirty sects mentioned above; cf. note 177.
363. That is to say, the calm which is the result of the Arhat state, free from *kleśa;* but the *Cm.* makes it clear that at this stage there is still the illusion of the existence of the *skandhas*. That is why one cannot as yet possess the true Pure Heart of Bodhi. This is the condition of the lotus flower which has sprouted out of the mud (the *skandhas*) but has not yet emerged from the water surface (Taishō, Vol. XXXIX, p. 601b[16]).
364. That is to say, the heart which has shaken off the *kleśas*. Cf. above, note 353.
365. According to the Tibetan version, *blo,* which = *mati*.
366. That is to say, to perceive the vacuity of the five *skandhas*.
367. *Phena*. This example and those which follow illustrate vacuity, the non-selfness (*nairātmya*) of the *dharmas* and, it goes without saying, of the *skandhas*. The order would have to be as follows: [1st] *phena,* which corresponds to the aggregate of formation (*rūpaskandha*).
368. *Budbuda,* which corresponds to the aggregate of feelings (*vedanā*-s.)
369. *Kadalī,* which corresponds to the aggregate of motivations (*saṃskāra*-s).
370. *Marīci,* which corresponds to the aggregate of ideas (*samjñā*-s).
371. *Māyā,* which corresponds to the aggregate of perceptions. In the text of the

Sūtra the "banana tree" is placed before the mirage caused by solar flames. One cannot take into account the reality of the *saṃskāra-skandha,* any more than it is possible to find hardness in the trunk of the banana even if it is peeled fibre by fibre.

372. *Vimukti, vimokṣa;* Tib. *rnam par grol ba.*
373. *Āyatana;* Tib. *skye mched.*
374. *Dhātu;* Tib. *khams.*
375. *Grāhaka;* Tib. *'dzin pa.* Cf. above, note 122.
376. *Grāhya;* Tib. *gzung ba.* Cf. above, note 123.
377. The *skandhas,* places, etc., are devoid of existence, denuded of reality in themselves; they are therefore far removed from the essential reality, the *dharmatā.*
378. *Śāntidhātu;* Tib. *zhi ba'i dbyings.*
379. This is a moment of capital importance. One is about to give up the way of the Śrāvakas and of the Pratyekabuddhas, proposing to enter the Mahāyāna. The *Cm.* contains the (following) comparison: The lotus flower is not yet ready to be in full bloom, but its shoot is already above the water surface. The practising (devotee) will not henceforth fall in the mud (of the *skandhas*). He has come out of it (*ibid.,* p. 601c[17]).
380. I [Japanese] (but) according to the Tib. text, *phyin ci log pa = viparyāsa;* cf. Ikeda Chōtatsu, *Lexique annexe: Tibetain elementaire* (Tokyo, 1933), p.29.
381. JUN; the Tib. text has *phyin ci ma log pa = aviparyāsa* (cf. *Mvtp.,* ed. Sakaki, No. 1716). Eight kinds of conformist hearts are distinguished. These conform to the popular beliefs of the world. (Besides, there are) eight kinds of deviant hearts (I-SHIN) which discard all these popular beliefs so as to become convert to Buddhism. The *Cm.* says: "As has been explained above, when the heart passes from the stages of the seed, sprout, etc. (see above, notes 210-16), completely, places itself under the care of the Three Jewels (*triratna*) and observes for (the profit to the cult) of mankind and the devas the excellent practices which consist of abstinence and charity, it is called the eight conformist (or, non-deviant) hearts. If in the Three Vehicles (*triyāna*) someone causes the *bodhicitta* to be born, let him extirpate the stumps of *karma* and of *kleśa*, and the seeds of *avidyā* which produce the twelve sequences (cf. above, note 359). This is what has been called the eight non-conformist (or, deviant) hearts" (*ibid.*, Taishō, Vol. XXXIX, p. 601c[20]).
382. The *Cm.* says: "The word *yoga* is rendered in translation by conformity (to the innate truth) (SŌŌ); in the feminine (gender) it gives *yogi (sic.*[for *yoginī*]). Thus *yogi* (= yogin) designates a man who practises meditation in conformity with his innate nature" (*ibid.*, p. 601c[28]).
383. "According to the current Buddhist explanation," says the *Cm.*, "the Bodhisattvas, after having aroused the Heart of Bodhi, experience the 'realm of calm' (*śāntidhātu*) only when they have traversed a great 'immeasurable eon' (*asamkhyeyakalpa*)..But according to the esoteric doctrine, it suffices them to traverse the first 'erroneous attachment' (MŌJŪ = *parikalpana-parāmarśa*), that is to say, to jump over the 'great measurable eon' (*mahāsamkhyeyakalpa*)" (*ibid.*, p. 602a[1]). The erroneous attachment to which the *Cm.* refers is the one (called) gross (*sthūla*, cf. above, note 352). In his incisive essay on the ten steps of the Heart (JŪJŪSHIN), Kōbō daishi thinks that this first *kalpa* comprises the first five degrees. All that precedes these degrees corresponds to the popular moral teachings and to the Lesser Vehicle.

384. MU-EN-JŌ = *aparālambana-yāna.* The Tibetan version has *gzhan gyi dring (la) mi 'jog pa* = *a-para-praṇeya* ("not owing submission to others"). The *Cm.* explains: "The Sanskrit word *apara* signifies 'without the other' (*a-para*) or else 'others' (*apara*). The Vehicle which has others for object (TA-EN-JŌ = *aparālambana-yāna*) consists in producing the grand vow of Equality, cultivating the path of the Bodhisattvas in favor of all beings of the *dharmadhātu,* and reducing to submission (all beings) as far as the *icchantikas* (who cannot be saved) and others who have entered upon the stage of the two inferior Vehicles so as to bring them to the (great) Vehicle.... It is placing oneself wherein is the view of Great Compassion without (particular) object (i.e. without distinguishing oneself from others: MU-EN-NO-DAIHI = *aparālambana-karuṇā*) that one speaks of the "Vehicle having others for object" (TA-EN-JŌ, *aparālamabana-yāna*). On the other hand, is the Vehicle without object (without distinction of 'I' and other, *a-parālambana-yāna*). It is only when one has entered the 'immeasurable' that one understands well in detail the profundity of the (appropriating consciousness) *ādāna-vijñāna* (Tib. *len pa'i rnam par shes pa*) as also the non-existence of the three worlds, namely, *kāma, rūpa,* and *arūpa,* and of the *dharmas* outside the Heart. It is then that one can profit by the thought of *a-parālambana-yāna* and practises the path of the Grand Bodhi. From this (comes) the other name of Vehicle without object (without distinction of 'I' and others) (*ibid.,* p. 602a[14]). On the meanings of *apara, a-para,* cf. Wogihara Unrai in Okada Kaishō, *Kōbō daishi no kyōgi* (Tōkyō, 1932, p. 1711).

385. The *Cm.* states: "One examines the *ālaya* of the *skandhas* in conformity with the study practised by the Bodhisattvas of yore. In the *Laṅkāvatāra, Saṃdhinirmocana,* and other *sūtras,* the eight *vijñāna...* The meaning of the word *ālaya* is 'storehouse that contains'; to translate it exactly, it is a room. It is there that all the *skandhas* are born and disappear; it is the 'nest', 'the den' of the *skandhas* wherefrom the name *'ālaya'*. But *ālaya* (also) has the three senses to wit, (1) FUMBETSU, particularization; (2) INNEN, sequence; and (3) SHINJITSU, truth" (*ibid.,* p. 602a[29]-b[5]). The practising (devotees) of former times imagined that the three spheres were nothing but Heart (*citta*)—SANGAI-YUI-SHIN ; that is to say, that they have no existence outside the Heart.

386. Another expression for "mirage"; castles built in the air.

387. The *Cm.* (states): "The sovereign Heart is the heart-king (*cittarāja*)...This sovereignty and this liberty mark a novel illumination of the Pure Heart of Bodhi which prevails over what has been obtained in the first *kalpa*" (*ibid.,* p. 603a[23]).

388. The *Cm.* explains that "the purity of the heart-king is similar to the original and fundamental nature of a tank; the purification of the 'numbers' of the heart (diverse and multiple spiritual phenomena) being similar to the purification of the adventitious (particles of) dust (which sullies the basic purity of the tank). When one has the feeling of the fundamental purity (of the heart-king) one understands that basically the heart is without origin (uncreated)" (*ibid.,* p. 603a[26]).

389. The *Cm.* states: "..in the same way as the waves in the ocean, because they are produced by the effect of conditions (*pratyaya*): (The wind) exists neither before nor after (the precise moment of its occurrence) but it is not so with regard to the nature of water. Thus the waves (of the heart) are produced and disappear by the

effect of conditions, but the nature of the heart is without production and without disappearance. Understanding this fundamental non-produced character of the heart, one gradually has access to the discipline of the letter '*a*' (*ibid.*, p. 603a[29]).

390. "This is to explain the heart of the third *kalpa* that the praise of the doctrine of Shingon is now sung with a view to reinforcing the faith and respect of the listeners" (*Cm., ibid.*, p. 603b[18]).

391. *Prajñā* [sic. for *jñāna*] = Tib. *ye shes.*

392. *Puṇya*; Tib. *bsod nams.*

393. In Buddhism there are many ways of counting the big numbers. The detailed count which mostly prevails is as follows: *koṭi* = 10,000,000. 100 *koṭi* = 1 *ayuta* = 1,000,000,000. 100 ayuta = 1 niyuta = 100,000,000,000. 1 niyuta × 1 niyuta = niyuta^2 = 1 nayuta = 10,000,000,000,000,000,000,000 (namely, 22 zeroes after the numeral 1). Cf. Sakaki, *Kaisetsu Bongoaku, Funkan* (Glossary appended to the *Elements of Sanskrit*).

394. *Upāya.* The means which the Great Compassion utilizes for converting and rescuing the beings.

395. The *Cm.* explains that this devotion is similar to that one feels at the time of the birth of a crown prince who will inevitably become king. He unto whom the Bodhi has come to manifest itself is revered because he will surely become a Buddha (Taishō, Vol. XXXIX, p. 603b[1]).

396. *Śūnyatā.* The *Cm.* explains it as the Mind identified with the void.

397. *Nirlakṣaṇa* or *animitta.*

398. *Viṣaya.*

399. *Prapañca*; Tib, *spros pa.*

400. The *Cm.* states: "After the destruction of the seeds of *karman* and of life which the *kleśas* of the 160 hearts constitute under their subtle aspect (the third category of erroneous attachment), the sprouts of the tree of Buddha, infinite as space, appear once again in a series (in succession)" (*ibid.*, p. 604a[11]).

401. *Saṃskṛta.*

402. *Asaṃskṛta.*

403. "The *dharmatā* of the *dharmas* baffles all principles of 'fabrication', of creation, of production, because it subsists as such whether a Tathāgata appears in the world or doesn't appear at all" (*Cm. ibid.*, p. 604a[16]).

404. The six *indriyas.*

405. *Niḥsvabhāvacitta.* "When all the *dharmas*, pure and blemished, are examined with the help of infinite *prajñā* (which has just been obtained), (one realizes) that, even if it is only an atom, it owes its birth to causal sequence. If it is something which is due to causal sequence, it cannot have a nature (*svabhāva*). And if it has no personal nature, it cannot also originally possess any nature. Therefore, the veritable nature of the heart is to be without nature in itself and consequently the nature in itself is a thing impossible to obtain" (*Cm.*, p. 604a[23]).

406. The heart at the very moment when it has caught hold of Bodhi for the first time.

407. "The heart (of the third *kalpa*)—if comparison is made with that of the first and the second *kalpa*—is the fully blossomed lotus flower (see above, note 379). And if comparison is made with the two hearts which will be born afterward, it is the fruit which provides the seed (from which fruits will later emerge) (the *Cm. ibid.*, p. 604a[26]). The heart of the third *kalpa* is called IN-SHIN (*hetucitta*): the following

ones are called KON-SHIN (*mūlacitta*) and KUKYŌ-SHIN (*niṣṭhācitta*) (respectively). (On the three *citta,* see below, note 410).

408. When one is liberated from *karman* and *kleśa,* these cease to be obstacles and become virtualities of the Heart of Bodhi (*bodhicitta*). "After being liberated from *karman* and *kleśa,* the practising (devotee) understands that *karman* and *kleśa* are attributes of the Buddha". This is, the *Cm.,* continues, like poison which when properly applied by the physician becomes a remedy. (*ibid.,* p. 604b[2]).

409. SHINGEGYŌJI; *śraddhādhimukticāryabhūmi.* According to the Tibetan version, *mos pa spyod pa 'i sa; adhimukticaryābhūmi* (cf. *Mvtp.,* ed. Sakaki, No. 897). This is another name of the "Ten Earths". In tantrism, when the Bodhisattva is in the "First Earth" of these (Ten Earths), that is to say, when he has arrived at the state of Tathāgata, his faith is indestructible, whence the term "stage of the practice of profound faith". The whole of this paragraph is concerned with the stage of the Ten Earths which is that of the practices observed by the Bodhisattva of the Shingon. These practices must be observed from the first earth and from it alone! These "Ten Earths" fall within the competence of Buddhas and, in spite of the analogy of the names, have to be carefully distinguished from the "Ten Earths" of exoteric Buddhism. In the Shingon these Ten Earths are nothing but the symbols of the virtualities (*guṇa*) of the heart, and as such no qualitative distinction between them can be made (*cf.* next chapter, section "F. The ten earths").

410. It concerns the three *citta* called *hetu, mūla, niṣṭhā.* The *Cm.* says that the Ten Earths are made to correspond to the three expressions of the Threefold Formula. The first Earth corresponds to the expression: "The Heart of Bodhi is the first cause"; the second Earth and the following ones up to the seventh (included) correspond to the second formula: "The Great Compassion is the root"; the three last ones (i.e. Earths) correspond to the third formula: "The means of liberation is the outcome" (*ibid.,* p. 604c[20]).

411. The "ten Pāramitās" are meant.

412. *Catvāri saṃgrahavastūni:* (1) *dāna,* giving; (2) *priyavāditā,* agreeable speech; (3) *arthacaryā,* benevolence; and (4) *samānārthatā,* mutual help.

413. Always for the same reason, namely, it falls within the competence of the Buddhas.

414. The *Cm.* says, "According to the *Avataṃsaka,* after uttering the ten grand vows, one obtains (the Ten Hearts), to wit, the heart that causes profit to others, the heart of tenderness, the heart of obedience, the heart of quietude, the subdued heart, the appeased heart, the heart of humanity, the heart of benevolence, the unshakable heart, and the unblemished heart" (*ibid.,* p. 605a[5]).

415. The stage of the First Earth, that is to say, of the profound faith. After having penetrated this stage, one surpasses the subtle category of the 160 *cittas* which are marked by defilements (*sūkṣmakalpa*) and constitute the third *kalpa* (*ibid.,* p. 605.b[11]).

416. Besides the three hearts (cf. note 410, above) there is also distinguished in the Ten Earths a marginal stage called JŌJŌHŌBEN-SHIN, "heart of the supreme Middle". The moment one arrives at this stage, one attains the omniscience of definitive outcome (*niṣṭhā-sarvajñāna, ibid.,* p. 605b[21]).

417. *Lakṣaṇa* (or *nimitta*).

418. *Nirbhayasthāna.* We are now concerned with the topic of the "Six Non-Fears". The term designates the stages through which the practising (devotee) of the

Shingon must pass during the three *kalpa* which precede the entry into the Ten Earths. These are the six which precede the appearance of the pure Bodhicitta. The latter manifests itself only at the moment of entry into the Ten Earths. With regard to the "cases of non-fear", the *Cm.* says, "The Sanskrit (word) *āśvāsa* may be translated precisely as "recovering breath". This is like the man whose throat is tightly grasped by a strong man and feels the grip relaxing just at the moment when he was about to suffocate. In the same way, the beings tied up by *karman* and the *kleśas* seem about to pass out; but when they go through the six events of Non-Fear, it is as if they are resuscitated" (*ibid.*, p. 605c[10]). It may be noted that the text has ROKU-MUI-SHO which seems to correspond to *Ṣannirbhayasthāna,* while the *Cm.* explains the expression *āśvāsa,* which is translated by SOSOKU-SHO. For the *Cm.* explanation for each of these *nirbhaya,* see the next chapter, section "G. The six non-fears".

419. It is understood that the three worlds are a manifestation of the mind and there is nothing outside it.

420. This is to say that one no longer allows oneself to be attracted by anything: one has freed oneself from attachment to the *dharmas*.

421. *Pañcaskandhāḥ.*

422. *Aṣṭādaśadhātavaḥ.*

423. *Dvādaśāyatanāni.*

424. *Grāhaka,* see above, note 122.

425. *Grāhya,* see above, note 123.

426. *Ātman.*

427. *Jīva*; concept of a heterodox school.

428. MU-EN; cf. above, note 384.

429. *Pratīyasamutpāda.* With this paragraph begins another section called "the ten formulas of production due to causal sequences". All things are the products of sequences of causality. In themselves they are without proper nature. The remaining part of the paragraph is consecrated to a demonstration of this affirmation (statement) with the help of ten examples. Mystic success (*siddhi*) is obtained by the practising (devotee) when he observes the Three Mysteries, but he (also) realizes that this is a manifestation which is as illusory as the ten "phenomena" to be discussed below. Now it concerns the method which would enable one to be liberated from these illusions which amount to so many obstacles (*Cm.*, p. 606b[10]).

430. *Māyā;* Tib. *sgyu ma.*

431. *Marīci;* Tib. *smig rgyu.*

432. *Svapna;* Tib. *rmi lam.*

433. *Pratibimba;* Tib. *gzugs brnyan.*

434. *Gandharvanagara;* Tib. *dri za'i grong khyer.*

435. *Pratiśrutka;* Tib. *brag cha.*

436. *Udakacandra;* Tib. *chu'i zla.*

437. *Budbuda;* Tib. *chu'i chu bur.*

438. *Khapuṣpa* ; Tib., *nam mkha'i me tog.* The non-existing flower which forms itself before the eyes of people afflicted by cataract (*timira*). The Tibetan text gives *'khrul pa* (*bhrānti*), "fault, illusion".

439. *Ālātacakra;* Tib. *mgal me'i 'khor lo.*

440. *Rūpa-bimba.*

441. That is to say, because the *dharmas* are without nature, essence, or existence of their own.

442. The miraculous phenomena (irradiation, levitation, etc.) which take place during the tantric practices under the effect of the mantras, and the *siddhi* resulting from them, are conditioned by the incantations and drugs which the magician applies. Therefore they do not have any real existence (or) autonomous (independent) 'nature', and the practising (devotee) must not be attached to these because they are only secondary 'transformations' of the original and pure *bodhicitta,* of "primordial nature" (*Cm.* p. 606b).
443. Upon reciting the *mantras* (shingon).
444. The devotee practising *yoga* cannot let himself be swayed by the apparitions which he sees during the religious exercises. He knows that they are fallacious and without real basis (*prajñapti [mātra]*).
445. The practising (devotee) knows that the apparitions which come to him during his meditations are the manifestations of this heart (*citta*) and they do not exist outside this *citta*.
446. The realization of the goal of religious exercises.
447. More precisely, the reflection of the face comes, in an absolute sense, neither from the mirror itself nor from the individual himself who looks at the mirror.
448. The reflection in the mirror is only manifestations of the Pure Body of the Tathāgata, i.e. tantric practices accomplished by the practising (devotee).
449. The *Cm.* distinguishes three kinds of domains (or "Buddha fields". *buddhakṣetra*), to which *siddhi* provides access: (1) superior ones (MITSUGON-BUKKOKU; esoteric and ornamented Buddhakṣetra—this is the paradise of Vairocana); (2) middling ones (JIPPŌ JŌGON-BUKKOKU, the Buddhakṣetra pure and ornamented in all directions—these are the pure terrains of the other Buddhas and Bodhisattvas in the *maṇḍalas*); (3) inferior ones (SHOTEN-SHURA-GŪ, palace of the Devas and of the Asuras—these are the domains of the divinities situated in the *maṇḍala* of the external enclosure). The meaning of this passage is as follows: Only the knowledge of the unreality of the manifestations which occur during the practice of *yoga* and consequently the attitude of detachment which the practising devotee of the *yoga* shows for them permits the realization called *siddhi* (*ibid.,* p. 608a).
450. During the practice of the *yoga* it may happen that the practising devotee believes that he hears the voice of the Buddha preaching the Dharma, but should realize that it only amounts to an echo so has the value of an unreal object. He does not allow himself to be misled by this illusion.
451. *Vidyādhara.* This epithet designates the practising devotee of the Shingon.
452. The *Cm.* says that when the water is pure, the brightness of the moon may be reflected (in it) but that this does not take place when the water is troubled. It is only when the practising (devotee) has purified his heart by the religious practices that the Buddha can project himself in him (the devotee) (*ibid.,* p. 608b[7]).
453. Just as the bubble cannot be, and is not, separated from water, out of which it is born, so the practising (devotee) of the Shingon arriving at the *siddhi* does not let himself be carried away outside of himself. Avoiding all illusions he remains in his purity and futile attractions have no power over his heart.
454. The *Cm.* says that the (supposed) living beings and their (assumed) creator in space (which children, diseased persons, etc. imagine to see) are only names without reality; for space is not at all visible, and following an optical illusion from a distance, one imagines to see them in space (*ibid.,* p. 608c[14]).
455. *Jīva*; Tib. *srog.*
456. *Kāraka*; Tib. *byed pa po.*

457. Just like persons afflicted by cataract whose illusory flowers (cf. above, note 438)
458. *Ālāta.*
459. The practising (devotee) of the *mantras* who has attained the supreme goal (*siddhi*) and is in possession of new virtualities knows that all phenomena come out of the letter *a,* the symbol of the *bodhicitta* and that they are as illusory as the figures (circle, triangle, etc.) traced in the air by a burning torch following the rotating or other movement that its holder may communicate to it (*ibid.*, p. 609a[3]).
460. The names of the six *pada* (in the *Cm., ku = pada*; Tib. has *gzhi*) which follow are the eulogistic epithets attributed to the "Ten Comparisons", "the Ten Formulae of production due to causal sequences" enumerated above inasmuch as they render it possible to accede to the Great Vehicle, a true heart, the unequalled omniscience, etc. (cf. above, note 429).
461. The ten comparisons given above form a "very profound" part of the Buddhist teaching, that is closed to the Śrāvakas and the Pratyekabuddhas. They belong to the doctrine of the Great Vehicle (*ibid.*, p. 607a[21]).
462. That is to say, the stage of the truth which cannot be communicated (or) expressed and the revelation which one can obtain only by oneself (*ibid.*, p. 607a[24]).
463. *Asamasama*; that is to say, the supreme wisdom of the Buddha.
464. *Dhruva,* Tib. *nges pa.* The Buddhas use these ten comparisons to explain the veritable, determined, invariable *citta* of the Tathāgatas (*ibid.*, p. 607b[1]).
465. *Samyaksaṃbodhi,* because thanks to these comparisons, *bodhi* can be obtained.
466. Progressive, because truth is profound like the sea whose profundity increases as one moves farther way from the coast. The more one penetrates the deep meaning of the ten comparisons, *pratītyasamutpāda,* the deeper one goes into the wisdom of the Buddha (*ibid.*, p. 607b[8]).
467. *Dharmādāna.* Thus one obtains a perfect and complete knowledge of the nature of Buddha which is in us.
468. According to the Tibetan text, *sems kyi bye brag = cittaviśeṣa,* distinctive varieties of the heart.

PART IV

DOCTRINAL ANALYSIS OF THE FIRST CHAPTER, DAINICHIKYŌ

A. THE TITLE OF THIS CHAPTER

The commentary states: "The chapter entitled 'Access to the discipline of the Shingon (which) installs (the being) in the heart (of Bodhi)' has two Sanskrit titles, viz. 'On the Practice of the Shingon'[1] and 'Access to the discipline of the Shingon (which) installs (the being) in the heart (of Bodhi)'. We say that the terms 'access' and 'installs' both convey the sense of 'practice'.[2] That is why, in short, only one of these titles need be retained."[3]

The Tibetan translation calls it the 'Chapter of the distinctions of the heart',[4] which does not at all correspond to the titles given above.

The commentary then explains the expression 'Shingon' as follows: " 'Shingon' is a Sanskrit mantra which signifies 'true speech', speech as such, the sound without error or distortion.' "[5] The Shingon is one of the Three Mysteries of Mahāvairocana in Dharmakāya; and each of these mysteries is necessarily accompanied by the two others. The commentary explains them this way: "To accede to the discipline of the shingon there are, in short, three things. One is the rubric of the Body Mystery, the second the rubric of the Speech Mystery, and the third the rubric of the Heart Mystery. The practising (devotee), after having purified the three kinds of acts (*karma* of body, speech, and heart by this threefold means (*upāya*) receives the empowerment (*adhiṣṭhāna*) of the Tathāgata's Three Mysteries; and even in the present life may achieve the (ten) stages (*bhūmi*) and the (ten) perfections (*pāramitā*), thus without needing to pass through many eons (*kalpa*) exercising fully all the practices which serve to counteract the defilements)."[6]

From the second chapter onwards the *sūtra* exposes the manner of developing, with the help of the Three Mysteries, the virtues and omniscience which are innate in us at all times. In a way the present chapter is an initial digest of this doctrine: "This chapter summarizes the main idea of the *sūtra*, viz. the true Heart of beings is nothing else than Omniscience itself. He who knows all in conformity with the reality is called omniscient. In this sense it is taught here how all the bodhisattvas on entering by way of the gate of true speech produce *bodhi* in their own hearts.[7] It is in their very own heart that all the practices turn out to be included. In their own heart they witness the perfect enlightenment. They prove the great Nirvāṇa in their own heart. They engender in their heart the means of helping sentient beings. It is in their own heart that they decorate and purify the Buddha field (*buddhakṣetra*). Starting from the 'cause' and going up to the 'fruit' (or, finality), without any installation they are installed in the Heart (of Bodhi).[8] That is why the chapter is called 'Access to the discipline of the Shingon (which) installs (the being) in Heart (of Bodhi).'"[9]

B. GENERAL ANALYSIS OF THE CHAPTER

In his Palace of the Vajradhātu, surrounded by the numberless retinue. Mahāvairocana explains to them eternally in the three times, the law of the equality of the Three Mysteries. A distinction is made between the internal retinue and the great retinue. The first one symbolizes the merits of the Tathāgata's compassion. The second represents his merits of compassion for converting sentient beings. The *sūtra* represents the internal retinue by the nineteen *vajra*-holders. One of them sums up in himself, the person of all the others; he is Vajrapāṇi.[10] He presides over the supernatural and miraculous Three Mysteries of Mahāvairocana. That is why he is called the 'Master of Mysteries'. In his capacity as representative of the Beings he continually puts questions to the Buddha. The great retinue has as representatives the four Bodhisattvas, Samantabhadra, Maitreya, Mañjuśrī, and Sarvanīvaraṇaviṣkambhin. In particular, Samantabhadra represents the universality of the heart of Bodhi; Maitreya, compassion for the Beings: Mañjuśrī, the science which explains the Dharma; Sarvanīvaraṇaviṣkambhin, the merit of eliminating all the obstacles (of defilement, etc.).

What is the topic of the preaching? The *sūtra* posits the equality of Body, Speech, and Thought. In this regard, the commentary declares: "The three acts of the Tathāgata, of whatever kind they be, have as a finality the primordial and supreme reality. Body equals

Speech; Speech equals Thought. It is like the ocean which extends to all places and which has everywhere the same saline taste . . . The empowerment by the Three Mysteries of Body, Speech, and Thought is the gate of entry. It may be said that the Body equality is the secret *mudrā,* the Speech equality is the *mantra,* and the Thought equality is the contemplation. These Three Mysteries are the means by which the vision of Sambhogakāya of empowerment is arrived at.[11] Now, this Sambhogakāya of empowerment is the omnipresent Body of Vairocana, and this omnipresent body is nothing else than the Body of knowledge of the Equality of the practising (devotee). This is why he who resides in this vehicle goes without going, arrives without arriving. This is the essential state of Equality, but all Beings who have penetrated it have neither penetrated nor been penetrated. That is why it is called Equality. The doctrine of Equality is the principal idea of this *sūtra.*"[12]

Our true nature is not in the least different from that of the Buddha; only because it is hidden by our defilements we lose sight of it. But as the Three Mysteries are fundamentally the same in the Buddha and in the Beings, thanks to the assisting Buddha and by the practice of this 'Three Mysteries' we may come to realize the Buddha in ourselves.[13] This true nature which stays in the depths of ourselves is what is called the 'pure Heart of Bodhi'. This is the *sūtra's* explanation from its beginning to its end.

The contents of this chapter may be analyzed as follows:

1. *The Triple Formula* (SANKU). Comparison with the growth of plants explains the progress of the disciple from the re-awakening of the Heart of Bodhi up the Buddha-state.[14]
2. *Bodhi and Omniscient Knowledge* (BODAI TO ISSAI-CHICHI). Definition of Bodhi and Heart of Bodhi (*bodhicitta*) identified with omniscience knowledge (*sarvajña-jñāna*).[15]
3. *The Nine Formulas* (KUKU). This is a sub-division of the Triple Formula.[16]
4. Thirty kinds of Heterodoxy (SANJUSSHU-GEDŌ). So as to clarify how the Heart of Bodhi blossoms, the text enumerates the heterodox errors relating to ego which are opposed to this blossoming.[17]
5. *The Eight Successive Stages of the Heart* (HASSHIN-SŌZOKU). How the profane evil-doer sets himself in the practice of the good on the profane level, then by the belief in the *devas* manages to awaken in himself the religious spirit by a

succession of stages which is compared with the development of the plants from seed to the fruit.[18]

6. *The Sixty Hearts* (ROKUJUSSHIN). The good heart which is still of a mundane order, but which improves little by little, is beset by bad impulses which jeopardize this improvement and which should be gotten rid of. There is enumeration of sixty of these bad impulses.[19]
7. *The Three Kalpas* (SANGŌ). Thanks to the elimination of the mundane errors, the heart becomes extra-mundane and enters into Buddhism by the Lesser Vehicle, after which it has access to the exoteric Great Vehicle and finally penetrates the esoteric doctrine.[20]
8. *The Ten Stages* (JŪJI). There is enumeration of the stages which the practising (devotee) of the Shingon passes through.[21]
9. *The Six Non-fears* (ROKUMUI). By the exercise of the Three Mysteries, the practising (devotee) of the Shingon pursues little by little the development of his Heart of Bodhi.[22]
10. *The Ten Formulas of Dependent Origination* (JU-ENSHŌ-KU). The *dharmas* which are constructed, the outcome of dependent origination, are here objects of ten comparisons, such as illusions, mirages. The practising (devotee) must guard himself so that his contemplative exercises are not troubled by the intrusion in his mind of delusions related to these *dharmas.*[23]

In the following pages, we shall give a more detailed explanation of some of the principal doctrinal points of the chapter.

C. THE TRIPLE FORMULA

Vajradhara admires the omniscience of the Tahtāgata and wants to know what its cause, root, and outcome are. The Buddha answers that the Heart of Bodhi is the cause of omniscience, the Great Compassion its root, and the means (*upāya*) bringing salvation are its outcome. This is what is called the 'Triple Formula' (SANKU).

The commentary says: "This Triple Formula sums up the entire doctrine of the Buddha".[24] And Kōbō daishi in his work *Unjigi* ("On the meaning of the syllable Hūṃ", Taishō, No. 2430) also declares: "The *sūtras,* notably the *Dainichikyō* and the *Kongōchōkyō,* do not teach any other thing than the Triple Formula which makes the Heart of Bodhi the cause, the Great Compassion the root, the means of salvation the outcome. To sum up the elaborated and pull back the ramification it may be said that all the doctrines are nothing but this Triple Formula which may be condensed in the single syllable *Hūṃ*... Were there even a thousand *sūtras* and ten thousand *śāstras,* they would not have anything which could not be included in the Triple Formula and the unique syllable."[25]

The *Dainichikyō* teaches us how our innate pure Heart of Bodhi is to be developed and how we can achieve the Buddha state. This teaching may be summed up in the Triple Formula. The commentary uses a comparison to explain the relation between each of the expressions of the Triple Formula: The Heart of Bodhi is like the seed which is conditioned by the four elements; Compassion, like the root which emerges from the seed; and the Means, like the fruit which is the final outcome of the vegetal evolution.[26]

The whole purpose of the Buddhist doctrine is the attainment of the Buddha state or of Bodhi. The primary source of Bodhi is the pure Heart of Bodhi, innate in each one of us and always identical no matter whether it is in a Buddha or in any other being. The single profound difference between a Buddha and an unenlightened being is that the former has 'attested' realized the pure Heart of Bodhi while we have still to awaken this Heart in ourselves so as to become Buddha. That is why the commentary says: "The Heart of Bodhi signifies faith, pure and immaculate".[27]

But once this immaculate faith is awakened, it is still necessary to consolidate and develop our Heart of Bodhi, just as the seed of plants requires the help of external forces, e.g. the sun rays and water, to develop a root. This is how the second term of the formula, the Great Compassion as root, is explained.

The commentary says: "Compassion (*karuṇā*) along with Great Love (*maitrī*) is the topic of discussion here. When a practising (devotee) presents an offering, whether he offers a flower or rubs some (powdered) perfume with the pure Heart of omnipresent Bodhi, he raises the cloud of offerings, worships the Buddhas everywhere, expresses his vow of compassion, transfers his merits (EKŌ = *pariṇāmana*) to all (sentient) beings, delivers them from all suffering imparting them an infinite joy. By the effect of our own 'root of merit' (*kuśalamūla*), by the empowerment (*adhiṣṭhāna*) of the Tathāgata, and by the force of the Dharmadhātu, all the good actions which we may perform enable us to achieve the accomplishment (of the Buddha state). The stage (JI = *bhūmi*) of universal omniscience and the terrain (KAI = *viṣaya*) of the totality of beings cause the roots (of Compassion, etc.) to arise everywhere."[28]

The second term of the Triple Formula has its application in the practice of the Three Mysteries (of Body, Speech, and Thought), which has evidently the achievement of the Buddha state as the goal. But the Bodhisattvas of the Mahāyāna can attain their own salvation only in assuring the salvation of the other beings because the ego is identical with the non-ego. When we seek enlightenment, it is essential to seek the same for others at the same time. This resolution is expressed by the phrase, "makes the Great Compassion the root". As a result of practising the Three Mysteries, illusion is completely removed, and the true nature of Bodhi is revealed at the same time as when one is conducting all beings to the Buddha state. For this case we have the third phrase of the formula: "makes the means of salvation the outcome", which the commentary explains as follows: "The innumerable practices (which are brought to a finality), in their full plenitude leaving nothing to be added, enable all works to be accomplished completely and in accordance with the circumstances of the beings...The fruit of omniscience which results from all the practices is what is called the means."[29]

Thus the Triple Formula is essentially related to the development of the pure Heart of Bodhi which is innate in us. It has already been seen above that according to another traditional scheme this development is sub-divided into five stages, themselves corresponding to five seed-syllables (*bījākṣara*). The esoteric exegesis establishes the following table of correspondence between the scheme of the Triple Formula and that of the five stages (fivefold evolution of the syllable 'A', AJI-GOTEN):

TRIPLE FORMULA	FIVE STAGES	SEED SYLLABLES
Bodhicitta (cause)	*Cittopāda*	A
Mahākaruṇā (root)	*Caryā*	Ā
	Bodhi	AṂ
Upāya (outcome)	*Nirvāṇa*	AḤ
	Upāya	ĀṂḤ

D. BODHI AND THE OMNISCIENT KNOWLEDGE

The Triple Formula comprises an explanation of the Heart of Bodhi. But the question arises: What is Bodhi? What is its definition? The *sūtra* answers these (questions) in these words: "What is Bodhi? It is to know one's heart as it is."[30]

The commentary comments this way upon the passage: "It is the revelation of the place where the treasure of the Tathāgata's merits is found. Where can one find this Dharma—the Dharma which is supreme, very profound, subtle and marvellous, and which none but omniscient persons can explain? Simply in the Heart of the faithful. When proceeding with an exacting examination, the faithful will be able to prove it and to recognize it in all clarity. This is what is called the realization of Bodhi. For truly speaking, one cannot comprehend it from the doing of another or obtain it from another. And if it be asked, since Bodhi is nothing else than the very Heart of being why they cannot become a Buddha even while coursing in transmigration? —we shall reply: because they do not know their Heart exactly as it is (*yathābhūta*)."[31]

Then the *sūtra* explains that Bodhi has a nature without a character and compares it to space: "The nature of Bodhi is that of space. It is not an object of either knowledge or comprehension. Why so? Because Bodhi is non-characterized."[32] The commentary explains this in these terms: "Since space is omnipresent and—by dint of its ultimate purity is non-characterized, immobile and undifferentiated, unmovable and indestructible, it may be compared with the non-characterized Heart of Bodhi in this resemblance... Moreover, space being exempt from all verbal elaboration (*prapañca-viśeṣa*), has no character of knowledge or of comprehension. Now, it is important to know that it is the same with *sambodhi* that is attested to by all the Buddhas. Only the Heart itself attests to the Heart; the Heart itself comprehends the Heart; but there is in it neither an object of knowledge nor a subject that knows."[33]

The Tibetan translation renders these notions with simplicity and clarity: "The Buddha is of the nature of space. In Bodhi there is in no way a subject or an object."[34]

Vajrapāṇi poses the next question so as to make the Buddha speak: "Who seeks omniscient knowledge? Who becomes as Saṁbuddha by dint of Bodhi? What produces this omniscient knowledge?"[35]

In the Heart of Bodhi can be distinguished a subject which seeks and an object which is sought, to wit, the omniscient knowledge. But according to the esoteric doctrine, such a duality does not exist. The Heart of Bodhi innate in all beings and the omniscience of the Buddhas in the depth are identical. The commentary states: "What is called the Heart of Bodhi is exclusively omniscient knowledge. But omniscient knowledge is precisely this Heart of Bodhi. How can it be said that there is subject who seeks and an object that is sought? Where is the awakened; where is he who awakens? Besides, outside of the Heart, there is no Dharma at all. Where is then he (the agent) who can produce this Heart (of Bodhi) and make it attain the supreme fruit?"[36]

This is why the Buddha responds to the question in these terms: "Master of Mysteries, Bodhi and omniscient knowledge must be sought by each individual in his own Heart. And why so? Because our original nature is pure."[37]

In connection with this reply the commentary says: "The true heart of all beings is Bodhi. Whether a Buddha arises or does not arise, it is always decorated and pure. But due to the fact that we do not know ourselves as we really are... on account of the defilements (*kleśa*)... we suffer all sorts of aching pains. It is necessary to know that outside of our heart there is no *dharma.* The practising (devotee) of the *yoga* or he who contemplates the truth of the three laws (Three Mysteries) will be able to see the Heart in its true aspect. It is this true aspect of the Heart which is Bodhi non-characterized; it is also called omniscient knowledge."[38]

The *sūtra* then explains the non-characterized state of this true aspect of the heart in these terms: "The Heart is neither interior nor exterior (to the beings). It is also not to be found in between these two. Master of Mysteries, the Tathāgata, Arhat, Samyaksambuddha is neither blue, nor yellow, nor red, nor white... Its nature has nothing in common with the realm of desire; the Heart is not in the realm of Space and Bodhi. These three things are at bottom just one thing."[39]

That summarizes the development of the first term of the Triple Formula, namely, what concerns the Heart of Bodhi. Immediately the *sūtra* adds: "These (three things) have Compassion as root, and perfection belonging to the Means as accomplishment", which are the second and the third terms of the Triple Formula. Finally, as though concluding the Triple Formula, the *sūtra* continues in these words: "Master of Mysteries, I explain the *dharmas* in this way so that all these assemblies of Bodhisattvas may take cognizance (of it) for purifying the Heart of Bodhi, (their true) Heart. In short, Master of Mysteries, if a man of good birth, and a woman of good birth, desires to take cognizance of Bodhi, they must (at the outset) take cognizance in this manner of their own Heart."[40]

The objective of the Buddha in promulgating the *Dainichikyō* is to reveal the "truth of the Heart". Indeed, the *Dainichikyō,* from its beginning to its end, reverts to the exposition of what is the true Heart of all the beings.

E. THE THREE KALPAS

The doctrine of Trikalpa (SANGŌ), along with that of the Triple Formula, amounts to one of the most important tenets of the first chapter. Let us quote the text of the *sūtra*: "Master of Mysteries, the hundred and sixty (kinds of) hearts (are obtained) in multiplying by two (the five fundamental defilements, *kleśa*) once, twice, thrice, four times, (and) five times. If one overcomes the three erring and worldly attachments (*laukika-kalpa*), then the extra-mundane heart is born."[41] A little later (it states): "Master of Mysteries, it is this initial Heart that the Buddha has explained to be the cause (enabling one) to attain the Buddha (state). Thanks to it, one is delivered from *karma* and *kleśa* (defilements), although throughout (the past) was relying on *karma* and *kleśa.* To him (in that Buddha state) the world will make worship and constantly present offerings."[42]

This passage shows that after having overcome deviance, the practising (devotee) of the Shingon must pass through the three steps. This is the basis of the esoteric method for rapidly becoming a Buddha.

This Trikalpa sums up the *Trimahāsaṅkhyeyakalpa* which ordinarily signifies a triple period of time, the length of which cannot be measured. According to popular Buddhism which conceives of *kalpa* as a duration of time, the practices of the three *mahāsaṅkhyeya-kalpa* are necessary for becoming a Buddha. According to esoteric Buddhism, which interprets *kalpa* as deviant attachment (*parikalpana-parāmarśa*), the period of a single thought may suffice to cross those steps and to achieve the Buddha state.

In the commentary we read: "The term 'supramundane Heart' is applied to the pure Heart of Bodhi of one who has transcended the three deviant attachments of the world and has (thus) instigated the birth of the supramundane Heart. He who has crossed the three *kalpas* is a yogin. In Sanskrit the word *kalpa* has two meanings: it is a period of time (JIBUN) and is also deviant attachment (MŌJŪ). According to the ordinary explanation, at the end of three great incalculable eons (*asaṅkhyeyakalpa*) one may arrive at the Buddha state. But, according to the esoteric explanation, crossing a *kalpa* is an exercise of the yogin who leaves behind this first level of deviant attachments called 'gross'. In this first 'incalculable eon' there may occur a hundred and sixty hearts, and so on. Crossing the second *kalpa* is to overcome a second level of deviant attachments called 'subtle'. There are also present the hundred and sixty hearts, and so on. The practising (devotee) who crosses one more *kalpa* and triumphs over a third level of attachments called 'very subtle', comprising the hundred and sixty hearts, and so on, can achieve the initial Heart of the Wisdom of the Buddhas. This is why one may say that the 'three incalculable eons' is nothing else than the accomplishment of Bodhi. But if in the course of one life one can cross the three levels of devious attachments, one can become a Buddha in a single life. In this case, what is the use of discussing (the duration of a *kalpa* in terms of) the period of time?"[43]

Let it be noted that in Sanskrit normally the term *kalpa* does not signify "deviant attachment"; the terms *kalpana* or *parikalpa(na)* are what are used for "deviant imagination". Possibly to synthesize popular and esoteric Buddhism, the translator-commentator has imagined that *kalpa* may signify also "deviant attachment". It bears witness to a happening in the evolution of the esoteric doctrine in China. The Tibetan translation retains the word as such: "Master of the Mysteries, since it is so, in multiplying [the five passions] by two once, twice, thrice, four times and five times, there are a hundred and sixty hearts of worldly men. After crossing the three *kalpas* one gives birth to the supramundane heart."[44]

Whatever [else] it be, the *trikalpa* are the three steps which the practising (devotee) of the Shingon crosses when he keeps away from the tenebrous passions which envelop and render obscure the splendor of the Pure Heart of original Bodhi. The first *kalpa* consists in conquering the gross (*sthūla*) devious attachment which overshadows the splendor of the Pure Heart of Bodhi when it begins to shine. The second *kalpa* consists in conquering the subtle (*sūkṣma*) deviant attachment which covers it (i.e. the Pure Heart of Bodhi) when it is about to bloom. The third *kalpa* (consists) in conquering the most subtle (*prasūkṣma*) deviant attachment which obscures the splendor of the Great Wisdom in its full radiance.

This division into three *kalpas*, thus interpreted, may be applied also to the steps of popular Buddhism. In fact the gross deviant attachment of the first *kalpa* must be suppressed by the doctrine of the non-existence or vacuity of the 'I', a personality in the personal aggregates (*skandha*); the more subtle deviant attachment of the second *kalpa*, by the doctrine of vacuity of every real *dharma* in the five personal aggregates themselves (all the *dharmas* being only transformations of the *ālaya*). The third *kalpa* consists in abandoning all attachment to the belief (in) and a duality between the subject and the object, and finally in recognizing the complete vacuity, the absence of own nature (*svabhāva*) of all the *dharmas* and of our own heart.

On the basis of the facts contained in the Sūtra and the commentary, it could be concluded that the first *kalpa* corresponds to the doctrine of the Hīnayāna, the second to that of the Mahāyāna and the third to the esoteric doctrine. But in the scholastic classification (HANGYŌ) of Kōbō daishi, the first *kalpa* corresponds to the Hīnayāna, the second to the Triyānavāda,[45] (and) the third to Ekayānavāda[46] which includes the beginning of the esoteric teaching.

F. THE TEN EARTHS (DAŚABHŪMI)

In exoteric Buddhism in general the state of Buddha can be attained only after passing through the fifty steps of 'degrees' (i=?*avasthā*), namely, ten degrees of faith (*śraddhā*), ten degrees of residence (*vihāra*), ten degrees of practice (*caryā*), ten degrees of dedication (of one's merit to others) (*pariṇāmana*) and the ten earths (*bhūmi*). He who has entered the state of Buddha further attains equal awakening (TŌGAKU = ?*sambodhi*) and marvellous awakening (MYŌGAKU = ?*abhisambodhi*). But in esoteric Buddhism the course of redemption comprises only two steps called "before the ten Earths" and "the ten Earths".

The step (called) "before the ten Earths" is accessible to the non-Buddhists; the subject still cannot fully perceive the truth of the Pure Heart of Bodhi. It corresponds to the *Trikalpa* and to the step of six Non-fears.

The step of "the ten Earths" is one where the truth of the Pure Heart of Bodhi is perceived. This is the stage of one who has already attained the state of Buddha (Buddhahood).

The ten Earths bear the same names as they do in exoteric Buddhism but a totally different significance is given to them. Indeed, in popular Buddhism the ten Earths are the ten degrees of asceticism, but in esoteric Buddhism they represent the sub-division of the merits of the Pure Heart of Bodhi in ten branches. That is why in the ten Earths there is no (idea of) progress.

The first of these ten Earths, called 'Joyful' (*pramuditā*) is associated with the following passage of the Sūtra: "Master of the

Mysteries, this rubric, Pure Heart of Bodhi of the Bodhisattvas, bears the name of 'Path', along which one begins to be enlightened on the *dharmas*. If the Bodhisattvas devote themselves to its exercises and study, even without long ascetic practices they will easily obtain *samādhi* which removes all the obstacles. He who obtains this *samādhi* will occupy the same ranks as the Buddhas and the Bodhisattvas. Thanks to the force of his fervent conviction, he will accomplish all the Buddha natures (*dharma*), and that without long religious exercises, etc."[47]

The commentary explains the passage in the following terms: "To enter into the Wisdom of the Buddha there are innumerable disciplines of the Means (*upāya*). According to this (esoteric) sect, one may enter directly into the discipline of the Pure Heart of Bodhi. He who enters into this discipline penetrates by this very (act) the domain of all the Tathāgatas."[48] This explanatory note means to say that the ten Earths are identical with the state of Buddha.

"The Path (on which) one begins to be enlightened on the *dharmas*" (*prathamadharmālokamukha*) is the step where one bathes in the splendor of the wisdom of the very Pure Heart of Bodhi. "The *samādhi* which wards off the obstacles" (*sarvanīvaraṇavis-kambhi-samādhi*) serves to eliminate the residue (*vāsanā*) of the three deviant attachments, more or less subtle, which one has already discarded in the triple *kalpa*. A little later the Sūtra says: "and then, O Master of the Mysteries, (having arrived at) the stage of the practice of profound faith (*śraddhādhimukticaryābhūmi*), one examines thoroughly the three hearts (*citta*) and with the knowledge of the incommensurable perfections (*pāramitā*) meditates on the four persuasions (= means of attracting sentient beings). The stage of the profound faith is absolute, incommensurable, (and) inconceivable. The ten hearts are established there, and this gives birth to infinite knowledge, etc."[49]

The commentary explains that passage as follows: "For the doctrinal position of this Sūtra the ten Earths of residence (*vihāra-bhūmi*), beginning from and above the Pure Heart of Bodhi are all in the practice of the profound faith (*śraddhādhimukti*); it is the domain of only the Buddhas. It is called the Earth of Omniscience of outcome accomplishment (*niṣṭhasarvajñānabhūmi*)."

The "three hearts" referred to in the Sūtra are placed in relation with the three terms of the Triple Formula, and the commentary (p. 604, c20-26) divides the ten Earths in such a way as to make them correspond to the three terms. The first Earth corresponds to the first term: "To develop the Heart of Bodhi which is the first cause". The following Earths from the second to the seventh correspond to the second term: "Great Compassion is the root". Finally, the three last (Earths) correspond to the third term: "The means leading to salvation are the outcome".[50]

Thus considered in the light of the Triple Formula, the Earths of the second (sub-division) mentioned above come within the altruistic discipline. They have for goal the redemption of others, and thus is explained the allusion of the Sūtra to the "four persuasions (of sentient beings)", viz. giving (*dāna*), agreeable speech (*priyavāditā*) performing of aims (*arthacaryā*), and common goals (*samānārthatā*).

This is the next passage of the Sūtra: "The wise man must also reflect at this stage the profound faith in omniscience; then crossing the (third) *kalpa* he elevates himself into this stage". This passage of the Sūtra signifies that the practising (devotee) of the Shingon before penetrating the ten Earths must leave behind the three *kalpas* or devious attachments, gross, subtle, and very subtle.

According to the commentary, the ten Earths, though identical with the state of Buddha, do not yet constitute the final step of the veritable "marvellous Awakening". Indeed, as a sequel to the passage just quoted from the Sūtra it adds: "He elevates himself into this stage (of the profound faith), one of whose four divisions surpasses the profound faith". The commentary explains this as follows: "Beyond the three *citta* corresponding to the three terms of the Triple Formula, there is still (in this stage of the profound faith) an Earth of the Buddha to be discovered. This is the Heart of the Supreme Means (*?uttarottara-upāya-citta*). When this fourth Heart is attained, one obtains what is called the Earth of omniscience of outcome. This is why the Sūtra says that of the four divisions (of the stage of profound faith), it is the fourth *citta* (lying beyond the first three) and surpasses (even this stage of) the profound faith."[51]

G. THE SIX NON-FEARS (ṢAṆNIRBHAYA)

The *Dainichikyō* explains that to destroy the illusions of our passions and to retrieve the original Pure Heart of Bodhi, two ways have been imposed on us. The first is that of Trikalpa (SANGŌ) which consists in overcoming the three kinds of passionate attachment. The second is that of the six Non-Fears, which we shall now examine. These two ways simultaneously precede the entry into the first of the ten Earths. These constitute the discipline which is called "Before the Earths (see the preceding section). What is the relation between the Trikalpa and the six Non-Fears? The Trikalpa is the passage from popular Buddhism to esoteric Buddhism. The six Non-Fears, on the other hand, belong to esoterism from the very beginning. All the divinities of the *maṇḍala* are adored; and helped with the practice of the Three Mysteries (body, speech, and mind), the road leading once more to the original Pure Heart of Bodhi is opened. The Trikalpa is the negative aspect. It is explained as representing principally the complete destruction of the illusions born of our passions. (On the other hand) the six Non-Fears are rather the positive aspects. They stand for the augmentation of the splendor of the Pure Heart of Bodhi as a result of this destruction (of illusions). The commentary presents successively the points of view of popular Buddhism and of the practising (devotee) of the Shingon regarding each of the six Non-Fears.

(1) Non-Fear of the Good (*ṣaṇnirbhaya,* ZEN-MUI):[52] From the popular viewpoint, it concerns a worldly being, a simple man, or a god, who is plunged into evil but who after he has re-awakened himself to moral good by the practice of the five Prohibitions and the ten good actions, is capable of avoiding the sorrows of evil destinies and of (thus) gaining peace. For the faithful of the Shingon, this step consists in penetrating into the *maṇḍala* and undertaking the observance of the Triple Mystery (*triguhya*).

(2) Non-Fear of the Body (*kāyanirbhaya,* SHIN-MUI): Meditating on the impurity of his body, the worldly being gives up the attachment he feels in regard to the 'I' and arrives at (the stage where) he has no more any sentiment of fear. He has become a *śrāvaka*, a Buddhist. (On the other hand), by the practice of the Triple Mystery, the Faithful follower of the Shingon comes to see the form of divinity with the eyes of the heart.

(3) Non-Fear of non-'I' (*nairātmyanirbhaya,* MUGA-MUI): Knowing that his body is a momentary combination of the five personal aggregates (*pañcaskandhasamudaya*), the *śrāvaka* conceives of the absence of all human personality, the vacuity of *pudgala* (NINGŪMUGA). He becomes an arhat. (On the contrary,) by the exercise of *yoga* the faithful follower of the Shingon meditates upon the unconditioned nature of this heart (and) himself comes to destroy the attachment to, and the pride in his 'I'.

(4) Non-Fear of *dharmas* (*dharmanirbhaya,* HŌ-MUI): The arhat conceives a part of the vacuity of the *dharmas* of the five personal aggregates. He becomes a Pratyekabuddha. The faithful

H. DOCTRINAL SCHEME OF THE FIRST CHAPTER

trikalpa
- 1st kalpa —
  - (1) sat (the good)
  - (2) kāya (body)
  - (3) nairātmya (non-self)
  - (4) dharma (natures)
- 2nd kalpa
  - (5) dharmanairātmya (non-self of natures)
- 3rd kalpa
  - (6) sarvadharmasamatā (sameness of all natures)

(1)–(6): ṣaṇnirbhaya (six Non-Fears)

Daśabhumi
1. Pramuditā (Joyful) — bodhicitta (hetu) (Mind of Enlightenment, cause)
2. Vimalā (Pure)
3. Prabhākara (Light-giving)
4. Arcismatī (Radiant)
5. Sudurjayā (Difficult-to-conquer)
6. Abhimukhī (Facing)
7. Dūramgamā (Far-going)

2.–7.: mahākaruṇā (mūla) (Great compassion, root)

8. Acalā (unmoving)
9. Sādhumatī (Good-mind)
10. Dharmameghā (Cloud-of-doctrine)

8.–10.: upāya (niṣṭhā) (Means, outcome)

bodhicitta, mahākaruṇā, upāya: tripada (three terms)

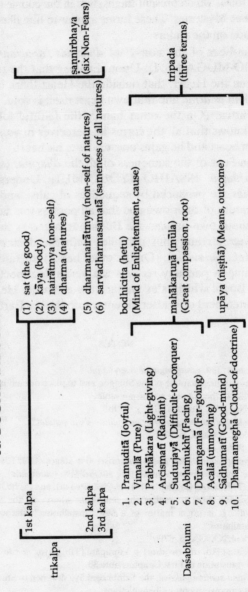

follower of the Shingon understands the independent non-existence of all the forms which present themselves in the course of the exercise of the Three Mysteries. These forms appear to him like the reflection of the moon on the waters.

(5) Non-Fear of the non-'I' of *dharmas* (*dharmanairātmyanirbhaya,* HŌ-MUGA-MUI): Upon realizing that the triple world is nothing but the Heart, that outside the Heart there is not a single independent *dharma* and that own heart itself is void, one becomes a Bodhisattva. (On the other hand,) the faithful follower of the Shingon knows that all the forms he perceives in *yoga* are aspects of his own heart and he gains mastery over his heart.

(6) Non-Fear of the sameness of all the *dharmas* (*sarvadharmasamatānirbhaya,* ISSAIHŌ-BYŌDŌ-MUI): Understanding that all *dharmas* are produced by sequences of cause and effect, have never a nature of their own and that all possess this same nature of being without own-nature, the Bodhisattva grasps the equality of all the *dharmas* and thus complies with the doctrine of 'Single Vehicle' (*ekayānavāda*). (On the other hand,) the faithful follower of the Shingon partially realizes the veritable aspect of the Pure Heart of Bodhi which is as immaculate as Space. He will attain a full enlightenment only after his entry into the ten Earths.

NOTES

1. *Mantracaryā*; Tib. *gsang sngags kyi spyod pa.*
2. For access to the discipline of the Shingon and to place oneself in the *bodhicitta,* the practice of the *mantras* is indispensable.
3. Taishō, No. 1796, Vol. XXXIX, p. 579b[16].
4. *Sems kyi khyad par rim par phye be = citta-viśiṣṭa-paṭala*(?).
5. Taishō, Vol. XXXIX, p. 579b[19].
6. *Ibid.,* p. 579b[27].
7. This development of the *bodhi* comprises five stages (GOTEN) for which the Japanese formula is as follows: (1) HOSSHIN (*cittotpāda*), (2) SHUGYŌ (*caryā*), (3) BODAI (*bodhi*), (4) NEHAN (*nirvāṇa*), and (5) HŌBEN (*upāya*).
8. It suffices for them to realize the *bodhicitta* where, all the while, they are "installed". It is not a matter of a new "installation" succeeding a state of "non-installation".
9. Taishō, Vol. XXXIX, p. 579b[21].
10. Vajradhara (Tib. *rdo-rje 'dsin*) = Vajrapāṇi (Tib. *phyag na rdo rje* or *lag na rdo rje*), cf. translation of First Chapter, note 30.
11. *Adhiṣṭhāna-sambhogakāya,* the Sambhogakāya destined to 'initiate' the beings with his empowerment, his benedictions.
12. Taishō, Vol. XXXIX, p. 583a[13].
13. Cf. above, "A. The title of this chapter", with note 7.

14. The translation of the first chapter, with notes 76-78.
15. *Ibid.*, with note 81.
16. *Ibid.*, with note 145.
17. *Ibid.*, with note 173.
18. *Ibid.*, with note 207.
19. *Ibid.*, with note 264.
20. *Ibid.*, with note 352.
21. *Ibid.*, with note 414.
22. *Ibid.*, with note 418.
23. *Ibid.*, with note 429.
24. Taishō, Vol. XXXIX, p. 586c^{7}.
25. Taishō, Vol. LXXVII, p. 407c^{16}.
26. Taishō, Vol. XXXIX, p. 586c^{119}.
27. Taishō, Vol. XXXIX, p. 587a^{4}.
28. Taishō, Vol. XXXIX, p. 587a^{16}.
29. Taishō, Vol. XXXIX, p. 587a^{28}.
30. Taishō, Vol. XVIII, p. 1c^{1}; the translation of 1st chap., with note 84.
31. Taishō, Vol. XXXIX, p. 587b^{11}.
32. Taishō, Vol. XVIII, p. 1c^{3}.
33. Taishō, Vol. XXXIX, p. 587c^{2}.
34. Edition of Narthang. *rgyud sde,* bundle Ta, f. 303b^{5}.
35. Taishō, Vol. XVIII, p. 1c^{6} tr. of 1st chap., with note 91.
36. Taishō, Vol. XXXIX, p. 588a^{3}.
37. Taishō, Vol. XVIII, p. 1c^{1}; tr. of 1st chap., with notes 92-93.
38. Taishō, Vol. XXXIX, p. 588a^{9}.
39. Taishō, Vol. XVIII, p. 1c$^{9\text{-}19}$; tr. of 1st chap., right after note 93.
40. *Ibid.*, 1c^{20}; tr. of 1st chap., with notes 108-110.
41. Taishō, Vol. XVIII, p. 3a^{28}; tr. of 1st chap., with notes 351-353.
42. *Ibid.*, p. 3b^{22}; tr. of 1st chap., with notes 406-408.
43. Taishō, Vol. XXXIX, p. 600c^{19}.
44. Edition of Narthang, *rgyud sde,* bundle Ta, f. 310a^{4}.
45. That is to say, according of the HOSSŌ and SANRON sects which distinguish between the Śrāvakayāna, Pratyekabuddhayāna, and Bodhisattvayāna.
46. That is to say, according to the TENDAI sect with the *Saddharmapuṇḍarīka-sūtra,* and the KEGON sect with the *Avatasakasūtra*..
47. Taishō, Vol. XVIII, p. 1c^{26} tr. of 1st chap., with notes 128, 129 and 141.
48. Taishō, Vol. XXXIX, p. 590a^{9}.
49. Taishō, Vol. XVIII, p. 3b^{25}; tr. of 1st chap., with notes 409-414.
50. Taishō, Vol. XXXIX, p. 604c^{12}.
51. Taishō, Vol. XXXIX, p. 605b^{21}.
52. See the translation of 1st chap., with note 418.

PART V

SUMMARY OF CHAPTER II AND FOLLOWING

CHAPTER II. ACCESSORIES AND MANTRAS NECESSARY FOR ACCESS TO THE MAṆḌALA[1]

This chapter explains the correct manner of executing the *maṇḍala* (Tib. *dkyil 'khor*) and performing the initiation (*abhiṣeka*) so as to realize effectively the teachings contained in the first chapter on the access of the officiant to the Heart of Bodhi. To construct the *maṇḍala* and perform the *abhiṣeka* all the circumstances and materials are to be prepared. First, it is indispensable to proceed to the empowerment (KAJI = *adhiṣṭhāna*) with the mantras (Tib. *gsang sngags*) of the Buddha. Hence the title of this chapter.

The *maṇḍala* with which we are concerned here is called GUEN MANDARA,[2] *maṇḍala* relating to the accessories, as against "the esoteric *maṇḍala* in the heart" which has been explained in chapters XI and XIII. Originally, the true thought of the Buddha was to explain that the esoteric *maṇḍala* is in the heart of all the beings. Now the question is to render it effectively visible. This is a kind of subterfuge for the good of all beings.[3]

The contents of this chapter may be broadly divided into three parts: the first part related to the preparation of the emplacement lasting seven days; the second, to the consecration belonging to the ceremony; the third, to the mantras for the consecration.

We shall summarize below these three parts in the presented order.

In the beginning of the chapter, following a question posed by the Vajra-Holder, the Buddha pronounces the words: "Now I explain the theme (*dharmaparyāya*) of omniscient knowledge which fully suffices for the practice of the execution of a *maṇḍala*".

There is definition of the abilities which qualify one to become an *ācārya* (Tib. *slob dpon*) who will make the preparation for the emplacement and its consecration; as well as definition of the requisite qualifications of the person who wants to become a disciple. As to the place that may be chosen for emplacement of the *maṇḍala*.

From this place of land are to be removed gravel, potsherds, insects of all kinds, rubbish, etc. A favorable day has to be chosen, and worship made to the local deity.[4] There are questions and answers concerning the motives behind making the *maṇḍala*. After consolidation of the ground with cow-dung (*gomaya*) and urine of cows (*go-mūtra*), it is purified with perfumed water, (the proficient) concentrating himself (all the while) on the thought of the five Buddhas.[5] Then with sandal powder one draws an outline sketch of the *maṇḍala* comprising nine emplacements reserved for the five Buddhas, the other Buddhas, the Bodhisattvas, the "Mother of Buddha", Gaganalocanā (=Buddhalocanā),Padmapāṇi, Vajrapāṇi, Acala, Trailokyavijaya, and for the *ācārya*. This is what is called "the *maṇḍala* with nine emplacements in sandal powder" (BYAKU-DAN-KUI-MANDARA). This is a preliminary and provisional sketch.[6]

Next are explained once again the qualities required of the disciple and how many persons may be allowed (to view) the *maṇḍala*-construction. There follow questions and answers on the denomination of this *maṇḍala*.

After this, with a view to conferring on the disciple the mastery of *samaya* he is given a tooth-pick (SHIMOKU = *dantakāṣṭha*. Tib. *so shing*), a thread of *vajra* (KONGŌSEN = *vajrasūtra,* Tib. *rdo rje'i skud*) composed of threads of five colors symbolizing the five Wisdoms of Buddha.[7] Then, after interpreting the dreams which the disciple has had, it is judged whether or not he is endowed with the gift of *siddhi*; and he is conferred the *śīla* of knowledge without obstacle of the three times. To purify the heart of the disciple, he is made to drink water containing pure perfume.

These preliminary explanations on the manner of making the *maṇḍala* and performing the consecration being over, the Sūtra explains how the emplacement is measured and how the compartments of the different Buddhas are separated and, in a detailed manner, how the forms of all the divinities are sketched.

Then it explains that even when one has the possibility of knowing the doctrine of the Shingon, it is difficult to penetrate into the *maṇḍala*. There is question and answer regarding the coloring of the *maṇḍala*. (Then,) the way of the five kinds of *samaya* (GOSHU-SAMMAI-DŌ), i.e. of the Buddhas, Bodhisattvas, Śrāvakas, Pratyekabuddhas, and Loka (human beings). (Also,) the five kinds of mantras; the mystic significance of the letters of the Sanskrit syllabary. (As well as) eulogy of the superior virtue of the Shingon doctrine; enumeration of offerings that may be made to the *maṇḍala*; the kinds of flowers, perfumes, food, (and) lamps.

The ceremony of initiation (*abhiṣeka*): The disciple is brought near the enclosure of the *maṇḍala* (MANDARA-DŌJŌ); how he will be introduced there; how the operation of the *homa* of *śāntika* (SOKUSAI-GOMA), propitiatory rite to eliminate all the faults of the disciple, will take place; how to erect next to the *maṇḍala* a second "altar of *abhiṣeka*" (KWANJŌDAN or SHŌGAKUDAN), where consecrated water (KAJI-SUI) is to be poured on the disciple's head. This "unction", properly called, is followed by curious rites of which the following is noteworthy: The *ācārya* points at the disciple's eyes a metallic wand (KONCHŪ, also called KOMPI); the Tibetan text of the Sūtra has *gser gi thur* ("wand of gold"), in the form of a *vajra* with rounded points and besmeared with drugs, which is supposed to operate symbolically, like the surgeon's probe (*śalākā*) for the troubled vision (*timira*), which is nescience.[8] Then he gives him a brilliant mirror,[9] in which he is reflected and which symbolizes the absence of own-nature (*niḥsvabhāva*) of the *dharmas*. Finally he puts before him a metallic wheel (HŌRIN = *dharmacakra*), and makes him whistle through a conch (HŌRA=*śaṇka*) which signifies that he must preach the Doctrine to others in order to rescue them. While extending these various objects to the disciple, the master recites many *gāthā*. Finally, he advises the disciple to not spare even his own life in dedication to the Dharma for the well-being of others, and not to hold back the Doctrine. Thus he is conferred the *śīla*[10] and the ceremony of unction comes to an end.

Thereafter the Sūtra explains the merits of the unction received on entering the great *maṇḍala* (NYŪDAN-KWANJŌ). Then follow the sixteen *mantras* recited in this ceremony.

This chapter, which extends from the middle of the first volume (KWAN) to the middle of the second volume is by far the longest chapter of the Sūtra.

In his commentary the translator Śubhakarasiṃha describes in detail the concrete methods effectively practised in India for the construction of the *maṇḍala* and for the ceremony of unction. His explanatory notes on these form an indispensable complement to the Sūtra.

The maṇḍala described in this chapter is the Mahākaruṇāgarbha *maṇḍala* which includes the personages mentioned below:

	Divinities	Followers
Central Lotus	9	
First enclosure:		
Quarters of universal knowledge	3	
— of Avalokiteśvara	7	
— of Vajrapāṇi	5	4
— of Vidyādhara	2	
Second enclosure:		
Quarters of Mañjuśrī	7	5
— Sarvanīvaraṇaviṣkambhī	9	2
— Kṣitigarbha	6	
— Ākāṣagarbha	6	
Third enclosure:		
Quarters of Śākyamuni	45	
	99	11

There are 110 divinities in all.

The commentary adds 43 others to this list, making the total 164 (*sic.*for 153). But the GENZU-MANDARA (the *maṇḍala* of present iconography) = we have examples of it executed in Japan from the time of Kōbō daishi = represents a much higher number of them. One counts here 414 divinities.

CHAPTER III. ON THE SUPPRESSION OF THE OBSTACLES[11]

At the beginning of this chapter Vajrapāṇi puts three questions to the Buddha: (1) When the rite of initiation is celebrated, how can obstacles of all sorts be avoided? (2) What *mantras* are to be recited? (3) What is the fruit (result) that may be obtained? The present chapter contains the reply to the first question.

When one makes a *maṇḍala* or celebrates the initiation, it easily happens that in spite of everything obstacles of all sorts present themselves. These are of two kinds, viz. spiritual and metereological. Among the spiritual obstacles the principal one is the agitation that may take place in the heart of the practising (devotee). The Sūtra says: "Obstacles are born in our own hearts. They are the consequence of our cupidity in the past. To get rid of the causes (of obstacles), it is necessary to concentrate on the Heart of Bodhi".[12] And it is necessary to invoke Acala-vidyārāja (FUDŌ-MYŌŌ) who personifies the firmness of the Heart of Bodhi. The metereological obstacles are the inconveniences caused by rain, wind, etc. As formerly the initiation (*abhiṣeka*) used to be performed in open air, these obstacles were unavoidable. In such cases, consecration (KAJI) and meditation (KWAN-NEN) are recommended.

CHAPTER IV. STOREHOUSE OF CURRENT MANTRAS[13]

Thanks to the original vow of the Buddhas and the Bodhisattvas, there is a miraculous power in the *mantras* so that in pronouncing them one acquires boundless merit. In reply to the second question of Chapter III, "What mantras are to be recited," Samantabhadra and the other Bodhisattvas adoring Mahāvairocana each enter into *samādhi,* and while entering the Great Maṇḍala of the 'womb' of the Great Compassion (*mahākaruṇāgarbha*) through the unblemished door of the *dharmadhātu,* recite their mantras. Since the Bodhisattvas and the other personages have well entered the world of the Knowledge as realized by the Tathāgata, the practising (devotee) who would penetrate the mantra of each of these personages will end up in finding access to the Knowledge of the Tathāgata. The mantras cited in this chapter number 118.

CHAPTER V. THE WORLDLY SIDDHI[14]

That which is 'worldly' (SEKEN = *laukika,* Tib. *'jig rten pa*) is opposed to the supramundane (SHUSSEKEN = *lokottara,* Tib. *'jig rten las 'das pa*). The supramundane domain disallows all expression as such; the Buddha takes recourse to phenomena of this lowly world to explain supramundane varieties. Humanity is familiar with these phenomena. It is only by miraculous action that the Buddha could penetrate the domain of the supramundane truths.

This chapter contains the reply to the third question of the Vajra-Holder (cf. Chapter III): "How can the fruit be attained?" The fruit is obtained as the result of the practice of the mantras. This practice involves four operations called 'recitation' [of the mantras], (NENJU = *jāpa,* Tib. *bzlas brjod*):

(1) SHINSŌ NENJU, contemplative recitation sub-divided into four exercises:

(a) The Heart of Bodhi: to recite while contemplating in his heart the form of the letters of the mantras.
(b) The practice of the sounds: (consisting) in distinguishing well the sound of the mantras.
(c) The practice of the sentences: by understanding properly the significance of the words of the mantras.
(d) The practice of respiration: (consists) in regulating the breath while contemplating the mutual penetration of the faithful (= the officiant) and the Buddha.

(2) SENJIJIHŌ NENJU, preliminary recitation of the mantras which accompany the worship made before the actual offering with perfumes, flowers, etc.

(3) GUJI NENJU, recitation accompanying real offerings. Thus, different objects like perfumes, flowers, etc. are effectively offered.

(4) SAJŌ NENJU, recitation of realization. It is with this that one realizes the *siddhi* by the force of the mantras.

The practices numbers 2, 3 and 4 are called "practices of the three moons".[15] It is a comparison between the moon reflected in the waters and in contemplations, namely, in the "Water of the Heart" of the (original) purity of *samādhi*.

CHAPTER VI. MANIFESTATION OF SIDDHI[16]

The Sanskrit word *siddhi* (Tib. *dngos grub*) signifies the "accomplishment of desires". To 'manifest' *siddhi* is to render this accomplishment visible. There are two kinds of desires, viz. mundane and supramundane. In the preceding chapter the Sūtra dealt with mundane *siddhi*. In the present chapter it will be the question of supramundane *siddhi*.

To explain all the manifestations of this *siddhi* the Sūtra states that the mantras possess "in a natural fashion, and after the manner of the *dharma*" (HŌNI) virtues which are inherent in them and which are due to the empowerment (*adhiṣṭhāna*) of the Buddha which exerts upon them a profound and unimaginable process.

Next is explained the "omnipresent" mantra (MUSHO-FUSHI NO SHINGON) which is very important in this Sūtra. This is the mantra: *Namaḥ sarvatathāgatebhyo viśvamukhebhyaḥ sarvathā a ā aṃ aḥ*.

Next is explained that thanks to the triple power (SAN-RIKI) of his own merits (*puṇya*, Tib. *bsod nams*), the empowerment (*adhiṣṭhāna*) by the Buddha and by the *dharmadhātu,* the faithful one practising the mantras finds all his vows fulfilled.

The mantra of Mahāvairocana Buddha can conquer the four Māra-s, deliver the beings from the six destinies (*gati*), and procure omniscience. This is the formula: *Namaḥ samantabuddhānām a vi ra hūṃ khaṃ*. These syllables *a, vi, ra, hūṃ, khaṃ* correspond to the seed syllables (*bīja*) of the five elements, namely, *a*=earth; *va*=water; *ra*=fire; *ha*=wind; *kha*=space (*ākāsa*).[17]

Next is explained the *maṇḍalas* of the five elements and how the practising (devotee) by identifying in contemplation his own body with the five elements can make himself so perfect as to attain even the state of the Buddha Mahāvairocana. Though there exists mantras of many kinds, it is the letter *a* (the first letter of the Sanskrit alphabet) which constitutes the fundamental mantra of Mahāvairocana. That is why by the contemplation of only the letter *a* the practising (devotee) comes to attain the intuitive knowledge of the real essence of his own heart and at the same time raises himself as far as supreme *siddhi*.

CHAPTER VII. THE ACCOMPLISHMENT OF SIDDHI[18]

The two preceding chapters have explained mundane and supramundane *siddhi*. The first is called "characterized *siddhi*" (USŌ NO SHIJJI),[19] and the supramundane siddhi "*siddhi* without a particular character" (MUSŌ NO SHIJJI).[20] The "formal *siddhi*" is limited, having certain characters without having others. The "*siddhi* without form" has nothing relative in it; its character comprises all the characters. The characters of the two (kinds of) *siddhi* being thus defined, the present chapter explains from where come the *siddhis* of the Shingon.

The Vajra-Holder eulogizes the Shingon, the doctrine of the mantras which sum up all the letters and is like the ocean where rivers lose their identity. He would like to know the original of *siddhi* of the Shingon, to which the Buddha replies in the following terms:

> "The *maṇḍala* is called the mental site (ISHO) of Mahāsattva (the practising devotee of the Shingon); when the heart of all the mantras is known, the fruit of *siddhi* may be attained... When the practising (devotee) of the Shingon knows the radiant way of the heart [of the Shingon], colors (that is to say, the objects of the six kinds of perception, *vijñāna*) become resplendent, and the practising (devotee) comes to see the perfect Buddha, the

venerated Biped, and while contemplating him, obtains the eternal body of the first (type of) *siddhi*."[21]

It is then stated that the contemplation of the letters *aṃ* and *ra* enables one to attain *siddhi*. The principal objective of this chapter is to explain that the *siddhi* is a possibility to originate in the heart of every being.

CHAPTER VIII. MAṆḌALA PRAXIS BY SETTING IN MOTION THE WHEEL OF SYLLABLES[22]

Setting the wheel of syllables in motion (*cakrākṣaraparivartana*) consists in meditating on the cycle of the syllables of the *dhāraṇī* in a circular order. By this means, one can practise a sort of [interior] *maṇḍala*. The preceding chapter has explained the interior *siddhis*. To make (the discussion) complete, the present chapter shows that one may contemplate the syllable *a* which is empowered by all the Tathāgatas:

> "Master of the Mysteries! If all the Bodhisattvas who cultivate the practices of the Bodhisattvas according to the doctrine of the Shingon desire to see the Buddha, if they desire to make offerings to him; if they desire to prove the Heart of Bodhi, participate in the assemblies of the Bodhisattvas, be of service to beings, seek *siddhi* and omniscient knowledge—it will be necessary for them to apply themselves with zeal to this heart of all the Buddhas [that is to say, to the Syllable *a*]."[23]

The Sūtra then explains how to draw a square *maṇḍala* in color showing three circular enclosures and consisting of twelve quarters. The twelve quarters are: (1) the central platform with Mahāvairocana; (2) the quarters of omniscience (HENCHI); (3) Avalokiteśvara; (4) Vajrapāṇi; (5) Vajradhara-s [retinue of Vajrapāṇi]; (6) Vidyādhara; (7) the four great [female] guardians; (8) Śākyamuni; (9) Mañjuśri; (10) Sarvanīvaraṇaviskambhī; (11) Kṣitigarbha; and (12) Ākāsagarbha.

This *maṇḍala* is very much simpler than that described in Chapter II. For each one of the quarters, the text gives precise information only for the principal divinity, his seed syllable (*bīja*) symbolic attribute (SAMAYA-GYŌ), whose image is the object of detailed prescriptions; but the secondary divinities are not described. The seed syllables are of particular importance because the interior contemplation rests particularly on them. From this *maṇḍala* the Sūtra equally prescribes a very simple rite of initiation (*abhiṣeka*).

CHAPTER IX. THE MYSTIC MUDRĀS[24]

Along with the symbolic attributes (SAMAYA-GYŌ), the seed syllables, etc., the *mudrā*-s (Tib. *phyag rgya*) are one of the perceptible manifestations of the *samaya* characteristic of the Buddhas. When the practising (devotee) of the Shingon makes an empowerment of himself with the help of the mystic *mudra*-s of the Tathāgata he is assimilated to the body of *dharmadhātu* of the Buddha. This chapter first states the merits of these mystic *mudrā*-s:

"Master of the Mysteries, there are symbolic indications[25] which are identified with the ornaments of the Tathāgatas and with the orientation (SHU = *gati*) of the *dharmadhātu* (that is to say, with the body of the Tathāgata that is oriented towards the *dharmadhātu*). If the Bodhisattva [the faithful follower of the Shingon] adorns his body with these, he makes himself conspicuous in the great assemblies of all the Buddhas by virtue of his great banner of *Bodhi*, even if he resides in *samsāra* and moves on through the destinies (*gati*). All the Devas, Nāgas, Yakṣas, Gandharvas, Asuras, Garuḍas, Kinnaras, Mahoragas, human and non-human beings, etc., adore him, turn towards him, receive their instructions (from him) and put them into practice."[26]

Next are enumerated the thirty-one mudrā-s and mantras of the Tathāgatas, symbolizing their virtues, attributes, ornaments, the conch, the seat, the *uṣṇīṣa,* etc., and the fifty-seven mudrā-s and mantras of all the divinities beginning from Bodhisattva Maitreya and the forty-five mudrā-s and mantras of the other gods.

CHAPTER X. THE WHEEL OF SYLLABLES[27]

When it does not move, the *akṣara* (Tib. *yi ge*) (wheel) represents the immobility of the Heart of Bodhi. Moreover, being without end, it represents the production of all the syllables beginning with *a* which is the seed syllable of Mahāvairocana. Just as the *cakra* (Tib. *'khor lo*) when in movement breaks everything, so our Heart of Bodhi breaks (i.e. annihilates) all the defilements (*kleśa*) and nescience (*avidyā*). Furthermore, the character *a* of the Buddha is at the basis of the essence of *bodhi* and hence the revolution of the wheel is profitable for all beings.

The wheel of the syllables is so called because all the syllables proceed from the seed syllable *a*, just as the spokes branch out from the nave. This chapter explains the manner of contemplating all these syllables.

According to esoteric teaching the letter *a* signifies the "Heart of Bodhi"; *ā*, the exercise of the career of *bodhi; aṃ*, participation in Enlightenment; *aḥ*, the entry into *nirvāṇa*.

The gods mentioned in the *Dainichikyō* are grouped into three clans (BU =*kula*, Tib. *rigs*), namely, Buddha, Padma, and Vajra. The seed syllable of the Buddha clan is *a*. The seed syllable of the Padma clan is *sa*. And that of the Vajra clan is *va*.

To the practising (devotee) the present chapter prescribes the way of contemplating on four regions of his own body the cycle of the syllables or the letters in the written form *siddham*. For example, in contemplating the syllables *kạ, kha, ga, gha,* etc. on the forehead, he comes to understand the Heart of Bodhi of the various gods of the three clans. In contemplating the same syllables in the lengthened form, i.e. *kā, khā, gā, ghā* in his throat, he fully realizes the practices of *bodhi* in the three clans. When he contemplates these syllables in a nasalized form, i.e. *kaṃ, khaṃ, gaṃ, ghaṃ,* in his heart, he participates in *bodhi* itself. When he contemplates on his navel the syllables *kaḥ, khaḥ, gaḥ,* and *ghaḥ,* he is a similitude of *nirvāṇa*. Finally, he arrives at (a stage when he is able) to make the Wheel (Disc) of Dharma rotate as is done by the Tathāgata Mahāvairocana. This is called the contemplation of the Wheel of the Three Clans on four regions [of the body] (SAMBU-SHISHŌ-RIN-KWAN).

CHAPTER XI. THE ESOTERIC MAṆḌALA[28]

This chapter expounds that Mahāvairocana enters the *samādhi* of the *Dharmadhātukośa*, then the *samādhi* called 'stretching of the lion', of the store-house of ornaments of the equality to the Tathāgata.[29] Thus he comes to accomplish the grand vow of rescuing the world of innumerable beings.

The essential insistence of the chapter is to admonish the faithful follower to contemplate in his body the five 'circles' of the elements, namely, earth, water, fire, wind and space, and liken his body to a *stūpa* of the *dharmadhātu* (*stūpa* of the five elements).[30] Next is given the "king of the mantras" in twelve syllables which serves in contemplating the equality of the *dharmadhātu,* that is to say, the identity of beings with the omniscient Tathāgata.[31]

With a view to resolving all doubt, the Vajra-Holder then asks forty-nine questions concerning the *Mahākaruṇāgarbha-maṇḍala* (described in Chapter II). The interpretation as given in Chapter II is still of a 'mundane' order. It is based chiefly on the 'grand compassion' (*mahākaruṇā*) for the novice for whom the master wants to procure access to the *maṇḍala*. The *maṇḍala* with which we are concerned in this chapter is what the *ācārya* profoundly versed in the doctrine reveals when he enters into *samādhi* after having obtained the *siddhi* of *yoga*. Here the initiation is of a greater spiritual order: it is an "ablution by the heart" (ISHIN-KWANJŌ).

Each of the twelve quarters receives an interpretation of the grand *maṇḍala* under the following names: Esoteric *maṇḍala* of Mahāvairocana, esoteric *maṇḍala* of the Buddha clan, of the clan of Padma, of the clan of Vajra, of the Vidyādharas, of the mother of the Buddhas (Buddhalocanā), of all the Bodhisattvas, of Śākyamuni, of Mañjuśrī, of Nīvaraṇaviṣkambhī, of Kṣitigarbha, and of Ākāsagarbha.

These *maṇḍalas* serve to promote the merits which lie hidden in our own heart. That is why they receive the epithet HIMITSU, 'secret, esoteric, mystic' (*guhya,* Tib. *gsang ba*).

CHAPTER XII. METHOD OF ACCESS TO ESOTERIC MAṆḌALA[32]

This chapter sums up in a few stanzas called *udāna* (Tib. *ched du brjod pa'i sde*) the reflections (or, remarks) on the way of entering the esoteric *maṇḍala* described in the preceding chapter. These stanzas are expanded in the Commentary. The master who is very familiar with this esoteric *maṇḍala* introduces his disciple there. And by the contemplation of the cycle of syllables that the disciple makes on his own body, he shakes off internally all the obstacles and he causes to be born and show life in him the *bodhi* of innate purity. Thanks to the syllables which the disciple imagines on the different parts of his body, he succeeds in contemplating the "king of the mantras in twelve syllables" and (thus) in realizing his equality with the Buddhas.

CHAPTER XIII. ACCESS TO THE STATUS OF ESOTERIC MAṆḌALA[33]

In conformity with the explanations given in the preceding chapter, this chapter elucidates the status in which one finds oneself in equality with the Buddhas in Dharmakāya. The "access to the status of maṇḍala" consists in contemplating on the "king of lotus" which has eight petals and which blooms in our own heart and symbolizes the identification of our heart with the *maṇḍala* itself.

To explain this process, the Sūtra says the following:

Then the World-Honored One spoke to the Vajra-Holder: "O man of good birth (*kulaputra*), listen carefully to (what I say about) the *maṇḍala* of the Interior Heart. O Master of Mysteries this depth of ourselves is the nature of Dharmadhātu. By the empowerment of mantras and mudrā-s, create the empowerment of your heart! It is pure by nature; and protecting it with the *karmavajra* (*vajra* with four branches, i.e. cruciform), purify it and cleanse it of all blemishes!..... The maṇḍala [of the Interior Heart] is square (and has) four doors. One enters it facing to the West; it being completely surrounded by circumference paths. In the interior there is the Grand Lotus-king with eight petals which blooms in our spirit.[34] From the stalk emerge pistils and stamens that are ornamented and very beautiful. In the center of this lotus is seen the Tathāgata. He has the most excellent body in the whole world. He has surpassed the depth of body, speech, and mind, and has arrived at the depth of his heart. He has obtained the supreme and delicious fruit. There stands on the eastern side [of Mahāvairocana] Hōdō Nyorai (Ratnaketu Tathāgatas); on the southern side, Kaifukeō Nyorai (Samkusumitarāja Tathāgata); on the northern side, Koin Nyorai (Divyadundubhimeghanirghoṣa Tathāgata); on the western side, Muryōju Nyorai (Amitāyus Tathāgata); on the south-eastern side. Fugen Bosatsu (Samantabhadra Bodhisattva); on the north-eastern side, Kwanjizai Bosatsu (Avalokiteśvara Bodhisattva); on the south-western side, Myōkichijō Dōji (Mañjuśrī Kumāra); and on the north-western side, Jishi Bosatsu (Maitreya Bodhisattva). Among all the pistils and stamens is placed the mother (Buddhalocanā) of the Buddhas and Bodhisattvas, as well as the [Bodhisattva] followers of the *samādhi* of the six Perfections (*pāramitā*). Below is arranged a large number of angry *vidyādhara-s*. Vajra-Holder Bodhisattva, who constitutes the stalk (of the flower), is placed in the middle of an exhaustible and grand ocean. All the devas who are earth inhabitants (JIGOTEN = *bhauma*),[35] and an infinite number of others, surround the flower."[36]

This *maṇḍala* has the form of the corolla of an eight-petalled lotus which constitutes the center of the *Mahākaruṇāgarbha-maṇḍala*. But in the representation of this latter *maṇḍala* called GENZU-MANDARA, the positions of Avalokiteśvara and Maitreya are interchanged.

CHAPTER XIV. THE EIGHT ESOTERIC MUDRĀS[37]

This chapter explains the esoteric eight mudrās and eight mantras relating to the *maṇḍala*, having the form of an eight-petalled lotus, described in the preceding chapter.

The eight esoteric mudrās correspond respectively to the four Buddhas of the cardinal directions, namely, Ratnaketu in the East, Saṃkusumitarāja in the South, Amitābha in the West, and Divyadundubhiṃeghanirghoṣa in the North; and to the four Bodhisattvas of the intermediate directions, namely, Samantabhadra in South-East, Mañjuśrī in the South-West, Maitreya in the North-West, and Avalokiteśvara in the North-East. The reason that the mudrā and the mantra of Mahāvairocana are not explained is that Mahāvairocana sums up in himself all the Buddhas and the Bodhisattvas.

The Sūtra states: "All this is what is called the esoteric mudrās of the Tathāgata Mahāvairocana. These supreme esoteric mudrās must not be communicated to men right away. They may be communicated to one who is already initiated (*abhiṣikta*), whose nature is under control and submissive, who has much application and firmness, who has taken the supreme vow, who respects his master, is not ungrateful, is pure internally and externally, and is ready to sacrifice his life in the pursuit of the Dharma."[38]

CHAPTER XV. OBSERVANCES PRESCRIBED FOR THOSE PRACTISING THE VIDYĀ[39]

This chapter narrates the observances imposed on those who practise the recitation of the *vidyā*-s (Tib. *rig sngags*) or the *mantras* (Tib. *gsang sngags*) for six months (MUTSUKI-NENJU). These mantras are the syllables *a, va, ra, ha, kha;*[40] whether *a* + *va* [earth and water] or *ra* + *ha* [fire and wind] are pervaded by *kha* [space]. One recites each one of these syllables for a month, with the mudras, maṇḍalas, suitable foods, and contemplation on each of the five Buddhas whose syllables are the 'seed' (*type*) (*kha* twice for Mahāvairocana). Of the rest, it is not necessarily a question of actual months; thus the expression "one month" may be understood in the sense of "one recitation". During this practice one must exercise complete control over one's own self and abstain from doing anything bad, with a view to obtaining *siddhi*. The observances thus prescribed are called 'restrictions' (SEIKAI = vrata, Tib. *brtul zhugs*) and are distinguished from the observances which are connected with the profound nature of the subject, his 'mind of enlightenment' (*bodhicitta*) and which are the *śīla*-s properly called (Tib. *tshul khrims*), described in Chapter II.

CHAPTER XVI. TRUE WISDOM OF THE ĀCĀRYA[41]

All the mantras of the maṇḍala are summed up in the syllable *a*. It is the 'heart' of these. This chapter states that the letter *a* is called the true wisdom of the *ācārya*. In fact, all sounds proceed from the syllable *a*. If it did not exist, no other sound would exist. When we contemplate in our heart (*hṛdaya*, Tib. *snying po*), whose nature is fundamentally pure, the letter *a*, the "heart of all the mantras", we shall succeed in realizing the true wisdom of the Tathāgata.

CHAPTER XVII. PLACEMENT OF THE SYLLABLES[42]

The Pure Heart of Bodhi (*śuddhabodhicitta*) is the site of all the syllables (of the Sanskrit syllabary). This chapter states how the practising (devotee), after having installed in the profoundest depth of his Heart of Bodhi the syllable *a* and having arranged all the Sanskrit letters on the various points of his own body, the practising (devotee) transforms his body into a *dharmadhātu-maṇḍala*. Thus he provokes the blossoming of the Buddha's virtues which pre-exist in himself. The conclusion of this chapter on omniscience as the 'principal thing' always present in our heart has been cited in the Introduction.

CHAPTER XVIII. POINTS OF INSTRUCTION AS A MEANS[43]

This chapter deals with the "points of instruction" (*śikṣāpada*, Tib. *bslab pa'i gzhi*), that is to say, the rules which all Bodhisattvas of the Mahāyāna must observe in the course of a wisely conducted discipline and which the practising (devotee) of the Shingon must equally observe as 'means' (*upāya*, Tib. *thabs*), accessories. For them, the fundamental observances consist in those which, on the one hand, make the most of this 'principal thing' of *bodhi*, which is the 'Thought of Enlightenment' (*bodhicitta*) always present in their profound nature (HONSHŌ-KAI or BODAISHINKAI), and besides which are practised in esoterism for a determinate period so that *siddhi* may be obtained (cf. Chapter XV).

The "points of instruction" mentioned here are the following:

(1) Those which consist in avoiding the ten major sins. They are what the Sūtra calls the ten good paths of action (JŪZENGŌDŌ, *daśa-kuśala-karma-patha*). The ten sins are those of the body (murder, theft, lust), those of speech (untruth, rudeness, calumny, verbiage) and those of the mind (greediness, malevolence, heresy).

(2) The five lay moral rules (GOKAI = *śila*) which the lay worshipper (*upāsaka*) Bodhisattva must observe and which consist in avoiding taking life, theft, lust, untruth, and false doctrine.

(3) The four prohibitions (KINKAI = *saṃvara*), which are an innovation of the esoteric school. They relate respectively to blaming the Dharma, abandonment of the *bodhicitta*, miserliness (consisting in not teaching the Dharma), and evil done to living beings. These are, according to the Sūtra, the four fundamental transgressions, against committing which one must guard oneself even at the cost of life. These four prohibitions are defined in Chapter II of the Sūtra[44] as the 'pledge rules' (*samayaśīla*); and in the Commentary[45] as the four 'defeats' (*pārājika;* Tib. *phas pham pa*) of the Tantra canon. He who observes them possesses life in Mantrayāna; he who violates them resembles a corpse. For the religion he is dead.

CHAPTER XIX. EXPLAINING THE PRODUCTION OF THE HUNDRED SYLLABLES[46]

This chapter has explained the syllable *aṃ*, "mantra of the universal radiance of the Hundred Splendors" and how from this syllable *aṃ* the hundred syllables proceed. Being the king of all the mantras, this mantra *aṃ* has the potency of destroying the darkness of all nescience. In this it resembles the disc of the sun which is seen on all sides.

The Buddhas of the three times can obtain enlightenment by contemplating this syllable. That is why this mantra is the direct way to the state of Buddha.

The method of production of the hundred syllables from one syllable is as follows: The five syllables of each of the series *ka*, *ca*, *ṭa*, *ta*, and *pa*, make in all twenty-five syllables. Three other syllables are derived from each of these syllables. For example, from *ka* are derived *ka*, *kaṃ* and *kaḥ*, or the four syllables which symbolize the awakening of the Heart of Bodhi, the religious practices, the obtaining of Bodhi, and the entry into nirvāṇa. In this way, finally the total becomes a hundred syllables. But they are all developments of *a*. They are not separate from *a*. Now the relation between *a* and *aṃ* is this: *a* symbolizes the cause and *aṃ* the effect. That is why, if the hundred syllables are conjoined as the outcome *aṃ*, they symbolize the effect which is the attainment of the state of Buddha.

CHAPTER XX. EFFECT WHICH CORRESPONDS TO THE HUNDRED SYLLABLES[47]

The preceding chapter has explained the practice comprising the contemplation of the "universal radiance of the splendor of the Hundred Syllables". The present chapter sets forth the innumerable virtues of the state of Buddha which are acquired in consequence of the practice of the Hundred Syllables. The Sūtra says:

> "Next seek the rank (*pada*) of Right Complete Enlightenment (*samyaksambodhi*). Knowing the infinity (*apramāṇa*) of the mind, thou shalt know the infinity of the body. Knowing the infinity of the body, thou shalt know the infinity of knowledge. Knowing the infinity of knowledge, thou shalt know the infinity of beings. Knowing the infinity of beings, thou shalt know the infinity of space. O Master of Mysteries, since the mind is infinite, thou canst obtain the four kinds of the infinite. After having obtained them, thou shalt acquire the incomparable Right Complete Enlightenment, possess the ten forces of knowledge, triumph over the four species of Māra; and, free from all fear, roar like a lion."[48]

This passage defines the state of enlightenment that may be obtained with the help of the hundred syllables.

CHAPTER XXI. FULFILMENT OF THE STATE OF HUNDRED SYLLABLES[49]

This chapter describes the state of the person who has acquired the total virtues of the "universal radiance of the Hundred

Splendors" of the syllable *aṃ* that was treated in the preceding chapter. The faithful follower who has acquired these virtues by the empowerment (*adhiṣṭhāna*) attached to the syllabe *aṃ* and by dint of contemplating the Pure Heart of Bodhi innate in himself, will finally realize that he is not different from Mahāvairocana or from his *maṇḍala*. The Sūtra says:

> "If the Great 'I' (*mahātman*) of the internal heart is known well, each person sees that his own heart is the habitation of the Guide (*nāyaka,* Tib. *'dren pa* = Buddha). The eight-petalled lotus which is born in the mind (*manas*) becomes splendid. It is like the pure mirror which is the immaculate disc of the full moon. Installed for all times in this orb of the moon is the Respected of the Shingon who is willing to help the world, has the color of god, emits flames, is absorbed in *samādhi*, and destroys the poison (of the defilements, *kleśa*). His face is like that of the sun which is difficult to look at. And it (operates) the same toward all beings of whatever kind. By the empowerment (*adhiṣṭhāna*) which penetrates them continually from all sides, both interior and exterior, all beings may know with the help of the eye of wisdom the brilliant mirror of their spirit, exactly in the same way as Mahāvairocana does. The practising (devotee) of the Shingon contemplates this pure mirror with the help of this eye of Insight; and it is in this way that finally he is able to come to the vision of his own face perfectly illumined by the contemplation of his [apparent] formal being."[50]

A little later (the Sūtra states):

> It is as if the contemplation of the maṇḍala which is in our mind has cured the fever. It cures immediately and without doubt the fever of all beings. The maṇḍala is not different from our mind, and our mind is not different from the maṇḍala, because this maṇḍala is only one with our mind."[51]

The Sūtra explains that the maṇḍala in its concrete formation is in itself only an exteriorization, like a magical metamorphosis, of this spiritual maṇḍala which is our Heart of Bodhi.

CHAPTER XXII. RECITATION PRESERVING THE ACCOMPLISHMENT BY THE HUNDRED SYLLABLES[52]

This chapter narrates the rules necessary for the 'up-keep', i.e. memorization (*dhāraṇa*) and recitation (*vācana*) of the syllable *aṃ,* which is the king of the mantras of the "universal radiance of the

Hundred Splendors". In this connection the Sūtra says:

"This mantra [the syllable *aṃ*], helpful to the world, does not differ, whether for [the practitioner's impure] body or for [the Buddha's pure] body. The [impure] mind born of the [pure] mind may indeed get purified; that is to say, in the universal radiance, wherein [the pure mind] takes issuance, and which afterwards is distributed to all parts of the body."[53]

In this way the idea of non-duality between the pure and the impure, between the (moving) beings and the Buddha, has been posited.

Next it is said that in contemplating all the syllables as not separate from the syllable *a,* one can acquire by dint of this syllable *a* the linkage (*samaya*) of non-two between the pure and the impure, between the (moving) beings and the Buddha. By contemplating the thirty-two syllables proceeding from the syllable *aṃ* [which are the Sanskrit alphabet minus the vowels and nasals but including *a, sa, va* (seed syllables of the three clans) and the composite *kṣa*] can be acquired the thirty-two principal characteristics of the Buddha (*mahāpuraṣalakṣaṇa*); by the meditation on the five nasals *ṅa, ña, ṇa, na* and *ma,* can be acquired the eighty secondary marks (*anuvyañjana*).

CHAPTER XXIII. THE MANTRA METHOD OF THE HUNDRED SYLLABLES[54]

This chapter exposes the virtues of the syllable *a* which is the origin of the syllable *aṃ*, the mantra of the "universal radiance of the Hundred Splendors".

To the syllable *a* is attributed the sense of "voidness, without original production, non-apprehensible" (*ādyanutpādā anupalambhyā śūnyatā*). The Sūtra says:

"In this discipline of linkage (*samaya*) [the practitioner] who has undergone empowerment (*adhiṣṭhāna*) with voidness (*śūnyatā*) [that is to say, with the syllable *a*] becomes master of all the dharmas [that is to say], understands them and accomplishes the supreme enlightenment. Indeed, this syllable is the venerated principal [Mahāvairocana]."[55]

Since from the beginning, non-apprehensible voidness (*śūnyatā*) has been the truth of all the dharmas, the faithful follower will be able to arrive at the universal comprehension of the dharmas, if he identifies his heart with the significance of the syllable *a*.

CHAPTER XXIV. EXPLAINING THE NATURE OF BODHI[56]

This chapter comments on the profound meaning of the nature of *bodhi*. Taken as a written letter, it is nothing else than the syllable *a*. As a dharma, it is the *bodhicitta* which is innate in us. Personified, it is Mahāvairocana Tathāgata who is enthroned in the center of the Mahākaruṇāgarbha-maṇḍala. As a matter of fact, we read in the first chapter, "What is Bodhi? It is to know one's own heart as it really is;"[57] and "the heart, the sphere of space, and Bodhi—these three things constitute only one thing."[58]

The present chapter explains the nature of *bodhi* in the following terms: As space eternally extends in the ten directions and on all sides without any point of support, so the mantra which helps the world that is to say, *a*, the mantra of Mahāvairocana, as also the mantras derived from it, has no point of support in any dharma.[59]

CHAPTER XXV. THE TRIPLE SAMAYA[60]

The term *samaya* (Tib. *dam tshig*), very much in use in esoterism, has been applied in various senses. Properly speaking, it signifies "convention, concordance, correspondence, identity, communion". It is generally translated by BYŌDŌ 'equality', which is also equivalent to *samatā*. Chapter IX of the Chinese Commentary[61] attributes to *samaya* the following four meanings: (1) *Samaya* is equality (BYŌDŌ = *samatā*) between beings and the Buddha. (2) It is the fundamental vow (HONZEI = *mūlapraṇidhāna*) by which the Buddha, seeing that all beings have the nature of *bodhi*, swears to enable them to attain *bodhi*. This is the pledge which all beings in their turn take with regard to other beings. (3) It is the destruction of the obstacles (JOSHŌ = *āvaraṇa-viṣkambaṇa*) by the Buddha, that is to say, the elimination of nescience (*avidyā*) which impedes the beings' realization of *bodhi*. (4) It is the re-awakening (KYŌGAKU) in the sense that the Buddha re-awakens the sentient beings from the slumber of nescience in which they have lost the knowledge of their *bodhi* nature, or reminds the Bodhisattvas of the duties of their state.

In esoterism the "triple *samaya*" (SANZAMMAYA = *trisamaya;* or SAMBYŌDŌ) signifies the identity between all sorts of triads; e.g., our heart, the Buddha, sentient beings; Heart, Insight, and Compassion; *dharmakāya, saṃbhogakāya,* and *nirmāṇakāya;*

Buddha, Dharma, Samgha; the actions of body, speech, and mind; and so on.

The present chapter defines the "triple *samaya*" first of all in prose as (1) the sprout of the Dharma (HŌSŌZOKU = *dharmasamtāna*), that is to say, the serial production, the gradual development of the *bodhicitta* in the mind of the faithful follower; (2) the destruction of the obstacles (JOSHŌ); (3) the *yoga* (SŌŌ), that is to say, the identification of the faithful follower with the Buddha.

Next, it is defined in verses as (1) the initial *bodhicitta*, that is to say, the Buddha who resides in the innermost depth of ourselves; (2) the Dharma; (3) the Samgha, that is to say, the totality of the faithful followers who gradually realize the Dharma.

CHAPTER XXVI. EXPLANATION OF THE TERM 'TATHĀGATA'[62]

This chapter contains the reply to Vajrapāṇi's question, as follows: "Why the names Tathāgata, Narottama, Bodhisattva, Saṃbuddha, Nāyaka, Mahāmuni?"

One calls 'Bodhisattva' he who seeks the undifferentiated *bodhi* as space (*ākāśa*). One calls 'Saṃbuddha' he who, having accomplished the ten Stages (*bhūmi*), comprehends with mastery the voidness of all dharmas and who knows the orientation of all the sentient beings of the world. One calls *saṃbodhi* the obtaining of the ten forces (*daśabalāni*) of the Buddha by anyone who comprehends the non-duality of the dharmas which are like space. One calls 'Tathāgata' he who, being all-insight, and having destroyed the darkness of nescience, realizes by himself the insight of which the true nature is ineffable.

CHAPTER XXVII. THE MANNER OF CELEBRATING MUNDANE AND SUPRAMUNDANE HOMA[63]

The *homa* (GOMA, Tib. *sbyin sreg*), an oblation to fire, is originally a Brahmanical sacrifice. Esoteric Buddhism has adopted this rite but has given to it a very different interpretation. Indeed, the *homa* of esoteric Buddhism represents the destruction, burning into flames of our passions and illusions in the fire of the Tathāgata's Insight.[64]

First, the Sūtra enumerates 44 varieties of 'worldly' *homa*. These varieties are, says the text, those which "the brahmacārins cultivating and studying the Vedas transmit and read." The Sanskrit names of these are given in transcription. As regards the *homa* called 'supramundane', that is to say, something exclusive with Buddhism, it is explained that there are two kinds of it, viz. external *homa* (GE-GOMA) and internal *homa* (NAI-GOMA). The first comprises twelve different varieties. Internal *homa* is a rite of meditation which consists in contemplating on the identity of fire, the divinity to whom the offering is made, and the officient. This is the most important rite. The flame of knowledge innate in our heart is nothing else than the fire of the Buddha's Insight which destroys our passions.[65].

CHAPTER XXVIII. EXPLAINING THE SAMĀDHI OF THE MAIN DEITY[66]

By the practice of the mystic contemplation (*samādhi*), the faithful follower of the Shingon perceives that the divinity and himself are but one; that is to say, the divinity penetrates him, and he penetrates the divinity. This is what is called "entry (of the Buddha) in us, and our entry (in the Buddha)" (NYŪGA-GANYŪ). This chapter expounds that the divinity may present itself in three kinds, and that the *siddhi* it procures is of two sorts:

"Master of the Mysteries! All divinities have three kinds of body, viz. the syllable, the 'gesture' (*mudrā*), and the figured representation. The syllable is of two kinds: on the one hand, the sound [the external syllable perceptible to the ear]; and on the other, the Heart of Bodhi [the syllable in our heart]. The *mudrā* is of two kinds: 'with form' and 'without form'. The body of divinity [figured in image] is also of two kinds, pure and impure.[67]

Each of the three forms of the divinity is sub-divided into two categories according as the contemplation (*samādhi*) of the practising (devotee) is 'possessed of characteristic' (USŌ= *salakṣaṇa*) or is 'devoid of characteristic' (MUSŌ = *nirlakṣaṇa*). To the first category correspond the sound of the syllable, the formal *mudrā*, and the impure image; to the latter, the Heart of Bodhi, the *mudrā* without form, and the pure image. According as the practising (devotee) devotes himself to one or the other of these two varieties of contemplation, he acquires one or the other of the two varieties of *siddhi* (about these, cf. Chapter VII).

CHAPTER XXIX. EXPLAINING THE SAMĀDHI WITHOUT SIGNS[68]

This chapter discusses how the faithful follower of the Shingon must devote himself to the *samādhi* 'without signs', with a view to acquiring the *siddhi* 'without signs'; and defines this *samādhi* as follows:

> "Master of the Mysteries, the Heart taken as having no nature of its own (*niḥsvabhāva*) eludes all conception (*samjñā*). That is why it is necessary to meditate on the voidness of its nature. O Master of the Mysteries, this Heart is non-apprehensible in the three times, because it is beyond the three times. Its proper nature is exempt from all signs."[69]

This *samādhi* without signs consists in contemplating the voidness and non-existence of 'I'. This contemplation is nothing else than that of the syllable a which is "without original production".

CHAPTER XXX. MUNDANE AND SUPRAMUNDANE RECITATION[70]

This chapter describes the esoteric recitation[71] of the mantras which entails two methods: The 'mundane' (*laukika*) recitation is formed in the mouth and consists of pronouncing the mantra of the divinity while regulating the respiratory rhythm (inhalation and exhalation). The 'supramundane' (*lokottara*) method is mental recitation of the mantra with concentration of the mind on the divinity with a view to identifying itself with it (the divinity). The first method corresponds to the particularized *samādhi*, while the second corresponds to the *samādhi* without characteristic. It is indispensable to cultivate the two methods simultaneously so as to assure the success of the recitation and the obtaining of *siddhi*.

CHAPTER XXXI. THE TRANSMISSION[72]

At the end of the Sūtra, the Buddha enjoins his listeners to transmit this teaching to select and tested disciples only: "Then the Bhagavat proclaimed to all the assemblies [listening to the Sūtra]: 'Do not be in the least negligent in what concerns this doctrine (*dharmaparyāya*); it must not be transmitted to others whose nature you do not know'." To be worthy of receiving this teaching, it is necessary to possess all sorts of qualifications which the text enumerates in detail, viz., birth under auspicious astrological signs, high ambitions, sharp intelligence, and so on; 'blue-white' or white complexion, large head, long neck, wide and even forehead, straight nose, etc. This chapter terminates with the usual conclusions of the Sūtras, viz., joyous acceptance by the listeners who adore the Buddha and request him to pronounce one last *dhāraṇī*.

NOTES

1. Taishō, Vol. XVIII, pp. $4a^{10}$- $12b^{3}$.
2. The word EN generally corresponds to Sanskrit *pratyaya* and GU to the prefix *sa*. The Commentary glosses GUEN by GU-SHŪEN-SHIBUN, "furnished with all the *pratyaya-anga*" (?)
3. Cf. Finot, ed., "Manuscrits sanscrits de Sādhana retrouves en Chine." *Journal Asiatique,* July-September, 1934, p. 21, where a distinction is made between *jñāna-maṇḍala* and *mantra-prayoga-maṇḍala.*
4. This is the divinity of the site.
5. Mahāvairocana, Ratnaketu, Saṃkusumitarāja, Amitābha, Divyadundubhimeghanirghoṣa.
6. Cf. the scheme of this *maṇḍala* in the Commentary, Taishō, No. 1796, Vol. XXXIX, p. 623b.
7. *Ādarśa-jñāna, samatā-j., pratyavekṣaṇā-j., kṛtyānuṣṭhāna-j., dharmadhātusvabhāva-j.*
8. Cf. image in *Mikkyō daijiten,* p. 740.
9. Cf. quotation in the Introduction, with note 22.
10. Cf. chapter XVIII, and there the five *śīla.*
11. Taishō, Vol. XVIII, pp. $13b^{4}$-$14a^{3}$.
12. *Ibid.*, p. $13b^{13}$.
13. *Ibid.*, pp. $14a^{4}$-$17b^{8}$.
14. Taishō, Vol. XVIII, pp. $17b^{14}$-c^{20}.
15. MITSUKI-NENJU, literally, "recitation (of the mantras) during three months". Cf. Mutsuki-nenju, p. 323.
16. Taishō, Vol. XVIII, pp. $17c^{21}$-$21c^{12}$.
17. See *infra,* with note 30.
18. Taishō, Vol. XVIII, pp. $21c^{23}$-$22a^{19}$.
19. Tib. *mtshan ma dang bcas pa'i dngos grub,* probably *salakṣaṇasiddhi.*
20. Tib. *mushan ma med pa'i dngos grub,* probably *nirlakṣaṇasiddhi.*
21. Taishō, Vol. XVIII, pp. $21c^{23}$-$22a^{20}$.
22. Taishō, Vol. XVIII, pp. $22b^{4}$-$24a^{21}$.
23. *Ibid.*, p. $22c^{11}$.
24. Taishō, Vol. XVIII, pp. $24a^{26}$-$29a^{23}$.
25. HYŌJI, literally indicator of posts and banners.
26. Taishō, Vol. XVIII, p. $24b^{1}$.
27. Taishō, Vol. XVIII, p. $29b^{5}$-c^{22}.
28. Taishō, Vol. XVIII, pp. $30a^{23}$-$36a^{17}$.

29. *Tathāgata-vijṛmbhita-samatā-vyūha-kośa-samādhī* (?).
30. Cf. above, with note 17.
31. Cf. Chapter VI summary; perhaps the last 12 syllables of that *mantra*.
32. Taishō, Vol. XVIII, pp. $36a^{18}$-b^{3}.
33. *Ibid.*, p. $36b^{6}$-b^{26}.
34. ISHO = *yid las byung ba.*
35. Rākṣasa, Vāyu, Agni Vaiśravaṇa, etc. (Cf. *Mikkyō daijiten*. p. 1717).
36. Taishō, Vol. XVIII, p. $36c^{1-16}$
37. *Ibid.*, pp. $36c^{27}$-$37b^{17}$.
38. *Ibid.*, p. $37b^{14}$.
39. *Ibid.*, pp. $37b^{18}$-$38a^{16}$.
40. Cf. ch. VI summary, *bīja*-s of the five elements.
41. Taishō, Vol. XVIII, pp. $38a^{16}$-c^{5}.
42. *Ibid.*, p. $38c^{6-21}$.
43. Taishō, Vol. XVIII. pp. $39a^{3}$-$40a^{20}$.
44. Taishō, Vol. XVIII, p. $12b^{1}$.
45. Taishō, Vol. XXXIX, p. $67a^{9}$.
46. Taishō, Vol. XVIII, pp. $40a^{21}$-b^{9}.
47. Taishō, Vol. XVIII, p. $40b^{10}$-c^{4}.
48. Different from the four ordinary *apramāṇas* which are friendliness (*maitrī*), compassion (*karuṇā*), joy (*muditā*), and indifference (*upekṣā*).
49. Taishō, Vol. XVIII, pp. $40c^{5}$-$41a^{29}$.
50. *Ibid.*, p. $40c^{20}$.
51. *Ibid.*, p. $41a^{18}$.
52. *Ibid.*, pp. $41a^{28}$ -c^{27}. The term JIJU (lit., to take to heart and to recite) we translate by 'up-keep'.
53. *Ibid.*, p. $41b^{1}$.
54. *Ibid.*, p. $41c^{29}$-$42a^{14}$. For HŌ the Tibetan text gives *cho ga* which may correspond to Sanskrit *vidhi, vidhāna,* etc. The Chinese Commentary also clearly states that HŌ does not render here the Sanskrit dharma but is a synonym for GIKI = *vidhi, vidhāña,* etc. and that this term is applied to virtues of all sorts born of the hundred syllables (Taishō, Vol. XXXIX, p. $776a^{4}$.
55. *Ibid.*, p. $41c^{28}$.
56. Taishō, Vol, XVIII, p. $42a^{15}$-b^{4}.
57. *Ibid.*, p. $1c^{1}$; cf. Translation of the Chapter One, note 81.
58. *Ibid.*, p. $1c^{18}$.
59. *Ibid.*, p. $42a^{16}$.
60. Taishō, Vol. XVIII, p. $42b^{5}$-c^{4}.
61. Taishō, Vol. XXXIX, p. $674c^{3}$.
62. Taishō, Vol. XVIII, p. $42c^{5-24}$.
63. Taishō, Vol. XVIII, pp. $42c^{25}$-$44a^{8}$.
64. Cf. the Commentary, Ch. XX, Taishō, Vol. XXXIX, p. $781c^{19}$ and Introduction, near end of "Shingon Esoterism".
65. Cf. *Ibid.*, $782c^{15}$.
66. Taishō, Vol. XVIII, pp. $44a^{9-25}$. For HONZON, literally "the principal respected person", the Commentary (Taishō, Vol. XXXIX, p. $783a^{12}$) gives a Sanskrit equivalent in Chinese transcription: so-ye-ti t'i-fo-to. The three last syllables correspond to the word *devatā*, "divinity". The equivalent of the first three syllables is not clear. Mr. Kambayashi, in his work on esoterism (*Mikkyōgaku,*

Tokyo, 1929, p. 192), gives the restoration *satyādhidevatā,* but the transcription lacks the *-t-*. The Tibetan text of the Sūtra simply gives *lha* = *deva(tā).* The word HONZON is used in Japanese Buddhism to designate the sacred personage who is the true object of worship or of a given rite or the principal personage in an iconographic assembly in contrast to his acolytes.

67. Taishō, Vol. XVIII, p. 44a$^{16-19}$.
68. *Nirlakṣaṇa-samādhi. Ibid.*, p. 44a^{26}-b^{18}.
69. *Ibid.*, p. 44b^{11}
70. Taishō, Vol. XVIII, p. 441b^{19}-c^{4}.
71. JIJU, lit. "to retain and to recite". The Commentary gives NENJU "to memorize and to recite". The Tib. *bzlas brjod* = *jāpa.* Cf. Ch. V, *supra,* discussion of 'recitation'.
72. Taishō, Vol. XVIII, p. 44c$^{5-26}$. ZOKURUI = *anuparīndāna*?

PART VI

BIBLIOGRAPHY

EDITOR'S INTRODUCTION

For the Bibiography part of Tajima's work it is necessary to clarify a few matters.

The use of the term 'volume': The term 'volume' is properly applied to volumes of the Taishō Buddhist canon, or to volumes of the Japanese Buddhist canons in their national language. However, the use of the term 'volumes' in regard to individual works may be confusing. A better English equivalent would be 'fascicules', and sometimes the word 'chapters' fits.

The transcription of Chinese: Tajima employs the European system used in France. The American Sinological school generally employs the "Wade-Giles" system of transcription into European alphabets. Modern China has devised a still different system of transcription.

Sino-Japanese studies: One may gain a comprehensive idea of the large scope of Sino-Japanese studies, published over twelve centuries (724-1931) from the *Daibirushana-Jōbutsu-jinben-kaji-kyō-kaidai* (Introductory notes of Dainichikyō) by Dr. Ryūjo Kambayashi. Kokuyaku Issaikyō, Mikkyō-bu, Vol. 10, pp. 26-34, Tokyo, 1931.

In more recent years modern Japanese scholars have published various helpful reference works. One may derive a bare idea of the numerous Japanese studies on this Sūtra and other tantric topics from Hajime Nakamura's chapter on Esoteric Buddhism in *Acta Asiatica,* 7 (The Toho Gakkai, Tokyo, 1964). The one-volume *Mikkyō Jiten* (ed. by R. Sawa and Y. Matsunaga, Kyoto, 1975) lists all the main commentaries on this Sūtra up to 1942. Among materials recently supplied us by the Rev. Shorei Nakayama of Narita-san Institute of Buddhist Studies, we can especially point to the reference work, *Mikkyō kankei bunken mokuroku* (Index of references about Tantra) (Shuchiin Daigaku Mikkyō-Gakkai, Kyōto, 1986); and can also point to the posthumous essays (Studies on

Dainichikyō) in the supplemental Vol. II, also to the *Kongōchōgyō no kenkyū* (Studies on *Kongōchōkyō*) Vol. III, from the *Toganoo shōun zenshū* (the collected works of Toganoo Shōun) edited by his son Shōzui Toganoo (Kyoto, 1985). Just as a suggestion of the kinds of articles published, may I mention, "(Dainichikyō)-ni-mieru-Indo-tetsugaku-shiso" (Indian philosophical thoughts found in the *Dainichikyō*), by Yūsho Miyasaka in *Bukkyō shisō ronshū* (collected essays on the history of Buddhist thought), Vol. I (Naritasan, 1988). And there are many many other such published essays.

Editor

BIBLIOGRAPHY

Mahāvairocana-sūtra

1. CHINESE DOCUMENTS

(a) Chinese texts of the Sūtra

Daibirushana-jōbutsu-jimben-kaji-kyō (Ta p'i-lou-tchö-na tch'eng fo chen pien kia tch'e king), 7 volumes (KWAN): usual abbreviations: *Daibirushanakyō,* Dainichikyō (Chinese version of the *Mahāvairocana-sūtra*). Translated by Śubhakarasimha and Yi-hing in 724-725, Taishō No. 848, Vol. XVIII; Nanjō, No. 530.

Daibirushana-bussetsu-yōryaku-nenju-kyō (Ta p'i-lou-tchö-na fo chouo yao lio nien song king). 1 Vol.: usual abbreviation *Yōryaku-nenju-kyō* (corresponds to the seventh volume of the version of Śubhakarasimha and Yi-hing). Translated by Kongōchi (Vajrabodhi) between 720 and 741, Taishō, No. 849.

(b) Chinese commentaries

Daibirushana-jōbutsu-kyō-sho (Ta p'i-lou-tchö-na teh'eng fo king chou), 20 vols.; usual appellation: *Dainichikyō-sho.* Daisho (Commentary of the Chinese version of the *Mahāvairocana-sūtra*).[1] Edited by Yi-hing after the oral teaching of Śubhakarasimha, between 725 and 727. Taishō, No. 1796, Vol. XXXIX.

Daibirushanakyō-kuyō-shidaibō-sho (Ta p'i-lou-tchö-na king kong yang ts'eu ti fa chou), 2 vols. usual appellation: *Dainichi-kyōkuyōbō-sho, Fushigino-sho* (Commentary on the seventh volume of the *Dainichikyō*). Edited by Fukashigi (Pou-k'o-sseu-yi) after the oral teaching of Śubhakarasimha towards 728. Taishō, No. 1797, Vol. XXXIX.

Dainichikyō-gishaku. 14 vols. (Modification of the Commentary of Yi-hing, Taishō, No. 1976. By Tche-yen (Chigon) and Wen-kou (Onko) between 728 and 735. *Dainihonzokuzōkyō* ("Supplement of the Tripiṭaka, Kyōto edition"), bundle XXXVI, fascicules 3-4.

Dainichikyō-gishaku-emmitsu-shō, 10 vols. (Commentary on

the *Dainichikyō-gishaku*). By Kio-yuan in 1076. Supplement of the Tripiṭaka, edition of Kyōto, bundle XXXVII, fasicicule 1.

II. JAPANESE DOCUMENTS

(a) General studies on the Sūtra and the Commentary

Dainichikyō-kaidai (Bibliographic notice on the *Dainichikyō*), 7 recensions. By Kūkai (Kōbō Daishi, 774-835), Taishō, No. 2211, Vol. LVIII.

Dainichikyō-sho-monshidai (Analysis of the Chinese Commentary on the D.) By Kūkai. Kōbō Daishi-zenshu, Vol. III.

Dainichikyō-sho-yomonki Notes on the Main Passages of the Commentary). By Kūkai, Vol. III.

Daibirushanakyō-shiki. 1 Vol.; usual abbreviation: *Dainichikyō shiki* (Guide to the *Dainichikyō,* after the interpretation of the Taimitsu school). By Chishō Daishi (Enchin, 815-862), Taishō, No. 2212, Vol. LVIII.

Daibirushanakyō-shimmoku, 1 Vol.; usual abbreviation: *Dainichikyō-shimmoku* (Summary of the D.). By Chisho Daishi in 858. Taishō, No. 2212, Vol. LVIII.

Dainichikyō-sho-shō, 4 vols; usual abbreviation: *Hannyajishō* (Interpretation of the Chinese Commentary in dialogue form). By Kwanken (853-925). Ed. Dainihon Bukkyōzensho.

Daikyō-yōgi, 7 vols. (Doctrinal quintessence of the D.) By Jippan (—1144). Dainihon Bukkyōzensho.

Dainichikyō-sho-gendan. 1 Vol. (Introduction to the Chinese Commentary on the D.) By Gōhō (1306-1362).

Himitsu-innen-kwangen-sōjō-gi, 2 vols.; usual abbreviation: *Kwangen-sōjō-gi* (Summary of the Chinese Commentary of the D., tending to harmonize the traditions of the Kogi and Shingi schools). By Hōjū (1723-1800) in 1785. Taishō, No. 2541, Vol. LXXIX.

Daibirushana-jōbutsu-jimben-kaji-kyō-kaidai (Introduction to the Japanese translation of the Chinese version of the *Mahāvairocana-sūtra* with complete Sino-Japanese bibliography in the *Kokuyaku Issaikyō,* Mikkyo-bu ("Translation into the national language of the Chinese Buddhist Canon, Esoteric Section") [Introduction] by Kambayashi Ryūjo, Tokyo, 1931.

Dainichikyō-kyōshu-gi (Edition of the 19 short ancient treatises on the question of who is the preacher of the D.). Edited by

Hayashida kōzen. Kyōto, 1921.
Daisho-hiki-shū, 2 vols. (Edition of 38 short ancient exegetical texts on the Commentary of the D.). Editors: Hase Hōshū and Toganoo Shōun, Kyōto, 1912.

(b) Special studies on the first chapter of the Sūtra and its commentary

(*Dainichikyō-jūshin-bon-sho-shiki,* 16 vols.; abbr.: *Daisho-shiki, Daisho-shō* (Detailed textual commentary on the Chinese Commentary of the first chapter of the D.). By Saisen (1025-1115). Taishō, No. 2215, Vol. LVIII.

Dainichikyō-sho-shishinshō, 16 vols.; abbr.: *Daisho-shishinshō* (Commentary on the Chinese Commentary of the first chapter of the D.; this work is taken as authoritative by the Shingi school, especially in regard to interpreting the preacher of the D. as Kajishin, *adhiṣṭhānakāya*). By Raiu (1226-1304). Taishō, No. 2217, Vol. LIX.

Dainichikyō-sho-shō, 29 vols.; usual title: *Daisho-gōhō-shō* (Detailed textual commentary on the Chinese Commentary on the first chapter of the D.). By Gōhō (1306-1362).

Dainichikyō-sho-shō, 85 vols; usual title; *Kuchi-no-sho-yūkai-shō* (Detailed textual commentary of the Chinese Commentary on the first Chapter of the D.). By Yūkai (1345-1416). Taishō, No. 2218, Vol. LX.

(*Daisho-shinan-shō-tsurimono,* 9 vols. Commentary on the Chinese on the first chapter of the D.). By Innyū (1435-1519).

Kuchi-no-sho-kachū, 6 vols. (Commentary on the Chinese Commentary of the first chapter of the D.). By Ryōtai (1622-1680).

Jūshin-bon-sho-yōge, 7 vols. (Commentary on the Chinese Commentary of the first chapter of the D.). By Eshō (about 1673).

Jūshin-bon-sho-ryakuge, 8 vols. (Commentary on the Chinese Commentary of the first chapter of the D.). By Jōgon (1639-1702).

Dainichikyō-jūshinbon-sho-gyokushin-shō, 10 vols. (Commentary on the Chinese Commentary of the first chapter of the D.; it is accepted as an authority in the Shingi school). By Hōjū (1723-1800).

Jūshin-bon-sho-shiki, 3 vols. (Commentary on the Chinese Commentary of the first chapter of the D.). By Sōken (1832-1898).

Daibirushanakyō-jūshin-shō, 7 vols. (Commentary on the Chinese Commentary of the first chapter of the D.). By Shinshō (1086-1142).

Zokugen-hikyoku, 5 vols. (Interpretation of the Chinese Commentary of the first chapter of the D.; it is inspired by the *Himitsu-innen-*

kwangen-sōjō-gi of Hōjū, cf. supra). By Gonda Raifu (1846-1934). Tōkyō, 1921.

Dainichikyō-kōyō (Summary of the first chapter of the D. in the Grand Manual of the Japanese Religions, Vol. VII). By Kanayama Bokushō, Tōkyō, 1930.

(c) *Detailed textual sub-commentaries on the Chinese Commentary as a whole*

Daisho-gijitsu, 31 vols. usual appellation: *Jōfuni-shō* (Commentary on the Chinese Commentary of the D.). By Yushō: preface of 1321.

Dainichikyō-myōin-shō, 80 vols.; abbr.: *Myōin-shō* (Commentary on the Chinese Commentary of the D.). By Yūhan (1270-1352), Taishō, No. 2213, Vol. LVIII.

Dainichikyō-myōin-shō-kuden 10 vols. (Commentary on the Chinese Commentary of the D.; oral sub-commentary of the preceding work). By Yūhan in 1331. Taishō, No. 2213, Vol. LVIII.

Dainichikyō-sho-ennō-shō, 36 vols.; abbr.: *Daisho-ennō-shō, Ennō-shō* (Commentary on the Chinese Commentary of the chapters II, ff. of the D., of which chapter II has an especially detailed treatment). By Gōhō (1306-1362). Taishō, No. 2216, Vol. LIX.

Dainichikyō-sho-shiki, 85 vols. (Commentary on the Chinese Commentary of the D.). By Donjaku (1674-1731). Taishō, No. 2219, Vol. LX.

(d) *Doctrinal questions; dialogue discussions on questions about the Sūtra and the Commentary*[2]

Daisho-gusō (or *Dainichikyō-sho-gusō*) 24 vols. (Dialogue discussion comprising 433 questions and answers on the controversial passages of the Commentary on the first chapter of the D.). By Raiyu (1226-1304).

Dainchikyō-kyōshu-honji-kaji-fumbetsu, 1 vol. (Dialogue discussion about the preacher of the D., conceived of here as HONJISHIN, "fundamental body" and not as **KAJISHIN,** *adhiṣṭhānakāya;* it is regarded with authority in the Kogi school). By Gōhō, as above, Taishō, No. 2452, Vol. LXXVII.

Daisho-hyakujō-daisanjū, 10 vols; abbr.; *Daisho-daisanjū* (Dailogue discussion on the hundred doubtful points of the first-chapter Commentary of the D.; it is accepted as an authority in the Shingi school). By Shōken (1307-1392). Taishō, No. 2538, Vol. LXXIX.

Jishō-seppō (or *Jishō-seppō-jūhachi-dan*) 1 vol. (Discussion in the dialogue form and in 18 articles as to the preacher of the D.: Can

Vairocana in *JISHŌ-I "svaprakāśa-sthāna"* preach? The conclusion is negative. It is regarded as authoritative in the Shingi school). By Shōken, as above. Taishō, No. 2539, Vol. LXXIX.

Daisho-keimō, 59 vols. (Commentary on the *Daisho-hyakujō-daisanjū*), by Unshō (1614-1693).

Daisho-shinan-shō, 9 vols. (90 questions and answers on certain points of the Commentary on the first chapter of the D.). By Chokāku (1340-1416).

Daisho-dangi, 10 vols. (100 questions and answers on the Commentary of the first chapter of the D.). By Unshō (1614-1693). Taishō, No. 2540, Vol. LXXIX.

Senpo-inton-shō, 20 vols. (Dialogue discussion comprising 100 questions and answers on the doctrines after the Sūtra and the Commentary). By Innyū (1435-1519).

Shosō-tōgo-shiki, 1 vol. (Dialogue discussion on the Chinese Commentery). By Takugen (1639-1712).

Daisho-daisanjū-hyōki (Critique of the *Daisho-daisanjū*). By Eigaku (1639-1712).

Jishō-seppō-jūhachi-dan-shiki, 1 vol. (Notes on the *Jishō-seppō-jūhachi-dan;* Taishō, No. 2539). By Ryōtei (1648-1719).

III. TIBETAN DOCUMENTS

(a) Tibetan text of the Sūtra and the Commentaries

Rnam par snang mdsad chen po mngon par rdsogs par byang chub pa rnam par sprul pa byin gyis rlob pa shin tu rgyas pa mdo sde'i dbang po rgyal po zhes bya ba'i chos kyi rnam grangs; Sanskrit title: *Mahāvairocanābhisambodhivikurvitādhiṣṭhānavaipulya-sūtrendrarājanāmaparyāya* (Tibetan version of the *Mahāvairocana-sūtra*). Translated by Sīlendrabodhi and Dpal-brtsegs. Editions: Narthang, bundle Ta, 301-455; Sde-dge, bundle Tha, 151-260; Peking, bundle Tha, 115-260. Cf. Otani, No. 126; Tohoku, No. 949; Catalogue of Beckh, p. 95.

Rnam par snang mdsad mngon par rdsogs par byang chub pa'i rgyud kyi bsdus pa'i don; Sanskrit title (according to the Catalogue of Cordier, Part II, p. 290): *Vairocanābhisambodhitantrapiṇḍārtha.* (Concise Commentary of the Tibetan version of the *Vairocanābhisambodhitantra*). By Buddhaguhya, translated by Śīlendrabodhi and Dpal brtsegs rakṣita. Tohoku. No. 2662.

Rnam par snang mdsad mngon par byang chub pa'i rgyud kyi'grel pa; Sanskrit title (according to the Catalogue of Cordier, Part II, p. 290): *Vairocanābhisambodhitantravṛtti* (Commentary on the *Vairocanābhisambodhitantra*). By Buddhaguhya. Translator(s) not known.

Rnam par snang mdsad mngon par rdsogs par byang chub pa rnam par sprul pa byin gyis rlob pa'i rgyud chen po'i 'grel pa; Sanskrit title (after the Catalogue of Cordier, Part II, p. 291): *Vairocanābhisambodhivikurvitādhiṣṭhānamahātantravṛtti* (Commentary on the *Vairocanābhisambodhitantra*). By Buddhaguhya. Revision of the Tibetan text by Gzhon-nu-dpal. Tohoku Nos. 2663 and 2664.[3]

Rnam par snang mdsad chen po mngon par byang chub par gtogs pa'i rgyud kyi mchod pa'i cho ga; Sanskrit title (after the Catalogue of Cordier, Part II, p. 291): *Mahāvairocanābhisambodhisambaddhatantrapūjāvidhi* (Ritual offering of tantra related to the *Mahāvairocanābhisambodhi*). By Dpal-bzang rabs-dga' (Srībhadranandana). Translated by Padmākaravarma and Rin-chen bzang-po. Tohoku, No. 2665.

Zobun Dainichikyo (Collation of the variants in the various editions of the Tibetan version of the *Mahāvairocanasūtra* with a glossary). By Hattori Yūtai; Hannō, 1931.

(b) Japanese translations of the Tibetan version of the Sūtra

Zōbun wayaku Dainichikyō (Japanese translation of the Tibetan version of the Sūtra). By Kawaguchi Ekai, Tōkyō, 1934.

Zōkan taisho wayaku Daincichikyō (Japanese translation of the Tibetan version of the Sūtra) in the journal *Misshū gakuhō*, Nos. 32-61, 1916-1918; the work is still unfinished and has stopped at Chapter V of the Tibetan text. By Toganoo Shōun.

Zōkan taiyaku Dainichikyō-jūshin-bon (Japanese translation of the first chapter of the Tibetan version of the *Mahāvairocana-sūtra* along with Tibetan and Chinese texts on opposite pages). By Tajima Ryūjun, Tōkyō, 1927.

(c) Studies on the Tibetan version of the Sūtra

Kan-zō ryōyaku Daibirushanakyō-no-hikaku (The *Mahāvairocana-sūtra:* Comparison between the Chinese and Tibetan versions) in the journal *Mikkyō kenkyū* (Researches on Esoterism), I,1. By Kawaguchi Ekai. Wakayama, 1918.

Dainichikyō-zōkan-ryōyaku-hikaku-kenkyū-gaikwan (comparative researches on the Tibetan and Chinese versions of the D., in the light of information in the Chinese Commentary about the original Sanskrit text). By Tajima Ryūjun. Tōkyō, 1927.

Nyoraishō-daimandara-kaji-hon ni tsuite (Analysis of Chapter VII of the Section "External" of the Tibetan text of the D.: *"de bzhin gshegs pa 'byung zhes bya ba'i dkyil 'khor chen po byin gyis rlob* pa"). In *Taishō Daigaku gakuhō,* No. 2. By Tajima Ryūjun, Tokyo, 1928.

IV. THE SHINGON DOCTRINES

(a) General works

Kongōchō-issai-nyorai-shinjitsushō-daijō-genshō daikyōō-gyō (Kin kang ting yi ts'ie jou lai tchen che chö ta tch'eng hien tcheng ta kiao wang king); usual abbreviation: *Kongōchōgyō*, 3 vols. Translated by Fukū (Amoghavajra). Taishō, No. 865, vol. XVIII; Nanjō No. 1020.

Kongōchō-yugachū-ryakushitsu-nenju-kyō (Kin kang yu k'ie tchong lio tch'ou nien song king); abbr. *Ryakushitsu-nenjukyō*. 4 vols. Translated by Kōngochi (Vajrabodhi). Taishō, No. 866, Vol. XVIII; Nanjō, No. 534.

Kongōchōgyō-daiyuga-himitsuo-shinji-hōmon-giketsu (Kin kang ting king ta yu k'ie pi mi sin ti fa men yi kiue), 1 Vol.; usual abbreviation: *Kongōchō-giketsu* (Commentary on the *Kongōchō-yugachu-ryakushitsu-nenju-kyō,* Taishō, No. 866). Edited by Amoghavajra after the oral teaching of Vajrabodhi. Taishō, No. 1798, vol. XXXIX.

Kongōchō-yugachū-hotsu-anokutara-sammayaku-sambodai-shin-ron (Kin kang ting yu k'ie tchong fa a neou to la san mao san p'ou t'i sin louen), 1 vol.; usual abbreviation: *Bodaishin-ron.* Taishō, No. 1665, Vol XXXII. Nanjō, No. 1319.

Taishō Daizōkyō, Mikkyō bu; vols. XVII-XXI, Nos. 448-1420 (Buddhist Canon, edition of Taishō, Esoteric Section). Tōkyō, 1928.

(b) Works in Japanese

Shingonshū-shogaku-kyōritsuron-mokuroku: usual appellation: *Sangakuroku.* 1 vol. (Catalogue of the sūtras, treatises of *vinaya* and the *śāstras* which the Shingon sect studies). By Kūkai (Kōbō Daishi, 774-835) in 823. *Kōbō Daishi zenshu,* vol. I.

Himitsu-mandarakyō-fuhōden: usual appellation: *Kō-fuhōden.* 2 vols. (The tradition of the school said to be Esoteric Maṇḍala: History of the patriarchs of the Shingon sect) in the *Dainihon bukkyo zensho,* "Thesaurus of Buddhist Literature of Japan". By Kūkai.

Shingon fuhōden; usually called *Ryaku fuhōden* (The tradition of the Shingon; in the "Thesaurus of Buddhist Literature of Japan"). By Kūkai.

Kōbō Daishi zenshū, 16 vols. (Complete Works of Kōbō Daishi). Edited under the direction of Hase Hōshū; Tōkyō, 1910.

Kōgyō Daishi zenshū, 1 vol. (Complete Works of Kōgyō Daishi, Kakuban Shōnin, 1095-1134). Edited by Kobayashi Shōsei, Tomita Kōjun, and Araki Ryōsen; Tokyo, 1910.

Taishō Daizōkyō, Zokukyōsho-bu, vol. LXI, Nos. 2291-2245 (Buddhist canon, edition of Taishō, Section of the Commentaries of the Sūtras, supplementary part). The volume contains the texts of esoteric exegesis.

Taishō Daizōkyō, vol. LXIX, Nos. 2284-2290 (Commentaries on *Shakumakaenron,* Taishō, No. 1668).

Taishō Daizōkyō, vol. LXX, Nos. 2281-2295 (Commentaries on *Bodaishin-ron,* Taishō, No. 1665).

Taishō Daizōkyō, vol. LXXV, Nos. 2385-2408 (Works of the Taimitsu school).

Taishō Daizōkyō, vol. LXXVII, Nos. 2425-2460 (Works of the *Tōmitsu* school).

Taishō Daizōkyō, vol. LXXVII, Nos. 2461-2509 (Works of the Tōmitsu school).

Taishō Daizōkyō, vol. LXXIX, Nos. 2510-2542 (Works of the Shingi School).

Kongōchō-yugachū-ryakushitsu-nenju-kyō-kaidai (Introduction to the Japanese translation of *Kongōchō-ryaku-shūtsu-kyō,* Taishō, No. 866) in *Kokuyaku Issaikyō, Mikkyō-bu, "Translation* into the national language of the Chinese Buddhist Canon, Section on Esoterism". By Kambayashi Ryūjō. Tōkyō, 1931.

Mikkyō-hattatsu-shi, 5 vols. (The Development of Esoterism). By Omure Seigai; Tōkyō, 1918.

Mikkyōgaku "Esoterism". By Kambayashi Ryūjō; Tōkyō, 1929.

Shingon Mikkyō no okoru made (Lecture entitled "Up to the development of Shingon Esoterism"). By Matsumoto Bunzaburō; Kyōto, 1925.

Mikkyō Daijiten, 3 vols. (Great Dictionary of Esoterism). By Kichijō Shinyū, Oda Jishū, Kodama Setsugen, Hattori Nyojitsu, Ueda Shinjō, Kyōtō, 1933.

Himitsu jirin (Esoteric Dictionary). By Tomita Kōjun, Tōkyō, 1911.

(c) Works in French

Hobogirin (Encyclopaedic Dictionary of Buddhism according to the

Chinese and Japanese sources, published under the direction of Sylvain Lévi and Takakusu Junjiro. Chief Editor: Paul Demieville, 3 vols. Tōkyō, 1929-1931.

Quelques pages de l'histoire religieuse du Japon (A few pages on the religious history of Japan). By Anesaki Masaharu, Paris, 1921.

Le Bouddhisme japonais (Japanese Buddhism). By Fujishima Ryōōn, Paris, 1889.

NOTES

1. Except otherwise indicated, this is the work we shall cite under the simple reference of "Commentary" or "Chinese Commentary". In Japan this Commentary enjoys an authority equal to that of the Sūtra and nearly always the Sūtra is studied through it. As a matter of fact, it adds to the Sūtra complements which are considered to be indispensable. It is divided into two parts: The first part consists of vols. I-III (pp. 579-609). It comments on the first chapter of the Sūtra and forms what is called KUCHI-NO-SHO,"the entrance". This part gives a general initiation to the esoteric doctrine. The second part, extending from Vol. III, p 609, up to the end of the Commentary, is called OKU-NO-SHO,"the secret" (lit. the inner part of the house). It is related to diverse practices the teaching and application of which are reserved only to the initiated.
2. Most of these texts are recited in the ceremony called RONGI, "doctrinal discussions".
3. [Editor's note:] The Tohoku catalogue is for the Derge edition of the Tibetan canon, which does not include the former version ('the unrevised version'), but only includes the revision by Gzhon-nu-dpal, which runs over two Tibetan 'bundles', thus the Nos, 2663 and 2664.
   The Peking edition includes both the 'unrevised' and the 'revised' versions of Buddhaguhya's great commentary on the words of the *Vairocanābhisaṃbodhi-tantra*.

PART VII

APPENDIX ESSAY BY THE EDITOR

The editor invites the indulgence of the reader for adding some personal observations to Tajima's splendid effort to communicate this remarkable Buddhist system to the reader. The following remarks are not in the nature of a 'book review', but rather aim to provide more information inspired by Tajima's account, since the editor did not attend to Tajima's work until after completing his own study based mainly on the Indo-Tibetan materials.[1] It did not seem feasible to arrange such observations in the form of editor's notes to Tajima's work due to the great wealth of notes already in the Sino-Japanese *Study* just completed. There are some difference of renderings of terms, e.g. for *bhūmi* I use 'stage(s)', and Tajima 'earth(s)'; for *citta* (especially in *bodhicitta*) I accept 'mind' or 'thought', and Tajima 'heart'. However, it is not right for me to challenge these renditions, since we have written individual works and made individual decisions about these terms. My comments will be in three parts: I. The text, II. Esoterism, III. The wider context.

I . THE TEXT

The greater Mahāvairocana-sūtra: Tajima's chapter on "Original Study of the Dainichikyō" deals in section B, "Three Alleged Sources of the Dainichikyō" with the theoretical resources for the text as presently preserved in Chinese translation, with title pronounced in Japanese *Dainichikyō*. He claims that Kōbō daishi has an original creation of the first source, the HŌNI-JŌGŌ-NO–HON (the eternal specimen which is in accordance with the Dharma). Then Tajima refers to a second source, which is indeed part of the Chinese tradition, the BUNRU-NO-KŌHON (the developed copy, bifurcating), which is the Sūtra in one hundred thousand verses (32 syllables counted as a verse), that was recovered and transmitted by Nāgārjuna, according to the legend that Tajima reports in C, "The Legendary Origins of the Dainichikyō". The third source is the presumed Sanskrit text that was translated into three thousand-odd verses to constitute the present text in Chinese and in Tibetan.

But is it true that Kōbō daishi made up that first 'alleged' source? The Brahmins anciently believed that their Dharma came from the sky. So in the *Īśa Upaniṣad,* K.15, when the prayer is addressed to the solar deity Pūṣan so that the devotee who has truth (*satya*) as his Dharma, may see it. And our Sūtra, in its Chapter Two, verse 23, states: "My Dharma is fully enlightened. It arises from the sky. Foolish beings, who range in wayward imagination, do not know it." Since the Tathāgata is represented as presenting his Dharma in this Sūtra, and this cited verse places the source in the sky-realm, this may well be what Kōbō daishi alludes to. Such a finding does not require 'unction' (*abhiṣeka*). It does require an appreciation of significance when reading the scripture. But it may be that some other reader learned in the Shingon can come up with a better explanation.

Then, as to the second alleged source, the form in one hundred thousand verses, perhaps this number is given in the light of the largest *Prajñāpāramitā-sūtra*, the 'one hundred thousand' one. In fact, the figure is just about correct, if one looks at it as follows: Tajima concludes his Introduction by pointing out that this Sūtra is permeated with ideas known from principal Mahāyāna scriptures, the *Saddharmapuṇḍarīka*, the *Avataṃsaka,* and the *Prajñāpāramitā.* If we add the Bodhisattva-piṭaka Literature, such as the *Akṣayamatinirdeśa,* earlier works dealing with the *homa* and other tantric rituals, probably also Asaṅga's *Mahāyāna-saṃgraha;* plus whatever other sources the commentators Śubhakarasiṃha and Buddhaguhya had to utilize for their commentaries on individual terms of the Sūtra, it does seem reasonable that it would amount to one hundred thousand verses in round numbers—meaning that the Sūtra composer was an avid reader of Mahāyāna scriptures and was determined to so write the scripture as to reflect all of them. This evident fact was stated in a somewhat mythological form as though the Sūtra had concretely existed in that larger version.

Then the third alleged source, the three thousand-odd verse edition, is of course the very Sanskrit text which was translated into both Chinese and Tibetan, with the difference that there are some extra chapters in the Tibetan version and some differences in the arrangement of chapters between the Chinese and the Tibetan versions. Western language translations are from this source.[2]

So perhaps some other word than 'alleged' should have been used to describe the sources of this Sūtra. Except that the term 'alleged' is properly applied to the story of Nāgārjuna's recovery of the Sūtra from the 'Iron Tower' of South India. There were probably three Nāgārjuna's—first the famous Buddhist author of the Mādhyamika-Kārikā, then an alchemist, finally the tantric author of the *Pañcakrama* and some other works of the *Guhyasamājatantra* cycle. The famous Mādhyamika Nāgārjuna lived before the composition of the *Mahāvairocana-sūtra*; and there is no evidence that the tantric Nāgārjuna had anything to do with our Sūtra. However, it is true that the commentary on the *Guhyasamājatantra* called *Pradipoddyotana,* by the tantric Chandrakīrti, contains a citation from our Sūtra.[3]

II. THE ESOTERIC TRADITION

Tajima in his Introduction asserts that the kind of esoterism found in the Shingon goes back to the Buddha, "not that the Buddha wanted to hide it, but that mankind is not able to understand it." This is a challenging remark, which is difficult to defend—even if one wants to, as does the present editor—because if it be true that "mankind is not able to understand it"—and both Tajima and this editor are included—we cannot understand it, and so on what grounds assert it, and how defend it? So let us admit at the outset Tajima's point that esoterism can go back to the Buddha, and that at all times there were those who could understand it, and those who could not.

Then there are two possibilities for this source of esoterism—the Buddha and the Buddha's doctrine. As to the Buddha's doctrine, it always had the esoterism of the difficult, as when 'dependent origination' (*pratītyasamutpāda*) was termed 'profound' (*gambhīra*), forcing a differentiation of the students into those of 'weak faculty' and those of 'keen faculty'. At all periods of Buddhism, the difficulty of certain tenets has been acknowledged, and teachers rendered their opinions, which sometimes led to differentiated tenets of Buddhist sects. Besides, the Shingon preserves a tradition that the *Mahāvairocana-sūtra* is "difficult on purpose", which further differentiates the students. Then, it could be asserted that the entire Buddhist canon of early scriptures is a secret code, that requires a clarification. For so declares Asanga in his *Yogācārabhūmi* (PTT, Vol. III, p. 18-5-4, 5): "Among them, the 'secret explanation' is generally any explanation of the Śrāvakapiṭaka" (*de la gsang ba bshad pa 'di lta ste phal cher ni nyan thos kyi sde snod bshad pa gang yin pa 'o*); "the 'open explanation' is generally any explanation of the Mahāyānapiṭaka" (*rnam par phye ba bshad pa ni 'di lta ste phal cher ni theg pa chen po'i sde snod bshad pa yin pa'o*). Asaṅga appears to intend by these remarks that the early Buddhist canon has a concealed meaning—hence the secret explanation of it; while the later, Mahāyāna Buddhist canon has an obvious meaning—hence the open explanation of it, or belonging to it. However, in the course of explaining the notion of *trikalpa* (*infra.*) the Shingon declares this Śrāvaka-piṭaka to be 'Hīnayāna' and that the esoteric code is subsequent and superior. It follows that esoterism—at least the kind preserved in the Shingon school—cannot be traced back to the Buddha's doctrine (the Dharma).

Then, how about the Buddha himself? This seems a probable source, as in the "Miracle of Śrāvasti"; here the form in the *Mahāvastu,* III, 115 (end):[4]

> atha khalu bhagavāṃ nyagrodhārāme tālamātraṃ vaihāyasam antarīkṣe sthitvā vividha-vicitrāṇi yamakaprātihāyāni karoti / heṣṭhimaṃ kāyaṃ prajvalati / uparimāto kāyāto śītasya vārisya paṃca dhārāśatāni śravanti / uparime kāye prajvalite heṣṭhimāto kāyāto śītasya vārisya paṃca dhārāśatāni śravanti /
> They, you should know, the Bhagavat, when in the Banyan Grove, stood in the air at a palm-tree's height in the intermediate realm (*antarīkṣa*) and performed various kinds of miraculous pairs. While the lower part of his body was in flames, from the upper part 500 torrents of cold water streamed forth. While the upper part of his body was in flames, from the lower part 500 torrents of cold water streamed forth.

One may notice that such a practice of yoga is based on a contrast of two principles—the hot and the cold, besides indicating corporeal locations—the upper and lower parts of the body. If one adopts the second form of the miracle, to wit, upper part in flames, lower part issuing cold water—this goes with the body as a *stūpa* according to the Sūtra's Chapter V and commentarial expansion. Thus, the Shingon's exposition (given in my own *Study* and by other authors) is that the yogin with interwined legs has a square base of yellow earth, has the round white water at the belly, the triangular red fire at the chest, the half-moon blue wind at the face, and the colorless *bindu* of *ākāśa* at crown of head. The color blue is presented in the Sūtra's Homa chapter (see my translation of the chapter six *Study*): "They are all my sons who are colored greenish blue, with handsome face..." (passage just before the final protective *mantra*).

But if we should grant the possibility of this Shingon *stūpa* going back so far to the beginning with the Buddha as a model, we should grant the same for Tibetan Buddhism (although Tajima denies it for this kind of Buddhism), because Tibetan teachings stress the employment of contrasting principles, e.g. the 'means' (*upāya*) constituting the first five 'perfections' (*pāramitā*) and 'insight' (*prajñā*), insisting that both are necessary.[5]

The reason that such kinds of esoterism as are exemplified in the Shingon system and the Tibetan kind as well, could only have arisen some time after the passing of Gautama Buddha, is that it was by reason of "remembrance of the Buddha" (*buddhānusmṛti*)—as contrasted with "remembrance of the Dharma" and "remembrance of the Sāmgha"—a situation could ensue promising to ultimately bring on a basic tantric position, since the "remembrance of the Buddha" constituted a presence in an absence. Much later in tantrism, the master must ascend to the void and there imagine a germ syllable (*bīja*), which can change into the body of a deity—again a kind of presence within an absence. This swing to the Buddha as a model took place after the downgrading of the Arhat, who was the finest fruit of the Sāmgha. Then arose a theory of practice modelled after the example of the Buddha, so there emerged a large Jātaka literature on past lives of the Buddha and then a formulation of Budhisattva path with the premise that a person so practising could arrive at Buddhahood. Then the early Prajñāpāramitā scriptures set forth that there are advanced Bodhisattvas who cannot be turned back, and beginning Bodhisattvas who could still back-slide.[6] This division of Bodhisattvas implicated a difference of instruction, which could hardly be traced back to Gautama Buddha's Dharma. Then tantras began to vie with one another on which set forth the practice attaining enlightenment quicker, perhaps even in one life. The *Mahāvairocana-sūtra* entered this fray on an exalted level of control of Buddhist positions early and later, while presenting its own solution for success by crossing over the three *kalpa* reinterpreted as deviant mental functions (*infra*).[7]

The term 'esoteric' is also employed in this literature for the tantric, other worldly secrets which the guru can only transmit to qualified students. According to Kōbō daishi, as Tajima reports both in his Introduction and in his chapter "General Introduction to the Dainichikyō", section F, Śākyamuni taught only exoteric doctrines for converting beings. It is the Dharmakāya of the Tathāgata which teaches the esoteric doctrine which is revealed to his retinue, and so on until it becomes the esoterism of the Shingon, a name which renders the Sanskrit word *mantra*—wherefor 'Shingon school' is equivalent to the Mantrayāna. At first reading it might be thought that the Sūtra tells it differently in Chapter Two, verse 126: "Moreover, Śākyamuni explains mantra and mudrā in the maṇḍala according to all streams of consciousness (*samtati*)." But if we recall the usage of the term *'mantra'* to apply to hymns of the *Ṛg-vdea* that are directed to deities—it may well be that the Sūtra's use of the term *'mantra'* here may be along the same lines, as even the Pāli canon, e.g. the beginning of the Samyutta-nikāya, shows discourses between the Buddha and deities. The term *mudrā* need not be the numerous ones listed in one of the Sūtra's chapters, but presumably gestures used when teaching, extending confidence to the audience and so on. And it was already agreed above that the Buddha in his lifetime did not teach the 'esoteric doctrine'. But that the Buddha's speech is empowered as *'mantra'* by dint of his 'merit' and 'knowledge' is probably intended by the Sūtra's verse.

III. THE TEXT IN WIDER CONTEXT

Crossing the Trikalpa: This topic is the theory advanced by the tantric movement that it is possible to become enlightened in one life, although Gautama started in that direction by working toward that goal during three incalculable eons (*kalpa*). The work which F.D. Lessing and I translated with title *Mkhas grub rje's Fundamentals of the Buddhist Tantras* starts out by giving various theories about how Gautama attained enlightenment in terms of eons, and so on. The *'śrāvaka'* theory is presented in Vasubandhu's *Abhidharmakośa*, Chapter IV, 110. According to this theory, Gautama Buddha started the process by taking a vow from an ancient teacher named Śākyamuni, and began to collect merit (*puṇya*) and knowledge (*jñāna*). At the end of the first incalculable eon (*asaṃkhyeya-kalpa*) there appeared the Buddha Ratnaśikhin; at the end of the second one, the Buddha Dīpamkara; at the end of the third one, the Buddha Vipaśyin. Then for one hundred eons (*kalpa*) he collected the equipment that caused his thirty-two characteristics and eighty minor marks, and then was born as Prince Siddhārtha, son of King Śuddhodana.[8]

The unknown author of the *Mahāvairocana-sūtra*, which I assign to the mid-sixth century A.D., must have heard various theories about how all this could be accomplished in one life. Some of these theories were probably of an oral nature in tantric lineages. So he gave a theory of his own (or that in a lineage he was following), and it involved a reinterpretation of the term *kalpa*. Thus the 'three *kalpas*' are three kinds of mental functions; and to cross over these is to proceed on a supramundane path. This is a theory advanced by this Sūtra in its chapter One. Tajima, in his chapter "Doctrinal Analysis of the First Chapter", section E, treats the three *kalpas,* with this summation: "On the basis of the facts contained in the Sūtra and the Commentary, it could be concluded that the first *kalpa* corresponds to the doctrine of the Hīnayāna, the second to that of the Mahāyāna,[9] and the third to the esoteric doctrine. But in the scholastic classification (HANGYŌ) of Kōbō daishi, the first *kalpa* corresponds to the Hīnayāna, the second to the Triyānavāda, and the third to the Ekayānavāda which includes the beginning of the esoteric teaching."

Without intervening in what may be a slight difference between Tajima's presentation and Kōbō daishi's classification, I am happy to report finding some evidence about the three *kalpa* in a Mahāyāna scripture entitled *Akṣayamatinirdeśa* with comments in the Tanjur commentary dubiously attributed to Vasubandhu. This is in the part of the scripture devoted to 'insight' (*prajñā*), and the scripture includes a treatment of the "16 non-companions of insight". Among these 16, the one which I count as number 10 is devoted to 'knots' (*mdud pa;* Skt. *grantha*) and 'superimpositions' (*sgro btags pa;* Skt. *āropa*), a list headed by three kinds of *kalpa* the (three 'knots'). The Tibetan terms of the scripture are *rtog pa, rnam par rtog pa,* and *yongs su rtog pa,* for which the original Sanskrit without doubt is: *kalpa, vikalpa,* and *parikalpa*.

The Tanjur commentary explains these as follows: "Kalpa is the positing of existence or non-existence of personal entities such as eye, ear, etc." (*mig dang rna ba la songs pa nang gi dngos po rnams la yod pa 'am med par 'dsin pa ni rtog pa 'o*). Vikalpa is the positing of existence or non-existence of external objects such as form, sound, etc." (*gzugs dang sgra la sogs pa phyi 'i yul rnams la yod pa dang med par 'dsin pa ni rnam par rtog pa 'o*). "Parikalpa is the positing of existence or non-existence of the two, viz. outer and personal entities". (*phyi dang nang gi dngos po gnyi ga la yod pa dang med par 'dsin pa in yongs su rtog pa 'o*).[10]

Accordingly, the first *kalpa* of personal deviance is overcome by the Hīnayāna emphasis on non-self or voidness of the personal aggregates. The second *kalpa* of exterior deviance is overcome according to Tajima by the Mahāyāna, or according to Kōbō daishi by the Triyāna (of Śrāvakas, Pratyekabuddhas, and Bodhisattvas).[11] The third *kalpa* of dualistic deviance is overcome by the Ekayāna, also the beginning of esoterism, stressing the non-two.[12] The Sūtra itself in Chapter One supports this approach, because it states: "One transcends the three eons of the 160 mundane minds by arousing the supramundane mind", and explains this kind of mind by the one that observes non-self in the personal aggregates, rejecting an agent, etc. It follows that all three countering movements, Hīnayāna, etc., signify kinds of "supramundane mind", in the context of gaining enlightenment in one life.

There is little doubt that the *Mahāvairocana-sūtra* has employed the expression *trikalpa* in this significance of three deviant mental traits while not losing sight of the other attested meaning, "three eons", as though to teach that these three deviant mental traits—*kalpa, vikalpa,* and *parikalpa*, have been 'knots' in the stream of consciousness for incalculable eons. And the Sūtra taken as a whole shows the way of crossing over these three deviant mental conditions and attaining enlightenment in one life

The triangle: The eminent Japanese Shingon scholar Toganoo studied Buddhaguhya's commentary and decided that while the Sūtra's triangle was pointing 'downward', the commentary can be construed as having it pointed 'upwards'.[13] The 122-deity *maṇḍala* that is number 20 in the Ngor Collection published by Kodansha, Japan, shows this triangle of the Abhisambodhi Vairocana Maṇḍala also pointed 'downward'. Before going further with this matter, it is well to point out that since this *maṇḍala* has three ranks, a triangle that is pointing 'downward' is in fact pointing inward, directly toward the central deity, who is Vairocana. But as I studied Buddhaguhya's commentary, I could find no evidence that he was changing the Sūtra's direction of the triangle. Let us see just what he did say, which is not without interest. The Sūtra, Chapter Two verses, 77-78, mentions: "...the 'seal (*mudrā*) of the Buddhas, the triangle all whitish green, on a lotus and surrounded by white rays". In my notes to translation of Chapter Two, Buddhaguhya in my n. 40: "In the East, one should place the 'seal of the Dharmakāya," and in **note** 42 : the direction in which it is placed, i.e. the East, is in Sanskrit *pūrva* which also means 'past' or 'former'. The suggestion that the Sanskrit word for 'East' is being employed with another meaning is significant. Then in Chapter X (of the Tibetan version), on the Speech *maṇḍala*, PTT version, p. 257-2-7, the scripture places in the East the "Dharmakāya of all the Buddhas" which therefore is the triangle. Then in Chapter XIII of the Tibetan ("Secret maṇḍala"), PTT, p. 264-1-4, 5, "with the color of the lunar orb, in its middle like conch, is the triangle of all the Buddhas, marked with *vajra*, and emitting two lights". Commenting on this, Buddhaguhya on Chapter XIII ('unedited version'), writes (PTT, p. 185-3-7): "triangle of all the Buddhas, placed above the white lotus" means above the water circle; "marked with *vajra*" means one draws inside the five-pronged *vajra*; "sending out two lights" means that from two vertices of the triangle come two lights, i.e. from the Dharmakāya come the Sambhogakāya and the Nirmānakāya. The foregoing information enables us to make some important conclusions. First, we decide that the 122-deity *maṇḍala* in Ngor Collection was based on this Chapter XIII, because it shows the five-pronged *vajra* and also omits the four Buddhas around the central Vairocana. Next, we can notice why Buddhaguhya pointed out two meanings for *pūrva* (the direction East and the meaning 'earlier'): he means that the triangle, placed by the scripture in the East, also has the meaning 'earlier' in a generative sense, since it stands for the Dharmakāya which is earlier than, and gives rise to, the other two Buddha bodies, the Sambhogakāya and the Nirmāṇakāya.[14]

Japanese and Tibetan esoterism: Tajima's Introduction claims that Indian tantrism was especially centered at Nālandā and at Vikramaśīla—two well-known north India monasteries; that the one at Nālandā was based on Vinaya while the one at Vikramaśīla was not and so became degraded into esoterism of the left (SADŌ-MIKKYŌ), the source of Tibetan esoterism.

Now, as to Tajima's differentiation between the two monasteries, as though Nālandā had founded esoterism on the Vinaya, but Vikramaśīla not so—the most famous Indian pandit to come to Tibet, and who came from Vikramaśīla, namely Atīśa, tells it quite in contrast to what Tajima claims. In his well-known Light on the Path to Enlightenment (*bodhipathapradīpa*) he says (verse 20): "When one continually holds the other vow belonging to the seven orders of the Prātimokṣa, he has the potentiality of the Bodhisattva vow, not otherwise." And he continues in verse 21: "Among the seven orders of the Prātimokṣa the Tathāgata explained the glorious pure life to be the best. (I) maintain (this) to be the vows of the *bhikṣu*."[15] Then we must speak of another Buddhist author, very influential on Tibetan Buddhism although he never came to Tibet, namely,

Ratnākaraśānti. He was one of the six gate-keeper-paṇḍitas of Vikramaśīla, that of the eastern gate. When the translator Rin-chen-bzang-po (958-1055) was nearing the age of fifty, the Tibetans 'Brog-mi and sTag-lo gzhon-nu brtson-'grus were sent to India to interview Rantākaraśanti. 'Brog-mi stayed eight years at the pandita's residence and heard the exposition of the Vinaya from him.[16] And if Tibetan Buddhism comes from Vikramaśīla, as Tajima thought to be the case; and if moreover this monastery had an esoterism divorced from Vinaya, how is it that we find in the Tibetan canon the translation of the entire Vinaya of the Mūlasarvāstivādins, taking up a lot of space?

Besides, Tajima himself presents as a profoundly true esoteric teaching what some others, finding it said in a tantra followed by the Tibetans, might have called 'left-hand'.

He says, "Popular Buddhism states that our defilements (*kleśa*) are the principal obstacles to Bodhi; and consequently it is necessary to suppress them completely. On the contrary, esoteric Buddhism declares that the defilements are of the same nature as Bodhi. It proceeds in the same way as a physician who derives the healing remedies from the most deadly poisons." And yet when Snellgrove wrote his Introduction to his edition and translation of the *Hevajra Tantra*—which some persons refer to as an example of a so-called "left-hand Tantra"—at that time anyway he thought it was natural to dislike the Tantras for their theory "to remove like by like".[17] Sometimes, it was stated in the manner, that the very thing which binds us to *samsāra,* liberates us from it. Since defilement binds us to *samsāra*, if it is identified with Bodhi (enlightenment), this has horrified some as a tantric teaching.

Previously I mentioned that the teaching of the priority of the Prātimokṣa vow to the Bodhisattva vow, was brought to Tibet under auspicious circumstances that stressed the point. Besides, there was the stipulation that the Bodhisattva vow is required for the Mantra vow (of the Diamond Vehicle, or Tantra).

It can be pointed out that the *Mahāvairocana-sūtra* itself stresses the requirement of having the Bodhisattva vow as a preliminary for the tantric instruction. This is said more than once, but a place worth citing is in Chapter Two (part B, on the "Several Means"), verses 238-39, for which I shall present the Tibetan in transcription with my translation:

/ de ring phan chad bu khyod kyis /
/ dam pa 'i chos dang byang chub sems /
/ srog gi phyir yang da phyin chad /

/ yongs su btang bar mi bya 'o //
/ khyod kyis ser sna dang ni gang /
/ sems can gnod pa mi bya 'o /
/ dam tshig 'di dag sangs rgyas kyis /
/ brtul zhugs bzang po khyod la bshad /
/ ci ltar rang gi srog bsrung ba /
/ de ltar khyod kyis 'di dag bsrungs /

'From this day on you, son, must not abandon the
Illustrious Dharma and the Mind of Enlightenment,
even for your life. You must not have envy, or
do harm to sentient beings. O well avowed one,
these pledges are given to you by the Buddha.
In the same way as you would guard your life,
so you must guard these.'

The vocative "O well avowed one" shows that the disciple has the Bodhisattva vow, and so can hold the tantric pledges (*samaya*).

It appears that Shingon Buddhism and Tibetan Buddhism can agree on this requirement of the Bodhisattva vow as a basis for the Mantra vow.

NOTES

1. Of course, Tajima is usually repeating views of his Shingon school, rather than putting forward novel theories of his own. So also is the case with Buddhaguhya in his commentary on the Sūtra. Therefore, I need not expatiate upon certain striking differences between the two lineages. Among these differences is Buddhaguhya's explanation that the Vairocana of the 2nd chapter's *maṇḍala* is the Sambhogakāya, while the Shingon, following Kūkai, explains this Vairocana as the Dharmakāya. Besides, the Sūtra's second chapter, which I have translated in my *Stūdy*, shows five Buddhas on petals of the central lotus, with the four petals bare; while Tajima, following the Sino-Japanese approach, fills up the four petals with four Bodhisattvas.
2. Probably the first English translation of the *Sūtra's* Chapter One to be published in English is that of Minoru Kiyota, within his booklet, *Tantric Concept of Boddhicitta* (Madison, 1982). The Chinese Commentary on this first chapter was translated with many notes by Wilhelm Kuno Müller in 1976 Ph. D. dissertation at UCLA. Both these works are based on the Sino-Japanese tradition. Tajima's is therefore the first translation into English to make extensive use of the Tibetan translation of the scripture while being based primarily on the Sino-Japanese tradition. My own translation of the scripture's second chapter is the first into English. so also some later chapters of the scripture in my own *Study*. In my case, the principal reliance was on the Indo-Tibetan tradition, and my study is the first in English to make extensive use of the Buddhaguhya commentary extant in the Tibetan canon.

3. Cf. Alex Wayman, *Yoga of the Guhyasamājatantra* (Delhi, 1977), p. 41.
4. I employ the edition by Radhagovinda Basak, *Mahāvastu Avadāna,* Vol. III (Calcutta, 1968).
5. Besides this well-known pair, see A. Wayman, *Yoga of the Guhyasamājatantra* (Delhi, 1977), p. 281, for the *yoga* of 'contraction' and 'expansion'; and rendering the stationary and the moving life into the 'Clear Light'.
6. For the signs of the Bodhisattva who is irreversible, see the *Aṣṭasāhasrikā prajñāpāramitā,* Chapter 17 (Conze tr., p. 121, ff.). This is probably the earliest of the Prajñāpāramitā scriptures.
7. Cf. H. Inagaki's Introduction to his translation, *Kūkai's principle of Attaining Buddhahood with the Present Body* (Ryukoku Translation Center, Ryukoku University, Kyoto, 1975).
8. Ferdinand D.Lessing and Alex Wayman, *Mkhas grub rje's Fundamentals of the Buddhist Tantras* (The Hague, 1968), pp. 18, ff.
9. The basis for Tajima's claim is that the Chinese Commentary brings in Mahāyāna for the second *kalpa*. See Müller's translation at p. 209 (as available from University Microfilms International, Ann Arbor), for this 'Mahāyāna' association; but notice the remark immediately following, "having others as condition". This is the clue to the meaning, and as I suppose, the reason that Kūkai preferred the explanation 'Triyāna' (the three vehicles).
10. I employ the Peking edition, PTT, Vol. 34, for the Kanjur version, the "16 non-companions" at p. 51-4-7, ending at 52-2-6; for the Tanjur commentary, PTT, Vol.104, at p.188-4-5, ending at 193-5-3. In the Kanjur, the 'knots' are presented at p. 51-1-4, ff.; and in the Tanjur commentary at p. 191-5-5, ff.
11. If one examines the Chinese Commentary attentively (Müller, pp. 209, ff.), it appears to agree with *vikalpa* as the second *kalpa*. It should be noticed that the *vi-* of this term seems to go back to the Vedic usage of 'going apart', thus the consciousness going apart in sense objects.
12. The 'non-two' in the Shingon formulation is especially with their two chief scriptures, the *Mahāvairocana-sūtra* and the *Tattvasamgraha-sūtra.* Cf. Yūkei Matsunaga, "Tantric Buddhism and Shingon Buddhism", *The Eastern Buddhist* (New Series), Vol. II, No. 2, Nov. 1969, for a well-formulated exposition pointing out (p. 5) that both these scriptures fuse Buddhist ritual (including *mantras*) with the philosophical ,system of Mahāyāna.
13. Cf. the posthumous publication essays of Shōun Toganoo, Vol. II (Kyōto, 1984), edited by Shōzui Toganoo, first two frontispieces.
14. The point about the two generative lights is still somewhat mysterious, even with Buddhaguhya's comment. It seems that the light which generates the Nirmānakāya is from the 'base line' of the triangle which is directed toward the bounding circle, and therefore directed outwards, and so in effect, downwards to the second rank where according to the Sūtra's chapter two (see the translation of it in my *Study*), Śakyamuni is the East and so is the Nirmānakāya of the Buddha Vairocana.
15. Cf. Alex Wayman, *Calming the Mind and Discerning the Real,* from the *Lam rim chen mo* (New York, 1978), pp. 10-11.
16. See George N. Roerich, *The Blue Annals,* Part One (Calcutta, 1949), pp. 205-6.
17. D.L. Snellgrove, *The Hevajra Tantra,* Part I (London, 1959), p. 42.

A FINAL NOTE

After the foregoing was put into page galley by Motilal Banarsidass, Indological Publishers, Delhi, two works have come to hand that should be mentioned:

I. We have received from Prof. J. Ochi, Kōyasan University, the four-volume collected works (*chōsaku shū*) of the late Prof. Sakai Shinten, published by Hōzōkan, Kyōto, 1983-1989. These volumes are 1. Studies on the *Dainichikyō* (13 essays); 2. Complete translation from Tibetan of Buddhaguhya's commentary on *Dainichikyō*; 3. Studies on the *Kongyōchōgyō*; 4. Miscellaneous essays on texts of the Yoga and the Anuttarayoga Tantras. Prof. Sakai was President of Kōyasan University, up to March 15, 1983, and became Grand Abbot of Kōyasan in 1989.

II. There is now an English version of the scripture: Chikyo Yamamoto, *Mahāvairocana-Sūtra* (International Academy of Indian Culture and Aditya Prakashan, New Delhi, 1990). One cannot dispute the term 'translation' applied to the version; yet it should be mentioned that the 'translation' is entirely in prose, although the scripture itself (whether original Sanskrit, Tibetan, or Sino-Japanese) is in verses and prose (cf. our Book One, rendering Chap. Two with verses numbering 244). As to the claim that it is a 'milestone', the reader can decide, e.g. by comparing the 'translation' of Chap. V (its p. 71) with our study of Chap. V and the preliminary service.

INDEXES

Introduction to the two indexes

The first of the following indexes is a combined subject index to the two preceding books, *Study of the Vairocanābhisaṃ- bodhitantra* by A. Wayman, and *Study of the Mahāvairocana-sūtra* by R. Tajima. This combined index was prepared by A. Wayman. It makes minimal use of Tajima's first index (on subjects) in his original French work. The reason is that this present index must serve for both our works. It observes these abbreviations: *dh.* for *dharma;* DD for *dharmadhātu;* Bo. for Bodhisattva; Praj. Pār. for Prajñāpāramitā; and V-scripture for the text that underlies both two books.

Tajima's original second index on Sanskrit terms and third index on Tibetan terms are not included here, since the interested readers can find these terms mainly at the appropriate places in the notes to Book Two.

To make the present work more useful to Sino-Japanese readers, a second index has been prepared on the basis of Tajima's fourth index by Toshio Sako. He successfully studied in the graduate school of Tokyo University, and is now in the doctoral program at Columbia University. Any additions to Tajima's index will be exhibited between square brackets.

I. *Subject Index*

63-4; of wind, water, and earth 65; earth and water *maṇḍalas* perfected by two mudrā 67; five streams of water descending from a hand gesture 101; 3rd initiation in earth-*maṇḍala* 86; Kūkai identified HŪṂ with wind 184; space goes with Vairocana's mudrā 102; enlightenment has the character of space 256; as to fire: dwelling in it 27, 161; Pāvaka the first mundane one 189; called Māruta when entering womb 189, 194; Pāvaka parent of the Āsura fire 190, 193; and acts of the P-fire 203; the forty-four (*sic.* for thirty-six) son-fires of Brahmā 191; mental one 197; flesh-eating one 198; Buddhist *homa* fire symbolical 219.

Ellora (an art center) 8-12, 36.

Enchin (a Japanese monk) 94, 221.

Enlightenment, is to know one's *citta* as it is 256; a being does not attain *bodhi* by an external cause, e.g. teacher, but in himself alone 273; right complete, has four kinds of infinite 326. See Onmiscience.

eons (*kalpa*), three 16, 44; *samvartakalpa* 63. See *kalpa*.

esoterism, was not unified in India 215-6; had centers in Nālandā and Vikramaśila 218; slowly decomposed in India 216; flourished with bulk of translations during the T'ang in China 216-7; bloomed in Japan as the Shingon 217, Tibetan and Japanese forms differ 218; that of both shingon and the Tibetan forms later than the Buddha 353; in the Japanese schools Shingon and Tendai 220; Buddha did not teach an esoteric doctrine, but his speech was empowered as *mantra* 354; Buddha's miracles as though his body was a *stūpa* 352; there was always esoterism of the difficult 351; Āsaṅga took the Srāvaka canon as the secret one 351; there is the pure aimed at the supramundane and the mixed for mundane aims 219; insists on oral transmission from master to disciple 220; this V-scripture the most esoteric of all 221; this V-scripture reevaluates the term *kalpa* 353.

eyes, five 271.

fear, i.e. six non-fears, 266-7.

Gandhāra 216.

garbha, its three meanings 4.

gates, first rank of Body-*maṇḍala* has one in West 87; 2nd rank two in East and West 87; 3rd rank has four 88; assisting the disciple at a gate 136; gate protectors 90; four female guardians as presumable gate protectors (for Speech) 106-7, 318; of all *dharmas* 133-4.

Gzhon-ngu-dpal (n. of a Tanjur 'editor') 29-31.

hair, style going with Akaniṣṭha heaven 101.

heart(s). See *citta*.

heresies (of ordinary persons) 259.

hero 31; 'Great Hero' (for Buddha or Complete Buddha) 130.

homa, Buddhist kind differs from the Brahmanical 219 its chapter 189-205; chapters of 'continuation tantra' 24; geometrical forms of 27; its performance 7-9, 29, 136-7 (Chap. II, k. 208-16); distinction between inner and outer 199-200; inner 192, 200-2; outer 199-200; for appeasing 193; for controlling 194; for prosperity 195; for drastic acts 195-6.

illusion, ten similes of 267-8; its words for each of the five personal aggregates (*skandha*) 285; restoration of vigor by so regarding one's body 161.

Indra (a Vedic deity) 83; 'great Indra' (*mahendra*) n. of earth 86; King Indra 235.

initiation (*abhiṣeka*), the result, *ācārya* the cause, the rite intermediate 90, 142; the ancient ceremony 222; in the *maṇḍala* reserved to Mahāyānists 110; a 'various means' 107; place and rite for 138-9; for the sprinkling (in subsidiary *maṇḍalas*) four pitchers are empowered by four Bos. Samantabhadra, etc. 91; in the Caryā-tantra 111; the *ācārya's* 154; in sequence of the three *maṇḍalas* 85; both with and without external ritual for the M-K-G-*maṇḍala* and Speech-*maṇḍala;* 3rd kind avoids space and time 86; that of the Speech-*maṇḍala* 318.

jñāna, the four. See Wisdom.

Jñānagupta, 216.

Kālidāsa 10.

has its own interpretation of it 321.
Mañjuśrī 5, 14-5, 37-8; his entourage 90; on S.W. petal in 'secret *maṇḍala*' 65; his insight 69; venerated 269; also called Mãñjughoṣa 67.
Mañjuśrīmūla-tantra or *-kalpa* 7-8, 35.
Mañjuśrī-nāma-saṃgīti 36; contains the n. Mahāvairocana 68, 80.
Mañjuśrī-nāmasaṃgīti-lakṣabhāṣya 80.
mantra(s), its character not made by the Buddhas 61; mantra character of mantras 132; 'speech' the best reality when it is one 134; questioned whether they succeed by their own nature 63; arise through dependent origination 170; require morality of the group in order to succeed 171; have four features 168-9; their power of three degrees 168-70; Gautama's words as mantra 143; imagination of eating violates them 145; may be muttered or whispered 162; of the four Bos. 155; 'heart' ones, the four 56-7; the one of omniscience A vīra HŪṂ KHĀṂ 13, 74; RAṂ of the DD and colored white 66; vow of Buddhas and Bos. lends power to mantras 315. See syllables.
Manusmṛti 169.
Māras, four 13, 74; their destruction 151; four mantra syllables that destroy them 158.
master or hierophant 17. See *ācārya*.
means (*upāya*), its correspondences 87.
Mind, is mind-produced 181; perfected by two mudrā 67; is intrinsically pure 69; two kinds of mental purity 161; the supramundane explained 166; the battleground for the fight between the gods and demons 85; three kinds of 70-2, 75, 187; ten kinds of 70-1, 76; three correlated to the ten stages 77-8.
Mind of enlightenment, is the unchanging (*akṣara*) 160; its correspondences 87; with the 'bright mind' 65; also 45-6, 55, 61.
mirror, one in the mind 181; master shows the disciple a clear one 139; pure one of the mind witnessed by the eye of wisdom 327.
Mitra, Debala 12, 16.
moonlight, circle of 50.
morality (*śīla*), constructed 47, 74; unconstructed 48, 74.
mother, of the Buddhas 86, called 'Space-eye' 87; her hall or quarters 88; who is Prajñāpāramitā 89, 103; why she is 'mother' 148; in Speech-*maṇḍala* is in N.E. with germ syllable GA 92; drawn with golden color, fiery, wearing white clothes 123.
mudrā ('seal'), of two kinds, without form and with form 331; with form of two kinds, similar and dissimilar 66; as 'distinctive marks' 56; the mark of comprehending the DD 66; usually associated with a mantra to be recited 67, 85; of body, speech, and mind 66; that arise from the DD 136; the Dharmacakra kind empowered by Vajrasattva 67, 136; Vairocana's as commented upon 102; eight esoteric ones go with four Buddhas and four Bos., as in the 'secret *maṇḍala*' 323; the term *mahāmudrā* 55, 66-7.
Munimatālaṃkāra (by Abhayākaragupta) 73.
muttering, four members of 31, 38, 89; 'mental muttering' expressed by mind and discursive thought 162.

Nāgabodhi, a disciple of Nāgārjuna 228; identified with Dharmagupta 228; but Taimitsu tradition denies this identity 233.
Nāgārjuna, legendary association with V-scripture 237-8, 240.
Nakayama, shorei 39, 337.
Nālandā 15-6, 218, 229.
Nirvāṇa, with and without remainder 48-9; without fixed abode 1, 17; quiescent or else of no fixed abode 61, 75; and Seventh Bo. Stage 74.
Niṣpannayogāvalī 67.

obstacles (*āvaraṇa*), five are recognized 276.
omens, superior good ones from sky 87; middling good ones from intermediate space 87; inferior good ones from earth 88; good ones in early morning 117; illustrations of the good omens 143; dream omens also of three kinds 121, 145; for *siddhi* 167. See throwing.
omniscience, exists in our own hearts 223; its two modes 17; three things stipulated for omniscient wisdom 2, 4, 19; three Wisdoms are forms of it 63; its three sets of correspondences 87; omniscient knowledge 70-1, 133; its fulfilment is 'great void' of the complete Buddha 108.
Orissa, its three principalities, Oḍra, etc. 12-4.

pada (as word), also means, foot (of stanza)

II

Sino-Japanese Index

The Chinese pronunciations are underlined. The doubtful Sanskrit equivalents are marked with an asterisk. We have not recorded in this index the titles of Chinese or Japanese works cited according to the Taishō Daizōkyō. Our work always indicates the numbers attached to these works in the Taishō Daizōkyō. It suffices to refer to a table of the Taishō Daizōkyō to find the Chinese characters for the titles in question.
